The Market and the Environment

INTERNATIONAL STUDIES IN ENVIRONMENTAL POLICY MAKING

General Editor: Frank J. Convery, *Heritage Trust Professor of Environmental Studies and Director of the Environmental Institute at University College Dublin, Ireland*

This important series makes a significant contribution to the development of policies to combat environmental problems. It is the result of Europe-wide study of the use of market-based instruments to formulate environmental policy and reduce degradation. International in scope, it addresses issues of current and future concern across the globe, in both East and West and in developed and developing countries.

This series provides a forum for the publication of a limited number of innovative, high quality volumes which extend and challenge the current literature. It demonstrates how economic analysis can make a contribution to understanding and resolving the environmental problems confronting the world in the twenty-first century.

Titles in the series include:

International Competitiveness and Environmental Policies
Edited by Terry Barker and Jonathan Köhler

Pollution for Sale
Emissions Trading and Joint Implementation
Edited by Steve Sorrell and Jim Skea

The Market and the Environment
The Effectiveness of Market-based Policy Instruments for Environmental Reform
Edited by Thomas Sterner

The Market and the Environment

The Effectiveness of Market-Based Policy Instruments for Environmental Reform

Edited by

Thomas Sterner

Professor of Environmental Economics, University of Göteborg, Sweden

INTERNATIONAL STUDIES IN ENVIRONMENTAL POLICY MAKING

Edward Elgar
Cheltenham, UK - Northampton, MA, USA

Published by
Edward Elgar Publishing Limited
Glensanda House
Montpellier Parade
Cheltenham
Glos GL50 1UA
UK

Edward Elgar Publishing, Inc.
136 West Street
Suite 202
Northampton
Massachusetts 01060
USA

A catalogue record for this book
is available from the British Library

Library of Congress Cataloguing in Publication Data
The market and the environment : the effectiveness of market based policy instruments for environmental reform / edited by Thomas Sterner.
(International studies in environmental policy making series)
1. Environmental policy—Economic aspects. 2. Environmental policy—International cooperation. 3. Environmental protection––Taxation. 4. Tax incentives. I. Sterner, Thomas, 1952–
II. Series: International studies in environmental policy making.
HC79.E5M3577 1999
333.7—dc21 99–19520
CIP

ISBN 1 85898 906 X

Printed and bound in Great Britain by Bookcraft (Bath) Ltd.

Contents

Figures

Tables

Contributors

Paula Antunes

Paula Antunes is professor of environmental management at the Faculty of Sciences and technology of the New University of Lisbon. She has published several papers on environmental policy analysis, environmental management and environmental impact assessment. She has been guest researcher in Dartmouth College, Free University of Amsterdam and the International Institute for Applied Systems Analysis.

Yoram Avnimelech

Yoram Avnimelech is professor of Water and Soil Sciences, Faculty of Agricultural Engineering, Israel Institute of Technology. Avnimelech holds a Ph.D. from the Hebrew University, Jerusalem. Main Research experience: Dissolution of calcium phosphates by soil, fertilizers evaluation development. Transformations of nitrates in peat, problems related to the pollution of Lake Kinneret. Research on solid waste: composting and use of compost, waste management. Research on aquatic sediments and surface water management, sediment-water relationship, water quality, water management and aquaculture. Earlier positions include Chief scientist, Ministry of the Environment, Israel 1989-1994.

Ofira Ayalon

Ofira Ayalon, M.Sc. in Agricultural Engineering is a Ph.D student working on Environmental accounting as a means for the development of solid waste management policy in Israel. Main research experience: Studies on the effect of municipal solid waste compost on the fertility of soils. Studies on biofilters for the separation of hazardous wastes from industrial sludge. Distribution of heavy metals in leachates of municipal wastes. Slow release fertilizers. Municipal Solid Waste Management, research on the economic, technological and environmental aspects of MSW management. Life Cycle Analysis research of packaging and MSW.

Collins Ayoo

Collins Ayoo is a lecturer in the Department of Economics and Business studies at Maseno University College, Kenya. The courses he has taught are microeconomics, macroeconomics and development economics. His research interests are in the areas of sustainable resource use and poverty issues in developing countries. He is currently doing doctoral work in economics at the University of Guelph in Canada.

Randall A. Bluffstone

Randall Bluffstone is a development associate with the Harvard Institute for International Development at Harvard University. He has been with the institute since 1993 when he received his Ph.D. in economics from Boston University. From 1994–1997 he was an environmental policy advisor to the government of Lithuania

Runar Brännlund

Runar Brännlund is Associate Professor at the Department of Economics, University of Umeå, Sweden. He has published articles and books within environmental and resource economics. He has been a guest researcher at the International Institute of Applied System Analyaia in Vienna and University of California Berkely. He has also been head secretary to the Swedish Green Tax Commission.

Fredrik Carlsson

Fredrik Carlsson is research associate at Göteborg University, where he also received his Ph.D. in economics. His research interests include transport economics, environmental regulation, and stated preference techniques. Recent published work deals with optimal environmental taxation under imperfect competition, environmental regulation of domestic civil aviation and willingness to pay for improved air quality in Sweden.

Peter Cramton

Peter Cramton is a Professor of Economics at the University of Maryland. His research focuses on economic exchange in markets with few parties. Most of his recent work has addressed design and incentive questions in auctions and bargaining. He has served as an auction expert for numerous companies in spectrum auctions. He has advised the FCC and several foreign governments on the design and implementation of spectrum auctions.

Crampton has designed electricity auctions in New England, and has advised bidders in electricity auctions. Before joining the Maryland faculty in 1993, he was an Associate Professor at Yale University and National Fellow at the Hoover Institution at Stanford University. He has published numerous articles on auction theory, auction practice and bargaining in major journals. Cramton received his B.S. in Engineering from Cornell University and his Ph.D. in Business from Stanford University.

Francesco Ferrante

Francesco Ferrante holds a Ph.D. from the University of York, U.K. He is lecturer in Economics at Cassino University, Italy. Before taking his Ph.D. he spent a short period as research assistant at the Stockholm Environment Institute (York branch) working on the control of acid rain. He has published papers in the fields of technical change and environmental policy modelling, the efficient control of global warming and industrial economics. He is a member of a Research Group on Environmental Taxation of the Italian Ministry of Finance.

Henk Folmer

Henk Folmer is Professor of Economics at the Wageningen Agricultural University. He served as first President of the European Association of Environmental and Resource Economics from 1987-93. He also served on the EC Task Force on the Single Market and the Environment. He has written a large number of publications in a wide variety of international outlets in the field of environmental and resource economics, econometrics, labour economics and regional economics. He is co-editor of the International Yearbook of Environmental and Resource Economics: a Survey of Current Issues.

David Gee

David has worked for over two decades on occupational and environmental risk reduction with UK Trade Unions (AUEW, TUC & GMB), with the Environmental group, Friends of the Earth, where he was Director, and as a consultant. Since December 1995, he has been working for the European Environment Agency, an EU information providing body, in Copenhagen, where he is responsible for "Information Needs Analysis and Scientific Liaison". He has specialized on several subjects, such as the risks and uncertainties arising from chemicals, radiation, asbestos; on clean production; on ecological tax reform; and on communicating scientific complexity and uncertainty to nonspecialists. He is currently working on the links between environment and health, particularly of children; recourses use; eco-efficiency and associated indicators; sectoral integration; the externalities of agriculture; and the precautionary principle.

Dominic Hogg

Dr Dominic Hogg is Senior Consultant at ECOTEC Research and Consulting. He has managed a range of projects for UK Government Departments and the European Commission concerning economic instruments for environmental policy. He has a special interest in the factors which determine the behavioral responses of actors to economic instruments (and hence their potential limitations). His Ph.D. (from Cambridge University) concerning processes of lock-in within agriculture, is due to be published shortly.

Mohamud Abdi Jama

Mohamud Abdi Jama was awarded a Fulbright great fellowship in agricultural economics, specialisation in resource economics at Washington State University. He is currently the Co-ordinator for Environmental Economics Network for Eastern and Southern Africa region (EENESA). He is also a research associate (on leave) in the Institute for Development Studies, University of Nairobi. Dr Jama´s research interest canters on the ways in which energy costs, taxation and policies influence standards of living, overall economics performance and the economics of water

Tim Jeppesen

Jeppesen is an assistant professor of environmental economics and welfare economics at Odense University in Denmark Tim. He has recently submitted his Ph.D. thesis on institutional arrangements for environmental policy in a federal system. His research areas are environmental policy in federal systems with emphasis on the European Union.

Olof Johansson-Stenman

Olof Johansson-Stenman is an assistant professor at Göteborg University, where he also received his Ph.D. in economics. His research interests include ethics and welfare analysis, public economics, environmental economics, and externalities associated with road transport. Recent published work deals with distributional weights in CBA, economics of altruism, and the welfare foundations and behavioral assumptions in economics.

Péter Kaderják

Peter Kaderják is Associate Professor of Economics at the Budapest University of Economic Sciences in Hungary. Between October 1997 and September 1998 he was Environmental Policy Advisor of the Hungary Environmental Economics Program of the Harvard Institute for International Development. After HIID he was nominated for Cabinet Chief of the Ministry of Economy in Hungary. His recent work includes environmental valuation, environmental tax reform and the environmental aspects of economic transition.

Godius Kahyarara

Godius Kahyarara is a young Tanzanian Economist who is currently at the Economic and Social Research Foundation, working on various economic research projects. He is the author of one book and several articles on Environmental economics, Labour, International Trade and Finance, Econometrics, Poverty and other Macro-economics issues.

Suzi Kerr

Suzi Kerr holds a Ph.D. from Harvard. She is with Motu Economic research in New Zealand. and has earlier worked as an Assistant Professor at the University of Maryland at College Park, and at Resources for the Future. She is currently working on a variety of climate change related issues, buyer vs. seller liability for international emissions credits, measurement of carbon sinks and assignment of risk within permit markets. She has also done empirical work on the responsiveness of technology diffusion to environmental regulation and the efficiency of permit markets in the presence of transaction costs.

András Kis

Between December 1994 and October 1998 András Kis was a Research Associate at the Budapest office of the Hungary Environmental Economics Program of the Harvard Institute for International Development. Since October 1998 he is a researcher of the Hungarian Environmental Economics Center in Budapest. His main specialties include product charges and environmental expenditure accounting.

Marinus H. C. Komen

Marinus H.C. Komen is a Ph.D. student at Wageningen Agricultural University. He has published various articles on the consequences of environmental policies for agriculture and firm/capital location and the relation between income and pollution. His dissertation deals with environmental and agricultural policy analysis using an applied general equilibrium approach for the Netherlands.

Bengt Kriström

Bengt Kriström is professor of resource economics at SLU Umeå and a member of the Economic Council of Sweden. He has published various articles and books on valuation of environmental goods, CGE-modelling, resource accounting including a recent textbook on environmental economics. He has been research associate at University of California, Berkley and has been teaching at e.g. Universitat d´Autonoma, Barcelona, Stockholm School of Economics, Stockholm, Swedish School of Economics, Helsinki. He has been consultant to several organizations, including the World Bank and the Stockholm Environmental Institute.

Sandra Martinho

Sandra Martinho is an economist and works in ECOMAN centre – Ecological Economics and Management Centre – at the Department of Environmental Sciences and Engineering, Faculty of Sciences and Technology – New University of Lisbon. Sandra has been involved in scientific research and consultant in the domains of economic evaluation of environmental resources and analysis of the economic implications of environmental policy instruments in Portugal.

Glenn Morris

Glenn Morris has conducted economic analyses of environmental, energy and other natural resource policies and programs for over twenty years and is currently a consultant in environmental and resource economics. He recently completed a three year assignment with Harvard Institute for International Development during which he served as a Senior Environmental Policy Advisor in Hungary. Dr Morris's recent work includes analyses of a variety of environmental policy innovations in central and eastern European countries including design and implementation of product charges, environmental funds and emission load fees.

Åke Nordlander

Åke Nordlander is first secretary at the Budget Department in the Swedish Ministry of Finance. He has a long experience working with energy and environmental taxes. Between 1995 and 1998 he was seconded to the European Commission working with energy and environmental taxes. Prior to that he was working with economic analysis of energy and environmental taxes in the division for tax policy analysis in the Swedish Ministry of Finance. He has also been acting as deputy secretary to the Swedish Green Tax Commission.

Andy Park

Andy Park is a research fellow at the University of Edinburgh, currently working on an economic analysis of negotiation procedures in civil justice. His previous research includes computable general equilibrium modeling of the distributional effects of energy pricing policies.

John C.V. Pezzey

John Pezzey is a lecturer in environmental and resource economics at the University of York, after holding research fellowships at the University of Colorado, Bristol and London. He has published various articles on the theory of sustainable development and the political economy of environmental policy instruments, among other topics.

Mihaela Popovici

Dr Popovici is executive director of the Center for Environmentally Sustainable Economic Policy in Bucharest, Romania and guest lecturer at the Polytechnics University of Bucharest, Romania. She was a water sector expert and principal legislative drafter in the Water Department of the Government of Romania for twenty-five years, prior to becoming Harvard's water sector economist from 1993 to 1998 under Dr Zinnes.

Maria Teresa Ribeiro

Maria Teresa Ribeiro is currently working at the European Environment Agency as a Project Manager for the areas of Scenarios and Policy Instruments. She has published several articles in the field of policy analysis. She has worked in this area in Norway, Brussels and Portugal where she was formerly working with CEEETA, a center for economics studies of the Higher Institute of Economics of the University of Lisbon.

Eirik Romstad

Eirik Romstad is Sr. Research Fellow and Head of Research at the Department of Economics and Social Sciences, Agricultural University of Norway. His main research area is environmental regulation, focusing on game theory, risk and uncertainty and concepts from the recourse allocation mechanism literature. He has been a visiting professor at The Ohio State University and The Swedish University of Agricultural Sciences.

Rui Santos

Rui Santos is Professor of Environmental Economics at the Faculty of Sciences and Technology of the new University of Lisbon. He has published several articles, namely on the use of market based instruments in several fields such as water resources, solid waste management and oceans management. He has also undertaken several environmental policy studies for the Portuguese Government and the European Commission among others.

Kai Schlegelmilch

Kai Schlegelmilch is project manager of economic instruments in environmental policy of the Climate Policy Division in Wuppertal Institute for Climate, Environment and Energy. He has published many articles and has carried out several studies on ecological tax reform and green budget reform. Recently he has edited a book on "Green Budget Reform in Europe. Countries at the Forefront, Springer: Heidelberg 1998. He has been working with the European Environment Agency in Copenhagen in 1996/7.

Mordechai Shechter

Mordechai Shechter, Ph.D. in Agricultural Economics, Iowa State University. Professor, Department of Economics, University of Haifa. Founder and Director of the Natural Resources and Environmental Research Center of the University of Haifa. Served as University Rector 1994-97. He held visiting positions at Resources for the Future, Washington D.C., University of Pennsylvania, Royal Agricultural University, Denmark, Agricultural University, Wageningen, the Netherlands, C.V. Starr Center for Applied Economics, New York University, University of Wollongong, NSV, Australia.

Paul Steele

Paul Steele is an environmental economist specializing in developing country issues. He is a Director of EFTEC Ltd., an environmental consultancy based in London and of Development Options Pvt Ltd, an environmental consultancy based in Sri Lanka. He recently completed a two year assignment funded by the World Bank as Environmental Economics Advisor to the Sri Lankan Ministry of Environment. His publications include work on market based instruments in both Asia and Europe.

Thomas Sterner

Thomas Sterner is Professor of Environmental Economics at the University of Gothenburg. He has written over 30 articles in the fields of industrial, energy, transport, development and environmental economics. His more recent work has focused largely on policy instruments for environmental and resource issues. He has started the Environmental Economics Unit at Göteborg University and served on numerous councils and boards currently including that of the EAERE, (European Association of Environmental and Resource Economists) and the Swedish Society for Nature Conservancy and Chairman of the Research Board of the Environmental Economics Network for Eastern and Southern Africa region (EENESA). He has held visiting positions at the World Bank, Resources for the Future and been a guest researcher at Universities of Grenoble, Cambridge, (UK) and Mexico (UNAM).

Cornel Tarhoaca

Professor Tarhoaca is an assistant professor of economics at the Academy of Economic Studies, Bucharest, Romania. He was part of the Harvard environmental economics policy team under Dr. Zinnes from 1993 to 1998. He has also served over the last decade as an economic advisor to the president of the Council of Economic Reform and to the minister of finance of Romania, and as a staff economist at the World Bank mission in Romania.

Tom Tietenberg

Tom Tietenberg is the author or editor of 10 books and over 70 articles and essays on environmental and natural resource economics. He is a former President of the Association of Environmental and Resource Economists (1987-8) and in 1990 he was named "Maine Professor of the Year" by the Council for Advancement and Support of Education, Washington D.C. He has served as a consultant to the World Bank, U.S AID, the United Nations and several national governments on the use of economic incentives to produce sustainable development.

Clifford Zinnes

Dr Zinnes is a development economist and Institute Associate at the Harvard Institute for International Development at Harvard University. From 1993 to 1998 he was the senior policy advisor for sustainable development to the Government of Romania in Bucharest, where he also directed the country's first environmental economics think-tank. During this period, he and his team co-authored numerous environmental regulations and the country's privatization law and water law. He has also taught economics at Harvard University and the University of Pennsylvania.

Series Editor's Preface

When economists address themselves to the analysis of policy choice, they typically think in terms of some variations of the following criteria: static efficiency, connoting optimization of net benefits, given existing technologies, or minimizing costs to achieve a given objective; dynamic efficiency, conveying the sense of endogenous innovation, an ongoing process of some combination of quality improvement and cost reduction; equity, addressing the extent to which those less or better endowed benefit, or bear costs; concordance or feasibility, focusing on the extent to which options are likely to be engaged, adopted and sustained by the policy processes and institutions at issue. In the case of environmental policy analysis, an additional criterion is often added, namely, that of environmental effectiveness the extent to which the environmental objectives at issue are achieved.

But it is clear that a judgement if environmental effectiveness is a necessary, if not sufficient, condition of static and dynamic efficiency are to be evaluated, and indeed can be central to matters of equity and political and administrative feasibility. And yet we find that this most fundamental of tasks is little addressed, either in concept or in practice.

This fulcrum, about which all serious policy analysis must be levered, is what this book is about; it begins to redress this lacuna in the analytical and empirical literature.

As such, it is consistent in philosophy with the other books in this series which attempt in a sense to 'benchmark' what is happening on the ground and in research relating to the mobilization of markets to achieve environmental economic objectives.

Europe is a very fruitful space in which to undertake such research, because it contains both a wondrous variety of ecosystems and environmental challenges in a relatively small space, and a remarkable range of policy responses to same. In its Climate Change and Environment research programme, the European Union has taken advantage of this diversity in physical nature and policy response to mobilize a wide range or research which aspires to demonstrate that there are great opportunities for mutual learning, that the whole can be more than the sum of the parts. Our endeavours of which this book is one product via the Concerted Action on

Market-based Instruments for Sustainable Development have been undertaken in this spirit. We are grateful to the European Commission, and, in particular to Jonathan Parker, Andrew Sors and Bill Watts for nurturing our endeavours with an effective combination of approbation, exhortation and the occasional critique. The usual disclaimer applies.

Frank J. Convery
Environmental Institute, University College, Dublin

Preface

Thomas Sterner

The complexity of many environmental issues requires knowledge of natural sciences ranging from ecology to chemistry and engineering which very few of us possess. This makes it unfortunately easy to believe whatever you want to believe and the disparity of views is enormous. According to the pessimists, there is hardly any hope for humanity at all while the majority of people are still optimistic and complacent to the point of even being skeptical about doing anything serious at all to deal with environmental issues. Most of the authors of this book would probably agree that even if Doomsday isn't just round the corner, the World does face some environmental challenges that require serious action. The importance of large-scale policy making in the environmental area has dawned on us at a time when large chunks of public policy making itself are being called into question. We have seen in other areas, such as employment and income distribution, that policy making is no easy matter. When it comes to most environmental issues we are still in the early phases of policy making (at least in most countries of the World). We thus have the opportunity to consider carefully our first experiences in order to improve on policy design for the future when really large-scale policies will be needed. The European Research Network on Market-based Instruments for Sustainable Development is funded by DGXII of the European Union under the Concerted Action initiative. The network aims to bring together researchers in a number of theme areas to exchange results, develop new research initiatives and disseminate results to the policy community. The network comprises 14 groups from nine member states of the EU, and is coordinated by Dr Frank Convery of University College, Dublin. It has held a large number of workshops and conferences throughout Europe and produced numerous books and policy briefs over the past couple of years. The present book is largely the result of a workshop held by the Research Network in November 1997 in Gothenburg, at the Department of Economics. I would particularly like to thank Frank Convery and the other network members who have worked with me on these issues in a most stimulating way for several years. I would also like to thank the DG XII for its financial and intellectual support. Furthermore I would like to thank Runar Brännlund, Umeå University, who was the main author of the Swedish Green Tax Commission and who co-organized this conference. Åsa Löfgren and Henrik Hammar did a very good job in managing the conference and in this connection I would particularly like to thank both of them and all the other participants, speakers and others who participated in that very inspiring workshop. Some of them such as Knut Rexed, Hans Vos, Terry Barker and Jonathan Köhler did not have the opportunity to contribute papers but they did provide useful input in the discussions, some of which is reflected in the revisions that various authors have undertaken. In the last couple of years, we have witnessed a number of green tax commissions, and as already mentioned we have had considerable input from the Swedish Commission. The public debate has sometimes come to focus almost exclusively on the so-called 'double dividend' issue – which basically purports that environmental taxes are free of charge since they would imply numerous side-benefits apart from their environmental effect. In this form, the claim is clearly misplaced and has in our mind done more harm than good to the debate. We have wanted to stay clear of this focus and concentrate on the many other vital issues related to environmental policy instruments. Thus our main focus in this book is on the environmental effects of environmental policies.

Still, there has to be an exception to every rule and we have one chapter, by Andy Park and John Pezzey, which we think does in fact deal in a very pedagogical fashion with the issue. The rest of the book deals with an exciting range of important issues. Among the theoretical issues are information provision, monitoring and enforcement, habit formation and the effects of restricted competition on the formulation of optimal policies. Among the empirical issues are waste management, energy, transport and distributional issues. While the formulation of our own policies is our most immediate concern in this book we need always to bear in mind that we represent only a small fraction of humanity and that the conditions, economical, political and environmental in the rest of the World are very distinct. At the same time we are interdependent in numerous ways – both economically and environmentally. Therefore, we have a particular interest in, and responsibility for, opening up a dialogue with environmental economists from the formerly planned economies and the emerging economies of the Third World. I am very grateful to the Swedish International Development Cooperation Agency, Sida, which has helped finance the participation of some colleagues from developing countries both in the workshop and in this book.

Finally I would like to thank numerous colleagues who have helped in various ways with the preparation of this book. All the authors have been asked to act as referees for other chapters and in spite (or because?) of the reciprocal nature of this assignment they have generally done it with great care. Some friends, Fredrik Carlsson, Henk Folmer, Mario Zejan, Wlodek Bursztyn, Daniela Roughsedge, Panchali Guha, Henrik Hammar, Bill Hyde, Olof Johansson-Stenman, Mathias Klang, Åsa Löfgren, Edwin Muchapondwa, Gbadebo Oladosu, Björn Olsson and Tom Tietenberg have all gone out of their way to provide considerable help with both practical and academic issues such as additional reviewing of various chapters. Mathias Klang and Gabriela Gitli Antunez have done a very professional job of copy editing, Ulla Mellgren has also helped me and Edward Elgar has been very patient in waiting for a delayed manuscript.

This job was finished while I was in Washington, and I would also like to thank my colleagues at the Resources for the Future and at the Environment Department of the World Bank for support.

Thomas Sterner
Washington, October 1998.

1. Introduction

Thomas Sterner

The design of policy instruments for environmental policy making is a complex mix of science and art. Economists are sometimes presumed, automatically, to promote market-based instruments. In fact these are sometimes called 'economic' policies to distinguish them from regulatory or legal policies but this is partly misleading. In fact economists have many of the tools needed to analyze which (combination of) policies are best and in many instances economists might in fact recommend simple regulation as a result of the particular circumstances (character of the damage function, monitoring capacity or costs or market structure). This book sets out to study the design of policy instruments for environmental development, focussing on environmental policy making at the national level.

Different countries have distinctly different experiences of policy making. Standards are the base for policy making in practically all countries. They have been complemented in many European countries by taxes and charges while the experience in the US has been that substantial environmental taxes are politically unfeasible. The US has instead pioneered such instruments as the Tradable Emission Permit, which on the other hand has found hardly any applications in Western Europe. Generally speaking, the Eastern European and formerly planned economies have little experience in implementing consistent environmental policies although ironically enough there were some very 'advanced' schemes in Russia and the Baltic republics (principally Estonia). They used environmental taxes and charges in the setting of a planned economy. Although these instruments looked appealing at a first glance, one of their main drawbacks was the pervasive feature of soft-budget constraints which in the end implied that companies were reimbursed (by ministries) for their costs – including such items as environmental taxes! After market reforms many of these countries are keeping and developing their environmental tax systems but some are also experimenting with tradable emission permits and other schemes.

Developing countries also, generally speaking, have less-advanced environmental policy making but there are some interesting experiences in individual cases. This applies both to some of the richer countries such as Chile and some East Asian 'tigers' but also to some poorer countries and to such areas as natural resource management and protection of the commons where innovative local policies have evolved as a mixture of tradition and modern policy thinking concerning property rights.

The selection and development of instruments is an important area for policy makers and central to environmental economics. It has also turned out to be a richer and more complex area than many researchers at first suspected with many different policies, evaluation criteria and other considerations to take into account.

In the first substantial chapter, Tom Tietenberg provides a systematic review of what he calls the third phase of policy making. After simple control and regulation (phase 1) had been shown to be both costly, inefficient and sometimes ineffective, it was gradually complemented by the traditional market-based instruments such as tradable emission permits, environmental taxes or fees, deposit-refund schemes and so on. This constitutes phase 2 which has greatly improved on policy making but, according to Tietenberg, these instruments may still not suffice to deal with all the very diverse environmental problems that face us, particularly in the face of constraints on the resources available to regulators. The latter point may be particularly relevant in developing countries. Phase 3 would then be information disclosure in various forms which appears to be a policy that places relatively little burden on the regulator and indeed little immediate burden on the polluter, either. Information is, however, a prerequisite for other policies and the idea here is that information availability will trigger other processes, ranging from compensation claims by exposed workers to caution among investors and suits from environmental action groups.

It would seem that information disclosure is often a set of policy options that supplement rather than replace other policy instruments but in some cases the policies may indeed be supplements. The author of this chapter takes great care to analyze systematically the different types of social context and interaction through which polluters and victims are related. This may, for instance, be through contractual relationships on the product or labor market, through financial relationships or simply as neighbors. For each of these different categories of relationship the incentives of polluters, victims and other parties are analyzed and this forms the basis for analyzing the various roles that could be played by public authorities and the structure of policy instruments.

The chapter includes quite an extensive review of examples, including the Toxic Release Inventory in the US, voluntary reduction programs and green labeling programs in various countries (including an interesting case from Indonesia). It also features a section on papers analyzing the effectiveness of information disclosure policies. This is a very new field and it is still very early to draw definite conclusions, but preliminary findings suggest that there is great potential in these types of policies. This applies particularly to settings where the firm has many contacts with the victims (for instance through selling products of mass consumption) and where authorities have limited competence for traditional policy making.

The fact that increased attention is being given to information disclosure, green pricing and labeling does not mean that the 'traditional' controversies concerning the relative merits of command and control versus incentive-based market-type instruments are in any way resolved or unimportant. Quite to the contrary, for many types of environmental problem and many socioeconomic settings, the main choices continue to be some combination of these more traditional instruments or some development thereof. In Chapter 3, Eirik Romstad provides some theoretical considerations concerning the effectiveness of these different policy instruments that may guide the policy maker in the choice between them. He discusses in some detail not only the static and dynamic efficiency of various instruments but also their distributional and political implications as well as transaction costs and informational aspects concerning the actual implementation and monitoring of policies.

His main conclusions point to the superiority of incentive-based mechanisms (except perhaps when firms have very similar abatement costs and/or very heterogeneous environmental costs depending on location and nonpoint source pollution).

Another important theoretical issue that touches on the basic fundamentals of neoclassical economics is the relationship between preferences and consumption. We generally assume that the preferences (and utility function) exist separately from and so to speak 'prior to' consumption. It is assumed that preferences govern our choice of consumption goods and the latter give us utility. In Chapter 4, Francesco Ferrante analyzes some consequences of modifying these assumptions to make room for the (likely) possibility that experience with some consumption goods will influence our expectations of these goods and other goods in asymmetrical ways. He provides a method for studying the formation of preferences through consumption experience. This turns out to be somewhat akin to spatial discounting – in the space of consumption goods or to putty – semiputty functions in production theory. Ferrante goes on to show that this has considerable consequences for environmental economics. In the area of contingent valuation the presence of feedbacks from consumption experience to preferences is clearly relevant for the validity and design of valuation survey instruments. This also has an effect on the optimal level of a Pigouvian tax. In the face of persistence in consumption habits, pricing might be less effective than generally presumed and this may provide arguments in favor of control and command or environmental standards in some cases. In the case of global warming and energy efficiency it has been seen by many economists as a paradox that there could exist any opportunities for increased energy, environmental and economic efficiency that are not currently exploited. This might, again, be attributed to persistence and myopia in consumption patterns due to the fact that we lack experience of consumption options that are 'far away' from those we are accustomed to. Ferrante draws the conclusion that price-based instruments will not suffice in this area.

Another common assumption in many studies concerning the relative efficiency of various policy instruments is that the various policies adopted have no effect on the geographical allocation of capital and hence production patterns. This implies that these studies might neglect the possible costs associated with capital flight caused by environmental regulation – if such flight does indeed occur. Since there is considerable anecdotal evidence of such flight – or at least of concern about and threats of capital flight – the matter is certainly worth thorough investigation. This is carried out in Chapter 5 by Tim Jeppesen, Henk Folmer and Marinus H.C. Komen who review both the theoretical and empirical literature. They start by pointing out that while a simple model might predict environmentally determined capital flight, more complex and sophisticated theoretical models give a much more complex picture with generally small and ambiguous results depending on many different parameters. The empirical studies generally confirm the latter picture, finding little evidence that environmental policies have actually provoked capital flight other than perhaps in rather special cases where there may have been some influence in industries with particularly high environmental abatement costs. The authors point out, however, that measurement and definition problems are sizeable and that in the future, with even greater mobility and perhaps tighter environmental legislation in some areas, environmentally determined capital relocation could become more important.

Another couple of issues that might complicate the choice of policy instrument are uncertainty and restricted competition. In Chapter 6, Fredrik Carlsson analyses both of these in a specific setting. Taking the perspective of the firm and concentrating on the uncertainty for the firm concerning the policy maker's actions, he analyses the outcome of environmental taxes for investments in emissions-reducing capital in the setting of an oligopoly. Ultimately the seminal work for this kind of approach is the article 'The Pigouvian Tax Rule under Monopoly', by Barnett (*American Economic Review*, **70**, p. 1037–41, 1980) showing that the optimal tax for a monopolist is lower than marginal damage costs because the monopolist has a tendency to underproduce anyway. Naturally an oligopoly is much more complex and the variety of games firms can play with each other and with the regulator is very large indeed. Thus the results will generally be ambiguous and in many cases more detailed information about the structure of the industry, technology choices and so on is needed to draw definite conclusions. One general conclusion shown by Carlsson is, however, that the effect on capital investments of increased uncertainty depends on whether capital increases or decreases flexibility. Another important conclusion is that strategic effects can be very important (depending on the character of the game). In the absence of strategic effects a higher expected environmental tax will always result in more investment in emission reduction. With strategic effects the result is ambiguous, which implies an important contrast to environmental standards the imposition of which does not create strategic effects.

The choice of policy instruments can be complicated for a number of other reasons. A good example of this is road transport externalities which are the subject of Chapter 7, by Olof Johansson-Stenman. Here we are confronted by a large number of different externalities such as congestion, local, regional and global air pollution, accidents, noise, wear and tear of roads and barrier effects. These externalities are characterized by different properties but since they are caused by the same agents it is logical to consider policy making and policy instruments in a unified context. Some of the external costs are very location- and time-specific such as congestion, local air pollution or noise while others, notably global air pollution are quite independent of these specificities. However, the latter problems are riddled by the complexity of potential free riding between nations since the atmosphere may be seen as a global common where each nation would receive only a small fraction of the benefit of its own abatement efforts. Furthermore some of the problems are characterized by severe non-convexities, one example of which is (night-time) noise where a small number of vehicles might be just as bad as a larger number (with a more even pattern of noise) leading in some cases to the optimality of complete bans on traffic for some combinations of time of day and location. Increasing returns to scale in manufacturing can also in some cases provide a rationale for the use of standards rather than the apparently first-best tax-type instruments. Rapid and unpredictable technological progress both in emission control and in monitoring costs further complicate the picture but the author uses a combination of theoretical insights and stylized facts about the orders of magnitude of various parameters to give the reader a good overview of the main problems and to argue for a mix of policy options including both standards and market-based instruments.

Chapter 8 provides yet another angle at the choice between policy instruments by analyzing the notorious double dividend debate. This single question has during the last few years come to dominate the discussion, particularly in Europe, concerning the choice of instruments. We believe this is unfortunate since there are so many other factors that affect the choice of policy instrument. In the popular debate however, the existence of a so-called 'double' dividend (decreased tax burden, increased employment, increased welfare and various other definitions) has almost become the main reason for having environmental taxes – even to the point of obscuring the obvious 'first benefit' of an improved environment! It was therefore one of the main objectives of this book not to concentrate on this issue but on the many other environmental, social and economic issues concerning environmental policy instruments. One such chapter is, however, clearly needed and Chapter 8 by Andy Park and John C.V. Pezzey does a fine job of presenting a structured overview and summary of the whole debate in a pedagogical manner. They conclude that few doubt the existence of a 'weak' double dividend which simply means that a tax scheme is more attractive if the revenues are considered than if they are ignored (the latter alternative might seem overly casual but we should remember that this is often the case in textbooks and other literature on 'Pigouvian' taxes). The contention concerns the 'strong' double dividend hypothesis which essentially says that the environmental benefits can be attained free of charge since the tax reform is desirable in itself and for other reasons (of efficiency and so on). The debate does of course become much more complex when it takes into account employment and other dynamic effects, for example. The various definitions of double dividend abound (and are nicely structured by the authors) but the essence of at least part of the debate can be summarized by saying that many tax theorists maintain that there can be no strong double dividend by definition since then the suggested tax reform would already be part of the optimal tax regime to which it is presumed we are comparing our reform. Many empiricists have, however, disregarded the notion of 'optimal' taxes and suggest that there may exist some form of 'double' dividend when comparing with actually existing (and clearly non-optimal) tax systems in various countries. Park and Pezzey add to the debate by pointing out that great care must be taken when defining what goal function we are assuming or what measure of desirability: welfare, employment or others. Also a number of specific features of the individual pollutant need to be addressed. As shown in other chapters of this book, there are a number of other considerations concerning the choice of instrument. Finally we should be careful in our choice of baseline: the relevant comparison for an environmental tax is not generally an absence of policy altogether but another policy – such as command and control standards. One of the crucial (and of course correct) criticisms of the free-lunch double dividend concept is that environmental taxes distort consumption choices which implies an excess burden. This may be motivated by overall environmental concerns but this should not obscure the fact that this adjustment of our consumption basket implies a true welfare cost to the individual. However, it should be equally obvious that environmental standards will have to cause a similar loss of individual utility (for the benefit of the common environment) if they are to be successful. Thus the comparison should not be between optimal taxes and distorting environmental taxes but between different combinations of real tax systems and various mixes of environmental policy instruments, including both standards and various types of market-based instruments.

This closes the methodological and theoretical part of this book, and opens up the empirical part. We start with two survey chapters, followed by a number of individual case studies. In Chapter 9, Maria Teresa Ribeiro, Kai Schlegelmilch and David Gee summarize their main message in the title of their contribution: 'Environmental taxes seem to be effective instruments for the environment' and this piece is in fact one of the first systematic attempts to summarize the empirical evidence to date. However, as shown in their chapter, the experience with environmental taxes is still scant, the criteria for evaluation uncertain and the methodological obstacles quite formidable. Clearly we are at the inception of a new area of study and therefore we must to some extent rely on impressions and approximations. Chapter 10 by Åke Nordlander is a highly useful complement to the previous chapter and in fact to the whole book since it summarizes neatly the actual level of energy and other environmental taxes in the Organization for Economic Cooperation and Development (OECD) countries. This kind of information is clearly vital for correct analysis. However, the chapter goes beyond the actual data and provides an insight into the legal and political forces behind these taxes and particularly focuses on harmonization within the European Union (EU). Chapter 10 also goes beyond taxes to provide some discussion of the effect of these taxes on final prices to the various categories of consumer (for instance, household and industrial). The chapter ends with a brief overview of the tax proceeds in various countries from environmental taxes. This overview shows as expected that the Nordic countries have a somewhat larger share of environmental taxes in overall tax revenue than the EC or OECD countries on average. A somewhat more surprising – and very telling – fact is that a country like Luxembourg has very high environmental tax revenues – not because of high tax rates but because of low ones! The country does thereby indeed constitute an example of the trade and environment connection sought for in Chapter 5! We should note, however, that this is a special case due to its extremely small size: the fact that German and other motorists' gasoline consumption makes a big difference in Luxembourg does of course not mean that it makes a big difference to the German economy.

As noted in the international surveys and evaluations, Sweden is one of the countries with the greatest experience of environmental taxation to date. It is therefore natural to dedicate a particular chapter to the Swedish case. This is done in Chapter 11 by Runar Brännlund and Bengt Kriström, who draw heavily on the experience of the recent Swedish Green Tax Commission. The chapter gives an overview of Swedish environmental policies in general and taxation in particular. The authors show that these taxes are 'working' in the sense that they do tend to decrease emissions, and most of them do generate revenues. Still the authors find that there appears to be little room for a 'double dividend': the fact that Sweden has a high overall tax level should not be taken to imply that reducing labor taxes as part of an eco-tax reform is necessarily going to be beneficial. The fact that general taxes are high can in fact imply the opposite: that the excess burden of additional 'distortions' (environmental taxes) is particularly high, making these more costly (in welfare terms) than expected. The role of tax exemptions is also used to illustrate the complexity of the second-best situations which inevitably govern real-World tax systems.

Tax exemptions also play an important role in the next chapter, where Peter Cramton and Suzi Kerr analyze carbon regulation and particularly the distributional effects of various policy instruments. Clearly the reduction of carbon emissions is one area where very sizeable rents are involved and hence it is no coincidence that this is a very contentious issue. Vested interests in the US can be counted on to lobby strongly in favor of the traditional American use of grandfathered permits while European firms will spend their energy on seeing to it that they get tax exemptions. Cramton and Kerr clearly see taxes as the most efficient and equitative mechanism overall but make the point that if permits are preferred then auctions can give the same allocative outcome as environmental taxes. The authors discuss various auction mechanisms, their efficiency and the distributive effects of various instruments. They show that auctions are feasible and note that permits have the advantage of allowing for trade at various levels (secondary markets within countries and inter-country trade). Permits may also easily permit partial 'buying off' of vested interests (through some limited grandfathering). Finally the chapter also dispels the notion that firms in countries where permits are grandfathered would be at a competitive advantage compared to other countries whose governments opt for taxes (or auctioned permits). Grandfathering does imply (an irrational) transfer of wealth but no lasting competitive advantage since marginal costs are not affected. In fact to achieve the same reduction in carbon emissions their marginal cost will inevitably be roughly the same, irrespective of the mechanism chosen.

If the institutional settings are different when comparing the US to Europe they are clearly much more different when we come to developing countries. Chapter 13 reviews the recent experience in Sri Lanka and the author, Paul

Steele, starts by pointing out a number of salient features that need to be taken into consideration:

* The prevalence of subsidies that are both economically and environmentally damaging which need to be remedied before we can even start to talk of any more sophisticated policies.
* Political opposition (often based on vested – and sometimes wealthy – interests but invariably presented under the heading of unacceptable consequences for the poor). In Sri Lanka as in many other societies with large rural communities, there are many poor people heavily dependent on local common property resources. Unfortunately there has been a legacy of central political interference with these resources which has had no respect for local collaboration or knowledge and hence alienated the very people it should have helped. This has earned environmental policy making and particularly natural resource management a very bad reputation.
* The revenue-raising potential of environmental taxes might make them extremely attractive to policy makers in economies where it is practically impossible to raise fiscal revenue.

The chapter then goes on to consider and describe the rather numerous steps actually taken in Sri Lanka to implement various environmental policies. Non-compliance fees have been raised, damaging subsidies and duties removed or at least diminished, user charges for water, energy, timber and so on introduced and a number of other instruments including deposit refund systems for paper, glass and mining areas as well as the use of subsidies for environmental clean-up or abatement. Various property right reforms have also been tried that are intended to reaffirm local communities' rights to manage certain common property resources such as beach fisheries. The author finishes by saying that although some progress has been made, there should be much more room for market-based instruments in environmental policies. The argument that such policies are regressive is often used and could of course in some cases be correct but often it is the urban middle class (consisting partly of civil servants who make the policies) that benefits from subsidies that are actually detrimental to the interests of those who are really poor by local standards. This is illustrated quite effectively in the last table of the chapter, which shows the relatively small percentage of the population that actually enjoys the subsidized services for water, electricity, sewage and so forth.

Chapters 14 and 15 are companion chapters in that the authors review the experience of economic instruments for environmental policy making in two neighboring countries, Kenya and Tanzania. Seen from afar these might appear similar cases and indeed some of the geographical preconditions are pretty similar. The two countries do, however, have quite different economic history with Kenya being more market oriented while Tanzania has had a more socialist orientation. This has implied that Tanzanian policy making has been more interested in distribution issues and at least in the past it has been less open to the World market. Neither of the two have much experience of environmental policy instruments and both are struggling to reform their fiscal systems and their economies in structural adjustment programs. Both rely rather heavily on distortive taxes such as import duties and have difficulty in widening their tax base. Both are predominantly rural economies but Tanzania somewhat more so than Kenya. As shown in Chapter 14, by Collins Ayoo and Mohamud Jama, Kenya has introduced some natural resource taxes on heads of cattle, forest products, sand, water, hunting and fishing. This is definitely a start although as the chapter suggests there is a long way to go before nature degradation can be dealt with adequately. There are some, but few, taxes on energy, sewage and other purely environmental hazards. In Tanzania, there appears from Chapter 15, by Godius Kahyarara, to be a somewhat more elaborate system of taxes for the energy and transport sector including vehicle, energy, fuel taxes and a road management levy. An interesting innovation when it comes to Kenya is the beach management levy earmarked for the protection and conservation of the coastal environment which means so much for Kenyan tourism.

Chapters 16–18 are likewise a block in that they analyze the use of policy instruments in formerly planned Eastern European countries. When we discuss the relative merits of 'command and control' versus 'market' instruments in the West we take for granted that even the 'market' instruments are backed by a certain amount of 'control' – at least enough to actually make people pay their fees. In fact people tend to overlook that the 'market' cannot work without a state strong enough to monitor, control and enforce regulations and contracts. The irony of many Eastern European countries is that old state institutions still have a strong control over some sectors but the main problem is perhaps that the state has not got enough power to enforce the rules of the market in many other sectors! In Chapter 16, Clifford Zinnes, Cornel Tarhoaca and Mihaela Popovici look at the role of enforcement and economic instruments in the water sector in Romania. They find that non-payment of environmental fees and so on is quite common, particularly among the companies with a large share of state ownership. Privatization will for this and other reasons (greater attention to cost minimization) imply that policy instruments become more effective. The authors also find that pollution fees are more effective than subsidies which were not found to affect investments at all. The fees are, however, still very low in Romania. Randall A. Bluffstone, in Chapter 18, also finds that enforcement of fines and fees is very variable when studying pollution charges at the firm level in Lithuania. In fact it is the very variation in these charges that makes his chapter possible since the econometric estimations would otherwise not have been possible! His results (which focus rather on air than on water emissions) show that firms are responding to environmental fees. Since both the fees and the elasticities are low, however, the results are still not too impressive. In order to achieve 25 percent reductions the charges would have to be raised in the order of 50-100 percent.

In Chapter 17, the authors begin by reminding the reader how policies that looked like environmental taxes were actually popular under the planned economy. The only snag was that with soft-budget constraints, the fees did not really have much effect on allocative decisions in the firm. The main purpose seems to have been the collection of funds for environmental protection and this is still an important feature of many Eastern European systems. The chapter gives an overview of the experiences with environmental charges on tires, batteries and air emissions. As in the earlier chapters on formerly planned and developing country economies, experience shows that monitoring and enforcement is crucial to the success of any of these policies. At present, enthusiasm appears to be leading policy makers to adopt more measures than they can effectively control, which may well be counterproductive.

Chapters 19–21 are again companion chapters in that they all deal with waste management. The study of several different countries helps underline the rather obvious point that a number of country-specific characteristics are very important for the design of policy instruments and as pointed out in Chapter 19 on Israel, by Ofira Ayalon, Yoram Avnimelech and Mordechai Shechter, there cannot be one single correct policy option for all countries. Municipal solid waste in Israel contains more organic waste and less paper than in other OECD countries and hence the authors of this study find that both mandatory recycling and bans on landfilling are counterproductive. They recommend an integrated approach to waste management and show that 'pay-per-bag' schemes are likely to be the preferred policy instrument to persuade households to sort (and compost) their waste. Chapter 20, by Thomas Sterner, is on waste management and recycling in Sweden and again it is indicated that recycling is not always optimal. Society must be clear over why recycling is to be promoted and what types of waste should be recycled. The main argument is that the toxicity of the waste is much more important than the value (which is often negligible or negative – almost by definition). When society has decided to recycle it needs to consider which policy instruments to use. Chapter 20 shows that economic incentives, such as deposits, can be one important instrument but that information as well as ease and comfort of collection are just as important. Chapter 21, by Dominic

Hogg, studies the effectiveness of the UK landfill tax which, being a tax only on waste that is actually deposited in a landfill, brings out some of the problems of designing single (and simple) instruments for complex problems. The risk is clearly that other forms of waste disposal may be encouraged that could be just as bad as, or worse than, landfilling. Examples might include (illicit – or other) incineration, dumping and so forth. Other problems related to the landfill tax concern the funding of waste management at the local level. Furthermore, the authors observe considerable differences in performance between best and worst practice but this may partly be due to the fact that the policy is new and there has not yet been sufficient time to see its full effects.

Finally, Chapter 22, by Rui Santos, Paula Antunes and Sandra Martinho, looks at market-based instruments in Portugal and particularly the sulfur (S) and lead (Pb) content of fuels on the one hand and volatile organic compounds (VOCs) on the other. Public policy has aimed at promoting cleaner fuels by lower tax levels on cleaner fuels (with lower S and Pb content) but the tax differentials appear to have been rather small so that they were dwarfed by differences in cost (or profit margin!). Hence the final consumer prices were still more expensive for the cleaner fuel. In spite of this there has been some increase in the use of the latter but naturally it is not too easy to judge how much of this is due to the policy followed. When it comes to VOCs, this is a European priority, and a case study was undertaken to study its effects in a number of Portuguese industries: ink, printing, pharmaceutical and paint. Naturally, price sensitivities vary considerably but on the whole the proposed VOC tax is expected to be quite effective. The authors emphasize, however, that instrument design with respect to local conditions (such as imperfect market structures, other instruments, technology and so on) will be crucial for the ultimate success of the policy.

The chapters of this book have been selected to give a feeling for both the theoretical and empirical flavor of our subject. The first seven chapters concentrated mainly on various theoretical concepts although several of them did contain some overview of empirical evidence. The remaining 15 chapters have given a large number of applications taken from various areas. Some of them covered wealthy industrialized countries while others focussed on formerly planned or developing countries. Some focussed on waste management while others gave an overview of a country's policy or compared the outcomes of numerous different policies. A couple of chapters were directly comparative in their layout, others were not but the purpose has all the time been comparative. Since environmental policies and the realities they address are complex issues, it is often hard to disentangle which results really depend on the policy and what would have happened anyway (in its absence). This is the reason why comparisons can be particularly helpful. It is our belief that there are many lessons to be learned that may carry over from one policy area or country to another and that it is not necessarily the most obvious comparisons that are the most useful. Sometimes policy making in one area in country A may have more to learn from policy experiences in a completely different field in country B: in spite of the apparent differences between, say, fisheries in Australia and leaded gasoline in the US, both cases involved with some form of tradable emission permit. Similarly a policy that works in one application in one country is not necessarily suitable in another one. Refineries, steel plants and cement factories might be regulated by market-based instruments like tradable permits in a large country but in a smaller one, heavy industries of this type often enjoy substantial market power or are monopolies which may make that instrument unsuitable. The same instrument might still, however, be suitable for another application. The variety of instruments is much larger than generally realized and the number of circumstances in which they are to operate is, of course, enormous. The criteria by which they are to be judged are complex and all this makes the choice, design and evaluation of policy instruments into a large new area of which we are still just discerning the first outlines.

2. Disclosure Strategies for Pollution Control

Tom Tietenberg*

1. THE DEMAND FOR DISCLOSURE STRATEGIES

The first phase of pollution control involved applying traditional legal remedies such as emission standards. Over time, however, it became clear that these traditional regulatory approaches to pollution control were excessively costly in some circumstances (Tietenberg 1985) and incapable of achieving the stipulated goals in others (Tietenberg 1995). In response to these deficiencies, in the second phase the use of market-based approaches such as tradable permits, emission charges, deposit refunds and performance bonds have become much more common (Hahn 1989; OECD 1989, 1994, 1995; Tietenberg 1990). In some instances they have substituted for traditional remedies, but in most cases they have complemented them. In general these approaches have added both flexibility and improved cost-effectiveness to pollution-control policy.

Even the addition of market-based approaches has not, however, fully solved the problems. In the industrialized countries the system remains over-burdened by the sheer number of substances to be controlled. Neither staffs nor budgets are adequate for the task of regulating all of the potentially harmful substances which are emitted by firms and households.

In many of the developing countries the regulatory infrastructure is insufficiently developed and/or subject to corruption. In either case it is incapable of adequately handling the burden of designing, implementing, monitoring and enforcing an effective pollution-control system.

Phase three in the evolution of pollution-control policy involves investment in the provision of information. This increasing role for disclosure strategies seems to emanate not only from the increasing perceived need for more regulatory tools (as described above), but also from the falling cost of

* An earlier version of this chapter was first presented at the Eighth Annual Conference of the European Association of Environmental and Resource Economists at Tilburg University, The Netherlands, June 26–28, 1997.

information collection, aggregation and dissemination. Rising benefits and falling costs imply that however inefficient their use may have been perceived to be in the past, changed circumstances merit another look.

The disclosure strategies considered in this chapter involve public and/or private attempts to increase the availability of information on pollution to workers, consumers, shareholders and the public at large. Provision of greater information may either complement or replace traditional regulation strategies. Disclosure strategies seek to enlist market forces in the quest for efficient pollution control. And in so doing they interact in sometimes complex ways with traditional standard setting and enforcement strategies. Whether they complement phase one and two strategies or substitute for them, they involve a rather different role for government – one which seems to offer the possibility of fulfilling the large and growing need for control despite limited budgets and staffs. But how real is this promise?

2. THE CONCEPTUAL FOUNDATION FOR DISCLOSURE STRATEGIES

The starting point for thinking about information approaches to pollution control is the Coase Theorem (Coase 1960). In that landmark essay, Coase pointed out that pollution-control situations have a certain symmetry. Inefficient pollution imposes costs on victims which exceed the costs of controlling that pollution. In other words the marginal benefits of pollution control exceed the marginal costs. The existence of inefficient pollution damage therefore provides a motivation for the victims to take corrective action even in the absence of any such incentives by the polluters.

What economists have learned rather recently is that the list of victims can be very large indeed, much larger than originally thought. The list of potential victims includes not only the traditional categories of those harmed directly by the pollution, but also those who may be disturbed by it even if they are not directly affected. The fact that this 'nonuse' value of pollution control can be quite large has become a familiar result to those conducting contingent value surveys. The pressure to control pollution therefore can arise from victims experiencing both use and nonuse damages.

One standard precondition for decentralized processes to work efficiently is for the decision makers to have full information. In the case of victims taking action to control pollution, this precondition is not likely to be met.

Information about environmental risks is asymmetrically distributed. In a typical case the best knowledge about emission profiles is held by the polluters, not the victims. Furthermore, the polluters are unlikely to share the information with victims in the absence of outside pressure to do so.

Even if information on emissions is provided, this may not be sufficient for victims to understand the severity of the risk they face. Such understanding can only occur when knowledge of emission levels is combined with information on exposure and on the exposure/risk relationship.

In the past the Coasian insight has been dismissed as a foundation for policy[1] for two reasons.

- In multiple-victim circumstances it ignores the public good nature of information. When coupled with the very real transaction costs associated with the collection and dissemination of information, this characteristic tends to undermine the incentive of any individual to derive and to share information on the nature and extent of pollution damage with the other victims.
- The approach appears to force the victim to pay for controlling pollution damage which he/she did not cause, an outcome which violates the well-established 'polluter pays' principle of pollution control.

Since, as discussed below, both of these flaws turn out to be remediable, the traditional lack of interest in these approaches may have been misplaced.

2.1 Overview

While disclosure strategies (particularly labeling) have become common in natural resource settings (organic agriculture and forest certification programs, for example), they are less familiar in a pollution-control context. Yet the number of applications in this new arena is increasing in both OECD and developing countries.

Generally these disclosure strategies are justified on ethical grounds. Victims were seen as having the right to know the environmental risks to which they were exposed. In this chapter we explore quite a different justification – whether providing greater information might be part of a larger strategy to promote efficient pollution control.

This chapter will review what we know and do not know about the use of disclosure strategies to control pollution. It is important to note that this review will not cover two related fields. First, we shall not examine the rather large literature on the relationship between regulator and polluter when the stakeholders have private information (Lewis 1996). Second, we shall not examine the literature on the role of strategies (for example, auditing) for increasing the amount of information available to the firm itself (Sinclair-

[1] I was one of those who was quick to dismiss it. See Tietenberg (1992).

Desgagné and Gabel 1997). Our focus is rather on information made available to consumers, workers, shareholders and the public at large.

Following a review of the conceptual foundations for disclosure strategies, the chapter will consider how the policy setting influences the type of information strategy employed. Examples of innovative disclosure strategies (US, Latin America, Indonesia and so on) and the channels through which they operate will be followed by a review of the empirical research on their effectiveness. The chapter will close with the author's sense of what we have learned and where further research would be particularly helpful.

2.2 The Context

Tailoring disclosure strategies to the specific context requires an understanding of the various types of situations that can arise and the policy-relevant characteristics which differentiate them. For the purposes of this study we shall consider two broad pollution types (product pollution and process pollution) and four specific settings (the household setting, the consumption setting, the employment setting, and the community setting).

Pollution can arise either from the consumption or use of products ('product' pollution) or the production of those products ('process' pollution). Examples of the former include the consumption of foods contaminated with pesticides, the use of aerosol sprays with ozone-depleting chemicals, driving automobiles, heating homes with polluting fuels and so on. Examples of the latter include water pollution from pulp and paper mills, air pollution from steel mills, hazardous waste pollution from chemical plants, radiation from nuclear power plants and so on.

The point of departure for disclosure strategies is understanding the economic incentives which face the relevant parties. Do the parties to an environmental pollution situation have incentives to take actions to control pollution? Are these incentives compatible with an efficient outcome or do the incentives create a bias toward too little or too much control?

Analyzing the answers to these questions begins with isolating the role of information in this process. In the absence of government intervention will the efficient amount of information be generated? Or will the amount of information supplied normally be inefficiently large or small? Will it normally be made available to victims?

Given the answers to the above questions what possible role for government is involved? Does this role complement or substitute for traditional regulation?

2.3 The Household Setting

Indoor pollutants, though increasingly recognized as significant contributors to human health problems, have not traditionally been addressed by conventional regulation. Two classic examples of dangerous indoor pollutants are radon gas[2] and lead paint.[3]

Do homeowners have an incentive to control these forms of pollution? Assuming they have full information, homeowners have three major possible responses when confronted with the possible risk of radon or lead contamination. They can decide not to control; they can undertake some control, or they can attempt to solve the problem by selling the house to someone else.

For the first two choices, homeowner incentives are compatible with efficiency. Because those who would bear the damage and those who would pay for the control are in the same household, theory would lead us to expect an efficient balancing of the benefits and the costs. Control would be undertaken until the marginal cost of additional control equaled the value of the marginal damage reduced by the expenditure.

The third choice, however, opens the possibility of an inefficiency. The cheapest solution may well be selling the home to an unsuspecting buyer, thereby passing any control costs on to them. This is a clear externality; what is cheapest for the homeowner is not cheapest for society as a whole.

How about the incentives for households to invest in information? Information on radon or lead has one of the characteristics of a public good – indivisibility. Information shared with one party does not diminish the stock of information available to be shared many other parties. Information about radon or lead, however, does not automatically have the second characteristic of a public good – nonexclusivity. The establishment of exclusive rights could be possible, at least in principle.

What does this suggest about the role for government? For the externality case it seems necessary to assure that only full information transfers of property take place. It would be expected that an informed buyer would reduce the offer price by an amount which reflects the cost of controlling the radon or lead. Linking the selling price to the pollution situation by full

---

[2] The Environmental Protection Agency (EPA) has estimated that between 5,000 and 20,000 lung cancer deaths per year in the United States can be attributed to exposure to radon gas. This colorless, odorless gas (a product of natural radioactive decay) tends to enter homes from the ground or through the water supply.

[3] The USEPA has also estimated that more than 1.7 million American children under the age of six have unsafe blood-lead levels, making lead poisoning a significant environmental health hazard for young children. Most of those children are poisoned by deteriorated lead-based paint and the contaminated soil and dust it generates. Children with too much lead in their bodies can experience lowered IQ, reading and learning disabilities, impaired hearing and other problems. More than 80 percent of the US housing stock built before 1978 – some 64 million residences – is estimated to contain lead paint.

disclosure would restore efficient incentives and offer the seller a choice – controlling the pollution (and raising the price) or accepting a lower selling price.

In fact, current policy in the US corresponds closely to this recommendation. As of December 6, 1996, all home buyers and tenants have the right to know about potential lead-based paint hazards before they buy or rent older housing under a program jointly sponsored by the US Environmental Protection Agency and the US Department of Housing and Urban Development. Prospective tenants or buyers of pre-1978 residential dwellings – including single-family-home owners – can ask for and receive information on known lead-based paint and lead-based paint hazards before purchasing or renting.[4]

With respect to the provision of public information, the US government has historically provided one type of information, leaving the provision of the other type to the market. Specifically the government has conducted the basic research to discover appropriate risk thresholds for lead and radon[5] and has widely disseminated this information. It has also made sure that low-cost test kits are available. It is now up to the market to supply the test kits at a reasonable price and up to the households to decide what they should do with the results.

This is a very different policy than would be implied by traditional regulation. The regulatory solution would involve the definition of a standard which would then have to be applied, with appropriate monitoring and enforcement, to every 'at risk' household. Even if physically possible, which is doubtful, this approach would not normally be expected to produce efficient outcomes. The homeowner would not generally be free to balance the benefits and costs of remediation.

2.4 The Product Setting

Consider now a situation of product pollution in which the pollution is inflicted directly on consumers of that product. Examples might include fruit or vegetables with residues of pesticides, heating systems that leak harmful gases, carpets or dry cleaning which emit toxic fumes left over from the manufacturing or cleaning process, and so on.

---

[4] In the case of sales transactions, home buyers can also request up to ten-days to conduct a lead-based paint risk assessment or inspection at their own expense prior to finalizing a sales contract. The new requirements apply to sales and rentals of residences built before 1978, the year the sale of residential lead-based paint was banned. Specific notification and right-to-know language must be included in the contract or lease, along with signed statements from all parties verifying that the requirements have been met.

[5] For the analysis behind the radon standard, see Marcinowski and Napolitano (1993).

Here we have a case when the polluter and the pollutee are different. Yet the apparent conclusion that an externality is present is not necessarily valid.

Since consumers and producers are linked by the purchase decision, pollution inflicted on consumers is not necessarily an externality. Consumers who are aware of products which are exposing them to an environmental risk will either not purchase the risky product (if, for example, an acceptable substitute which poses no environmental risk is available) or will purchase the product only if the price is lowered to reflect either the damage caused or the costs of preventing or mitigating the damage. In any of these cases the producer has an incentive to be concerned about the pollution and to balance the potential loss of sales against the costs of eliminating or mitigating the problem.

Will the market supply the proper amount of information about the risk to assure that consumers are fully informed? Not necessarily. Since producers have something to lose by providing this information (a loss of sales or lower prices), they will provide it only if prodded by some outside force.[6] Consumers normally do not have an incentive to derive the information since their *individual* gains are so small (even when *societal* gains are large) in comparison to the costs of the testing program which would be necessary to uncover the cases where a problem existed.[7] Hence even in cases where the costs of assuring informed consumers can be justified on efficiency grounds, private incentives will not necessarily produce that outcome.

What is the implied role for government? If the environmental risk is so large that rational consumers would not purchase the product, the government typically bans the product. A common case, however, arises when the environmental risk exceeds the benefits of the product for some consumers, but not for others. One obvious answer here is for the market to provide products posing various levels of environmental risks, leaving the market to sort out the market share going to each type of product. As long as the products are produced by several producers, the competitive process will normally supply the requisite information by means of labeling. Vegetable producers who use no pesticides will label their produce as 'organic', thereby affording consumers the opportunity to make an informed choice. In general, produce labeled as organic has been able to command a price premium for the lower environmental risk it poses.

---

[6] In principle one such outside force could be liability law. If producersare held liable for the pollution damages caused by their products, they would have an incentive to balance the expected liability costs against the costs of controlling the pollution. In practice, however, this channel does not work very well. For a detailed assessment of why not, see Dewees (1992).

[7] Another interesting possibility would be for a competitor to supply the information, thereby diverting sales to his/her own product. One example of this involves milk. Distributors who have specifically prohibited their suppliers from milking cows injected with growth hormone advertise the absence of this hormone in their milk, thereby assigning significance to the silence of their competitors.

Governments also have a role in assuring the reliability of provided information. While producers of energy-efficient appliances, for example, have an incentive to communicate the efficiency of their products, less-efficient competitors have an incentive to make the same (but in this case incorrect) claim if they can get away with it. Here the government may have a role in standardizing the information provided and sanctioning those who disclose deceitful information.

A different sort of information is needed when the pollution arises from the use of the product. For example, pesticides are clearly toxic by design, not default. As long as the use of pesticides makes sense, banning them simply because they are toxic is not practical. The key to government policy in this case is recognizing that how the pesticides are applied can influence the likelihood and severity of damage caused. In response, government policy typically mandates labels which explain in detail 'proper' (damage-minimizing) application procedures. Application of especially risky pesticides may be limited to licensed applicators who are required to undergo special training.[8] Disclosure strategies in the consumption setting share with those in the household setting the characteristic that they provide an alternative to traditional regulation. In some cases, disclosure strategies can substitute for traditional regulation (as when private labeling produces informed consumers) and in some cases can complement traditional regulation (as when pesticides posing an unacceptable risk are banned, but the others are controlled by requiring precautionary labels or licensed applicators).

2.5 The Occupational Setting

Whereas the consumption setting involves one relationship where pollutees can put pressure on polluters to control their pollution, the employment setting provides quite a different opportunity. Occupational environmental risks are jointly controlled by employees and employers. While employers typically control the overall production process, which includes decisions about the toxicity of the substances employees face, employees control the amount of precaution they exercise in working with those substances.

What incentives do fully informed employers and employees have with respect to controlling those risks? Are those incentives likely to be compatible with efficiency? Consider first the incentives of the employee. To

---

[8] This strategy will not be sufficient if the risky chemicals are readily available to nonlicensed applicators. In the US the state of Mississippi had to evacuate a record 281 households in response to the spraying of methyl parathion, a toxic farm pesticide, in hundreds of Gulf Coast homes and businesses. Five day-care centers, a motel and a restaurant have also been closed. Two men face charges of spraying commercial pesticides without a license (*Greenwire*, 11/18/96).

the extent that they bear both the cost of taking precautions and the expected damage from the environmental risk, employees will maximize their welfare by taking all cost-justified precautions to reduce risk and seeking wage increases to compensate for the remaining risk.[9]

The employer faces a choice of how much to invest in risk reduction. Since fully informed employees will demand compensation for any remaining environmental risk, the employer must balance the cost of increased wages with the cost of reducing the risk which gives rise to those increased wages. Through the wage mechanism, the employer is induced to balance the cost of risk reduction with the benefits to the worker, a balancing which is compatible with an efficient outcome.

All of this, however, depends on fully informed workers. Will normal market processes guarantee the efficient generation and sharing of occupational risk information?

The answer seems to depend on the nature of the employment situation. Individual employees are unlikely to be willing to bear the cost of acquiring the information about the risk since their individual benefits are likely to pale in the face of their individual costs. When employees band together, however, as in labor unions, providing that information becomes possible. In this case the collective benefits may be sufficient to justify the collective costs.[10]

How about employers? In general if employers do not pay the damages suffered by employees, they do not have an incentive to assure that employees are fully informed about the occupational risks. Fully informed workers are likely to demand higher wages; workers who are ignorant of the risks they face are not.

What role does this suggest for the government? It suggests a limited, but growing role at least in the United States. Since unionization seems to be a key in producing fully informed workers, the fact that unionization is on the decline in the US implies a growing need for other sources of information. The original thrust of US government policy (in 1970) was strictly regulatory. The government promulgated thousands of very detailed standards, which in many cases prescribed the specific action to be undertaken by the employer. Empirical analysis performed up to the mid-1970s clearly indicated that this approach was ineffective (Viscusi 1992, pp. 181–205). In response to that lack of success, major reforms were proposed

[9] Not all occupational risk situations, however, fit this description. In some cases the cost of taking precautions may be borne by the employer (as when special equipment is involved). In others the damage may be borne by other workers insteadof, or in addition to, the worker who controls the risk. In either case no presumption of efficient behavior would be forthcoming.

[10] Unions would be expected to produce more efficient information flows since they represent many workers and can take advantage of economies of scale in the collection, interpretation, and dissemination of information. Available evidence suggests that the preponderance of wage premia for risk are found for unionized workers. See Viscusi (1983).

during the Carter and Reagan administrations. The evidence on that period is more mixed. While some statistically significant effects of the Occupational Safety and Health Act (OSHA) on worker safety were derived from this period, these effects were neither dramatic in terms of the magnitude nor robust across different measures of risk (Viscusi 1992, pp. 206–22).

Risk communication became an important element of the policy in 1983 when the 'Hazard Communication Standard' was introduced. This policy established uniform hazard communication requirements for manufacturers. Each employee who is, or may be, exposed to hazardous chemicals in the workplace must receive information and training tailored to the nature of the risk. The act prescribes three different types of risk communication instruments: container labels, material safety data sheets (MSDS)[11] and training sessions. In this case risk communication is designed to complement, rather than substitute for, other policies.

2.6 The Community Setting

From an economic point of view the most difficult setting to incorporate disclosure strategies involves situations where the polluter and pollutee have no obvious contractual relationship. Whereas disclosure strategies could build upon the purchase relationship for consumption-related pollution, and the wage relationship for employment-related pollution, no such behavioral linkage exists in this final category.

In addition to the public good characteristics of information provision which plague the other types of pollution problems, in this case another source of market failure arises. To the extent that the failure to provide the requisite information increases the amount of pollution, the damage caused is another form of externality (Kennedy, et al. 1994). It represents the purest case of externality. Examples would involve ambient air and water pollution.

In this case the pollutees still have some incentive to take action to reduce the environmental risk to which they are exposed, but the action has to be indirect. This case raises some fundamental problems about how the information would be generated, distributed and used.

[11] MSDS are required of all chemical manufacturers and importers. Employers using such substances must obtain the relevant sheets from their suppliers and make them available to employees. These sheets contain information on the characteristics of the substance, proper handling procedures and emergency and first-aid procedures.

3. DISCLOSURE STRATEGIES FOR THE COMMUNITY SETTING

The typical information strategy involves four separate functions: (i) establishing mechanisms for discovering environmental risks, (ii) assuring the reliability of the information, (iii) publicizing or sharing the information, and (iv) acting on the information.

3.1 Detecting Environmental Risks

The necessary first step in an information approach is discovering the extent and magnitude of environmental risks. Environmental risks will normally be detected only after some investment in information is made. Who should make that investment? What incentives do they face?

The degree of environmental risk faced by a community is determined by a somewhat complex causation process. How much of the substances are emitted, the degree of exposure to the substances, and the sensitivity of the population to this exposure are all highly relevant considerations. Full information about those risks requires knowledge about all of the links in that process, but notice that the types of information involved are quite different. Some of the information is general – it applies to the population at large – while other information is specific to the polluter. General risk information might include, for example, dose–response relationships for substances and how these relationships can be used to define a socially acceptable level of risk. This information is useful for all citizens who may be exposed to the chemicals.

Polluters themselves are an obvious source of the firm-specific components of the risk. They have the best access to information about the substances they are using, the processes which rely upon those substances and the exposure of third parties to those substances, but they normally do not have the proper incentives to detect or to reveal these risks in the absence of the threat of liability or some other outside force.

The government may be in the best position to identify the general elements of the risk. These elements are of interest to the largest number of citizens. Collecting this information once by a central body eliminates the duplication of effort which would result if every firm had to derive this information independently on its own.

The polluters are not the only possible source of firm-specific information. In the US, for example, an alternative approach to monitoring places some responsibility for monitoring on private enforcers. The US system of 'riverkeepers' provides an example of how this might work. Typically hired by associations of citizens who live along the river, these riverkeepers constantly oversee, usually with the help of a large number of volunteers, a network of monitoring stations. These associations are funded by voluntary dues from the members.

3.2 Assuring Reliable Information

Information has both a quantity and quality dimension. Effective risk communication assumes not only that the requisite information is forthcoming, but also that it is reliable. Inaccurate or partial information could be worse than no information at all to the extent that it promotes either a false sense of security or unjustified fears. And firms have incentives to mislead the public either by overstating their environmental accomplishments or by selective omission (noting the positive outcomes and ignoring or burying the negative ones).

Accurate information can be promoted by standardizing the method of collection (specifying acceptable collection instruments and procedures, for example, as well as the nature of the information to be gathered) and by making the penalties for falsifying information appropriately large.[12] The ISO 14,000 process, a set of voluntary environmental management standards crafted by the International Standards Organization, represents one international attempt to standardize the requirements for certification of good environmental practice.

When allegations of a potentially actionable environmental risk are raised from the community, a process must be established to verify and validate the claim. Lodging a complaint does not assure its validity. The organization which receives the complaint may be the control authority, a court, or perhaps a special commission set up for the specific purpose of dealing with these claims. Its function is to determine whether the claim is valid by establishing whether the party bringing the claim has met the required burden of proof.

3.3 Disseminating the Information

For a disclosure strategy to work, the necessary information must reach the pollutees in a usable form. This step may be automatically satisfied by information raised by the community itself, but for information produced by the government or the polluter it is not. Transparency is the key to assuring the availability of useful information.[13] In practice this means that the

[12] This may be one area where criminal penalties may be justified. See Segerson and Tietenberg (1992).

[13] In the United States the Center for Environmental Information and Statistics became operational and open to the public early in 1998. The Center provides easy access for the public to the EPA's massive environmental information resources through computers and other means.

information must be in a form which can be used by the community and the community must have access to it.[14]

Information disclosure can be either voluntary or mandatory. With respect to the products from organic farms, for example, the tradition has been to let those farms providing the 'green' product identify themselves, subject to certification procedures. No requirements are placed on conventional farms to list the pesticides used and the amounts. This is a voluntary system. On the other hand most community-right-to-know approaches (such as the Toxic Release Inventory described below) require all firms to provide emission information.[15]

With respect to complaints against public officials, the necessary information will be available to private enforcers only if the relevant decision processes are sufficiently open to public scrutiny. For example, community leaders may wish to assure that environmental impact assessments filed by developers in preparation for project construction comply with procedural requirements and are truthful. Timely access to the assessments is especially important to prevent the process from proceeding too far before its consequences become clear. Nearly completed projects are more difficult to enjoin. In practice, timely access may be the exception rather than the rule.[16]

With respect to complaints against polluters, at least some degree of monitoring the activities of the polluter is a prerequisite for a claim to be initiated. In most cases this monitoring is done by the regulated entity itself. Transparency is assured when the mandated periodic reports submitted to the public enforcer are also accessible to the public. When publicly available,

[14] The Sector Facility Indexing Project (SFIP) initiated by the USEPA is a community-right-to-know and data integration pilot project that provides environmental performance data for facilities within five industrial sectors: automobile assembly, petroleum refining, pulp mills, iron and steel and primary nonferrous metal production (aluminum, copper, lead and zinc). The ultimate goal of the SFIP is to publish information regarding each profiled facility, and provide a publicly accessible database of current information which would allow for customized data searches (62 Federal Register 19573).

[15] The mandatory versus voluntary dimension is becoming an important issue in a US proposal to provide pollution information on electric utilities as part of the deregulation process. This proposal would attempt to provide consumers with information on the emission profiles of each of the utilities from which they would be able to secure power, thereby enabling them to choose on environmental as well as economic grounds. An unresolved issue is whether it would be sufficient to let the 'green' utilities identify themselves or to require all utilities to disclose their emission profiles.

[16] In commenting on the Mexican system, Alanis-Ortega (1995, p. 9) states 'While government bodies may let you consult a document, obtaining a copy is generally more difficult. Not all offices have copy machines and most often it is prohibited to take a document out of the government office to make copies. Another limiting factor is that many government offices in Mexico do not have an organized document system, a place to store their documents that is readily available to the public or to the staff, to manage and organize such information. At times documents are not even available to the very government officials that are legally responsible for the information'.

they can be used by private enforcers as the basis for raising noncompliance claims.[17]

3.4 Acting on the Information

Once the information is generated about an environmental risk, the next step is to define what can be done with it. The options range from letting the information generate its own pressure through preexisting channels to establishing new channels for pressure to be applied.

Existing channels can be used in many different ways.

- In the product market, consumers may choose less environmentally harmful products when effective information makes the choices clear. In addition to the obvious case where consumers may be directly harmed by the product (such as pesticides) this channel can also be used by consumers who choose to buy 'green' products even if they are not directly harmed by the pollution (such as those who pay more for chlorine-free paper). Product market effects are enhanced when disproportionately large buyers (large chains or the government, for example) decide to take environmental considerations into account in their purchasing decisions.
- In the capital market, owners of shares of common stock in polluting firms may decide to invest in companies with a 'greener' record either for moral reasons or because they believe that ultimately environmentally benign firms will face fewer clean up-costs and therefore will be more competitive. Some evidence suggests that 'green' firms may have higher rates of return.[18] The ability of green investors to make these choices has been facilitated by the rise of several 'green' mutual funds where the investment advisors carefully screen the firms using well-defined criteria. In the Netherlands the government subsidizes green funds by exempting their income from taxation.
- In the labor market, environmentally responsible employers may find it easier to hire employees, and to retain employee loyalty. These situations could result either because employees perceive that environmentally responsible employers are likely to be more financially stable over the long run or because they have a moral preference for the types of activities they support with their labor.

---

[17] For an analysis of the consequences of various rules for making regulatory information available to private enforcers, see Che and Earnhart (1997).

[18] A study conducted by RichardClough of Duke University indicated that portfolios invested in 'environmental responsible' companies generally return one to three percentage points more annually than the holdings of 'irresponsible' companies (*Investor's Business Daily*, 5/27/97).

- In the legislature when existing legislation seems inadequate, the information may build community support for additional legislation.[19]
- In the judicial system, parties directly harmed by the pollution seek redress through a variety of different channels.
- Victims can recover compensatory damages by suing polluters (called 'tort law' actions).
- In addition, judicial 'oversight' actions can be brought against public enforcement authorities which are not fulfilling their statutory responsibilities.[20] Furthermore the results of these judicial actions can also be made available to the public.
- Following the United Nations Conference on the Human Environment at Stockholm in 1972, many countries incorporated environmental considerations in their constitutions. These constitutional principles were in general related to the following basic ideas: the State and all its citizens are responsible for environmental protection; all humans have the right to a healthy environment; the State and all citizens must foster development that is environmentally appropriate. Some constitutions, such as those in Colombia, Ecuador and Chile, contain the right of people to live in an unpolluted environment. As a result of these constitutional provisions the right to a clean and safe environment has become a fundamental right for each individual, enforceable through judicial action.
- The public can be given certain enforcement powers. Private enforcement actions differ from more conventional liability actions in that in private enforcement the initiator of the action is not seeking compensation for pollution-related damages. Rather, the private enforcer is seeking to bring a noncomplying polluter into compliance or to prevent pollution which is perceived as violating individual rights to a clean environment. Private enforcement actions can either be direct, where the private enforcer is empowered to bring claims before the judiciary on its own behalf (called 'citizen suits') or indirect, where the enforcer is only allowed to file complaints with a designated legal authority (called 'complaint actions').[21]

---

[19] Hamilton (1997), for example found that US legislators were more likely to vote for disclosure strategies when they had a large number of Superfund sites in their district.
[20] In January, 1997, France's largest water distribution company,Lyonnaise des Eaux, filed an 'unprecedented' lawsuit against the French government for failure to meet European Union directives regulating permissible nitrate levels in one of the country's rivers.Lyonnaise had been fined after Brittany residents sued the firm for supplying water that contained high nitrate concentrations. The company seeks $900,000 in compensation for damage to its reputation and for the cost of maintaining a special water-treatment plant to meet the standards (Andrew Jack, *Financial Times*, 1/24/97).
[21] Private enforcement mechanisms are currently being actively used in both the United States and Europe to enforce environmental standards as well as in Latin America(Tietenberg 1996). In the US, some 14 statutes authorize citizen suits and some thousands of claims have been

4. SELECTED FUNCTIONING PROGRAMS

How these principles can be put into practice can be illustrated by reference to a small number of representative programs.

4.1 The Toxic Release Inventory Program

The Toxic Release Inventory (TRI) was enacted by the US Congress in January, 1986 as a part of the Environmental Protection and Community Right to Know Act (EPCRA). It is designed to provide information to the public on releases of toxic substances into the environment. Most of the substances involved are not themselves subject to release standards.

TRI states that firms who use 10,000 pounds or more of a listed chemical in a given calendar year, or firms who import, process or manufacture 25,000 pounds or more of a listed chemical must file a report on each of the chemicals in existence within the plant if they also have ten or more fulltime employees.

Reporting of emissions or use of listed chemicals is accomplished annually. The reports include such information as the name of the company, name of the parent company if it exists, toxic release and frequency of release as well as the medium in which the chemical is released.[22] The information is available to the public. Firms must also separately report emissions to their state and local authorities as well as to fire and emergency officials.

Has it resulted in reduced releases of toxic emissions into the environment? Apparently it has. According to official EPA data total releases are down by a bit over 44 percent (Table 2.1).

---

initiated (Naysnerski and Tietenberg 1992 a&b) According to Sand (1991), in Europe the number of public and private environmental complaints filed rose from about ten in 1982 to 460 in 1989. More than half of these have been filed by private individuals or organizations.

[22] Polluters must also report the scientific as well as the common name for the chemical being addressed by that form and give the amount a rating. The ratings go as follows; immediate (acute) health hazard, delayed (chronic) health hazard, fire hazard, sudden release of pressure hazard, and reactive hazard (40 C.F.R. § 370.2).

Table 2.1. Total releases

	1988	1992	1993	1994	1988–94 Change	
	(Number)	(Number)	(Number)	(Number)	(Number)	(Percent)
Total Facilities	21,046	22,593	21,938	21,336	+ 290	1.38
Total forms	66,571	70,238	68,567	66,777	+ 206	0.31
	(Million pounds)	(Million pounds)	(Million pounds)	(Million pounds)	(Million pounds)	(Percent)
Total air emissions	2,253	1,560	1,385	1,341	-912	-40.48
Surface water	177	196	203	47	-130	-73.40
Underground injection	622	366	295	307	-319	-51.01
On-site land releases	480	328	274	282	-198	-41.25

Source: The 1994 TRI Data Release report (EPA publication 745-R-96-002) available on-line at http://www.epa.gov/opptintr/tri/ttintro.htm

4.2 The 33/50 Program

To complement and reinforce the TRI Program the EPA initiated the 33/50 Program in February, 1991. This program set national goals of 33 percent reduction in 17 priority toxic chemicals by 1992 and 50 percent reduction by 1995. These reductions were to be achieved voluntarily by program participants,[23] and compliance with the guidelines was to be measured using the TRI reports. The program emphasizes pollution prevention rather than end-of-pipe control.

The initial invitation list, which contained the names of 555 companies with substantial chemical releases, was subsequently expanded to 5,000. Some 1,300 corporations ultimately signed up to participate in the 33/50 Program. Participants collectively reduced their emissions by more than 50 percent, a total of 757 million pounds of pollutants, by 1994 – a year ahead of schedule.

[23] Aside from good publicity, there seems to be little evidence of any other *quid pro quo* for participation. Apparently participants, for example, faced no diminished enforcement pressure from their participation. See Arora and Cason (1996).

4.3 Proposition 65

Proposition 65 was established in the state of California by popular vote in November of 1986 after the inception of the Toxic Release Inventory by the EPA. Prop 65 requires companies producing, using, or transporting one or more of the 480 listed chemicals to notify those who are potentially impacted by the substance. Substances are listed as carcinogenic or causing reproductive harm, and when the use or potential exposure levels of these chemicals exceed what has been determined by a group of approved state scientists as an unacceptable risk threshold, the impacted people or person must be notified. The risk threshold is uniquely determined for each chemical and depends upon its intrinsic potency or the potency of a released mixture.

Notification (by means of warning labels) must be placed on all products which will cause adverse health effects when used for a prolonged period of time. Notification must also be made in the case of a company exposing a surrounding community to toxins released to the air, ground or water system above what is deemed a safe level after prolonged exposure.[24]

The third group which must be notified of exposure includes the workers in the plant emitting the toxins. If the use of certain chemicals used in manufacturing a product, created as a byproduct of production, or the chemical is the product, are unhealthy as defined by Prop 65, then workers must be warned of the potential danger.

Only companies with ten or more fulltime workers are required to notify endangered people of exposure. Non-profit organizations like hospitals, recycling plants, and government organizations, which make up over 65 percent of California's pollution, are not required to participate in Prop 65.

Under the Proposition, private citizens, other industry members and environmental groups can sue companies who fail to notify people of exposure in an appropriate fashion. Plaintiffs who make a successful legal claim get to keep a substantial portion of the settlement, which serves to encourage private enforcement of the law and reduce government monitoring. Other industry members also have a strong incentive to monitor themselves so that one company does not cheat and come out looking greener than its rivals.

---

[24] Notification on labels has in practice sometimes been so small as to attract little attention from the consumer. Notification of community-type risks has frequently been accomplished via the classified advertisement sections of the newspapers, which few people read. An increasing body of research suggests that the form of the risk communication matters. See Magat and Viscusi (1992).

4. 4 EPA Audit Policy

What incentives can the government provide for encouraging the discovery of private environmental information? One possibility is to suggest that firms reporting environmental problems before they are detected by regulatory authorities might face lower sanctions.

On December 22, 1995, USEPA issued an ambitious new policy to provide incentives for companies that audit or otherwise voluntarily discover violations, and where the companies promptly disclose and correct such violations (60 Fed. Reg. 66706). As of 1997, 24 states had passed environmental-auditing laws, while 16 states were still considering such legislation (*Greenwire,* 8/14/97).

EPA's policy encourages self-audits, but fines are reduced, not waived, and USEPA believes that audits should be made public. About 100 companies had taken advantage of the EPA program by February of 1997 (*Greenwire*, 2/18/97).

Achieving a balance between the desire to encourage firms to disclose private information and the desire to punish wrongdoing has not been easy. Some of the states have carried this policy beyond EPA's 'comfort zone', granting immunity from prosecution rather than reduced fines.[25]

Despite these problems, data provided by the Agency show that the Audit Policy is having some effect on corporate behavior. One hundred and five companies have disclosed violations at more than 350 facilities under the policy. EPA already has settled matters with 40 companies and 48 facilities, waiving all penalties in most cases. In some cases even criminal penalties have been waived.[26]

4.5 Private Enforcement Actions

One increasingly common form by which citizens follow up on the availability of greater information gives citizens the right to bring an

---

[25] In one, for example, the EPA ruled that Idaho must revise its 'controversial' environmental audit law to ensure it does not interfere with the state's authority to enforce air pollution regulations. The Idaho Audit Act grants immunity from civil and criminal penalties to companies that disclose and correct environmental problems during self-audits (*Lewinston Morning Tribune*, 12/4 as cited in *Greenwire*, 12/4/97).

[26] For example, in one such case, on February 7, 1996, the United States Department of Justice announced that Chiquita Brand International was not prosecuted due to its voluntary disclosure that its subsidiary, John Morrell and Company, had illegally dumped slaughterhouse waste into the Big Sioux River in Sioux Falls, South Dakota for years and had deliberately submittedfalse discharge monitoring reports to conceal its crimes. John Morrell and Company and several of Morrell's corporate officials now stand convicted of conspiracy and various Clean Water Act felonies, but the government declined to prosecute Chiquita, citing the parent company's voluntary disclosure and cooperation as the prime factors (http://es.inel.gov/oeca/ epapolguid..html (March 21, 1997)).

environmental complaint to some kind of administrative or judicial board.[27] In Latin America and the Caribbean, for example, frequently the complaint is triggered by a perceived violation of some procedural requirement or of some fundamental right to a clean environment which is not related to specific legal discharge standards. In the US and European contexts the action is more likely to be related to a violation of a specific discharge standard.[28]

Administrative actions may result in the imposition of a civil penalty, the creation of a compliance order, or both. Successful negotiation between the control authority and the violator typically produces a consent decree, which creates compliance schedules and/or provides for the collection of civil penalties. Civil penalties may be imposed to ensure that violators receive no economic benefit by failing to comply with environmental standards. Sometimes the citizens who brought the action will even receive monetary rewards, though that is currently the exception rather than the rule.[29]

The next possible step beyond a complaint process involves giving private enforcers power to do more than simply raise complaints. [30] When empowered by statutes as private attorney generals, citizens are authorized to initiate civil proceedings against any private or public polluter violating the terms of its pollution permit. In the US, these proceedings may be initiated by 'any person'. A 'person' is defined as an 'individual, corporation, partnership, association, state, municipality, political subdivision of a state and any agency department or instrumentality of the U.S. or any officer, agent or employee thereof'.[31]

Under several US statutes, citizens may sue for appropriate civil penalties as well as an injunction. The civil penalties assessed in citizen suits are calculated to remove any 'significant economic benefits' which resulted from noncompliance with federal environmental statutes. When determining the

---

[27] This section draws upon Tietenberg (1996).

[28] Complaint processes have also been established in both China and India. In India, for example, an 'environmental audit' procedure has been developed for the 500 megawattDahanu Thermal Power project. The authorities in charge of the project distribute summaries of the results of environmental monitoring to the local community. Community groups can then check emissions against legal standards and seek redress through the courts as necessary(World Bank 1992).

[29] On February 7, 1997, the EPA approved monetary awards to 20 citizens who helped the Agency take successful enforcement actions under the Clean Air Act (CAA). These were the first monetary awards given under the CAA, which authorizes the EPA to make awards of up to $10,000 after an enforcement action is concluded for reporting violations or assisting the Agency in enforcement proceedings. The Agency awarded the $10,000 maximum to a citizen who helped the EPA conclude a major asbestos enforcement case. The citizen learned that children were playing with bags of a powdery substance in an abandoned industrial building and suspecting that the material was asbestos, warned the children, contacted the local air pollution control agency, and provided other information about the large quantity of asbestos improperly stored there.

[30] This section is based on Naysnerski and Tietenberg (1992 a&b).

[31] 42 U.S.C. 7602(e).

magnitude of the penalty, the agency considers such aspects as: the amount and types of costs a defendant has delayed paying through noncompliance, the savings gained by failing to operate and to monitor the proper pollution-control equipment, the advantage gained over competitors who have installed the required pollution-control equipment, the amount and toxicity of the pollution, the length of time the violation continued, and the sensitivity of the environment affected.

With only a few exceptions, under the American Rule each party in a court case must bear its own litigation expenses. The 'private attorney general' theory, created during the 1970s, extended the common benefit theory by allowing reimbursement for actions performed in the general public interest. Otherwise, the court ruled, few people would have an incentive to protect the public good. Congress followed and affirmed the private attorney general theory when they included attorney fee reimbursement procedures in the citizen suit provisions of the environmental statutes (Jordan 1987).

Citizen groups are reimbursed only for successful or partially successful claims. When an action against defendants is proved to be harassing or frivolous, attorney fee awards can also be made to them. That is apparently a rare occurrence.

4.6 Indonesia's Public Disclosure Program[32]

Indonesia's regulatory structure for controlling pollution is weak due to budget constraints and staffing deficiencies. Faced with a growing industrial sector, Indonesia's National Pollution Control Agency (BAPEDAL) decided to initiate a program, called PROPER (Program for Pollution Control, Evaluation and Rating), for rating and publicly disclosing the environmental performance of Indonesian factories.

Indonesia has chosen a single-index approach to the provision of information. Under this approach the authority compiles the various raw pollution information and aggregates it into a single (hopefully easy-to-interpret) index.

Under the Indonesian scheme, each polluter is assigned a color rating based on BAPEDAL's evaluation of its environmental performance.

- A Black rating is assigned to factories which have made no attempt to control pollution and are causing serious damage.
- A Red rating is assigned to factories which have some pollution control, but which fall short of compliance with local standards.

[32] This section is based upon Afsah et al. (1996). This paper is available on the web at http://www.NIPR.org/work_paper/1672/index.htm.

- A Blue rating is assigned to factories which are in compliance with national regulatory standards.
- A Green rating is assigned to factories whose emission control and environmental management procedures significantly exceed those needed for local compliance.
- A Gold rating is reserved for world-class performers, those which rank among the cleanest plants of that type anywhere in the world.

In the pilot phase of PROPER, 187 plants were rated. When the program was officially launched in June 1995, only the names of the five Green plants were publicly announced. The 121 plants rated as Red or Black were privately notified, and given until December 1995 to improve their performance. Full disclosure was implemented on December 29; the pilot-phase results are displayed in Table 2.2.

Table 2.2. Number of firms in each classification category (Various Dates).

Color	June 1995	December 1995	September 1996
Gold	0	0	0
Green	5	4	5
Blue	61	72	94
Red	115	108	87
Black	6	3	1

Source: Data provided by the World Bank site: http://www.NIPR.org/proppres/sld036.htm.

These data suggest that PROPER's short-term impact in the below-average category has been substantial. Before full disclosure in December, half the Black plants made successful efforts to upgrade their status, along with a substantial number of Red plants. No short-term impact is observable in the overcompliance range, but this is not surprising. Attaining Green or Gold status will require longer-term investments, while rapid installation of basic abatement equipment can be sufficient to promote escape from a Black rating.

The concept is spreading. The Philippines' Department of Environment and Natural Resources (DENR) is introducing a public disclosure program called EcoWatch modeled on Indonesia's PROPER program. EcoWatch will soon have its first disclosure of factory performance ratings. The program started on a high note last year when President Fidel Ramos publicly introduced EcoWatch along with the leaders of about 20 Philippine Business Associations. The Associations signed an agreement with DENR to support

EcoWatch by providing information for program development and encouraging participation by members (*Manila Bulletin*, April, 1997 as cited in http://www.NIPR.org/comrole.htm#ecowatch).

Table 2.3. Green electricity pricing in the US

Sponsor and Program	Year	Type	Capacity	Market	No of participants	Funding	Monthly consumer cost $
City of Austin Electric Utility: Solar Explorer	97	PV	219 kW	R & B	NA	Fixed Payment	7
Detroit Edison: Solar Currents	95	PV	28.4 kW	R	195 R*	Fee per 100 W (– elec. credit)	9.89 (avg.)
Florida Energy Extension Service and Gulf Power: Solar for Schools	96	Solar, thermal and PV	100 W PV (for lights)	R	513	Fixed payment	1.75
Fort Collins (Colorado) Light & Power: Wind Power Pilot Project	96	Wind	750 kW	R & B	NA	Fee per kW (R) Fee per MWh block (B)	10 (R) (est.)
Gainesville Regional Solar Project	93	PV	10 kW	R & B	657	Contribution	3.27 (avg.)
Hawaiian Electric Co and subsidiaries Sun Power for Schools	96	PV	8–16 kW	R & (min.) B	NA	Contribution	NA
Northern States Power: EnergyWise Solar Advantage for Homes	95	PV	34 kW	R	17*	Fixed payments (- elec. credit)	36 (est.)
Portland General Electric: Renewable Energy Supply	96	Wind	NA	Large C & I	NA	Fee per kW	NA
Public Service of Colorado: Renewable Energy Trust	93	PV	13 kW	R	14,000	Contribution	1.77 (avg.)
Sacramento Municipal Utility District: PV Pioneers	93	PV	1,200 kW	R	350*	Fixed payment	4
Traverse City (Michigan) Light & Power: Green Rate	94	Wind	600 kW	R & B	145 R & 20 B	Fee per kW	7.58 R 27 B (avg.)
Wisconsin Electric Power: Energy for Tomorrow	96	Hydro and Biomass	5 MW	R & B	NA	Fee per kW	3, 6 or 12 depending on option
Wisconsin Public Service: SolarWise for Schools	95	PV	36 kW	R	2,600	Contribution	1.64 (avg.)

Notes: R = Residential, B = Business, C = Commercial, I = Industrial.
*Participation limited by project size.

Source: Ed Holt & Associates, Harpswell, Maine as cited in Lamarre (1997, p 8).

4.7 Green Electricity Pricing[33]

As of 1997, some 13 electric utilities (Table 2.3) in the United States had adopted some form of green pricing. Under a green pricing scheme the customer is asked to pay a premium of up to 15 percent of the normal bill.[34] In return the utility acquires renewable energy sources according to a set formula.

Surveys consistently reveal that from 56 to 80 percent of respondents to polls indicate a willingness to pay more for environmentally friendly energy sources. Green pricing attempts to tap this willingness to pay as a means of financing renewable energy sources which are not quite cost effective (the cost-effective sources would presumably be added to the mix even without green pricing).

Green pricing provides an example of a voluntary information disclosure strategy. Utilities prepared to offer green options to consumers willing to pay a price premium can advertise that fact, but utilities which are not prepared to offer that option do not have to.

5. EMPIRICAL ANALYSIS

The literature on economic analysis of disclosure strategies is rather young, but it does contain some useful, if partial, information.

5.1 Doyle et al. (1990)

In the early stages of this study, a review of the literature on risk communication and motivating self-protective behavior found that traditional information and awareness programs (such as advertising campaigns and public service announcements) were likely to fail when they are targeted at the general population.

- To test this hypothesis for the radon context this study sent a mail survey to 920 households that had purchased radon test kits as part of an intensive information and awareness campaign in the Washington, DC area. Over 100,000 test kits were purchased as a result of this campaign. Although about 33,000 homes in this area exceeded the EPA action level for radon by a factor of five or more (had a radon reading of 20

[33] This section is based upon Moscovitz (1993) and Lamarre (1997).
[34]Despite the fact that in Detroit Edison's Solar Currents plan customers pay an average of 14 percent more, the program quickly became oversubscribed. Some 70 customers are currently on a waiting list (1997).

picocuries per liter or higher), the survey results indicate that only 1.2 percent of this group had taken convincing remedial action as a result of the campaign. In addition, only about a third of the homes in this 1.2 percent group conducted a post-mitigation retest to confirm that mitigation had been effective.

- In contrast, a separate telephone survey of 303 home buyers in Boulder County, Colorado found that over 40 percent of recently purchased homes were tested for radon gas at the time of home sale and that this testing was often motivated by information provided by the realtor. Even though no intensive information and awareness campaign has been conducted in Colorado and currently no state laws are in effect concerning radon, 54 percent of tested homes in their sample that had radon levels above the EPA action level underwent mitigation (with 87 percent of those completing follow-up testing) as part of the home sale transaction.

The authors believe that these results suggest that a radon information and awareness program targeted at the point of home sale, when the transaction context provides a strong economic incentive to repair any problems a home might have, could be highly effective in comparison to information targeted at the general population.[35]

5.2 Magat and Viscusi (1992)

This was one of the first studies to examine the potential role of hazard warnings. Through a series of carefully defined experiments the authors attempted to discern not only the value of hazard warnings, but also how the structure of the warning might influence its effectiveness. The authors suggest several conclusions from their work.

- Consumers did react to warning labels and their reactions implied benefit levels to the individual which implied that warning labels were valuable.
- Information overload is a potentially serious problem. Due to cognitive limitations in processing information, more information is not always better. This suggests that complete information will rarely be efficient, not only because of the marginal cost of providing additional information, but also because the marginal benefits of additional information apparently decline after some point and may even become negative.

---

[35] This study was subsequently published in concise form as Fisher et al. (1991).

- Making information available to consumers is insufficient to guarantee that they will respond to it. The information must be organized in such a manner as to be able to be processed efficiently. Label design matters.[36]

5.3 Arora and Cason (1996)

Using an econometric model, this study attempts to isolate the factors which influence a firm's decision to participate in the EPA's 33/50 Program. The study draws the following conclusions:

- The largest firms with the greatest toxic releases were the most likely to participate in this voluntary program.
- The authors found no evidence that firms either free ride on emission reductions prior to the program's initiation or that they participate to divert attention away from poor compliance with mandatory regulation.
- Firms in industries with more contact with final consumers (proxied by normalized advertising expenditures) were more likely to participate in the program.

5.4 Naysnerski and Tietenberg (1992 a&b)

The data used in this analysis included 1,205 citizen actions. The database included information regarding plaintiffs, defendants, filing dates for notices and/or complaints, penalties, and statutes involved in the claim. The analysis examined the effects of various incentives on the types of claims filed. The following conclusions emerged from this study:

- Disclosure plays a key role in determining the effectiveness of private enforcement since the disclosed information was the basis for bringing the actions. The effectiveness of citizen suits has been greatly affected by the magnitude of the burden of proof environmental groups are forced to bear. Proof of violation is relatively easy to establish under the Clean Water Act because of the publicly available Discharge Monitoring Reports that regulated firms are required to file. Lacking the government's power to conduct on-site inspections, citizen groups are heavily dependent on the self-monitoring reports filed by those subject to the regulations.

[36] The USEPA is in the 'early' stages of considering whether to require 'talking labels' on products like pesticides and herbicides. Under a proposal being circulated among interested parties, computer chips like those found in toys and greeting cards would play brief warnings when activated by a button (Mike Magner, Newhouse/*S.F. Examiner*, 12/31/96 as cited in *Greenwire*, 12/31/96).

- The effectiveness of the citizen suit process is affected to a large degree by the incentives offered private enforcers in the program. In particular, allowing private enforcers to extract penalties which are earmarked for environmental improvement and to be reimbursed for legal expenses increases the attractiveness of the private enforcement process for private enforcers.
- For one class of polluters, public facilities, citizen suits seem a distinctly superior form of enforcement.
- Since citizen suits are typically based on proving noncompliance with specific effluent/emission standards determining that citizen suits have led to greater compliance does not necessarily indicate that they have led to greater cost effectiveness. Complete compliance is not necessarily cost effective if the effluent/emission standards are not themselves cost effective.
- Since the evidence suggests that private enforcers respond to specific incentives, if the incentives are not applied uniformly to the various pollution problems' a bias will be created. Those problems which treat private enforcers favorably will be preferred whether or not they represent the most serious problems.

This study suggests that coupling disclosure with private enforcement can be effective, but whether this combination is efficient depends crucially on the way the program is designed.

5.5 Muoghalu et al. (1990)

This study examines the capital market impacts of hazardous waste mismanagement lawsuit filings and settlements for the 1977–86 period. The sample contained 128 initial lawsuits against firms and 74 case settlements which were announced in the print media (generally the *Wall Street Journal*).

- Although significant results were obtained for the day of the announcement, no significant results were obtained for the two control periods: from 2 to 5 days prior to and 1 to 5 days after the announcement.
- The results indicate that stockholders suffered on average a statistically significant loss in market value of 1.2 percent at the filing of the lawsuit, but no significant abnormal returns at the disposition of the suit.

5.6 Laplante and Lanoie (1994)

This study examines the capital market effects on Canadian firms of some 47 announcements of environmental events, including environmental regulation violations (12), initiation of legal action (9), settlement of suits (13), and investments in emission control (13) covering the 1982–91 period.

- Announcements of incidents and the filing of lawsuits did not trigger any significant abnormal stock market returns.
- Announcements of suit settlements which resulted in fines resulted in a decline in value of about 2 percent.
- Announcements of investments in emission control equipment resulted in an abnormal loss on the day of the announcement of about 1.2 percent.

These results contrasted with the earlier result discussed above involving American firms (Muoghalu et al. 1990). That study found that the American stock market reacted to the announcement of the initiation of a law suit. The authors attribute the difference to the less credible enforcement of environmental regulations in Canada; Canadian investors are seen as influenced only by the outcome.

5.7 Badrinath and Bolster (1996)

This article examines stock market reactions to 730 EPA judicial actions for a sample of publicly traded firms from 1972–91.

- The market value of the average affected firm dropped 0.43 percent during the week of settlement.
- While high relative fines appear to affect stock market prices, the analysis uncovered no consistent relationship between the magnitude of relative fines and prices.
- The estimated market penalty was larger for more recent actions and for repeat offenders.

The authors note that while these results reflect an environment where no special attention is paid to providing public information about enforcement actions, they also appear to support the possibility of substantial social benefits from providing more systematic information.

5.8 Hamilton (1995)

An event study is performed on 436 publicly traded companies to ascertain whether the announcement of the information compiled under the Toxic Release Inventory (TRI) affected stock prices. This is complemented by a study of media coverage of this information compiled by searching the Nexis database and the *Wall Street Journal* index for 1989.

- Holding emissions constant, the more dispersed its pollution across facilities and the more information available to the public about the company's pollution patterns prior to the TRI, the less likely journalists were to treat the firm's TRI releases as news.
- Most of the publicly traded firms in the sample did not receive any coverage of their TRI releases in the print sources traced by this study.
- For those companies which reported TRI data to the EPA, the average abnormal return on the day the information was made public was negative and statistically significant.
- These effects were smaller for firms where investors had previous information about pollution patterns (such as companies with exposure at Superfund sites).

This study suggests that disclosure does have stock market impacts, but the magnitude of the impacts depends on the treatment of the disclosure by the press and how much knowledge investors already had.

5.9 Konar and Cohen (1997)

Comparing the 40 firms with the largest abnormal reductions in their stock prices to a control group of otherwise similar firms, this analysis examines differences in the behavior of firms in these two samples. In general they find:

- The top 40 firms were found to be among the top third of polluting firms (per dollar revenue) in their industries, but not necessarily the largest emitters in terms of overall emissions.
- The top 40 firms subsequently reduced their emissions more than other firms in the industry (including those firms with the largest TRI/$revenue prior to the disclosure of TRI levels).
- The top 40 firms made more significant attempts at improving their environmental performance by reducing the number and severity of oil and chemical spills.

- The top 40 firms had a lower likelihood of receiving higher fines from the government in subsequent years.

This study suggests that stock market effects are ultimately translated into real environmental improvements.

5.10 Khanna et al. (1997)

This study also examines stock market and waste management responses to disclosure of the Toxic Release Inventory, but in this case the sample period is 1990–94 and the focus is on the chemical industry.

- Chemical firms incur statistically significant losses in market value during the one-day period following the disclosure of the TRI.
- These losses have a significant negative impact on subsequent on-site releases and a significant positive impact on wastes transferred off-site for recycling and treatment, but their impact on total toxic wastes generated by these firms is negligible.

The key aspect of this study was the deeper analysis of the nature of the changes in environmental behavior which followed the capital market effects of disclosure. While it promoted a reduction in on-site releases and off-site recycling, it did not encourage pollution prevention.

5. 11 Khanna and Damon (1997)

This paper examines the motivations for participating in the voluntary 30/50 Program and its implications for toxic releases. It demonstrates that benefits due to potentially avoided costs of liabilities and compliance provide strong incentives for participation.

- After controlling for sample selection bias and the impact of other firm-specific characteristics, this paper shows that program participation led to a statistically significant decline in toxic releases over the period 1991–93.
- Participation also had a statistically significant impact on short-run profits of firms, but it had a positive and statistically significant effect on market value, indicating that investors expect the costs of participating and improving environmental performance to be more than offset by lower future environmental liabilities.

This study suggests that the short and long-run effects on the firm of participating in voluntary pollution reduction programs may be different. It finds that the adverse effect on short-run profits is reversed in the long run.

5.12 Dasgupta and Wheeler (1996)

This study examines environmental complaints lodged in China by citizens over the 1987–93 period to discover the factors that seem to explain the number of complaints. The results indicate:

- The incidence of complaints does mirror abatement benefits and the intensity of exposure for visible pollutants, but not less visible, but potentially equally harmful, pollutants.
- Regions with higher education levels tend to initiate many more complaints, all other things being equal. This implies that a reliance on complaints alone would result in inappropriately low allocation of inspection resources to less-educated, relatively 'silent' regions.

This study raises the specter that complaint processes may be biassed against poorer and less-educated communities.

6. SUMMARY AND CONCLUSIONS

The information that we have in hand at this point is too sketchy to allow us to draw firm conclusions. It is possible to use the available information, however, to generate some hypotheses which are consistent with the evidence we currently have before us. If and when these hypotheses are upheld by other studies, they could form a basis both for understanding information approaches and for enhancing their effectiveness.

6.1 Overall Effectiveness

- Disclosure strategies can be effective in motivating environmental improvement; some evidence raises the possibility that the improvement to date may involve diversion of pollutants rather than pollution prevention.
- When information disclosure is coupled with voluntary compliance programs the evidence suggests that the largest firms with the greatest toxic releases were the most likely to participate and there is no evidence to suggest that firms either free ride on emission reductions prior to the program's initiation or that they participate to divert attention away from

poor compliance with mandatory regulation. In other words voluntary compliance programs can result in real, not merely reported, environmental improvement.

- For one class of polluters, public facilities, combining disclosure with the empowerment of private enforcers, has apparently provided a form of enforcement that is superior to traditional public enforcement.
- Public announcements do seem to affect stock market valuations of firms, but these effects seem lower for known polluters. The different results for Canada and the US suggest that the enforcement culture may determine whether it is the announcement of the initiation of the action or the final settlement of the action which affects value.
- Large declines in stock market value seem to motivate firms to improve their environmental performance.
- The green pricing information suggests that at least some consumers are willing to pay higher prices for products which were produced with a lower negative impact on the environment even when the consumers may not be directly affected by that pollution.
-

6.2 The Determinants of Effective Strategies

- The quality and quantity of information conveyed can have a large effect on the effectiveness of the program. Due to the possibility of cognitive overload, more information does not always produce lower risk and the form in which information is conveyed can matter a great deal.
- The experience with providing US homeowners with information about radon suggests that how the information is targetted may make a considerable difference in its effectiveness.
- Incentives created by complementary aspects of disclosure programs can also be important. Private enforcers, for example, seem to respond to incentives such as earmarking penalties for environmental improvement and the reimbursement of legal costs. Their effectiveness has apparently also been affected by the magnitude of the burden of proof environmental groups are forced to bear in bringing claims against polluters. Properly designed disclosure strategies can lower this burden of proof significantly.

6.3 Biases in Disclosure Strategies

- Firms in industries with more contact with final consumers (proxied by normalized advertising expenditures) were more likely to participate in the voluntary compliance programs which were accompanied by disclosure.

- Complaint processes seem to reflect damages for visible pollutants, but not for less-visible pollutants.
- Complaints processes seem to work quite well in areas with relatively high education levels, but they work less well in areas with lower education levels.
- Although citizen suits have apparently led to greater compliance, that is not sufficient to demonstrate that they have led to greater cost effectiveness. Complete compliance is not necessarily cost effective if the effluent standards are not themselves cost effective.
- Since the evidence suggests that private enforcers respond to specific incentives, if the incentives are not applied uniformly to the various pollution problems a bias will be created. Those problems which treat private enforcers favorably will be preferred whether or not they represent the most serious problems.

6.4 Remaining Questions

- The current level of evidence provides no guidance on whether disclosure strategies are producing efficient outcomes or not. The fact that they are effective does not necessarily mean that they are efficient. Reaching that conclusion requires much better information than we currently have on both the marginal benefits and marginal costs of information provision strategies.
- We currently do not have enough information to begin to assess where the next investments in information provision should be made. Do these investments yield rates of return that compare favorably with other investments or not? Which types of information provision yield the highest rates of return?

REFERENCES

Alanis-Ortega, Gustavo (1995), 'Private Enforcement of Environmental Regulations: El Tamarindo in Jalisco, México: A Case Study', A report to the Inter-American Development Bank, Washington, DC (September).

Afsah, S., B. LaPlante and Wheeler (1996), *Controlling Industrial Pollution: A New Paradigm*, Washington, DC: World Bank Policy Research Department.

Arora, S. and T.N. Cason (1996), 'Why Do Firms Volunteer to Exceed Environmental Regulations? Understanding Participation in EPA's 33/50 program', *Land Economics*, **72**(4), 413–32.

Badrinath, S.G. and P.J. Bolster (1996), 'The Role of Market Forces in EPA Enforcement Activity', *Journal of Regulatory Economics*, **10**(2), 165–81.

Che, Y.-K. and D. Earnhart (1997), 'Optimal Use of Litigation: Should Regulatory Information Be Withheld to Deter Frivolous Suits?', *Rand Journal of Economics*, **28**, 120–34.

Coase, R. (1960), 'The Problem of Social Cost', *Journal of Law and Economics*, **3**(October), 1–44.

Dasgupta, S. and D. Wheeler (1996), *Citizen Complaints as Environmental Indicators*, Washington, DC: World Bank.

Dewees, D. (1992), *Tort Law and the Deterrence of Environmental Pollution. Innovation in Environmental Policy*. T.H. Tietenberg. Cheltenham, UK: Edward Elgar, 139–64.

Doyle, J. K., Gary H. McClelland, William D. Schulze, Paul A. Locke, Steven R. Elliott, Glenn W. Russell and Andrew Moyad (1990), *An Evaluation of Strategies for Promoting Effective Radon Mitigation*, Washington, DC: US Environmental Protection Agency.

Fisher, A., G.H. McClelland, W.D. Schultz and J.K. Doyle (1991), 'Communicating the Risk from Radon', *Journal of the Air and Waste Management Association*, **41**(11), 1440–45.

Hahn, R.W. (1989), 'Economic Prescriptions for Environmental Problems: How the Patient Followed the Doctor's Orders', *Journal of Economic Perspectives*, **3**(2), 95–114.

Hamilton, J.T. (1995), 'Pollution as News: Media and Stock Market Reactions to the Toxics Release Data', *Journal of Environmental Economics and Management*, **28**(1), 98–113.

Hamilton, J.T. (1997), 'Taxes, Torts, and the Toxics Release Inventory: Congressional Voting on Instruments to Control Pollution', *Economic Inquiry*, **35**(4), 745–762.

Jordan, S.J. (1987), 'Awarding Attorneys' Fees to Environmental Plaintiffs Under a Private Attorney General Theory', *Boston College Environmental Affairs Law Review*, **14**, 287–311.

Kennedy, P.W., B. LaPlante, et al. (1994), 'Pollution Policy: The Role for Publicly Provided Information', *Journal of Environmental Economics and Management*, **26**(1), 31–43.

Khanna, M. and L. Damon (1997), 'EPA's Voluntary 33/50 Program: Impact on Toxic Releases and Economic Performance of Firms', Environmental and Resource Economics Working Paper #8, Program in Environmental and Resource Economics, University of Illinois at Urbana-Champaign.

Khanna, M., W.R.H. Quimio, et al. (1997), *Toxics Release Information: A Policy Tool for Environmental Protection*, Urbana-Champaign: Department of Agricultural and Consumer Economics, University of Illinois.

Konar, S. and M.A. Cohen (1997), 'Information as Regulation: The Effect of Community Right to Know Laws on Toxic Emissions', *Journal of Environmental Economics and Management*, **32**(1), 109–24.

Lamarre, L. (1997), 'Utility Customers Go for the Green', *EPRI Journal*, **22**(2), 6–15.

LaPlante, B. and P. Lanoie (1994), 'Market Response to Environmental Incidents in Canada', *Southern Economic Journal*, **60**, 657–72.

Lewis, T. (1996), 'Protecting the Environment When Costs and Benefits are Privately Known', *Rand Journal of Economics*, **27**(4), 819–47.

Magat, W.A. and W.K. Viscusi (1992), *Informational Approaches to Regulation*, Cambridge, MA: MIT Press.

Marcinowski, F. and S. Napolitano (1993), 'Reducing the Risks from Radon', *Air and Waste*, **43**, 955–62.

Moscovitz, D. (1993), 'Green Pricing: Why Not Customer Choice?' *Electricity Journal*, **6**(8), 42–9.

Muoghalu, M.I., H.D. Robison and Glascock (1990), 'Hazardous Waste Lawsuits, Stockholder Returns and Deterrence', *Southern Economic Journal*, **57**, 357–70.

Naysnerski, W. and T. Tietenberg (1992a), *Private Enforcement. Innovation in Environmental Policy*. T.H. Tietenberg, Cheltenham: UK, Edward Elgar, 109–36.

Naysnerski, W. and T. Tietenberg (1992b), 'Private Enforcement of Environmental Law', *Land Economics*, **68**(1), 28–48.

OECD (1989), *Economic Instruments for Environmental Protection*, Paris: Organization for Economic Cooperation and Development.

OECD (1994), *Applying Economic Instruments to Environmental Policies in OECD and Dynamic Non-member Countries*, Paris: Organization for Economic Co-operation and Development.

OECD (1995), *Environmental Taxes in OECD Countries*, Paris: Organization for Economic Cooperation and Development.

Sand, P.H. (1991), *International Cooperation: The Environmental Experience. Preserving the Global Environment: The Challenge of Shared Leadership*, J.T. Mathews, New York: W.W. Norton & Co, 236–79.

Segerson, K. and T. Tietenberg (1992), 'The Structure of Penalties in Environmental Enforcement: An Economic Analysis', *Journal of Environmental Economics and Management*, **23**(2), 179–200.

Sinclair-Desgagné, B. and H.L. Gabel (1997), 'Environmental Auditing in Management Systems in Public Policy', *Journal of Environmental Economics and Management*, **33**(3), 331–46.

Tietenberg, T.H. (1985), *Emissions Trading: An Exercise in Reforming Pollution Policy*, Washington, DC: Resources for the Future.

Tietenberg, T.H. (1990), 'Using Economic Incentives to Maintain Our Environment', *Challenge*, **33**(2), 42–6.

Tietenberg, T.H. (1992), *Environmental and Natural Resource Economics*, New York: HarperCollins Publishing Co.

Tietenberg, T. (1995), *Design Lessons from Existing Air Pollution Control Systems: The United States. Property Rights in a Social and Ecological Context: Case*

Studies and Design Applications. S. Hanna and M. Munasinghe. Washington, DC: World Bank.

Tietenberg, T. (1996), *Private Enforcement of Environmental Regulations in Latin America and the Caribbean: An Effective Instrument for Environmental Management?*, Washington, DC: Inter-American Development Bank.

Viscusi, W.K. (1983), *Risk By Choice: Regulating Health and Safety in the Workplace*, Cambridge, MA: Harvard University Press.

Viscusi, W.K. (1992), *Fatal Tradeoffs: Public and Private Responsibilities for Risk*, New York: Oxford University Press.

World Bank (1992), *World Development Report 1992: Development and the Environment*, Washington, DC: Oxford University Press.

3. Theoretical Considerations Regarding the Effectiveness of Policy Instruments

Eirik Romstad

1. INTRODUCTION

It is widely accepted among economists that incentive-based (IB) regulations generally provide lower average and marginal abatement costs than command and control (CAC) type regulations. Even though other professionals may accept the cost argument, they often challenge the environmental performance of IB regulations. This was partly the reason for a study by Oates et al. (1989) where they compared the environmental performance and the abatement costs of IB and CAC regulations. In this study they arrived at the following conclusion:

> IB policies designed to achieve prescribed regulatory standards may not be so obviously superior to CAC approaches as supposed. This will be the case when CAC policies are designed with at least one eye on cost savings – as they sometimes are, and when reductions below the level of relevant environmental, product or workplace standards result in beneficial effects. In these cases the overcontrol that makes CAC policies more expensive also makes them more efficacious. (Oates et al. 1989, p. 1240)

One of the important qualifiers for this argument to hold is that it is based on the comparison of suboptimal regimes. Oates et al. (1989, p. 1241) argue that this should not be held against their conclusion for devising practical regulations as it is extremely complicated to devise optimal policies in a multi-product multi-pollutant setting.

The findings of Oates et al. should be interpreted with some care for several reasons, including:

1. Their result is based on an empirical study in a particular region. Questions remain regarding the heterogeneity of firms.[1]
2. They have only investigated the static efficiency, something they also acknowledge (Oates et al. 1989, p. 1242).
3. Other empirical studies that have been undertaken indicate that the abatement costs of IB regulations could be considerably less than those of CAC (see, for example, Brännlund et al. 1996; Vatn et al. 1997).

In this chapter I therefore aim to take a closer theoretical look at the economic and environmental performance of various regulatory regimes. I shall consider the effects of the informational structure, agent heterogeneity, transaction and monitoring costs. The ensuing analysis will show that the choice of IB regulatory instrument depends on the interaction of these factors.

The next section delineates the difference between CAC and IB regulations, exemplified through non-tradable and tradable emission permits. In Section 3 some key criteria for regulatory policy are addressed, the so-called resource allocation mechanism requirements. Section 4 gives an overview of the four classical IB regulations – emission taxes, tradable emission permits, taxes and tradable permits on polluting input factors – pointing to the advantages and disadvantages of these regulatory regimes.

2. COMMAND AND CONTROL VS. INCENTIVE-BASED REGULATIONS

2.1 Cost Considerations

Consider a 50 percent emission reduction requirement. Assume that two policies are available to the regulator: (i) non-transferable emission permits, and (ii) tradable emission permits. These two policies are depicted in Figure 3.1 for a stylized situation with two types of firms. Figure 3.1 shows that the cost savings to society of the tradable permit system over the non-tradable system with an equal share of the two firms is the sum of the areas C_1 and C_2. True savings equal these areas less the difference in the costs of operating the two systems. Using an emission tax instead of a fixed standard, the cost savings to society would equal the same amount as for a tradable permit system, but with some other deduction from the costs of operating the tax system, and with different distributional effects.

[1] The general economic insight is that the larger the heterogeneity of firms or the informational advantage held by firms, the larger the relative benefits of IB regulations over CAC regulations.

Figure 3.1. Non tradable and tradable permits

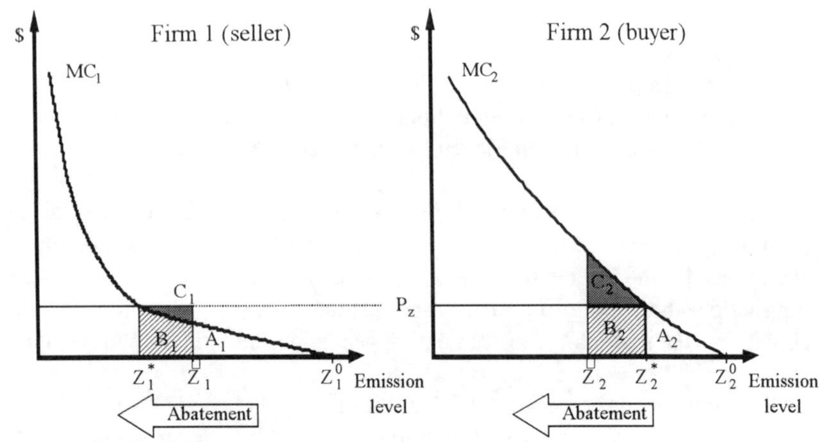

Note: z_i^0 : initial emission level; $\bar{Z}_i$: 50 percent. emission reduction; Z_i^* : optimal emission level.

Generally, the costs of operating a tradable permit or tax system are assumed to exceed the operating costs of a system of fixed standards. This implies that for an emission tax or tradable emission permits to lead to any cost savings over the fixed standard, the additional transaction costs of the IB systems must be less than the cost savings to firms (C_1 + C_2). Basically this means that there must exist some heterogeneity among firms for taxes or tradable permits to provide cost savings for the regulated firms compared to a CAC system in a static setting. This is illustrated in Figure 3.2.

In a situation where firms have superior information *vis-à-vis* the regulator, private information *vis-à-vis* other firms, and they are reluctant to reveal their abatement costs, the regulator will not know the true abatement costs. The only way the regulator will know the degree of cost heterogeneity among firms is to observe the amount of trade going on,[2] or how individual firms choose to adjust their emissions to an emission tax (in terms of Figure 3.1, set the tax equal to the permit price, P_Z).

[2] Care must be taken in designing the permit market so that firms do not benefit from manipulating the market. See Romstad and Bergland (1997) for details on how this can be done.

Figure 3.2. Costs associated with CAC and IB regulatory regimes

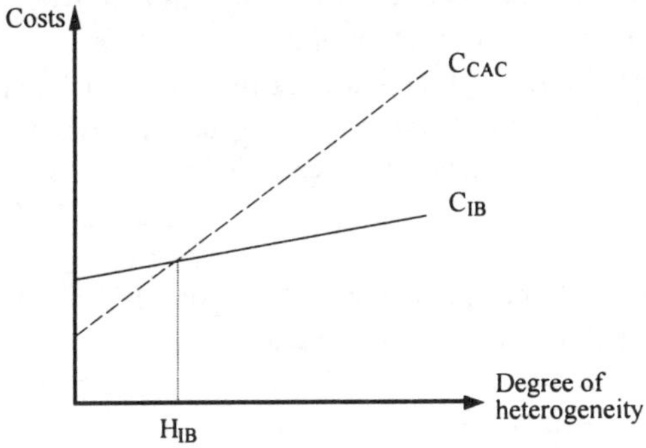

Note: H_{IB}: degree of cost heterogeneity when *IB* regulations become less costly; C_{CAC}: costs of *CAC* regulation; C_{IB}: costs of *IB* regulations).

2.2 Environmental Performance and Monitoring Issues

It is only under extreme assumptions about homogeneity of the cost structure of the regulated firms, or when the transaction costs of the alternative IB schemes are high, that CAC schemes will provide less costly solutions than IB regulations. Still, many question the ability of IB regulations to provide the desired environmental standard. This is of particular concern when the marginal environmental damage curve is steep, so that even small variations in (aggregate) emission levels may have large harmful effects. Romstad (1997b) argues that there is no principal difference between a system of tradable permits and fixed standards in terms of being able to meet an overall emission target. The key question here is to devise cost-effective monitoring systems that induce firms not to exceed their individual emission quota, irrespective of whether this quota is tradable or non-tradable.[3]

There is an important distinction between emission taxes and tradable emission permits, following from Weitzman (1974). Suppose that the marginal environmental damage curve exhibits some marked curvature change (going from fairly flat to very steep in a short interval), while marginal abatement costs are reasonably flat, wrongful assessment of these abatement costs on behalf of the regulator could lead to excessive emission levels using a tax instrument. Under such conditions, Weitzman showed that

[3] See Romstad and Bergland (1993) for details on how to set up such monitoring systems.

quantity restrictions are preferred over tax instruments, the so-called Weitzman proposition.[4]

Several scholars have indicated that because of the implicit overcompliance inherent in CAC regulations, the environmental performance of these regulations exceeds that of IB regulations (Atkinson and Tietenberg 1982; Oates et al. 1989). Barring the *ex-ante–ex-post* argument[5] by Atkinson and Tietenberg (1982), this view rests on several simplistic and erroneous presumptions:

1. That IB regulations automatically involve a more lax perspective on overall emission targets. This is very much a question of how the IB regulations are devised, confer with the Weitzman proposition (Weitzman 1974). In brief, the ability to maintain high environmental standards depends on the monitoring and enforcement regimes put in place.
2. That IB regulations are more difficult to implement than CAC regulations. A look at some of the theoretical and empirical evidence suggests the converse:
   a. Theoretically, one would expect firms to lobby harder against more costly policies. Here it should be noted that some IB regulations – in particular grandfathered tradable permits – entail lower costs for firms, and hence would meet less resistance in the business community than nontradable permits and emission taxes (for details, see Romstad and Kriström 1994).
   b. The empirical evidence suggests that strict CAC regulations are rare. Rather, regulations are modified in each individual case, indicating that the regulatory authorities make implicit assessments of firms' abatement costs when introducing regulations and setting environmental standards (see, for example, Brännlund et al. 1996).

The latter point – that environmental protection agencies consider costs to the regulated firms when setting the firm-specific emission standard – actually suggests the converse: all other factors assumed the same, a less costly (IB) policy *vis-à-vis* firms would allow for more stringent environmental standards. This aspect becomes even more important in a dynamic setting, as regulations providing stronger incentives for firms to lower their marginal abatement costs lead to optimal emissions decreasing

[4] Weitzman (1974) also demonstrated that the converse holds, that is, if the marginal abatement-costs curves are much steeper than the marginal damage curves, tax instruments are preferred over quantity restrictions. Baumol and Oates (1988) extend Weitzman's analysis, and provide a summary of the debate that Weitzman's seminal paper created.

[5] The gist of the *ex-ante–ex post* argument is that when location of emissions matters, it becomes extremely difficult to ensure that after-trade emissions do not exceed location-specific emission limits.

over time, as illustrated in Figure 3.3, by the counter-clockwise rotation of the marginal abatement-cost curve from MAC_1 to MAC_2

Figure 3.3. Optimal emission levels (Z_t) with decreasing marginal abatement costs over time, MAC_t, t = {1,2}

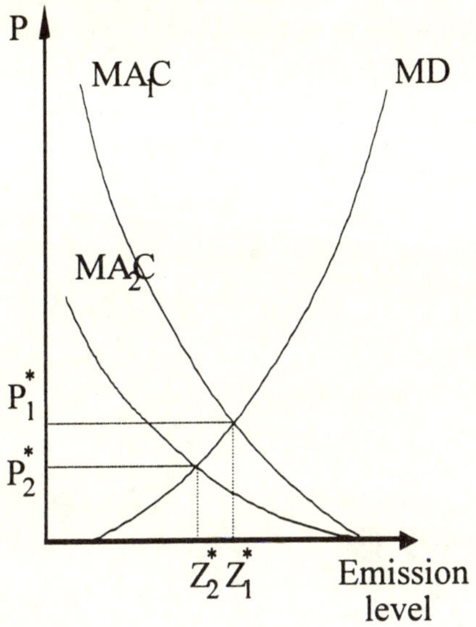

2.3 Static and Dynamic Efficiency

Another key distinction between CAC and IB regulations is how well they induce the development and adoption of new abatement technologies. The dynamic efficiency properties of emission taxes and tradable emission permits are well documented (for an overview, see Baumol and Oates 1988).

In the case of CAC regulations, one needs to distinguish between (i) very specific regulations mandating certain technologies and abatement solutions, and (ii) regulations setting a location-specific target, in terms of ambient standards or emission loads. While the former may entail substantial cost increases, the latter may in some cases be reasonably comparable with respect to costs in a static setting (for further elaborations on this, see Cropper and Oates 1992).

While the difference between CAC-ii and IB regulations may be minor in a static setting, this is not the case in a dynamic setting. With a fixed standard, the regulatory agency receives no information regarding the optimality of this standard over time when firms are reluctant to disclose their cost information. This implies that any tightening of the environmental standards would be *ad hoc*, and would be met with opposition from firms as such changes in the standards imply a less predictable business environment.

In terms of emission taxes, the development of less-costly abatement technologies would result in lower emissions for a fixed emission tax rate. Unfortunately, finding manipulation-free adjustment rules for the tax regime is difficult, which implies that it is hard for the regulator to assess the optimality of the aggregate emission levels that evolve over time under an environmental tax system.

Figure 3.4. Aggregate emissions under transferable quotas

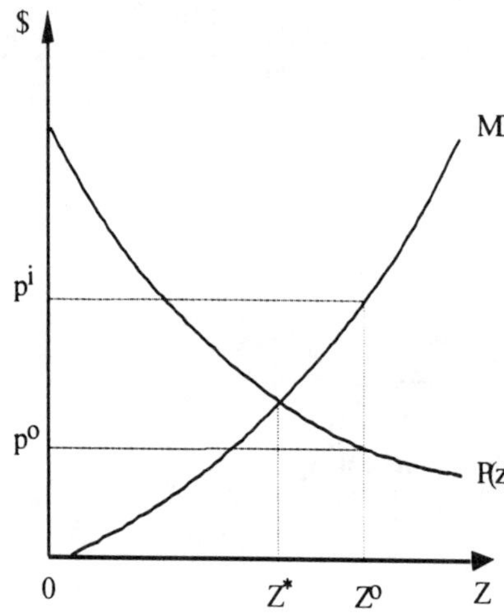

Note: The issued aggregate emission quota (Z^o) is too large (p^i:price implied from the marginal damage curve at emission level Z^o, p^o: observed price at emission level Z^o, and $P(Z)$ the price curve of emission permits at various emission levels). Z^* denotes the optimal aggregate emission level.

This consistency problem is less for tradable emission permits. Allowing the regulatory agency to become an actor in the emission permit market, Romstad and Bergland (1990) showed how the regulator could achieve optimal aggregate emission levels by buying permits if the inferred price is above the observed emission permit price, and selling permits under the converse situation. A situation where the aggregate emission quota is too high is depicted in Figure 3.4.

The converse situation would arise if $Z^0 < Z^*$, as $p^0 > p^i$. This discrepancy between the implied price from the damages of pollution and the observed (actual) price for pollution permits signals to the regulatory agency whether the aggregate quota, Z^0, of a particular pollutant is too small or too large. Note that under the proposed scheme the regulatory agency does not need to know the firms' abatement costs. The only problem with this scheme is to avoid manipulative behavior on behalf of firms, that is, that firms attempt to act in the emission permit market in a way to 'rig' the emission permit price to allow for an overall larger quota. Romstad and Bergland (1997) have shown how such manipulative behavior can be avoided by providing incentives to firms for truthful revelation of their abatement costs. One major advantage of this system of tradable emission permits over standards or emission taxes is that the rules for adjusting the aggregate emission level are part of the mechanism design.

3. RESOURCE ALLOCATION MECHANISMS

When comparing CAC and IB regulations, it is also important to bear in mind the insights gained from the mechanism design literature. One of the biggest caveats of CAC schemes is that they tend to overlook the informational asymmetries that exist between regulators and those subject to the regulations.

Any economic system or mechanism is a communication process, where each agent transmits messages to which other agents respond according to their self-interest. A successful resource allocation mechanism (RAM) utilizes this, so that each agent without necessarily understanding the complete process, is induced to cooperate in the determination of a satisfactory bundle of goods and services (Campbell 1987).[6]

Campbell lists the following desirable properties of RAMs; (i) individual rationality, (ii) informational viability and efficiency, (iii) incentive compatibility and (iv) Pareto optimality. The importance of these properties, and necessary modifications due to conflicts between them will be demonstrated.

Individual rationality requires that the suggested RAM generates allocations that make all the firms, $n \in N$, and all consumers, $i \in I$, at least as well off as they were initially. This property is also called the participation constraint (Rasmusen 1989).

Informational viability is important because RAMs which do not satisfy this property have informational requirements that exceed the available

[6] Formally (i) is called the privacy preserving property of the RAM, implying thatonly public information about one agent can be used by the other agents. A convenient way of formalizing (ii) is that the message space of the proposed RAM must be finite in Euclidian space. This means that the vector of information exchanged between the agents has a finite dimension.

information. Any RAM that is not informationally viable may therefore not yield its intended outcome(s). Informational viability requires (i) that agents use only accessible information about the other agents, and (ii) that the amount of information is such that it can be treated (Campbell 1987).

Informational efficiency means that there exists no known RAM which satisfies the stated objectives at less cost of gathering and processing (Campbell 1987).

Incentive compatibility means that it should be in the self-interest of the firms to act in the prescribed way. Unfortunately joint incentive compatibility and Pareto optimality are not always possible, because of the problems of manipulation (Hurwicz 1972). An important implication of this is that incentive compatibility must be attained before welfare comparisons are made between different RAMs.

Informational viability and efficiency and incentive compatibility are required for the proposed RAM to yield a predictable outcome. To evaluate any RAM, a welfare indicator other than Pareto optimality is needed. Without going into a lengthy discussion on the choice of welfare criteria, I would like to point to:

1. Spulber (1989), who suggests replacing Pareto optimality with second-best Pareto optimality, as it does not rule out incentive compatibility.
2. Poe (1997), who argues for seeing several policy objectives in conjunction, ruling out cost minimization as an operational criterion. Poe suggests using social welfare maximization to rank policy options.

To sum up, the key aspects of any RAM are individual rationality, informational viability and efficiency, and incentive compatibility. In addition, some welfare criterion is needed which is jointly attainable with incentive compatibility. Second-best Pareto optimality is one such welfare criterion. Pure CAC regulations are not designed with these aspects in mind. Hence, it would only be under special cases that CAC regulations will yield outcomes that are efficient or even approach maximizing societal welfare.

4. INCENTIVE-BASED REGULATIONS REVISITED

The informational structure is detrimental to the applicability of the policy options available to regulators. An excellent example in this connection is the distinction made between nonpoint and point source pollution. One important characteristic of nonpoint source (NPS) pollution is the technological difficulties and often prohibitive high costs[7] of measuring pollution loads, and hence enforcement (see, for example, Shogren 1993; Tomasi et al. 1994). This has led NPS pollution research in the direction of policy instruments that do not depend on measuring emissions, that is, input-oriented policies (see, for example, Braden and Segerson, 1993; Vatn et al. 1997).

Another issue pertains to the ability of tailoring regulations toward local conditions, that is, the possibility of differentiating the regulation to the state of local recipients. With respect to CAC schemes this has been relatively non controversial as fixed emission standards can be differentiated easily. In the next subsections I shall discuss these issues in more detail for various IB schemes.

4.1 Emission Taxes

Emission taxes have several desirable features, such as (a) incentive compatibility provided that emissions can be monitored, (b) cost efficiency (equimarginal abatement costs among agents), (c) low informational requirements on behalf of the regulator, and (d) low transaction costs. The major disadvantage with emission taxes is that they are difficult to implement as they increase firms' overall costs (breach of individual rationality in the sense that other regulatory options cost less for the regulated firms).

Emission taxes can easily – in principle – be tailored to capture local differences in the marginal environmental damage functions, simply by operating with varying tax rates from one location to another.

4.2 Tradable Emission Permits

Tradable emission permits exhibit the same three first advantages as emission taxes, namely (a) incentive compatibility provided that emissions can be monitored, (b) cost efficiency (equimarginal abatement costs among agents), and (c) low informational requirements on behalf of the regulator. Transaction costs are generally assumed to be somewhat higher than is the case for emission taxes. Organizing the emission permit trading in a low-cost fashion, for example in terms of a permit exchange, helps to reduce transaction costs to the firms. This, however, requires some trading volume, which again implies that firms must be somewhat heterogeneous.

Tradable permits are not so easily implemented if there are few prospective trading partners, which for example is the case when one deals with local pollutants. The primary reason for this is that it is easier to obtain price-

---

[7] In the sense of rendering the externalities Pareto irrelevant, compare Dahlman (1979).

taking behavior in the emission permit market if the number of participating firms is large. This limits the applicability of tradable emission permits when pollutants mainly have local effects, and environmental damages vary between locations, as the emission permit market may become 'thin'.

The issue of avoiding locally high emission levels through the concentration of permits on a few firms, has been addressed by altering the trading rules, including:

- ambient permits, that is, that trades cannot take place if ambient standards are exceeded (Montgomery 1972), and
- pollution offset permits, that is, that increased emissions[8] for one firm cannot occur unless similar reductions take place for other firms emitting to the same receptor (Krupnick, et al. 1983; McGartland and Oates 1985; McGartland 1988).

The empirical experience from these and other alterations of the basic tradable emission permit scheme are generally negative, resulting in few trades taking place (for a summary, see Hahn 1989). In the same article, Hahn concludes that the lesson from this is a need to keep trading schemes simple, predictable and transparent.

4.3 Taxes on Polluting Inputs

Taxes on polluting inputs are generally suggested when there is a clear linkage between input use and environmental damages. A nice feature of such taxes is that it alleviates the need for (costly) monitoring. It should also be noted that taxes on polluting inputs generally do not yield equimarginal abatement costs. Hence, in theory, less-costly options exist.

The primary example of such taxes are found in NPS settings, for example with taxes on fertilizers in agriculture.[9] The environmental performance of such taxes are mixed. For example a recent study by Vatn et al. (1997)[10] concluded that to reach the necessary reductions in nitrogen leaching, nitrogen taxes needed to be 150 percent or more of the original nitrogen price. Such high taxes had undesirable distributional consequences with the tax penalizing grain farmers – with generally lower nutrient leakages – more than intensive livestock units generating higher nutrient leakages. At such high nitrogen tax rates this policy was not the least-costly policy option.

---

[8] Irrespective of whether standard, emission taxes or tradable emission permits are chosen, individual firm compliance needs to be monitored. In the case of taxes, knowing the emission level of individual firms is the base from which a firm's emission tax payment is issued.

[9] A recent discussion of issues linked to nutrient leakages in agriculture is Romstad et al. 1997.

[10] These results emerged from a five-year research program on NPS in Norwegian agriculture, involving both economists and natural scientists.

However, combining a 100 percent nitrogen tax with a 50 percent catch crop requirement yielded the desired reductions in nitrogen leakages at lower costs in private as well as societal terms in some regions. This combination of policies also provided substantial reductions in the variability of nutrient leakages between years (Vatn et al. 1997).

It should also be noted that it is difficult to vary input taxes between regions, as this would result in trade leakages between regions.[11]

4.4 Tradable Permits on Polluting Inputs

Tradable permits on polluting inputs works the same as taxes on polluting input factors at the margin. This also includes a breach on the theoretical efficiency criterion requiring equimarginal abatement cost. As is the case for emission taxes and tradable emission permits, tradable permits on polluting inputs reduces firm profits less than its tax counterpart. Another desirable feature of tradable input factor permits over input taxes is that they can easily be varied between regions.

4.5 Extensions of the Basic NPS Models

In particular for the NPS setting, the basic IB models exhibit several undesirable features including:

- breach of the efficiency criterion requiring equimarginal abatement costs,
- insufficient capabilities of reducing variability in emissions, and
- difficulties in adjusting policies to varying local environmental damages.[12]

I have already mentioned the finding by Vatn et al. (1997) regarding the possibility of combining tax measures with other policies such as catch crops. Other interesting IB policies include making the NPS problem into a point problem.

One such approach is found in Millock et al. (1997). They suggest providing farmers with a menu of contracts, where farmers adopting self-monitoring practices face different regulations from those with traditional

[11] With differences in input factor permit prices exceeding transportation costs between regions, one would expect trade leakages to occur. This is easily countered by reducing aggregate permit levels in 'export' regions.

[12] It is self-evident that the costs of environmental damages from nutrientloadings to a highly valued (say Norwegian) salmon river exceed those of having the same nutrient loadings flow into a less valuable (say a Swedish) river.

farming practices. With prices for such monitoring equipment set to drop in the future, this becomes an interesting possibility.

Another such approach is Romstad (1997a).[13] He suggests monitoring nutrient loads or ambient standards at the watershed or river-stretch level, hence reducing monitoring costs compared to monitoring nutrient leakages from farm fields. With the borders of farm operations rarely following watershed or river-stretch boundaries, this requires producing incentives for farmers to work in teams.

Both these approaches (Millock et al. 1997; Romstad 1997a) employ menus to generate separating equilibria, and this increases the possibilities of tailoring policies in relation to local environmental damages. Another common feature of these approaches entails potential gains in efficiency and environmental performance over traditional NPS solutions by transforming the NPS problem into a point source. This highlights the effect of information on efficiency.

5. CONCLUDING REMARKS

This chapter delivers a strong case for incentive-based regulations over command and control regulations, provided:

1. that firms are sufficiently heterogeneous in their marginal abatement-cost schedules, and
2. that the geographical location of emissions is not so restrictive that the *ex-ante–ex-post* problem noted by Atkinson and Tietenberg (1982) becomes more important than cost considerations.

If neither of these two conditions is violated, the most important argument in this chapter is that the demarcation between IB and CAC regulations regarding environmental performance is not the regulation itself, but how regulations are enforced. Exploiting the parallels between tradable and non-tradable emission permits, it is shown that CAC regulations do not lead to improved environmental performance over IB regulations. On the contrary, in a dynamic setting it is argued that regulations that have strong incentives for reducing marginal abatement costs over time, result in lower aggregate emission levels.

Another important result is that for IB regulations to yield cost savings over CAC regulations, there needs to be a certain heterogeneity among the regulated firms. More specifically, increased heterogeneity increases the cost

[13] Romstad (1997a) is downloadable from Internet, http://www.nlh.no/institutt/IOS/publikasjoner/d9701.htm.

savings of IB schemes over CAC regulations in incomplete information settings. In this context it should also be noted that if the regulator has incomplete information on firms' abatement-cost structures, it is only through carefully designed IB regulations that the degree of heterogeneity is revealed to the regulator.

The third major insight from this chapter is that IB schemes can be tailored to reduce variability in emissions and to account for local and seasonal variations in environmental sensitivity to emissions. In this connection it should be noted that it is more difficult to make such considerations for nonpoint than point sources. When local or seasonal considerations are important, transforming nonpoint source problems to point source problems appears a promising avenue for further research.

REFERENCES

Atkinson, S.E. and T.H. Tietenberg (1982), 'The Empirical Properties of Two Classes of Designs for Transferable Discharge Markets', *Journal of Environmental Economics and Management*, **9**(2): 101–21.

Baumol, W.J. and W.E. Oates (1988), *The Theory of Environmental Policy*, Cambridge University Press, Cambridge.

Braden, J.B. and K. Segerson (1993), 'Information Problems in the Design of Non-point-source Pollution Policy', in Russell, C.S. and J.F. Shogren (eds), *Theory, Modeling and Experience in the Management of Nonpoint-source Pollution*, Kluwer Academic Publishers, Boston, MA, pp. 1–36.

Brännlund, R., L. Hetemäki, B. Kriström and E. Romstad (1996), *Command and Control with a Gentle Hand: The Nordic Experience*, Final report from the NERP project 'Economic Instruments in Environmental Policy: The Nordic Forest Sector', Swedish University of Agricultural Sciences, Umeå, Sweden.

Campbell, D.E. (1987), *Resource Allocation Mechanisms*, Cambridge University Press, Cambridge.

Cropper, M.L. and W.E. Oates (1992), 'Environmental Economics: A Survey', *Journal of Economic Literature*, **30**(2): 657–740.

Dahlman, C.J. (1979), 'The Problems of Externality', *Journal of Law and Economics*, **22**: 141–62.

Hahn, R.W. (1989), 'Economic Prescriptions for Environmental Problems: How the Patient Followed the Doctor's Orders', *Journal of Economic Perspectives*, **3**(2): 95–114.

Hurwicz, L. (1972), 'On Informationally Decentralized Systems', pp. 297-336 in McGuire, C.B. and R. Radner (eds), *Decisions and Organizations*, North Holland, Amsterdam, The Netherlands, pp. 297–336.

Krupnick, A., W.E. Oates and E. Van De Verg (1983), 'On Marketable Air-pollution Permits: The Case for a System of Pollution Offsets', *Journal of Environmental Economics and Management*, **10**(3): 233–47.

McGartland, A.M. (1988), 'A Comparison of Two Marketable Discharge Permits Systems', *Journal of Environmental Economics and Management*, **15**(1): 35–44.

McGartland, A.M. and W.E. Oates (1985), 'Marketable Permits for the Prevention of Environmental Deterioration', *Journal of Environmental Economics and Management*, **12**(3): 207–28.

Millock, K., D. Sunding and D. Silberman (1997), 'An Information-revealing Incentive Mechanism for Nonpoint Source Pollution', manuscript, Department of Agricultural and Resource Economics, University of California, Berkeley, CA.

Montgomery, W.D. (1972), 'Markets in Licenses and Efficient Pollution Control Programs', *Journal of Economic Theory*, **5**: 395–418.

Oates, W.E., P.R. Portney and A.M. McGartland (1989), 'The Net Benefits of Incentive Based Regulation: A Case Study of Environmental Standard Setting', *American Economic Review*, **79**(5): 1233–42.

Poe, G.L. (1997), 'Extra-market Values and Conflicting Agricultural Environmental Policies', *Choices*, **12**(3): 4–8.

Rasmusen, E. (1989), *Games and Information: An Introduction to Game Theory*, Basil Blackwell, New York, NY.

Romstad, E. (1997a), *Team Approaches in Reducing Nonpoint Source Pollution*, Discussion Paper #D01/1997, Department of Economics and Social Sciences, Agricultural University of Norway, Ås, Norway.

Romstad, E. (1997b), *Environmental Performance: An Extension of Weitzman*, Discussion Paper #D16/1997, Department of Economics and Social Sciences, Agricultural University of Norway, Ås, Norway.

Romstad, E. and O. Bergland (1990), *Principles for Obtaining Optimal Emission Levels When Abatement Costs Are Private Information*, Oregon State Graduate Faculty Working Paper No. 90-103, Oregon State University, Corvallis, OR.

Romstad, E. and O. Bergland (1993), 'Inducing Individual Firm Compliance to Emission Quotas When Abatement Costs are Private Knowledge', paper presented at the Fourth Meeting of the European Association of Environmental Economics at Fontainebleau (June 29–July 3, 1993), France.

Romstad, E. and O. Bergland (1997), 'Manipulation of Emission Permit Markets', in Nau, R., E. Grønn M. Machina and O. Bergland (eds), *Economic and Environmental Risk and Uncertainty*, Kluwer Academic Publishers, Dordrecht, The Netherlands, pp. 75–86.

Romstad, E. and B. Kriström (1994), *Environmental Regulations and International Competitiveness*, Department of Economics and Social Sciences Discussion Paper #D04/1994, The Agricultural University of Norway, Ås, Norway.

Romstad, E., J.W. Simonsen and A. Vatn, eds (1997), *Controlling Mineral Emissions in European Agriculture: Economics, Policies and the Environment*, CAB International, Oxon, UK.

Shogren, J.F. (1993), 'Reforming Nonpoint Pollution Policy', pp. 329-345 in Russell, C.S. and J.F. Shogren (eds), *Theory, Modelling and Experience in the Management of Nonpoint-Source Pollution*, Kluwer Academic Publishers, Dordrecht, The Netherlands, pp. 329–45.

Spulber, D.F. (1989), *Regulation and Markets*, MIT Press, Cambridge, MA.

Tomasi, T., K. Segerson and J. Braden (1994), 'Issues in the Design of Incentive Schemes for Nonpoint Source Pollution Control', in Dosi, C. and T. Tomasi (eds), *Nonpoint Source Pollution Regulation: Issues and Analysis*, Kluwer Academic Publishers, Dordrecht, The Netherlands, pp. 1–37.

Vatn, A., L.R. Bakken, P. Botterweg, H. Lundeby, E. Romstad, P.K. Rørstad, and A. Vold (1997), 'Regulating Nonpoint Source Pollution from Agriculture: An Integrated Modelling Analysis', *European Review of Agricultural Economics*, **24**(2): 207–29.

Vatn, A. and D.W. Bromley (1997), 'Externalities – A Market Model Failure', *Environmental and Resource Economics*, **9**(1): 131–51.

Weitzman, M.L. (1974), 'Prices vs. Quantities', *Review of Economic Studies*, **41**: 477–91.

4. Locally Rational Affection and the Choice of Environmental Policy Instruments

Francesco Ferrante*

For I would almost say that this very thing,
self-knowledge, is wisdom and I am at one with who
put up the inscription of those words at Delphi
(Plato, Charmides, 160 D-E)

1. INTRODUCTION

The consensus view of economists is that the formation of wants does not fall within the province of economic analysis: it is contended that the objective of economic analysis is to observe the *consequences* of choices which reveal underlying preference structures, not to question the psychological and physiological causes of wants or to investigate the mechanisms governing the formation of preferences. Building on this, it is assumed that one can always derive a preference ordering, which may be incorporated in well-behaved utility functions, from actual market behaviour.

The legitimacy of this operation becomes questionable if one admits that wants may be internal to the socio-economic process and influenced by market dynamics. Habit formation due to past consumption experience is now a widely discussed case in which people's choices affect their future preferences. The idea that preferences may be malleable has led to a reconsideration of how economic agents' behaviour is to be understood; specifically, consumption analysis is being rethought in many respects.

* Universita' di Cassino, Facoltà di Economia, Dipartimento Economia e Territorio, Via Mazzaroppi s.n., 03043 Cassino (FR) Italia; tel. 39 0776 299440; fax: 39 0776 312035; email: f.ferrante@caspur.it. I would like to acknowledge valuable comments from Paul Burrows, Neil De Marchi, Alistair Munro, Charles Perrings, Kerry Smith and participants at various seminars. The usual disclaimer applies. Financial support from Ministero dell' Universita e della Ricerca Scientifica e Tecnologia is gratefully acknowledged.

Preferences conditional on market dynamics are a serious problem for welfare economics, even though they may not be for empirical analysis (Hogarth and Reder 1986; Pollak and Wales 1992).

On purely theoretical grounds, within traditional consumer theory, two main strands of research can be identified, reaching quite different conclusions on the relevance of this form of time dependence to economic analysis.

The first approach originates from well-known contributions on 'rational habit formation' (Stigler and Becker 1977; Becker and Murphy 1988), whereby 'rational' habit formation is said to be the result of a non-myopic dynamic optimization process (that is, the agents know the marginal rate of substitution of current for future consumption). The second approach takes a less sanguine view of agents' awareness and ability to learn the psychological mechanisms governing habit formation and reaches the opposite conclusion, namely that contingent choices are affected by the dynamics of preferences in a way that is not anticipated by agents (Pollak 1970, 1976, 1978). On this view, agents take their consumption history into account but are not able to recognize the impact of present consumption on future tastes (that is, they do not know the marginal rate of substitution of current for future consumption).

The present contribution can be placed within the so far empty intersection between these two approaches on the role of habit in consumption, since it posits that agents are 'locally rational', that is, they form 'rational expectations' on habit formation but that the underlying learning process is centred on the actual consumption choices that they have experienced. For this reason, I refer to Becker and Murphy's concept of global rational learning, as opposed to local rational learning as the product of experience.[1]

On more general grounds, the idea of inter-temporal rationality underlying economic analysis and the postulate of consistency have been more strongly attacked by psychologists (for example, Thaler 1980; Loewenstein and Thaler 1989; Loewenstein 1988, 1992; Kahneman and Snell 1992) on the basis of the empirical evidence showing biases in the ability of individuals to predict their future tastes. This strand of analysis has progressively gained reputation within the economics profession, but its results are still rejected as a scientific proof of failure and a clear demonstration that the concept of intertemporal rationality and consistency being used by economists needs serious scrutiny. In this context, *procedural* as opposed to *substantive* rationality is recommended as a viable methodological option to build a consistent theory of decision (Simon 1978, 1986). Within this psychologist-led research area, contributions from *prospect theory* provide helpful insights

[1] The expression 'habit formation' will be replaced by 'affection', in that this seems to better reflect the psychological process underlying the formation of habits in consumption.

about the role of hedonic consumption habits in that they can be seen as *frames* that affect people's preferences and choices. The basic intuition is that people evaluate the hedonic consequences of choices as differences from a reference point. In this context, the endowment of consumption experience should be seen as a potential source of reference-dependent preferences[2] (Tversky and Kahneman 1986, 1990, 1991).

This recognition of the powerful connection between short-sighted choices and long-run outcomes should prompt rethinking of the normative implications of consumption theory. In particular, if one does not consider rational habit formation as a plausible account, locally rational (dis)affection may undermine the basis of standard welfare economics.

As Pollak suggests (1978), in a world characterized by myopic habit formation and the endogeneity of tastes, the competitive equilibrium does not guarantee that, given technological constraints and unconditional preferences, everyone gets what he/she wants but rather the converse; namely, that people come to want what they get. In this chapter, I suggest that one does not need to introduce myopia in habit formation to generate these disturbing results and that given habits, one should distinguish between unobservable unconditional preferences and observable preferences conditional on past choices.

The analytical framework presented here does not pretend to give a full account of the factors affecting consumers' intertemporal choices. My far more limited aim is to offer a coherent description of the effects of assuming that learning from experience is an idiosyncratic process. In particular, I investigate how locally rational affection or disaffection may generate persistence or, alternatively, discontinuity in the experienced patterns of consumption. Building on this, I identify two main types of agents, distinguished by different attitudes towards repetition in consumption.

Section 2 discusses the role of locally rational affection or disaffection in inter-temporal choices. Section 3 discusses the main implications of assuming existence of an affection process in environmental economics. Section 4 considers the implications of behavioural inertia for the analysis of the efficient control of global warming. Finally, Section 5 draws the main conclusions.

2. LOCALLY RATIONAL (DIS)AFFECTION PROCESSES

The logic behind locally rational affection or, alternatively, disaffection is very much akin to the idea of local learning, applied to the analysis of

[2] *Loss aversion* and *diminishing sensitivity* are two main features of the model that one can find in the model of (dis)affection.

technical change, developed by Atkinson and Stiglitz (1969) and David (1975). Whereas in the latter what is affected by local learning is the technical coefficient of the production function, in the former it is the parameters of the utility function.

As in firms' technological learning, in the presence of locally rational (dis)affection, the consumer's affection or disaffection for consumption patterns is assumed to be locally rational within an appropriate neighbourhood of the current consumption choice. *By 'appropriate neighbourhood' I mean the space of consumption possibilities that is the actual object of hedonic experience.* Conversely, goods or services that are not consumed or that are sufficiently remote from the current consumption choice in terms of embodied characteristics are supposed not to generate affection or disaffection. It is worth emphasizing here that the assumption of locally rational (dis)affection does not imply myopia in the strong form assumed in the literature. Notably, I assume that the households recognize the impact of current choices on future preferences, that is, learn from their choices and form correct expectations. The contention is that the opportunities for this learning process are restricted to the actual consumption choices, so that the untried choices are excluded from the learning process and do not generate correct expectations on (dis)affection.[3]

The idea that familiarity may affect choices is not new in the psychological literature and is consistent, in particular, with the idea that utility from consumption depends not only on direct experience but also on the memory of past and the anticipation of future consumption. In fact, one should expect that the actual extent of both these intertemporal consumption spillovers is affected by the level of familiarity of consumption: 'The impact of memory and anticipation on current utility lead to a type of triple counting of experience. A single event can influence utility first through anticipation, then through direct experience, and finally through memory' (Elster and Loewenstein 1992, p. 214). Most important, the role played by past consumption experience in determining future choices is crucial in that

> unlike the future, the past cannot be altered, so that its effects on the present are largely determined by prior decision. Our current selves are largely at the mercy of past selves, although we have some limited capacity to direct our thoughts toward or away from the past or even to represent the past as we wish. But if past selves have endowed us with an overly rich or lean stock of memories, there are limits to our capacity to cognitively amend them without lapsing into autism (Elster and Loewenstein 1992, p. 214)

---

[3] The relevance of this point will be made clearer later in the discussion of the model.

There are different ways of modelling the impact of experience on consumer behaviour. One may consider individuals who are initially nonconsumers of a commodity who become consumers thanks to the information acquired through consumption. Another strategy is based on the idea that consumption generates experience and skills (for example, mountain climbing). In this chapter I follow an intermediate strategy based on the idea that consumption generates both information and hedonic experience which affect the level of effective satisfaction delivered by commodities.

The mechanism leading to the building up of (dis)affection in consumption can be more fruitfully set forth through the analysis of household choice in the space of commodities' characteristics[4] (Lancaster 1971) by assuming that the households get (dis)affected to the set, combinations and intensity of characteristics which are present in the commodities or appliances they consume or use most. Thus, they attach decreasing or increasing utility over time to those patterns of consumption which embody the same packages of characteristics or similar ones. For simplicity, I abstract from all considerations of risk and uncertainty. This may discontent those who think that the essence of dynamic problems is ignored. But I contend that this is not the case, in that the model captures the main features of the choice problem and that issues of uncertainty may be introduced later on.

In the spirit of the household production model, let us assume that agents have well-behaved utility functions $U_t = F(\boldsymbol{Z}_t)$ defined over a finite set of weakly separable consumption services $\boldsymbol{Z}_t = (Z_{1t}, \ldots, Z_{st}, \ldots, Z_{mt})$. The homogeneous flow of services Z_s can be provided by different commodities: there are 'n' such commodities in the economy which embody two characteristics, c_1 and c_2, in different combinations (speed and comfort, say, for transportation services).

As $n \rightarrow \infty$ one can display isoquants yielding the flow of homogeneous services Z_s defined over characteristics through standard continuous curves. One can think of each pair (c_{1i}, c_{2I}) as the arguments of a fixed-coefficient Leontief-type consumption technology:

$$Z_{sit} = \text{Min}(\omega_{Iit}c_{1it}, \omega_{2it}c_{2it}) \tag{4.1}$$

where ω_{1it} and ω_{2it} for $I = 1, \ldots, n$ determine the level of efficiency in the provision of service 's' by using consumption technology 'i' at time 't' (that is, the effective quantity of characteristics per unit of the commodity that

[4] I shall use the term 'commodity' (and not 'good') which is more consistent with the household production model.

provides services[5] '*s*'). Notably, according to this formulation, the assumption of Leontief consumption technology over characteristics allows for *ex-ante* substitutability through the availability of a continuum of commodities that embody different combinations of characteristics[6] Now, let us suppose that whenever a commodity is chosen, affection or disaffection builds up according to the following specification:

$$\omega_{kit}^{h} = \omega_{ki}^{h*} + f\left(\delta_i^h, \mu_i^h, \Omega_i^h, t\right) \tag{4.2}$$

for $k = 1, 2$ characteristics, where $i=j$ is the commodity chosen, and

$$\omega_{kit}^{h} = \omega_{ki}^{h*} + \phi_i^h\left(\theta_{i-j}\right) f\left(\delta_i^h, \mu_i^h, \Omega_i^h, t\right) \tag{4.3}$$

for $i \neq j$. The arguments of the (dis)affection function play the following role: $\mu > 0$ is the rate of decay of experience or the gross rate of disaffection, $\delta > 0$ is the gross rate of habit accumulation, $\Omega>0$ is the maximum level of (dis)affection formation and $0 < \phi(\theta) < 1$ determines the actual amount of consumption experience that spills over on to the untried consumption technologies, where θ_{i-j} is the distance (for example, the Euclidean distance in the characteristics space[7]) between commodity '*i*' and '*j*'. The following conditions are assumed to hold: $f_\delta > 0$, $f_\mu < 0$, $f_\Omega > 0$, $f_t > 0$. In addition, for $\delta - \mu > 0 \Rightarrow f_{\delta-\mu} > 0$, and repetition in consumption yields affection where, $\lim_{t \to \infty} f\left(\delta_i^h, \mu_i^h, \Omega_i^h, t\right) = \Omega_i^h$ and, of course, $\lim_{t\to\infty} \phi_i^h\left(\theta_{i-j}\right) f\left(\delta_i^h, \mu_i^h, \Omega_i^h, t\right) = \phi_i^h\left(\theta_{i-j}\right)\Omega_i^h$ for $i \neq j$. Conversely, for $\delta-\mu < 0 \Rightarrow f_{\delta-\mu} < 0$ repetition yields disaffection: in the latter case, one may reasonably suppose that the lower bound of the disaffection is '0' in that the household would withdraw from consumption if it yields zero utility. The rationale behind this formulation of preferences is that the extent to which (dis)affection builds up varies among different types of commodities and, for some commodities, repetition may yield decreasing benefits.[8] On the other hand, some households may like repetition and others dislike it.

The idea of diminishing consumption spillovers, as portrayed here, has its counterpart in the property of diminishing sensitivity discussed by Kahneman and Tversky in their analysis of reference dependent preferences. 'The impact of a difference [between two consumption bundles, measured on a given dimension] is attenuated when both options are remote from the

[5] In order to economize in notation, the subscript '*s*' has been suppressed.
[6] The isoquant map at time '0', which is just a continuous approximation of the set of discrete consumption technologies, can be generated through a standard Cobb–Douglas function defined over characteristics, that is, $Z_{s0} = c_{1s0}^{1-\beta} c_{2s0}^{\beta}$.
[7] A suitable measure is the Euclidian distance.
[8] The idea of decreasing inter-temporal benefits must be distinguished from the concept of diminishing marginal utility.

reference point for the relevant dimension' (Tversky and Kahneman 1990, 1040).

In Figures 4.1 and 4.2, below, the generic commodity is represented, in the characteristics space, as ray-vectors '$0T_i$' of equation $c_{1it} = (\omega_{2it}/\omega_{1it})c_{2i}$. Given the choice of technique $0T_i$ at time '0' for $\delta - \mu > 0$ the unitary isoquant moves down towards the origin over time (Figure 4.1) whereas for $\delta - \mu < 0$ the opposite holds (Figure 4.2).

There are five main differences between this formulation of the (dis)affection function and Pollak's: here (i) habit formation is a bounded process and its upper limit depends on the specific consumption experience (that is, the consumption technology chosen at the reference point), whereas Pollak derives this limit by imposing stationarity; (ii) the (dis)affection process does not depend on the absolute amount of each characteristic/commodity consumed but on the time spent in using a particular commodity; (iii) the build-up of consumption experience is defined over characteristics and is locally neutral with respect to the latter, namely, the rate of (dis)affection formation over time is the same for both the characteristics; this implies that we move down on a commodity-ray over time (that is, $c_{1it} = (\omega_{2it}/\omega_{1it})c_{2it} = \omega_i{*}c_{2it}$); (iv) the model allows for affection as well for disaffection; (v) finally, the model is not based on the strong albeit plausible assumption that the household does not learn over time from experience: it suggests that learning is an idiosyncratic process.

The connections between this model and the model of reference-dependent preferences are strong. But, while the basic intuition is the same, the latter provides a general explanation of why people display a *status quo* attitude, whereas the model of local (dis)affection offers a specific interpretation of the mechanisms linking idiosyncratic hedonic consumption experience to preferences. Moreover, in addition to *loss aversion*, the model considers the possibility that, due to disaffection, the endowment of consumption experience generates *aversion to repetition.*

An alternative interpretation of the impact of past consumption experience on preferences, consistent with that offered here, is based on the concept of *spatial discounting*, that is, the idea that, in addition to discounting utility over time, people discount utility according to the proximity – in terms of hedonic experience – of the objects that yield utility. If this is the case, the household discounts current consumption according to the time-dependent level of familiarity with past consumption choices. Zero discount rates would be used by the households that like repetition on the replicated familiar choice, and increasing rates would be charged on less familiar commodities. Conversely, households that dislike repetition would charge negative and increasing discount rates for less familiar commodities. Positive or negative discounting, in the space of commodity characteristics, would depend on people's attitude towards repeat consumption. Of course, in this context, the rates of (dis)affection formation in (4.2) and (4.3) should be seen as discount rates.

This interpretation of the impact of experience on consumer preferences can also be developed within a model of choice under uncertainty. In a world of uncertainty, familiarity with consumption should be expected to affect the *ex-ante* subjective distribution of hedonic experience from consumption and, hence, the expected utility from consumption: if, plausibly, the variance of the distribution is inversely correlated with familiarity, risk-averse individuals would tend to undervalue unfamiliar consumption bundles, risk-prone individuals the opposite.

Going back to the model, at this point, one can define the unconditional consumption function as the one in which the efficiency coefficients are not affected by past consumption experience, that is,

$$Z_{sit} = \mathrm{Min}[\omega_{1i0}c_{1it}, \omega_{2i0}c_{2it}] \tag{4.4}$$

I assume that the set of unconditional consumption technologies is well-behaved, so that the isoquants map showing the *ex-ante* combinations of characteristics that yield the same level of service satisfies the usual convexity property.

The corresponding conditional consumption technologies are the time-dependent consumption technologies conditional on past consumption experience, that is, $Z_{st} = \mathrm{Min}[\omega_{1it}c_{1it}, \omega_{2it}c_{2it}]$, where '$\omega_{kit}$' is given in (4.2). In addition, agents' conditional consumption technologies are explicitly defined over the parameters of the learning function, notably, the decay rate 'μ', the rate of affection 'δ', the potential for (dis)affection 'Ω' and the spillover function $\phi(\theta)$. The intuition behind this specification is that although *ex ante* one can treat the consumption possibilities as a continuous set displaying the usual desirable properties, *ex post* this operation becomes unfeasible, in that the building up of experience is idiosyncratic, that is, specific to a certain consumption technology (namely, a particular commodity–ray in the characteristics space). Nevertheless, this assumption on the diffusion of experience does not lead to the extreme outcome of a putty-clay specification of the consumption technology in that, by introducing spillovers, I allow also for *ex-post* substitutability, in the spirit of a putty–semiputty technology[9] (Fuss 1977).

[9] In the semi-putty technology, the *ex- post* substitutability is always less than the *ex ante* and the former is a choice variable affected by the expected price level; see Fuss (1977) and McFadden and Fuss (1978).

Figure 4.1. Locally rational effect

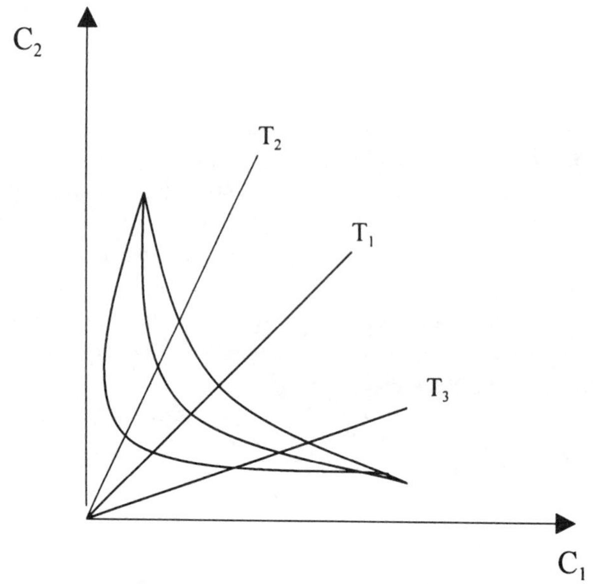

As a preliminary classification, one can distinguish different types of (dis)affection-generating technologies, respectively in terms of rate of (dis)affection accumulation and total potential for (dis)affection. One may also classify the (dis)affection-generating technologies by degree of localization and therefore, on the basis of the *ex-post* degree of substitutability they confer on consumption technologies, a concept that will become clearer later in the discussion. In particular, the latter classification is based on the shape of the consumption spillover function: convex functions are associated with weaker localization and identify potentially more flexible technologies/households, whereas quasi-concave functions are associated with strong localization and identify less flexible technologies/households. In the case of complete spillovers, that is, $\phi(\theta) = 1 \; \forall \; i = j$, *ex-ante* and *ex-post* substitutability coincide; when spillovers are zero *ex-post* substitutability tends to zero as time goes to infinity.[10]

A useful classification can be drawn also for the case where $\delta - \mu < 0$ that is, when repetition of consumption yields decreasing satisfaction. The spillover function in this case determines the extent to which the untried

[10] In the terminology of Fuss (1977), convex spillover functions would yield putty--putty technologies (that is, *ex-ante* and *ex-post* substitutability) whereas concave spillover functions would generate putty–clay technologies (that is, *ex-ante* substitutability and *ex-post* zero substitutability).

consumption technologies, owing to their similarities with that adopted, generate less disaffection over time than that adopted. This case will be more thoroughly investigated in the context of the analysis of innovative behaviour in consumption discussed below.

Let us focus now on the dynamics of affection, that is, $\delta - \mu > 0$. Suppose that within the interval t=[0,t*], given the constant price vector, properly redefined over the characteristics,[11] and constant income, the representative agents optimally consume the bundle $[c_{1j}^*, c_{2j}^*]$ embodied in commodity-ray 'j' of equation $c_{1jt} = (\omega_{2jt}/\omega_{1jt})c_{2j} = \omega c_{2j}$.

How would the indifference map look at time $t^* > 0$ under the assumption that $\delta - \mu > 0$? The intuitive answer is that it will show increased curvature around the actual consumption choice and, hence, reduced substitutability between characteristics that the household could obtain through changes in the commodities purchased.

This case is depicted in Figure 4.1 where the shape of the unitary level of service takes on larger curvature around the actual consumption bundle ($0T_1$).

The implication of this pattern of locally rational affection is straightforward: as time passes, the household gets locked into the space of characteristics that belong to an appropriate neighbourhood of the characteristics embodied in the commodity actually consumed. The main consequence is that own-demand price elasticity for that specific commodity will decrease over time.

Another implication of the model is that a convex isoquant map may not be retained over time if the spillover function displays strong concavity, that is, if the affection process is highly localized.

The extent of localization of the consumption experience and the consequent locking-in effect will presumably differ among households and commodities. Households that display a 'conservative' attitude, that is, that have, *ceteris paribus*, a higher 'memory' parameter, will follow a more localized consumption pattern and will eventually be more locked in. The same applies to commodities that generate more idiosyncratic affection through consumption, that is, that are characterized by concave spillover functions for example, because of their complexity, perhaps, or the tacit nature of the knowledge required to use and enjoy them at their full potential.[12]

The main conclusion is that with local affection, changing prices[13] may lead the household to regret previous choices and *reverse* its *preferences*. In fact, the household may realize the availability of better affection technologies –

---

[11] If p_1 is the price of commodity 'one', then the unit cost of characteristic 'two', purchasing commodity 'one' is p_1/ω_{21}.

[12] For instance, durable goods, electric and electronic equipment.

[13] See Appendix 4A for the derivation of demand function.

relative to those experienced in the past – through the consumption of previously untried commodities induced by a new set of prices. In this context, regret may arise from looking back at one's consumption experience and seeing lost opportunities for larger affection gains from consumption. The consumer can be likened to a mountain climber who, on his/her way towards the peak, surveys the landscape below and realizes that he/she could have chosen an easier way. Contrary to this, in the case of disaffection, shown in Figure 4.2, the consumer that has adopted technology $0T_1$, would be induced to change the consumption technology under unchanging prices, as soon as it becomes inferior.

Figure 4.2. Locally rational disaffection

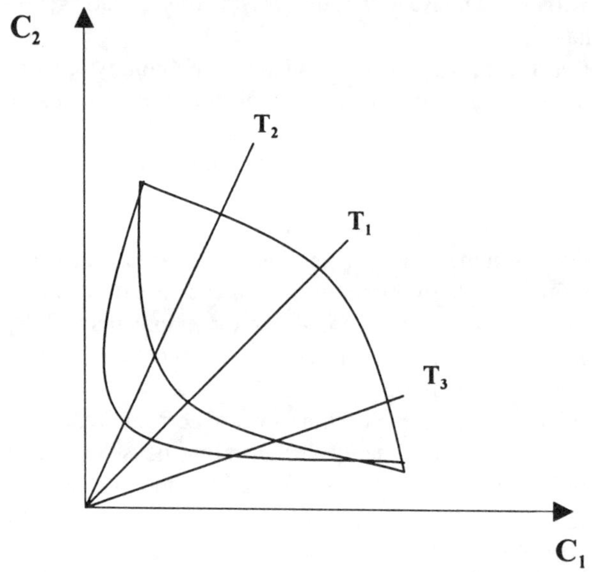

Hence, conditional consumption technologies may differ not only in ability to provide homogeneous services at the minimum cost at the reference point but also in different (dis)affection-generating technology,[14] and a specific pattern of (dis)affection (that is, a different 'memory' parameter) is associated with each consumption choice. The distinction drawn above between types of agent helps to predict different attitudes towards innovation in consumption and efficiency implications. In this respect, one may

[14] As a matter of simplification, I have intentionally left out from this the existence of consumption externalities due to interdependent utility functions. Naturally, the pattern of social interaction, through its 'demonstration effect', should affect the behaviour of people over time. Hence, one should add a further element to the previous picture, the link between agents' (dis)affection and aggregate consumption patterns.

distinguish two types of innovations in consumption: (i) *subjective innovations*, induced by changing prices with a given set of commodities; (ii) *objective innovations*, that is, those induced by the introduction of new commodities with given prices. According to this distinction we can identify:

1. Conservative agents (type 'C'), characterized by $\mu - \delta < 0 \ \forall \ t$ and/or very concave spillover functions,[15] one should expect that for this type of agent the incentive to carry over subjective innovations will be absent and the inclination to adopt objective innovations will be relatively small and will shrink over time.
2. Innovative agents (type 'I'), such that at least for some interval Δt, $\mu_{\Delta t} - \delta_{\Delta t} > 0$ and/or $\phi(\theta)$ is convex for $\mu_{\Delta t} - \delta_{\Delta t} < 0$ and concave for $\mu_{\Delta t} - \delta_{\Delta t} > 0$;[16] these agents will be more prone to innovations.

It is possible to show that, in the case of *subjective innovations*, the following propositions hold.

Proposition I:
Under the condition $\delta - \mu > 0$ conservative households will choose globally optimal consumption profiles only in the specific case where the unconditional cost-minimizing consumption technology also yields the highest level of total affection (the largest area under the affection curves).

Proof: For simplicity, since utility is a monotonic increasing transformation of the flow of services, we can refer to the latter. Let us assume that, *if they are adopted*, the flow of services provided over life by two affection-generating consumption technologies is given by $Lz_{si} = \int_0^T Z_{sit}\, dt$ (where i= *a*, *b*). Moreover, the two technologies, *if adopted*, satisfy the conditions: $Z_{sa0} = \text{Min}[\omega_{1a0}c_{1a0}, \omega_{2a0}c_{2a0}] > Z_{sb0} = \text{Min}[\omega_{1b0}c_{1b0}, \omega_{2b0}c_{2b0}]$ and $LZ_{sb} > LZ_{sa}$ which, of course, implies that for $t > t^*$ $Z_{sat} < Z_{sbt}$. Since the household will choose the short-run cost-minimizing technology '*a*', because affection spillover is smaller than 1, '*b*' will never cross '*a*' from below, that is, $Z_{sat} > Z_{sbt}$ for all *t*'s. Hence, only when $a = b$ will the cost-minimizing household choose the statically efficient technology that also yields the higher level of utility over the entire life. This proof can easily be extended to the case of '*n*' technologies.

The intuition behind Proposition I is straightforward: households that enjoy repetition will do best if they commit to an intertemporal consumption

[15] For example, $\phi(\theta) = 1 - \theta^2$.

[16] For example, $\phi(\theta) = 1 - \theta$.

profile that provides the higher level of total affection. Notably, in this case, short-run and long-run optimal choices coincide.

Proposition II:
Under the condition $\delta - \mu < 0 \; \forall \; t$, *innovative households will always choose the optimal consumption path.*

Proof: This proof is symmetric to Proposition I. Let us assume that the flow of services Z_{st} provided by two consumption technologies i = a, b for which $\mu > \delta$, satisfy the following condition: $Z_{sa0} = \text{Min}[\omega_{1a0} c_{1a0}, \omega_{2a0} c_{2a0}] > Z_{sb0} = \text{Min}[\omega_{1b0} c_{1b0}, \omega_{2b0} c_{2b0}]$. Since the household will choose the short-run cost-minimizing technology 'a', because affection spillover is smaller than 1, 'b' will cross 'a' from below, that is, there is a $t = t^* < T$ such that $Z_{sat} < Z_{sbt}$ for all $t > t^*$. Hence, the household will optimally switch to 'b' at t^*. This proof can be easily extended to the case of 'n' technologies: if these technologies are ordered such that $Z_{sh0} < ... < Z_{sh0} < ... < Z_{s10}$ the household will switch to another technology whenever Z_{sht} crosses Z_{sh+1t} for $t < T$ ('a' is the optimal intertemporal consumption profile if 'b' crosses 'a' for $t > T$).

In this case, continuous dissatisfaction generates flexibility and inclination towards innovation. Given the consumption possibilities open to them, households will minimize the adverse impact of repetition, thereby maximizing total satisfaction.

Figure 4.3. Locally rational affection

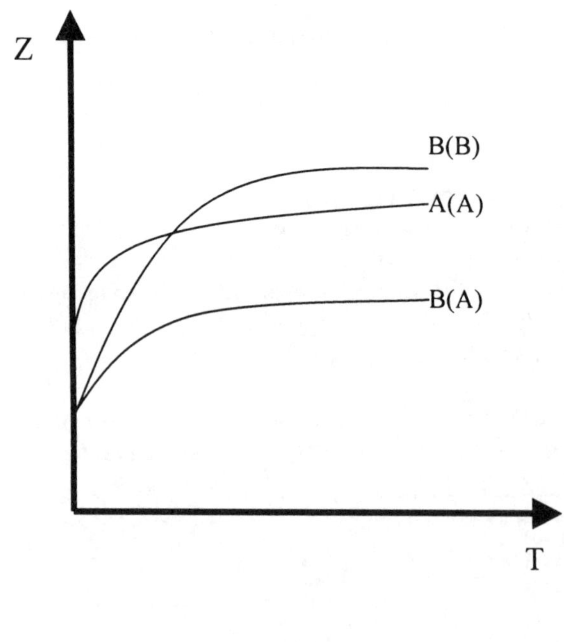

A graphical example may help to clarify these arguments. Suppose that there are just two commodities, which generate the flow of services Z_{sit} where i = A, B, and A(A), B(B) are the levels of service under adoption of, respectively, A and B, and B(A) is the level of service of B conditional on the adoption of A. Because of the monotonic concave shape of $U_t = (\boldsymbol{Z_t})$, the associated consumer utility would display the same concave shape. Figure 4.3 plots the levels of services over time stemming from the direct consumption of each of the two commodities (that is, if it is chosen). In this particular case, owing to the fact that commodity 'B' presents a stronger affection process (that is, the integral under 'B' is larger than under 'A') it should be preferred even though 'A' yields a higher level of utility over the interval [0, t*].

Figure 4.4 illustrates the case of monotonic disaffection; for i = C, D at t = 0, C is adopted and at t = t* the consumer switches from C to D. By doing so, it also switches to the new disaffection formation technology D. One should expect that under the assumptions made, the consumer will keep switching back and forth between C and D over time.

Figure 4.4. Locally rational disaffection

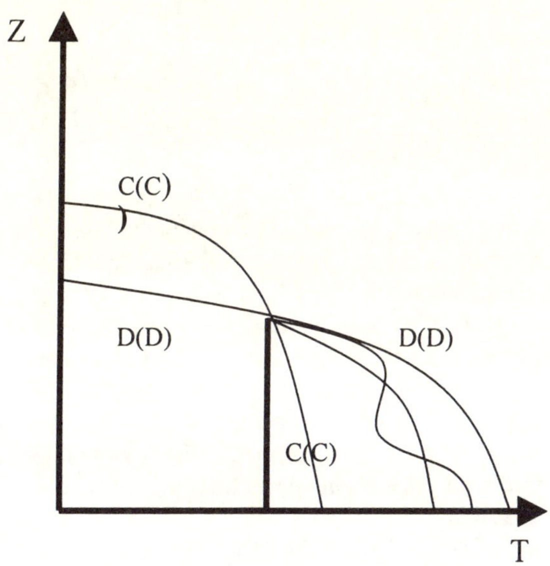

Building on these results, one may argue that a conservative attitude limits the household's ability to follow an intertemporally optimal consumption profile whereas an innovative attitude (or alternatively, a tendency to easy disaffection) leads it to search for the optimal intertemporal path. This is hardly comforting for the innovative households, in that their inability to enjoy repetition may well imply that over their entire life cycle they will get a lower level of total effective services than the conservative non-optimizers! But of course, they cannot choose which type they wish to be.

A limiting but interesting case is one in which $\delta - \mu < 0$ and the slope of the disaffection technology is so steep that this highly innovative household quickly exhausts all its consumption opportunities and withdraws from consumption (if no sufficiently radical innovations are introduced in the meantime). I shall call this the 'Oblomov case'. I am sure that sociologists and psychologists alike can provide examples proving that this is no mere theoretical curiosity.

The main working hypothesis deriving from the interpretative framework presented here is that, owing to locally rational affection, under the condition that $\delta - \mu > 0$ people's preferences may show a quite stable intertemporal pattern within the boundary of an appropriately defined subset of choices. As has been shown, this stable pattern needs to be correctly defined over choices as well as over the associated affection processes. Conversely, if the opposite condition holds, one should observe an unstable pattern of intertemporal preferences and choices, which should be not interpreted as a signal of inconsistent behaviour (on dynamic consistency see, for example, Strotz 1956; Hammond 1976).

3. LOCALLY RATIONAL AFFECTION (LRA) AND ENVIRONMENTAL ECONOMICS

Economists have traditionally been suspicious of endogenous tastes. Yet this attitude appears untenable in the light of empirical evidence and experimental studies on the role of experience in preference formation. The recent impetus to incorporate taste formation and change into economic analysis has come primarily from those interested in household behaviour rather than welfare, and the principal focus of this work has been empirical demand analysis. Indeed, taste formation and change pose more difficult problems for welfare analysis than for demand analysis. Most important, preferences are necessary for environmental economics, but cannot be inferred from market behaviour.

The main implications of the model of LRA that I intend to discuss here pertain to specific methodological issues, that is, the reliability and predictive validity of non-market valuation in the presence of feedbacks from experience to choices, and general implications for environmental policy concerning the feasibility and cost effectiveness of market-based instruments.

As far as the methodological issues are concerned, I shall touch on the following aspects:

1. The need to consider the specific characteristics of the object of investigation in non-market valuation in relation to the potential for experience and (dis)affection.
2. The role of information provision as a substitute for consumption experience in CV (contingent valuation).

3.1 The Revelation of the Demand for Environmental Quality and LRA

I have shown that under 'locally' rational affection, unconditional preference ordering may not coincide with long-run preference ordering. This is a serious challenge to non-market valuation in that the preference ordering revealed through the integration of market data on demand may not reveal the 'true' underlying structure of people's preferences. Substantial methodological changes are required, in empirical work, along the lines envisaged, by Cameron and Englin (1996) among others, to account for the role of experience in preference formation.

Decades ago, Harsanyi suggested that when one faces changing tastes 'the operational meaning of the proposed concepts of "taste" and of "utility" cannot be defined in terms of the consumer's market behaviour alone but must involve a reference to his verbal and expressive reactions' (1954, p.207).

The paucity of the studies which address the role of experience in CV does not permit one to draw conclusions on its actual impact. Empirical support for the conclusion that experience matters emerges from the studies[17] by Munley and Smith (1976) and Cameron and Englin (1996). They suggest that if one controls for consumption experience and familiarity, estimated willingness to pay (WTP) appears to be larger and more reliable. Moreover, the authors find that there are discrete jumps in resource values as experience increases from zero and that more-experienced respondents have smaller conditional variances.[18]

Contrasting results are achieved by Kealy et al. (1990), who compare two commodities that lie at the extreme of the private/public good continuum (a brand-name chocolate bar and a deacidification programme for lakes). The authors test the hypothesis that familiarity and experience generate more reliable contingent values for the private good. They finally conclude that the nature of the good may have little influence on the reliability and predictive validity of the CVM.

[17] On the role of habit formation, see also Adamowicz (1994).
[18] On the role of experience and familiarity in CVM, see also Kealy et al. (1990); Kealy et al. (1988).

Much richer is the psychological literature addressing a related issue, namely, the extent to which people are able to predict their future tastes. For instance, Loewenstein and Adler (1995) provide empirical support for the hypothesis that predictions of future tastes are substantially biased.

The model of locally rational (dis)affections has clear implications for analysis regarding (i) the need to account accurately for experience in consumption in connection also with the nature of the commodity that is being valued and (ii) the ineffective role of information provision in CV.

The reasonable assumption that hedonic experience and the potential for affection is not purely subjective but depends also on the nature of the commodity implies that analysts should construct appropriate CV surveys that account for this. Turning to the second question raised, the main practical consequence of affection is that the researchers' provision of information should not be considered as a good substitute for consumption experience since the accumulation of the latter is a time-consuming process. The attempts to put actual users and potential users of environmental goods in the same position by providing the latter with information about the goods that they have not experienced will not, in general, yield reliable results.

While estimating existence values does not appear to pose particular problems – since the researcher is interested in assessing WTP when consumption is zero – the option value should be substantially affected by experience and familiarity, in that what is measured is the value that people attach to the option of consuming in the future.[19]

3.2 LRA and the Choice of Policy Instruments

It is reasonable to suppose that the absence of markets for the environment and the resulting underpricing of pollution, which still characterizes developed and underdeveloped societies alike, has generated *locally* rational affection for pollution. The presumption is that locally rational cost-minimizing choices have led to inherently polluting consumption habits (Harsanyi's 'civilized prejudices'; Harsanyi 1954) that disregard the availability of consumption choices based on a higher level of consumption of environmental quality. If this is the case, in present conditions, the market-determined willingness to pay for environmental quality may systematically understate society's long-run true valuation of environmental quality and the corresponding level of efficient *Pigouvian* pricing.

Moreover, under persistence of consumption habits, only drastic relative price movements, to be achieved through environmental costing, would

[19] On this issue see, for example, Whitehead et al. (1995).

induce households to change their consumption habits to achieve sustainable consumption patterns.

It appears that, under these circumstances, a *contractual* approach to long-term environmental planning, based on the revelation of social demand for environmental quality through the markets, is neither feasible nor desirable. Most important, under the persistence of consumption patterns induced by affection the use of economic incentives may be less efficient and cost effective than is generally claimed. Conversely, command and control instruments such as technology-based environmental standards may be less inefficient than is suggested by economic theory. This intuition finds some support in a few empirical studies showing that technology-based environmental standards may heighten firms' and consumers' awareness of unexplored opportunities for cost-effective pollution control (Porter and Van der Linden 1995). These arguments appear very relevant to the debate on the efficient control of global warming.

4. THE EFFICIENT CONTROL OF GLOBAL WARMING IN THE PRESENCE OF INERTIA

Environmental policy in the energy sector offers an opportunity to debate the role of behavioural inertia of energy users in connection with the choice of policy instruments. Debate on the cost of climate changes is locked in two critical difficulties: on the one hand, the assessment of the short- and long-term flexibility of the production and consumption systems; on the other, the choice of cost-effective incentive mechanisms to increase flexibility and abate emissions of greenhouse gases. The connection between these two points of contention is evident in the debate on the role of price-induced and autonomous technical change in reducing energy intensity. Adopting a high value of the potential for autonomous energy efficiency improvements, envisaged by bottom-up analyses, reduces the cost of abatement strategies and stresses the influence of research and development (R&D) and technology policies on energy demand and supply. Conversely, a conventional top-down model assuming fixed technology and no major market failures takes price signals as the sole policy variable and concludes that the cost of abatement will be higher (Wilson and Wisher 1993).

The model of LRA provides a rationale for the findings of the many empirical studies suggesting that, because of market barriers, there are opportunities in the energy sector that only government action can exploit. Market barriers to energy efficiency are implied by engineering calculations when a device based on proven technology saves energy at or below the price of energy and is not being adopted after being on the market for several years. In addition, there must be no hidden costs and the input parameters used for the calculation must capture the range of possible physical situations and the usage characteristics throughout the economy. (Sanstad et al. 1993, p. 2)

Along the same lines, market barriers to the development of eco-efficient technologies are implied when the rate of return on the R&D capital employed in an energy project is higher, according to engineering calculations, than the rate which is obtained on energy projects of equivalent riskiness and this project is not carried out for several years. There is an intrinsic linkage between market barriers, which limit the potential size of the market for innovations, and the generation of R&D barriers.

The emerging evidence *that there are free lunches* in the energy sector[20] that should be explored through policy action does not imply the strong conclusion that agents are irrational but simply, according to the model, that they are locally rational and lack subjectively reliable information about their consumption opportunities (Porter and van der Linden 1995; Sanstad et al. 1993; Ferrante 1996).

The explanation offered in the economic literature of why households may not invest in more efficient energy technologies yielding favourable rates of returns is that the rate of time preference of these households is particularly high (Hausman 1979) so that they attach a small weight to financial benefits occurring far in the future through savings in the energy bill. The estimated implicit very high discount rates seem to suggest that the latter is not a very convincing interpretation. There is a more plausible story suggested by the model of locally rational affection relying on the idea that the household may discount not only in time but also in space. *That is to say, when they compare tried/familiar with untried/unfamiliar energy technologies – in terms of embodied characteristics – in addition to time discounting, they apply a positive and decreasing spatial discount rate to the flow of energy services according to the level of familiarity of the technology.*

On the other hand, analyses based on market barriers suggest that price-induced changes in the structure of energy production and consumption to achieve a sustainable pattern of CO_2 emissions, are not feasible, at least on political grounds, because price changes of the size required to overcome these barriers cannot be implemented. *Non-price* modifications, which may eventually counteract market barriers, should be considered as well. The

[20] The idea that there are unexplored opportunities to improveeco-efficient technologies in the energy sector is supported by several technical studies showing that the rates of return on these R&D projects are higher than on projects of equal risk (on this point see, for example,Rubin et al. 1993).

same indication emerges from other analyses showing that the carbon taxes that would have to be implemented to stabilize the global emissions would be invariably very high, reaching intolerable levels early in the next century. For example, according to the European Commission estimates, a tax of $10 per boe on all energy sources (excluding renewable) would be needed in Europe to achieve just half the abatement target required to stabilize emissions of CO_2 at the 1990 level. Indeed, these conclusions are very much in line with the model's implications about the incentives to subjective innovations in consumption.

Environmental policy in the energy sector and, specifically, the attempts in the European Union to introduce measures of energy taxation are very good examples of policy failure induced by behavioural and institutional rigidity. The major emphasis posed in the debate on the need to switch from *command and control* to a *market-based* approach to the control of emissions declined promptly when the discussion moved to practical implementation issues. The level of taxation required to achieve the emission control targets of SO_2 and CO_2 have been, so far, invariably considered too high and unsustainable on economic grounds by the interest groups that lobby in the political arena at national and European levels. The groups and countries supporting deregulation and free market opposed energy taxation and favoured the more familiar command and control approach to emission control.

The findings strengthen the case on behalf of the idea that the level of energy taxation required to induce technological switching is not feasible and that a politically feasible energy tax alone would not suffice to make individuals alter their behaviour significantly. Other incentive schemes are required which may reduce the costs of switching to eco-efficient energy technologies (according to the model, by reducing the cost of eco-efficient technologies, these measures would ease innovations in consumption).

The list of measures is well known. The specific role of the available instruments in the pursuit of institutional and behavioural flexibility[21] is discussed in Ferrante (1998).

5. CONCLUSION AND QUALIFICATIONS

The model of locally rational affection developed in this chapter is not based on the strong – albeit very plausible assumption – of myopia in learning through experience, but it reaches the same conclusion as the myopic habit models (Pollak 1978); notably, that given technological constraints and

[21] On the preference for *preference* flexibility, see, for example, Koopmans (1964); Kreps (1979).

unconditional preferences, the household may come to want what it gets rather than to get what it wants.

This result is derived under the assumption that the opportunity for rational learning processes is restricted to the actual consumption choices so that the untried commodities do not generate rational expectations on habit formation.

According to a 'prospect theory' interpretation of this story, in the presence of psychic decision costs, localized learning and habit formation can be viewed as rational protocols developed by consumers to reduce decision costs in uncertain environments. On the other hand, utility and preferences in this context, as suggested by Kahneman and Snell (1992, p.187), appear to be 'a characteristic of experienced outcomes, not an inference from observed decisions'.

Indeed, the results derived from this simple model are quite disturbing for environmental economics in that short-run optimal choices governed by unconditional preferences and rational expectations may well lead conservative households to inefficient intertemporal choices. Moreover, behavioural inertia may delay desirable markets and institutional adjustment processes.

In the previous sections I have shown that the model of locally rational affection provides a convincing explanation for the institutional and behavioural inertia in the energy sector which block the implementation of schemes of carbon taxation. There is a now wide body of literature suggesting that a policy mix should be preferred to single instruments in the pursuit of pollution control, notably, carbon taxation. This is not a new story in that environmental policy around the world, in practice, is a collection of economic and command and control interventions that may appear, in *ex post* terms, a policy mix. Unfortunately, in most of the cases, this historical sedimentation of measures appears hardly cost effective in that it lacks political, administrative and economic coherence. Conversely it seems that, to generate good performance, the adoption of an environmental policy mix requires an explicit *ex ante* coordination of the measures concerned. In particular, measures should be coordinated internally and they should also be consistent with other measures of economic policy.

In this context, the principle of *neutrality of carbon taxation* should imply that the revenues raised through a *politically feasible* carbon/energy tax should be used to finance demand-side management and technology policies and that the use of an economic approach to the control of emissions is not to be confined to the final source of market failure – the emissions – but should be extended to its original cause, that is, the production and consumption energy technologies.

Finally, to come to political feasibility, a mix based on energy taxation, technology and demand-management policies has a substantial advantage over single instruments in that it can contribute significantly to institutional flexibility: in fact, by redistributing the costs of technological switching, it reduces the incentive for lobbying by those groups that would otherwise have to bear most of the adjustment costs.

REFERENCES

Adamowicz W.L. (1994), 'Habit Formation and Variety Seeking in a Discrete Choice Model of Recreation Demand', *Journal of Agricultural and Resource Economics*, **19**(1), 19–31.Atkinsonand Stiglitz, J. (1969), 'A New View of Technical Change', *Economic Journal*, **79**, 573–8.

Becker G.S. and Murphy, K.M. (1988), 'A Theory of Rational Addiction', *Journal of Political Economy*, **96**, 675–700.

Cameron T.A and Englin, J. (1997), 'Respondent Experience and Contingent Valuation of Environmental Goods', *Journal of Environmental Economics and Management*, **33** (3), 296-313

David, P. (1975), *Technical Choice, Innovation and Economic Growth*, Cambridge: Cambridge University Press.

Elster, J. and Loewenstein, G. (1992), 'Utility from Memory and Anticipation', in Loewenstein G. and Elster J. (eds), *Choice over Time*, New York: Russell Sage Foundation, 213–34.

Ferrante, F. (1996), 'Mercati Incompleti, Incertezza e Politica Ambientale', *Società Economia e Istituzioni*, n.1, 205–26.

Ferrante F. (1999), 'Localised Technical Change and the Efficient Control of Global Warming', forthcoming in J. Van Der Straaten, C Spash and D. Requier Desjardens (eds) *Environmental policy and Societal Aims*, Kluwer Press

Fuss, M.A and McFadden, D.(1978), 'Flexibility vs. Efficiency in *ex ante* Plant Design', in Fuss, M.A and McFadden, D. (eds), *Production Economics: a Dual Approach to Theory and Applications*, Amsterdam: North-Holland.

Fuss, M.A. (1977), 'The Structure of Technology over Time: A Model for Testing the "Putty-clay" Hypothesis', *Econometrica*, **45**(8), 1797–1821.

Hammond, P.J. (1976), 'Changing Tastes and Coherent Dynamic Decisions', *Review of Economic Studies*, **43**(3), 159–73.

Harsanyi, J.C. (1954), 'Welfare Economics of Variable Tastes', *Review of Economic Studies*, **21**(3), 204–13.

Hausman, J.A. (1979), 'Individual Discount Rates and the Purchase and Utilization of Energy-using Durables', *Bell Journal of Economics*, **10**, 33–54.

Hogarth, R.M. and Reder, M.W. (1986), 'Editors' Comments: Perspectives from Economics and Psychology', *Journal of Business*, **59**(4), S185–S207.

Kahneman, D. and Snell, J. (1990), 'Predicting Utility', in Hogarth, R.M. (ed.), *Insights in Decision Making*, Chicago and London: University of Chicago Press, 295-310

Kahneman, D. and Snell, J. (1992), 'Predicting a Changing Taste: Do People Know What They Will Like?', *Journal of Behavioral Decision Making*, **5**, 187–200.

Kahneman, D. and Tversky, A. (1979), 'Prospect Theory: An Analysis of Decision Under Risk', *Econometrica*, **47**, 263–91.

Kahneman, D., Knetsch, J.L. and Thaler, R. (1990), 'Experimental Tests of the Endowment Effect and the Coase Theorem', *Journal of Political Economy*, **98,** 1325–48.

Kealy, M.J., Dovidio, J.F. and Rochel, M.L. (1988), 'Accuracy in Valuation is a Matter of Degree', *Land Economics*, **64**, 158–71.
Kealy, M.J., Montgomery, M. and Dovidio, J.F. (1990),'Reliability and Predictive Validity of Contingent Values: Does the Nature of the Good Matter', *Journal of Environmental Economics and Management*, **19**, 244–263.
Knetsch, J. (1989), 'The Endowment Effect and Evidence of Nonreversible Indifference Curves', *American Economic Review*, **79**, 1277–84.
Knetsch, J. and Sinden, J.A. (1984), 'Willingness to Pay and Compensation Demanded: Experimental Evidence of an Unexpected Disparity in Measures of Value', *Quarterly Journal of Economics*, **99**, 507–21.
Koopmans, T.C. (1964), 'Flexibility of Future Preferences' in Shelly M.W. and Bryan G.L. (eds), *Human Judgements and Optimality*, Wiley, 243-254.
Kreps, D.M. (1979) 'A representation Theorem for Prefernce for Flexibility' *Econometrica*, **47**(3), 565-577
Lancaster, K.J. (1971), *Consumer Demand: A New Approach*, New York: Columbia University Press.
Lamb, W. (1964), *Plato with English Translation*, London: Harvard University Press.
Loewenstein, G. (1988), 'Frames of Mind in Inter-temporal Choice', *Management Science*, **34**(2), 200–14.
Loewenstein, G. (1992), 'The Fall and Rise of Psychological Explanations in the Economics of Intertemporal Choice', in Loewenstein, G. and Elster, J. (eds), *Choice over Time*, New York: Russell Sage Foundation, 3–34.
Loewenstein, G. and Adler, D. (1995), 'A Bias in the Prediction of Tastes', *Economic Journal*, **105**, 929–37.
Loewenstein, G. and Thaler, R.H. (1989), 'Anomalies. Inter-temporal Choice', *Journal of Economic Perspectives*, **3**(4), 181–93.
Munley, V.G. and Smith, V.K. (1976), 'Learning-by-Doing and Experience: The Case of Whitewater Recreation", *Land Economics*, **52**(4), 545-553
Pollak, R.A. (1970), 'Habit Formation and Dynamic Demand Functions', *Journal of Political Economy*, **78**, 60–78.
Pollak, R.A. (1976), 'Habit Formation and Long-run Utility Functions', *Journal of Economic Theory*, **13**, 272–97.
Pollak, R.A. (1978), 'Endogenous Tastes and in Demand and Welfare Analysis', *American Economic Review*, **68**, 374–79.
Pollak, R.A. and Wales, T.J. (1992), *Demand systems specification and estimation*, Oxford, New York, Melbourne, Toronto: Oxford University Press.
Porter, M.E. and Van der Linden, C. (1995), "Toward a New Conception of the Environment-Competitiveness Relationship', *Journal of Economic Perspectives*, **9**, 97–118.
Rubin, E., Cooper, R., Frosch, R., Lee, T., Marland, G., Rosenfeld, A. and Stine, D. (1993), 'Realistic Mitigation Options For Global Warming', Working Paper.
Sanstad, A.H., Koomey, J.G. and Levine, M.D. (1993), 'On the Economic Analysis of Problems of Energy Efficiency: Market Barriers, Market Failures and Policy Implications', Technical Report, Lawrence Berkeley Laboratory, Technical Report, LBL-32652/UC-350.
Simon, H.A. (1986), 'Rationality in Psychology and Economics', *Journal of Business*, **59**(4), S209–S224.
Simon, H.E. (1978), Rationality as Process and Product of Thoughts', *American Economic Review*: P&P, **68**, 1–16.
Stigler, G.J. and Becker, G.S. (1977), 'De Gustibus Non Est Disputandum', *American Economic Review*, **67**(2), 76-90
Strotz, R.H. (1956), 'Myopia and Inconsistency in Dynamic Utility Maximization', *Review of Economic Studies*, **23**(3), 165–80.
Thaler, R. (1980), 'Toward a Positive Theory of Consumer Choice', *Journal of Economic Behavior and Organization*, **1**, 39–60.

Tversky, A. and Kahneman, D. (1986), 'Rational Choice and the Framing of Decision', *Journal of Business*, **59**(4), S251–S278.

Tversky, A. and Kahneman, D. (1990), 'Rational Choice and the Framing of Decisions', in Cook, K.S and Levi M. (eds), *The limits of rationality*, Chicago and London: University of Chicago Press, 60–89.

Tversky, A. and Kahneman, D. (1991), 'Loss Aversion and Riskless Choice: A Reference Dependent Model', *Quarterly Journal of Economics*, **106**, 1039–61.

Whitehead, J.C., Blomquist, G.C., Hoban, T.J. and Clifford, W.B. (1995), 'Assessing the Validity and Reliability of Contingent Values: A Comparison of On-site Users, Off-site Users, and Non-users", *Journal of Environmental Economics and Management*, **29**(2), 238–51.

Wilson, D. and Wisher, J. (1993), 'Exploring the Gap. Top-down vs. Bottom-up Analyses of the Cost of Mitigating Global Warming', *Energy Policy*, March, 249–63.

APPENDIX

The derivation of the household's short-run demand functions associated with the utility function and the consumption technology is straightforward. Assuming M to be the agent's income, under standard assumptions on the shape of the utility function $U_t = F(\mathbf{Z}_t)$ and its weakly separable and homothetic[22] form, one can compute the optimal weights 'α_s' of the flow of services in the total household expenditure budget (Pollak and Wales 1992). Then, the demand for the flow of services Z_s at time 't' is:

$$Z^*_{st} = \frac{a^*_s M}{\underset{i=1,\dots,n}{\mathrm{Min}}\left[p_{it}\left(\frac{1}{\omega_{1it}}+\frac{1}{\omega_{2it}}\right)\right]} \tag{4A1}$$

where, $\underset{i=1,\dots,n}{Min}\left[p_{it}\left(\frac{1}{\omega_{1it}}+\frac{1}{\omega_{2it}}\right)\right]$ is the minimum cost of getting one unit of homogeneous services 's' and, of course, the time-contingent efficiency parameters 'ω' are given in (4.2) and (4.3). The long-run demand functions under the steady-state condition $\omega_{kit} = \omega_{kit-1} = \omega_{ki}^*$, reflecting the fact that the build-up of (dis)affection has been exhausted, for k=1,2 and i=1,...,n can be derived as:

$$Z^*_{st} = \frac{\alpha^*_s M}{\underset{i-1,\dots,n}{\mathrm{Min}}\left[\lim_{t\to\infty} p_{it}\left(\frac{1}{\omega_{1it}}+\frac{1}{\omega_{2it}}\right)\right]} \tag{4A2}$$

It is worth remarking that the limit for the steady-state condition[23] should be more correctly computed over the household's life span. It is reasonable to suppose that, as a general case, the two limits will not differ significantly. Conversely, one should expect that relevant differences could occur in the case of very slow rates of (dis)affection and a high potential for (dis)affection. On the other hand, the household's planning horizon is not

[22] For non-homothetic functions the weight should be expressed as a function of income.
[23] These demand functions are not Marshallian in that prices are not exogenous.

relevant, in that the assumption of locally rational (dis)affection implies that short-run and long-run maximization would yield the same optimal choices, so that one can restrict attention to the former, simpler case.

5. Impacts of Environmental Policy on International Trade and Capital Movement: A Synopsis of the Macroeconomic Literature

Tim Jeppesen, Henk Folmer and Marinus H.C. Komen

1. INTRODUCTION

The notion of efficiency has received a lot of attention in environmental economics. Research has focused primarily on a comparison of policy instruments in terms of costs of achieving policy targets, including costs that various subjects of the policy incur as well as costs associated with implementation and enforcement. The standard result is that economic instruments, that is, taxes and tradable permits, are superior to command and control.

Efficiency analysis is usually performed under the assumption that environmental policy does not lead to relocation of capital and, hence, the costs associated with relocation are ignored. In recent policy debates, however, capital flight has become a major issue and forms an important impediment to the implementation of environmental policy. Capital flight and relocation of firms were major arguments launched by opponents in the discussions about the introduction of environmental and energy taxes in Denmark, Sweden and the Netherlands. They have also played a role in the discussion about an EU CO_2 tax. Because of possible capital flight the Dutch energy tax applies only to consumers and small producers (see, for example, Komen and Peerlings 1998). An EU CO_2 tax is still under discussion and it is unlikely that it will be introduced at all. Moreover, some of the larger industries in Denmark and Sweden are exempted from the CO_2 tax because of possible capital flight.

The likelihood of capital movement and firm relocation has undoubtedly been facilitated by trade liberalization and harmonization of regulations and product norms, both regionally (the enlargement of the European Union (EU) and the creation of the North American Free Trade Agreement (NAFTA)) and at the world scale (World Trade Organization (WTO)). As a consequence of these developments, firms that relocate may still have access to the market they have left. In this context international mergers are also relevant because they may make it possible to shift production without physical relocation of production facilities. Moreover, as a consequence of the opening up of new markets in developing countries and Eastern Europe, regions have emerged with environmental policies that are substantially more lax than the ones prevailing in most Western countries. Finally capital movement and relocation of firms have been facilitated by new communication techniques such as the Internet.

Capital movement and relocation behaviour have received quite some attention in recent environmental economics literature. A distinction can be made between macro and micro approaches. The latter focuses on location behaviour of firms while the former concentrates on aggregates in the form of trade and international capital movement. Trade and capital movement are closely related and therefore form the main subject of macro studies.

This chapter gives a concise[1] review of the literature dealing with the impacts of environmental policy on capital movement and international trade.[2] The organization of the remainder of this chapter is as follows. In Section 2 we summarize the Heckscher–Ohlin model, some models of international capital mobility, and some models that combine trade and international capital mobility. These models form the framework within which the effects of environmental policy on international trade and capital flight are analysed. Section 3 deals with theoretical analyses of the impact of environmental policy while Section 4 presents an overview of empirical studies. Conclusions follow in Section 5.

2. THE GENERAL THEORETICAL FRAMEWORK

In the analysis of capital flight induced by environmental policy, extensive use is made of the Heckscher–Ohlin (HO) model of international trade and the theory of international capital movements. Both theoretical frameworks are summarized below. Moreover, a model that combines both approaches is discussed.

---

[1] We do not intend to give a complete overview. However, the selection is made in such a way that all relevant aspects are dealt with from all angles of incidence.

[2] It should be observed that the related problem of strategic environmental policy is not dealt with in this chapter. This problem relates to the possibilities that governments may wish to distort their environmental policies to achieve trade and capital movement objectives rather than deal with the consequences of such policies which is the focal point of this review chapter. For details on strategic environmental policies, see Ulph (1997) and the references therein.

2.1 The Heckscher–Ohlin Model

In the HO model, international trade is explained by differences among countries in terms of resources, such as land, capital and mineral resources. In the standard HO model two commodities are produced in two countries using two factors of production (that is, capital and labour). It is assumed that factors of production are mobile between sectors but immobile between countries, there are no transport costs, and there is free trade and perfect competition.

A country is abundant in a resource if it has a large supply of the resource relative to the supply of other resources. The country will tend to produce more of the commodities that use the more abundant resource intensively. In the absence of trade, capital will earn less in the capital-abundant country than in the labour-abundant country and labour will earn more. The capital-abundant country would have a lower relative price of the capital-intensive commodity than the labour-abundant country. Further, the difference in relative prices of commodities implies an even larger difference in relative prices of factors.

In the presence of trade the country will increase its production of the product in which it has a comparative advantage. The result is the HO theorem: countries tend to export commodities that are intensive in the factors with which they are abundantly supplied. Under the assumptions that: (i) production functions are identical in both countries and homogeneous of degree one, (ii) one commodity requires a greater proportion of one factor than the other commodity at any factor price at all points on any production function, and (iii) trade does not bring about complete specialization, the relative prices of commodities converge which leads to convergence of the relative prices of capital and labour. In the HO model, factor prices will be completely equalized. The capital-abundant country increases its production of the capital-intensive commodity and trades this commodity for the labour-intensive commodity of which the labour-abundant country has increased production. That is, more capital is embodied in the capital-abundant country's export than in its import. In this way the capital-abundant country exports some of its capital to the labour-abundant country. This is not done by a physical movement of capital (capital is assumed to be internationally immobile), but it is done by exporting the product which embodies the abundant factor. Hence factor price equalization is obtained through international movements of commodities. The classic references are Heckscher (1919), Ohlin (1933) and Samuelson (1948 and 1949). Recent references are, for instance, Krugman and Obstfeld (1997) and Gandolfo (1987).

2.2 International Capital Mobility

We shall now turn to capital location in a model with international mobile capital and no trade. Jasay (1960), MacDougall (1960) and Kemp (1964) (referred to as the MacDougall–Kemp model) examine the costs and benefits of foreign investment. It is assumed that there are two countries, two factors, unimpeded capital imports, perfect competition, constant returns to scale, external economies, no taxation and full employment. In each country the capital stock is owned partly by the native population and partly by foreigners. In this model, capital will flow to whichever country offers the greatest marginal return. Therefore, this model has the same property as the HO model, and factor prices will be equalized.

Important features of the model are diminishing average return on capital and the fact that capital-rich countries tie up too great a proportion of their resources in the foreign country. One argument for the latter is that there is divergence between the social and the private optimum. A capital investment in a country lowers the marginal product of capital but raises the marginal product of labour. The private investor does not consider the influence his/her investment has on domestic productivity; he/she considers only his/her private average rate of return. From the country's point of view, the optimum is attained when the marginal product of capital at home is equated to the marginal earnings abroad. Therefore, foreign investments tend to be excessive and should be curbed. This leads to the MacDougall–Kemp Theorem (Ruffin 1984): it pays the capital-exporting country that is large enough to influence the world interest rate to restrict incipiently its capital exports if the rest of the world does not retaliate.

For the analysis of environmental capital flight the general equilibrium neoclassical model developed by McLure (1970) is very important. He uses this general equilibrium neoclassical model to examine the sensitivity of capital location to various taxes levied in only one country. The model assumes that two countries use two factors, capital and labour, to produce one product under perfect competition. Taxes on production, labour and capital are considered and mobility parameters describe the degree of interstate factor mobility. They express the tendency of factors to migrate in response to differences in their earnings. The locational response of capital to a tax on production depends upon the elasticity of demand for the product. The higher the elasticity in the country that levies the tax, the higher the propensity to migrate to the non-taxing country. In addition to the elasticity of demand, the ease of substituting the untaxed for the taxed factor has to be taken into account. Thus, the model implies that capital migrates more in response to taxation of capital or production: (i) the easier labour can be substituted for capital in the taxing state, (ii) the easier capital is absorbed in production in the non-taxing state, and (iii) the better commodities from different states are substitutes in consumption.

2.3 Trade and International Capital Mobility

The HO model is an extreme case with unrestricted trade and factor immobility. The theory of international factor movements is the opposite extreme, which assumes perfect factor mobility but no trade. The real world is found in between these extreme cases. Mundell (1957) develops a theory for international factor mobility and describes the effects of introducing factor mobility into the HO model. His starting point is the HO model, that is, two countries, two commodities and two factors. One of the countries is well endowed with labour and poorly endowed with capital relative to the other country. One of the products is labour intensive relative to the other. Under the assumption that factors are immobile and trade impediments are absent trade will arise and commodity- and factor-price-equalization occur.

When we leave the classical HO model, and assume that all impediments to the movement of capital are removed and that the marginal product of capital is the same in both countries, no capital movement will take place. When the labour-abundant country under these conditions introduces a tariff on the capital-intensive commodity, the price of the capital-intensive commodity will rise relative to the labour-intensive commodity (in the labour-abundant country). Factors will move out of the labour-intensive industry into the capital-intensive industry. At constant factor prices the production shift creates an excess supply of labour and an excess demand for capital because factors are moving away from the labour-intensive industry. According to the Stolper–Samuelson tariff argument (Stolper and Samuelson 1941), the marginal product of labour must fall and the marginal product of capital must rise. This is due to the fact that the capital intensive sector becomes less capital intensive due to the inflow of labour from the labour-intensive sector. But since capital is assumed to be mobile, its higher marginal product in the labour-abundant country induces a capital movement into the country from the capital-abundant country. This will change the factor endowments so as to make the labour-abundant country more capital intensive. With linear, homogeneous, and identical production functions, as in this model, the mobility of capital results in equalization of prices as well as marginal products of both capital and labour. The tariff has eliminated trade, but after the capital movement there is no longer any need for trade;

capital movements have had the same effect as trade would have had. In this model, capital mobility is a perfect substitute for trade.[3]

3. IMPACTS OF ENVIRONMENTAL POLICY: THEORETICAL APPROACHES

For more than 25 years the impact of environmental policy on trade and capital movement has been in the limelight of literature on environmental economics. Some important references are: Baumol (1971), D'Arge and Kneese (1972), Walter (1974), Siebert (1974, 1977, 1979 and 1985), Markusen (1975), Asako (1979), Siebert et al. (1980), McGuire (1982), Rubin and Graham (1982), Merrifield (1988), Krutilla (1991), Rauscher (1991, 1992, 1995a, 1995b and 1997), Dean (1992), Zaelke et al. (1993), Cameron et al. (1994), Chichilnisky (1994), Copeland (1994), Copeland and Taylor (1994 and 1995), Steininger (1994), Wang (1995), Beghin and Potier (1997) and Ulph (1997). Any of these works has its own peculiarities and there is no easy way to summarize them. We continue the structure, laid down in the preceding section. We start with a model combining international capital movements and environmental policy. This type of approach is relatively simple because international capital movements can be dealt with in a framework with only one commodity. International trade models are more complicated and include at least two commodities. Most of the work has been done in the second category, connecting environmental policy and trade. From a policy perspective, the most interesting models are the third category, which is a combination of the two extremes. It is an unrealistic description of reality when either imperfect mobility of capital or absence of trade is assumed. There are, however, relatively few approaches that include both trade and international capital mobility.

As we shall show in the sequel, when the restrictive assumptions are relaxed in the HO model or in the models of international capital movements, the results become rather ambiguous. This may give some explanation for the limited number of studies dealing with trade and international capital movements simultaneously.

3.1 International Capital Movements

Rauscher (1997) develops a two-country static general equilibrium model with only one commodity produced and consumed. The model is based on the classic MacDougall–Kemp model. Capital stocks owned by the citizens

[3] Markusen (1983), Ruffin (1984) and Wong (1986) consider situations where they are complements.

of the home and foreign country are exogenously given and fixed. Capital in both countries is a composite of domestic and imported capital. Factors are assumed to be immobile across sectors but internationally mobile. Commodities are not internationally mobile so there will be no trade and transport activities. Pollution is caused by domestic and foreign emissions and stems from production as well as consumption. Income is composed of domestic output plus the return on capital invested abroad minus interest payments made to the owners of foreign capital. Welfare is a function of consumption and environmental quality is a function of emissions.

In this model there is a direct and an indirect productivity effect of emissions. The direct effect, which relates to emissions as a production factor, increases the productivity of capital. The indirect or external effect is that emissions may reduce the productivity of capital via production losses. The fact that the direct and the indirect effects have opposite signs generates ambiguities. This can be illustrated by also considering Rauscher (1992), of which Rauscher (1997) is an extension in the sense that Rauscher (1992) does not have consumption externalities or external effects on production.

In both models the central question is: what happens when a government relaxes its environmental policy? Two situations must be distinguished: (i) the country is small, that is, the marginal productivity of capital is fixed via the world market, and (ii) the country is large, that is, the home country's environmental policy has an impact on the foreign marginal productivity of capital. In the small-country case, Rauscher (1992) derives the unambiguous result that imposing a restrictive environmental policy repels mobile capital. Rauscher (1997), however, leads to more ambiguous results. The effects of a change in environmental policy on mobile capital consist of two effects, a productivity effect and an effect dependent upon consumption externalities. If the sum of the productivity effect and the consumption externality effect is positive (negative) capital tends to be attracted (repelled). For the overall productivity effect to be positive, the direct positive productivity effect needs to be larger than the negative indirect production effect. Decisive for the sign of the consumption externality effect is the size of the elasticity of substitution between capital and emissions. The elasticity of substitution is inversely related to the external effect on the marginal productivity of capital. The smaller the external effect on production, the larger the substitution effect, and a large elasticity of substitution gives a positive consumption externality effect. Therefore, a country may either attract or repel capital by imposing a restrictive environmental policy. The overall result is highly dependent on the typical parameter configuration representing the productivity effect and the consumption externality effect. It follows that under certain parameter constellations, the pollution heaven hypothesis holds, while under other parameter constellations, an 'environmental heaven' hypothesis holds. In the latter situation, countries can attract capital by introducing a tight environmental policy. This may, for instance, be the case when employees are unwilling to live in pollution heavens.

If the country under consideration is large, matters become even more complicated. Now we have to distinguish between the situation where the foreign emissions are given and the situation where they are variable. In the simple model without consumption externalities and external effects on production and under the assumption that foreign emissions are given, Rauscher (1992) shows that the large country can attract capital by loosening its environmental policy. This effect is the same as in the small-country case. However, it is weaker because it influences both the domestic and the foreign rates of return on capital.

If we assume that foreign emissions are variable,[4] then the effect of implementing a lenient environmental policy is also affected by an effect from the foreign country, which is induced by a change in emissions in the large country. Also in this situation a country can attract capital by implementing a more lenient environmental policy. However, the result is amplified because the capital flight from the foreign country reduces the marginal productivity of emissions and, since it is now lower than the emission tax, the foreign firms will react by reducing their emissions.

When consumption externalities and external effects on production are included, interaction effects of the consumption externalities and the pollution effects on production are generated and a great variety of results may occur. To derive results the analysis is simplified in two ways. First it is assumed that the foreign emissions are either given or are variable. Second, it is assumed that there is either no consumption externality, or no external effect on production.

If the foreign emissions are given and there is no consumption externality, we get the result that the effects of a change in environmental policy on mobile capital may be positive or negative. As in the small-country case, it is the direct and the indirect production effects that cause the ambiguities. The direct effect of increased emissions on the marginal productivity is positive. But the indirect effect is that increased emissions have detrimental effects on both domestic and foreign capital productivity. If the direct effect dominates, the country can attract mobile capital by imposing a lenient environmental policy. If the indirect effect dominates, it repels capital. If there are no external effects on production and foreign emissions are still given, we get the unambiguous result that a country can attract capital by imposing a lenient environmental policy. This result is similar to the results obtained in the simpler model in Rauscher (1992).

---

[4] Foreign emissions might be variable because the country has implemented emission taxes.

If foreign emissions are variable and there is no consumption externality, all effects of a more lenient environmental policy on capital location are ambiguous. The introduction of emission taxes adds further complexities to the model and hence, many of the effects become indeterminate.

Under the assumption that there is no external effect on production (but there are consumption externalities) a country can attract capital by implementing a more lenient environmental policy. Increased domestic emissions increase the productivity of capital and therefore foreign direct investment is increased. The foreign country now employs a smaller capital stock and if productivity is not affected by the externalities, the foreign country will have a reduction in the marginal productivity of emissions. With a given emission tax, foreign producers will reduce their emissions.

3.2 Trade

In some early papers, D'Arge and Kneese (1972), Walter (1974) and Siebert (1974) discuss how environmental policy influences commodity prices and thereby comparative price advantages. Siebert (1974) considers a two-country, two-sector model with only one production factor (natural resources). Production generates a pollutant that affects the ambient quality of the environment. The environment is considered as a receptor of pollutants. An environmental protection agency imposes an effluent charge and maximizes its 'profit' in terms of environmental quality.[5] From this maximization an expression for the scarcity price of the environment is obtained. Siebert (1974) finds a positive relationship between the scarcity price for the environment and commodity prices. If the two countries have different scarcity prices for the environment, it follows that the commodity prices will also differ. If country 1 has a lower scarcity price for the environment, the environment is relatively abundant in that country. Moreover, if country 1 has a relative price advantage in commodity 1, it will export that commodity. This leads to the theorem: the country richly endowed with the environment will export the commodity with a high pollution content. Similar conclusions are reached in D'Arge and Kneese (1972) and Walter (1974). In summary: when environmental policy is included in trade models, relative commodity prices are not only determined by relative marginal productivities, but also depend on (i) the marginal tendency to pollute, (ii) the marginal social damage caused by one unit of pollutant, and (iii) the total supply and demand of environmental services.

Environmental policy is not explicitly taken into account in the literature quoted above. Pethig (1976) relates trade theory to environmental policy and

---

[5] Alternatively, it can be assumed that the agency maximizes a social welfare function with the three arguments: the output from the two countries and environmental quality.

he explicitly rationalizes and qualifies environmental scarcity in a general equilibrium model. The model consists of two sectors where only one production factor (labour) is used in the production of two commodities (X1 and X2). X1 is relatively environment intensive and X2 is relatively labour intensive. Pethig assumes a fixed consumption ratio, which ensures that the international production ratio of X1 and X2 cannot change. Only the volume of production can change.

Production generates a pollutant that is released into the environment. In Pethig's model, pollution is not internationally mobile but is indirectly imported or exported in the two commodities. In this way trade affects the countries' environmental quality. Pethig (1976) first analyses a situation where the supply of environmental resources is large relative to demand, and no environmental controls are enforced in the two countries. These could be two developing countries. This situation leads to the Ricardian result as if labour were the only production factor. The countries' endowment of environmental services has no impact on trade. However, the countries' capacity of environmental services does affect the welfare in the countries. The country that specializes in the production of the environment-intensive commodity may suffer a welfare loss from trade, because additional pollution damages might offset the usual material gains from trade. The other country gains from trade. Next, Pethig considers the situation of two countries that have implemented pollution control differently; that is, pollution control is more restrictive in country 1. Then country 2 exports and specializes in the production of the environment-intensive commodity. This implies that the Ricardian case is replaced by a factor endowment basis for trade. This is the standard HO result, and is in accordance with D'Arge and Kneese (1972), Walter (1974) and Siebert (1974).

If an environmental standard is implemented, Pethig (1976) shows that the country with the lowest shadow price for pollution becomes the relatively well endowed with the pollution factor. The two countries' welfare is interdependent, because a change in one country's environmental policy will affect the volume of production and hence welfare in both countries.

In summary, Pethig shows that if environmental scarcity is explicitly taken into account, it may or may not affect trade depending on the scarcity of the environment. Further it is shown that the usual gains from trade do not always materialize. Welfare may decrease if the exported commodity is the more polluting commodity. Asako (1979) also obtains this result. Siebert et al. (1980) and McGuire (1982) extend Pethig's analysis to the case of two primary factors. Environmental policy in these models is, however, exogenous. By endogenizing environmental policy, patterns of trade are explained as a function of the underlying technology and endowments, rather than as merely reflecting exogenous environmental policy differences. This has been done in many different ways: (i) whether a country is small (for example, Copeland 1994) or large (for example, Krutilla 1991), (ii) whether pollution is local (for example, Copeland and Taylor 1994, Steininger 1994) or transboundary (for example, Markusen 1975, Copeland and Taylor 1995), or (iii) whether or not consumption externalities are taken into account (for example, Steininger 1994 and Rauscher 1992). In the sequel we shall analyse aspects of environmental policy and trade following Rauscher (1997). This model can be seen as a unified framework in which the different factors can be taken into account. Furthermore, he includes transport externalities and external effects on production, which are not dealt with in the other papers.

Rauscher (1997) considers a model with trade in final consumption commodities, and internationally immobile, but inter-sectorally mobile, factors. A country is producing two commodities with two factors, capital and an environmental resource. Perfect competition prevails. The foreign country is the rest of the world of which only its import demand or export supply functions are considered. Commodity one is the numéraire and its consumption does not cause any pollution. The consumption of commodity two, however, is causing pollution. Finally, environmental quality affects production, but not demand. In this model it is possible to vary the environmental policies and the pollution-impact parameters[6] and to analyse the effects on comparative price advantages and thereby competitiveness, specialization and trade. Three types of environmental policy are considered: an emission tax, a consumption tax and a trade tax. A distinction is made between the small-country case and the large-country case.

In the small-country case the country cannot affect the world market prices and cannot use its environmental policy to improve its terms of trade. The analysis is therefore reduced to the way in which environmental policy affects the volume of trade and changes in imports and exports. Since there are transport-specific externalities in the model, a trade tax becomes an environmental policy instrument as well. It is assumed that the country is net exporter of commodity one and net importer of commodity two, and that foreign pollution does not affect the domestic environment. In this model the effects of environmental policy on international trade are ambiguous. The reason is again the external effect on production mentioned in the preceding section. In the more simple version of the model where external effects on production are ignored, the ambiguities are reduced, but not eliminated as the following examples show:

1. A higher emission tax in sector two increases the comparative disadvantage in the production of this commodity. The country will

[6] Pollution-impact parameters reflect the capability of the country's natural resources to assimilate or withstand environmental disruption.

therefore specialize even more in the production of commodity one and import of commodity two is increased.[7] A higher emission tax may therefore increase trade and the pollution impact of transportation may dominate the effect of more strict environmental policy.

2. A tax on the consumption of commodity two reduces trade because consumers substitute towards commodity one, which may lead to overall reduction of pollution both via the production and transportation effect. Hence, in a small open economy the impacts of changes in environmental policy are in general ambiguous because the regulation of a pollution activity has spillover effects to other pollution activities. Moreover, the effect may vary along with the policy instrument.

In the large-country case the country has an impact on world market prices and can use its environmental policy to improve its terms of trade. It is now assumed that trade interventions are restricted, for instance because the country is part of a free-trade agreement. Moreover, transport externalities are ignored and contrary to the small-country case, pollution is assumed to be transboundary. Further, in order to avoid indeterminate results it is assumed that foreign import demand is not too inelastic. This model leads to unambiguous price effects, but ambiguous effects on pollution. If a tax is levied on the consumption of a commodity, its demand will be reduced and the world market price goes down. If emissions in one sector are taxed, the supply of the final commodity in that sector is reduced and the world market price is increased.

The ambiguous pollution effect of a change in environmental policy arises because of the transboundary externality that generates leakage effects. Leakage effects occur, for instance, if the consumption tax rate is increased. The direct effect is that pollution decreases. However, since terms of trade change,[8] the foreign country might be induced to increase its emissions. This leakage effect may outweigh the direct effect from an increasing consumption tax.

A somewhat different approach to the analysis of environmental policy and trade than the one in Rauscher (1997) can be found in the literature on trade between a rich region (North) and a poor region (South) (Copeland and Taylor 1994, 1995, Chichilnisky 1994, (1995) and Beghin and Potier 1997). These models assume a sufficiently asymmetric distribution of human capital endowments and absorptive capacities between North and South. These

[7] Non-homothetic preferences reverse this effect.

[8] In the large-country case, tighter environmental policy in the export industry improves the terms of trade and tighter environmental policy in the import industry worsens the terms of trade (Rauscher 1997).

endowment differences will be translated into income differences and a lower valuation of the environment in the South than in the North. The result is that the North implements a more stringent environmental policy than the South. In Copeland and Taylor (1994), the income-induced differences in pollution taxes are the sole determinant of trade flows. The model is a static two-country general equilibrium model with a continuum of commodities differing in their pollution intensity of production. Pollution is local. The result is that free trade shifts pollution-intensive production to the human-capital-scarce South and raises world pollution. Nevertheless, there is no market failure because pollution stays within the country of origin and it is assumed that governments regulate pollution optimally. Consequently, trade always increases welfare.

In a subsequent paper, Copeland and Taylor (1995) extend their 1994 model and allow for transboundary pollution. In order to focus on income effects they have maintained that income-induced differences in attitudes towards the environment are still the sole motive for trade. The result is that if the distribution of income is highly skewed, then free trade harms the global environment, but if the distribution of income is even, then free trade has no adverse effect on the environment. Because low-income countries have a strategic advantage in setting pollution levels in a free-trade regime, they have an incentive to delay international pollution negotiations until multilateral trade liberalization has been achieved.

Chichilnisky (1994) considers another reason for differences in environmental policy between North and South. She considers the difference in institutional capacity between North and South to define property rights on natural resources and the environment. The differences in institutional capacity provide a basis for trade, driven by ill-defined property rights and a tragedy of the commons. The North overconsumes underpriced resource-intensive products imported from the South. In this case the implementation of environmental taxes in the South may be inappropriate, basically because taxes decrease the price of the resource and lead to more extraction. Property right policies may be more effective.

3.3 Trade and International Capital Movements

McGuire (1982) discusses what happens when regulation is incorporated into the standard HO model with international factor mobility. He alters the HO model to accommodate the environment by assuming that the environment is a production factor that is used in industrial processes. Being a production factor, the environment will be used up to the point where its marginal product equals its price that, in the absence of any regulation, is equal to zero. The environment is a factor in only one of the industries, so there is a regulated and an unregulated industry. McGuire further assumes that capital, labour and emissions are equally substitutable. Thus when environmental regulation occurs, the shape of the production function is not altered. In this way environmental regulation, which constrains the allowable level of pollution to some given marginal product, is equivalent to negative neutral technological progress.

With respect to trade it is important to distinguish between coordinated and uncoordinated environmental regulation. Under coordinated environmental regulation, both countries face the same shadow price of pollution. The qualitative implications of the HO model still hold and so does the factor price equalization. However, with uncoordinated environmental policy, factor price equalization is lost. For a small country, facing given world commodity prices, environmental policy depresses the world commodity price of the regulated product and the released factors have to be absorbed by the unregulated industry. When international factor movements are possible it is clear that labour and capital will have an opportunity to relocate according to factor rewards. In the HO model with identical technologies but international mobile factors, factor price equalization cannot be restored until all of the polluting industries have left the country with the strictest environmental policy. The regulated country will be driven out of production of the regulated commodity. Thus international factor mobility and uncoordinated environmental regulation lead to complete specialization in at least one of the countries and perhaps in both.

Merrifield (1988) develops a model inspired by McGuire (1982). The general equilibrium model allows commodity and input prices to be determined endogenously. Commodities, pollution and capital are internationally mobile. He considers the economic impact of tighter abatement equipment standards. The model considers two countries (A and B) which produce one composite commodity each (X1 and X2, respectively). Country A consumes some of X1 and exports the balance to country B and vice versa for country B. The model incorporates a production function in which the scarcity of capital services varies directly with the pollution flow in order to capture the positive impact pollution has on input, production procedures, commodities and so on. Thus, the production factors are capital, labour, emissions, pollution-abatement equipment and transboundary pollution. Two pollution-abatement strategies are analysed: (i) an equipment standard strategy (command and control approach), and (ii) production tax strategy (economic approach). Due to internationally mobile commodities, capital and pollution, the production tax has an ambiguous impact. The production tax may actually increase pollution because the change in pollution flows, due to a reduction in the emissions of one country, may be more than offset if capital movements increase the output and emissions of the other country. In other words: a production tax in country A may induce the polluting industries to move to country B, which reduces country A's emissions by a certain amount, but increases the emissions in country B by an even larger amount. This result is similar to the result in Rauscher (1997). The change in pollution flows, which results from the production tax, depends on which country produces the most pollution intensive commodity. If country A's output is relatively more pollution-intensive than country B's, then a production tax on country B's output will result in a net increase in pollution flows because capital movement increases country A's output and emissions. However, a production tax on A's output reduces pollution flows. In this case, the capital movement from country A (and the increased pollution in country B) is not enough to offset the emission reduction in country A. This ambiguity is not present in case of an equipment standard.

Wang (1995) analyses the impacts of a production pollution tax on environmental capital flight and national product in a two-country static general equilibrium model with two-way foreign investment. There is only one produced commodity that is tradable and produced using labour and capital. The endowment of labour is fixed and internationally immobile. Endowment of capital is fixed but internationally mobile. Capital is a composite of domestic and imported capital, and the analysis allows for different degrees of substitutability between domestic and imported capital. Pollution is assumed to originate in the production process, and the productivity of capital can be negatively or positively affected by domestic or foreign emissions. Production pollution taxes in both countries are designed to optimally mitigate environmental degradation by reallocating capital and national product. In this way, the investment decision is influenced by the pollution tax because the equilibrium rates of return on capital and national products in both countries are affected. The result is that when a tax is levied in country A, it initially decreases the rates of return on inputs and then production. Capital tends to flee out of the country (labour is immobile). Domestic capital outflows increase, and foreign capital inflows decrease if elasticities of substitution between labour and capital are sufficiently high in both countries. This is due to the fact that for high elasticities of substitution between labour and capital, country A will adopt a more labour-intensive input combination, while country B will adopt a more capital-intensive input combination in production. An additional result of the model is that negative transboundary externalities will affect the tax impact on production. An increase in the domestic pollution tax reduces domestic production and increases foreign production because capital has moved to the foreign country. Negative transboundary externalities affect domestic productivity negatively and domestic production decreases. Hence, negative transboundary externalities exacerbate the decrease of the domestic product.

This escalates environmental capital flight and thus enhances the increase in foreign production.

4. EMPIRICAL STUDIES

The conclusion reached above from the theoretical discussion was rather blurred. Under some parameter constellations strict environmental policy may lead to environmental capital flight; under other parameter constellations this may not be the case. We now turn to empirical studies. This section consists of two parts. The first deals with the effects of environmental regulation on trade. In the second we discuss studies of international capital movement and changes in foreign direct investment as a response to environmental policy.

4.1 Trade Models

There are two approaches in which to analyse empirically the relationship between environmental regulation and trade: the Leontief approach and the HO approach. Leontief (1954) measured whether American exports were labour or capital intensive relative to imports. Contrary to what was expected, Leontief found that the US exports were less capital intensive than its imports. If environmental policy is introduced into Leontief's model, one measures whether the export of a country is more or less pollution intensive than its import.

Walter (1973) uses the Leontief approach to measure whether US environmental policy is 'trade neutral' or export or import biased. He estimates the 'overall environmental control loadings' (OECL) which measures the proportion of the product's final value attributable to environmental regulation. This measure is then multiplied by the value of the US imports and exports to obtain the environmental cost component of US trade. The result is that the average annual OECL of US exports during 1968–70 was about 1.75 percent of total exports. The US average annual OECL of imports is estimated to be 1.52 per cent of total imports or 13 per cent lower than the exports. Walter concludes that this difference does not appear to be very significant and the result suggests that environmental control measures bearing on the respective suppliers of US exports and imports will be trade neutral, or at worst only marginally biased against the US trading partners. However, on the level of individual industries there may be basis for a loss in competitiveness as a consequence of a more strict US environmental policy. The most sensitive industries turned out to be ordnance and accessories, construction and mining equipment, and plastics.

It is difficult to say something about differences in environmental policy between the US and its trading partners. An indicator could be the difference in OECL. In 1968–70, US exports to Japan had an OECL value of 1.70, whereas imports had a value of 1.50. The corresponding values for Canada were 1.75 and 1.70, respectively. Thus, relative to imports from Japan, US exports to Japan appear to be relatively pollution-intensive, which is much less the case for US–Canadian trade.

More recent data for several years were analysed by Robison (1988). By means of a partial equilibrium model similar to Walter (1973), Robison measured the impact of marginal changes in industrial pollution-abatement cost on the US balance of trade in general and the balance of trade with Canada in particular. Walter (1973) measured price changes caused by environmental regulation by multiplying the abatement-cost vector by the total requirements matrix. Robison (1988) notes that this approach misses the abatement costs implicit in capital goods used in the production process. Robison takes this into account by adding a capital flow coefficient to the total requirements matrix. By means of this model, the average abatement content of US trade is estimated for the years 1973, 1977 and 1982. The ratio of abatement content of imports to abatement content of exports rose from 1.151 in 1973 to 1.389 in 1982. From this it is concluded that a more stringent environmental policy in the US has changed the comparative advantage in such a way that more high-abatement-cost commodities have been imported and more low-abatement-cost commodities exported. There is no significant change in the abatement content ratio for US–Canadian trade, implying no major shift in trading patterns between these two countries.

Sorsa (1994) analysed the links between environmental expenditures and trade in environmentally sensitive commodities in seven countries that have high environmental standards – Austria, Finland, Germany, Japan, Norway, Sweden and the US. Two approaches were used. First, she compared world trade shares in environmentally sensitive commodities in the period 1970–90. Second, revealed comparative advantage (RCA) indices were calculated for the seven countries within the sensitive industries. The RCA measures changes in the share of a country's exports of a product in world exports of the product, compared to changes in the country's total share in world exports, that is, relative to the size of the country. If this ratio is more (less) than unity it means that the country is at a comparative (dis)advantage in the trade of the product.

With respect to the first, the analysis shows that world market shares in environmentally sensitive commodities have not changed much over the last two decades. The industrialized countries' share in the world trade of environmentally sensitive commodities was 81.3 percent in 1970 and 81.1 percent in 1990. However, at country level there have been some changes.

Austria, Finland and Germany have increased their share, while Japan, Norway, Sweden and the US have decreased their shares. Correlation coefficients based on time series for Austria, Germany, Japan and the US, between changes in world trade shares of the sensitive commodities and changes in environmental expenditures, confirm that there is no significant impact of higher environmental expenditures on trade performance in environmentally sensitive commodities. For Germany, Japan and the US the correlation coefficient was statistically insignificant. Austria was the only country for which the correlation coefficient was significant. However, it was found to be positive.

With respect to the second approach, a comparison of RCAs also showed that stricter environmental policy in the countries has not decreased their comparative advantage in pollution-intensive commodities. The RCA for the industrialized countries was 1.1 in 1970 and 1.0 in 1990. Thus, they have roughly maintained their comparative advantage in environmentally sensitive commodities. The same is true for the developing countries. Their RCA in 1970 was 0.8 and 0.9 in 1990. Again there is more divergence at the country level. Austria and Finland have a comparative advantage in environmentally sensitive commodities and have actually increased their competitiveness from 1970 to 1990. Norway has a comparative advantage, but the RCA has dropped from 2.3 in 1970 to 1.5 in 1990. Japan has lost its comparative advantage in the period. Sweden has a comparative advantage that has not changed over the period. The German and US RCAs are 1.0 and 0.8, respectively, and have not changed from 1970 to 1990. The decrease in Japanese and Norwegian RCAs may be due to other factors than stricter environmental policy. In the case of Japan, the decline in RCA might be caused by the increase of other exports. The reason for the decline in Norwegian RCA may reflect the increase in oil revenues in total exports.

Low and Yeats (1992) focused on secular changes that occurred in developed and developing countries' actual trade, and on (RCA) in heavily polluting industries. This approach is quite similar to Sorsa (1994). Low and Yeats (1992) computed RCA indices for some 109 countries and provided an almost complete profile of changing national comparative advantages within polluting industries. The results suggest that 'dirty' industries account for a growing share of exports of some developing countries. This has occurred against the background of a reduction of such exports in world trade. However, the study does not identify the different factors underlying this development. Differences in environmental policy could be just one out of a large array of other significant factors. For instance, for metal manufactures the relative labour intensity could explain 'dirty' industry location. Natural resource endowments turned out to be an important factor for industries such as pulp and waste paper, petroleum refining, cement and non-ferrous metals.

There are some drawbacks of the Leontief approach. First, the three studies mentioned do not take into account differences in strictness of environmental policies between countries, and second, it is a bivariate analysis. We now turn to the HO approach, which may overcome the problems inherent in the Leontief approach. In the HO model it is possible to include several factors which might influence trade patterns. Further, if it is possible to construct a measure indicating the stringency of environmental policy applicable in all countries, cross-country comparisons can be made.

Murrell and Ryterman (1991) developed a procedure that can be used when some variables of interest are difficult to measure or unavailable, which frequently occurs in the case of measuring effects of environmental policy. The approach is an omitted variable procedure based on Ryterman (1988). The procedure is applied to test whether high environmental damages in Eastern Europe can be explained by a tendency to export pollution-intensive commodities. The basic assumption is that Eastern Europe has a more lax environmental policy than its trading partners have, and should therefore have a comparative advantage in pollution-intensive products. The authors use 1975 statistics on imports and exports of pollution-intensive commodities, defined as commodities the production of which produces more than average levels of pollution or requires more than average amounts of pollution-abatement cost. The trade statistics relates to nine East European countries, seven low-income Organization for Economic Cooperation and Development (OECD) countries and ten Latin American countries. The null hypothesis is that differences in environmental policy do not affect the structures of trade. The test comes down to a comparison of each group to the seven OECD countries. The null hypothesis was accepted for all nine East European countries. Thus the relatively lax environmental policy in Eastern Europe does not show up in a tendency to export commodities intensive in pollution.

Kalt (1988) examines the power of domestic regulatory costs in explaining aggregate trade performance. He focuses on the environmental control costs because these are the bulk of the regulatory costs. His point of departure is that the imposition of stringent environmental regulations in the US can be viewed as a decline in the relative abundance of environmental resources. According to the HO model, the US exports of environment-intensive products would decline. In the regression analysis the dependent variable is the net exports from a specific industry and among the five independent variables are expenditures on pollution services by each industry. These expenditures are defined as the annualized capital, operating, and administrative costs of pollution abatement in 1977, representing the direct impact of environmental regulation. Kalt notes that an indirect impact of environmental regulation arises when direct pollution-control costs are not entirely absorbed by the directly spending industry and become embodied in the output of industries that purchase the output of the directly spending industries. A cross-section analysis for all 78 industries shows that pollution-abatement regulations have an insignificant influence on net exports in 1977. However, for the 52 manufacturing industries the influence is negative and significant. This result is also obtained if the dependent variable is specified alternatively as the change in net exports over the period 1967–77 and the independent variable is specified as the change in expenditures on pollution services over the same period. In order to obtain an estimate of the total pollution-abatement costs, that is, both the direct and the indirect, Kalt multiplies the direct abatement costs by the total requirements 1977 input–output matrix. The analysis shows that including the indirect costs as well does not change the conclusion. Pollution-abatement regulations have an insignificant influence on net exports in 1977 when all industries are included but a negative and significant influence when the analysis is narrowed by including only manufacturing industries.

Tobey (1990) tests whether trade patterns for pollution-intensive commodities, which are produced by the world's 'dirtiest' industries, are affected by environmental policy. The test is conducted by using a cross-section Heckscher–Ohlin–Vanek (HOV) model, which is a multi-factor, multi-commodity extension of the classic HO model. Pollution-intensive products are defined as the products of industries in the US where the pollution-abatement costs are greater than or equal to 1.85 per cent of total costs. In 1977 there were 34 such industries which Tobey divides into five commodity groups. Net export in a specific commodity is regressed on country characteristics. Data are from 1975 and are obtained from a mix of 13 OECD countries and ten developing countries. The test is applied in two ways. First, trade is regressed on country characteristics including an index measuring the stringency of pollution-control measures. This measure is based on a 1976 United Nations Conference on Trade and Development (UNCTAD) survey, ranking the countries in seven categories, from 'strict' (7) to 'tolerant' (1). The measure of environmental policy stringency is not found to be statistically significant in the regressions of polluting industries' exports. The second approach is the omitted variable test based on Ryterman (1988) and is quite similar to Murrell and Ryterman (1991). The idea is that if the stringency of environmental policy affects exports, it will affect the constant and disturbance term if it is omitted. The result is similar to the first approach: the stringency of environmental policy does not affect HOV trade patterns. Tobey (1990) also relaxes two of the HOV assumptions. First, non-homothetic preferences are allowed. Then consumption is a function of population and income. Second, scale economies are allowed. None of these extensions make the stringency of environmental policy significant. Hence,

Tobey does not find any support at all for the hypothesis that environmental policy affects trade. The negative results may be due to a time lag between the introduction of environmental policy and the subsequent effect on trade. Therefore, he conducts a 'fixed effects' test where he examines the change in trade patterns before and after the introduction of environmental measures. In this test, Tobey finds a significant effect in only one of the five commodity groups. However, the sign is positive.

At a first glance Kalt (1988) and Tobey (1990) obviously derive contrasting conclusions. However, the conclusions from the two approaches are not directly comparable because the dependent and the independent variables are not defined in the same way. Kalt defines his dependent variable as net exports of all industries, or alternatively net exports of the manufacturing industries. The dependent variable in Tobey is a subset of Kalt's because he concentrates on the net exports from the 24 most pollution-intensive industries. Also the environmental policy variable differs between the two studies. Kalt uses expenditures on pollution-abatement services as a proxy for environmental policy. Tobey uses a qualitative variable measured on a scale from one to seven. The purpose of Kalt's study was to examine the power of domestic regulatory costs in explaining aggregate trade performance. Hence, the perspective is much broader than the one in Tobey which is more focused on environmental policy.

Van Beers and Van den Bergh (1997) is in several respects an extension of Tobey (1990). First, a disadvantage of the multilateral approach in Tobey is that effects of differences in environmental policy on trade flows may cancel out because multilateral trade is an aggregate of bilateral trade flows. Therefore Van Beers and Van den Bergh analyse bilateral trade flows made up of imports and exports from one country to another measured in thousands of US dollars. Second, the results may be strongly dependent upon the choice of the indicator measuring strictness of environmental policy. Van Beers and Van den Bergh use two such measures. The first measure reflects a large array of environmental indicators, including ones that do not directly reflect private environmental costs. The second is a narrow measure that more adequately reflects private environmental costs. In terms of both measures countries are ranked between 0 (weak environmental policy) and 1 (strict environmental policy). Moreover, the UNCTAD environmental policy measure used in Tobey is an input-oriented indicator, whereas Van Beers and Van den Bergh use an output-oriented environmental policy measure. The former is an *ex-ante* measure that does not take into account counterbalancing financial assistance, such as export rebates and import surcharges, and therefore may exaggerate the costs of environmental regulations. The output-oriented policy measure takes these counterbalancing financial compensations into account. The third difference compared to

Tobey is that three types of dependent variables (bilateral trade flows) are used. The first is an aggregate bilateral trade flow including all industries. The second is bilateral trade flow in highly pollution-intensive sectors. The third is bilateral trade flow in highly pollution-intensive sectors that are not resource based. The non-resource-based industries (the 'footloose' industries) are highly mobile industries that are very sensitive to inter-country differences in environmental policy. Naturally, these industries are of great interest here.

The first group of regression analyses, which Van Beers and Van den Bergh (1997) perform, is quite similar to the Tobey regression, but now the three bilateral trade flows are used as the dependent variable. As in Tobey, data are from 1975 and includes 14 OECD countries and nine developing countries. The result is that the environmental policy indicator is significant for the exports, but has a positive sign. Hence, more strict environmental regulation increases the export of the country. A possible explanation is that in this regression the environmental policy indicator is input oriented because Van Beers and Van den Bergh wanted to approximate the Tobey regression as closely as possible (except from the bilateral trade flows as the dependent variables). By using the input-oriented environmental policy indicator possible effects from subsidies are not captured. The environmental policy indicator is insignificant for the imports.[9]

If a distinction is made between industries according to their capability to relocate, the analysis shows that the environmental policy indicator is significant and positive for exports, but only for the footloose industries. The environmental policy indicator is insignificant for imports.

The second group of regression analyses is related to 1992. Data is obtained from 21 OECD countries. Both the broad and the narrow environmental policy measures are used. The former has an insignificant effect on exports as well as imports, irrespective of which trade flow is used. The narrow measure is significant and negative for exports if aggregate trade flows and trade flows from the footloose sectors are used. It is insignificant if trade flows from the highly pollution-intensive sectors, including both footloose and non-footloose industries, are used. The impact on imports is significant and negative for all types of sectors. This is in contrast to what trade theory would predict and may indicate the presence of import barriers.

There are, however, some problems with the operationalization of strict environmental policy. The most important problem is that the main indicator used is energy use, while others relating to, for example, waste, are ignored. According to the energy use indicator, countries like Norway and Sweden are

[9] One might expect that domestic consumers would substitute domestic products for foreign ones because a strict environmental policy is expected to raise domestic production costs and hence prices. The result indicates that this substitution effect does not take place.

found to have lax environmental policies. This can be explained in terms of the availability of hydropower in these countries. As is well known, the environmental impacts of hydropower are quite different from the impacts of coal. Hence, it is doubtful if energy use is a correct indicator. Moreover, the negative impact on exports from the footloose sectors raises some questions. Because of its very nature, for the long run one would expect this sector to locate in regions with lax environmental policies. Hence, if there was to be a significant policy effect one would expect it for the resource-based rather than the footloose sectors.

4.2 International Capital Movements

In this section, capital migration in the form of foreign direct investment is analysed. This form of investment is characterized by a relatively strong commitment and a relatively long time horizon and, hence, is expected to be sensitive to environmental policy.

Walter (1982) examines whether differences in environmental policy between countries will favour incremental industrial restructuring. Three types of data are used. First, data about plant closures, based on a US Department of Commerce sample survey, is examined. In the period 1974–76 130 plants were closed in the US. In 87 cases the entire establishments closed down permanently. In 80 per cent of the cases, air pollution requirements were given as the main pollution-related reason to the plant closure. Naturally, other factors, such as age or obsolescence, also contributed to the plant closures, but unfortunately it is not possible to determine the relative weight of the environmental considerations. However, plant closings for environmental reasons seem to differ widely for US industries. In the mining industry the shutdown rate was 8.72 per cent and in the chemical industry it was 0.79 per cent. Walter concludes that the results suggest that no significant migration of productive capital may be expected to result from closures. This conclusion, however, seems to rest on a slender foundation. Data for more than three years are needed and more precise evidence for the importance of environmental regulations relative to other factors is necessary. The second type of statistics examines whether environmental control costs give a relocation 'push'. An indicator of the 'push' is a comparison between domestic and overseas investments in pollution control. For seven major pollution-intensive industries in 1974–75, the percentage capital investment required for pollution control abroad is significantly lower than in the US. Thus, in the US there is a strong 'push' for the polluting industries to relocate. However, it does not say whether they actually relocate. An indicator of this could be the flows of foreign direct investment. Walter examines the regional differences of the capital expenditures of US companies. Data of domestic and overseas capital expenditures of US companies are examined for the period 1970–77. Overseas investments are also differentiated by regions. The data shows that the industries vary greatly in the direction of their foreign direct investment. However, there is no significant increase in foreign direct investment by pollution-intensive industries in developing countries. In summary, Walter's analysis does not find support for the hypothesis that pollution-intensive industries have moved towards less-regulated countries.

Leonard (1988) seeks to establish some recent trends in foreign investment by US industries that might ascertain whether industries with high pollution-control costs have recently increased investments in countries with low environmental standards. Based on pollution-abatement expenditures and the extent of the ease with which industries can relocate, he selects the chemical and the mineral processing industries for further analysis. The aggregate investment and trade figures indicate that the years immediately following emergence of stringent environmental regulations in the US did not witness widespread relocation of industries to countries with drastically lower environmental regulations. Nor in the long run could Leonard find any significant effects, and not even when countries have tried to attract 'dirty' industries. The few industries that moved out of the US had few incentives to improve production facilities because demand for their products was reduced as a result of product obsolescence or hazards. There are no examples of healthy and growing US industries that have been forced to move abroad because of environmental regulations. In recent years, however, among pollution-intensive industries, some trends, which could be related to increased environmental regulations, seem to occur. Of greatest potential significance, Leonard remarks, are the large increases in recent years in overseas investment and refined imports by US mineral processors.

Rowland and Feiock (1991) do not consider international migration, but migration across states in the US. The purpose is to investigate to what extent the interstate allocation of new Chemical and Allied Producers (CAP) capital can be accounted for by interstate variance in CAP pollution-abatement costs. The federal states in the US differ greatly from each other in terms of environmental regulation of the CAP as well as share of new CAP capital. Rowland and Feiock come to the opposite conclusion of Walter (1982) and Leonard (1988): pollution-abatement costs have a significant negative influence on the states' ability to attract new CAP capital in the period 1977–81. However, this relationship is non-linear. There appears to be a threshold. Capital relocates if a state exceeds the threshold, but below it there is no relocation. This means that while states that impose high pollution-abatement costs tend to compete unsuccessfully for new capital, those states with the lowest marginal pollution-abatement costs are not necessarily the most successful in attracting new CAP capital. Rather, there seems to be a pollution abatement expense threshold. When a state exceeds it, the state loses capital to states that remain below it. Rowland and Feiock do not discuss whether or not their result can be generalized to an international setting.

Hettige et al. (1992) and Lucas et al. (1992) examined whether environmental regulation in the OECD countries has displaced toxic industrial production towards less-regulated less developed countries (LDCs). They find support for the replacement hypothesis by studying measures of the toxic intensity of manufacturing in 80 countries from 1960 to 1988. The data are divided into subsets for each decade and show that in the 1960s, toxic intensities grew most quickly in high-income countries. After the introduction of stricter environmental regulation in the OECD countries in the 1970s and 1980s, the pattern was sharply reversed: toxic intensity in the LDCs grew most quickly. Further, the authors conclude that pollution intensity has grown most rapidly in developing countries, which are relatively closed to world market forces. The same conclusion is reached in Birdsall and Wheeler (1992), who find that in Latin America, pollution heavens are to be found in the most protectionist economies. Openness promotes cleaner industries. However, a major drawback of Hettige et al. (1992) and Lucas et al. (1992) is that the regressions do not include any environmental policy variables. Thus, one cannot be certain of a causal connection between the decade patterns and the shifts in OECD environmental policies.

5. CONCLUSION

The purpose of this chapter is to review the literature on capital flight and trade impacts due to environmental policy. The theoretical analysis starts from the general HO model of international trade and from models of international capital movements. In the HO, model international trade is explained by differences in factor endowments. The model predicts that the relative prices of commodities converge, which leads to the convergence of relative factor prices. According to the theory of international capital movements, in the absence of trade, capital relocates internationally on the basis of marginal return. Consequently, factor prices converge. It follows that in these standard models with perfect competition and no scale economies, international trade and factor movements are substitutes.

The simplest possible model with environmental effects included assumes international capital movements and ignores consumption externalities and external effects on production. In this model, the result is obtained that a country repels mobile capital by imposing a restrictive environmental policy. However, in a more realistic model with consumption externalities and external effects on production, results become ambiguous. Then no clear-cut relation between the strictness of environmental policy and capital movement can be found. The same is true for trade models. The trade models are more complicated than the models with international capital movements because trade models include at least two commodities. If environmental policy is introduced in the simplest possible trade model, the standard HO result is obtained: the country well endowed with environmental resources exports the environmentally intensive produced commodity. However, in more realistic models with different technologies or external effects on production, the impact of stricter environmental policy on trade flows becomes ambiguous and dependent on specific parameter constellations.

The empirical studies also give mixed results. This applies to the Leontief approach, which focuses on the problem whether or not strict environmental policy gives a comparative disadvantage in the production of pollution-intensive commodities. Robison (1988) finds that a comparative disadvantage will occur; Walter (1973) and Sorsa (1994) do not. On the contrary, Sorsa finds that in some instances, more strict environmental policy results in a comparative advantage.

There are some drawbacks of the Leontief approach. First, this type of study does not take into account differences in strictness of environmental policies between countries. The second major drawback is that it is bivariate. It is assumed that environmental costs are the only factor that explains the patterns of specialization.

The empirical studies using the HO model do not find much support for the claim that strict environmental policy in a country has a negative influence on the country's export of the pollution-intensive commodities. Tobey (1990) finds an insignificant output-oriented environmental policy measure for 1975 data, using both the standard HO model, and a modified model with scale economies and non-homothetic preference. For the same data, Van Beers and Van den Bergh (1997), who use bilateral trade flows and an input-oriented environmental policy measure, confirm these results. They even find a significant and positive relationship between strictness of environmental policy and exports. However, on the basis of 1992 data, and an environmental policy measure that better reflects the private environmental costs of production, they find a significant and negative relation between the stringency of environmental policy and trade. This applies in particular for industries that relocate relatively easy.

Empirical research with respect to international capital movement does not provide much evidence for the hypothesis that more strict environmental policy has affected international capital movements. Walter (1982) and

Leonard (1988) reject the hypothesis. Rowland and Feiock (1991) find support for the hypothesis, but only consider capital movements within the US. There seems to be some evidence that LDCs have a growing share of the toxic industrial production. It is, however, not clear whether changes in environmental policy have induced this change.

The general conclusion that emerges from the literature reviewed is that highly simplified theoretical models of international trade and capital movements support trade effects and large-scale capital flight. However, when these models are made more realistic, the clear-cut conclusions disappear. If, for instance, several different externalities are included, or other differences between the countries than environmental policy are considered, then more strict environmental policy does not necessarily lead to trade effects or capital flight. The empirical studies are also somewhat mixed in their conclusions. The majority of the studies find an insignificant relationship between environmental policy and environmental capital flight. Some studies even find a significant positive relationship. Other studies, however, do find a significant negative relationship.

The empirical studies show that there are many methodological problems. First of all, there is a scarcity of data. Second, some of the studies relate to years when environmental policy was in its infancy and costs of environmental regulation were relatively small. This leads to the more general hypothesis that the costs of environmental regulation need to exceed a certain threshold in order to have an impact on capital flight and trade. Although several of the empirical studies find that in general there is little support for trade effects or environmental capital flight, this does not hold for industries where the environmental cost component is much larger than average. This supports the hypothesis that with a continued increase in the strictness of environmental policy in the future, trade effects and environmental capital flight may occur.

REFERENCES

Asako, K. (1979), 'Environmental Pollution in an Open Economy'. *Economic Record* **55**: 359–67.

Baumol, W.J. (1971), *Environmental Protection, International Spillovers, and Trade.* Stockholm: Almkvist & Wicksell.

Beghin, J. and M. Potier (1997), 'Effects of Trade Liberalization on the Environment in the Manufacturing Sector'. *The World Economy* **20**(4): 435–56.

Birdsall, N. and D. Wheeler (1992), 'Trade Policy and Industrial Pollution in Latin America: Where are the Pollution Heavens?'. In P. Low (ed.) *International Trade and the Environment.* World Bank Discussion Papers 159. World Bank, Washington, pp. 159–71.

Cameron, J., P. Demaret, and D. Geradin (1994), *Trade and the Environment: The Search for Balance.* London: Cameron May.

Chichilnisky, G. (1994), 'North-South Trade and the Global Environment'. *American Economic Review* **84**(4): 851–74.

Copeland, B.R. (1994), 'International Trade and the Environment: Policy Reform in a Polluted Small Open Economy'. *Journal of Environmental Economics and Management* **26**: 44–65.

Copeland, B.R. and M.S. Taylor (1994), 'North–South Trade and the Environment'. *Quarterly Journal of Economics* **109**: 755–87.

Copeland, B.R. and M.S. Taylor (1995), 'Trade and Transboundary Pollution'. *American Economic Review* **85**(4): 716–37.

D'Arge, R.C. and A.V. Kneese (1972), 'Environmental Quality and International Trade'. *International Organization* **26**: 419–65.

Dean, J.M. (1992), 'Trade and the Environment: A Survey of the Literature'. In P. Low (ed.) *International Trade and the Environment.* World Bank Discussion Papers 159. World Bank, Washington, pp. 15–28.

Gandolfo, G. (1987), *International Economics I. The Pure Theory of International Trade.* Berlin: Springer-Verlag.

Heckscher, E.F. (1919), 'Utrikeshandelens Verkan på Inkomstfördelningen: Några Teoretiska Grundlinjer'. *Ekonomisk Tidskrift* **21**: 497–512.

Hettige, H., R.E.B. Lucas, and D. Wheeler (1992), 'The Toxic Intensity of Industrial Production: Global Patterns, Trends, and Trade Policy'. *American Economic Review* (Papers and Proceedings) **82**: 478–81.

Jasay, A.E. (1960), 'The Social Choice Between Home and Overseas Investment'. *Economic Journal* **70**: 105–13.

Kalt, J.P. (1988), 'The Impact of Domestic Environmental Regulatory Policies on U.S. International Competitiveness'. In A.M. Spence and H.A. Hazard (eds) *International Competitiveness.* Cambridge, MA: Ballinger Publishing Company.

Kemp, M.C. (1964), *The Pure Theory of International Trade.* Englewood Cliffs: Prentice-Hall, pp. 221–62.

Komen, M.H.C. and J.H.M. Peerlings (1998), 'Energy Taxes in The Netherlands: What are the Dividends'. Manuscript, forthcoming in *Environmental and Resource Economics.*

Krugman, P.R. and M. Obstfeld (1997), *International Economics. Theory and Policy.* Fourth edn, Reading Addison-Wesley.

Krutilla, K. (1991), 'Environmental Regulation in an Open Economy'. *Journal of Environmental Economics and Management* **10**: 127–42.

Leonard, H.J. (1988), *Pollution and the Struggle for the World Product.* Cambridge: Cambridge University Press.

Leontief, W. (1954), 'Domestic Production and Foreign Trade: The American Capital Position Re-examined'. *Economia Internazionale* **7**: 9–45.

Low, P. and A. Yeats (1992), 'Do "Dirty" Industries Migrate?'. In P. Low (ed.) *International Trade and the Environment.* World Bank Discussion Papers 159. World Bank, Washington, pp. 88–103.

Lucas, R., D. Wheeler, and H. Hettige (1992), 'Economic Development, Environmental Regulation and the International Migration of Toxic Industrial Pollution: 1960–1988'. In P. Low (ed.), *International Trade and the Environment.* World Bank Discussion Papers 159. World Bank, Washington, pp. 67–88.

MacDougall, G.D.A. (1960), 'The Benefits and Costs of Private Investment from Abroad'. *Economic Record* **36**: 13–35.

Markusen, J.R. (1975), 'International Externalities and Optimal Tax Structures'. *Journal of International Economics* **5**: 15–29.

Markusen, J.R. (1983), 'Factor Movements and Commodity Trade as Compliments'. *Journal of International Economics* **14**: 341–56.

McGuire, M. C.(1982), 'Regulation, Factor Rewards, and International Trade'. *Journal of Public Economics* **17**: 335–54.

McLure, C.E. Jr. (1970), 'Taxation, Substitution, and Industrial Location'. *Journal of Political Economics* **78**: 112–32.

Merrifield, J.D. (1988), 'The Impact of Selected Abatement Strategies on Transnational Pollution, the Terms of Trade, and Factor Rewards: A General Equilibrium Approach'. *Journal of Environmental Economics and Management* **15**: 259–84.

Mundell, R. A. (1957), 'International Trade and Factor Mobility'. *American Economic Review* **47**: 321–35.

Murrell, P. and R. Ryterman (1991), 'A Methodology for Testing Comparative Economic Theories: Theory and Application to East–West Environmental Policies'. *Journal of Comparative Economics* **15**: 582–601.

Ohlin, B. (1933), *Interregional and International Trade*. Cambridge, MA: Harvard University Press.

Pethig, R. (1976), 'Pollution, Welfare and Environmental Policy in the Theory of Comparative Advantages'. *Journal of Environmental Economics and Management* **2**: 160–69.

Rauscher, M. (1991), 'Foreign Trade and the Environment'. In H. Siebert (ed.) *Environmental Scarcity: The International Dimension*, Tübingen: Mohr, pp. 17–31.

Rauscher, M. (1992), 'Environmental Policy and International Capital Movements'. Paper prepared for the Task Force Meeting in Stockholm, 12–14 June 1992.

Rauscher, M. (1995a), 'Environmental Regulation and the Location of Polluting Industries'. *International Tax and Public Finance* **2**: 229–44.

Rauscher, M. (1995b), 'Environmental Policy and International Capital Mobility – An Aggregate View'. Paper presented at the workshop: 'Environmental Capital Flight', Wageningen Agricultural University.

Rauscher, M. (1997), *International Trade, Factor Movements, and the Environment*. Oxford: Oxford University Press.

Robison, H.D. (1988), 'Industrial Pollution Abatement: The Impact on Balance of Trade'. *Canadian Journal of Economics* **21**: 187–99.

Rowland C.K. and R. Feiock (1991), 'Environmental Regulation and Economic Development: The Movement of Chemical Production Among States'. In M.J. Dubnick and A.R. Gitelson (eds), *Public Policy and Economic Institutions*, Greenwich, CT: JAI Press: 205–18.

Rubin, S.J. and T.R. Graham (eds) (1982), *Environment and Trade. The Relation of International Trade and Environmental Policy*. Totowa: Allanheld & Osmun.

Ruffin, R.J. (1984), 'International Factor Movements'. In R.W. Jones and P.B. Kenen (eds) *Handbook of International Economics*, Vol. I. Amsterdam: Elsevier Science Publishers.

Ryterman, R. (1988), 'Technological Flexibility and the Pattern of East–West Trade'. Ph D Thesis, University of Maryland.

Samuelson, P.A. (1948), 'International Trade and Equalisation of Factor Price'. *Economic Journal* **58**: 163–84.

Samuelson, P.A. (1949), 'International Factor Price Equalisation Once Again'. *Economic Journal* **59**: 181–97.

Siebert, H. (1974), 'Environmental Protection and International Specialization'. *Weltwirtschaftliches Archiv* **110**: 494–508.

Siebert, H. (1977), 'Environmental Quality and the Gains from Trade'. *Kyklos* **30**: 657–73.

Siebert, H. (1979), 'Environmental Policy in the Two-country Case'. *Zeitschrift für Nationalökonomie* **39**: 259–74.

Siebert, H. (1985), 'Spatial Aspects of Environmental Economics'. In A.V. Kneese and J.L. Sweeney (eds), *Handbook of Natural Resource and Energy Economics*, Vol. 1. Amsterdam: North-Holland, pp. 125–64.

Siebert, H., J. Eichberger, R. Gronych and R. Pethig (1980), *Trade and Environment: A Theoretical Inquiry*. Amsterdam: North-Holland.

Sorsa, P. (1994), *Competitiveness and Environmental Standards. Some Exploratory Results*. World Bank Policy Research Working Paper 1249. World Bank, Washington.

Steininger, K. (1994), 'Reconciling Trade and the Environment: Towards a Comparative Advantage for Long-Term Policy Goals'. *Ecological Economics* **9**: 23–42.

Stolper, W.F. and P.A. Samuelson (1941), 'Protection and Real Wages'. *Review of Economic Studies* **9**: 58–73.

Tobey, J.A. (1990), 'The Effects of Domestic Environmental Policies on Patterns of World Trade: An Empirical Test'. *Kyklos* **43**(2): 191–209.

Ulph, A. (1997), 'International Trade and the Environment: A Survey of Recent Economic Analysis'. In H. Folmer and T. Tietenberg (eds), *The International*

Yearbook of Environmental and Resource Economics 1997/1998. A Survey of Current Issues, Cheltenham: Edward Elgar, 205–42.

Van Beers, C. and J.C.J.M. Van den Bergh (1997), 'An Empirical Multi-country Analysis of the Impact of Environmental Regulations on Foreign Trade Flows'. *Kyklos* **50**: 29–46.

Walter, I. (1973), 'The Pollution Content of American Trade'. *Western Economic Journal* **11**: 67–70.

Walter, I. (1974), 'International Trade and Resource Diversion: The Case of Environmental Management'. *Weltwirtschaftliches Archiv* **110**: 482–93.

Walter, I. (1982), 'Environmentally Induced Industrial Relocation to Developing Countries'. In S.J. Rubin, and T.R. Graham (eds) *Environment and Trade. The Relation of International Trade and Environmental Policy.* Totowa: Allanheld & Osmun, pp. 67–101.

Wang, L.-J. (1995), 'Environmental Capital Flight and Pollution Tax'. *Environmental and Resource Economics* **4**: 273–86.

Wong, K.Y. (1986), 'Are International Trade and Factor Movements Substitutes?'. *Journal of International Economics* **21**: 25–43.

Zaelke, D., P. Orbuch, and R.F. Housman (1993), *Trade and the Environment.* Washington, DC: Island Press.

6. Effects of Uncertainty over Environmental Taxes on Emission-reducing Capital in an Oligopoly*

Fredrik Carlsson

1. INTRODUCTION

Policy uncertainty from a firm's perspective has received little interest in environmental economics. The focus has been more on the policy maker's perspective and the choice between different policy instruments under uncertainty.[1] However, environmental policies have changed over time, and they will continue to change. This implies that there could be an uncertainty over future policy from the firm's perspective, although it does not necessarily have to be that way. A recent analysis of this problem is in Larson and Frisvold (1996), which investigates how uncertainty over an emission tax affects investments in resource conservation, and how these investments in turn affect demand for the polluting input. This is an important contribution to the discussion on policy instruments and incentives for the development of emission-abatement technologies.[2] The uncertainty over an emission tax could reflect genuine uncertainty, for example due to the political process, or difficulties for a firm to observe the correct tax, for example because of a time lag between decision and implementation. Larson and Frisvold (1996) assume perfect competition, and they find that the effect on investments, among other things, depends on input-price elasticities, and how investments affect these elasticities. Here we instead emphasize imperfect competition and the strategic aspect of capital investments, that is, the fact that investments might affect the behaviour of the competitors, see, for example, Brander and Spencer (1983), Vives (1988), Spencer and

* The author would like to thank Dinky Daruvala, Peter Frykblom, Mattias Lundbäck, Peter Martinsson, Thomas Sterner, and an anonymous referee for useful comments. Financial support from the Swedish Civil Aviation Administration is gratefully acknowledged.

[1] This discussion originated from the seminal paper by Weitzman (1974).

[2] For examples on models without uncertainty over the environmental regulation, seeDamania (1996), Downing and White (1986) and Milliman and Prince (1989).

Brander (1992) and Simpson and Bradford (1996). In our model, investments in emission-reducing capital/technology affect both emissions and production costs. At the time of the investment decision, the firms do not know the true emission tax, but at the time of the output decisions the true tax is known. The purpose is to investigate how uncertainty, in a two-stage Cournot model, affects the investment decision and output and emission levels. In Section 2, the basic model is outlined. In Section 3, a comparative static analysis of uncertainty is presented. In Section 4, we compare the emission tax regulation with a standard regulation. Finally, in Section 5 we discuss the implications of our results.

2. THE MODEL

We consider an industry with two firms, producing a homogeneous good q^i. Both firms can invest in emission-reducing capital, k^i, at cost r per unit. Investment affects both intercept, $\theta(k^i)[t+\varepsilon_s]$, and slope, $\gamma(k^i)$, of the marginal cost function. The cost function for firm i is

$$C^i(k^i,\varepsilon_s,q^i)=\theta(k^i)q^i[t+\varepsilon_s]+\gamma(k^i)\frac{(q^i)^2}{2}+rk^i, \tag{6.1}$$

where $i = 1, 2$, $\theta(k^i) > 0$, $\theta'(k^i) < 0$ and $\gamma(k^i) \geq 0$. The first part of the cost function is the cost of the emission tax, $t + \varepsilon_S$, where $\theta(k^i)q^i$ are emissions from firm i. Thus, emissions are increasing in output, q^i, and decreasing in capital, since $\theta'(k^i) < 0$. The emission tax consists of a deterministic, t, and a random, ε_S, part, where $E[\varepsilon_S] = 0$ and $\mathrm{Var}[\varepsilon_S] = \sigma_s^2$. We assume that the regulator sets a fixed tax per unit of emission, and that the tax is not a function of output and capital.[3] Several writers have used this type of cost function, for example, the plant-design model in Vives (1989), and the flexibility model in Spencer and Brander (1992). However, the specification with an emission tax, and emission-reducing capital, has not previously been employed. The sign of $\gamma'(k^i)$ represents the effect on the firm's flexibility of capital investments. We allow for two types of investments: flexibility

---

[3] We do not consider the regulator's problem of setting an optimal emission tax. For a discussion on this problem, see Simpson (1995) and Carlsson (1997).

increasing, $\gamma'(k^i) < 0$, and flexibility reducing, $\gamma'(k^i) > 0$.[4] Let $p(Q)$ denote the inverse demand function, then the profit function for firm i is

$$\Pi^i = p(q^i + q^j)q^i - [\theta(k^i)q^i[t + \varepsilon_s] + \gamma(k^i)\frac{(q^i)^2}{2} + rk^i], \qquad (6.2)$$

where $i = 1, 2$ and $i \neq j$. We impose the following restrictions on the profit function

$$\begin{aligned} \left|\Pi^i_{ii}\right| > \left|\Pi^i_{ij}\right| &\Rightarrow \Omega = \Pi^1_{11}\Pi^2_{22} - \Pi^1_{12}\Pi^2_{21} > 0\text{, and} \\ \left|\Pi^i_{k^ik^i}\right| > \left|\Pi^i_{k^ik^j}\right| &\Rightarrow \Phi = \Pi^1_{k^1k^1}\Pi^2_{k^2k^2} - \Pi^1_{k^1k^2}\Pi^2_{k^2k^1} > 0, \end{aligned} \qquad (6.3)$$

where subscripts denote partial derivatives with respect to output and capital. These conditions are sufficient for the Nash equilibrium to be locally stable. Given cost function (6.1), a linear demand function is a sufficient condition for (6.3), and we assume that the inverse demand function is linear, $p = \alpha - Q$. Finally, we assume that the firms are risk neutral.

It is reasonable to assume that firms know the emission tax when they make their output decision, but that there is an uncertainty when they make their investment decisions. Therefore, the problem is analysed in two stages. In stage 1, each firm chooses its level of emission-reducing capital. At this stage there is uncertainty over the emission tax and, for simplicity, we assume that the expected tax is the same for both firms. In stage 2, each firm chooses its level of output. At this stage the actual emission tax is known. Further, the firms cannot change the level of capital in the second stage.[5] In the chapter, we refer to a symmetric equilibrium (SE), defined as equilibrium where

$$k^{1N} = k^{2N} \wedge q^{1N}(k^{1N}, k^{2N}, \varepsilon_s) = q^{2N}(k^{1N}, k^{2N}, \varepsilon_s),$$

where N denotes the Cournot–Nash equilibrium levels of capital and output. By backward induction, we first solve the second stage. Given the optimal levels of output at that stage, we analyse the optimal investment problem at stage 1. We analyse both the open- and closed-loop equilibrium of the first stage, in order to clarify the effects of strategic behaviour.

---

[4] This concept of flexibility, where steeper marginal cost curves represent less-flexible technologies, was first described by Stigler (1939).

[5] We assume that the realized emission tax is sufficiently small that both firms have positive outputs.

2.1 The Second Stage

At the second stage, the actual emission tax is known, that is, ε_S is known. Each firm maximizes its profit with respect to output, given its rival's output. First-order conditions are therefore

$$\Pi_i^i = p'(Q)q^i + p(Q) - \theta(k^i)[t+\varepsilon_s] - \gamma(k^i)q^i = 0\,. \tag{6.4}$$

Solving the first-order conditions for the linear demand function yields the equilibrium output levels,[6]

$$q^{iN} = \{[\alpha - \theta^i(t+\varepsilon_s)][2+\gamma^j] - [\alpha - \theta^j(t+\varepsilon_s)]\}\Omega^{-1}\,, \tag{6.5}$$

where $\Omega = [2+\gamma^i][2+\gamma^j]-1$. From (6.5) we have that $E[q^i(k^i,k^j,\varepsilon_s)] = q^i(k^i,k^j,0)$, that is, expected output is independent of the variance, or any higher moment, of ε_S. For future use, differentiate the first-order conditions, at the equilibrium levels of output, with respect to k^i

$$q_{k^i}^{iN} = C_{ik^i}^i \Pi_{jj}^j \Omega^{-1} > 0;\ q_{k^i}^{jN} = -C_{ik^i}^i \Pi_{ji}^j \Omega^{-1} < 0.^7 \tag{6.6}$$

If we assume that marginal cost at the equilibrium is decreasing in capital investments, then firm i's output is increasing in its own investment and decreasing in its rival's investment. Furthermore, industry output is increasing in capital investment.[8] Clearly, the assumption about marginal costs restricts the number of possible cases in the analysis. However, the assumption is realistic for several types of emission-reducing investments, for example investments in more fuel-efficient engines. The assumption is made solely for analytical convenience, and we can easily extend the analysis to, in capital, increasing marginal costs.

---

[6] If we substitute q^j from firm j's first-order condition, firm i's first-order condition is $\alpha - \Pi_{ij}^i(\alpha + \Pi_{ji}^j q^i - \theta^j[t+\varepsilon_s])(\Pi_{jj}^j)^{-1} - \theta(k^i)[t+\varepsilon_s] + \Pi_{ii}^i q^i = 0$. Solving this yields (6.5).

[7] Differentiating (6.4) with respect to k^i we have, $\begin{bmatrix} \Pi_{ii}^i & \Pi_{ij}^i & -C_{ik^i}^i \\ \Pi_{ji}^i & \Pi_{jj}^j & 0 \end{bmatrix} \begin{bmatrix} q_{k^i}^{iN} \\ q_{k^i}^{jN} \\ 1 \end{bmatrix} = \mathbf{0}$. Using Cramer's rule and solving yields (6.6).

[8] Combining the expressions in (6.6), we have that $Q_{k^i}^N = C_{ik^i}^i(\Pi_{jj}^j - \Pi_{ji}^j)\Omega^{-1} > 0$ by (6.3).

2.2 The First Stage: Open Loop

In an open loop, each firm takes output of the second stage as given. Therefore at this stage it chooses the cost-minimizing level of capital, given its rival's level of capital. Using the first-order conditions from the second stage, (6.4), and the linear demand function, first-order conditions are[9]

$$E[\Pi^i_{k^i}] = E[\Pi^i_i q^i_{k^i}] - E[C^i_{k^i}] = \\ -\{\theta'(k^i)tq^i(k^i,k^j,0) + \frac{\gamma'(k^i)}{2}E[(q^i)^2] + r\} = 0\,, \tag{6.7}$$

since Π^i_i will be set to zero by maximization of the profit function at the second stage.

2.3 The First Stage: Closed Loop

In a closed loop, each firm takes into account the effect of capital investment on output in the second stage. Using the first-order conditions from the second stage, (6.4), and the linear demand function, first-order conditions are

$$E[\Pi^i_{k^i}] = E[\Pi^i_j q^j_{k^i}] - E[C^i_{k^i}] = \\ -\theta'(k^i)tq^i(k^i,k^j,0)(1+\Omega^{-1}) - \gamma'(k^i)E[(q^i)^2](1/2+\Omega^{-1}) - r = 0\,. \tag{6.8}$$

Note that the closed-loop equilibrium involves a higher level of capital than the open-loop equilibrium, and for an SE each firm's level of capital is higher in the closed-loop case.[10] This difference in investments in emission-reducing capital reflects the strategic effect of the investments.

3. UNCERTAINTY AND THE CHOICE OF CAPITAL AND OUTPUT

In this section we conduct a comparative static analysis of the uncertainty in emission-reducing capital and investments in this capital. We analyse the effect of increased uncertainty on the choice of investments in emission-reducing capital in terms of increased variance and changes in the expected emission tax.

Beginning with increased variance, note that from (6.5) we have that

---

[9] Note that $E[q^i(k^i,k^j,\varepsilon_s)] = q^i(k^i,k^j,0)$ and $E[\varepsilon_S] = 0$.

[10] This follows directly from Spencer and Brander (1992), and it is a standard result in the certainty case. See, for example, Brander and Spencer (1983).

$$E[(q^i)^2] = (E[q^i])^2 + V[q^i] = \\ q^i(k^i, k^j, 0)^2 + [(\theta^i)^2(2+\gamma^j)^2\sigma_s^2 + (\theta^j)^2\sigma_s^2]\Omega^{-2}. \tag{6.9}$$

Thus $E[(q^i)^2]$ is increasing in σ_s^2. From (6.7) and (6.8) we therefore have that an increased variance of the tax increases k^i if $\gamma'(k^i) < 0$, and decreases it if $\gamma'(k^i) > 0$, since the profit function is concave in capital.[11] Thus, the effect of an increased variance depends, in both the open- and closed-loop cases, on whether capital investments are flexibility increasing or reducing. Greater variance increases the investments only if investments increase flexibility of a firm by making the marginal cost curve flatter, that is, a greater variance results in firms preferring a more flexible technology. The result is similar to that in Larson and Frisvold (1996), but here it is flexibility on the output market, and not demand on inputs, that determine the effect of an increased variance. Note that if $\gamma'(k^i)$ is zero, that is, if investments only shift down marginal cost curves without affecting the slope, then an increased variance will not affect investments. However, even if the variance has no effect on the investments, the expectations of the tax have an effect. Therefore, we now consider the effect of the expected emission tax. Here we must distinguish between the open and closed loop. For the open-loop case, differentiating the first-order conditions of the first stage with respect to the tax, at the equilibrium levels, we find that

$$k_t^{iN} = \{\theta'(k^i)E[q^{iN}]E[\Pi^j_{k^jk^j}] - \theta'(k^j)E[q^{jN}]E[\Pi^i_{k^ik^j}]\}\Phi^{-1} \tag{6.10}$$

For the closed loop, differentiating the first-order condition of the first stage with respect to the tax, at the equilibrium levels, we find that

$$k_t^{iN} = (1+\Omega^{-1})\{\theta'(k^{iN})E[q^{iN}]E[\Pi^j_{k^jk^j}] - \theta'(k^{jN})E[q^{jN}]E[\Pi^i_{k^ik^j}]\}\Phi^{-1}. \tag{6.11}$$

The difference between the open and closed loop is due to the strategic effect of investments. However, the sign of the effect of the tax on investments is the same in both cases. If investments are strategic complements, that is, $\Pi^i_{k^ik^j} > 0$, then both firms' investments are increasing in the expected tax. If investments are strategic substitutes,[12] that is, $\Pi^i_{k^ik^j} < 0$, the sign of (6.11) is undetermined. Therefore, the effect on the individual firm's investment is, without further assumption, not determined. However, industry level of

[11] Note that this proposition applies only in the linear demand case.
[12] For strategic substitutes, an increase in k^j induces a decrease in k^i, and conversely for strategic complements (Bulow et al. 1985).

investments is, in both the open and closed loop, increasing in t.[13] Consequently, for an SE each firm's level of capital is increasing in the tax. In the closed loop case the effect on capital also depends on the strategic effect of capital. A firm's investments is decreasing in the tax if the effect of investments on the firm's own emissions is small, the effect on the rival's emissions is large, and the cross-effect of the rival's investments on marginal profits exceeds the rival's own effect (Carlsson 1997). The last effect can be expressed in terms of the slope of the reaction curves in investment-space. If the cross-effect, $|\Pi^i_{k^i k^j}|$, is large, then firm i is sensitive to a change in the rival's investments. If the rival's own effect, $|\Pi^j_{k^j k^j}|$, is small, then the rival is sensitive to a change in firm i's investments. It is therefore difficult to reach any general results, since they depend on several effects. However, from the properties of the SE we know that the more equal the two firms are, the more likely it is that they behave in the same manner, and that both firms' investments are increasing in the expected tax.

One important observation is that the effect on emissions of increased investments is not determined. The direct effect of increased investments is that emissions are reduced. Increased investments have at the same time an effect on output; from expression (6.6) we have that a firm's output is increasing in its own and decreasing in its rival's level of capital. For an SE, increased investments of both firms result in increased output of both firms, and consequently increased emissions due to increased output. If we instead assume that marginal costs are increasing in investments, then the effects are reversed. This means that industry output is always decreasing in investments, but one firm's output can still be increasing in investments. Without further assumptions, the effect of an increased variance on emissions is not clearly determined. We believe that this is an important property of these models, that the effect on emissions of, for example, an increased emission tax might not create incentives for reduced emissions.[14]

It is also interesting to analyse how uncertainty affects the output decision in the second stage. The interesting aspect here is what happens when the firms over- or underestimate the emission tax, the sign and size of ε_S reflects this. A high realisation of ε_S means that the firms have underestimated the emission tax. If we differentiate first-order conditions of the second stage with respect to ε_S, at the equilibrium levels, we have

$$q^{iN}_{\varepsilon_s} = [C^i_{i\varepsilon_s}\Pi^j_{jj} - C^j_{j\varepsilon_s}\Pi^i_{ij}]\Omega^{-1}. \tag{6.12}$$

[13] $K^N_t = (1+\Omega^{-1})\Phi^{-1}[\theta'(k^{iN})q^{iN}(E[\Pi^j_{k^j k^j}] - E[\Pi^j_{k^j k^i}] + \theta'(k^{jN})q^{jN}(E[\Pi^i_{k^i k^j}] - E[\Pi^i_{k^i k^j}])]$ > 0 by (6.3).

[14] This result is also obtained in oligopoly models under certainty, see Carlsson (1997).

Note, given the assumptions about demand and cost functions, firms' outputs are strategic substitutes, that is, $\Pi^i_{ij} < 0$. The sign of (6.12) is therefore undetermined, thus the effect on the individual firm's output is undetermined. However, industry output is decreasing in ε_S. Thus at an SF, the output of both firms is decreasing in ε_S,[15] that is, output is decreasing in the underestimation of the emission tax. Again, this reflects the nature of the Cournot model, since equilibrium levels of output also depends on the behaviour of the rival.

4. COMPARISON WITH AN EMISSION STANDARD

It is interesting to compare a tax regulation with an emission standard, where there is uncertainty about the standard in stage 1. Let the emission standard be $d + \varepsilon_d$, where $E[\varepsilon_d] = 0$ and $\mathrm{Var}[\varepsilon_d] = \sigma_d^2$. In the second stage, both firms know the true emission standard, and they face the following maximization problem

$$\max_{q^i} \Pi^i = p(Q)q^i - C^i(k^i, \varepsilon_d, q^i) = p(Q)q^i - [\gamma(k^i)\frac{(q^i)^2}{2} + rk^i] \qquad (6.13)$$
$$\text{s.t. } \theta(k^i)q^i \le d + \varepsilon_d .$$

If we assume that the standard restriction is binding, we have that $q^i = [d + \varepsilon_d]\theta(k^i)^{-1}$. This implies that $q^i_{k^i} > 0$, and that

$$E[q^i(k^i, k^j, \varepsilon_d)] = q^i(k^i, k^j, 0) = d\theta(k^i)^{-1}. \qquad (6.14)$$

Thus, output is increasing in capital, and output is not a function of the rival's capital investment. Consequently, the open and closed loop will generate the same result, since there is no strategic effect of investments. At the first stage, each firm chooses its level of emission-reducing capital, and there is an uncertainty over the emission standard. If we assume that the expected standard restriction is binding, the first-order conditions of the first stage are

15 $Q^N_\varepsilon = [C^i_{i\varepsilon}(\Pi^j_{jj} - \Pi^j_{ji}) + C^j_{j\varepsilon}(\Pi^i_{ii} - \Pi^i_{ij})]\Omega^{-1} < 0$ by (6.3).

$$-(\frac{\gamma'(k^i)}{2}E[(q^i)^2]+r)-\mu^i\theta'(k^i)q^i(k^i,k^j,0)=0\text{, and} \tag{6.15}$$
$$g^i=\theta(k^i)q^i(k^i,k^j,0)-[d+E[\varepsilon_d]],$$

where μ^i is the Lagrangian multiplier. From (6.14) and (6.15) we have that the effect of an increased variance of the emission standard is the same as in the tax case, that is, it depends on the flexibility effect of capital investments. However, the effect of the expected emission standard is different from the effect of the expected emission tax. Although this is a straightforward result of the model, differentiating the first-order conditions from the first stage we have that

$$k_d^i=\begin{vmatrix}0 & g_k^i\\ 1 & 0\end{vmatrix}|J|^{-1}=-[\theta'(k^i)q^i+\theta(k^i)q_k^i]/[-(g_k^i)^2], \tag{6.16}$$

where the Jacobian is the determinant of the bordered Hessian for the cost-minimization problem. Thus, the effect on capital depends on the effect of investments on emissions. If emissions are decreasing in capital then an expected stricter regulation, that is, a lower d, results in increased investments. Conversely, if emissions are increasing in capital then the investments are reduced. Note that this result only holds when the standard restriction is binding.

5. DISCUSSION

We have, in a very simple model, shown how uncertainty affects the choice of capital and output. Instead of focusing on the underlying technology as Larson and Frisvold (1996), we focus on the strategic aspect of investments. We find that the effect on capital of an increased uncertainty depends on whether capital increases or decreases the flexibility. Further, the effect of uncertainty over the emission tax depends on strategic effects of capital investments. The effect on output of over- and underestimation of the tax is also ambiguous. These ambiguities arise since equilibrium levels of capital and output depend on the behaviour of the rival. We also show that for an SE, these two effects are clearly determined. This result is intuitively reasonable: the more equal the two firms are, the more likely it is that they behave in the same manner. We could also, by specifying a functional form of the cost function, derive explicit conditions for the effects on capital investment and output. The model also reveals that the effect of increased investment in emission-reducing capital does not necessarily mean that the emissions decrease. This is because investments also affect the marginal costs-inducing changes of the equilibrium levels of output.[16] Again, to derive explicit conditions of the effect on emissions, we would have to specify a functional form of the cost function.

We also show that there is a fundamental difference between a tax regulation and an emission standard, since the latter does not create any strategic effects of capital investment. Consequently, the effects of uncertainty are different for the two types of regulation.

The simplicity of the model has allowed us to point out the distinguishing features of regulation and uncertainty under imperfect competition. Consequently, it is difficult to reach any general results or conclusions, as the results depend on functional forms of demand and cost functions. However, we believe that this model adds to the knowledge of how uncertainty over future environmental policy affects investments in capital or technology that reduce emissions. In addition, the model itself, and the analysis, can be extended to several other interesting cases. For example, interpreting the strategic variable as R&D, we can allow for knowledge diffusion between the firms. It is also possible to analyse entry deterrence, and the issue of commitment of capital versus flexibility.

REFERENCES

Brander, J. and B. Spencer (1983), 'Strategic Commitment with R&D: The Symmetric Case', *Bell Journal of Economics* **14**, 225–35.

Bulow, J.I., J.D. Geanakoplos and P.D. Klemperer (1985), 'Multimarket Oligopoly: Strategic Substitutes and Complements', *Journal of Political Economy* **93**, 488–511.

Carlsson, F. (1997), 'Environmental Taxation and Strategic Commitment in Duopoly Models', Working paper 1997:11, Unit for Environmental Economics, Department of Economics, Gothenburg University.

Damania, D. (1996), 'Pollution Taxes and Pollution Abatement in an Oligopoly Supergame', *Journal of Environmental Economics and Management* **30**, 323–36.

Downing, P.B. and L.J. White (1986), 'Innovation in Pollution Control', *Journal of Environmental Economics and Management* **13**, 18–29.

Larson, B.A. and G.B. Frisvold (1996), 'Uncertainty Over Future Environmental Taxes', *Environmental and Resource Economics* **8**, 461–71.

Milliman, S.R. and R. Prince (1989), 'Firm Incentives to Promote Technological Change in Pollution Control', *Journal of Environmental Economics and Management* **17**, 247–65.

[16] Note that this is also true for the case when marginal cost is increasing in investments, because then firm *i*'s output is increasing in its rival's investment.

Simpson, R.D. (1995), 'Optimal Pollution Taxation in a Cournot Duopoly' *Environmental and Resource Economics* **6**, 359–69.

Simpson, R.D. and R.L. Bradford III (1996), 'Taxing Variable Cost: Environmental Regulation as Industrial Policy', *Journal of Environmental Economics and Management* **30**, 282–300.

Spencer, B.J. and J.A. Brander (1992), 'Pre-Commitment and Flexibility', *European Economic Review* **36**, 1601–26.

Stigler, G. (1939), 'Production and Distribution in the Short Run', *Journal of Political Economy* **47**, 305–28.

Vives, X. (1989), 'Technological Competition, Uncertainty, and Oligopoly', *Journal of Economic Theory* **48**, 386–15.

Weitzman, M.L. (1974), 'Prices vs. Quantities', *Review of Economic Studies* **41**, 477–91.

7. Regulating Road Transport Externalities: Pricing Versus Command and Control

Olof Johansson-Stenman*

1. INTRODUCTION

Road transport is a sector where the presence and importance of externalities are obvious. For a long time, most emphasis was put on the road congestion problem, that is, that each road-user on a congested road or network imposes time costs for other road-users. As noted by many, this was the example considered by Pigou (1920) in his classic treatment of external costs. Congestion is still considered as one of the most important externalities, but the focus has now largely switched towards other externalities as well, including air pollution (local, regional and global), accidents and barrier effects, noise, and road wear and tear.[1]

Until now, the problem of regulating road transport externalities has in most countries largely been handled by so-called command and control (CaC hereafter) policies of various kinds. Economists, on the other hand, have often advocated market-based instruments, such as pricing solutions, since these in stylized models appear to be more cost efficient than CaC measures. However, in a more complex world with many different kinds of market failures, non-convexities, and large transaction costs, the value of such general advice may be quite doubtful. The aim of this chapter is to discuss, based on economic theory, when economists appear to have a point in advocating market-based solutions, in particular pricing, and when they do not. Hence, the aim here is not primarily to try to quantify these external

* I am grateful for useful comments from Eirik Romstad, Thomas Sterner and Erik Verhoef, and for financial support from the Swedish Communications and Research Board (KFB). The usual disclaimer applies.

[1] In principle, external benefits should of course be included as well. However, as argued by Rothengatter (1994) and others, there are no obvious non-negligible *external* benefits from road transport, at least not in developed countries. See Gramlich (1994) for a critical review of studies (for example, Aschauer 1989) which claim that there are large additional benefits from infrastructure investments which are not covered by standard micro-based cost-benefit analysis.

effects; for such attempts, see Greene et al. (1997), Hansson (1997), Kågeson (1993), Maddison et al. (1996), Mayeres (1993), Mayeres et al. (1996), Newbery (1988a, 1990), Rothengatter and Mauch (1994), Small and Kazimi (1995) and Verhoef (1994).

Tradable permit systems have often been considered unsuitable to deal with road transport problems due to the obvious large transaction costs which would occur if road-users were to simultaneously trade with each other. However, there are other possibilities such as auctioning a limited number of licenses or 'driving rights' in an area, or emission trading between car manufacturers; see Verhoef et al. (1997) and Walton (1997) for recent contributions. However, tradable permits seem to be more difficult to differentiate with respect to the circumstances compared to charges, and the transaction costs are still likely to be large. Their main advantage compared to taxes seems instead to be that they in some countries (or areas) may be easier to implement politically, but we shall not discuss tradable permits further here.

In this chapter, we shall first discuss (by necessity rather briefly) each externality and the associated specific problems separately and then discuss the simultaneous treatment of them, as well as the simultaneous treatment of different policy instruments. In Section 2 the congestion problem is discussed; Section 3 deals with global, regional and local air pollution from cars; and Section 4 discusses the noise problem. Sections 5 and 6 discuss the accident and barrier effects, and road wear and tear, respectively; Section 7 discusses the treatment of these externalities simultaneously; and Section 8 provides a summary and conclusion.

2. CONGESTION

CaC policies to deal with congestion have, in most large cities all over the world, proved rather unsuccessful. To an economist, this is not surprising, since the absence of any kind of pricing implies that the scarcity of road space is not taken into account. Consequently, there are often too many road-users simultaneously in an urban road network, especially at rush hour. Attempts to increase capacity in larger cities have often been quite unsuccessful too, which sometimes seems to have offered unpleasant surprises for the policy makers. Still, economists have been able to explain this phenomenon for a long time. The standard economic argument goes as follows: congestion increases the travel time, and hence the generalized cost for the road-users. Utility-maximizing road-users are assumed to travel (by car) if and only if the (expected) benefits of the trip exceed the (expected) costs. Increased capacity for a given vehicle flow increases the (average) speed, and hence decreases the travel time and the generalized costs for the road-users. Since the costs have decreased, more road-users will travel and the congestion and costs will increase again. If the time cost is a large part of the overall generalized cost, we may end up with a similar traffic situation in terms of congestion as initially; see Mogridge (1997) for a recent survey of traffic generation from infrastructure improvement and similar related effects. A general conclusion appears to be that it is very difficult in practice to solve the congestion problems in major cities by building more roads with larger capacity.

Congestion is one of the areas where pricing instruments have the largest allocative efficiency potential compared to CaC policies; see, for example, Walters (1961) and Vickrey (1963, 1969) for classic contributions to the road-pricing literature, and Button and Verhoef (1998), Hau (1992), Lewis (1993) and Morrison (1986) for surveys. Studies which try to quantify the welfare gains from various measures typically conclude that the possibility of differentiating the charge between peak and off-peak is especially important; see, for example, de Borger et al. (1997). In spite of this, no real road-pricing system exists anywhere in the world where the charges are differentiated in time and space in order to reflect the external time costs.[2] Why this is so has been discussed extensively in the literature and the answers are often focussed on political feasibility and distributional issues; see, for example, Emmerink et al. (1995), Langmyhr (1997), Lave (1994) and Verhoef (1995) for recent contributions. Other reasons include the large technological difficulties and the corresponding large monitoring and administration costs, and the risk associated with investments in new technology which may be insufficiently tested in practice, and which may soon be out-competed by other technological solutions; see, for example, Johansson-Stenman and Sterner (1998).

Nevertheless, given the very large potential efficiency gains and the rapid development of information technology, it seems likely that road pricing will be considered a necessary strategy to deal with urban traffic problems in a not too distant future, despite the serious implementation problems.

[2] The system in Singapore appears currently to be the case which comes closest; see Phang and Asher (1997) and Seik (1997).

3. AIR POLLUTION

3.1 Global Pollution Problems

At a first glance, global warming may seem to be the easiest problem to deal with from a policy instrument perspective, since the environmental damage is independent of where and when the emission occurs. Furthermore, it is not possible to cope with CO_2 emissions by using catalysts or other emission-control techniques, so the emissions are roughly proportional to the fossil fuel used. A simple fuel tax appears then to be perfectly targeted to the global warming problem, and hence to be an efficient policy instrument.

However, looking around in the world, the successful treatment of the global warming problem is hardly the most striking impression. Instead we are very far from what the Intergovernmental Panel on Climatic Change (IPCC) and others have recommended regarding CO_2 emission levels. An important reason for this is probably that the atmosphere is a global common property resource, so that each country will bear all the costs associated with CO_2 reductions, but receive only a very small fraction of the benefits. Consequently, global CO_2 reductions will tend to be inefficiently small. The standard economic solution to this type of problem is of course cooperation and international agreements. However, in waiting for these perhaps far-reaching international agreements, each country will have to make decisions on its own. It will then, for example, have to decide whether or not it should take further steps on its own. One argument in favor of doing so is provided by the possibility of lower adjustment costs in the future, if the global warming problem turns out to be more serious than expected.

More important, however, seems the possibility of some kind of national altruism (or perhaps individual altruism aggregated to a national level), that is, the fact that single countries may choose to reduce CO_2 emissions (and other greenhouse gases) further beyond current international agreements even though the national costs may be larger than the benefits, simply because the country to some degree also values the consequences for other countries, or because of some social norms against free-riding. Indeed, it is typically found in prisoner's dilemma experiments that quite a large fraction of individuals tend to choose the cooperative alternative, even though they would individually benefit from choosing the non-cooperative alternative (Thaler 1992). Similar behavior has frequently been observed in experiments with finite repeated prisoner's dilemma games, that is, that many individuals will not choose the non-cooperative solution based on backward induction, which conventional rational-choice based game theory would propose. The social value of such social norms that promote cooperation in prisoner's dilemma situations may, naturally, be very large. It seems, then, important for economists to emphasize and study these possibilities further in international decision making; see Elster (1989 a, b), and Sugden (1989) on how and why such social norms occur, and Zamagni (1995) for a good overview of published work on economics and altruism. Sen (1977) denoted people who are always selfishly rational as 'rational fools' since such behavior will often imply a sub-optimal outcome for all involved. As argued by Thaler (1992, p. 20): "Perhaps we need to give more attention to 'sensible cooperators'".

In addition to the global 'tragedy of the common' situation, a serious problem in many countries (such as the US) is the apparent political difficulty of raising fuel taxes (and to some extent other taxes as well). In such situations there may be high motivation to introduce various forms of standards such as the so-called CAFE (Corporate Average Fuel Economy) norms, a system of fuel-efficiency standards directed at car producers introduced in the US in 1978. The mean fuel intensity of the passenger car stock has since then decreased much more rapidly in the US than in other OECD countries (Schipper 1995). Johansson and Schipper (1997) estimated that CAFE may have decreased mean fuel intensity by as much as 2 per cent per year in the US between 1979 and 1993, although they emphasized that uncertainties are large and that it may partly be the case that the uncertainty of the international oil situation has affected the US car market more than other car markets, and that this has instigated the additional intensity reductions more than the CAFE standards themselves; see, for example, Greene (1990) and Crandall et al. (1992) for discussions on the implications of the CAFE standards.

According to conventional economic theory, standards such as CAFE are (of course) inferior to fuel taxes since such standards do not directly affect the distance driven. Thus, only one component of fuel demand is considered. Further, in a situation where these standards vary between different kind of vehicles one may even get perverse consequences due to substitution effects. For example, in the US car market the share of light trucks (which have much less restrictive standards than passenger cars) has increased rapidly in recent years and is currently above 50%! It appears likely that this development is at least in part a result of the (differentiated) CAFE norms.

However, there are other second-best arguments supporting various standards in addition to the political feasibility issue, such as problems with cross-border shopping if the fuel prices differ too much. Furthermore, there may be problems associated with the fact that consumers tend to apply an inefficiently large discount rate when they choose a new car (or other energy-consuming durable goods). If so, it would be efficiency improving to tax fuel intensity (liter/km) *per se*, for example, as a type of 'gas-guzzler' tax.[3] The empirical evidence on this point is, however, not unambiguous; see Hausman (1979) for an often quoted paper supporting the view that consumers tend to apply an inefficiently high internal discount rate.

3.2 Regional and Local Environmental Problems

If it is true in principle that a fuel tax is well-targeted at dealing with the global warming problem, this is very far from true concerning regional and, in particular, local environmental problems. Instead these corresponding external costs vary strongly with respect to space (for example, city center versus countryside) emission characteristics of the car (for example, catalytic converter or not), weather situation (there are larger marginal health costs during inversion), driving behavior, and traffic conditions (there are larger emissions during congestion). As shown by Johansson-Stenman and Sterner (1998), these regional and local environmental costs, per liter fuel consumed, may easily vary by several orders of magnitude. Thus the cost of uniform environmental improvements such as requiring ultra-clean cars and very clean fuels all over the board may seem to be very large, compared to the rather limited environmental benefit in, for instance, rural areas. In an environment of rapid technological progress, and great diversity in performance, there appears to be considerable gains from a policy instrument which would guide the environmentally best vehicles to the most sensitive areas, such as the city centers, but still allow cheaper (older and less environmentally sophisticated) vehicles to be used in less sensitive areas.

From a first-best theoretical point of view, the only policy instrument which appears to be possible to differentiate with respect to the circumstances (time, space, vehicle characteristics and so on) is an advanced road-pricing system. But, as mentioned, no such system exists yet anywhere in the world. Instead, the by far most frequently used and important policy instruments until now, to deal with local and regional traffic air-pollution problems, are various kinds of emission standards. This leads to the following question: would it be better to replace emission standards with differentiated charges on distance driven? Theoretically, in a first-best world with no control and operation costs and with exogenous technical change, the

[3]On the contrary, one could of course argue, based on consumer sovereignty, that if consumers wanted to apply a particularly high discount rate for durable goods, they should be free to do so, without governmental intervention. The key point is, then, whether the consumers' actions fully reveal their true preferences, or whether they partly reflect cognitive limitations which may imply systematic deviations from their 'true' preferences.

answer would clearly be yes.[4] In reality, however, there are several factors which may make it unwise to abandon emission standards, including possible economics of scale in the production of cars and emission-control equipment, costly monitoring, search costs for the consumers, and uncertainties about the actual effects of (non-optimal) road pricing.

For an advanced road-pricing system to be a socially profitable way to deal with local and regional air pollution, environmental costs must vary strongly with respect to variables not considered by conventional policy instruments. As already discussed, this criterion seems to be fulfilled. Second, the environmental costs must be sufficiently large for the allocative efficiency gains in turn to be sufficiently large to outweigh the investment and operational system costs. This seems less clear, at least in a not too distant future due to likely time-dependent reduction of the emission factors; see Johansson-Stenman and Sterner (1998). Preliminary and rough calculations by Johansson-Stenman and Sterner indicate that it seems unlikely that local and regional air pollution problems per se would justify an advanced road-pricing system. However, since road pricing is virtually the only policy instrument to deal with congestion in an effective way, the *additional* investment and operational cost for including some environmental aspects in the system need not be very large. Moreover, the additional cost of more technologically advanced systems (compared to pure congestion pricing) will probably decrease in the future.

In addition to environmental road-pricing, there are also a number of second-best policy instruments which could be environmentally differentiated, such as sales taxes, annual taxes, fuel taxes, and scrapping subsidies; see, for example, Acutt and Dodgson (1997). Many of these instruments seem better targeted than fuel taxes in order to deal with local and regional environmental problems. In Section 7.3 we shall discuss some of these in relation to systems of environmental classes.

Finally, one cannot rule out that local and regional environmental problems from road transport may be solved almost completely by 'technical fixes' at a modest cost in a few decades, and it may be important to realize that this 'corner solution' may be socially optimal (including various kinds of transaction costs) when considering suitable policy instruments in the long run.

[4] For example, with emission standards we would theoretically have non-optimally clean cars in the countryside, and not sufficiently clean cars in the city centers. With optimal environmental charges per distance driven, it would be much more expensive to drive in the city center and an optimal mix of vehicles would result.

4. NOISE

Noise from traffic is considered by many to be the most serious road transport external effect, and surveys by the OECD typically report that a large fraction of the population are disturbed by traffic. Apart from decreased 'quality of life', transport noise is also responsible for productivity losses caused by an inability to concentrate at work or fatigue from disrupted sleep. The external noise costs are typically estimated by hedonic prices or by survey-type methods such as the contingent valuation method (Soguel 1995). Traffic noise can be divided into low-speed noise, where the engine sound dominates, and high-speed noise where the sound from the tires dominates almost entirely. Because of stricter noise norms, and corresponding technological development, there has been a decrease in the low-speed noise levels from cars during the last 20 years. However, high-speed noise has typically increased since the speed has generally increased and the high-speed low-profile tires make more noise than conventional tires (Swedish Department of the Environment 1993).

Following Lamure (1990), the average noise level in dB(A) can be approximated as follows:

$$L = a + 20\log v - 10\log d + 10\log q \tag{7.1}$$

Where L is the noise level, a is a constant, v is the speed of traffic, d is the distance from the road, and q is the traffic flow per time unit. The most common strategy of estimating the external cost of noise is by using the hedonic pricing method, that is, by estimating the impact from noise on property (mainly houses) values (for example, Nelson 1982). A common functional form is a linear cost relation between noise levels and property prices beyond a certain level, for example, 50 dB(A).[5] Assuming a threshold level of 50 dB(A), where the cost is zero below this level, we have that

$$TC^{noise} = \begin{cases} b(L-50) & L > 50\,\mathrm{dB(A)} \\ 0 & L < 50\,\mathrm{dB(A)} \end{cases} \tag{7.2}$$

where b is a constant. If we are going to use pricing to deal with this cost, it is well known that the optimal tax t is the short-run marginal external cost. Substituting (7.2) into (7.1) and differentiating with respect to q gives:

[5] The percentage price decrease per additional dB(A) is typically denoted the Noise Depreciation Sensitivity Index (NDSI). Surveys by CSERGE/EFTEC (1994) and Nelson (1982) reported mean values on NDSI equal to 0.67 and 0.4, respectively.

$$t = \begin{cases} \dfrac{\partial(b10\log q)}{\partial q} = \dfrac{\partial(b10\ln q/\ln 10)}{\partial q} = \dfrac{10}{\ln 10}\dfrac{b}{q} & L > 50\text{dB(A)} \\ 0 & L < 50\text{dB(A)} \end{cases} \tag{7.3}$$

Hence, this functional form implies that the tax is zero for the corresponding vehicle flow where the noise level is less than 50 dB(A). At a larger flow, the tax is positive but decreasing in flow; the tax goes asymptotically to zero and infinity when the flow goes to infinity and the flow corresponding to 50 dB(A), respectively. This extreme discontinuity at 50 dB(A) seems rather counter-intuitive, and it is of course a result of the rather *ad hoc* (but frequently used) assumption of a linear damage noise intensity curve starting at 50 dB(A).

Alternatively, applying a common 'rule of thumb' it is often assumed that an increase by 10 dB(A) implies that the perceived noise level Lp is doubled (for example, Alexandre et al. 1980). Thus, the perceived noise level Lp would then be an exponential function of the noise level L (as measured in dB(A)), which in turn is a logarithmic function of the traffic flow. Next, it is not necessarily obvious that the total noise cost is proportional against the perceived noise level either, but for algebraic simplicity we assume that the relation can be given by an exponential relationship. We can then write the total noise cost as a general exponential function of the noise level:

$$TC^{noise} = \alpha e^{\beta L} = \alpha e^{\beta(a+20\log v-10\log d+10\log q)} = \gamma q^{\frac{10\beta}{\ln 10}} \tag{7.4}$$

where α, β and γ are constants and where the last step holds when we hold everything but the flow (and the corresponding noise) constant. The noise tax is then given by:

$$t = \frac{10\beta\gamma}{\ln 10} q^{\frac{10\beta}{\ln 10}-1} = \frac{\beta\gamma}{\mu} q^{\frac{\beta}{\mu}-1} \tag{7.5}$$

This function is decreasing in q as long as $\beta < \mu = \ln 10/10 \approx 0.23$, which corresponds to the case where the total cost is doubled per additional 3 dB(A) increase. Naturally, the tax (= marginal noise cost) is constant with respect to the flow if the total noise cost is proportional to the flow. This, however, appears to be a quite extreme assumption even if the total cost increases more than proportionally with the noise level. Instead, it seems reasonable that in most cases the marginal noise cost decreases with the flow, at least in some intervals. If, for example, the total noise cost is proportional to the perceived noise level *Lp*, and this level is doubled for a noise level increase of 10 dB(A), then $\beta = \ln 2/10 \approx 0.07$. The tax can then correspondingly be written:

$$t = \gamma \frac{\ln 2}{\ln 10} q^{\frac{\ln 2}{\ln 10}-1} \approx \rho q^{-0.7} \tag{7.6}$$

where ρ is a constant. Hence, the tax decreases strongly in vehicle flow q.

Figure 7.1. Non-convexity generated by decreasing marginal social costs

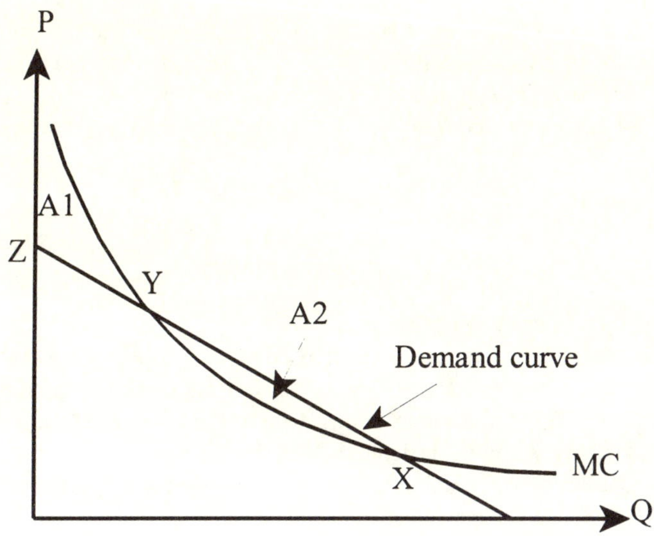

Point X in Figure 7.1 then fulfills both the first- and the second-order conditions for a local maximum of the net benefit. Point Y satisfies the first-order, but not the second-order condition (and is then a local minimum). Point Z (that is, flow equal to zero) does (normally) not satisfy the first-order condition, but it may still be a social optimum. The criterion for this is that area A1 (the area between the marginal external cost curve, the demand curve, and the vertical axis) in Figure 7.1 is larger than area A2.[6] Hence,

[6] Ignoring possible income effects and changes in relative prices.

marginal cost pricing which would result in point X may not imply a social optimum.[7] That this is the case with decreasing marginal external cost curves has recently been pointed out by Jansson (1997); see also Baumol and Bradford (1972) and Baumol and Oates (1988) on non-convexities caused by externalities. Now, intuitively, why is this so? Why does the first-order tax solution at X, when each road-user is paying the marginal external noise cost, fail to be a social optimum? Consider a homogeneous town. Either the traffic in this town is spread out evenly over all roads, or it is concentrated on half of the roads.

Since the marginal noise cost is decreasing in flow, clearly the total noise costs are lower if we concentrate the traffic on half of the roads. (This effect must then of course be weighted against demand effects and other externalities, such as congestion which is typically strongly increasing in traffic flow.)

Note, however, that the result is not due to an assumption that the marginal external cost is decreasing in the noise level L. Instead, total noise cost is marginally *increasing* in L, that is, the marginal noise cost with respect to the noise level L is an increasing function of L. Differentiating (7.4) with respect to L gives

$$\frac{\partial TC^{noise}}{\partial L} = \alpha\beta e^{\beta L} \tag{7.7}$$

which is clearly increasing in L (since α , $\beta > 0$).

The conclusion is thus that it may perfectly well be socially optimal to ban traffic altogether on some roads, also in a first-best world without monitoring costs and so on. This is in sharp contrast with some of the conventional economics wisdom. As will be demonstrated in the next section, there are also other road transport externalities where one would expect this non-convexity feature.

5. ACCIDENTS AND BARRIER EFFECTS

A common view is that there are no *external* risk costs associated with road transport since, according to some empirical evidence (for example, Vitaliano and Held 1991), the accident rate (number of accidents per vehicle kilometer) seems to be roughly constant, irrespective of the vehicle flow. Consequently, there should be no associated traffic-related tax from accident

[7] Still, Z is not incompatible with marginal cost pricing. If Z is optimal, a price equal to the marginal social cost at Z would then be larger than the marginal benefit from traveling.

risk. This is also the official view of the UK Department of Transport (1987) among others, and it implies that there would be no economic reason to intervene in the road safety market. There are a number of problems with this view, however. First, it is not obvious that this empirical relation is correct.[8] Second, even though this relation may be true, that is, the risk level may be independent of the traffic flow, this phenomenon needs an explanation. As argued by Newbery (1988a, p. 170) and Vitaliano and Held (1991) themselves, individuals most likely adapt their behavior in response to the changed flow. They will, for instance, lower their speed, or concentrate harder, and be more watchful when the traffic flow increases. Johansson (1997b) showed that if these adjustments were considered costly by the individual, there might still be external costs associated with accidents and the accident risk from road transport. Third, it may be that some types of road-users increase the risk of others, whereas others decrease the risk. These ideas have been formalized by Jansson (1994), who shows that under some conditions road-users should ideally be charged whereas some road-users (such as pedestrians) should be subsidized. Fourth, there exist a large number of safety regulations today (speed limits, seat-belt laws and so on), which have probably counteracted a flow-dependent accident risk. Fifth, individuals may not be perfectly rational and they may misjudge the risk of an accident, as noted by Viscusi (1992) among others. For example, Rothengatter (1993) quotes evidence that a large majority of drivers consider themselves to be better drivers than the average.[9] Sixth, there are large adaptation costs by pedestrians. For example, Bradshaw (1995) and Davis (1994) argue that parents now have a decreased willingness to let their children walk to school because of the increased traffic. There are also problems associated with the crossing of big roads which may cause time delays, feelings of insecurity, and a deterioration of social networks. These types of phenomena are sometimes denoted barrier effects.

It seems likely that the marginal costs associated with barrier effects often are decreasing in traffic flow. For example, parents would not allow small children to play on the street in the presence of car traffic, irrespective of the

[8] For example, Vickrey (1968, 1969) argues that the accident risk generally increases with the flow and he cites evidence suggesting that the marginal increase of the number of accidents divided by the average number of accidents is approximately equal to 1.5.Newbery (1988a) proposes 1.25 as a compromise between Vickrey and the conventional engineering wisdom (suggesting a proportional relationship).

[9] Strictly speaking, all of them may be right, however. If the driving quality considered is measured by the probability of an accident per kilometer, it is likely that a small number of drivers (for example, alcoholics) have a several times as large accident risk as the average. Consequently, with a sufficiently skewed distribution, most people can be better drivers than the average. Still, many people probably do overestimate their own capacities in many respects, for example, due to cognitive dissonance; see Akerlof and Dickens (1982).

traffic flow. Hence, we seem to have a non-convexity problem here too, where it may be socially optimal to have corner solutions with car-free streets, and where a first-order pricing solution is not sufficient to achieve a social optimum. Because of the large number of effects which affect road safety, it seems reasonable to focus largely on various CaC measures in the future, even though some regulations such as speed limits and corresponding penalties could also be seen as part of a second-best pricing.

6. ROAD WEAR AND TEAR

Road damage is caused primarily by heavy vehicles (and weather and so on). Sweden used to have an odometer-based system for charging trucks per distance driven where the charge was quite heavily differentiated with respect to relevant variables such as the axle weight (Swedish Department of Communication 1987; Hansson 1993). From an economic point of view, this old system was in many respects superior to a fuel-tax based system. The system was, however, abandoned in 1993, officially as an adaptation to the rules within the European Community (Swedish Department of Finance 1992).[10] As a result, the correspondence between the short-run external marginal costs and the variable user charge decreased dramatically; the overall taxation on the use of heavy vehicles has also decreased substantially. There are currently discussions going on in many places in Europe concerning some kind of distance-related charge for heavy vehicles. Such a charge could then, if implemented, hopefully be extended to take other external costs into account as well.

Except for the costs related to repairing the roads, there are also costs related to the fact that the comfort of other road-users will be lower when the roads get damaged. Furthermore, the maintenance costs of the cars might also increase. However, Newbery (1988b) in his 'fundamental theorem' shows that these costs should not be reflected in an optimal externality correcting charge. The reason, in short, is that if the road is restored to its original state whenever the roughness, or some other quality indicator, reaches a predetermined level, then the average road surface quality will not be lower if the traffic flow is high. This is so since the road would then be restored at shorter time intervals.

In the absence of distance-related charges, one has to rely heavily on CaC strategies; for example, heavy trucks are forbidden on certain roads. Given administrative and control costs, it seems reasonable that CaC strategies will

[10] This was the main official argument. However, there are also indications supporting the view of successful lobbying by the Swedish road-carrier organization.

also be important after an introduction of distance-related charges. The fast technological development of information technology is obviously important for the possibility of a far-reaching distance-related charge for heavy vehicles. Such technology, however, is also important in order to check the observance of the laws more effectively.

7. SIMULTANEOUS ANALYSIS

7.1 Simultaneous Treatment of Different Externalities

In a first-best well-behaved world, the fact that one activity *A* may affect the demand for other externality-generating activities *B* and *C* should generally not affect the regulation or pricing of *A*; see, for example, Sandmo (1975). For example, in calculating the costs and benefits of a new public transport system one should not include the benefits of reducing the air pollution from cars which would be the result of the decreased demand for car transport (providing that public and private transport are substitutes). The reason is simply that if the price of the car traffic is socially optimal, there would be no social net benefit increase resulting from a reduction in car traffic.

We know, however, that this is quite far from the current situation. Instead, most studies indicate that urban car traffic is socially underpriced (see, for example, Maddison et al. 1996). In such situations, as shown by Sandmo (1976), one needs to take indirect demand effects into account. For example, in this case, there should be an additional benefit (roughly equal to the size of the under-price of car traffic times the car traffic demand change) in the cost–benefit analysis of the public transport system. However, this effect may not be very large, because of the relatively low cross-price elasticity between the generalized cost of public transport and demand of private car transport, that is, the demand effect on car traffic is often very limited. Furthermore, since public transport systems are most often characterized by increasing returns to scale, and decreasing marginal costs, there is an external cost associated with car traffic since increased car traffic increases the per unit (social) cost of public transport (see, for example, Jansson 1997).

There are other interdependencies, however, which are also relevant in a first-best world. As shown in Johansson (1997a), the fact that increased traffic (and the corresponding congestion) increases emissions and fuel consumption (and hence CO_2 emissions) per distance unit should ideally be reflected in a first-best road-pricing system. A road-user should then pay a charge corresponding not only to his/her own emissions, but also to the increased emission and fuel consumption of other road-users. It is further demonstrated in a numerical example that these 'system effects' may be significant. The reason these indirect effects should be considered, whereas the indirect effects through demand effects should not (in a first-best world), is basically identical to why 'technological' externalities should be considered and 'pecuniary' externalities should not; for the latter, see Baumol and Oates (1988).

7.2 Simultaneous Treatment of Different Policy Instruments

We have seen that market-based instruments seem to have large advantages over command and control measures for some types of externalities, notably congestion and climate change. However, we have also seen that command and control policies of various kinds most likely are part of a second-best strategy and, perhaps a bit surprisingly, are probably also part of a first-best strategy due to non-convexities in the markets (for example, for noise and safety). Still, given that we use CaC measures to regulate externalities such as air pollution, should we then still use economic instruments such as charges to reflect the external costs which are left? In the air pollution case, should one ideally charge road-users for their remaining (given the emission standards) emissions, or could one perhaps argue that given that the emission standards are designed to be socially optimal, then the externalities are already taken into account in an appropriate way, and that consequently an emission charge would be reducing the emissions to a socially too-low level?

In order to throw some light on this issue, consider the following simple model: a society consists of n identical individuals, with utility functions

$$u = U\left[q, x, E(Q, z), z\right] \tag{7.8}$$

where q is the individual distance traveled (per time unit), x is the consumption of a Hicksian composite good which also serves as a numéraire with a price equal to one, E is the emission level (which, for example, may cause negative health effects), Q (= nq) is the total of distance traveled in the society (per time unit), and z is some index of the emission standards of cars. An individual will maximize this utility function with regard to q and x and treat E and z as given (that is, the standard competitive assumption given that n is a large number) subject to a budget constraint

$$y + s = x + q\left[p_q(z) + t_q\right] \tag{7.9}$$

where y is private income (net of exogenous income taxes) s is a lump-sum transfer from the government, p_q is the price of travel (which depends positively on the emission standard index z), and t_q is the tax on car travel. The individual first-order condition is then given by

$$\frac{\partial U / \partial q}{\partial U / \partial x} = 1 + \frac{t_q}{p_q(z)} \tag{7.10}$$

The problem for the government is to choose t_q and z to maximize (7.8). In a first-best world, however, we are able to obtain the optimal quantities of x and q (and z). Hence, we can write the social maximization problem as a problem of choosing x and q for each individual subject to the social budget constraint that total income must equal total consumption, that is,

$$ny = nx + nqp_q(z) \tag{7.11}$$

or

$$y = x + qp_q(z) \tag{7.12}$$

The social first-order conditions for maximization of (7.8) subject to (7.12) with regard to q and x for an arbitrary individual can then be combined to

$$\frac{\partial U / \partial q}{\partial U / \partial x} = 1 - \frac{n}{\mu p_q} \frac{\partial U}{\partial E} \frac{\partial E}{\partial Q} \tag{7.13}$$

If we combine these social and the private maximization conditions (7.10) and (7.13) we have

$$t = -\frac{n}{\mu} \frac{\partial U}{\partial E} \frac{\partial E}{\partial Q} \tag{7.14}$$

Thus, the optimal tax on transport should exactly equal the actual marginal external cost, irrespective of whether there are any emission standards or not. (However, the amount of these external costs will of course depend on the emission standards.) Since this result holds for all emission standards, they will consequently hold also for socially optimal emission standards. This result also holds in cases where we have banned traffic on some roads for reasons related to the non-convexity property. Hence, in such cases we should still tax the traffic according to the standard Pigouvian tax level.

We have seen that it seems likely that we shall also rely heavily on various standards and regulations in the road transport sector also in the future. The design of these regulations in detail is of course far from trivial, but this is an issue which is beyond the scope of this chapter. However, some indications may be given. First, the most obvious decision criterion for an economist would be to weight costs and benefits of a standard improvement, and to choose the alternative where the social net benefit, that is, social benefits minus social costs, is maximized; for example, see Crandall et al. (1986) or Hahn (1995). Of course, this is easier in theory than in practice. First, the costs are generally unknown to the authorities, and car manufacturers have generally no incentives to reveal their true (or expected) costs. Second, there may be an important indirect benefit of improvements due to the (at least partly) irreversible technical progress. For this reason, it will be less costly to reach a future norm if some technical progress is made today. As recently shown by Smulders (1997), it may then under fairly general conditions be economically optimal to take further actions today, compared to the case with no general technical progress; compare Rosenbaum (1997).

7.3 Policy Instruments Which Are a Mix of CaC and Economic Policy Instruments

In addition to pure market-based instruments, such as charges or tradable permit systems, and pure command and control measures, there are also possible intermediate instruments which have both market based and command-and-control features. As argued, for example, by Johansson-Stenman and Sterner (1998), a system based on environmental classes for vehicles and fuels may be an interesting policy instrument to regulate emissions (other than CO_2). First, it would provide incentives for car manufacturers and oil companies to make cost-efficient improvements beyond the current emission standards. Although this system will theoretically be less efficient (in an allocative sense) than an idealized road-pricing system, or a system based on driving distance and actual emissions rather than on car ownership or fuel consumption, it will still provide important incentives at a probably rather modest administrative cost. It also seems likely to be cost efficient that some companies are on the technological front regarding emission and fuel technology, and some companies are 'followers', which will introduce similar technology a few years later.

Second, it may be part of a second-best strategy due to incomplete and asymmetric information. Since, as mentioned above, the authorities have very limited information concerning the costs of stronger emission standards, environmental classes may be a way of buying important information. For example, the tax on diesel fuel in Sweden has since 1992 been differentiated in three classes with respect to the contents of sulfur, aromatics, polycyclic aromatics and cetane indices (Sterner 1994). In 1992, the market shares were about 50 percent for class 1 (the strongest standard) and for class 2 taken together, and correspondingly about 50 percent for class 3 (corresponding to the standard before the introduction of different classes). The demand for the cleaner diesels has continuously increased, and in 1996 the market share of class 1 diesel was larger than 80 percent (Johansson and Sterner 1997, p. 155). Without this system of classes the government would probably not have taken the risk of introducing a much stronger compulsory standard, since it might suspect that the costs, and hence the consumer price, would increase drastically. On the contrary, given diesel taxes (in addition to the CO_2 tax and value-added tax (VAT)) of 1.61, 1.84 and 2.14 SEK/liter for environmental classes 1, 2 and 3, respectively (Johansson and Sterner 1997, p. 154; 1 USD = 8.5 SEK, May 1999), the government has strong reasons to believe that these tax differentiations are larger than the increase in production costs. There has been a similar purchase-tax differentiation of heavy trucks which, however, is generally considered rather unsuccessful.[11] For several years, not a single truck was sold in the 'better' classes 1 and 2. Since the expressed aim from the authorities was to promote cleaner technology, the strategy chosen in this case may seem to be a failure, as opposed to the case with diesel fuel.

However, one might actually see this the other way around. Since most of the diesel consumption has now switched to the cleaner versions, this indicates that a general standard increase of diesel may after all not have been that expensive to implement. On the other hand, the fact that no heavy trucks in classes 1 and 2 were sold indicates that the costs associated with a compulsory standard improvement might have been rather large.

As emphasized by Johansson-Stenman and Sterner (1998), the effectiveness of a system based on environmental classes would most likely be very scale dependent. Hence, the effectiveness would be much larger if implemented at a multinational level such as the European Union or the North American Free Trade Agreement (NAFTA). Currently, it is possible within the European Union to have a system with different environmental classes as long as the standards for the varying classes are equivalent to emission standards already decided for future implementation in the EU. Hence, the possibility of using these classes for buying information is currently strongly limited. However, if a system based on environmental

[11] There are two different standards for passenger cars, where the strongest standard (environmental class 1) is exempted from annual tax on car ownership for the first five years. The former tax differentiation between leaded and unleaded gasoline (16 percent higher tax on leaded gasoline) has contributed to the fact that leaded gasoline has been entirely out of the market since the second half of 1994 (lead was forbidden in petrol by January 1, 1995). However, there is still a tax differentiation between two classes of petrol with taxes (in addition to the CO_2 tax and VAT) equal to 3.61and 3.68 SEK/liter, respectively (Johansson and Sterner 1997).

classes were to be implemented in the European Union, the information from this system could be a very important input in the process of *deciding* the future emission standards. In a similar way, there could be different noise classes and different safety classes.

8. CONCLUSIONS

In this chapter it has been argued that economic policy instruments are most efficient in order to deal with some external effects, notably congestion and the global warming problem. In the congestion case, it seems that there are virtually no powerful alternatives to a road-pricing system. For all other externalities, however, it has been argued that CaC policy instruments are probably part of a second-best strategy, mainly due to various kinds of transaction costs. Furthermore, it is also shown that in some cases it seems likely that banning traffic altogether may be part of a first-best strategy due to decreasing marginal external cost curves, which in turn imply a non-convexity feature. This was particularly apparent in the case of noise and barrier effects. Hence, marginal-cost pricing would not imply a social optimum in these cases.

For some externalities, such as local and regional air pollution, a successful strategy may be to combine standards with economic policy instruments such as fuel taxes. In such cases it is shown that the optimal tax is equal to the marginal damage, irrespective of the fact that we have also used CaC measures to control the externality. Finally, it is argued that an intermediate type of policy instruments, such as a system based on environmental classes, may combine many of the benefits with an ideal road-pricing system at lower transaction costs. Such systems could also under asymmetric information and rapid technical change be an effective way of buying information for the government, which is important for an appropriate determination of future emission standards.

REFERENCES

Acutt, M.Z. and J.S. Dodgson (1997), 'Controlling the Environmental Impacts of Transport: Matching Instruments to Objectives'. *Transportation Research, part D*, **2**(1), pp. 17–33.

Akerlof, G.A. and T.W. Dickens (1982), 'The Economic Consequences of Cognitive Dissonance', *American Economic Review*, **72**, pp. 307–19.

Alexandre, A., J.-Ph. Barde and D.W. Pearce (1980), 'The Practical Determination of a Charge for Noise Pollution', *Journal of Transport Economics and Policy*, **14**, pp. 205–20.

Aschauer, D.A. (1989), 'Is Public Expenditure Productive?', *Journal of Monetary Economics*, **23**(2), pp. 177-200.

Baumol, W.J. and D.F. Bradford (1972), 'Detrimental Externalities and Non-convexity of the Production Set', *Economica*, **39**, pp. 160-76.

Baumol, W.J. and W.E. Oates (1988), *The Theory of Environmental Policy*, 2nd edition, Cambridge: Cambridge University Press.

Bradshaw, R. (1995), "Why do parents drive their children to school?." *Traffic Engineering and Control*, January, pp. 16-19.

Button, K.J. and E. Verhoef (eds) (1998), *Road Pricing, Traffic Congestion and the Environment: Issues of Efficiency and Social Feasibility*, Cheltenham: Edward Elgar.

Commission of the European Communities (1995), *Towards Fair and Efficient Pricing in Transport - Policy Options for Internalizing the External Costs of Transport in the European Union*, Green Paper, ISBN 92-77-99209-3, Catalogue no. CB-CO-95-774-EN-C.

Crandall, R.W. (1992), 'Corporate Average Fuel Economy Standards', *Journal of Economic Perspectives*, **6**, pp. 171–80.

Crandall, R.W., H.K. Gruenspecht, T.E Keeler, and L.B. Lave, (1986), *Regulating the Automobile*, Washington, DC: Brookings.

CSERGE/EFTEC (1994), 'A Survey of Noise Cost Estimates', Centre for Social and Economic Research on the Global Environment (CSERGE), University College London and University of East Anglia.

Davis, A. (1994), "The speed and mobility culture: the sacrifice of health and quality of life." *Traffic Engineering and Control*, October, pp. 568-72.

De Borger, B., S. Ochelen, S. Proost, and D. Swysen (1997), 'Alternative Transport Pricing and Regulation Policies – A Welfare Analysis for Belgium in 2005', *Transportation Research*, **2D**(3), pp. 177–98.

Department of Transport (1987), *Values for Journey Time Savings and Accident Prevention*, Department of Transport, London.

Elster, J. (1989a), 'Social Norms and Economic Theory', *Journal of Economic Perspectives*, **3**(4), pp. 99–117.

Elster, J. (1989b), *The Cement of Society*, Cambridge: Cambridge University Press.

Emmerink, R.H.M., P. Nijkamp and P Rietveld (1995), 'Is Congestion Pricing a First-best Strategy in Transport Policy – A Critical Review of Arguments', *Environment and Planning B*, **22**(5), pp. 581–602

Gramlich, E.M. (1994), 'Infrastructure Investment: A Review Essay', *Journal of Economic Literature*, **32**(3), pp. 1176-96.

Greene, D.L. (1990), 'Cafe or Price?: An analysis of Federal Fuel Economy Regulations and Gasoline Price on New Car MPG 1978-89', *The Energy Journal*, **11**, pp. 37–57.

Greene, D.L., D.W. Jones, and M.A. Delucchi (eds) (1997), *The Full Costs and Benefits of Transportation*, Heidelberg: Springer Verlag.

Hahn, R. W. (1995), 'Choosing Among Fuels and Technologies for Cleaning Up the Air', *Journal of Policy Analysis and Management*, **14**(4), pp. 532–54.

Hansson, L. (1993), *Vägtrafiken och det trafikpolitiska kostnadsansvaret*, The International Institute for Industrial Environmental Economics at Lund University.

Hansson, L. (1997), *The internalization of external effects in Swedish transport policy - A comparison between road and rail traffic*, Doctoral dissertation, IIIEE Dissertations 1997:2, International Institute for Industrial Environmental Economics at Lund University.

Hau, T. (1992), 'Congestion Charging Mechanisms for Roads', World Bank, Working Paper WPS 1071.

Hausman, J.A. (1979), 'Individual Discount Rates and the Purchase and Utilization of Energy-using Durables', *Bell Journal of Economics*, **10**(1), pp. 33–54.

Jansson, J.O. (1994), 'Accident Externality Charges', *Journal of Transport Economics and Policy*, January, pp. 31–43.

Jansson, J.O. (1997), 'Theory and Practice of Transport Infrastructure and Public Transport Pricing', in de Rus, G. and C. Nash (eds) Aldershot: *Recent Developments in Transport Economics*, Ashgate, pp. 74–134.

Johansson, O. (1997a), 'Optimal Road-pricing: Simultaneous Treatment of Time Losses, Increased Fuel Consumption, and Emissions', *Transportation Research*, **2D**(2), pp. 77–87.

Johansson, O. (1997b), 'Optimal Road Pricing with Respect to Accidents in a Second-best Perspective', *International Journal of Transport Economics*, **24**, October issue, pp. 343–65.

Johansson, O. and L. Schipper (1997), 'Measuring Long-run Automobile Fuel Demand; Separate Estimations of Vehicle Stock, Mean Fuel Intensity, and Mean Annual Driving Distance', *Journal of Transport Economics and Policy*, **31**(3), pp. 277–92.

Johansson, O. and T. Sterner (1997), 'Ekonomiska styrmedel' in Thoresson, S. (ed.) *Luftvård*, Göteborgs Universitet, ISBN 9188376109, pp. 146–58.

Johansson-Stenman, O. and T. Sterner (1998), 'What Is the Scope for Environmental Road Pricing?' in Button, K.J. and E. Verhoef (eds), pp. 150-70.

Jones-Lee, M.W. (1990), 'The Value of Transport Safety' *Oxford Review of Economic Policy*, **6**(2), pp. 39–58.

Kågeson, P. (1993), *Getting the Prices Right. A European Scheme for Making Transport Pay its True Costs*, Transport and Environment 93/6. ISBN 91 558 7721 4.

Lamure, C. (1990), 'Environmental Considerations in Transport Investments', in *Transport Policy and the Environment*, ECMT ministerial session, Paris: OECD, pp. 108–46.

Langmyhr, T. (1997), 'Managing Equity. The Case of Road-pricing', *Transport Policy*, **4**(1), pp. 25–39.

Lave, C. (1994), 'The Demand Curve Under Road Pricing and the Problem of Political Feasibility', *Transportation Research*, **28A**, pp. 83–91.

Lewis, C. (1993), *Road Pricing: Theory and Practice*, London: Thomas Telford.

Maddison, D., D. Pearce, O. Johansson, E. Calthrop, T. Litman, E. Verhoef, (1996), *The True Cost of Road Transport, Blueprint 5*, CSERGE, London: Earthscan.

Mayeres, I. (1993), 'The Marginal External Cost of Car Use – With an Application to Belgium', *Tijdschrift voor Economie en Management*, **38**(3), pp. 225–58.

Mayeres I., S. Ochelen and S. Proost (1996), 'The Marginal External Costs of Urban Transport', *Transportation Research, part D*, **1**(2), pp. 111–30.

Mogridge, M.J.H. (1997), 'The Self-defeating Nature of Urban Road Capacity Policy. A Review of Theories, Disputes and Available Evidence', *Transport Policy*, **4**(1), pp. 5–24.

Morrison, S.A. (1986), 'A Survey of Road Pricing', *Transportation Research*, **20A**, pp. 87–97.

Nelson, J.P. (1982), 'Highway Noise and Property Values: A Survey of Recent Evidence', *Journal of Transport Economics and Policy*, **16**(2), pp. 117–38.

Newbery, D.M. (1988a), 'Road User Charges in Britain', *Economic Journal*, **98** (Conference), pp. 161–76.

Newbery, D.M. (1988b), 'Road Damage Externalities and Road User Charges', *Econometrica*, **56**(2), pp. 295–316.

Newbery, D.M. (1990), 'Pricing and Congestion: Economic Principles Relevant to Pricing Roads', *Oxford Review of Economic Policy*, **6**(2), 22–39.

Phang, S.Y. and M.G. Asher (1997), 'Developments in Transport Policy: Recent Developments in Singapore's motor vehicle policies', *Journal of Transport Economics and Policy*, **31**(2), pp. 211–20.

Pigou, A. (1920), *The Economics of Welfare*, London: Macmillan.

Rosenbaum, E.F. (1997), 'Environmental Policy and Structural Change in the Passenger Transport Sector: Are Taxes Enough?' *Transport Reviews*, **17**(4), pp. 287–309.

Rothengatter, W. (1993), 'Externalities of Transport', in Polak, J. and A. Heertje (eds) *European Transport Economics*, Oxford UK: Blackwell, pp. 81–129.

Rothengatter, W. (1994), 'Do External Benefits Compensate for External Costs of Transport?' *Transportation Research*, **28A**(4), pp. 321–28.

Rothengatter, W. and S. Mauch (1994), *External Effects of Transport*, Project for the UIC, Union Internationale des Chemin de Fers, Paris.

Sandmo, A. (1975), 'Optimal Taxation in the Presence of Externalities', *Swedish Journal of Economics*, **77**, pp. 86–98.

Sandmo, A. (1976), 'Direct Versus Indirect Pigovian Taxation', *European Economic Review*, **7**, pp. 337–49.

Schipper, L. (1995), 'Determinants of Automobile Use and Energy Consumption in OECD Countries". *Annual Review of Energy and the Environment*, **20**, pp. 325–86.

Seik, F.T. (1997), 'An Effective Demand Management Instrument in Urban Transport: the Area Licensing Scheme in Singapore', *Cities*, **14**(3), pp. 155–64.

Sen, A.K. (1977), 'Rational Fools: A Critique of the Behavioural Assumptions of Economic Theory', *Philosophy and Public affairs*, **6**, pp. 317–44.

Small, K.A., and Kazimi, C. (1995), 'On the Costs of Air Pollution from Motor Vehicles', *Journal of Transport Economics and Policy*, **29**, pp. 7–32.

Smulders, S. (1997), 'Should Environmental Standards be Tighter if Technological Change is Endogenous', Working paper no. 9779, Center for Economic Research, Tilburg University.

Schweizerische-Zeitschrift-fuer-Volkswirtschaft-und-Statistik.1996 (March); 132:1: pp.109-123.

Soguel, Nils (1995), 'Contingent Valuation of Traffic Noise Reduction Benefits', *Swiss Statistical and Political Economic Review*, **132**(1), pp. 109-23.

Sterner, T. (1994), 'Environmental Tax Reform: The Swedish Experience', *European Environment*, **4**(6), pp. 20–25.

Sugden, R. (1989), 'Spontaneous Order', *Journal of Economic Perspectives*, **3**(4), pp. 85–97.

Swedish Department of Communication (1987), *DsK 1987:11 Den tunga vägtrafikens kostnader*.

Swedish Department of the Environment (1993), *SOU 1993:65 Handlingsplan mot buller*, Betänkande av utredningen för en handlingsplan mot buller.

Swedish Department of Finance (1992), *SOU 1992:53 Skatt på dieselolja*, Betänkande av utredningen om beskattningen av dieseldrivna fordon, Stockholm.

Thaler, R.H. (1992), *The Winner's Curse: Paradoxes and Anomalies of Economic Life*, Princeton: Princeton University Press.

Verhoef, E. (1994), 'External Effects and Social Costs of Road Transport', *Transportation Research*, **28A**., 273–87.

Verhoef, E. (1995), 'The Demand Curve Under Road Pricing and the Problem of Political Feasibility', *Transportation Research*, **29A**, 459–65.

Verhoef, E., P. Nijkamp and P. Rietveld, (1995), 'Second-best Regulation of Road Transport Externalities', *Journal of Transport Economics and Policy*, **29**, pp. 147–67.

Verhoef, E., P. Nijkamp and P. Rietveld, (1997), 'Tradeable Permits: Their Potential in the Regulation of Road Transport Externalities', *Environment and Planning B*, **24**(4), pp. 527–48.

Vickrey, W.S. (1963), 'Pricing in Urban and Suburban Transport', *American Economic Review*, **59**, 251–61.

Vickrey, W. (1968), 'Automobile Accidents, Tort Law, Externalities, and Insurance', *Law and Contemporary Problems*, Summer, pp. 467–68.

Vickrey, W. (1969), 'Congestion Theory and Transport Investments', *American Economic Review,* Papers and Proceedings, May, pp. 251–60.

Viscusi, W.K. (1992), *Fatal Tradeoffs, Public and Private Responsibilities for Risk*, Oxford: Oxford University Press.

Vitaliano, D.F. and J. Held (1991), 'Road Accident External Effects: an Empirical Assessment', *Applied Economics*, **23**, pp. 373-378.

Walton, W. (1997), 'The Potential Scope for the Application of Pollution Permits to Reducing Car Ownership on the UK. Some Preliminary Thoughts', *Transport Policy*, **4**(2), pp. 115–22.

Walters, A.A. (1961), 'The Theory and Measurements of Private and Social Cost of Highway Congestion' *Econometrica*, **29**, pp. 676–99.

Zamagni, S. (ed.) (1995), *The Economics of Altruism*, Aldershot: Edward Elgar.

8. Variations on the Wrong Themes? A Structured Review of the Double Dividend Debate

Andy Park and John C.V. Pezzey

1. INTRODUCTION

Since the early 1990s a large and complex body of literature has built up on the possible existence of a 'double dividend' from revenue-neutral environmental taxation. The original concept arose from the proposal to use the revenues from carbon taxation to reduce conventional distortionary taxes, in order to make the high rates of carbon taxation that would be necessary to significantly control global warming more politically acceptable (Pearce 1991). We offer here a structured review of the academic literature on the double dividend in recent years: what assumptions it has made, what conclusions it has reached, and perhaps most importantly, what issues it has usually ignored. These omissions are significant enough that we suggest that from the point of view of the environmental policy maker, the double dividend debate is putting rather too much emphasis into exploring seemingly endless variations on the wrong themes.

One immediately obvious conclusion is that popular debate on the double dividend (which is not the main focus of our review) is served only indirectly by the two main strands of the academic debate. Public debate focuses mostly on the ideal of 'environmental (or ecological) tax reform': shifting the tax base away from goods such as labour and capital to bads such as pollution or resource degradation in general. However, the empirical academic literature still almost always analyses only the case of carbon taxation. Such generalizing is questionable, since carbon emissions are different in many ways from many other forms of environmental degradation, as we show below by comparing them to sulphur emissions. By contrast, the theoretical debate almost always deals with a general pollutant, with no stylized empirical details at all, which is hardly any more satisfactory.

What largely drives all three debates (popular, empirical and theoretical) is the idea that the double dividend offers something for nothing: not only can the environment be improved, but also the tax system can be made less burdensome, even if the value of environmental improvement is completely ignored. This idea has become known as the strong double dividend hypothesis, and a striking feature of the academic literature is how much this is disputed. In very general terms, theoretical papers most commonly refute it, while empirical papers most commonly support it. However, there is plenty of disagreement on both sides, as well as between sides, and our review documents the wide range of detailed assumptions made which leaves so much room for reaching different outcomes.

Another feature which may help to explain this controversy is that double dividend debates are conducted in at least three different currencies. Improvements from (or costs of) tax reforms can be measured in terms of welfare, employment or output, and changes in different measures may be in opposite directions. Further explanation of the controversy may come from the omission by almost all theoretical analyses of two important determinants of any practical programme for using market-based instruments to control pollution: how diverse polluters are in terms of control costs, and how much any existing control policies recognize this diversity. Overlooking diversity (heterogeneity) of control costs will naturally underestimate the benefits of market-based controls which allocate control efforts at minimum overall cost. But equally, overlooking the cost sensitivity of existing regulatory policies will overstate the gains to be made from market-based control.

There are other surveys of the double dividend literature, notably Goulder (1995b, 1997) who looks at the issue in general terms, and Majocchi (1996) who considers employment effects. In addition, Bovenberg (1997) neatly summarizes his own and co-authors' work.

Our survey also highlights two further common omissions from both popular and academic debates. First, very little attention is paid to monitoring and enforcement costs, which can make all the difference to whether or not a policy instrument is workable in practice. Second, many writers have made the idea of the strong double dividend as a free lunch into the main purpose of environmental taxation. As stressed in a companion paper, Pezzey and Park (1998), this seems to us to underplay the political resistance to raising revenue in the first place. It seems better to emphasize the idea of the weak second dividend (see Section 2.1) as a palliative to raising revenue in cases, such as carbon control, where monitoring and enforcement costs make it impossible to introduce market-based instruments which do not raise revenue.

Another reason for writing this chapter is our belief that formally classifying the literature is a useful process in itself. It unearths issues that may have been neglected or forgotten. There is so much, often confusing, variation between authors in the voluminous double dividend literature that it is difficult to find a level playing field for comparisons to be made. It is thus helpful to classify the literature by several different criteria, in the hope that a clearer picture will emerge.

From a policy maker's perspective the most useful classification is by policy move[1] (Section 4); but from an academic perspective it is better to classify it first by academic criteria, between what can be broadly classed the theoretical and empirical literatures (Section 3). The classification can be practical again, in terms of the revenue-recycling instrument concerned (Section 5); it seems pointless talking about double dividends unless a specific revenue-returning instrument is specified. Finally, the classification can be technical, by the measure of desirability used by the authors concerned (Section 6). First, however, Section 2 looks at the definition of the double dividend and also considers a rather neglected but vital area, that of distributional concerns.

For simplicity in wording, we make the assumption that the double dividend hypothesis is being applied to classic revenue-neutral tax reform: the tax rate on an externality is increased, and the revenue is recycled by the reduction of another tax rate or rates. Very few writers consider whether the revenue to be recycled could come from auctioning tradable emission permits (Cramton and Kerr 1998 is a notable exception), so we neglect this issue here, although it is covered in Pezzey and Park (1998).

2. DEFINITION OF THE DOUBLE DIVIDEND

2.1 The Double Dividend Defined

This section borrows heavily from Goulder (1995b), who provides a comprehensive analysis of the definition of the double dividend. It consists of an environmental dividend (the first dividend) and a dividend from an increase in the efficiency of the tax system (the second dividend) and is best explained through the use of a diagram. In Figure 8.1 the vertical axis represents some notion of desirability (see Section 6), with A representing the desirability of the status quo with no environmental tax. Movements along the horizontal axis represent the two stages of revenue-neutral tax reform: the imposition of an environmental tax, and the recycling of revenue. Points B and C are intermediate stages in the process, points D and E are for

[1] We shall make the distinction between a policy and a policy move, the latter being a switch between policies. This is important as any existing regulation or environmental policy will have an impact on a newly introduced policy.

explanatory purposes and points F to I are possible outcomes. In Figure 8.1 vertical lines (BC, FG and HI) represent a change in the environment, and diagonal lines represent changes in the tax system.

The process of analysis begins with the move from A to B, which is simply the imposition of an environmental tax with the revenue being retained, without taking any environmental effects of the tax into account. It is, however, assumed that this tax change will cause an improvement in the environment, represented by the line BC. Thus the imposition of an environmental tax where the revenue is retained is desirable because of the environmental benefit, but undesirable because of the higher tax burden. It should be remembered, however, that the revenue raised does not disappear. The usual analysis is to assume that it is returned in lump-sum fashion.[2] A lump-sum return of revenue is non-distorting and would be represented by a horizontal line on the diagram.[3] Thus the imposition of an environmental tax is represented, in desirability terms, by a move from A to C.

So far we can say nothing about the double dividend hypothesis.[4] However, once the revenue raised by the initial environmental tax is used to reduce other, distortionary taxes, the nature of the second dividend becomes clear. The effect of the reduction in other taxation is represented by either of the heavy lines, BD and BE and the second dividend by AD and AE. In the case of BD, the loss of desirability caused by the environmental tax (AB) is offset, but not completely, by the reduction of other taxation. The fact that BD rises is the weak form of the second dividend, and is often referred to as an increase in the efficiency of the *rest* of the tax system. Goulder (1995b) also defines an intermediate second dividend, which specifies that there is at least one redistributive tax for which the strong form of the second dividend holds. We would argue that this is unnecessary, as the double dividend is not defined until the particular revenue recycling instrument is defined. See Section 5.

The move from point A to point E represents the strong form of the second dividend. In this case the loss of desirability caused by the environmental tax is more than offset by the rise in BE from the reduction of other taxation. In other words, there has been an increase in the efficiency of the *whole* tax system. This has important policy implications. The existence of the strong form of the second dividend can be seen as the holy grail of environmental tax reform as it represents a free environmental lunch. With the strong form,

---

[2] Revenue may, however, be retained and used to fund further publicexpediture or reduce government debt. Bovenberg and van der Ploeg (1996) include the optimum level of public spending in their analysis of revenue-neutral tax reform.

[3] A lump-sum redistribution, although neutral in tax efficiency terms, may be desirable if equity issues are important. See Section 2.3.

[4] It may be thought that BC represents the environmental dividend but, as will be seen, this is not the case.

the magnitude of environmental effects need not be considered, as the switch in the tax system (the move A to E) is desirable in itself. Given the difficulty in quantifying the value of environmental improvements, this would be a persuasive argument, if true.

Figure 8.1. Desirability of revenue-neutral tax reform

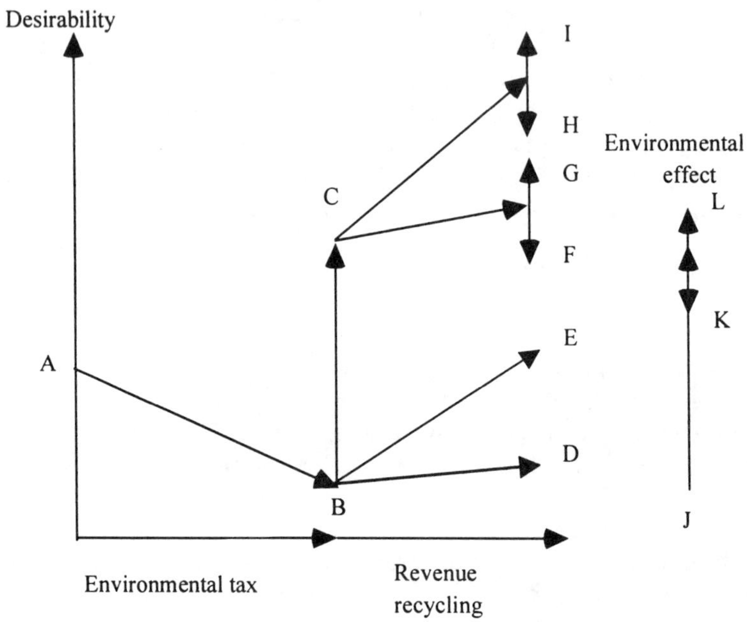

The story does not end here, however. So far we have considered the second dividend and the primary environmental effect of the environmental tax. Schöb (1996) makes the point that the recycling of revenue will also have an environmental effect. Whether this effect is desirable or not will depend on two factors. The tax rate that is reduced will be the primary influence, and its effect will depend on the relationship between the item that is subject to less taxation and the environment (see Section 5). It is also obvious, but may be overlooked, that the measure of desirability being used is vital (see Section 6). Thus, this second environmental effect is indeterminate. The overall environmental effect is represented to the right of the main diagram in Figure 8.1 by a line from J to between K and L.[5] Combining the two dividends we move from A to a point between H and I (the strong form) or between F and G (the weak form).

The rejection of the strong form of the second dividend by much of the literature often seems to be viewed as a reason for the rejection of revenue neutral environmental tax reform. This view should be tempered by careful consideration. The existence of the weak form of the second dividend is almost universally accepted and so revenue recycling is preferable to the case of revenue retention.[6] This is in addition to the standard benefits of taxation of externalities over other forms of control, in that taxation allows the achievement of a least-cost (in terms of abatement costs) solution (Pigou 1920; Downing and White 1986). This issue is considered in greater detail in Pezzey and Park (1998).

2.2 Distributional Issues

Distribution is an issue mentioned by the literature far more often than it is analysed, yet it may be the crucial factor in determining the acceptability of revenue-neutral tax reform to policy makers and politicians.

> Distributional issues are at the heart of the double dividend issue: Without distributional concerns, taxes would not need to be distortionary as governments could freely use lump-sum taxes to meet their revenue needs. (Bovenberg 1997, p. 98)

It is important to make the distinction between distribution in terms of equity, defined as some notion of 'fairness', and distribution in terms of equality, defined as a more even distribution of income. With any tax reform there will be a redistribution of welfare: some will gain, others will lose, and the losers will probably think this is unfair. Here we briefly address the equality issue by simply asking, will revenue-neutral environmental tax reform be regressive?

It would seem to be easy to analyse the problem theoretically. If the environmental tax is more regressive than the tax that is lowered using its revenue, then the change will be regressive overall. If the situation were reversed, the tax reform would be progressive and equality would be increased. This is a relatively simple analysis for environmental tax reform involving indirect taxation. The situation is made much more complicated with the introduction of labour taxes, since unemployment then enters the

[5] There is some evidence that this second environmental effect is so small as to be insignificant. See Bovenberg and Goulder (1996).
[6] Lump-sum redistribution is almost certainly impractical in reality.

equation, and also the question of which income groups are most at risk from unemployment, given a specific reform package. It would be possible, in terms of unemployment, for a strong second dividend to leave the poor much worse off, if employment was diverted away from sectors of the economy where those on low incomes are predominately employed.

As mentioned above, only a few papers have considered distribution explicitly. Bovenberg and de Mooij (1994b) and Bovenberg (1997) include workers and non-workers in their models, and find that a strong double dividend is possible only by cutting the real value of non-labour incomes, thus worsening equity. Proost and van Regemorter (1995) and Mayeres and Proost (1997) use several income groups and a social welfare function with an aversion to income inequality, and find that not just the strong double dividend hypothesis can fail, but even the weak one can, since reducing income taxes rather than giving out lump sums can worsen equity. Park (1997), in an extension of Schöb (1996), considering commodity taxation, finds conversely, that although the strong form of the second dividend fails for all revenue-recycling instruments except alcohol and tobacco, the overall effect in terms of equity depends on the distribution of environmental valuation. More specifically, the higher the level of environmental concern generally,[7] the less regressive and more progressive the tax reform.

3. THE ACADEMIC DEBATE: THEORY VERSUS EMPIRICISM

A distinction between those authors who tackle the double dividend question in a theoretical manner, and those who consider it empirically, is the most obvious way to classify the literature from an academic point of view. This distinction must be remembered whenever the double dividend is discussed, because the theoretical literature tends to reject the strong form of the double dividend, whilst the conclusions of the empirical literature are more mixed. The reasons for this distinction are not immediately apparent, but we shall attempt to suggest some explanations.

The key theoretical result is that of Bovenberg and de Mooij (1993, 1994a). A detailed analysis can be found in Goulder (1995b), so only a brief outline is given here. Assuming that the environmental tax is successful in reducing emissions, this success causes the erosion of the environmental tax base and hence a loss of revenue. This in turn means that other taxes cannot be reduced enough to compensate for the adverse effects of the higher pollution

[7] Park considers the issue of who will value the environment the most – poorer-income households who cannot isolate themselves from its effects, or higher-income households who can afford to be concerned. The answer will depend on the pollutant in question.

tax, from a consumption viewpoint. In addition, substitution between inputs, caused by the environmental tax, means that labour market distortions may actually increase. Thus, real wages and hence employment fall. Welfare effects depend on the separability assumptions between consumption, leisure and environmental quality. However, it is still preferable to return environmental tax revenues as lower distortionary tax rates rather than as lump-sum transfers. The weak form of the second dividend holds.

The empirical literature cannot be so neatly labelled as the results are much more mixed. Authors such as Brinner et al. (1992) and Goulder (1992 and 1995a) find that the strong form of the hypothesis fails, but many other authors, among them Capros et al. (1996) and Bossier and De Rous (1992), find in favour of the strong form.

These papers, and those examined in a policy context in Section 4.2.3, all share the distinction of being general equilibrium models of varying complexity. As such they may be picking up more of what is happening than the theoretical models, which by their nature are forced to be more simplistic. However, an important factor could be that the empirical models implicitly consider existing environmental regulation by their use of baseline scenarios for calibration purposes. As will be seen in Section 4, this issue is important and is generally ignored by theoretical work.

On the other hand, Goulder (1997), Bovenberg (1997) and de Mooij (1998) agree that theoretical results can show a strong dividend if the existing tax system is inefficient enough, but doubt whether the equity concerns which probably caused these inefficiencies in the first place can be swept aside. An alternative reconciliation of theory and empiricism would therefore be if it turned out that strong dividends are found in empirical models only when existing taxes are very inefficient, and when revenue-neutral carbon taxation results in significant redistributive effects. Further research is necessary to determine which is the better explanation for the divergence between the theoretical and empirical literature.

In mitigation, the empirical literature deals with carbon/energy taxation, which is obviously not subject to the regulatory standards, both technical and emission based, which are set for 'controllable' pollutants such as sulphur dioxide. However, there are still strong effects that must be considered. The key point is that any current baseline will be in compliance, or at the very least is supposed to be in compliance, with existing regulation. We would suggest that any form of energy-use technical standard will have some bias on the results generated by a model that does not include the standard. In addition, any form of environmental standard, be it for SO_2 or other pollutants, will have some impact on energy usage. Brendemoen and Vennemo (1996), although they do not explicitly consider the issue, probably analyse this effect most efficiently due to the extensive range of pollutants they include in their model.

This divergence between the theoretical and empirical literature was diminished somewhat by Bovenberg and Goulder (1996). The paper focuses on how the optimal environmental tax rate is usually less than from the Pigouvian ideal (that is, the marginal damage cost) when the existing second-best tax structure is taken in consideration. This point is stressed by Goulder et al. (1997), who also show that environmental control at the margin can be harmful if the marginal damage cost falls below a certain threshold. This analysis is undertaken both theoretically and empirically.[8] Although the double dividend is not explicitly examined, the theoretical and empirical results are very similar.

4. POLICY MOVE AND POLLUTANT

The first part of this section lays out the general policy framework in which the double dividend hypothesis should be considered. The second section then considers, in depth, the literature within this policy framework. As will be seen, as soon as one starts to consider policy, the actual pollutant concerned is of vital importance.

4.1 A Framework for Classification

There has been a tendency, in our view, for the academic debate on the double dividend hypothesis to stray from the original policy context. To this end it is useful to look at the possible ways in which governments can control environmental externalities that are relevant to the double dividend. The key, and in our view oft-neglected, point is that the most suitable policy will vary with the pollutant in question. And we consider this here in detail, using the practical differences between CO_2 and SO_2 to illustrate our points. The focus will be on those policy moves, or shifts, from one policy to another that are relevant to the double dividend.

Figure 8.2 shows four possible policy states that a government can take to control a pollutant plus the state of no control, and six possible moves between states. It is the policy moves that we are interested in, specifically those moves that allow a double dividend. We thus require a move from the current policy (which we assume does not include market-based instruments) to emission taxes. The current policy, assuming no market-based instruments are currently in use, is likely to be either no control, technology standards, or

[8] The theoretical model is an extension of Bovenberg and de Mooij (1994a), and the empirical general equilibrium model is that used in Goulder (1995a).

emission standards. This current policy is of crucial importance and is often overlooked in the double dividend literature. The taxes which are moved to may be at optimal or non-optimal rates. Other market instruments such as tradable emission permits are not considered here. Although they are of relevance to the double dividend debate, they are not considered in the literature. Pezzey and Park (1998) consider the double dividend in a wider policy framework, including other market instruments.

Figure 8.2. Possible policy moves giving rise to the double dividend

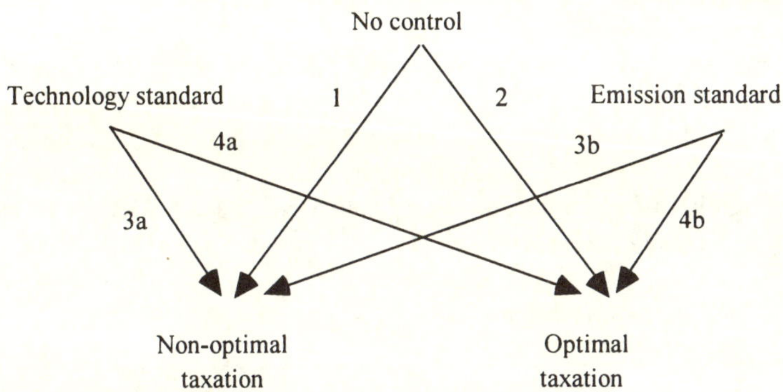

Crudely speaking, there are four criteria if any move away from current policy is to be first considered and then adopted, and the application of these criteria depends on the pollutant in question. First, it must be known that emissions cause environmental damage. The local damage caused by SO_2 has been known for decades, although awareness of its long distance damage via acid deposition is more recent. Confirmation that rising CO_2 concentrations will alter climate significantly has been very recent, and is still controversial.

Second, emissions must be controllable. Again, the nature of the pollutant is important. In terms of control of emissions, pollutants can be classified into two broad types or cases: those that are an unwanted byproduct of a production process, and those that are, in some sense, the goal of a production process. The first case, byproducts, covers most 'traditional' pollutants such as SO_2, particulates and so on. Here there must exist an affordable technology to control emissions; or in other words, it must be possible for producers to clean up after themselves. Technologies to control SO_2 emissions are commercially available, although there has been a long debate about whether the best technology is to use tall stacks to disperse and dilute the emissions, or flue gas desulphurization to reduce total emissions at source.[9] With this type of pollutant, the goal of environmental policy is the introduction of the appropriate control technology.

The second case, where the marketed output of a production process is or becomes a pollutant, is more complex. The most obvious example is CO_2 from fossil fuels, although in the recent past Chlorofluorocarbons (CFCs) also fell into this type. For pollutants of this type there is no control technology, and the goal of environmental policy must be to reduce or eliminate the usage of a product. In the case of CFCs this was achieved, in the developed world at least, by the introduction of non-environmentally damaging alternatives. Unfortunately, in the case of fossil fuels, no alternatives are immediately available, at least on a sufficiently large scale. So the goal of policy must be to limit use.

The third and fourth criteria are that it must be affordable for the government or agency to monitor the results of its policy; and there must be the political will to impose the costs of control on polluting firms (and their customers). Leaving aside the issue of political acceptability for the moment, there are big differences in monitoring costs between SO_2 and CO_2, as shown by the data in Table 8.1.

Table 8.1 Proportion of total emissions

	Proportion of total emissions coming from:	
Pollutant	Housing, commerce, transport and agriculture (%)	Power stations, refineries and other industry (%)
SO_2	11	89
CO_2	44	56

Sources: UK. Dept of Trade and Industry (1996), Digest of UK Energy Statistics, pp. 190-91.

The 44 percent of CO_2 emissions which come from small and often mobile emitters makes it prohibitively expensive to monitor a large majority of individual emissions. In addition, it is generally difficult to increase the energy efficiency of most existing equipment, so it is no surprise that there has been little political will to set efficiency standards for existing CO_2 technologies. Efficiency standards for CO_2 therefore apply only to new equipment. We observe later that the literature pays little explicit attention to such standards.

[9] One should also mention the introduction of smokeless zones in cities, which achieved a major reduction in SO_2 emissions by simply banning small-scale coal burning. Whether one calls this a technology standard or an input standard hardly matters, since the furnace type and the fuel type are jointly determined. The existence of alternative fuels such as gas was critical for this to be an acceptable policy.

Even if they are possible, technology standards have obvious disadvantages. They give no incentive to find alternative means of control, and they give no direct control over the level of emissions. It is therefore preferable to have emission standards,[10] provided that the information costs of so doing are reasonable, which is generally true for SO_2 given modern monitoring equipment.

The equivalent, indirect move for CO_2 would be to move from setting standards for new energy equipment, to fixing the amount of carbon energy actually sold (since CO_2 emissions are directly in proportion to this). This is obviously seriously impractical and incredibly costly. This is the origin of the idea of moving from (indirect) technology standards for CO_2, to control by carbon taxes. The latter will create a pervasive incentive to reduce CO_2 emissions in the most cost-effective way, without specifying which users are to reduce emissions, by how much, or with which technologies. But because monitoring CO_2 emissions directly is so costly, and because almost all carbon fuel used is burned,[11] the tax incentive is applied to carbon inputs instead. Without carbon taxation (which could be implicit, for example the reduction of any existing subsidies for carbon-energy use), many analysts cannot see how widely-agreed targets for CO_2 control can be achieved.

But why is there no equivalent literature on sulphur or SO_2 taxes, extolling the virtues of using the revenue from them to get a double dividend by lowering conventional, distortionary taxes? For there is virtually no literature solely on SO_2 taxes as such. The nearest one is in a recent empirical discussion of 'Ecological Tax Reform' (von Weizsacker and Jesinghaus 1992) – that is, a deliberate, macroeconomically significant move from taxing 'goods' such as income, labour and commodities towards taxing 'bads' such as pollution, congestion and resource depletion. This is because first, SO_2 emission standards are feasible and moderately effective. Second, thanks to much lower monitoring costs, a politically much more attractive alternative is available: grandfathered tradable permits for SO_2 emissions. Any concern about the inefficiency of emission standards (caused by their typical uniformity, which again is a result of the information costs of non-uniform standards) will therefore push policy in the direction of that alternative, not towards revenue-neutral SO_2 taxes.

As shown in Figure 8.2, revenue-neutral emission taxes can be set non-optimally. This is virtually inevitable for carbon taxes, given the near-impossibility of valuing the future environmental damage caused. To our knowledge only Nordhaus (1993) has attempted the numerous and highly

[10] Standards would ideally be set in terms of the total emissions from a site, often known as the 'bubble' policy in the US, rather than in terms of emissions from one stack, or emissions concentrations.

[11] Any problems of unfairness caused by taxing carbon which ends up locked up in products, for example, in plastics, are ignored here.

debatable empirical and ethical[12] assumptions needed to calculate an optimal carbon tax. Or, taxes can be set 'optimally', which is what the theoretical literature does. In all these cases, the policy move is not well defined until the means of revenue neutrality is specified: that is, which conventional tax is to be reduced using the emission tax revenue. See Section 5.

The 'No Control' situation in Figure 8.2 hardly exists in reality, at least for developed countries. In practice, some form of environmental regulation exists for all recognized pollutants, whether it is specifications of nuclear storage facilities, or regulations on the design of waste sources. More importantly, there are strong linkages between regulatory standards for any pollutant and energy usage. A simplistic example would be the mandatory fitting of catalytic converters on cars, having an effect on their (energy) efficiency. The theoretical analysis of the double dividend question does not tend to acknowledge the existence of existing regulatory standards, whilst the empirical literature does. In reality it is very likely that all pollutants are subject to both forms of regulatory standard (technology and emission based) either explicitly or, especially in the case of carbon, implicitly.

4.2 The Literature within the Framework

This section categorizes the double dividend literature into the framework outlined in Section 4.1. Because of informational difficulties we do not make the distinction between technology standards and emission standards, but consider them jointly as regulatory control.

4.2.1 No control to non-optimal taxes

This category, represented by policy move 1 in Figure 8.2, contains mostly theoretical papers and one, that of Schöb (1996), that attempts empirical analysis. Bonetti and Fitzroy (1996) set up a theoretical model and then produce simulation results, but the model is not calibrated, in the strictest sense, to real-world data.

The basic result here is the standard Bovenberg critique that the erosion of the environmental tax base results in an inability to reduce other taxes enough to compensate for the adverse effects of the higher pollution tax. The strong dividend fails, but the weak dividend holds. From a different perspective, Parry (1995), in a simplistic model, shows that by increasing marginal production costs, environmental taxes reduce GDP and this is not compensated for by a reduction in distortionary tax. A negative exception is Proost and van Regemorter (1995) who find that if the macroeconomic

[12] The prime ethical assumption is that the objective of policy is tomaximize the present value of welfare using a constant exponential discount rate applied over the lifetimes of several generations.

regime is one of flexible wages and fixed employment then the second dividend fails. This is because with fixed labour supply and their redistributive instrument, social security contributions, there is no reduction in distortions.

Labandeira-Villot and McCoy (1996) explicitly consider the issue of the first dividend (environmental improvement) depending on public finance considerations, in other words the redistribution of revenue. This is the issue raised in moving from J to either K or L in the right of Figure 8.1. Schöb (1996) also analyses this question, first from a theoretical perspective and then empirically. He uses commodity taxation as the revenue-returning instrument, and shows that the environmental dividend will depend on the complementarity or substitutability relationship between the polluting good and the revenue-returning instrument chosen. He uses a partial equilibrium model of the UK economy, based on Pashardes' (1991) 'Almost Ideal Demand System', and finds that the strong form of the second dividend fails.

Bonetti and Fitzroy (1996) show that a small, revenue-neutral energy tax will raise employment at constant wages if government expenditure is not large. Although the authors interpret their tax energy tax rise as an additional tax rise on fossil fuel energy, the simplistic nature of their model categorizes the paper into this section. The simulation results presented show that a substitution of energy taxation for labour taxation, which doubles the price of energy, increases output by 1 percent, employment by 6–9 percent and welfare by 5–13 percent if the net wage is held constant. To some extent, the result is driven by this assumption in that a constant net wage, given a lower income tax rate, means that gross wages fall and thus labour demand rises. Fitzroy (1996) also finds that there is the possibility of a strong dividend existing. Schneider (1997) shows that where involuntary unemployment exists, a second (employment) dividend may be possible if workers do not respond to lower unemployment by reducing their effort.

4.2.2 No control to optimal emission tax

This category of policy action is by far the most common theoretically, and is represented in Figure 8.2 by policy move 2. It is a shift to optimal taxes that has the most appeal intuitively. Optimal tax rates mean that pollution is optimally controlled, or in other words the environment receives the 'right' amount of help. However, there are obvious problems in quantifying optimal rates, as the monetary value of the environmental impact of the pollutant is required. We would argue that the very concept of 'optimal' environmental taxation is, for this reason, of little use to policy makers, particularly in the case of CO_2 taxation to curb global warming.

Policy move 2 represents most of the work of Bovenberg and co-authors. An in-depth analysis of theoretical methodology is not attempted here.

Rather, a few stylized facts are presented. Bovenberg and de Mooij (1993, 1994a) and Bovenberg and van der Ploeg (1994a, 1994b) all find that the strong form of the double dividend fails, although the weak form holds. Bovenberg and de Mooij's simplistic models of 1993 and 1994a are elaborated on by Bovenberg and van der Ploeg, who include variable labour supply in an open economy (1994b) and a closed economy (1994a).

However, Bovenberg and de Mooij (1994c, 1997) find that when the environmental externality has an impact on production, the strong form may hold if this externality is large. Also, the inclusion of involuntary unemployment in Bovenberg and van der Ploeg (1996) suggests more hope for the strong form. They use an analytical general equilibrium model of a closed economy, and also find that a third dividend, arising through the analysis of the optimal level of public spending, is possible. Employment will rise if the shifting of the tax burden of firms away from wages outweighs the effect of a fall in the marginal cost of public funds, encouraging the government to raise the overall tax burden. A welfare 'triple dividend' will occur if environmental concern is small, fixed factors account for a large share of production, substitution between fixed factors and resources is easy, and substitution between resources and labour is difficult. This result is qualified by the suggestion that it is less likely to hold in the long run, and is unlikely in the context of an open economy with internationally mobile capital.

Bovenberg and de Mooij (1997) use an endogenous growth model and find a second dividend may exist if either the environmental externality impacts on production (rather than the standard assumption of impact on consumption only) or if there is a shift in the tax burden from capital to profits.

4.2.3 Technical standards to non-optimal taxes

Policy move 3, a move from regulatory standards to non-optimal taxes, is the most common policy action studied empirically. Indeed, the literature surveyed in this section deals entirely with empirical models of carbon/energy taxes for two reasons. First, there is the implicit inclusion of regulatory standards, technical in the case of energy,[13] when one has reference to a baseline case. This is a natural process in computable (empirical) general equilibrium modelling, the way in which carbon/energy taxes are most commonly (and usefully) analysed. Second, in a general equilibrium setting, the use of non-optimal tax rates is the most natural way to proceed, especially when dealing with carbon/energy. Setting optimum tax rates to control greenhouse gases requires knowledge of the dynamic effect

[13] Although the point made previously with regard to the interaction between standards for any pollutant and energy use should not be forgotten.

of emissions on concentration of gases in the atmosphere, the effect of concentration on climate change, and the effect of climate change on the economy. Including these effects within an economic model is challenging to say the least. It has been attempted – the DICE (Dynamically Integrated Climate Economy) Model of Nordhaus (1993)[14] but the simplifying assumptions that have to be made about the underlying science are truly heroic, and the sensitivity of the results to these assumptions is large. The validity of his results for policy making is thus easily challenged. The large majority of the empirical carbon/energy literature avoids such heroism and focuses on non-optimal taxes. To a large extent, until climate–economy interactions are understood more fully, this is the most useful approach.

Brendemoen and Vennemo (1996) calculate the effect of the imposition of taxes on eight different pollutants (SO_2, NO_2, CO, CO_2, VOC, CH_4, N_2O and particulates), that appear primarily through their role as composites of fossil fuels. The authors calculate both a measure of the direct impact of tax changes (the second dividend) and a measure of both the direct effect and environmental impact (the overall dividend). Without including externalities, overall welfare increases when CO_2 tax rates are raised and income tax or Value-added tax (VAT) levels are reduced; remains approximately the same when gasoline and oil are taxed and income tax levels reduced; and falls for oil and gasoline taxes with VAT reduction. If externalities are included, then all the above tax changes are welfare increasing. They implicitly include regulatory standards for a wide range of pollutants in their base-case scenario.

Capros et al. (1996) use the GEM-E3 computable general equilibrium (CGE) model for the 12 EU member states linked through endogenous trade. They find that a carbon tax refunded by lower employers' social security contributions increases employment across the EU, with the exception of Greece which loses 12,000 jobs. The UK and Germany gain most, and GDP at market prices increases by between 3.3 percent (Belgium) and 1.2 percent (Greece). However, they make the critical assumption that the real wage elasticity of labour supply is relatively high.

Carraro et al. (1996) model a segmented labour market within a dynamic CGE model of the EU. They consider a carbon tax with the revenue used to reduce payroll taxes, paid by employers.[15] They find that employment rates rise in the short run, but stabilize to the baseline case in the long run, except in the UK where there is a positive effect in the long run. Brinner et al. (1992), although they use a less sophisticated methodology and do not explicitly analyse the double dividend, find the strong form exists in the long term in the US, if the revenues raised by a gasoline tax are again used to

[14] This model is not included as it uses lump-sum transfers.
[15] Equivalent to employers' National Insurance contributions in the UK.

reduce payroll (employer paid) taxes. Welsch (1996) finds that the strong dividend will hold, in terms of employment, if there are no increased wage claims.

These papers are in conflict with the studies by Goulder (1995a, 1992) that use a similar sophisticated methodology. Goulder (1995a) finds that the impact of a carbon tax on intermediate goods and its narrow base outweighs the benefit of the attendant labour tax reduction. In his 1992 paper, Goulder finds that although the welfare loss is lower if revenues are redistributed through income tax, corporation tax and/or payroll tax reductions, as opposed to a lump-sum fashion, there is still a welfare loss.

In the case of Bossier and De Rous (1992), revenue from carbon taxation is returned in the form of subsidies to investment in energy-efficient technology.[16] Unsurprisingly perhaps, their empirical results suggest that this policy, although it reduces GDP in the short term, increases GDP in the long run. This is due to the fact that energy-efficient technology takes time to come 'on-line'. Although the modelling of future technical change is fraught with difficulty, the result would seem sensible.

5. CHOICE OF REVENUE-RECYCLING INSTRUMENT

It is simple to list the available alternatives. Personal income taxes, corporate income taxes, employment taxes, specific commodity taxes, general commodity taxes (whether on sales or value added), and social security contributions are the main ones. The important point is that the choice of revenue-returning instrument will make a difference to the desirability of revenue-neutral tax reform.

The most common choice of instrument is labour or income taxes. It is interesting to note that with the exception of Brendemoen and Vennemo (1996), all papers that choose income taxes find that the strong form of the second dividend fails. The majority of the papers are theoretical so the points made in Section 3 may apply, but Brinner et al. (1992) and Goulder (1992) both find that whilst labour tax reductions do not give a strong second dividend, other tax reductions do. A problem may be that labour taxes are generally not modelled to a sufficient degree of accuracy. For example, most models view income tax as simply a proportion of income. This is technically necessary in general equilibrium modelling because a more realistic income tax structure with tax allowances and bands is discontinuous, and will result

---

[16] See also Carraro and Galeotti (1997). Returning the revenue through energy-efficiency subsidies, an example of what Pezzey and Park (1998) call an 'environment-subsidising' environmental tax, is rather outside 'standard' double dividend context.

in a general equilibrium model behaving unpredictably or not achieving solution.

Both the above papers in addition to Capros et al. (1996) and Carraro et al. (1996) find that a reduction in payroll taxes[17] is most likely to provide the strong form. This is perhaps because this is one tax reduction that may benefit both producers and consumers directly. We suggest that the way forward is more comprehensive modelling of realistic tax structures, and an examination of all possible redistributive instruments.

6. MEASUREMENT OF DESIRABILITY

Of fundamental importance to the double dividend hypothesis is how dividends are measured, or more specifically over what they are measured. Section 2.1 defined the double dividend purely in terms of its 'desirability'. The usual measures of desirability are employment, output and most commonly, welfare. Although an increase in any or all of these would, generally, be considered desirable, for a given policy change an increase in one measure may not necessarily mean an increase in the others. It is possible, for example, for output to increase following some change in the tax system, but for employment to fall.[18] Many authors impose this distinction within their work (Bonetti and Fitzroy 1996; Bovenberg and de Mooij 1993; Bovenberg and van der Ploeg 1996; Capros et al. 1996; Goulder 1992), but many others do not, which can lead to confusion, particularly in the popular debate.

The most common and obvious measure is some notion of aggregate welfare, usually measured as the change in some social utility function which depends on both total goods consumption and pollution, but not on the distribution of either. Welfare has the advantage of being the only measure of desirability that can directly capture environmental effects. The exact functional form of this welfare function will have a bearing on results and most of the literature, including this chapter, assumes that the effects of consumption and emissions on desirability are additively separable. This imposes the important restriction that the environment is a component of welfare, but does not affect any of the other components. But without additive separability, it is hard to agree on how decompose the effect of a revenue-neutral emissions tax into an environmental dividend and a second dividend from reduced tax distortion.

---

[17] Employers' National Insurance contributions in the UK.

[18] This could happen if there was a switch in the burden of taxation from capital to labour and the marginal productivity of capital was higher than the marginal productivity of labour.

Another common method of measurement is that of changes in employment (Capros et al. 1996; Carraro et al. 1996; Fitzroy 1996 and the majority of papers by Bovenberg and co-authors). The second dividend is then the effect of the revenue-neutral tax change on the labour market, and modelling of the labour market becomes crucial. Obviously one must not assume full employment if one wants to measure employment effects. This was illustrated in Section 4.2.2, where the inclusion of involuntary, unemployment in Bovenberg and van de Ploeg (1996) reversed the results of their earlier models. This should be contrasted with the work of authors such as Schöb (1996) who ignore labour market effects completely. There are obvious linkages between welfare and employment, but which measure is used can make a big difference to the way a theoretical model is constructed. This makes comparisons between models much more difficult.

This difficulty in comparison gets worse when one considers empirical models of revenue-neutral emission taxes, which are relevant to double dividend questions, even if their authors often do not explicitly recognize this. As mentioned above, virtually all such models are of carbon-energy taxation. The complex nature of general equilibrium models means that a comparison of even two models requires detailed scrutiny. Looking at the empirical literature as a whole, the measures of desirability used vary, and include output and growth in addition to welfare and employment. In this context, the problem of comparison of models is compounded by the problem of comparison of results.

7. CONCLUSION

We have considered the literature on the possible double dividend achieved by revenue-neutral environmental tax reform from several different aspects: type of policy change, theory versus empiricism, method of revenue recycling, and measure of desirability. Few writers, theoretical or empirical, doubt that the weak double dividend exists: that environmental taxation is more attractive than would be calculated if its revenue benefits were ignored. The main point of debate is that the divergence between the theoretical and empirical literature – the fact that the former usually finds no strong double dividend, whereas the latter often does – may be due to the non-specific nature of the theoretical literature in terms of pollutant, and its neglect of existing environmental regulation. On the other hand, the divergence may be caused by different treatment of distributional issues (can poor people afford coal for heating and so on, or who gains or loses from revenue-neutral tax reform). Strong double dividends may be found by empirical models only if the existing tax system is very inefficient, and if the adverse equity effects of reforming it are tolerable, since such results are found by a number of theoretical models. In that case, tax reform would be advisable in any case, without bringing in environmental taxation. Only further research can establish which explanation is more plausible.

Once one looks at the empirical literature on, or accidentally relevant to, the double dividend idea, one rapidly realizes how it is almost entirely restricted to the idea of taxing carbon and/or energy use (an important recent exception is Mayeres and Proost 1997). This is not surprising, because CO_2 is the only major pollutant where the costs of directly monitoring and controlling the large majority of emissions are prohibitive, and therefore directly revenue-neutral alternatives such as grandfathered tradable emission permits have not been considered. The outcome is that wider forms of the double dividend idea, such as the idea of reforming the whole tax system to tax 'bads' rather than 'goods' (ecological tax reform), are almost entirely untested empirically.

As well as addressing the subtler equity effects of revenue-neutral emission taxes that the theorists have highlighted, further empirical modelling also needs to address the practical and political realities of the pollutants under debate. Modelling taxes on SO_2, particulates or biochemical oxygen demand (BOD) effluent will produce very different numbers than for carbon. Attention needs to be paid to the starting point of current policy, to the administrative costs of monitoring, and it would help if the conventional tax which is to be reduced using emission tax revenue were to be more standardized. And above all, estimates, or at least lower bounds, of the non-market values of reduced emissions will have to be found, unless there is already a binding commitment to reduce emissions.

Finally, the proponents of wider-ranging 'ecological tax reform' must not lose sight of political realities. It may be better for aggregate welfare (though perhaps not for distribution) to return emission tax revenue as lower distortionary taxes rather than as lump sums. But that does not mean that it will be politically easy to raise environmental tax revenue in the first place. When polluters are few, and hence environmental property rights are practicable to administer, non-revenue-raising schemes which use such rights, like grandfathered tradable emission permits or taxsubsidies (Pezzey 1992), need to be considered instead. These still yield the static and dynamic efficiency benefits of controlling heterogeneous emissions by price rather than by regulation. Only if polluters are pervasive (as in the case of carbon) is revenue-neutral environmental taxation, probably at less than its full incentive level, likely to be acceptable politically.

REFERENCES

Bonetti, S. and Fitzroy, F.R. (1996), 'Welfare and Employment Effects of Energy Taxes: Theory and Simulations', Typescript, Department of Economics, University of St. Andrews.

Bossier, F. and De Rous, R. (1992), 'Economic Effects of a Carbon Tax in Belgium', *Energy Economics*, January 1992, pp. 33–41.

Bovenberg, A.L. (1997), 'Environmental Policy, Distortionary Labour Taxation and Employment: Pollution Taxes and the Double Dividend'. In C. Carraro and D. Siniscalco, (eds), *New Directions in the Economic Theory of the Environment*, Cambridge: Cambridge University Press.

Bovenberg, A.L. and Goulder, L.H. (1996), 'Optimal Environmental Taxation in the Presence of Other Taxes: General Equilibrium Analyses', *American Economic Review*, **86**(4), pp. 985–1000.

Bovenberg, A.L. and de Mooij, R.A. (1993), 'Do Environmental Taxes Yield a Double Dividend?', Center for Economic Research Discussion paper, no. 9369.

Bovenberg, A.L. and de Mooij, R.A. (1994a), 'Environmental Levies and Distortionary Taxation", *American Economic Review*, **94(**4), pp. 1085–89.

Bovenberg, A.L. and de Mooij, R.A. (1994b), 'Environmental Policy in a Small Open Economy with Distortionary Labour Taxes: a General Equilibrium Analysis'. In E.C. van Ierland, (ed.), *International Environmental Economics*, Amsterdam: Elsevier.

Bovenberg, A.L. and de Mooij, R.A. (1994c), 'Environmental Tax Reform and Endogenous Growth', Center for Economic Research Discussion paper, no. 9498.

Bovenberg, A.L. and de Mooij, R.A. (1997), 'Environmental Tax Reform and Endogenous Growth', *Journal of Public Economics*, **6**, pp. 207–37.

Bovenberg, A.L. and van der Ploeg, F. (1993), 'Does a Tougher Environmental Policy Raise Unemployment? Optimal Taxation, Public Goods and Environmental Policy with Rationing of Labour Supply", CEPR Discussion paper, no. 869, pp. 32.

Bovenberg, A.L. and van der Ploeg, F. (1994a), 'Environmental Policy, Public Finance and the Labour Market in a Second-Best World', *Journal of Public Economics*, **55(**3), pp. 349–90.

Bovenberg, A.L. and van der Ploeg, F. (1994b), 'Green Policies and Public Finance in a Small Open Economy', *Scandinavian Journal of Economics*, **96**(3), pp.343–63.

Bovenberg, A.L. and van der Ploeg, F. (1996), 'Optimal Taxation, Public Goods and Environmental Policy with Involuntary Unemployment', *Journal of Public Economics*, **62**, pp. 59–83.

Brendemoen, A. and Vennemo, H. (1996), 'The Marginal Cost of Funds in the Presence of Externalities', *Scandinavian Journal of Economics*, **98(**3), pp. 405–22.

Brinner, R.E., Shelby, M.G., Yanchar, J.M. and Cristofaro, A. (1992), 'Optimizing Tax Strategies to Reduce Greenhouse Gases without Curtailing Growth', *The Energy Journal*, **12(**4), pp. 1–14.

Capros, P., Georgakopoulos, T., Van Regemorter, D., Proost, S., Schmit, T. and Conrad, K. (1996), 'Using the GEM-E3 Model to Study the Double Dividend Issue', mimeo, National Technical University Athens.

Carraro, C. and Galeotti M. (1997), 'Economic Growth, International Competitiveness and Environmental Protection: R&D and Innovation Strategies with the WARM Model'. *Energy Economics*, **19**(1), pp. 2–28.

Carraro, C., Galeotti, M. and Gallo, M. (1996), 'Environmental Taxation and Unemployment: Some Evidence on the Double Dividend Hypothesis in Europe', *Journal of Public Economics*, **62**, pp. 141–81.

Cramton, P. and Kerr, S. (1998). 'The Distributional Effects of Carbon Regulation'. Chapter 12 this volume.

de Mooij, Rd A. (1998), 'The Double Dividend of an Environmental Tax Reform'. In J. van den Bergh (ed.), *Handbook of Environmental Economics*, Cheltenham: Edward Elgar, forthcoming.

Downing, P.B. and White, L.J. (1986), 'Innovation in Pollution Control', *Journal of Environmental Economics and Management* **13**(1), pp. 18–29.

Fitzroy, F.R. (1996), 'Green Taxes and Defensive Expenditure', Typescript, Department of Economics, University of St Andrews.

Goulder, L.H. (1992), 'Do the Costs of a Carbon Tax Vanish when Interactions with Other Taxes Are Accounted For?' National Bureau of Economic Research Working Paper, 4061.

Goulder, L.H. (1995a), 'Effects of Carbon Taxes in an Economy with Prior Tax Distortions: An Inter-temporal General Equilibrium Analysis', *Journal of Environmental Economics and Management*, **29**, pp. 271–97.

Goulder, L.H. (1995b), 'Environmental Taxation and the Double Dividend: A Reader's Guide", *International Tax and Public Finance*, **2**(2), pp. 157–83.

Goulder, L.H. (1997), 'Environmental Taxation in a Second-best World'. In H. Folmer and T. Tietenberg (eds), *The International Yearbook of Environmental and Resource Economics 1997/1998*, Cheltenham: Edward Elgar.

Goulder, L.H., Parry, I.W.H. and Burtraw, D. (1997), 'Revenue Raising vs. Other Approaches to Environmental Protection: The Critical Significance of Pre-existing Tax Distortion', *Rand Journal of Economics*, **28**(4), pp. 708–31.

Labandeira-Villot, X. and McCoy, D. (1996), 'Interaction Dividends from Environmental Taxation', Conference on Environmental Economics, Ambleside, England, August.

Majocchi, A. (1996), 'Green Fiscal Reform and Employment: A Survey', *Environmental and Resource Economics*, **8**, pp. 375–97.

Mayeres, I. and Proost, S (1997), 'Optimal Tax and Public Investment Rules for Congestion Type of Externalities', *Scandinavian Journal of Economics*, **99**(2), pp. 261–79.

Nielsen, S.B., Pedersen, L.H. and Sorensen, P.B. (1995), 'Environmental Policy, Pollution, Unemployment, and Endogenous Growth', *International Tax and Public Finance*, **2**(2), pp. 185–205.

Nordhaus, W. (1993), 'Optimal Greenhouse-gas Reductions and Tax Policy in the DICE Model', *American Economic Review* (Papers and Proceedings), **83**(2), pp. 313–17.

Park, A. (1997), 'Cigarettes and Alcohol: Distribution Implications of the Double Dividend Hypothesis', Typescript, Department of Economics, University of Edinburgh.

Pashardes, P. (1993), 'Bias in Estimating the Almost Ideal Demand System with the Stone Index Approximation', *Economic Journal*, **103**, pp. 908–15.

Parry, I.W.H. (1995), 'Pollution Taxes and Revenue Recycling', *Journal of Environmental Economics and Management*, **29**, pp. S64–S67.

Pearce, D. (1991), 'The Role of Carbon Taxes in Adjusting to Global Warming', *The Economic Journal*, **101**, pp. 938–48.

Pezzey, J. (1992), 'The Symmetry Between Controlling Pollution by Price and Controlling it by Quantity', *Canadian Journal of Economics*, **25**(4), pp. 983–91.

Pezzey, J. and Park, A. (1998), 'Reflections on the Double Dividend Debate: The Importance of Interest Groups and Information Costs', *Environmental Resource and Economics*, **11**(3–4), pp. 539–55.

Pigou, A. C. (1920), *The Economics of Welfare*. London: Macmillan.

Proost, S., and van Regemorter, D. (1995), 'The Double Dividend and the Role of Inequality Aversion of Macroeconomic Regimes', *International Tax and Public Finance*, **2**(2), pp. 207–19.

Rico, R. (1995), 'The U.S. Allowance Trading System for Sulphur Dioxide: An Update on Market Experience', *Environmental and Resource Economics*, **5**(2), pp. 115–29.

Sandmo, A. (1975), 'Optimal Taxation in the Presence of Externalities', *Swedish Journal of Economics*, **77**, pp. 86–98.

Schneider, K. (1997), 'Involuntary Unemployment and Environmental Policy: The Double Dividend Hypothesis', *Scandinavian Journal of Economics*, **99**(1), pp. 45–59.

Schöb, R. (1996), 'Evaluating Tax Reform in the Presence of Externalities', *Oxford Economic Papers*, **48**(4), pp. 537–55.

Terkla, D. (1984), 'The Efficiency Value of Effluent Tax Revenues', *Journal of Environmental Economics and Management*, **11**, pp. 107–23.

von Weizsacker, E.U. and Jesinghaus, J. (1992), *Ecological Tax Reform: A Policy Proposal for Sustainable Development*, London: Zed Books.

Welsch, H (1996), 'Recycling of Carbon/Energy Taxes and the Labor Market', *Environmental and Resource Economics*, **8**, pp. 141–55.

9. Environmental Taxes seem to be Effective Instruments for the Environment

Maria Teresa Ribeiro, Kai Schlegelmilch and David Gee[1]

1. DO ENVIRONMENTAL TAXES WORK?

1.1 Definitions of Effectiveness

Taxes might be called effective if they do what they are supposed to do. In theory, environmental taxation should attempt to improve the market efficiency of the environmental goods and services by imposing a price on such goods equal to the marginal costs of their use (marginal environmental damage costs). If authorities manage to calculate these costs, environmental taxation is inherently effective, provided that no other major imperfections distort the relevant markets. Good knowledge of marginal environmental damage costs is an exception, however. Only one example is known where authorities are explicitly basing the tax rate on an estimate of these costs.[2]

Environmental taxes can have different functions:

- cost covering;
- incentive effects; and
- revenue raising.

[1] The authors edited a recent report by the European Environment Agency (1996) as requested by the European Parliament. Evaluation studies of 16 environmental taxes have been identified and reviewed in this report of which those parts are presented here that deal with the evaluation of the environmental effectiveness. Given resource constraints, an inclusion of the findings of *ex-post* evaluation studies published after the report had been edited in late 1996 was not possible, though it is at least referred to some of these studies and their findings.

[2] The UK landfill tax, introduced in October 1996.

For these functions, the concept of 'environmental effectiveness' needs to be defined. For assessing the effect of taxes, two criteria may be substituted for the theoretical criterion of equality of tax rate and marginal environmental damage costs:

1. The effect of the tax on environmental pollution or the use of scarce resources ('environmental effect').
2. A comparison of the tax rate with the marginal pollution-abatement costs, or, as a proxy, average abatement costs of measures taken by taxpayers ('incentive effect').

These criteria can be used to assess a similar impact in different ways. The first criterion directly attempts to trace the contribution of the tax to the monitored pollution reduction, whilst the second criterion endeavors to establish incentives for taxpayers to change their behavior in a way more favorable to the environment often by adopting abatement measures or by saving on scarce resources.

Pollution-reduction goals are often not set explicitly, or price incentives are not explicitly intended. This may be the case for all types of taxes, but especially for fiscal environmental taxes and for cost-covering charges. This makes evaluation more difficult and qualitative rather than quantitative.

Assessing the cost effectiveness of policy instruments is even more difficult. As data is usually deficient, no such evaluation is attempted in this chapter. However, some overall observations on policy effectiveness are made in Table 9.1 (p. 182-184). In evaluating the environmental effectiveness of taxes, their functions need to be taken into account.

The main function of fiscal environmental taxes is raising income for government expenditures. Environmental effects are a side-effect. However, positive environmental impact may be expected because of the price effect on behavior. Consequently, evaluating the environmental effectiveness of this type of tax involves examining the environmental effects, for example, in terms of pollution reduction.

Incentive taxes are designed to achieve a specific environmental impact. So the evaluation of environmental effectiveness includes comparing pollution-reduction targets. It also involves measuring the incentive effect by comparing the differential between the tax rate and the cost of pollution reduction.

Cost-covering charges are designed primarily to raise funds for financing specific environmental systems, measures or programs. Two types have been defined:

- the user charge and
- the earmarked charge.

In both cases, funds raised are a major objective, so effectiveness evaluation involves assessing the money available for carrying out the environmental measures or programs. However, cost-covering charges may also have an incentive impact if charge rates for cost recovery reach substantial levels.[3] Incentive effects are sometimes aimed for in cases where formerly fixed rates for certain environmental services were differentiated according to the level of the service rendered.[4]

1.2 Review of Studies on Effectiveness

Drawing firm conclusions about actual environmental effectiveness of green taxes depends on the availability of *ex-post* policy-evaluation studies. The study for the OECD concludes that there is little tradition in policy evaluation (OECD 1997). A practical reason is its complexity. These studies normally have to cope with difficult methodological problems as well as with problems of data availability. Ideally they should also be independent of the institutions responsible for the design and use of the taxes.

Methodological issues include disentangling the tax effects from other elements in the baseline and the policy package, and answering the counterfactual question 'What would have happened without the tax?'. For these purposes a reconstruction is needed of all the relevant economic, environmental and societal factors and their mutual relationships in a quantitative or qualitative dynamic model. The reinforcing or possibly counteracting effects of other regulations on the tax scheme must be taken into account. New tax schemes almost always enter a policy field already crowded with other players: permits, standards, bans, agreements and so on, so isolating the exact contribution of the tax scheme requires an in-depth study which is rarely done: an exception is water pollution charges (Andersen 1994). More such studies are needed.

Data availability plays a crucial role in policy evaluation. Data is often difficult to retrieve retrospectively; it may not have been kept long enough, or is not detailed enough, or is simply not suitable because it has been collected for other purposes, such as tax registers. Reconstruction can be a laborious job.

The time factor is also crucial in evaluation. Both taxes and regulations can take up to a decade or more to be effective, so the time periods estimated – and needed in practice – to achieve a given level of impact need to be included in tax design and implementation.

---

[3] This has been reported by several authors who examined the Dutch water pollution charge.

[4] Variable charge rates for household collection (for example, 'pay-per-bag' schemes) are an example.

Despite these difficulties a number of evaluation studies of environmental taxation have been conducted, of varying quality and independence, but covering 16 environmental taxes, applied in at least six countries. However, judgments about the performance of green taxes remain at the level of best guesses.

1.3 Findings

Within the limitations discussed earlier, Table 9.1 summarizes the main findings in terms of effectiveness of the taxes/charges (environmental effectiveness and incentive effectiveness) and adds some remarks on the functioning of the taxes.

Table 9.1a. Summary of an assessment[1)] of selected environmental taxes[2)] (Fiscal environmental taxes)

Country	Instrument	Environ. function	Environmental effects	Incentive effects	Overall effectiveness
S	Sulfur tax	Penetration of low-S fuels and abatement	+++ Reduction of 6,000 tons of S (6% of total) reduction of S content of oil by 40%	+++ Average abatement costs about SEK 10, lower than tax rate of SEK 40	Although a fiscal tax, it had strong incentive effect, probably due to high tax rate
S	CO_2 tax	Reduced CO_2 emissions	?/+ Shift in district heating from fossil to bio-fuels; increased competitiveness of combined heat and power	? Unknown	Hard to evaluate due to short period of operation
N	CO_2 tax	To reduce CO_2 emissions	++ Some signs of reduction in CO_2 emissions 3–4% in 2–3 years (1991–93) from a rising trend	Price of heating oil increased 15% and price of petrol by 10%	
S	Tax on flights	Reduce emissions in transport	+ Some impact on acceleration of replacement of combustion chambers by one airline	? Unknown	
DK	Waste charge	To reduce waste generation and increase recycling and reuse	++ Reused fraction of demolition waste increased from 12% to 82%	? Doubles average cost of waste dumping and increases cost of incineration by 70%	

Table 9.1b. Assessment of incentive charge

Coun try	Instrum ent	Environ. function	Environmental effects	Incentive effects	Overall effectiveness
S	Tax rebate on un-leaded petrol	To increase penetration of unleaded petrol	+++ Emissions of lead dropped by about 80% between 1988–1993.	+++ Presently tax differential exceeds extra costs of unleaded petrol	Contributed to phasing out of lead tax
S	Tax rebate 'cleaner ' diesel	To increase penetration of low-pollution diesel fuels	+++ 75% reduction of S emissions by diesel cars; 95% in cities; reduced emissions of particles, smoke, NO_X, hydrocarbons and PAC expected but not quantified	+++ Tax differential higher than additional production costs	Dramatic increase of market share of 'cleaner' fuel
D	Toxic waste charge	To reduce the amount of toxic waste	++ Reduction of toxic waste production of 20-45% between 1991 and 1993	++ Increased average dumping and incineration costs by at least 5–15%	Planned capacities for incineration were consequently reduced
S	NO_X-charge	To speed up reduction of NO_X emissions from large combustion plants	+++ Main cause of the reduction by 9,000 tons in 1992 (35% of liable emissions)	+++ Charge rate of SEK 40 exceeds by far average abatement costs	Provided incentive for monitoring and abatement measures
S	Ferti-lizer charge	To reduce the demand for fertilizer	+ N down by 25%; P down by 65% from 1980 to 1992; charge was one of the factors	? Unknown	Contributed to decreased use of artificial fertilizers
F	Water pollu-tion charge	To stimulate adoption of in-plant wastewater treatment	+ Modest	+ Charge rate considerably lower than average abatement costs	Some positive environmental impacts; revenues are modest
D	Water pollu-tion charge	To support adoption of water pollution abatement in permit application process	+ Early announcement helped speed up wastewater treatment capacity	+ No relation between charge rate and marginal damage costs	Positive impact on applying for and issuing of lower-pollution permits

Table 9.1c. Cost-covering charges: user and earmarked charges

	Instrument	Environ. Function	Environmental effects	Incentive effects	Overall effectiveness
NL	Water pollution charge	To finance wastewater treatment plants	+++ Water pollution reduced	+ Average charge slightly lower than average pollution abatement costs	Incentive small but created funds for increase in treatment capacity
NL	Household waste charge	Fair distribution of waste management costs over users	+ 10–20% less waste in 'pay-per-bag' villages	?/+ Unknown	Fairer distribution of costs
Earmarked charges					
S	Battery charges	To cover costs of collection, disposal and information	++ Collection rate of lead-batteries 95%; decreasing share of small Hg and NiCd batteries	0 Charge makes recycling of Pb-batteries feasible	Effect for other batteries is still unclear
NL	Aircraft noise charge	To finance insulation and redevelopment programs around airports	+ Insulation of buildings around airport	0 Very low	Satisfactory in terms of fund-raising

Notes: +/++/+++ = small/medium/high, 0 = absent or negligible, ? = unknown.

The incentive effect evaluation is based on the evidence found on taxpayers being encouraged to reduce pollution, mostly due to significant differentials between the tax rate and the cost of abatement measures (or a proxy). The environmental effectiveness is based on the evidence on environmental benefits derived from the tax. The question marks indicate lack of evidence.

The diffusion of taxes over various environmental policy fields is widespread. Such instruments are found in water and air quality policy and in waste management. Their role in noise-abatement policy is marginal.

Half of the taxes/charges considered in this chapter were reviewed in a Swedish policy evaluation study. Water pollution charge systems (France, Germany and the Netherlands) have been reviewed quite thoroughly. A number of studies – for example, on the Danish waste charge, the Danish CO_2-tax scheme, the Dutch waste and groundwater taxes and the Swedish environmental taxes – have been published.[5]

[5] However, given resource constraints, findings could not be included in this chapter. The

As far as environmental effects are concerned, incentive charges and fiscal environmental taxes on air quality in Sweden, and on water pollution charges in the Netherlands, have worked well. The tax differentiation schemes for fuels have been particularly successful, as has the Swedish NO_x charge. For CO_2 taxes reviewed to date (Norway, Sweden and Denmark) a positive impact has been found (no detail findings of Erhvervsministeriet et al. 1999, Enevoldsen 1998, Togeby et al. 1998 and.the Swedish Environmental Protection Agency 1997 are provided here).

- The 'incentive effect' of taxes has been studied in a few cases only. It appeared from the Swedish evaluation study that the tariffs on sulfur dioxide and nitrogen oxides were at levels which encouraged less-polluting courses of action. In the water pollution charge schemes, provisions for financial assistance were reported to be of great importance for adopting wastewater treatment measures (France, Germany and the Netherlands). In the Dutch case the charges themselves were found to exert an incentive effect because of the high charge levels.
- 'Incentive charges' are of a variable nature. As shown in Table 9.1, several taxes such as the Swedish NO_x charge and the German toxic waste charge, are functioning quite well.[6] Most of the schemes also have a fund-raising capacity. Environmental effectiveness, then, is the result of incentive and revenue-raising effects. This is reported to be positive to variable degrees for the water pollution charge systems. The impact of the fertilizer charge (Sweden) is less clear.
- The 'overall effectiveness' of environmental taxes seems to be positive and even high in some cases. Policies on air quality in Sweden and water quality in the Netherlands have been well supported by taxes.
- As regards their functions, the performance of the various types of taxes is variable. The main function of 'fiscal environmental taxes' has not been studied. However, most of these taxes were reported to have a positive environmental effect. Little is known about the single reviewed fiscal tax with incentive purposes, the tax on domestic flights in Sweden.[7]
- Most cost-covering charges served their objectives, collecting money for pre-set purposes, quite well.

---

studies include Norwegian Green Tax Commission (1996), Swedish Environmental Protection Agency (1997), Swedish Government Commission on Green Taxation (1997), Enevoldsen (1998), Andersen (1998) and Schlegelmilch (1999).

[6] However, the latter has not been collected since early 1997, partly dueto its success, partly due to some redeclaration of waste that is said to have occurred.

[7] This tax had to be abolished by the beginning of 1997 because of the EU-Directive on mineral oil excises that requires a mandatory exemption of fuel used for commercial aviation.

2. DESCRIPTION OF INDIVIDUAL TAXES

2.1 Sulfur Tax (Sweden)

In 1991 a sulfur tax was introduced in Sweden in order to further the decrease of the emissions of sulfur. The tax applies for fuels (coal, oil, peat) that contain 0.1 percent of weight of sulfur or more. The tax amounts to SEK 40 per kg of S. if sulfur emissions are abated, the tax might be reimbursed. For light oils a tax differentiation scheme compensates indirectly for the cost of producing oils of class I (maximum S-content of 0.001 percent) and class II (maximum S-content of 0.005 percent) through tax exemption. The maximum allowable S-content in light oil is 0.2 percent (class III).

The sulfur tax should promote the use of cleaner fuels and the cleaning of flue gases from the use of fuels with a high S-content. An evaluation study of economic instruments in Swedish environmental policy[8] indicates that the tax may have had a considerable impact. The average S-content of fuel oil decreased from about 0.65 percent in 1990 (the legal maximum allowable content was 0.8 percent at that time) to 0.4 percent recently.[9] The S-content of light oils is lower than 0.1 percent on average which corresponds with levels for which no tax is due. Policy effectiveness is high.

About a quarter of the taxpayers have undertaken measures for the cleaning of flue gases and are receiving tax refunds. The reduction of sulfur emissions is 70 percent on average.

It is concluded that the tax has had an impact on the emissions of SO_2. The Swedish evaluation study assumed an environmental impact of 6,000 tons. Total SO_2 emissions were approximately 110,000 tons in 1991, but the share of emissions that could be influenced by the tax is considerably lower, as a consequence of the tax base – fuels for combustion purposes – and the tax threshold. The average costs of the measures taken after the introduction of the S-tax were about SEK 10 per kg, which is considerably lower than the tax rate of SEK 40. This suggests a high incentive impact of the tax.

2.2 CO_2 Tax (Sweden)

In Sweden a special CO_2 tax was introduced in 1991 as part of a fiscal reform. At the same time, value-added tax (VAT) on energy was introduced and general energy taxes were reduced. In 1993 the tax burdens were differentiated according to economic sectors: the total burden for industry was reduced through a decrease of the CO_2 tax and complete abolition of the

---

[8] MENS (1994).

[9] See OECD 1997.

general energy tax, and the burden for other sectors was increased through an increase of the CO_2 tax. Bio-fuels are exempt from these taxes.

The impact of the CO_2 tax is difficult to determine since this tax is part of a broader tax reform package. Furthermore, the period of application of the tax is rather short. In 1994, an evaluation study of applied economic instruments in Sweden was published.[10] This study concludes that some indications about the steering effects of the tax can be given. In many cases, energy production plants are said to have shifted fuels as a consequence of the tax. The tax relief for bio-fuels has led to an increased interest to convert existing plants. The use of wood fuel in district heating continues to grow. Combined heat and power production appear to having become more competitive, especially when coal and oil are used.

The report finds a tendency to a higher consumption of fuel oils in industry, while industrial production decreased slightly in the same period. This might be attributed to the tax relief for this sector after 1992. In particular, the consumption of fuels in the paper and pulp industry increased by more than 30 percent in one year, compared with about 20 percent for the industry as a whole. The other way round, this shows that exemptions might be environmentally counterproductive.

2.3 CO_2 Tax (Norway)

The CO_2 tax in Norway, in place for five years, has been evaluated.[11] The analysis is carried out for selected sectors on a sub-macro level. The focus is on emissions from stationary sources in mainland manufacturing industry and services and from stationary and mobile sources of households. In total it covers about 40 percent of taxable CO_2 emissions.

The methodology implies a comparison of the actual economic developments (with the CO_2 tax) and the fictitious developments (without the CO_2 tax). The price of heating oil and petrol increased by about 15 and 10 percent as a result of the tax. The total effect of the tax was a reduction of CO_2 emissions of 3–4 percent for the period 1991–93.

The largest effect was calculated for the paper industry. Oil consumption would have been 21 percent higher without the tax. The impact in the intermediate product sector and government services was 11 and 10 percent, respectively. The impact was much lower in other sectors.

The effect of the tax on household use of energy for heating was low because low share of oil was earmarked for this purpose (less than 10

[10] See OECD (1997).

[11] Larsen and Nesbakken (1996).

percent). Private car transport by households would have been 2–3 percent higher per year without the tax.

2.4 Tax on Domestic Flights (Sweden)

Domestic flights are subject to a tax based on emissions of hydrocarbons and nitrogen oxides. The tax rate is SEK 1 per kg for both pollutants. These taxes are additional to the CO_2 tax of SEK 0.32 per kg for aviation fuel used in domestic air traffic. Calculation of the taxes is based on standard emission figures for types of aircraft and on average flight distances.

The report that evaluates the tax scheme[12] states that the tax has resulted in 'thorough analysis of aviation procedures and exhaust emissions from the aircraft'. The tax is also said to have accelerated the change of combustion chambers of the aircraft by one of the airlines subject to the tax. The direct impact of the tax on aircraft emissions is unknown. However, it was abolished at the beginning of 1997 since the European Commission considered it not to be in line with the internal market.

2.5 Waste Charge (Denmark)

Denmark has applied a charge on the disposal (dumping and incineration) of non-hazardous waste since 1986. Current tariffs are DKK 195 per ton for dumping and DKK 160 per ton for incineration. The difference in tariffs reflects the aspiration to increase the share of waste incinerated and to decrease the share of waste for dumping. Tariffs will be further raised and differentiated in 1997. Waste incinerated in installations that recover heat or generate electricity will be charged at DKK 160 per ton. Otherwise a charge of DKK 210 per ton is due. Landfill waste will cost DKK 285 per ton.

Exemptions exist for certain types of waste. Any charge paid for waste that is shipped off the waste site is reimbursed. The revenues from the Danish waste charge go into the general budget. Since 1993 they have been used as a part of the green tax reform.

This fiscal tax has an explicit regulatory function. The intended environmental impact includes reduction of waste generation, increase of reuse and recycling and a larger share of waste incinerated. Reuse and recycling of waste increased from 21 percent to 50 percent of the total amount of waste offered for collection in the period 1985 to 1993. Dumping decreased from 57 percent to 26 percent. The share of waste incinerated remained constant.

[12] MENS (1994).

The financial effect of the waste charge is considerable. Eighty percent of the landfill tariffs (waste charge excluded) are between DKK 150 and DKK 250 per ton. The waste charge of DKK 195 results on average in doubling the costs of waste dumping. The tariffs for incineration are between DKK 150 and DKK 300 per ton. The charge of DKK 160 increases the costs of incineration by 70 percent on average.

The charge scheme has been under evaluation. The purpose of this study was to investigate the impact of the tax scheme on the changes in the disposal of waste mentioned above.

No results of this study are included here. [13] However, the Danish Environmental Protection Agency is of the opinion that the tax scheme has contributed significantly to a substantial increase of the reuse of demolition and construction waste. Total waste supply increased only slightly in the period 1988–93, by 2 percent. In 1985, 12 percent of the demolition waste was reused. The reused fraction increased to 82 percent in 1993. This result by far exceeds the target for the year 2000, which is 60 percent reuse. The Agency has based its opinion on statements made by representatives of the construction sector.[14]

2.6 Tax Differentiation on Leaded Petrol (Sweden)

In order to facilitate and accelerate the penetration of unleaded petrol, a tax differentiation of unleaded and leaded petrol was introduced in 1986 in Sweden, as in many countries. Phasing out leaded petrol was necessary for the reduction of lead emissions and to facilitate the use of cars equipped with catalytic converters, which was a parallel measure taken. The tax differential increased from SEK 0.10 in 1986 to SEK 0.51 in 1992. The share of leaded petrol decreased from 100 percent in 1986 to 40 percent in 1992 to practically zero in 1993.

This instrument was aimed rather at producers of car fuel than at consumers. Producers should be persuaded to start producing unleaded fuel by (partial) compensation of the additional production costs. Drivers of cars suitable for this fuel would comply quite readily, provided that the price of unleaded petrol is lower.

Originally, the tax differential was too small to cover the additional costs. After the increase to SEK 0.51 the differential appeared to be sufficient.[15] Another reason for the dramatic fall in the share of leaded petrol after 1992 (40 percent) was the replacement of leaded fuel for cars that continue to

[13] Andersen 1998 - findings are not included here

[14] Danish Environmental Protection Agency (1995).

[15] MENS (1994).

require this type of fuel by a fuel containing an alternative lubricant, sodium. Total emissions of lead dropped by about 80 percent between 1988 and 1993.

As to the incentive impact of the tax differential, oil producers stated that the differential was an important reason for starting to produce unleaded petrol. Whether the announced regulations, necessary in the framework of promoting cars with catalytic converters, were also an important incentive is unknown, but not improbable.

2.7 Tax Differentiation for Diesel (Sweden)

Reduced tax levels apply for types of diesel fuel that comply with environmental characteristics that are stricter than those required under environmental regulations. Three classes have been distinguished. Class III is the standard type of diesel for which a maximum allowable content for sulfur of 0.2 percent was set. Classes II and I comply with stricter requirements, not only for the contents of sulfur but also for the emissions of aromatics and other environmentally relevant characteristics.

Tax rebates were introduced for Classes I and II in 1991. In 1994, the levels of the rebates amount to SEK 457 per m^3 and SEK 260 per m^3 for Classes I and II, respectively. The tax rebates should encourage the production and market penetration of the cleaner fuels by compensating higher costs of production.

The Swedish evaluation study[16] describes the impact of the tax rebate scheme on the diesel market as 'dramatic'. In 1990, less than 1 percent of the diesel sold in Sweden would have qualified for Classes I or II. In 1994, 60 percent of all diesel fuels complied with Class II and 15 percent with Class I requirements. Emissions of sulfur from diesel cars decreased by 75 percent, and even by 95 percent in cities. The study attributes this apparent success to the combination of the tax rebate scheme and lower-than-expected production costs for cleaner diesel fuels. It appeared that, rebates included, the costs of production of Classes I and II were lower than the production cost of standard fuel. This induced producers to concentrate production and marketing on the cleaner products.

2.8 Toxic Waste Charge (Baden-Württemberg, Germany)

A charge on toxic waste was introduced in April 1991 in the south-western *Land* Baden-Württemberg, Germany, in order to cope with the increasing amount of toxic waste. Hence, the tax may be classified as an incentive tax, although it also raised substantial revenues. The tax rates were doubled in

[16] MENS (1994).

1993 up to a level of DEM 100, 200 or 300 per ton, depending on the potential danger and the expenditures for treatment.

In terms of environmental pollution it can be regarded as successful. The amount of toxic waste declined from 605,000 tons in 1991 via 430,000 tons in 1992 to 354,000 tons in 1993. At the same time the revenue rose from DEM 19.8 million in 1992 to DEM 36.7 million in 1993. According to an evaluation study carried out by the Eco-Institute in Darmstadt (Öko-Institut 1994), only half the 250,000 tons of reduced toxic waste may be classified as abated. The other half may be explained by using other terms, evasion or the recession. The tax has even led to a reduction of planned capacities of incineration. The consultants discovered that there was still a large potential for abatement. Thus, they recommended that residual substances also to be taxed in order to prevent evasion. However, this charge was abolished in 1996 for several reasons:

- the tax was very effective;
- some undesired effects, such as fraud and redeclaration of waste, continued to occur;
- the current level of toxic waste will now be monitored to keep it at this low level.

2.9 NO_x Charge (Sweden)

On 1 January 1992 a charge on emissions of NO_x was introduced in Sweden. About 185 large combustion installations for generation of energy are subject to the charge system. The charge is imposed on emissions which are calculated on the basis of continuous monitoring. Taxpayers may apply for a fixed charge rate. It is assumed in those cases that emissions amount to 600 mg NO_x per MJ input of fuel for gas turbines and 250 mg NO_x per MJ of fuel input otherwise. Since these parameters by far exceed actual emission factors (amounting to 112 mg/MJ on average for all fuels), subjects are encouraged to install monitoring equipment and pay the charge on the basis of actual emissions.

Plants with an input energy capacity of at least 10 MW and a total annual energy production of at least 50 GWh are subject to the charge. The production threshold was decreased to 40 GWh in 1995 and should be decreased further to 25 GWh in 1997.

The charge scheme is additional to the system of permits and its purpose is to accelerate the reduction of NO_x emissions. A reduction of 5,000 to 7,000 tons per year was originally aimed at. Total emissions of the liable plants amounted to 24,000 tons of NO_x in 1990, 21,000 tons in 1992 and 15,300 tons in 1993.

The tax rate is SEK 40 per kg NO_x emitted. The revenues (SEK 600 million in the first year of operation) are refunded to the taxpayers on the basis of a proportional share of the total energy produced by the plants.

According to an evaluation,[17] the charge has had an environmental impact that was noticeable from 1990 when the system was adopted by Parliament. The main portion of the reduction of 9,000 tons of NO_x, realized in 1992, is reported to be attributable to the charge. The average emission of NO_x per unit of energy input dropped from 159 mg per MJ to 103 MJ. Based on adopted projects by the liable subjects, emission reductions are expected to continue.

Reactions of subjects to the charge could be traced by comparing net payments with emission reductions, by sector. Table 9.2 shows the redistributive impact of the charge and NO_x reduction data for five sectors (figures for 122 plants).

The largest net payer is the waste incineration sector. This sector managed to bring about an emission reduction of 40 percent. The largest net receiver is the metal industry. Their emissions increased slightly. The results for the other three sectors are not conclusive in this respect.

Table 9.2. Net payments and emission reductions, by sector

	Number of installations	Net payment (reception) per GWh of energy produced (SEK/GWh)	NO_X emission reduction, 1992–1993 (%)
Waste incineration	5	9,763	42
Energy generation	53	(878)	23
Chemical industry	23	(94)	17
Pulp and paper ind.	39	1,304	13
Metal industry	2	(9,168)	–2
Total	122	176	20

Source: OECD (1997).

The charge rate was set at SEK 40 per kg of NO_x for incentive reasons. The costs of reducing emissions in the installations under the charge scheme were estimated at between SEK 20 and SEK 80 per kg. Many measures are reported to be cheaper than SEK 20 per kg, however. An average cost figure of SEK 10 per kg is considered to be likely by the Swedish Environmental

[17] MENS (1994); OECD (1997).

Protection Agency. This implies that the charge provides a strong incentive for finding and applying cost-effective solutions.

Since the primary objective of the charge system was to strengthen the permit policy, it can be concluded that the policy effectiveness was high.

2.10 Fertilizer Charge (Sweden)

A charge on the nitrogen (N) and phosphorus (P) content of fertilizer has been applied in Sweden since 1982. This charge was a 'price-regulating' charge aimed at providing financial support for the export of agricultural products (and skimming some of the farmers' rent due to low fertilizer prices). In 1984, an environmental charge on fertilizer containing P and N was introduced. The dual purpose of this charge is to raise the price and discourage the demand of fertilizer, and to create funds for financing measures to mitigate negative environmental effects of agriculture, such as manure treatment plants, counseling and information. The rates of both charges were raised to a level of about 30–35 percent of the sales value of fertilizers in 1991. The 'price-regulating charge' was dropped in 1992; the level of the environmental charge was about 10–13 percent in that year.[18] The rates are SEK 0.6 per kg for N and SEK 1.2 per kg for P.

The use of fertilizer has been reduced significantly since 1984. Even so, the impact of the charge systems on these reductions is hard to assess as a large agricultural reform program was undertaken during the same period. The Swedish evaluation report states that the impact on the use of nitrogen and phosphorus was noticeable. The reduction of N was largest when the charge rate reached a high level (1990). The use of P shows a continuous decrease during the period 1984–92, of 50 percent in total. The report states that this result was caused by the charge system and by growing awareness of the negative effects of phosphorus on the environment. The latter factor was assumed to be influenced by information campaigns financed from the charge funds.

2.11 Water Pollution Charge (France)

The purpose of the French water pollution charge system is to stimulate and partly subsidize the construction of wastewater treatment plants operated by municipal and industrial discharges. The responsibility for purification of wastewater remains with the polluters themselves; they pay the charge if they discharge to open water, and they are supported financially if they undertake treatment measures. The charge system is administered by the six Agences de

[18] MENS (1994); OECD (1997).

l'Eau. These public bodies formulate objectives, decide about the necessary funds and calculate the charge rates on that basis.

According to an in-depth evaluation study of the system,[19] the French charge is best described as earmarked. A major feature of the system is a tax-bounty scheme for firms and local authorities concluded in sector contracts and river contracts.

The amount of wastewater treated in public purification plants rose from 21 million in 1980 (30 percent of total wastewater emissions) to 32 million in 1992 (42 percent of total emissions). Industrial emissions of oxygen-binding substances, suspended solids and heavy metals decreased by 28 percent, 38 percent and 39 percent, respectively, in the period 1980–92.

Assessing the impact of the charge on pollution behavior is difficult since the charge system is part of the French water-quality policy that is dominated by permit issuing. This can be illustrated by some figures. Total expenses for water-quality policy in France amounted to FRF 44,000 million in 1992 (42 percent of total environmental expenses of FRF 105,000 million).[20] The funds created by the proceeds of the water pollution charges amounted to FRF 3,600 million, or 8 percent of the total water-quality expenses. Investments for prevention and treatment of wastewater were FRF 19,000 million in 1992. These figures indicate that most of the measures taken for a better water quality are geared by the permit policy, and by the willingness of local authorities to undertake water treatment projects and to pass on the costs (92 percent on average) to the inhabitants.[21] Of course, the sector and river contracts may have been the decisive factor in starting treatment works in individual cases.

The charge rates are modest, compared with the charges in Germany and the Netherlands. Consequently, the incentive impact of the charge on adoption of pollution-control measures – a refund takes place upon proof of adequate measures – is small (less than 10 percent of those in Germany and the Netherlands). The charge rate has also never been related to the marginal costs of abatement costs, and appears to be much smaller than the average costs of pollution control.

2.12 Water Pollution Charge (Germany)

The German water pollution charge system was introduced to reinforce the water quality policy which mainly is the competence of the German *Länder*. Although originally intended to be purely an incentive, the actual system has

[19] Andersen (1994).
[20] Chapuy (1995).
[21] Andersen (1994); de Savornin Lohman (1995).

been weakened, as a compromise between Federal authorities and the States.[22] The system contains some incentive elements, such as reductions for best available technologies (BAT) and lowered rates in expectation of investments. As the charge bill is based on discharge values in the permits and not on actual emissions, the objective of the charge could be described as encouraging applicants for a low-discharge permit. Funds of the charge accrue to the *Länder* and are added to their budgets for water-quality policy, financing monitoring and administrative structures.

As to the objective of the charge, the German system is probably best rated as an incentive charge, when it came into effect from 1981 onwards. Due to several changes, in particular after German reunification, it may now also be characterized as an earmarked charge.

Although lack of data impedes a proper evaluation of the charge system in terms of environmental impact, some evidence exists that the early announcement of the system induced municipalities and industry to undertake action aimed at reduction of wastewater discharges by treatment of effluent. One evaluation study observes that the decline in water pollution discharges began in 1981, the year the charge was actually introduced, though minimum requirements for discharges were also introduced around that time.[23]

The charge rate was calculated against the background of marginal abatement costs of different industry sectors. But the rate was then set rather to limit the financial consequences for the charge subjects than to reflect marginal pollution-abatement costs.

2.13 Water Pollution Charge (Netherlands)

The Dutch water pollution charge system is primarily geared towards financing collective wastewater treatment plants. It was introduced in 1970 in order to facilitate the building of wastewater treatment capacity for discharges into the large water bodies managed by the State (big rivers, estuaries, Ijssel Lake). The charge rates, as far as the non-state part of the system managed by the Water Boards is concerned (the other part is the state part of the charge, which is not evaluated here), is calculated on the basis of funds required for expenses for investment in and running of the plants in the coming period. The charge system accompanies a system of permit giving.

Available evaluations observe that the Dutch water-quality policy has been quite successful.[24] Treatment capacity increased from 52 percent in 1975 to

[22] Kraemer (1995); de Savornin Lohman (1995).
[23] Andersen (1994).
[24] de Savornin Lohman (1995); Andersen (1994).

95 percent in 1992, in terms of households connected with a public sewage treatment plant. Of all discharges, 74 percent was treated in 1991, against 51 percent in 1980. Emissions from the manufacturing industry fell from 19 million to 4 million in the period 1975–91.

Discharges from large emitters in the manufacturing industry decreased by 80 percent in the period between 1975 and 1991. Two studies attempted to disentangle the impact of the charges from the impact of the Dutch water-quality policy at large. One study[25] found a strong relationship between variations in charge rates of Water Boards and the rate of reductions of discharges within their jurisdiction. Another study[26] found that the majority of interviewed industry representatives (54 percent) claimed that the charge has been the decisive factor in decisions in favor of water pollution-abatement measures, whereas only 20 per cent pointed at the permit policy to be of main importance. This study also stated that the average charge rate – which varies substantially across Water Boards – was only slightly lower than the average pollution-abatement costs. Consequently, in some individual cases, the charge rate would exceed the average abatement costs.

2.14 Household Waste Charge (Netherlands)

Collection and removal of household waste and waste from small municipal enterprises is the responsibility of the Dutch municipalities. Many cities and villages have contracted out waste management tasks to private firms, but they remain responsible for financial aspects. The majority of municipalities pass on (part of) the costs of waste collection to the inhabitants by annually issuing fixed-rate waste bills. Increasingly, especially the smaller, rural cities are introducing variable charge rates. Three main systems are found. One or two municipalities actually weigh the contents of the dustbin at the moment of collection. A few villages apply a 'pay-per-bag' system. Finally, a number of municipalities base the charge bill on the size of the household or the frequency of collection.

The motivation for variable charge rates primarily includes the wish for a fairer distribution of the costs across households, in the framework of rapidly increasing charge bills. Explicit reference to the 'polluter-pays principle' is made. Furthermore, variable rates may have an incentive impact on households.

An evaluation study analyzed a number of 'pay-per-bag' systems and observed that indications for a positive impact on the waste supply by

[25] Bressers (1983), cited in de Savornin Lohman (1995).

[26] Schuurman (1988), cited in de Savornin Lohman (1995).

households can be found.[27] Municipalities operating a 'pay-per-bag' system produced 10–20 percent less waste per capita than comparable municipalities with traditional systems. Illegal dumping or dumping of waste in adjacent villages was reported to be of no major problem, provided that the price per waste bag did not exceed the level of NLG 2. This finding is similar to US studies of 'pay-per-bag' systems (OECD 1997).

2.15 Battery Charges (Sweden)

In 1991, charges on the sales of lead batteries over 3 kg and of small batteries containing over 0.025 percent of mercury and cadmium were introduced. The funds of the charges are allocated to finance collection and final deposition, which is not economically feasible without financial support, and information campaigns.[28]

Lead Batteries

The charge rate is SEK 40 per kg. A special company was established to administer the funds from the charge. As a consequence of producer responsibility, sellers of lead batteries have to take them back. The target for collection was 95 percent. In 1991 and 1992 the number of used batteries collected exceeded the number of sold batteries. In 1993 the collection rate was 95 percent.

Since the charge amounts to only 6–8 percent of the price of batteries and since consumers have no alternatives, the demand for lead batteries is hardly if at all influenced by the charge. The policy effectiveness of this user type of charge has to be measured in terms of the success of the collection system, which is very good.

Mercury (Hg) and Nickel-Cadmium (NiCd) Batteries

The charge rates for Hg batteries and NiCd batteries are SEK 23 per kg and SEK 25 per kg, respectively. The funds from the charges are used for financing final deposition of the collected batteries and for information, and to support recycling of NiCd batteries. The storage facility contains large unsorted amounts of old batteries with high Hg and Cd contents and many batteries are still in use. The funds from the charge are decreasing because Hg and Cd contents in today's batteries are falling below the level above which the charge is due. A deficit is expected.

---

[27] DHV Milieu (1993).

[28] MENS (1994).

The collection rate for batteries containing Hg was 89 percent in 1991, and only 49 percent for NiCd batteries, which is below the target of 75 percent set by the government. NiCd batteries have a long durability and a significant number of these batteries which are incorporated in consumer goods are sold outside the system of registration. A collection premium for this type of battery is under discussion.

The charge rates are too low to have a noticeable impact on the demand for batteries. The decreasing content of heavy metals is attributable to environmental awareness and international developments, rather than to price incentives. The policy effectiveness is good at the moment, but funds may fall short of the costs of disposal of batteries in the future due to less harmful substances in new batteries.

2.16 Aircraft Noise Charge (Netherlands)

Since 1983 a surplus has been imposed on landing fees for aircraft landing at Dutch airports. This aircraft noise charge is differentiated according to noise characteristics of the aircraft. The proceeds are earmarked for financing measures to reduce the noise nuisance caused by airports (insulation and redevelopment). The impact of the charge system in the Schiphol area was evaluated in 1991[29]. The main conclusions were that the charge was rather effective in terms of raising money for the purposes intended. The impact on noise nuisance by aircraft was assessed to be 'very limited'. The relationship between the charge level and the actual noise production of the aircraft appeared to be very weak.

[29] Berenschot (1991).

Table 9.3. Linked policy process and evaluation procedure

Stage	Policy process	Link	Stage	Evaluation procedure
1	Identifying and defining the environmental problem			
2	Discussing the need for policy intervention and setting objectives			
3	Designing and assessing effective and efficient options (instruments or instrument mixes)	→ ←	1	Description of the instruments and of the institutional context, definition of relevant internal and external factors; (baseline inventory)
4	Selecting, discussing and adapting instrument chosen	→	2	Definition of evaluation criteria
			3	Construction of evaluation model and definition of all data to be gathered
5	Introduction of instrument (mix), implementation of control and enforcement	→	4	Continuous collection of data and reassessment of influential factor, and *ex post* evaluation
			5	Possible adaptation of the evaluation model, evaluation criteria and data
6	Possible modification of instrument (mix) after evaluation	←	6	Conclusions, recommendations and feedback into the policy process

Source: OECD (1997, Table 9, p. 112).

3. FUTURE EVALUATION

It is clear from this brief review of the evidence on the evaluation of environmental taxes that evaluation needs to be built into the process of designing and implementing the taxes so that both methodological and data-availability problems can be minimized. The OECD has recently considered this question in some depth (OECD 1997) and Table 9.3 summarizes some of the information and design features that will help improve future evaluation studies.

REFERENCES

Andersen, M.S. (1994), *Governance by Green Taxes: Making Pollution Prevention Pay*, Manchester University Press, Manchester.

Andersen, M.S. (1998), *Assessing the Effectiveness of Denmark's Waste Tax*, Environment, May.

Berenschot (1991), *Rapport Audit Sanering Woningen in verband met Feluidshinder*, Schiphol.

Bressers, J. (1983), *Beleidseffectiviteit en waterkwa-liteitsbeleid,* dissertation, Enschede, Impacts and Future Solutions, Gland.

Chapuy, P. (1995), *Evaluation de l'Efficacité et de l'Efficience des Systemes de Redevance de Pollution de l'Eau: Etude de Cas de la France*, OECD, Paris.

Danish Environmental Protection Agency (1995), *The Danish Waste Charge Act* (note), Copenhagen.

De Savornin Lohman, A. (1995), *The Efficiency and Effectiveness of Water Pollution Charges in France, Germany and the Netherlands: A Synthesis of Available Evidence*, OECD, Paris.

DHV Milieu (1993), *Differentiatie van Tarieven voor Inzameling van Huishoudelijk Afval, Ministerie van VROM,* Publicatiereeks Afvalstoffen nr.1993/9, Den Haag.

Enevoldsen, M. (1998), *Joint Environmental Policy-Making and Other New Abatement Strategies for Industrial CO_2 Pollution*, Wageningen Agricultural and Aarhus University, Wageningen, Aarhus.

Erhvervsministeriet et al. (1999): *Evaluering af grønne afgifter og erhvernene*, Copenhagen.

European Environment Agency (1996), *Environmental Taxes – Environmental Effectiveness and Implementation*, EEA, Copenhagen (http://www.eea.eu.int, report in full).

European Environment Agency (1997), *Environmental Agreements – Environmental Effectiveness*, EEA, Copenhagen (http://www.eea.eu.int, report in full).

Gale, R., Barg, S. and Gillies, A. (1995), *Green Budget Reform*, International Institute for Sustainable Development (IISD)/Earthscan London.

Gee, D. (1996), *Economic tax reform in Europe: Opportunities and Obstacles*, in Ecotaxation, edited by O'Riordan, T., Earthscan, London.

Kraemer, R.A. (1995), *The Effectiveness and Efficiency of Water Effluent Charge Systems: Case Study on Germany*, OECD, Paris.

Larsen, B.M. and Nesbakken, R. (1996), 'Norwegian Emissions of CO_2 1987–1994', Statistics Norway, (mimeo), Oslo.

MENS (Ministry of the Environment and Natural Resources) (1994), *The Swedish Experience – Taxes and Charges in Environmental Policy*, MENS, Stockholm.

Norwegian Green Tax Commission (1996), *Policies for a Better Environment and High Employment*, Oslo.

OECD (1997), *Evaluating Economic Instruments for Environmental Policy*, OECD, Paris.

Öko-Institut (1994), *Bericht über die Auswirkungen der Abfallabgabe in Baden-Württemberg (Report on the Effects of the Charge on Toxic Waste in Baden-Württemberg)*, Öko-Institut, Darmstadt.

Schlegelmilch, K. (1999), *Green Budget Reform in Europe, Countries at the Forefront*, Springer, Berlin, Heidelberg, New York.

Schuurman, J. (1988), *De Prijs van Water*, Gouda Quint BV, Arnhem.

Swedish Environmental Protection Agency (1997), *Environmental Taxes in Sweden, Economic Instruments of Environmental Policy*, Stockholm.

Swedish Government Commission on Green Taxation (1997), *Skatter, miljö och sysselsättning (Taxes, Environment and Employment)*, Stockholm.

Togeby, M., Bjorner, T.B and Johannsen, K. (1998): *Evaluation of the Danish CO_2 Taxes and Agreements*, unpublished paper of AKF, Copenhagen.

Wuppertal *Bulletin on Ecological Tax Reform* (1994) several issues of the quarterly newsletter, published by the Wuppertal Institute for Climate, Environment and Energy, Wuppertal (http://www.wupperinst.org).

10. Energy and Environmental Taxes in the European Community and in OECD Countries

Åke Nordlander[1]

1. INTRODUCTION

The chapter presents an overview of energy and environmentally related taxes in the European Community and some other OECD countries. The focus of the survey is existing taxes in 1997.

In the late 1980s and the first half of the 1990s, environmental taxes were discussed within the OECD and the EU. In addition to energy taxes which have been used as revenue raisers for a long time, a number of environmental taxes have been introduced in different OECD countries in the last decade. Examples are newly introduced taxes on landfills, sulphur, plastic bags, certain disposables, tap water and waste water. Furthermore, existing taxes on energy products have in some countries been modified to also take account of environmental objectives, in addition to the traditional revenue-raising objective. Notably, the introduction of differentiated fuel taxes according to environmental criteria. The most widespread example is different tax treatment of unleaded and leaded petrol. Another example is different levels of taxation on diesel according to sulphur content. A handful of countries have also introduced carbon dioxide taxes on fossil fuels.

Environmental taxes introduced solely to improve the environment have not provided any substantial tax revenue. However, a number of environmentally related taxes yield substantial tax revenue, such as energy taxes on motor fuels and heating fuels, annual circulation taxes and sales taxes on motor vehicles. In principle they were introduced to raise revenue, but in the past few years such taxes have also been motivated by environmental policy.

---

[1] First Secretary, Department of Taxation, the Swedish Ministry of Finance, at present seconded to the European Commission, Directorate General XXI 'Customs and Indirect Taxation'. The chapter is an updated and modified version of Chapter 5 of the final report from the Swedish Green Tax Commission (SOU 1997, p. 11).

Within the European Community some harmonization applies in the field of indirect taxation. Section 3 of the chapter therefore gives a short description of existing Community legislation covering excise duties on energy products and other products. Section 4 gives an overview of energy taxes and energy prices for 1997 for Member States of the European Community and some other OECD countries. Section 5 gives a short description of taxes on motor vehicles. Section 6 lists a number of other environmentally related taxes introduced during the last decade. Finally, Section 7 presents the economic importance of energy and environmentally related taxes in OECD countries from 1965 to 1995.

2. DEFINITION OF ENERGY AND ENVIRONMENTALLY RELATED TAXES

In this chapter, the definition of what could be regarded as an energy or environmentally related tax has on purpose been set wide. The reason is to also include not only taxes introduced solely for the purpose of improving the environment but also taxes introduced for fiscal reasons but which have a direct effect on the environment through the price of the taxed product. In the survey the taxes have been divided into three groups. The first group contains all indirect taxes (except value-added tax (VAT)) levied on the quantity of energy product consumed, for example, traditional excise duties on motor fuels and heating fuels, carbon taxes, energy taxes and taxes on sulphur. The second group covers sales taxes on motor vehicles and annual circulation taxes. The third group covers the more purpose-designed environmental taxes, for example, taxes on fertilizers, pesticides, landfill, plastic bags, natural gravel and batteries.

3. COMMON RULES WITHIN THE EUROPEAN COMMUNITY

For a long time the European Community has been trying to create common rules in the tax area. Notably, the work has focused on harmonizing indirect taxation. This effort was intensified with the introduction of the internal market on 1 January 1993, which basically abolished all border crossing formalities for trade. Import duty, customs duty or indirect taxes can no longer be collected at borders. In preparation for the internal market in 1993, Member States (Council of Ministers) adopted a number of Directives which harmonized the VAT and excise duty on alcoholic beverages, tobacco products and mineral oils. In this context it is important to bear in mind that fiscal measures at Community level requires unanimous approval of the 15 Member States.

The harmonization of excise duties covers tax bases for the different products, taxation procedures and minimum levels of taxation. The driving force behind the 1993 legislation was the internal market and the need to secure Member States' tax revenue accruing from these products. European Community tax legislation does not restrict maximum tax rates. Member States are free to set whatever tax rates they wish, as long as those tax rates exceed laid-down minimum rates. In 1992, the Council of Ministers adopted three Directives concerning excise duty on mineral oils: Directive 92/12/EEC (movement of taxable goods), 92/81/EEC (tax structure) and 92/82/EEC (minimum tax rates). All Directives came into force as of 1 January 1998.

In addition to those taxes that are regulated by these Directives, Member States have a limited possibility to levy other taxes on mineral oils. Such taxes should be levied for specific purposes, and they must comply with the tax rules applicable for excise duty on mineral oils concerning determination of the tax base, calculation of the tax, chargeability, and monitoring of the tax.[2] Member States can also levy taxes on products other than those covered by Community legislation, provided that they comply with the Treaty of Rome and in particular do not prevent free movement of goods between Member States. That is, taxes must not require border crossing formalities.[3]

The basic principle is that all mineral oils used for heating purposes or as a motor fuel should be taxed. All fuels, including biofuels, which are used as a propellant, must be taxed at the same rate as the equivalent fuel (diesel, petrol or liquefied petroleum gas (LPG)). Mineral oils that are not used for heating or as motor fuel must be exempted from excise duty. Furthermore, Member States may not tax mineral oils used for commercial aviation or for navigation at sea, other than for private pleasure craft.[4] EC tax legislation allows Member States to apply total or partial tax exemption on mineral oils in the process of producing electricity and in combined power and heat plants. Exemptions are also allowed for pilot projects when developing more environmentally friendly products, for example in relation to biofuels used as motor fuels.

The Directives on excise duty on mineral oils lay down minimum rates (Table 10.1) of excise duty which as of 1 January 1993 must be respected by Member States. Member States are free to apply rates above these minima, but may only apply one rate per product type (for example, unleaded petrol, leaded petrol, diesel, LPG and so on). However, there is provision under Article 8 (4) of Directive 92/81/EEC whereby Member States can seek the

[2] Article 3.2 of Directive 92/12/EEC.
[3] Article 3.3 of Directive 92/12/EEC.
[4] Article 8.1 of Directive 92/81/EEC.

approval of the Commission and the Council to depart from the general rules in certain circumstances. This has been used in relation to motor fuels to apply rates below the minima in some cases (for example, public transport) and to apply differential treatment of fuels according to environmental criteria (for example, different rates for different grades of unleaded petrol). The derogations granted under this provision were to be reviewed by 31 December 1996 on the basis of a report and proposal from the Commission. Such a report and proposal were presented to the Council on 14 November 1996 (COM (96) 549 final).[5]

Table 10.1. Minimum excise duty rates on mineral oils in the European Community, as of 1 January 1993, ECU per unit.

Product	Unit	Excise duty ECU
Petrol		
Leaded	1,000 litres	337
Unleaded	1,000 litres	287
Diesel and gas oil		
Propellant	1,000 litres	245
Special purposes[1]	1,000 litres	18
Heating fuel	1,000 litres	18
LPG and methane		
Propellant	1,000 kg	100
Special purposes[1]	1,000 kg	36
Heating	1,000 kg	0
Heavy fuel oil	1,000 kg	13

Note: Special purposes laid down in Article 8.3 of Directive 92/81/EEC, e.g. stationary motors; concerning plant and machinery used in construction, civil engineering and public works; for vehicles intended for use off the public roadway or which have not been granted authorisation for use mainly on the public highway.

In the report, the Commission took account of the fact that it would shortly present proposals for an overall scheme of taxation of energy products.[6] Indeed, it recognized that some of these derogations should be prolonged pending adoption of a new scheme of taxation based on such proposals. It also acknowledged that there could be merit in giving Member States greater freedom to implement unilaterally some of the measures which are currently applied under derogations. These include, in particular, derogations granted

[5] Acting upon the proposal from the Commission, the Council has adopted a Council decision 97/425/EC (of 30 June 1997) authorizing Member States to apply and to continue to apply to certain mineral oils, when used for specific purposes, existing reduced rates of excise duty or exemptions from excise duty, in accordance with the procedure provided for in Directive 92/81/EEC.

[6] COM (97) 30 final Proposal for Council Directive restructuring the Community framework for the taxation of energy products.

in respect of public transport and differential treatment of unleaded petrol according to environmental criteria.

Under Article 10 of Directive 92/82/EEC, the minimum rates of excise duty must be reviewed every two years. These reviews must take account of the proper functioning of the internal market, the real value of the rates of duty and the wider objectives of the Treaty. In its first such review, in 1995, the Commission noted that significant increases in the minimum rates for petrol were warranted, even just to keep pace with national rates. The review (European Commission 1995a) also noted that there were grounds for narrowing the gap between the rates on petrol and diesel. However, presentation of proposals was deferred pending a wide-ranging consultation process. That process has now concluded and the Commission has put forward a new proposal for a new approach on taxation of energy products.

The new initiative from the Commission arises partially as a result of the conclusions of the first review of minimum rates and partially from the ECOFIN invitation to put forward new proposals, following the absence of agreement on the carbon/energy tax proposals.[7] As indicated above, it will also incorporate aspects arising from the review of the derogations granted under Article 8 (4) of Directive 92/81/EEC.

The broad thrust of the new proposal is to extend the scope of the existing Community-wide system beyond mineral oils to other competing fuels. This will be of greatest impact in the heating-fuel sector, as all motor fuels are already subject to excise duty at present. The proposal also covers not just excise duty but all indirect taxes on fuels (excluding VAT), by laying down minimum levels of taxation rather than specific excise duty minima. Member States will be free to construct their tax systems as they wish provided that the consequent tax incidences are not below the new minima. In addition, they will have greater freedom to differentiate duty rates above the minima. For motor fuels, the minimum levels proposed will be significantly higher than the existing excise minima. In addition, greater coherence between the minimum levels on different products is envisaged, as are periodic specified increases in the minima. The adoption of the proposal would, for example, increase the minimum rate on unleaded petrol by 45 percent by 1998 and diesel by 27 percent by 1998 and by 74 percent and 60 percent, respectively, in 2002. The increase by 2002 is only indicative and would require a future confirmation by the Council. But as most Member States apply tax rates above the existing Community minimum, direct impact of the proposed Directive would be limited. An economic assessment of the proposal is presented in a working paper from the European Commission (1997c). The

[7] COM (92) 226 final, Proposal for a Council Directive introducing a tax on carbon dioxide emissions and energy and COM (95) 172 final, Amended proposal for a Council Directive introducing a tax on carbon dioxide emissions and energy.

new minimum tax rates proposed by the Commission are presented in Table 10A.3.

4. ENERGY TAXES AND ENERGY PRICES

This section presents energy taxes and energy prices for the European Community and some other OECD countries. The survey covers leaded and unleaded petrol, diesel, heating gas oil, heavy fuel oil and electricity. As for natural gas and coal, the survey is limited to tax rates, since relevant information on price levels is not available.

In this survey, energy taxes and carbon dioxide taxes are not accounted for separately, but are simply grouped together under one heading; energy taxes. However, sulphur taxes are treated separately since they are refunded in relation to the level of emission control measures applied. When discussing the effect of taxes on energy products it is important to pay attention to the overall structure since it is the overall tax rate that determines the effect on consumer behaviour. The total tax burden on fuels will affect the total consumption of energy products while the relative tax burden between fuels will have an impact on what fuel is consumed. Carbon dioxide taxes apply only in Sweden, Finland, Denmark, Norway and the Netherlands. These countries also levy other taxes on energy products. Therefore a presentation of carbon dioxide taxes only would give an incorrect picture.

Table 10.2 shows that petrol and diesel are taxed in almost all OECD countries. A large number of countries also levy taxes on mineral oils used for heating purposes. Approximately 40 percent of the OECD members tax electricity and natural gas. Coal is taxed only in six countries. Generally, the lowest tax rates on motor fuels, heating fuels and electricity can be found in the US and Canada and the highest rates in Western Europe and Japan. However, widely different levels of taxation can be found in Europe.

International price comparisons suffer from some limitations and shortcomings. IEA[8] statistics contain average prices. Prices faced by different categories of users, however, can deviate significantly from these average prices. It applies particularly to electricity prices and fossil fuels used by energy-intensive industries. Furthermore, comparisons between countries are sensitive to shifts in exchange rates. The survey shows a large variation in energy prices. However, the entire difference is not attributable to energy taxes. To some extent the price differences are explained by the fact that energy products are liable to VAT in all countries but the US. Tax rates vary between 3 percent and 25 percent. Pre-tax prices also differ depending on

[8] International Energy Agency (IEA) is an autonomous body within the framework of the Organization for Economic Cooperation and Development (OECD).

such things as infrastructure, market structure (regulated or deregulated markets), and public regulations, for example on maximum allowable sulphur content in fuels.

Table 10.2. Taxation of energy products in OECD countries

Energy product	Energy products taxed in OECD countries (number)	Per cent of Total members
Motor fuels		
Petrol	27	96
Diesel	28	100
Heating fuels		
Heating gas oil, households	19	68
Heavy fuel oil, industry	19	68
Natural gas, households	12	43
Natural gas, industry	11	39
Coal	6	22
Electricity, households	12	43
Electricity, industry	7	25

Source: IEA (1997).

Generally, the lowest motor fuel prices can be found in the US and Canada, which have significantly lower prices than Western Europe and Japan. The US and Canada also have among the lowest heating fuel prices and electricity. However, the difference between the US and Canada on the one side and European countries on the other side is not as large as on motor fuels. Some European countries have heating fuel prices and electricity at the same level as in the US.

4.1 Value added Tax on Energy

In all OECD countries but the US and Australia, sales of energy products are liable to VAT. Tax rates vary from 3 percent (Japan[9]) to 25 percent (Sweden and Denmark). Value-added tax on energy implies that taxable persons – for example industry – are allowed to deduct tax on energy products in the same way as on other inputs. Households, on the other hand cannot deduct the tax and would pay the full tax. In principle VAT affects only the cost of energy for private consumption and not the cost of energy used as input in production of goods and services. Price statistics below include VAT only on energy products for private consumption. Some, countries apply restrictions to the right of taxable persons to deduct VAT on the purchase of petrol and diesel when used in passenger cars.

[9] In 1997 the VAT rate in Japan was increased from 3 to 5%

4.2 Motor Fuel

Taxes on motor fuels have a longstanding tradition as revenue raisers and all countries in the survey levy energy taxes on motor fuels. However, during the last decade we have seen a number of countries modifying their taxes on motor fuels to also take account of environmental objectives (see Figures 10.1, 10.2 and 10.3).

One example is the different tax treatment of unleaded and leaded petrol. Another example is the introduction of differentiated taxes on diesel according to sulphur content. Generally, the level of taxation on motor fuels is substantially higher than on other energy products. Furthermore, the tax rate on diesel is normally lower than on petrol, reflecting the fact that diesel is the main source of fuel used by commercial vehicles. The only exception is the United Kingdom where diesel is taxed at the same rate, expressed in volumetric terms, as unleaded petrol. Measured in relation to energy content, the UK still treats diesel more favourably than unleaded petrol. In the US, diesel is taxed at a higher rate than petrol. Leaded petrol must under Community law be subject to a higher excise duty than unleaded petrol. All countries but the US, Canada and Japan levy higher tax rates on leaded than on unleaded petrol. However, the US applies restrictions on sales of leaded petrol, and all passenger cars of model 1974 or later must be equipped with a catalytic exhaust emission control. Thus they can only use unleaded petrol. As can been seen in Figure 10.2, leaded petrol has been phased out from the market in Sweden, Finland, Denmark, Norway, Germany, Austria, the Netherlands, Japan, Canada and the US.

Figure 10.1. Tax incidence in retail price of unleaded petrol 1Q 1997 (ECU per litre)

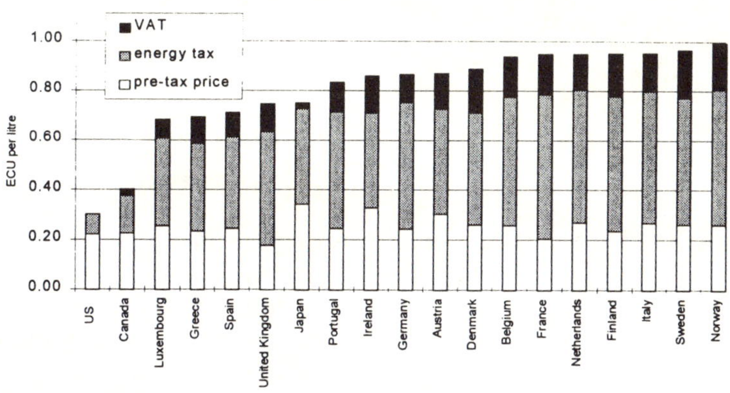

Source: IEA (1997).

Sweden and Finland differentiate the excise duty on diesel and petrol according to environmental criteria. Furthermore, the United Kingdom, Greece and Ireland apply tax differentials on unleaded petrol according to octane level, also for environmental reasons. Denmark operates a system with reduced excise duty rates when petrol is sold from stations equipped to recycle petrol fumes. These differentials have been authorized under the terms of Article 8(4) of Council Directive 92/81/EEC. The United Kingdom has recently introduced a lower rate on diesel with ultra-low sulphur content.

Figure 10.2. Tax incidence in retail price of leaded petrol 1Q 1997 (ECU per litre)

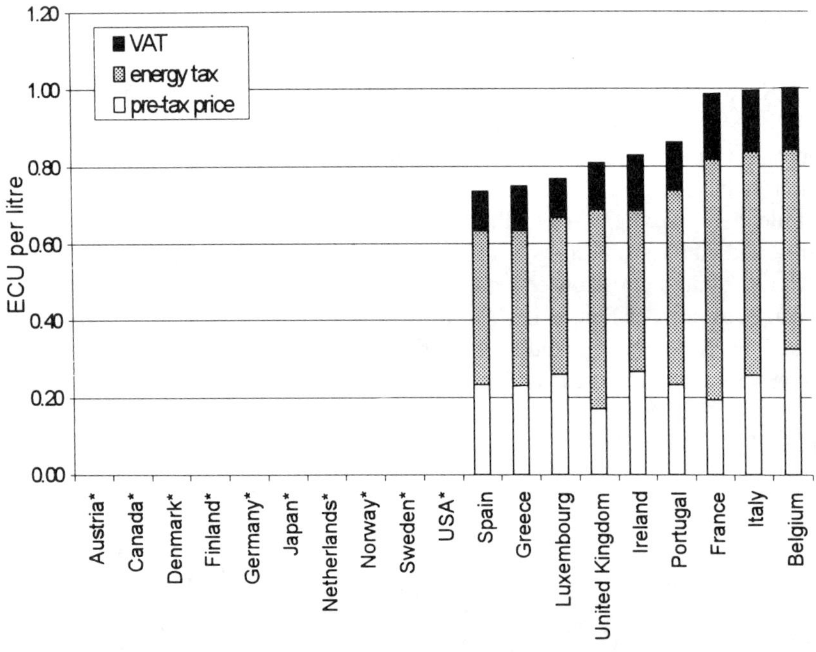

Source: IEA (1997).

Besides VAT and excise taxes, motor fuels are also subject to a number of special taxes in different Member States. These include environmentally related taxes such as carbon taxes (Sweden, Denmark, the Netherlands and Finland); fuel storage taxes (Finland, the Netherlands and Germany) and taxes to fund different industrial activities (France, Belgium). Appendix Table A.1 gives the total level of indirect taxation (excluding VAT) on diesel, and petrol applied in different countries. The quoted level of energy tax in the US represents an average of local and federal energy taxes and local sales taxes. There is a large difference in the level of taxation on motor fuels. The highest tax rates on leaded and unleaded petrol can be found in France, Finland, Norway and the Netherlands. The lowest levels are in the US and Canada.

Figure 10.3. Tax incidence in retail price of diesel 1Q 1997 (ECU per litre)

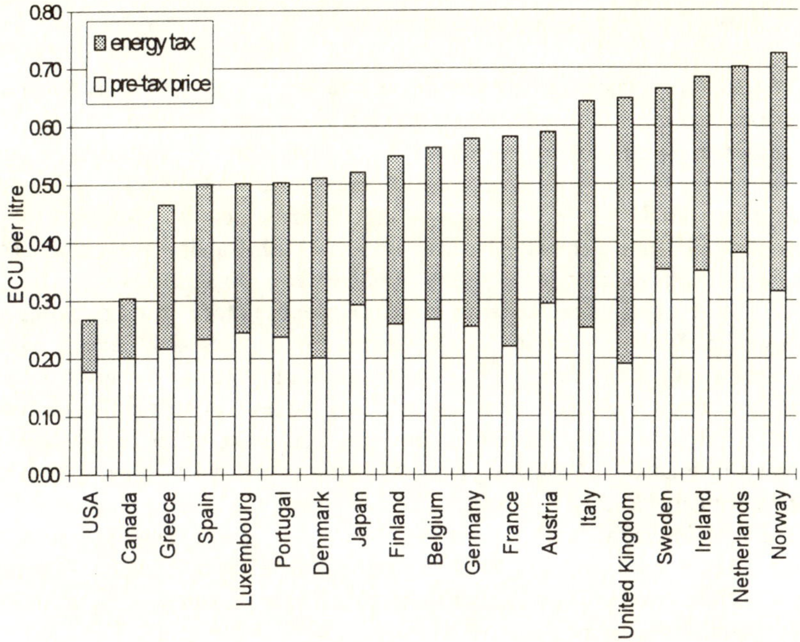

Source: IEA (1997).

The situation is somewhat different for diesel. The United Kingdom has the highest level of taxation, with almost ECU 50 per 1,000 litres higher than Norway, Italy and France who apply the second-highest tax rate. The lowest level can be found in the US and Canada.

Since taxes on motor fuel have a large impact on fuel prices, a wide spread in tax levels creates a corresponding large divergence in consumer prices between countries. The tax incidence in the retail price of unleaded petrol and diesel are presented in Figures 10.1, 10.2 and 10.3. In many countries, diesel-driven vehicles are used mostly for commercial activities. Therefore the pertinent comparison is price excluding VAT. In order to compare prices of diesel for private consumption, VAT must be included. Differences in consumer petrol prices and diesel depend on both differences in pre-tax prices and levels of taxation. Differences in net prices could be explained by different market structures and national regulations, for example, environmental regulations. The pre-tax price of low-sulphur diesel is normally higher than on standard diesel. However, caution is required when comparing diesel prices. Large consumers normally purchase their fuel direct from the producer at a price that can differ significantly from retail prices given in Figure 10.3.

4.3 Fossil Fuels for Heating Purposes

The traditional objective behind indirect taxation on heating fuel is revenue raising. However, in recent years a number of countries have modified their tax system to also pursue environmental objectives. A large number of countries in Europe (for example, Sweden, France, Belgium, Portugal and Italy) levy higher taxes on oil with high sulphur content. Countries like Sweden, Finland, Denmark, Norway and the Netherlands have introduced carbon dioxide taxes to promote low carbon emitting fuels.

The total level of indirect taxation levied on fuel used for heating purposes is shown in Appendix Table 10A.1. Except for the US and Canada most countries levy some form of energy tax on heating gas oil.[10] Only a small number of countries tax natural gas and coal. The level of taxation on heating gas oil differs widely. The tax incidence in retail price of heating gas oil is shown in Figure 10.4. Heating gas oil is most expensive in Italy, Denmark and Portugal, and cheapest in the United Kingdom, the US and Belgium.

The variation in the level of taxation on heavy fuel oil consumed by industry is smaller than on heating gas oil for households. The tax incidence in retail price of heavy fuel oil for industrial consumption is presented in Figure 10.5. The highest prices are found in Norway, Finland and Sweden.[11] The lowest prices are once again found in the US and Canada. However, in Norway the wood-processing and fishing industry only pay 50 percent of the energy tax. Furthermore, the Norwegian and Swedish sulphur taxes are refunded in relation to the level of emission control measures applied. In Sweden, fuels used in so-called soda boilers within the pulp and paper industry are exempted from the sulphur tax, and fuels used in cement and lignite production escape the sulphur tax.

[10] In the US, a charge of US$ 0.097 per barrel of light or heavy fuel oil is levied. The revenue from the charge is earmarked to finance cleaning-up of industrial sites.

[11] As of 1 July 1997, the tax rate on fossil fuels used by industrial consumers has been increased by 100 percent in Sweden. Figure 10.5 shows the situation before the tax increase.

Figure 10.4. Tax incidence in retail price of heating gas oil for households 1Q 1997 (ECU per 1,000 litres)

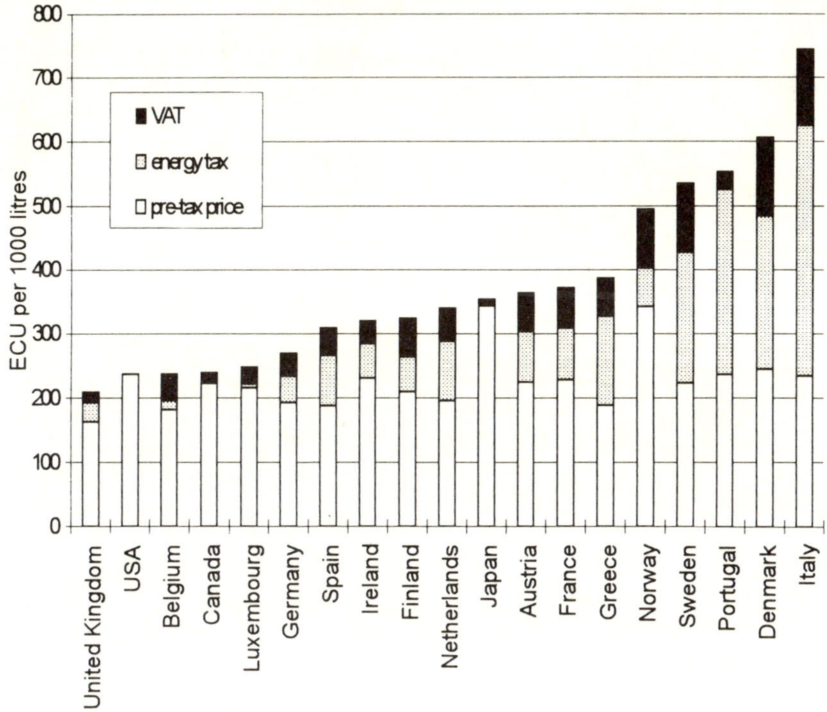

Source: IEA (1997).

For coal and natural gas, the survey is limited to information on energy taxes, since statistics on prices are not available. There are no harmonized EU tax rules on these products. Member States have complete freedom to tax or not. In the EU, coal is taxed only in the Netherlands, Finland, Denmark and Sweden. It is also taxed in Norway (see Appendix Table 10A.1). In Norway, the largest consumption of coal takes place within the cement industry, whose consumption is exempt from energy tax. However, the European Commission has recently presented a proposal for a new Directive restructuring the Community framework for taxation of energy products. The major thrust of this proposal is an expansion of the scope of taxation beyond mineral oils to also cover natural gas, electricity and coal. The proposal has not yet been adopted by the Council. A more in-depth description is given in Section 3 of this chapter.

Figure 10.5. Tax incidence in retail price of heavy fuel oil for industry 1Q 1997 (ECU per 1,000 kg)

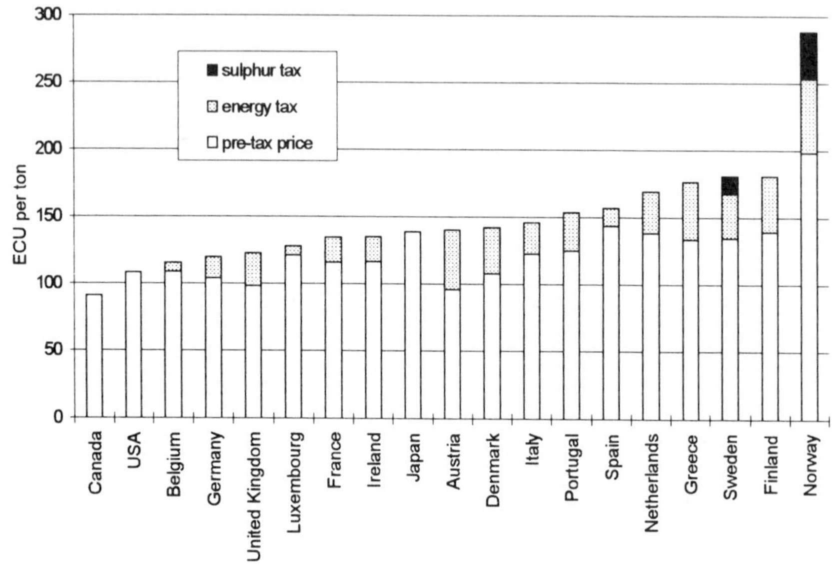

Source: IEA (1997).

Natural gas is taxed in Sweden, Finland, Denmark, France, Italy, Germany, Spain, the Netherlands, Austria, Belgium and Japan. However, in France the tax on natural gas is charged only to consumers with an annual consumption exceeding 500,000 m^3. The Netherlands apply a reduced tax rate equivalent to ECU 6 per 1,000 m^3 on consumption exceeding 10 million m^3. In Sweden, coal and natural gas consumed for non-industrial purposes are taxed five times higher than on industrial consumption. In Spain the natural gas tax is a municipal tax levied on non-industrial consumption. The tax rate is 1.5 percent of the natural gas price. In Belgium the tax is levied only on domestic consumption.

4.4 Electricity

Electricity is generated mainly in hydro, nuclear and fossil fuel power plants. Table 10.3 shows the structure of electricity production in some OECD countries in 1994.

The heading 'fossil fuel power etc.' also includes power production where biomass has been used as inputs. However, the share of electricity from biomass sources is insignificant. In the table we can see that the production structure differs enormously between countries. For example, hydro power plants make up 100 percent of electricity production in Norway, while approximately 97 percent of Denmark's electricity is produced in fossil fuel power plants.

In principle, there are two different approaches to the taxation of electrical power. In the first model, a tax is levied on the fuels used to generate electrical power or the tax is based on the type of generating plant, such as a hydro power station, a nuclear power plant or some other source. Taxes are thus levied at the generation stage with this approach. When electricity has reached the network, the nature of electrical power makes it impossible to distinguish between sources. In addition, it is also impossible to tell whether electricity is domestically generated or imported. It is not possible to differentiate the tax between end users within the first approach. However, it is possible to affect the choice of generation technology and/or the choice of fuel, which is an advantage. In practice, the first approach to the taxation of electrical power is the only one within which a pure environmental tax may be levied.

The second approach entails an energy tax in distribution. The level of tax can be varied among end users. A consumption tax is neutral, in the sense that it does not matter how electrical power is generated or who generates it. This implies that a consumption tax is neutral towards domestically generated and imported electrical power. In addition, a consumption tax does not affect the competitiveness of a particular fuel or method of generation. However, a consumption tax is not a first-best tax from an environmental point of view, because the tax is independent of fuel choice and/or generation method. On the other hand, a tax levied in the 'consumption stage' has the smallest disruptive impacts on electricity generation, in a country that trades significant amounts of electricity on international markets.

Table 10.3. Structure of electricity production in 1994 (% of total production)

Country	Hydro power, wind power	Nuclear power	Fossil fuel power plants, etc.
Belgium	0	56	44
Denmark	3	0	97
Finland	25	30	45
France	18	75	7
Greece	8	0	92
Ireland	7	0	93
Italy	23	0	77
Japan	7	28	65
Canada	60	20	30
Luxembourg	55	0	45
Netherlands	0	5	95
Norway	100	0	0
Portugal	35	0	65
Spain	19	35	46
United Kingdom	3	26	71
Sweden	42	51	7
Germany	5	29	66
US	8	20	72
Austria	66	0	34

Source: SOU (1997, p. 11).

In summary, the two approaches to electricity taxation have different properties and also imply different impacts, not the least on resource allocation. If the purpose of the tax is to generate revenues in the most efficient manner, then one should use the least distortive tax, that is, a 'consumption' tax. If, instead, one is interested in affecting the use of some particular energy good, the tax should be levied on the energy good used in the conversion stage. A carbon dioxide tax on fossil fuels, or a tax on uranium used in nuclear power plants, are two examples. If international trade is possible, the consequence of a production tax may be that domestic electrical power is replaced by imported electrical power. The global environmental impact then depends on how the imported electricity is generated.

A survey of some OECD countries' taxation of electricity production is presented in Table 10.4. In Appendix Table 10A.2, information is given on taxes levied on consumption. Internationally a large share of electricity is not taxed in the production process. However, within the European Community most Member States tax oil for generating electricity, whereas use of other fuels such as coal and natural gas are not taxed. Electricity production in hydro and nuclear power plants is rarely taxed either.

Table 10.4. Level of indirect taxation on electricity production in 1997 (ECU per MWh)

		Taxes on production plant		Taxes on fuels used as inputs	
Country	Hydro power	Nuclear power	Oil	Coal	Natural gas
Belgium	–	–	0.66	–	–
Denmark	–	–	–	–	–
Finland	–	–	–	–	–
France	–	–	1.86	–	–
Greece	–	–	4.38	–	–
Ireland	–	–	1.32	–	–
Italy		–	0.15	–	–
Canada	yes[1]	–	–	–	–
Luxembourg	–	–	–	–	–
Netherlands	–	yes[2]	2.96	–	–
Norway	1.9	–	–	–	–
Portugal	–	–	–	–	–
Spain	–	–	1.32	–	–
UK	–	–	3.18	–	–
Sweden	–[3]	2.41	1.10[4]	2.2	0[2]
Germany	–	–	2.85	–	2.19
USA	–	–	–	–	–
Austria	–	–	–	–	–

Source: IEA (1997).

Notes
1. Information of the tax level is missing.
2. A tax on uranium was introduced in the Netherlands as of 1 January 1997.
3. A tax levied on electricity produced in hydro power plants. It is designed as a real estate tax.
4. In Sweden a sulphur tax is levied on all fossil fuels used in electricity production. The sulphur content in natural gas, however, is so low that no tax is levied.

In most of these countries only a small percentage of the electricity is generated by oil. Most electricity is generated with other non-taxed fuels. There are exceptions to the rule. In Italy (1990), some 45 percent of the electricity output is generated by oil, and the corresponding figure for Greece (1990) is 20 percent. However, electricity markets in those countries are not open to the same level of competition from imported electricity as the Nordic ones.

Figure 10.6. Electricity prices for households 1Q 1997 (ECU per MWh)

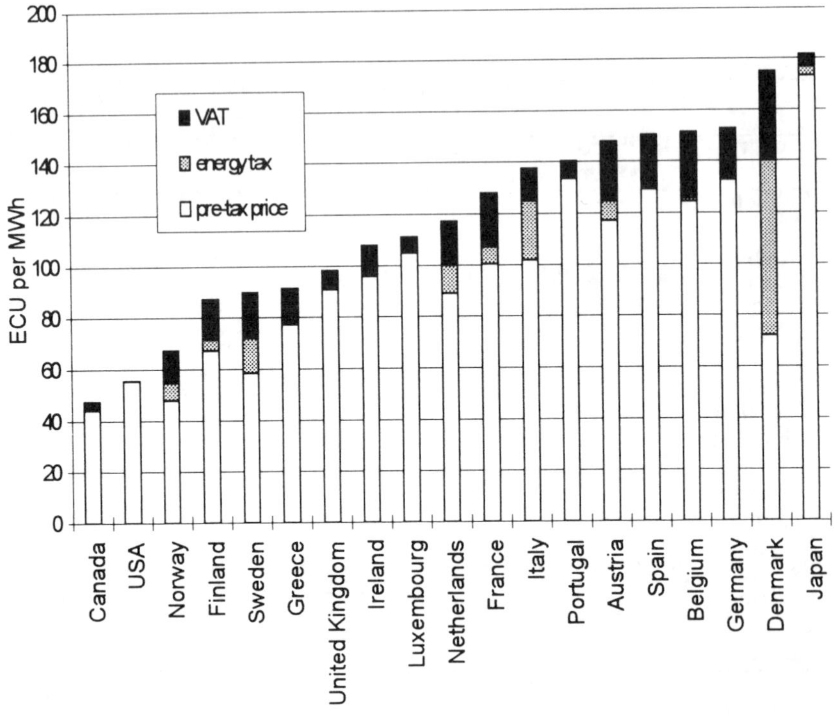

Source: IEA (1997).

Finland is another exception, where up until the end of 1996 all fossil fuels were taxed when used for electricity generation. However, this taxation system created serious problems related to importation of electricity from neighbouring countries with different tax systems, and as of 1 January 1997, all taxes within the production process have been abolished and replaced with an energy tax levied on final consumption. Sweden and the Netherlands levy a tax on electricity production in nuclear power plants. Moreover, Norway, Sweden and Canada levy a production tax on hydro power plants. The Norwegian and the Swedish production taxes on hydro power plants are constructed in a way that does not affect the marginal production cost. In Norway the annual tax paid by the producers is based on historical production and in Sweden the tax is designed as a tax on real estate.

Table 10.5. Electricity prices for industry, at 1 January 1995 (ECU per MWh)

Power	0.5 MW	2.5 MWh	10 MW
Utilization	2,500 h	4,000 h	7,000 h
Total consumption	1.25 GWh	10 GWh	70 GWh
Belgium	94	76	46
Denmark	52	51	46
Finland, Helsinki	63	52	32
France	79	66	46
Greece	60	56	39
Ireland	76	58	45
Italy	95	74	48
Japan, Tokyo	146	120	70
Canada, Montreal	50	33	22
Luxembourg	73	48	36
Netherlands, Rotterdam	90	63	47
Portugal	91	81	57
Spain	83	70	56
United Kingdom, London	78	68	59
Norway[1]	48	46	36
Sweden, Stockholm·	48	38	29
Germany	118	95	66

Note:. The price of electricity in Norway reflects the situation at 1 January 1994.

Source: SOU (1997, p. 11).

In addition to the above-mentioned production taxes, a number of countries apply taxes on electricity delivered to the consumer (Table 10.2 and Appendix Table 10A.2). These countries usually apply reduced tax rates or tax exemptions on industrial consumption. Norway, Denmark, Italy, Belgium, Sweden, Austria, Finland, the Netherlands and France levy a tax on electricity when delivered to the final consumer. However, in Sweden, Norway, the Netherlands and Belgium industrial consumption is exempt from the tax, and in France the tax rate on industrial consumption is levied only on low voltage consumption and amounts only to 0.5 percent of the retail price. In Austria industrial consumption is taxed with a reduced rate. Until the end of November 1995, Germany levied a special consumption tax on electricity. The revenue was used to subsidize the German coal industry, whose coal was mostly used to produce electricity. The 1997 consumption tax on electricity introduced in Finland has separate rates for industrial and non-industrial consumption. In Spain a local tax is levied on all electricity consumption. On average the tax rate is 1.5 percent of the retail price. The United Kingdom levies a small charge on electricity where the revenue is used to support non-fossil electricity production.

Where tax comparisons are relative easy, price comparisons are complicated. Statistics exist only for household consumption and for small and medium-sized industrial users. Statistics for the electricity-intensive industry, which consumes a large share of the total industrial consumption, are difficult to find.

Table 10.6. Electricity prices for electricity-intensive industry, 1995 (Index Sweden = 100)

Country	Index	Spread
Sweden	100	90-144
Belgium	157	
Brazil	139	91-273
Chile	102	
Finland	135	
France	133	100-153
Netherlands	149	
Iceland	86	
Canada	68	
Norway	49	28-110
Spain	315	
United Kingdom	178	
Czech Republic	156	
Germany	200	145-315
US	69	34-156
Austria	293	

Source: SOU (1995, p. 139).

Electricity prices for households vary widely among countries. Electricity for households is most expensive in Japan, Denmark and Germany, while electricity in countries like the US, Canada, Sweden, Finland and Norway is relatively cheap. It is interesting to note that a large part of the difference in consumer price cannot be explained by different levels of taxation. Instead it is driven by a large difference in pre-tax prices. Prices of electricity for certain industrial consumers are shown in Table 10.5.

Sweden, Norway and Canada are among those countries that have the lowest prices for medium-sized consumers. Unfortunately, Table 10.5 gives no information on prices for electricity-intensive industry. Prices for these users are not presented in the available international publications on electricity prices. The final report of the Energy Commission (SOU 1995, p. 139) presents information that could at least give some indication of the price level for electricity intensive-companies (see Table 10.6). Electricity-intensive industry is defined as companies with an annual use of at least 7,500 hours at an efficiency of 40 MW. This corresponds to a consumption of at least 300 GWh. The information in the survey is derived from records of a number of Swedish electricity-intensive companies with manufacturing in affiliated companies abroad. A number of the presented indexes are based on information from only one production plant, so the results cannot be statistically verified. The average electricity price in Sweden for electricity-intensive companies has been set at an index of 100. Foreign prices have been converted into Swedish currency at the currency exchange rates from 13 November 1995. From countries with information from more than three production plants a price interval is presented. The compilation in Table 10.6 shows a relative large spread among the countries. The lowest price levels can be found in the US, Canada and the Nordic countries.

5. TAXATION OF MOTOR VEHICLES

Most OECD countries levy three types of taxes on motor vehicles: value-added tax, sales tax (or registration tax) and annual circulation tax. Some countries also levy a tax on mandatory traffic insurance premiums. [12]

5.1 Value-added Tax

In all OECD[13] countries except the US and Australia, sales of motor vehicles are liable to VAT. Tax rates vary from 3 percent (Japan[14]) to 25 percent (Sweden and Denmark). In principle, VAT affects only purchase for private consumption. If a motor vehicle is purchased for business purposes, the tax is refunded. However, some countries apply restrictions to taxable persons' right to deduct VAT on the purchase of passenger cars.

5.2 Sales Tax or Registration Tax

A number of countries levy an extra sales tax or a registration tax[15] in addition to a general sales tax (VAT). Registration or sales taxes are normally payable in advance of, or at the time of, registration of a vehicle. They are normally charged only once, at the time of first registration.

[12] A more detailed description of the situation in each OECD country is presented in OECD (1995). A more detailed description of the situation within the EU is presented in the document 'Vehicle Taxation in the European Union', DG XXI, 1997.

[13] OECD members in 1993.

[14] In 1997 the VAT rate in Japan was increased from 3 to 5 percent.

[15] Since the introduction of the internal market in 1993, taxation of cars cannot be related to border-crossing formalities between two Member States. As a result, most Member States which previously applied an excise duty (sales tax) on cars modified existing taxes on motor vehicles, typically in the form of registration taxes, where the taxable event occurs when the vehicle is registered in the national vehicle register.

Countries apply various methods to calculate the tax. The calculation of the tax normally depends on weight, size of motor, fuel consumption or just a percentage of the retail price. The level of the sales tax differs widely among countries. In Denmark and Finland the sales tax amounts to 200 percent and 100percent, respectively. The sales tax in Norway is on the same level. Generally, sales taxes are highest on vehicles for private use, such as passenger cars, while vehicles for commercial use, such as heavy goods vehicles, face a lower tax. One exception is in the US, where heavy goods vehicles are taxed at a higher rate than passenger cars. It can be noted that countries with a domestic car industry tend to levy lower sales taxes than countries without a car industry.

5.3 Annual Circulation Tax

All countries levy some form of circulation tax. They are charged on a periodic basis, and usually confer the right to use the public road network. These taxes are charged according to various criteria, such as engine capacity, horsepower, fuel type, region of registration etc. In some countries the tax is a fixed amount per vehicle, while other countries relate the rate to the weight of the vehicle. Heavy goods vehicles are commonly taxed higher than passenger cars. Tax rates differ widely among countries. A number of countries apply a system where diesel powered passenger cars face a higher circulation tax than petrol powered cars to compensate for the lower diesel tax.

6. OTHER ENVIRONMENTAL TAXES

In the last decade a number of non-energy related environmental taxes have been introduced in a number of OECD countries. Table 10.7 lists some examples of newly introduced taxes. The list does not represent a comprehensive list of all new environmental taxes introduced, but should be regarded as an indicator of the most important taxes introduced.

Table 10.7. A few examples of non-energy environmental taxes in the OECD

Country	Type of goods taxed
Sweden	Natural gravel, pesticides, commercial fertilizers, batteries, landfill (to be introduced)
Denmark	Landfill, disposable tableware, extraction of sand and gravel, certain retail containers, insecticides, waste water, tap water, tyres, batteries
Norway	Certain retail containers, commercial fertilisers, Pesticides,
Finland	Pesticides, certain beverage containers
Netherlands	Waste water
UK	Landfill
US	Taxes on hazardous chemicals and tax on CFCs
Belgium	Disposable cameras and razors

7. TAX RECEIPTS, 1965–1995

This section shows revenue of energy and environmentally related taxes in most OECD countries. The presentation covers the period from 1965 to 1995, and is based on statistics from OECD (1997). Taxes have been divided into three groups: energy taxes; annual circulation taxes and sales taxes on motor vehicles; and other environmental taxes. The last group contains all environmentally related taxes that do not fit into any of the two first groups, for example landfill taxes (Denmark), tax on commercial fertilizers (Denmark and Sweden), tax on chlorofluorocarbons (CFCs) (USA) and various product taxes (pesticides and fertilizers).

Figure 10.7 gives the above taxes' share of GDP from 1965 to 1995. For the OECD as a whole these taxes' share of GDP shows little variation during the period. In the European OECD countries, the share of GDP has increased a little. In the Nordic countries the share of GDP is more than twice as high in 1995 as it was in 1965.[16] Figure 10.7 shows that, on average, the share of tax revenue in the Nordic countries is higher than the average for OECD-Europe and OECD-total.

Figure 10.8 illustrates revenue from energy and environmentally related taxes in 1995 as a percentage of GDP for all countries in the survey. As we can see, all Nordic countries are placed on the upper half of the list.

[16] The figures give a somewhat incorrect picture of the development. The fact that excise duties on energy and also sales taxes on motor vehicles are often part of the tax base for VAT increases the effect of excise duties. That is, abolish excise duties and the tax base for VAT would decrease and consequently the revenue from VAT. Therefore tax revenues as an effect of excise duties are significantly larger. Available OECD data does not contain enough information to calculate this extra effect. The international comparison is therefore made without the additional VAT component.

Figure 10.7. Energy and environmentally related tax receipts as a percentage of GDP, 1965–1995

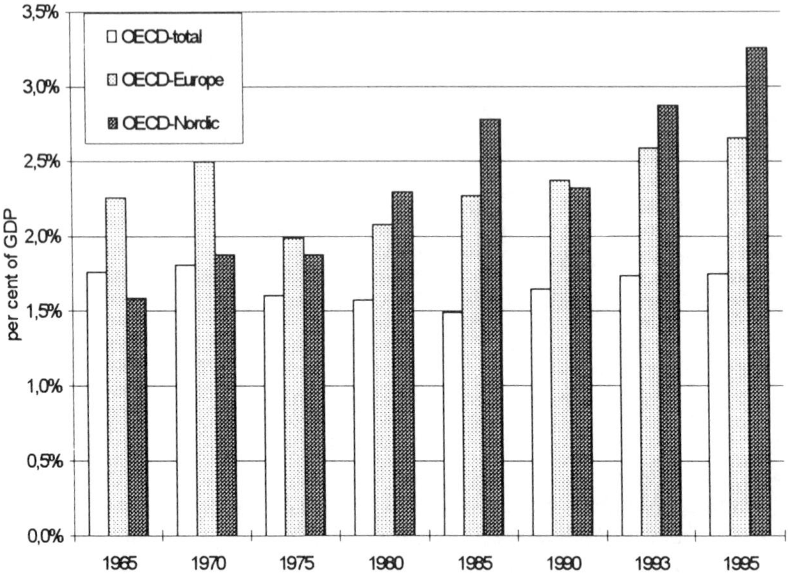

Source: Processing of OECD Revenue Statistics, OECD (1997).

Energy taxes, annual circulation taxes and sales taxes on motor vehicles all accrue substantial revenue, while other environmental taxes yield only a small amount of revenue. In most countries it is energy taxes that yield the most revenue. However, in some countries, for example the Netherlands, Denmark, Iceland and the US, revenue from energy taxes and vehicle taxes are of equal size. It is only in Denmark and the Netherlands where the other environmental taxes give revenue of any important size. In Denmark this 'other environmental taxes' is made up of tax on extraction and import of raw materials, tax on certain retail containers, tax on waste water and landfill group, tax on piped water, and tax on certain disposables. In the Netherlands this tax is made up of various charges on water and air pollution. It could be the case that some of these charges are paid to local sewage treatment works for services provided, and if so they do not belong in this survey.

Figure 10.8. Energy and environmentally related tax receipts as a percentage of GDP, 1995

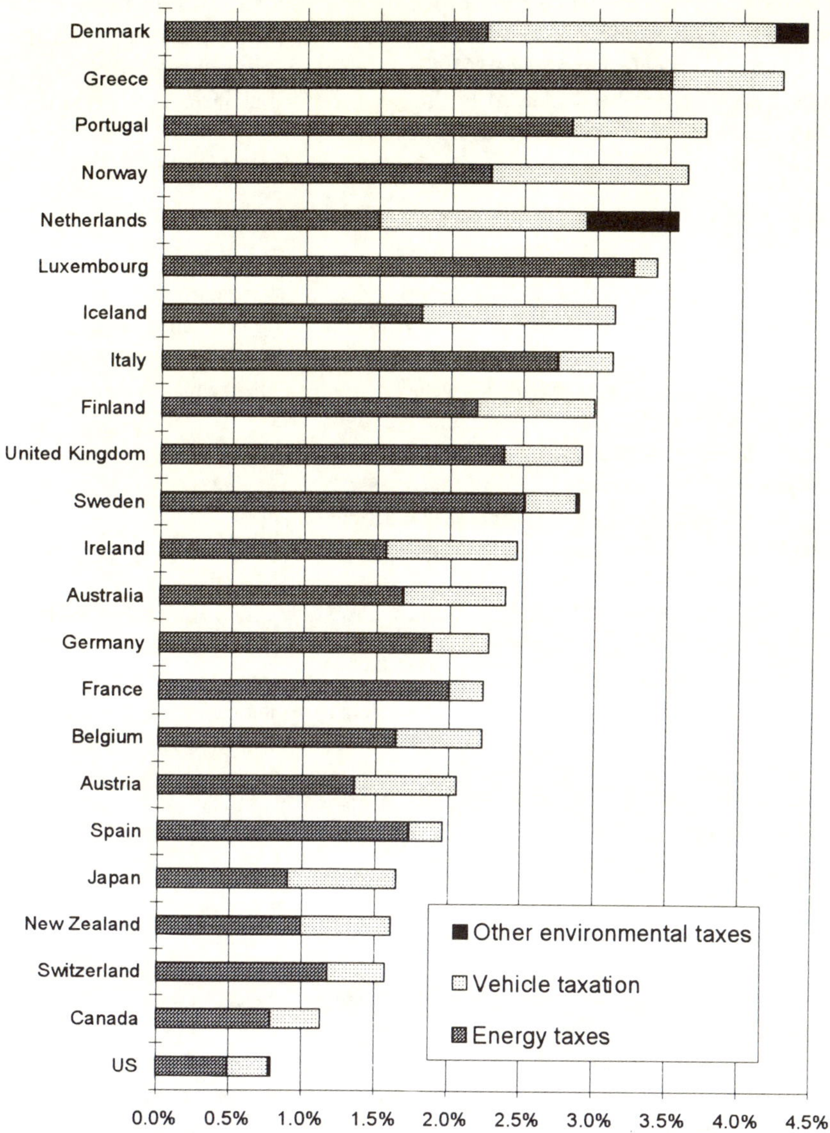

Source: Processing of OECD Revenue Statistics, OECD (1997).

The lowest level of tax revenue is found in the US, Canada, Japan and Switzerland. Somewhat unexpectedly Luxembourg also has large tax revenues in relation to GDP. This is not due to high tax rates in Luxembourg, but the fact that some 50 percent of petrol and diesel sold in Luxembourg is purchased by consumers from other countries who travel to Luxembourg to purchase cheap petrol and diesel. The high share of tax revenue in Portugal and Greece cannot be explained by high tax rates, but instead by high tax rates in relation to internal purchasing power.

REFERENCES

Council Directive 92/12/EEC of 25 February 1992 on the general arrangements for products subject to excise duty and on the holding, movement and monitoring of such products.

Council Directive 92/81/EEC of 19 October 1992 on the harmonization of the structures of excise duties on mineral oils.

Council Directive 92/82/EEC of 19 October 1992 on the approximation of the rates of excise duties on mineral oils.

European Commission (1992), 'Proposal for a Council Directive Introducing a Tax on Carbon Dioxide Emissions and Energy' COM (92) 226 final, European Commission, Brussels.

European Commission (1995a), 'Amended Proposal for a Council Directive Introducing a Tax on Carbon Dioxide Emissions and Energy', COM (95) 172 final, European Commission, Brussels.

European Commission (1995b), 'Commission Report to the Council and European Parliament on the Rates of Duty Laid Down in Council Directive 92/79/EEC of 19 October 1992 on the Approximation of Taxes on Cigarettes, Council Directive 92/80/EEC of 19 October 1992 on the Approximation of Taxes on Manufactured Tobacco Other Than Cigarettes, Council Directive 92/84/EEC of 19 October 1992 on the Approximation of the Rates of Excise Duty on Alcoholic Beverages and Council Directive 92/82 of 19 October 1992 on the Approximation of the Rates of Excise Duty on Mineral Oils', European Commission, Brussels.

European Commission (1997a), 'Proposal for Council Directive restructuring the Community framework for the taxation of energy products' COM (97) 30 final, European Commission, Brussels.

European Commission (1997b), 'Presentation of the New Community System for the Taxation of Energy Products – Part 1' Commission Staff Working Paper, European Commission, Brussels.

European Commission (1997c), 'Presentation of the New Community System for the Taxation of Energy Products Part 2 – Assessment of the Impact of the Proposal', Commission Staff Working Paper, European Commission, Brussels.

European Commission (1997d), 'Vehicle Taxation in the European Union 1997 – background paper', Directorate General XXI, Brussels.

IEA (1997), 'Energy prices and Taxes, 1st Quarter 1997', IEA, Paris.

OECD (1995), 'Environmental Taxes in OECD Countries', OECD, Paris.

OECD (1997), "Revenue Statistics 1965–1995', OECD, Paris.

SOU (1995), 'Omställning av energisystemet', Betänkande från Energikommissionen, Fritzes, Stockholm, p. 139.

SOU (1997:11), 'Skatter, miljö och sysselsättning', Slutbetänkande från skatteväxlingskommitten, Fritzes, Stockholm.

Swedish Green Tax Commission (1997), 'Taxation, Environment and Employment: A Report from the Swedish Green Tax Commission', Fritzes, Stockholm.

APPENDIX 10A

Table 10A.1. Level of indirect taxation in OECD countries (in ECU)[1]

	Leaded /ml	Unlead. /ml	Diesel /1000 l	Gasoil[2] /1000 l	Heavy fuel oil[3] /ton	Coal /ton	Nat. gas /1000 m3
Existing min.	337	287	245	18	13	–	–
Proposed 98	417	417	310	21	18 (22)	5	7
Belgium	577	518	296	14	6[4] (19)	–	14
Denmark[5]	535	451	311	239	282	162	32
Finland[6]	631	553	314	55	43	31	13
France	625	583	362	79	18 (25)	–	13[7]
Greece	419	366	254	139	43	–	–
Ireland	418	375	326	52	19	–	–
Italy	580	534	390	390	23 (47)	–	14 – 54[8]
Luxembourg	408	355	258	5	6[9] (14)	–	–
Netherlands[10]	605	538	325	93	31	11	40
Portugal	504	469	266	266	13 (28)	–	–
Spain	401	368	267	78	13	–	6.1[11]
UK	518	458	458	29	24	–	–
S – industry[12]	586	512	308	32	33	28	24
S – other users	586	512	308	205	216	143	120
Germany	568	516	328	46	20	–	22
Austria	489	422	295	77	37	–	50[13]
Norway	620	549	410	61	55[14]	52	–
Japan	386	386	228	–	–	–	4
Canada	148	148	104	–	–	–	–
US	80	80	91	–	–[15]	–	–

Notes:

1. Tax rates as at 1 January 1997, exchange rates as at 1 October 1996.
2. Member States which on January 1991 did not apply excise duty to gas oil for heating are authorized to continue to apply a zero rate provided that they levy a monitoring charge of ECU 5 per 1,000 litres (Article 5(3) of Directive 92/82/EEC).
3. Tax rates on low-sulphur fuel oil (< 1%). High-S fuel in brackets.
4. Under the provisions of article 8(4) of Directive 92/81/EEC, Belgium has been authorized to apply a rate below the minimum rate on low-sulphur fuel.
5. A special tax regime applies to industrial users, with tax rates lower than indicated above.
6. Reduced rates apply for reformulated diesel (–ECU 28) and petrol (–ECU 9).
7. Levied only on industrial users with an annual consumption of more than 500,000 m^3.
8. The tax rate depends on type of consumption (industrial/domestic) and by region.
9. Under the provisions of Article 8(4) of Directive 92/81/EEC, Luxembourg has been authorized to apply a rate below the minimum rate on low-sulphur fuel.
10. The Dutch energy tax system contains reduced tax rates for energy-intensive industries. The effects of these rules are not included.
11. A municipal tax levied on non-industrial consumption. The tax rate is 1.5 percent of the natural gas price.
12. In addition to the above, a sulphur tax of ECU 3.30 per kg of sulphur is levied if the sulphur content exceeds 0.1 percent of the weight. It can be refunded if sulphur emissions have been reduced. In view of the low sulphur content of most fuels, only heavy fuel oil and coal are in fact affected. The tax rate on diesel oil applies to urban-area diesel, which accounts for almost 100 percent of the market. As of 1 July 1997, the tax rates on oils, natural gas and coal used for industrial consumption have been increased by 100 percent. In addition, a special scheme has been introduced in order to reduce the extra tax burden on energy-intensive industry.
13. A special tax regime applies to energy-intensive industries.
14. In addition to the above rates a sulphur tax is levied. The rate is ECU 9 per 1,000 litres for each per cent sulphur content.

15. A number of separate excise taxes are levied on crude oil and oil products to cover damages from various kinds of petroleum spills. An excise tax is levied on hard coal but not on lignite or brown coal from US mines, to provide for the Black Lung Disability Trust Fund, to fund compensation to health-impaired coal miners. Tax rates as at 1 January 1997.

Sources: European Commission (1997c) and IEA (1997).

Table 10A.2. Overall level of indirect taxes (other than VAT) on electricity in certain OECD countries, (in ECU)[1] *and new minimum tax rate proposed by Commission*[2]

Country	Consumption tax (levied on the final consumption)		Production tax (levied on delivery into the grid)	
	Industrial ECU per MWh	Household ECU per MWh	Nuclear power plants ECU per MWh	Hydro Power plants ECU per MWh
Existing min	–	–	–	–
Proposed min for 1998	1.0	1.0		
Belgium	–	1.4	–	–
Denmark	12.2[3]	63.1	–	–
Finland	2.5	5.7	–	–
France[4]	0.2	8.5	–	–
Greece	–	–	–	–
Ireland	–	–	–	–
Italy[5]	14.5	24.4	–	–
Luxembourg	–	–	–	–
Netherlands[6]	13.7	13.7	–	–
Portugal	–	–	–	–
Spain[7]	0.9	1.9	–	–
UK[8]	1.1	2.2	–	–
Sweden	–	7.0–13.5	2.6	n.a.[9]
Germany	–	–	–	–
Austria	7.4	7.4	–	–
Norway	–	6.5	–	1.9
Japan	3	3	–	–
Canada	–	–	–	n.a.[10]
US	–	–	–	–

Notes:
1. Exchange rates as at 1 October 1996.
2. Source: European Commission, OECD and Nordic Council.
3. Reduced tax rates apply to energy-intensive industries.
4 Local taxes. The above tax rates represent the annual national average.
5. Tax rates shown are average annual national rates. Rates differ between regions and type of consumption.
6. The tax is levied on low energy consumption only and is therefore limited to consumption of 50,000 kWh for 12 months. In addition, the first 800 kWh consumed are tax free.
7. A municipal tax. The tax rate is 1.5 percent of the electricity price. Rates above show the national average.
8. The rates shown above are a national average resulting from the non-fossil fuel levy. It is estimated that the non-fossil fuel levy increases the price of electricity by an average of 2.2 percent.
9. Sweden levies a production tax designed as a real estate tax.
10. Canada levies a production tax on hydro power plants. No information of the tax rate is available.

Sources: European Commission (1997c) and IEA (1997).

Table 10A.3. Proposed minimum level of taxation (ECU per specific unit)

	Unit	1998	2000	2002
Motor fuels				
Petrol	kl	417	450	500
Gas oil	kl	310	343	393
Kerosene	kl	310	343	393
LPG	tn	141	174	224
Natural gas	Gj	2.9	3.5	4.5
Fuels used as provided in Article 7, paragraph 2				
Petrol	kl	32	37	41
Kerosene	kl	30	35	39
LPG	tn	41	48	53
Natural gas	Gj	0.3	0.6	1.1
Heating fuels				
Heating gas oil	kl	21	23	26
Heavy fuel oil (low sulphur <1%)	tn	18	23	28
Heavy fuel oil (High sulphur >1%	tn	22	28	34
Kerosene	kl	7	16	25
LPG	tn	10	22	34
Natural Gas	Gj	0.2	0.45	0.7
Solid Fuels	Gj	0.2	0.45	0.7
Electricity	MWh	1	2	3

Source: European Commission (1997a).

11. Energy and Environmental Taxation in Sweden: Some Experience from the Swedish Green Tax Commission*

Runar Brännlund and Bengt Kriström

1. INTRODUCTION

The Swedish Green Tax Commission has recently presented its final report (SOU 1997:11a). The recommendations from the Commission include a further 'greening' of the Swedish tax system, and a specific 'Green tax reform'. However, no specific proposals were put forward. This chapter sheds some light on why this might be the case, by combining a historical account of Swedish environmental policy, with various empirical analyses. The chapter is structured in the following way. The next section is devoted to the institutional setting concerning environmental policy in Sweden. We outline the general structure as well as give an overview of the areas which are currently subject to eco taxes. The work of the Swedish Green Tax Commission is presented in the third section. An analysis of some of the eco taxes currently at work in Sweden is presented in the fourth section of the chapter, as well as some simulations of hypothetical tax reforms. In the fifth section we present some results from a general equilibrium model for the Swedish economy, including an analysis of the current exemptions in energy taxation. Some concluding comments are given in the sixth section.

2. ENVIRONMENTAL POLICY IN SWEDEN

The early environmental problems were usually relatively local in character. They were, as in many other countries, a product of industrialization and

* The authors acknowledge valuable comments and suggestions from an anonymous referee.

urbanization. Local environmental problems became most accentuated in the form of water and air pollution in and around the major cities or in the vicinity of larger industries. As much as the forest industry and the metal-based industry contributed to the prosperity of the country, they were also responsible for a major part of the emissions from industrial sources. In urban areas, air pollution from heating houses and water pollution from the release of untreated waste water were major health hazards.

To a large extent, local environmental problems have been eliminated. For example, the levels of sulphur dioxide in cities have been reduced to 20 to 40 per cent of those levels that existed twenty years ago. Sulphur dioxide concentrations are today generally well below the guidelines and planning goals laid down by the Swedish National Environmental Protection Agency. Indeed, it is now difficult to find any detrimental health effects from local pollution.

Local water pollution mimics the history of local air pollution quite closely. In many cities it was not possible to bathe outdoors during the greater part of this century, because of the release of untreated waste water directly into water courses or the sea. Today, through the development of municipal waste-water treatment plants, the water is now fit to swim in even in the central part of Stockholm.

Some local environmental problems do remain. Traffic in densely populated areas and residuals from agriculture in the form of air and water pollution are two major challenges for the current policy. Thus, while sulphur emissions have diminished over time, nitrogen emissions have been fairly stable or have increased.

During the latter part of the 1960s, a series of research findings emerged which indicated that air pollution was not just a local problem, but could be transported from one country to another. Further research showed that many pollution problems were common to the whole of Europe or at least to a large part of the European continent. Sulphur and acid emissions attracted most of the attention. In Sweden, it was Svante Odén's compilation of changes in the pH values in precipitation and surface water from large parts of Europe and C. Brosset's measurement of pollutants along the Swedish south and west coasts, which revealed that acidity was a transboundary problem. It was shown that pollutants were transported to a considerable extent over national boundaries.

While sulphur has received a large amount of attention since the compilations of Odén and Brosset, research subsequently revealed that long-distance transportation was a phenomenon that did not apply just to sulphur; also, nitrates, photochemical oxidants, heavy metals and persistent organic material could be transported in a way analogous to that for sulphur.

The observations by Odén and others were quickly followed by research findings that demonstrated detrimental effects of sulphur on fish, and on human health. For example, in the early 1980s, 16,000 of Sweden's 85,000 lakes were severely acidified; sensitive species had decreased substantially or died out. An extensive liming programme has prevented death of most forms of life in 6,000 of those lakes. It should be noted, however, that several of the lakes that were considered damaged by anthropogenic emissions are now considered to be naturally acidified.

While sulphur emissions in Sweden have decreased substantially, sulphur deposition still exceeds the critical load. According to the government bill of 1991, sulphur deposition must be decreased by about 75 percent of the 1980 level in the south-western parts of Sweden to bring depositions below the critical load. Such a goal is complicated by the fact that emissions from foreign sources accounted for about 93 percent of sulphur deposition in Sweden in 1994.

The sulphur case explains why one of the main issues in current policy today is to foster international cooperation. The 1979 Convention on Long-Range Transboundary Air Pollution is a forum for European cooperation. A number of binding Protocols have also been developed under the 1979 Geneva convention. For example, the 1985 Sulphur Protocol established a minimum 30 percent reduction of sulphur emissions between 1980 and 1993.

At the end of the 1970s, the international problems in the marine environment became increasingly apparent. Eutrophication and pollution in the marine environment began to appear more and more as regional problems. This applied to both the Baltic Sea and the North Sea. The large-scale pollution of the oceans during the 1980s became an ever-increasing problem, one that has led to the drawing up of international plans of action for both the above-mentioned seas.

The risk for a global increase in temperature as a consequence of the increased emission of carbon dioxide was pointed out a hundred years ago by the Swedish chemist (and Nobel-laureate) Svante Arrhenius. The more serious alarms concerning a global effect on the earth's climate came first during the 1970s and have been further accentuated in the past decade. It was, however, first through the discovery of a significantly quicker breakdown than expected of the stratosphere's ozone layer over the Antarctic that global atmospheric pollution issues appeared on the agenda in international negotiations. A contributing factor was also the coverage these questions received in the Brundtland Report. One important feature of the current Swedish policy is to stabilize carbon dioxide emissions by the year 2000 to the 1990 level.

2.1 Organization

The organizational arrangement of environmental policy in Sweden is as follows. At government level, the Ministry of the Environment is responsible for matters relating to environmental policy. The Environmental Protection Agency (EPA) (Naturvårdsverket) is the central administrative authority and deals with matters such as air and water pollution control, noise abatement, and management of natural resources. At the regional level, the 24 county administrations are the regional supervisory authorities under the Environment Protection Act and the Health Protection Act. Together with the Labour Inspectorate they are also the supervisory authority under the Act on Chemical Products. The 284 municipalities are responsible for local environmental protection. Here, municipal board for environmental protection and health and the building boards have important functions.

With regard to the general construction of its control system for environmental protection, Sweden belongs to a north European model. It is characterized by individualized non-transferable permits to sources and the Best-Available-Control-Technology (BACT) principle. Sweden has utilized guidelines for air quality and applied general rules for assessing water quality. In the United States, and increasingly so in European countries, there exist explicit standards for environmental quality. A recent Swedish commission has investigated the feasibility of switching to this model.

2.2 Economic Instruments

Economic instruments in environmental policy have only very recently been generally accepted as viable instruments in Sweden. In the 1970s, large subsidies were given to firms and local government to facilitate and speed up environmental protection measures. In particular, municipal waste-water treatment plants were developed and extended during this period. This subsidization scheme explains a major part of the substantial improvements in local environmental quality. Subsidies play only a minor role today. There exist subsidies for development of new technology, subsidies for liming of lakes, and a subsidy for the preservation of the cultural landscape.

A major shift in emphasis came with the appointment of the Commission of Environmental Charges in 1988. It was a part of a major tax reform. A total of SEK 19,000 million was being transferred from income tax to environmental and energy taxes. The commission produced a large number of proposals in its interim reports (SOU 1989:21; SOU 1989:83) and in its final report (SOU 1990:59). The Commission was to analyse the scope for using economic measures in environmental policy on a large scale. Some of the proposals were accepted by the parliament, and a number of environmental charges came into play on 1 January 1991. Table 11.1 lists the most important environmental taxes in current use.

The tax on CO_2 was introduced on 1 January 1991, at the level of 0.25 SEK/kg of CO_2 released. It is levied on oil, coal, natural gas, liquefied petroleum gas, petrol and aviation fuel in domestic traffic. There are exceptions on ethanol/methanol/biofuels, peat and waste. As of 1 January 1996 the tax has risen to 0.37 SEK/kg of emitted CO_2, but after the energy tax reform in 1993, the manufacturing industry pays only 25 percent of the amount for competitive reasons. Note that the tax varies over fuels and that it is an input tax.

Table 11.1. Main environmental taxes in Sweden, 1996

Type of tax	Tax rate
Electricity tax	Industry: 0 Other: 0.09 SEK/kwh
Energy tax on fossil fuels	Petrol: 3.30 SEK/litre Oil for heating: 0.59 SEK/litre Industry exempted
Carbon dioxide tax	Industry: 0.09 SEK/kg Other: 0.37 SEK/kg (petrol:0.86 SEK/litre)
Sulphur tax	30 SEK/kg
Producer tax on electricity	Hydro: 0.04 SEK/kwh Nuclear: 0.012 SEK/kwh
Tax on nitrogen in fertilizers	1.80 SEK/kg
Tax on pesticides	20 SEK/kg
Tax on gravel	5 SEK/ton
Tax on domestic air traffic (no tax from 97/01/01)	CO_2 1 SEK/litre Hydrocarbons 12 SEK/kg Nitrogen oxides 12 SEK/NO_x
Charge on nitrogen oxides	40 SEK/kg NO_x (large-scale combustion)
Battery charge	Led: 40 SEK per battery Alk: 23 SEK/kg Nicd: 25 SEK/kg
'Junk' car charge	1,300 SEK/car

Source: Treasury of Sweden.

Invariably, environmental taxes are constructed as taxes on inputs, because of the difficulty of constructing a pure emission tax. Roughly, the CO_2 tax corresponds to about 200 US$/ton carbon. According to the Commission of

Environmental Charges (SOU 1990:59), US$200 is the marginal cost for achieving stabilization of CO_2 emissions at the 1988 level (a goal that, incidentally, has been abolished).

The sulphur tax of January 1991 focuses on sulphur content in oil, coal and peat (exceptions are crude oil and waste oil). The sulphur tax was introduced with the aim of reducing sulphur emissions by 80 percent, using 1980 as the baseline. This goal is likely to have been met. The sulphur tax is 30 SEK/kg S, which is roughly US$4.

Table 11.2. Revenues from environmental and environmentally related taxes 1996 (billion SEK)

Taxes and charges	1996
Energy tax on fossil fuels	23.77
Carbon dioxide tax on fossil fuels	12.90
Sulphur tax	0.19
Electricity tax (consumption tax)	6.72
Producer tax on hydro electric power	1.36
Producer tax on nuclear power	0.92
Tax on domestic air traffic	0.19
Total energy related taxes	46.05
Sales tax vehicles	1.37
Vehicle tax	4.95
Total vehicle tax	6.32
Tax on fertilizers and pesticides	0.32
Tax on gravel	0.11
Nitrogen oxides	0
Battery charge	0.03
Junk car charge	0
Total other environmentally related taxes and charges	0.45
Total energy and environmental taxes	52.82
Share of GDP (%)	3.2
Share of total tax revenues (%)	≈ 6.0

The tax on nitrogen oxide (NO_x) emissions is focused on reducing emissions by 30 percent, using 1985 as the base year. It is levied on domestic air traffic (12 SEK/kg NO_x, introduced in 1989) and large combustion plants (40 SEK/kg NO_x, introduced in 1992). The tax on domestic air traffic has, however, been abandoned from 1 January 1997. The NO_x charge on combustion plants has two interesting features. First, it is the only emission charge levied in Sweden; NO_x emissions are monitored at the large plants and taxed accordingly. Second, because monitoring all combustion plants is too expensive, the tax revenues have to be returned to the liable plants as a group to avoid unfair competition between small and large plants. The income from the charge is refunded to the large plants according to their energy efficiency.

In this way, the scheme provides the individual plant with incentives to invest in cleaner technology.

Tax differentiation on diesel fuels was introduced in January 1991 with the purpose of stimulating the use (and production) of environmentally superior grades of diesel oil. There are three environmental classes of diesel, where the parameters for classification are maximum sulphur content, maximum aromatic hydrocarbon content, maximum polycyclic aromatic hydrocarbons, and certain other parameters. Technically, it is the energy tax that differs between the classes. Class 1 has an energy tax of 90 SEK/m^3, class 2, 290 SEK/m^3, and 540 SEK/m^3 for class 3 diesel. From an environmental point of view this was a success. Already in 1992, 50percent of total diesel sales belonged to class 1 or 2. In 1993 the figure was 80 percent.

Table 11.3. Emission of some important substances, 1970–1995

Substance	1970	1975	1980	1985	1990	1995
CO_2, Mton	120	139.4	82	65.4	59.3	58
SO_2, kton	920	690	485	280	128.2	103
NO_x, kton	300	320	320	300	405.8	382.8[a]
VOC, kton	600	560	[c]	450	500	500
Mercury (air, ton)	18	7	6	6	1.4	1
Mercury (water, ton)	16	1	3	1	0.2	[c]
Cadmium (air, ton)	38	12	12	5	2	1[a]
Cadmium (water, ton)	12	4	6	2	2.1	[c]
Led (air, ton)	3,000	1,300	1,300	950	540	365[a]
Led (water, ton)	330	70	160	24	14	[c]
BOD[b], kton	790	490	280	220	210	210
Suspended solids (kton)	340	180	140	85	[c]	[c]
Phosphorous (water, kton)	16	13	8	5	3.5	3.5
Nitrogen, kton	127	[c]	135	135	90	90

Notes:

[a] 1992 value.
[b] BOD is biological oxygen demand.
[c] missing value.

Source: SOU (1997:11a).

It may also be of interest to note that the 1989 tax on domestic air traffic (volatile organic compound (VOC) and NO_x) has led the domestic airline (there was only one at that time) to change the combustion chamber of its Fokker F28 engines. This has reduced hydrocarbon emissions by about 90 percent.

Table 11.2 lists revenues from taxes that have a clear environmental profile, and some other excise taxes which are environmentally related. Among the 'pure' environmental taxes, the carbon dioxide tax is by far the most important. Note that most of the tax revenues are not earmarked, that is, they are not for any specific use. This fact has been the subject of some controversy, because the public's acceptance of new taxes is closely related to the way in which the revenues are to be used. When the Commission of Environmental Charges discussed the use of tax revenues (SOU 1990:59), a number of different solutions were proposed. In particular, two funds were suggested – the waste fund and the chemicals fund. Neither of these proposals were accepted by the parliament, however.

To conclude this section we ask whether Swedish environmental policy has been successful in a historic perspective. A partial answer can be found in Table 11.3 where it can be seen that the emissions of many dangerous substances have decreased in a dramatic way over the last twenty years.

3. THE SWEDISH GREEN TAX COMMISSION

3.1 Background and Terms of Reference

The Swedish Green Tax Commission was launched in the spring of 1995. From a Swedish perspective it is possible to identify two main reasons for launching the Commission. First, there has been a growing interest and concern about environmental problems for quite a long time in Sweden. Economic instruments, such as taxes, are now acceptable as a cost-efficient instrument to achieve specific environmental targets. It has been realized that not only would environmental taxes improve environmental quality, they also yield tax revenues. Second, the increasing unemployment rate in Sweden during the 1990s has been a serious concern, not the least in light of the low historical unemployment rates. The main reason for the increase in unemployment is the deficient demand. Another explanation put forward is that the high taxation of labour has created inefficient resource allocation in general and inefficiencies in the labour market in particular. The question posed to the Commission was: would it be possible to improve environmental quality, and as a second dividend get an efficiency improvement in resource allocation, which would lead to a reduction in unemployment? According to the terms of reference the Commission should analyse the effects of the energy and environmentally related taxes currently at work. Furthermore, the Commission was asked to analyse the conditions for and effects of different kinds of revenue neutral tax reforms.

3.2 Proposals and Recommendations from the Commission

One main conclusion from the Commission is that Sweden has secured environmental improvements in a number of areas. This has been accomplished in part by an increase in the use of economic instruments within a general reshaping of the Swedish tax system. The general recommendation from the Commission is that Sweden should continue this reshaping process.

The Commission does not propose any specific tax reforms. Instead, the Commission proposes some overarching principles which should guide future policy in this area. These overarching principles are as follows[1].

First, Sweden should pursue its active role in the international efforts to combat global and regional environmental problems, given that other countries follow suit. Second, is that the chosen policy can show up positive results on the national level. The Commission states that Sweden cannot be viewed as a 'good example' to the rest of the world if the measures taken in Sweden imply that production is moved to countries with less stringent environmental policy. More specifically, the Commission suggests increased joint action between countries, and promotion to research and development to promote the use of renewable energy sources. Sweden should actively use its European Union membership in this process.

The Commission states that a Swedish green tax reform has to take into consideration how investments, economic growth and equity are affected. Regional effects within Sweden have to be considered whenever environmental taxes are introduced or are subject to changes. One such measure is to target tax cuts to compensate for possibly negative distributional impacts.

The Commission also recommends that revenues obtained through environmental or other taxes should in general not be earmarked. Each dollar of tax revenue should be used where its utility is highest. A conclusion from the Commission is that additional revenues from energy and environmental taxes will not give room for any substantial general decrease of labour taxes. Revenues from a green tax reform should be used for selective cuts, that is, those which have the largest effects on unemployment.

---

[1] For a thorough presentation of the recommendations, see SOU (1997:11b).

4. ARE ECO-TAXES WORKING IN SWEDEN?

As has already been mentioned, one of the objectives for the Swedish Green Tax Commission has been to assess whether environmentally related taxes have been efficient or not. In this section we report some of the findings of background research done for the Commission. It should be pointed out that it is a difficult task to make such an assessment. Many green taxes have been introduced quite recently, which means that we have very little experience of the effects, especially the long-run effects.

Suppose that a tax, such as the CO_2 tax, or the sulphur tax, is equivalent to a consumer price increase on fossil fuels. One way to evaluate the effects of such eco-taxes amounts to an estimation of price elasticities. Thus, if a tax increase on fossil fuels leads to an increase in the consumer price by the same amount, which is a reasonable assumption for a country like Sweden, then the tax will have the intended effect, depending on demand sensivity to price changes.

4.1 Partial Equilibrium Model of the Industry

In order to analyse the sensitivity to price changes we employ a partial equilibrium framework. In this case this means that we shall analyse the industry and households separately, and that all prices are exogenous both to the industry and to the households. The industry is disaggregated into 16 manufacturing sectors, and each manufacturing sector is assumed to produce one good (y) using labour (l), fossil fuels (f), electricity (e) and capital (K) as inputs. The underlying assumption behind the derivation of goods supply and input demand is that each firm seeks to maximize its profits. Given this assumption we can derive the demand functions for all inputs as functions of all prices and the capital stock. Formally the derived supply and demand equations can be written as:[2]

$$y = y(\underset{+}{p_y}, \underset{?}{p_l}, \underset{?}{p_e}, \underset{?}{p_f}, \underset{?}{K}) \tag{11.1}$$

$$x_l = x_l(\underset{+}{p_y}, \underset{-}{p_l}, \underset{?}{p_e}, \underset{?}{p_f}, \underset{?}{K}) \tag{11.2}$$

[2] We shall not go into any details concerning the model here. The interested reader is referred to the appendix to SOU (1997:11b), Report No. 4.

$$x_e = x_e(\underset{+}{p_y}, \underset{?}{p_l}, \underset{-}{p_e}, \underset{?}{p_f}, \underset{?}{K}) \quad (11.3)$$

$$x_f = x_f(\underset{+}{p_y}, \underset{?}{p_l}, \underset{?}{p_e}, \underset{-}{p_f}, \underset{?}{K}) \quad (11.4)$$

Where p denotes prices and the sign under the argument the expected sign of the partial derivative. This system was estimated using data for each variable for 16 different industrial sectors over the time period 1974–93. The resulting price elasticities are presented in Table 11.4, where it can be seen that all own-price demand elasticity's have a negative sign, meaning that a price increase will decrease demand for that good.

Table 11.4. Average own-price and cross-price elasticities for the Swedish manufacturing industry (t-values in parentheses)

	Output price	Wage	Electricity price	Fossil fuel price
Goods supply	0.12	–0.08	–0.03	–0.01
	(4.34)	(–2.99)	(–9.42)	(–3.05)
Labour demand	0.14	–0.13	–0.02	0.008
	(2.99)	(–2.83)	(–2.66)	(0.97)
Electricity	0.64	–0.22	–0.26	–0.16
demand	(9.42)	(–2.66)	(–2.76)	(–3.10)
Fossil fuel	0.40	0.12	–0.19	–0.32
demand	(3.06)	(0.97)	(–3.10)	(–4.68)

Source: SOU (1997:11b, p. 217).

Table 11.1 should be read in the following way. If the price of fossil fuels increases by 10 percent, the demand for fossil fuels decreases by 3.2 percent. In addition, this will lead to a 1.6 percent decrease of electricity demand, and an almost unchanged demand for labour. Output will according to these estimates decrease by 0.1 percent. In other words, the effects are very small, suggesting that taxes on oil have a rather small impact on the environment. It should be pointed out that these elasticities should be interpreted as short-run elasticities since the capital stock is treated as fixed. In the long run we should expect that a price change does have an effect on capital formation in the industry. Thus we expect that the industry is more sensitive to price changes in the long run.

Furthermore, the results suggest that the tax base is fairly stable in the short run. Suppose, for example, that the policy makers decide that the industry should cut emissions of CO_2 by 25 percent. To achieve this goal, a 250 percent tax increase from today's level would do the job. This would amount to a tax increase from today's 0.09 SEK/kg CO_2 to approximately

0.34 SEK per kilo, which is equivalent to a 23 percent increase of the oil price.

4.2 Models of the Household Sector

The major part of energy consumption within the household sector in Sweden is through expenditure on transport and heating of houses. About 10 percent of total household expenditure on non-durable goods is allocated to expenditure on transport. Expenditure on energy for heating is of the same magnitude. Thus it should be quite clear that the household sector has to be considered when it comes to an analysis of energy and/or environmentally related taxes.

Household behaviour has been analysed through a system of demand functions, describing how the demand for a specific good changes when the price of some good, or the income, changes. The system of demand functions has been derived by assuming utility-maximizing households. Two versions of the model have been estimated. The first one is a 'two-stage budgeting' model which uses aggregate data from the national accounts. In this first model it is assumed that the household takes its consumption decisions in two stages.[3] In the first stage the household determines, given its total budget, how much to spend on transport, heating and other goods. In the second stage, the household allocates resources within each group. For example, given a specific amount of money to be spent on transport, the household determines how much of that should be allocated to expenditure on gasoline, public transport and other means of transport (taxi, train, airplane and so on).

In the same manner the household determines in the second stage how to use its budget for heating. In this case the household can choose between electricity for heating, oil for heating or district heating. In the second model, which is based on household survey data, it is assumed that the household makes all consumption decisions in one stage.[4] The advantage with the former approach is that it makes estimation easier since each 'group' consists of a separate system of equations. This is an advantage especially in the aggregate time-series model, where there are relatively few data points and problems with multicollinearity. The disadvantage with the 'two-stage' approach is that it places certain restrictions on consumer behaviour.

The results in Table 11.5 show that all own-price elasticities have a negative sign. In other words, a price increase of one specific good has a negative effect on consumption of the same good. It should also be noted that the own-price elasticities are between 0 and –1 for all goods, which implies that a higher price of one good increases its budget share in spite of lower

[3] For a more detailed description of the model, see Report No. 5 in SOU (1997:11b).

[4] See Hansson-Bruzewitz (1997).

consumption of that good. Another important result is that the two models give similar results.

If the price of gasoline increases by 10 percent, everything else being given, gasoline consumption decreases by approximately 1.5 percent. The corresponding figure for oil used for heating purposes is between 1 and 2 percent depending on model specification. A 100 percent increase of the Swedish CO_2 tax, from 0.37 to 0.74 SEK/kg implies that the consumer gasoline prices increase by approximately 13 percent, while the oil price for heating increases by 31 percent. The direct effect on gasoline and oil consumption is a 1.6 percent and 6percent reduction, respectively.

Table 11.5. Price and income elasticities for private consumption

Two-stage macro model			*price*				
Consumption	Gasoline	Public transport	Other travels	Electricity	Oil	District heating	Other goods
Gasoline	−0.12	−0.002	−0.002	−0.01	−0.006	−0.008	−0.70
Public transp.	−0.005	−0.25	−0.001	−0.01	−0.004	−0.004	−0.41
Other travels	−0.02	−0.007	−0.56	−0.05	−0.02	−0.02	−1.91
Electricity	−0.02	−0.008	−0.006	−0.09	−0.04	−0.04	−0.85
Oil	0.03	0.01	0.008	0.14	−0.19	0.06	1.09
District heat.	−0.03	−0.01	−0.009	−0.15	−0.05	0.00	−1.14
Other goods	−0.06	−0.02	−0.01	−0.03	−0.01	−0.02	−0.72

Income elasticities, private consumption			
	Transport	Heating	Other goods
Elasticity	1.04645	0.76604	1.01434

One-stage micro model			*price*		
Consumption	Gasoline	Public transport	Electricity	Oil	Income elasticity
Gasoline	−0.15	0.04	−0.32	0.03	0.609
Public transport	0.12	−0.39	0.12	−0.01	0.902
Electricity	−0.94	0.22	−0.32	0.28	0.337
Oil	0.08	−0.09	0.51	−0.10	0.220

Source: SOU (1997:11a).

Energy taxes may thus be efficient from a fiscal point of view, at least in the short run. In other words, such taxes will generate stable tax revenues, at least in the short- and medium-term perspective. On the other hand, if the objective for taxation is to reach a specified environmental target, an ambitious environmental target calls for dramatic changes of the corresponding taxes.

5. GREEN TAX REFORMS – A GENERAL EQUILIBRIUM ANALYSIS

A second objective of the Swedish Green Tax Commission is to evaluate and analyse various green tax reforms. In this section we shall report on some of the findings from this analysis. The tool used in the analysis is a general equilibrium model for the Swedish economy.

5.1 The Double Dividend Issue

Much of the recent discussion around green tax reforms has focused on revenue-neutral reforms and the scope for double dividends. The first dividend is due to the environmental benefits generated from a revenue-neutral tax change, whereas the second dividend arises when revenue from the environmental tax is used to lower distortionary taxes such as labour taxes. Thus, if there exists a double dividend, a revenue-neutral change in the tax mix will improve welfare no matter how small the environmental effect is. The intuition is that it must be welfare improving to tax 'good' things less and 'bad' things more, since taxes on 'good' things are distortionary and taxes on 'bad' things are corrective. But as Oates (1995) puts it, our economic intuition is not a very reliable guide when we enter the murky waters of second best. In the presence of existing distortionary taxes, the introduction of a green tax may very well exacerbate these distortions. This effect may very well outweigh the efficiency gains from recycling the revenues to reduce existing taxes.[5] One example where we can find a double dividend is given by Sandmo (1975), where the revenues from the environmental tax (equal to the marginal social damage) provide enough funds to finance the entire public sector. In that case, we do not need any distortionary taxes, which means that the introduction of the environmental tax necessarily leads to a double dividend. This case is not very realistic.

Total tax revenues in Sweden in 1995 amounted to approximately SEK 900 billion. Revenues from 'pure' environmental taxes amount the same year to approximately SEK 13 billion, where the CO_2 tax accounted for SEK 12 billion. If we use a broader definition of environmental taxes, by adding all energy and vehicle taxes, the total is about SEK 50 billion. Even if we raise energy and environmental tax rates substantially, and assume that the tax

[5] See Bovenberg and de Mooij (1994), Parry (1995) and Bovenberg and Goulder (1996).

bases for these goods are price inelastic, the scope for any major reductions in other taxes are limited. Substantial increases of energy taxes will likely have a negative effect on the real wage, which may have a negative incentive effect to supply labour; this, in turn, means lower tax revenues from labour taxes.[6] Since pre-existing taxes on labour are relatively high in Sweden, the erosion of revenues from labour taxes may be substantial even if the change in labour supply is small.

Most studies, both theoretical and empirical, indicate that there is little if any scope for a double dividend. It is an empirical issue whether any double dividends can be found. This will be the next issue.

5.2 A General Equilibrium Model for Sweden

Details of the Computable General Equilibrium model used by the Commission can be found in Harrison and Kriström (1997). Goods are produced using primary factors (real capital and different labour types) and intermediate inputs such as raw materials. The data allow us to distinguish between eleven different categories of labour, depending upon the length of education. Production factors can move freely across sectors, but with some exceptions such as the mining sector and the agricultural sector. Output is differentiated between goods destined for the domestic market and export markets, and exports are further distinguished depending upon which of seven foreign markets they are destined for. In addition, factors of production are not transferable across borders. These two assumptions make the construction of the model follow the trade theory developed during the 1920s by Eli Heckscher and Bertil Ohlin.

Because Sweden is a small open economy, increased costs in Sweden cannot be shifted to the world market. The model allows potential differences between trade restrictions and duties within the trade regions.

Households demand products from domestic markets and import markets (these are the same as the export markets). They receive income from the primary factors plus net transfers from the government.

The household expenditures data is based on the 1992 Household Expenditure Survey conducted by the Statistiska Centralbyrån (SCB). This survey uses a different categorization of goods, as compared to the definitions used in the national accounts. An official key that would permit linking of these two databases is currently not available. Information about expenditure patterns in other countries, together with other judgements, has

---

[6] We can also think of this as a case when the consumer consumes two goods: thegood which is subject to the environmental tax, and leisure. A higher environmental tax means that leisure becomes relatively cheaper which means that the consumption of leisure increases, and hence labour supply decreases (if the good and leisure are substitutes).

been used to link the data-sets.

Households divide their time between leisure and work. In the present version of the model there are no imperfections on the labour market. Consequently, there is no 'involuntary unemployment' in the model. Needless to say, this is not necessarily an accurate picture of the present state of the Swedish labour market.

An important part of the effort has been to obtain data on the finest level of aggregation available. The core part of the database is the input–output table published by the Swedish Statistical Office for 1992, covering 88 sectors. The data-matrix describes transactions between different sectors, as well as foreign trade, investment activity, public sector consumption and a wealth of other useful information.

It is important to note that all sectors, as they are conceived in the national accounts, are integrated in the database. Included are, for example, agriculture, forestry, manufacturing, electricity and heating, construction, transportation and a number of service sectors such as consulting, banking, insurance, hotel and restaurant.

The input–output tables have been supplemented with data on household expenditure patterns, as explained above. Data on labour income for different categories of labour has been obtained via the SCB.

A significant effort has been expended to describe trade patterns. No easily available data directly fits the core database, because the input–output table lacks country-specific destinations of imports and exports. Available statistics from customs have been used to determine exports and imports concerning Denmark, Finland, Japan, Norway, the rest of the EU countries, the US, and the rest of the world.

Public sector revenue consists of different taxrevenues including tariff revenues. Public sector costs include public consumption and various kinds of subsidies. Taxes on energy, social security taxes on labour, value-added, tariffs and corporate tax are all included. The tax on corporations (a tax on profits) has been set to 19.2 percent, using calculations presented in Andersson and Norrman (1987, p. 224).

The model utilizes the energy and environmental taxes for 1995, according to the Table 11.6.

The current energy-tax exemptions in manufacturing, as well as other components of the energy and environmental tax system, are handled separately in the model, using the tax code of 1 January 1996 as the benchmark. In short, those rules imply that fuels used in manufacturing and the horticultural industry are exempted from the energy tax, and that the carbon dioxide tax is only 25 percent of the general level. In addition to these general tax breaks, energy-intensive companies may obtain additional reductions, if tax payments exceed 1.2 percent of their revenues.

Table 11.6. Energy and environmental taxes and prices for different fuels (industry, vehicles), 1995 (%, SEK)

Fuel	Energy-tax % of price	CO_2 tax % of price	SO_2 tax % of price	PRICE
Gasoline	148	36	0	2,175[a]
Diesel	109	67	0	1,468[a]
Light oil (EO1)	48	82	0	1,203[a]
Heavy oil (EO2-EO5)	60	102	11	963[a]
Coal	77	268	56	319[b]
Coke	77	268	56	319[b]
Gasol	8	73	0	1,407[b]
Natural Gas	16	61	0	1,188[c]

Notes: [a] SEK/m^3, [b] SEK/ton, [c] SEK/1000 m^3

Source*: SCB.*

As far as possible, the tax system represented in the model obeys the current tax code, even though it has not been practical to integrate a complete description of the fairly complex energy taxation system of Sweden.

For technical modelling reasons it is easier to tax emissions ‘at the source’ rather than in later stages of the value-added chain and in private consumption, as is the case in practice. Technically, taxes in the model are constructed so that a sector that buys goods from the refineries pays the tax on those deliveries (gasoline, diesel and fuel oils). Refineries shift the tax burden to the buying sector. In the case of coal and coke, the tax has been assigned to one of the mining sectors (which in practice means that imports of coal are taxed, since there is no coal mining in Sweden). A similar construction has been used for the sulphur tax.

Data have been collected on the consumption of gasoline, diesel, light and heavy oils, coal, coke and natural gas for each sector. Emissions of carbon dioxide and sulphur dioxide have been calculated via the emission coefficients that are available for these fuels. The matrix published by Konjunkturinstitutet (KI), within the resource-accounting project for Sweden, was used to calibrate the calculations. The varying carbon content for imports depending on the import region has been integrated in the data.

The calculations show that the largest emissions are found in the transportation sector and the electricity and heating sector. This follows naturally in that the transportation and energy sectors use significant amounts of fossil fuels. In relation to the value of production, we find the largest emissions in the iron and steel sectors. Imports to Sweden contribute about 20 percent of the carbon dioxide emissions over and above those that are generated domestically.

The results are comparable to those presented in the 16-sector matrix compiled by SCB/KI, within the resource-accounting project. The largest difference is found in the iron, steel and metal-casting sectors, as the figures used here suggest much larger emissions. Overall, there is fair agreement between the data used here and official data.

A number of different tax scenarios are analysed by the Commission, using this model. Here we present only some of the basic scenarios. The basic scenario presented by the Swedish Green Tax Commission is called C100. It includes a 100 percent increase of the CO_2 tax and a revenue-neutral reduction of the payroll tax. In addition to this scenario we shall present a scenario with a 100 percent increase of the CO_2 tax but where the revenues are returned as a lump-sum transfer to the households. This latter scenario will be denoted C100LS.

Some general results for the two basic scenarios C100 and C100LS are given in Table 11.7.

Table 11.7. Effects on 'welfare', CO_2 emissions and tax revenues

SCENARIO	EV billion SEK*	Emissions CO_2, percentage change	Revenues from CO_2 tax, percentage change	Reduction of payroll tax, percentage points
C100LS	–4.6	–0.2%	+91%	
C100	–3.9	–0.1%	+92%	1.5

Note: * EV = equivalent variation. This can be interpreted as the change in real income.

Source: SOU (1997:11b).

The 'welfare' effect, equivalent variation (EV), is presented in the first column. Environmental benefits are not included in this measure. The total welfare loss under C100 is SEK 3.9 billion, or 0.4 percent of private consumption, which means that there is no double dividend. If we compare this figure with the figure obtained when revenues are returned as a lump-sum transfer we find that the welfare loss is larger in the latter case. In other words, the results support the idea of a weak double dividend, that is, that it is better to use the revenues to reduce distortionary taxes than return them as a lump sum.

The second column in Table 11.7 displays the reduction in CO_2 emissions, and as can be seen, the reduction is less than 1 percent, independent of recycling schemes.

A very crude idea of whether the reforms are socially desirable or not can be found by interpreting the figures in the first column as costs, and the emission reductions in the second column as benefits. According to the IPCC (Intergovernmental Panel on Climate Change) the social costs of CO_2 emissions can be estimated to US$5–125 per ton emitted carbon. Suppose now that a Swedish green tax reform leads to a reduction of CO_2 by 600,000 ton (1 percent of 60 million tons). This corresponds to 162,000 tons of carbon, which, according to the IPCC, has a value amounting to US$0.8–20 million. Given this valuation of the avoided damages, the reform is not socially desirable.

The third column displays the change in tax revenues. According to this figure, revenues will increase by approximately 90 percent, or SEK 12.4 billion.

As has already been mentioned, a tax reform such as C100 will change the relative price between labour and energy, which will affect different sectors differently depending on production structure. Figure 11.1 displays some of the 'winners', that is, examples of sectors in which value added has increased.

Figure 11.1. Sectors with an increase in value added

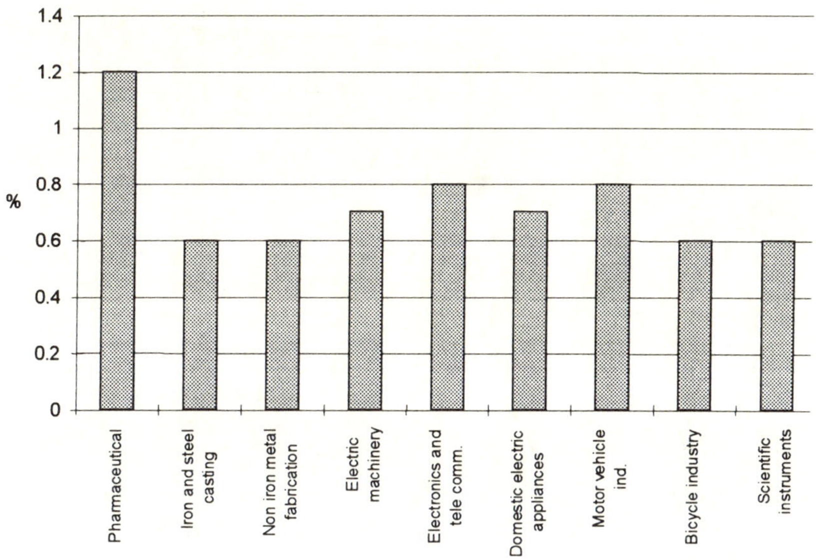

Source: SOU (1997:11a).

As can be seen from Figure 11.1, all changes are quite small in magnitude. The increase in value added is most pronounced in the pharmaceutical industry. This is not surprising since this industry is quite labour intense. At a first glance it might seem strange that value added in the motor vehicle industry (Volvo and SAAB) increases, since a higher gasoline price probably leads to a reduction in demand for cars in Sweden. The result, however, shows that labour costs are more important to the car industry than the costs of fossil fuels. Lower costs for the Swedish car industry give an opportunity to expand on the world market, which may compensate for the domestic reduction in demand. According to the calculations, car exports will increase by approximately 1 percent, while there will be a reduction in car imports. Perhaps even more peculiar is that the value added in the iron and steel industry increases. As we shall show later, this is due to tax exemptions when energy is used in industrial processes. The 'losers' from the tax reform are presented in Figure 11.2.

Figure 11.2. Sectors with a decrease in value added

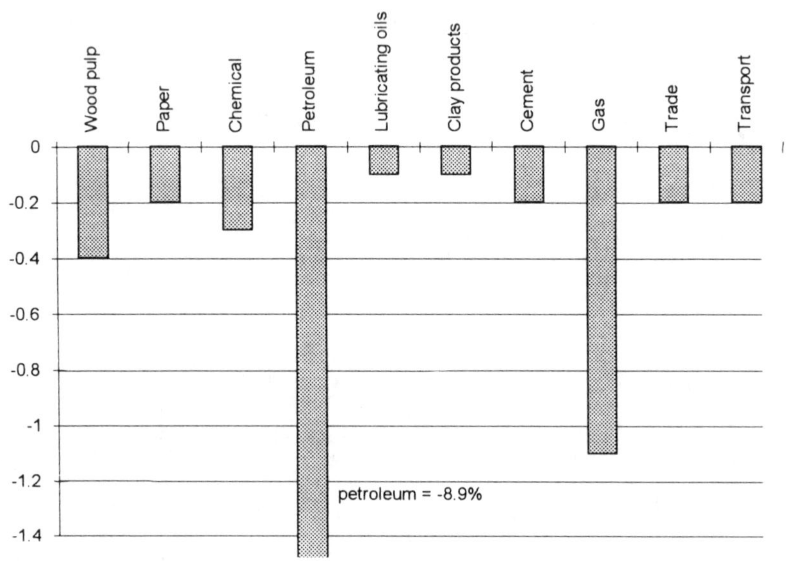

Source: SOU (1997:11).

As expected, the petroleum sector will have the largest loss in value added. Other losers, such as pulp and paper and the cement industry are also expected, since they all are relatively energy intensive.

Figures 11.1 and 11.2 show how different manufacturing sectors are affected by the tax reform. What is interesting in the end is how Swedish households are affected. The welfare effects on various types of households are depicted in Figure 11.3. It should be noted that the welfare effects in Figure 11.3 are the total, or 'net', effects, that is, they include all changes including the effects on the industry.

Figure 11.3. Distributional effects, C100

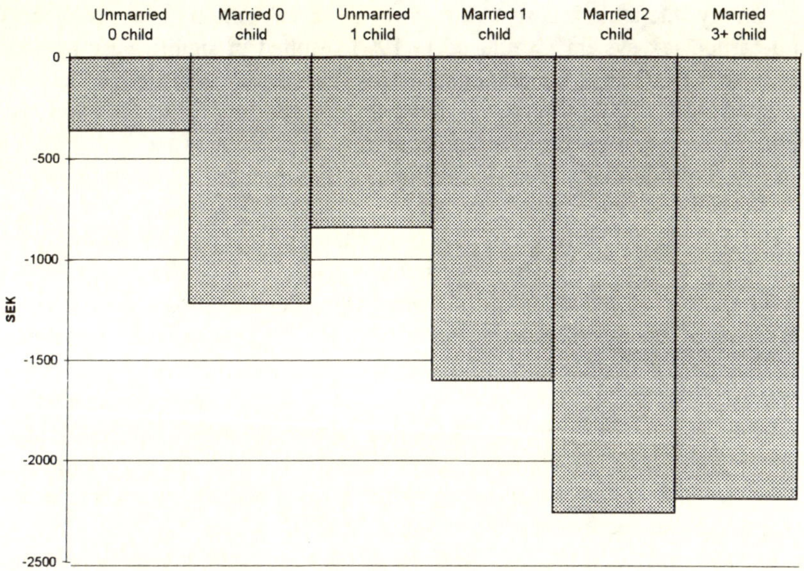

Source: *SOU (1997:11a).*

The figure shows that C100 leads to a welfare loss to all types of household, according to the model. This does not mean that every household will lose as a result of the reform. We could certainly find some households that will gain as a result of the tax reform. Furthermore, it should be noted that the results in Figure 11.3 correspond well to the results obtained in studies using micro economic data, where it is found that the cost increases by the number of children in the household (see Hansson-Bruzewitz 1997).

5.3 The Role of Exemptions

In an international context Swedish energy taxes are high. Because export-oriented industries are competing in markets with significant price elasticities, it is not surprising that several tax exemptions are used. Beginning in 1974, through the law on (partial) exemptions of the general energy tax, energy-intensive manufacturing industries and the horticulture industry have escaped some part of energy taxes. This, of course, is not unique in Europe. Similar exemptions have also been used in Denmark and Norway for manufacturing.

These exemptions for manufacturing are a key feature of the tax system.

In the tax system prior to 1993, approximately 100 energy-intensive firms were granted reduced tax rates on fuels and electricity. In 1992 the reduction for energy-intensive industry was worth SEK 1.3 billion. The new energy and carbon tax system introduced in 1993 resulted in significantly reduced tax rates for industry. The total amount of energy and carbon tax collections dropped from SEK 3.8 billion in 1992 to just SEK 0.5 billion in 1994. We approximate these exemptions as applying to manufacturing industries *in toto*, so that manufacturing industry and horticulture are assumed to pay 25 percent of the general carbon tax rate.

Before the 1993 change of the energy tax system, tax exemptions were essentially granted on a case-by-case basis. Thus energy-intensive industries could apply for a reduction of the energy tax on electricity and fuels. With a zero energy tax on electricity and fossil fuels, such applications are now redundant. There are still possibilities for deductions for fuel use, some of them of considerable importance for individual firms. These deductions are possible only for firms producing cement, lignite and glass. They apply only to the carbon tax on coal and natural gas, and not to the use of oil products. In 1995, less than ten energy-intensive firms could benefit from this rule, and the value of the reduced tax was less than SEK 50 million.

Suppose that a C100 type reform is contemplated, given the existing structure of the tax system. Because of the exemptions, we would argue that carbon emissions could increase in the exempted sectors. The logic is simple, although the empirical results may not comply with it, due to equilibrium repercussions. Still, the exempted sectors benefits directly through the across-the-board decrease of the labor tax. Consequently, we expect that they will expand and along with it the carbon emissions from those sectors. Table 11.8 displays the sectoral impacts on emissions under C100LS and C100.

Under the lump-sum replacement scenario, all sectors decrease their emissions, as intuition would suggest. True enough, the exempted iron and steel sectors increase their emissions under C100. Note that the increase swamps almost half of the decrease obtained in the other sectors. While the levels are uncertain in this kind of model, the mechanism is plain; the environmental benefits are smaller if the existing tax system has exemptions.

Table 11.8. Emission reductions in different sectors from a 100 percent increase of the CO_2 tax with different tax replacement schedules (thousands of tons)

Replacement	Transport	Iron and steel	The rest
Lump sum (C100LS)	60	4	59
Labour tax (C100)	65	–52	40

These results are 'obvious', to some extent, at least 'after the fact'.

Nevertheless, they highlight the complexity of the current energy tax system, which is supposed to cater for more than one political goal.

6. SUMMARY AND CONCLUDING REMARKS

Economic instruments, such as taxes and subsidies, are quite recent in Swedish environmental policy. The use of economic instruments started in the 1970s with the subsidies to municipal waste-water treatment plants. Environmental taxes were brought into focus with the Commission on Environmental Charges, which delivered its final report in 1990. The general tax reform in 1990 and 1991 was another milestone in Swedish environmental policy. In conjunction with the tax reform, a tax on the carbon content in fuels, the CO_2 tax, was introduced, as well as the sulphur tax. The Green Tax Commission, which delivered its final report in January 1997, recommends that Sweden should continue the process of reshaping the tax system. However, the Commission emphasizes that Sweden cannot solve global environmental problems on its own. Other countries must follow. The analysis of the eco-taxes presently at work show that they have the intended effect in the sense that they tend to reduce emissions. However, it is also shown that effects from further increases of carbon taxes probably have a moderate effect on Swedish emissions, at least in the short run. This should be seen in the light of the fact that the use of fossil fuels in Sweden has been considerably reduced during the last twenty years. A general equilibrium analysis of various green tax reforms shows that the scope for double dividends are rather limited. The impacts of current exemptions have also been highlighted. The empirical results tell a simple story; there is no free lunch – if we want to have more environmental goods, we must pay for them.

REFERENCES

Andersson, K. and Norrman, E. (1987), 'Capital Taxation and Neutrality. A Study of Tax Wedges with Special Reference to Sweden', Lund Economic Studies Number 41, Department of Economics, University of Lund.

Bovenberg, A.L. and de Mooij, R. (1994), 'Environmental Levies and Distortionary Taxation', *American Economic Review*, **84** (4), pp. 1085–89.

Bovenberg, A.L. and Goulder, L.H. (1996), 'Optimal Environmental Taxation in the Presence of Other Taxes: General Equilibrium Analyses', *American Economic Review*, **86** (4), pp. 985–1000.

Hansson-Bruzewitz, U. (1997), 'Höjd koldioxidskatt och höjd skatt på elektrisk kraft: effekter på hushållens välfärd och konsumtion', in, SOU 1997:11b, underlagsrapporter till Skatteväxlingskommitténs slutbetänkande, pp. 261–301.

Harrison, G. and Kriström, B. (1996), 'Effekter av olika skatteväxlingsalternativ enligt en allmän jämviktsmodell', in, SOU 1997:117.

Harrison, G. and Kriström, B. (1997), 'Carbon Taxes in Sweden', in, SOU 1997:11, underlagsrapporter till Skatteväxlingskommitténs slutbetänkande.

Oates, W.E. (1995), 'Green Taxes: Can We Protect the Environment and Improve the Tax System at the Same Time?', *Southern Economic Journal*, **61** (4), pp. 915–22.

Parry, I.W.H. (1995), 'Pollution Taxes and Revenue Recycling', *Journal of Environmental Economics and Management*, **29** (3), pp. 564–77.

Sandmo, A. (1975), 'Optimal Taxation in the Presence of Externalities', *Swedish Journal of Economics*, **77** (1), pp. 86–98.

SOU (1989:21), 'Sätt värde på miljön. Miljöavgifter på svavel och klor', Delbetänkande från miljöavgiftsutredningen, Allmänna förlaget, Stockholm.

SOU (1989:83), 'Ekonomiska styrmedel i miljöpolitiken', Delbetänkande från miljöavgiftsutredningen, Allmänna förlaget, Stockholm.

SOU (1990:59), 'Sätt värde på miljön. Miljöavgifter och andra ekonomiska styrmedel', Slutbetänkande från miljöavgiftsutredningen, Allmänna förlaget, Stockholm.

SOU (1997:11a), 'Skatter, miljö och sysselsättning', Slutbetänkande från Skatteväxlingskommittén, Fritzes, Stockholm.

SOU (1997:11b), 'Skatter, miljö och sysselsättning', Underlagsrappporter från Skatteväxlingskommittén, Fritzes, Stockholm.

12. The Distributional Effects of Carbon Regulation: Why Auctioned Carbon Permits are Attractive and Feasible

Peter Cramton and Suzi Kerr[1]

1. INTRODUCTION

The United States, the European Community, Japan and many other OECD countries agreed to restrict their carbon emissions to, on average, 5 percent below 1990 levels by 2008–2012 (subject to ratification) at the Climate Change Summit in Kyoto in December 1997. Binding domestic regulation is now a real possibility in the US and elsewhere.

Short-term policies in the US, including voluntary agreements, subsidies to energy-efficiency research and information programs, have been implemented since the Rio Conference. None of these is capable of controlling carbon emissions to the levels required. In fact, Department of Energy figures reveal that from 1990 levels US CO_2 output had climbed 9 percent by 1997. Further, they project that the increase will reach 14 percent by 2000. More effective, efficient policies are necessary for real progress on climate change. How can these best be designed?

CO_2 is the major current contributor to climate change. It is released whenever fossil fuels are burned and sequestered in the growth of trees. How can we reduce our consumption of fossil fuels at lowest cost? The major option for the United States, being discussed in Washington, is a tradable permit program, following in the footsteps of the successful acid rain trading program. European countries have traditionally proposed (and some have implemented) carbon taxes. In this chapter we consider the distributional implications of these options and how they depend on the allocation of permits. We then show that auctioning permits is feasible. This means that a permit market can mimic a tax on both efficiency and equity grounds.

The regulatory options we compare are a comprehensive carbon tax and an optimally designed, comprehensive carbon permit system with either

[1] Acknowledgements: Peter Cramton is grateful to the National Science Foundation for its financial support. Suzi Kerr would like to thank Boaz Moselle, Robert Stavins, Ian Parry, Larry Goulder and participants in the Centre for Clean Air Policy Greenhouse Gas Emissions Trading Braintrust. She gratefully acknowledges funding from the US Environmental Protection Agency. Many of the issues in this chapter are discussed in more detail in Resources for the Future Discussion Paper 98-32.

auctioned or grandfathered permits. CO_2 is a uniformly mixed pollutant with an extremely long lifetime in the atmosphere. For this chapter, we assume that the tax or permit system regulates carbon at the level of oil refineries, natural-gas pipelines, natural-gas liquid sellers, and coal-processing plants. This creates a comprehensive, administratively feasible system. Carbon emissions in all sectors of the economy will be indirectly controlled. From an environmental standpoint, neither the timing of emissions nor their source is important. Thus, permits are ideally defined in a homogeneous way over time and space. Permits allow a one-time use of one metric ton of carbon. They can be banked indefinitely for use in later years. Ideally, permits would be fully tradable internationally. Trade in the secondary permit market is completely unrestricted.

In the US, the political debate over permit markets focuses on how to allocate the permits. Powerful vested interests in the energy sector (electric utilities, coal and oil companies) are already lobbying that the permits be allocated to them in a way related to historical output. In countries that are considering tax systems, the equivalent debate is over exemptions from the tax. The permit debate only affects distribution. The vested interest group pressure on taxes has major efficiency implications if they lead the tax to be non-comprehensive, as all current carbon taxes are.

In a permit system, periodic auctions of permits are a simple and highly efficient alternative to grandfathering permits to vested interests. As with a carbon tax, auctions have the benefit that the revenue from the auctions can be refunded through tax cuts to all citizens. This 'revenue recycling' means that polluters are effectively buying the right to pollute from the public. If the target of 6 percent below 1990 emissions by 2010 is implemented, 1,260 million metric tons of permits will be issued each year in the United States (Energy Information Administration (EIA) 1997, *Annual Energy Outlook*). The marginal cost of this target will be in the range \$25 to \$150 if current estimates of the cost of carbon regulation are correct. If the marginal cost, and hence the permit price, is \$100 per metric ton, an efficient auction could raise \$126 billion annually. This is around 2 percent of GNP and around 10 percent of federal receipts in 1995. If permits are grandfathered, a 10 percent reduction in taxes will be forgone.

An active group of researchers is estimating the aggregate costs of carbon dioxide policy, both domestically and globally, and the optimal aggregate path for carbon emissions. Researchers have worked less on how to achieve those emissions paths. The arguments for carbon permit auctions have not been comprehensively addressed. Parry (1995) addresses the advantages of revenue recycling. Milliman and Prince (1989) have addressed the effects of regulatory form on incentives to innovate. In the context of the Acid Rain Program, Van Dyke (1991) argued that fairness required that SO_2 allowances be sold rather than given out for free. Researchers have considered the serious design problems in the SO_2 auction and its effects on the operation of the auction and market (Cason 1995; Cason and Plott 1996; Joskow et al. 1997) in previous work on environmental auction design. They have not considered the design issues in carbon permit auctions.

We begin by discussing the arguments in favor of auctioning permits or taxing rather than grandfathering permits. Then we describe how carbon permits should be auctioned. In the case of carbon we conclude that the arguments for auctions or taxes rather than grandfathering, on efficiency and equity grounds, are overwhelming. The ability to achieve identical efficiency and distributional outcomes with either auctioned permits or taxes provides greater regulatory and political flexibility. We conclude that, in a permit market, bankable, identical permits should be auctioned on a quarterly basis using a standard, ascending-clock design.

2. WHY COLLECT THE SCARCITY RENTS RATHER THAN GRANDFATHERING THEM?

Carbon regulation makes carbon a scarce resource and hence creates scarcity rents. Figure 12.1 illustrates, in a simple way, how the price of fossil fuels, and of goods directly or indirectly produced using fossil fuel, must rise to reduce the total demand for fossil fuel. This figure assumes only one fossil fuel, and that it is sold directly from producers to the ultimate consumers. $\underline{Q}$ is the carbon cap translated into a fossil fuel cap. The price buyers pay for the representative fossil fuel rises from P_0 to P_D and the price sellers receive falls to Ps. The permit price or tax is the difference between these prices.

These price changes occur under any efficient form of carbon regulation. The constraint on the quantity of fossil fuel (carbon) used creates a scarcity rent, the lightly shaded area in Figure 12.1. The regulatory design determines who receives these rents.

If permits are auctioned, or a tax is used, the government receives these rents on behalf of taxpayers. Alternatively, in a permit system, the government could give the permits away to specific groups. This alternative is known as 'grandfathering'. The government could allocate permits on the basis of past usage, on some measure of output, or to politically favored groups. The US has mostly chosen this option. Prominent examples are the Acid Rain Program, the phasedown of lead in gasoline and the Reclaim Program in Los Angeles. The traditional view in the United States is that grandfathering, while inefficient, is chosen because it provides greater political control over the distributional effects of regulation (Stavins 1997). Examples of auctioned permits are new quota allocations in the New Zealand

Individual Transferable Quota system for fisheries, the Federal Commerce Commission (FCC) auctions of the telecommunications spectrum in the US, and radio spectrum auctions in New Zealand. In Europe, taxation is generally the instrument chosen for environmental regulation.

We argue that auctioned permits or taxes are superior to any form of grandfathered permits, because they allow reduced tax distortions, provide more potential flexibility in distribution of costs, and reduce the need for politically contentious arguments over the allocation of rents. In addition, grandfathering has no effect on the 'competitiveness' of the industry that receives the permits. We recognize that these arguments do not mean auctions will be chosen in the US or elsewhere. We argue, however, that they may be more compelling in the case of carbon than they have been in SO_2 and other programs, and therefore may overcome the US political economy problems.

Figure 12.1. Price, scarcity rent and dead-weight loss from carbon regulation

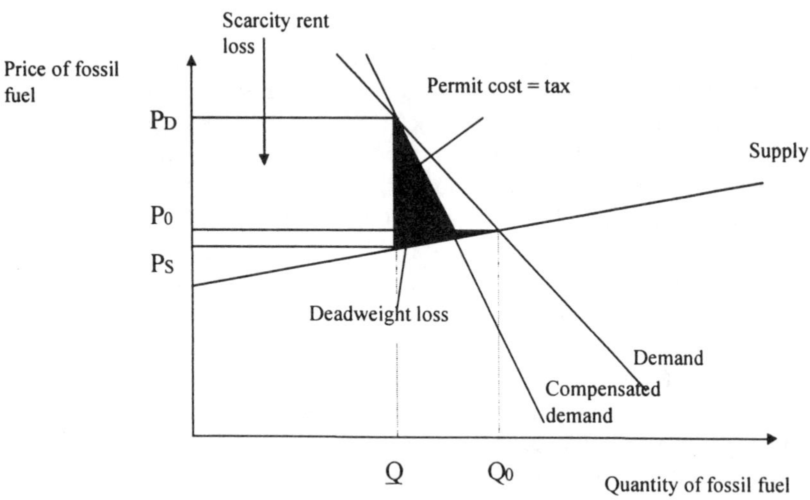

2.1 Reduced Deadweight Loss from Revenue Raising

Carbon taxes and auction revenue can replace distortionary taxes. Distortionary taxation creates a deadweight loss by inserting a wedge between marginal cost and price. The rise in marginal cost from carbon regulation implies a real cost of carbon regulation equivalent to the deadweight loss from distortionary taxation (see Figure 12.1). This unavoidable real welfare cost corresponds to a loss of US output estimated to be on the order of 0.8 percent of GDP which would have been $60 billion in 1995 (Repetto and Austin 1997). At the same time, in the US, the regulation of carbon creates scarcity rents on the order of $126 billion.

Careful use of this scarcity rent can significantly lower total costs. Ballard et al. (1985) estimate that each additional $1.00 of government revenue, raised through distortionary taxation, costs society $1.30. If we can gain revenue with no additional distortion, by auctioning rather than grandfathering, we can achieve significant efficiency gains. The revenue raised in the auction could be used to cut taxes and reduce the deficit. If the auction raises $126 billion annually, compensating tax cuts could increase US GNP by up to $40 billion. Parry et al. (1997) estimate that, if the emissions reductions are less than 23 percent, grandfathering permits, and hence losing the value of revenue recycling, would double the cost of regulation relative to a tax or auction system.

One criticism of the efficient revenue-raising argument is that government spending is not exogenous. Private sector actors often express concern that government will not use the revenue well. Raising revenue through carbon taxes or auctions may not lead to equivalent tax cuts. Preliminary work by Becker and Mulligan (1997) suggests that more efficient tax systems are associated with larger governments. If this is the case, the efficiency gain from auction revenue will depend on the actual size of the tax cuts and what is done with the additional government spending. With revenue of about $126 billion annually, Congress may be forced to use the revenue in transparent and hence relatively socially beneficial ways.

2.2 The Distributional Effects of Carbon Regulation

The distributional effects have two parts, the effects that arise through changes in prices and returns to factors, and the wealth effects of changing ownership of a resource. Ownership is being transferred from the commons to either the taxpayer, under taxes and auctions, or the recipients of grandfathered permits. The price effects, which are the most complex effects, are the same regardless of the form of carbon regulation. In particular, they are unaffected by whether permits are auctioned or grandfathered. The aggregate distributional effects depend on the sum of price and wealth effects.

2.3 Who Bears Taxes/Regulatory Costs?

Three groups ultimately bear costs: consumers, workers (owners of human capital), and capital owners, especially current owners of physical capital. Consumers suffer loss of consumer surplus, workers suffer a fall in income, and capital owners suffer a fall in the value of their capital. The legal incidence of the regulation does not affect prices or cost bearing.

Increased costs, due to the need to purchase a permit or pay a tax, are passed forward to consumers, and backward to factor suppliers, capital owners and workers. How the prices throughout the economy adjust depends on the elasticities of supply and demand at all levels in the economy. Prices will rise most where behavior is most inelastic. In Figure 12.1 we illustrate one possibility. The relatively inelastic demander faces a large price increase while the elastic supplier suffers only a small price decrease. Given a set of consumption price changes, consumers will bear costs in proportion to their expenditures on goods produced using fossil fuels.

In the short run, fossil-fuel-specific capital stocks such as oil-fired electric utilities, and the human capital and location of workers in industries such as coal mining, will tend to be inelastic. Thus capital owners and workers will suffer high short-term costs. How these price changes translate into distributional effects depends on the distribution of ownership of physical and human capital. The effects on physical capital will be diffused across many shareholders when the companies are publicly owned. The effects on workers tend to be heavily concentrated in relatively few individuals and communities.

In the long run, capital is mobile and workers will make appropriate choices of education and location. This will lower their costs as well as total costs. How long this requires depends on the rate of obsolescence of capital and how quickly individuals and communities can adjust. The outlook for some coal-mining areas is not promising. After capital and labor have adjusted, consumers bear the ongoing costs of carbon regulation.

3. WHAT DOES THE EMPIRICAL EVIDENCE SHOW?

All current US models of carbon tax incidence assume that the tax is fully passed through to consumers. Jorgenson et al. (1992) use a general equilibrium model to consider the lifetime incidence of carbon taxes through all possible channels. Dowlatabadi et al. (1994) allow for partial equilibrium responses to energy prices but consider only effects on fuel prices not on products that indirectly involve fuel use. Casler and Rafiqui (1993) consider the relative expenditure shares directly devoted to energy across the expenditure distribution. They also use an input–output framework to estimate indirect incidence through the purchase of goods produced using energy. Poterba (1990) looks simply at the relative expenditure shares on energy products.

All the models agree that the impact of the tax will be relatively, but not dramatically, regressive. The indirect effects tend to reduce the regressivity. Consumer incidence varies significantly by region. The Midwest bears the highest costs; the Pacific States bear the lowest. These models say nothing about loss of capital income and therefore loss of capital value. To do this a model would need to identify the mobility of capital in specific industries, and the owners of capital. None of the models say anything about the effects of carbon regulation on labor markets.

A number of studies of distributional effects have been done for other OECD countries using a variety of methodologies. These include Cornwell and Creedy (1996) in Australia, and in Europe, Johnson et al. (1990), OECD (1995), Smith (1992), and, in this volume, new work by Barker and Köhler. The weak regressivity of carbon regulation appears to hold across countries and modeling techniques.

Identifying the cost distribution is a non-trivial exercise. The empirical evidence suggests that costs will be slightly regressive across consumers. Theory suggests that carbon regulation will reduce the income of shareholders in parts of the energy sector, and will have impacts on immobile workers in the energy sector. Clearly more research is needed to clarify these relative effects on individuals.

3.1 How do the Distributional Effects Depend on the Choice of Auctioned Permits/Taxes vs. Grandfathered Permits?

The effect of regulation through consumer prices and factor returns distributes costs in the same way in a tax or auctioned permit program as in a grandfathered program. All efficient forms of regulation lead to a distribution of costs that is determined by general equilibrium cost incidence, factor endowments and consumption patterns. Those heavily dependent on fossil fuels in their consumption patterns or for capital or wage income will bear more costs. Groups that respond significantly and rapidly to the pressure to reduce fossil fuel use will be rewarded by lower shares of costs. The wealth effects from grandfathering and the use of tax/auction revenue determine how the ultimate distribution of costs varies among the options.

Auction/tax revenue can be used in a multitude of ways, benefiting many different groups. Labor, consumption, payroll or capital gains taxes could be cut. The deficit could be reduced. Expenditure could be targeted at afflicted workers and communities to compensate and assist during the transition to a less carbon–intensive economy. Only the political process and the normal constraints on redistribution limit the flexibility of compensation under auctions. In addition, the revenue-recycling benefits reduce total costs.

In contrast, grandfathering permits redistributes wealth only to shareholders. Only those who directly receive permits gain because it produces a pure wealth effect. Grandfathering is usually used to compensate some current owners of specific capital. These owners can be adequately and more efficiently compensated, through targeted tax breaks. These not only provide direct compensation, but also increase the efficiency of the industry by reducing tax distortions. It would be theoretically possible to grandfather the permits to a wide range of workers, consumers and capital owners. This would be costly and complex to administer, however, and would forsake the efficiency benefits of a tax/auction program that returns the revenues through broad–based tax cuts.

Taxes and auctioned permits are more likely to lead to equitable outcomes than grandfathered permits. Cost bearing is widely spread and, in the long run, all costs are borne by consumers. Therefore compensation should also be widely spread. Poorer people tend to be workers and consumers more than they are shareholders, so they are unlikely to benefit from grandfathering.

3.2 'Competitiveness' and Grandfathering

Within Europe, many believe that if US firms are grandfathered carbon permits rather than having to buy them in auctions, they will have a competitive advantage *vis-à-vis* European firms which are likely to face carbon taxes. Some in the US believe the same. This is based on a misunderstanding of permit markets and grandfathering.

Grandfathering gives permits to firms based on past behavior, not current or future. If a firm increases its production to export more, and uses more carbon in doing so, it must either pay more tax, or it requires more permits. If permits are auctioned, it will need to buy more or draw down banked reserves. If permits are grandfathered, it will need to use up some of the stock it holds. In every case, the opportunity cost of increasing output is the cost of the permit or equivalently, the tax. If the firm reduces production, it saves the opportunity cost of the permit price, it avoids the tax or need to buy permits, or can sell the permits it was grandfathered. The grandfathering of permits makes the owners of the firm wealthier, but does not change their marginal production costs.

In fact, the US economy as a whole will be disadvantaged if grandfathering is used because of the loss of efficiency gains that could be achieved through revenue recycling. This will lower US productivity and make it harder for US firms to compete.

3.3 How to Design Carbon Permit Auctions

Government often has two goals when designing an auction, first to allocate the permits efficiently, and second to maximize its revenue. Fortunately, these goals are closely aligned. An efficient auction will raise substantial revenues.

3.4 What is a 'Carbon Permit'?

With carbon permits it is easy to define the items being auctioned. Each permit is for one metric ton of carbon usage. Oil refineries, natural-gas pipelines, natural-gas liquid sellers and coal-processing plants require permits. All permits are the same after their date of issue, and permits are bankable; that is, a permit issued for the year 2000 can be used in any later year. There is no environmental loss in making permits bankable. Current carbon emissions are reduced to the extent that permits are banked. Given the long lifetime of CO_2 in the atmosphere, short-term voluntary banking is unlikely to have significant impacts on CO_2 concentrations.

Permits can and should be auctioned not only for the current years but also for future issue years. Thus, some permits for 2012 could be auctioned in 2008 even though they cannot be used to offset carbon emissions until after 1 January 2012. Early auctions would facilitate the development of an active futures and options market, thus improving risk allocation.

The homogeneity and bankability of permits makes the auction and secondary market very liquid. The more liquid the issue is, the lower is the transaction cost. Illiquidity not only costs the seller money, but it also reduces auction efficiency. Illiquidity increases the risk that some bidders may have market power in certain circumstances.

Market power should not be a concern in an auction for carbon permits. Even in an upstream program, there would still be more than 1,700 permit buyers. Most importantly, even the largest buyers would constitute just a tiny fraction of the market, as is seen in Table 12.1. The table shows the shares of permits each part of the energy sector would have demanded if an upstream permit market had been introduced in 1995. No one firm will control more than 6 percent of the market. In addition, in the active secondary market many more buyers will participate as speculators. It is inconceivable that any party would be successful in exercising substantial market power in the US market for carbon permits. This may not be true in smaller countries with more concentrated industries. Still, substantial distortions from market power are unlikely even with only a few traders (Tietenberg 1985), and will disappear completely with trading among developed countries.

3.5 Ways to Auction Many Identical Items

Auctioning many identical items is a common, relatively well understood situation. In the permit market setting, a seller is offering a fixed supply of identical items. The buyers submit bids at auction to express their willingness to buy various quantities at various price levels. Auctions need to be held frequently enough to reduce cash flow problems and ensure that firms will have a good idea of their likely needs. Quarterly auctions, as in Treasury auctions, would suffice. Of course, with an active secondary market, firms can buy almost any quantity of permits at any time.

Table 12.1. Carbon permit needs across US firms – direct permit market players

Carbon user	Total carbon produced in 1995 (million metric tons)	% of permit market
Oil industry[1] (175 refineries)	436	31.1
Largest oil company (Chevron)	31.1	2.3
Second largest (Exxon)	28.7	2.0
Largest 10 oil companies	226.7	16.2
Coal industry[2] (550 coal preparation plants)	610	43.5
Largest coal producer (Peabody Holdings)	79.3	5.6
Largest 3 companies	158.6	11.2
Natural gas industry[3] (250 natural gas pipeline companies and 725 natural gas processing plants)	356	25.4
Total	1,402	100

Notes: 1. US Department of Energy, Energy Information Administration (1996).
2. US Department of Energy, Energy Information Administration (1997).
3. US Department of Energy, Energy Information Administration.

We first discuss the more familiar sealed-bid auctions. We then explain the advantages of ascending-bid auctions, and specifically the standard ascending-clock auction.

3.6 Sealed-bid Auctions

In sealed-bid auctions, the bidders simultaneously submit demand schedules. The auctioneer adds these demand schedules to form the aggregate demand curve. A sample demand curve appears in Figure 12.2. The intersection of the aggregate demand curve and the supply curve determines the clearing price. All demands above this clearing price are filled, those at the clearing price are rationed, and those below are rejected.

The two most common pricing methods are uniform pricing and pay-your-bid pricing. Under uniform pricing, each winner pays the clearing price p^* for each permit. With pay-your-bid pricing, each winner pays its bid. The two approaches lead to quite different bidding behavior. With a uniform price, bidders with market power may bid below their true value in an attempt to influence the market price. With pay-your-bid pricing, the bidder attempts to guess where the clearing price is likely to fall and then bids slightly above it. Bids in excess of the clearing price are money left on the table. With uniform pricing, predicting the clearing price is less important, since every winner pays the clearing price regardless of how high it bids. Permits will not be fully efficiently allocated under either pricing rule. Buyers will not always truthfully reveal their valuations. This strategic bidding leads to inefficiency (Ausubel and Cramton 1996).

Figure 12.2. Sample demand curve

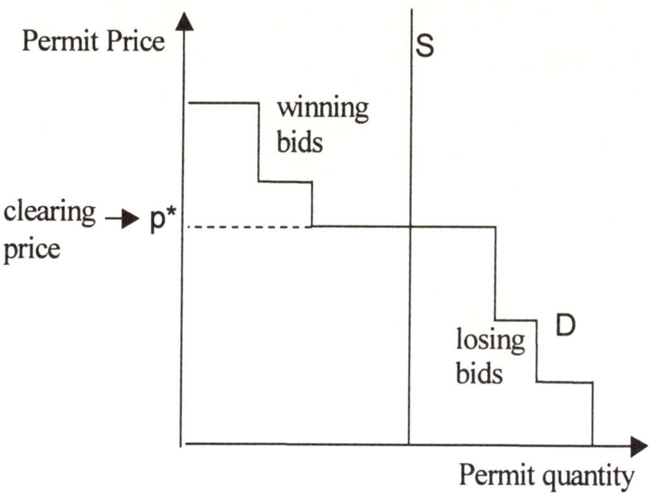

Comparing these sealed-bid auctions is difficult, even in the setting with private values. The inefficiency from uniform pricing depends on the extent of market power. When no bidder has significant market power, uniform pricing is nearly efficient in a private value setting. Relative to pay-your-bid pricing, uniform pricing has the benefit that everyone pays the same price. Uniform pricing is strategically simple for small bidders and they benefit from the demand reduction by the large bidders. This encourages participation by small bidders. In contrast, pay-your-bid pricing exposes small bidders to strategic risk, since they may be less able to gauge the probable level of the clearing price. Hence, among the sealed-bid auctions, a uniform-price auction probably is best for the case of carbon permits.

3.7 Ascending Auctions

A primary advantage of ascending auctions is a reliable process of price discovery. Both price and allocation are determined through a process of open competition. Each bidder has every opportunity to improve its bids, changing losing bids into winning bids. In the end, all buyers have good information about price and those willing to pay the most win the permits. An ascending process is especially desirable when bidders' valuations depend on information held by others. Then the bidding process reveals information, which improves the bidders' valuation estimates. In the early years of carbon regulation, when elasticities are uncertain, and the feasibility and cost of new technologies is changing rapidly, improved information will have major efficiency impacts. Despite its failures, one benefit of the government conducted SO_2 auction, in the US Acid Rain Program, was to focus attention on the permit price and reveal information (Joskow et al. 1996). The auction price was much lower than expected but ended up being a much better predictor of future permit prices than any of the model estimates.

Multi-unit ascending auctions can be conducted in two basic ways: with demand schedules or with an ascending clock. The demand schedule approach is a multi-round version of the sealed-bid auction. Iterations stop when no bidder is willing to improve its bids. Pricing can be either uniform or pay-your-bid as in sealed-bid auctions. Here, however, the market power problems arising from the use of a uniform price are exacerbated by the undesirable ability to use bids to signal during early rounds. The strategic risk arising from pay-your-bid pricing is diminished by the price discovery process. Thus, of the two, the pay-your-bid is preferred. The ascending-clock auction, however, is simpler and even more efficient in this situation.

3.8 Ascending-clock Auction

In each round, the bidders submit the quantity they are willing to buy at the price indicated by the clock. The clock is increased if the total quantity bid exceeds the quantity available. The bidding continues until the quantity available exceeds the quantity bid. The permits are then allocated at the prior price, and are rationed for those who reduced their quantity in the last round. An activity rule is needed to promote reliable price discovery. The activity rule forces the bidders to bid in a way that is consistent with a downward-sloping demand curve. This prevents bidders from holding back initially and then submitting large bids after the other bidders have revealed their information. The activity rule in this case is simply that each bidder cannot increase its quantity as prices rise.

This design shares all the price discovery advantages of all ascending auctions, avoids the undesirable bid signaling which is possible with uniform-price ascending auctions, and has several additional advantages relative to the pay-your-bid ascending auction. Because a buyer only bids a single quantity, rather than a schedule, it is easier to implement. It yields a single market-clearing price yet avoids the mechanism for collusion under a sealed-bid uniform-price auction. Rapid convergence is guaranteed, since the price increases by one bid increment with each round of bidding.

It is still not perfectly efficient, if there is market power, because buyers shade their bids to lower the price. They will shade them differently depending on their size. Large bidders win too little and small bidders win too much. However, in this setting where market power is apt to be slight, the inefficiencies from a standard ascending-clock auction are likely to be insignificant.

In conclusion, auctioning carbon permits is simple and efficient. As a result of communications advances, ascending auctions are now easy to implement through the Internet. We prefer the ascending-clock auction, primarily because of its advantages in price discovery, but a sealed-bid uniform-price auction will also operate well.

4. CONCLUSION

Different forms of regulation will suit different countries. To control climate change, and comply with the new commitments under the FCC, two efficient instruments can be used, taxes and permits. Because the climate agreement is framed as a quantity not price control, and because it has such a long time frame, the usual price/quantity distinction between taxes and permits is not so critical. Other distinctions remain. The political economy of taxes contrasts strongly with that of permits, particularly in the United States. Taxes and permits require slightly different administrative, and private sector, infrastructure. They have different inter-temporal and risk-sharing qualities.

The focus of this chapter has been on the revenue and distributional effects of carbon taxes and carbon permits. Carbon taxes raise revenue in an efficient way. In their most commonly used forms, taxes and permits have very different distributional effects. Carbon taxes, with compensating tax cuts or public expenditures are considerably more equitable than grandfathered permits. However, as we have shown, auctioned permits can achieve the same equitable distribution and can provide an equally efficient revenue source. In addition, we have shown that auctions are feasible.

The ability to use auctioned permits broadens the menu of instruments available to the regulator. In a country where taxation is politically unacceptable, or the specific political economy requires some amount of grandfathering to buy off vested interests, or the high level of private sector involvement of a permit market is desired, auctions allow the equity and efficiency benefits of a tax to be achieved within a carbon permit market. This may allow a country such as the US to regulate efficiently despite the political resistance to taxation. Even if permits were partially grandfathered in the short run, the mechanism to move toward broader distribution of costs through auctions would be available and could be phased in gradually.

In Europe, recognition of the possibility of auctioning the majority of permits may allow some countries to adopt permits rather than taxation. They may be able to buy off powerful interests with some grandfathered permits, while replacing the tax with auctioned permits in other sectors. This may solve some of the political problems that currently lead to exclusion of some important sectors from carbon taxes. Short-term losses from grandfathering may be rapidly outweighed by the efficiency advantages of a comprehensive regulation.

Finally, as the world moves toward some form of carbon trading among developed countries, and in the future developing countries, domestic permit trading may facilitate more efficient international trading. Countries that have begun regulation with taxation may be able to move relatively seamlessly to an auctioned permit system without serious concerns about redistribution. Recognition of the true effects of grandfathered and auctioned permits relative to taxes may reduce the concerns about competitiveness, which currently plague international trading negotiations.

REFERENCES

Atkinson A. and J. Stiglitz (1980), *Lectures in Public Economics*, New York: McGraw-Hill.

Ausubel, Lawrence M. (1996), 'An Efficient Ascending-bid Auction for Multiple Objects', Working Paper, University of Maryland.

Ausubel, Lawrence M. and Peter C. Cramton (1996), 'Demand Reduction and Inefficiency in Multi-unit Auctions', Working Paper No. 96-07, University of Maryland.

Back, Kerry and Jaime F. Zender (1993), 'Auctions of Divisible Goods: On the Rationale for the Treasury Experiment', *Review of Financial Studies*, **6**, 733–64.

Ballard, Charles L., John B. Shoven and John Whalley (1985), 'General Equilibrium Computations of the Marginal Welfare Costs of Taxes in the United States', *American Economic Review*, **75**, 128–38.

Barker, Terry and Jonathan Köhler (1997), 'Equity and Ecotax Reform in the EU: achieving a 10% Reduction in CO_2 Emissions Using Excise Duties', Environmental Fiscal Reform Working Paper No. 10, Department of Applied Economics, University of Cambridge, UK.

Becker, Gary S. and Casey B. Mulligan (1997), 'Efficient Taxes, Efficient Spending, and Big Government' Draft, University of Chicago.

Casler, Stephen D. and Aisha Rafiqui (1993), 'Evaluating Fuel Tax Equity: Direct and Indirect Distributional Effects', *National Tax Journal*, **46**(2), 197–205.

Cason, Timothy N. (1995), 'An Experimental Investigation of the Seller Incentives in EPA's Emission Trading Auction', *American Economic Review*, **85**, 905–22.

Cason, Timothy N. and Charles R. Plott (1996), 'EPA's New Emissions Trading Mechanism: A Laboratory Evaluation', *Journal of Environmental Economics and Management*, **30**, 133–60.

Center for Clean Air Policy (1997), 'U.S. Greenhouse Gas Emissions Trading: Description of an Upstream Approach' Draft Paper, Airlie Papers, September.

Cline, William (1991), *The Economics of Global Warming*, Washington, DC: Institute of International Economics.

Clinton, President (1997), 'Remarks by the President on Global Climate Change', National Geographic Society, Washington, DC, 22 October.

Cornwell, A. and J. Creedy (1996), 'Carbon Taxation, Prices, and Inequality in Australia', *Fiscal Studies*, **17**(3), 21–38.

Dowlatabadi, Kopp R. and Tschang (1994), 'Distributional and Environmental Consequences of Taxes on Energy', Resources for the Future Discussion Paper 94-19, March.

Feldstein, Martin S. (1977), 'The Surprising Incidence of a Tax on Pure Rent: A New Answer to an Old Question', *Journal of Political Economy*, **85**(2), April, 349–60.

Fischer, Carolyn (1997), 'An Economic Analysis of Output-based Allocation of Emissions Allowances', Draft Paper, Resources for the Future, Washington, DC.

Gaskins, D.W. and J.P. Weyant (1993), 'Model Comparisons of the Costs of Reducing CO_2 Emissions', *American Economic Review*, AEA Papers and Proceedings, **83**(2), 318–23.

Johnson, P., S. McKay and S. Smith (1990), 'The Distributional Consequences of Environmental Taxes', Commentary No. 23, London: IFS.

Jorgenson, Dale W., Daniel T. Slesnick and Peter J. Wilcoxen (1992), *Carbon Taxes and Economic Welfare*, Brookings Papers: Microeconomics.

Jorgenson, Dale W. and Peter J. Wilcoxen (1992), 'Reducing U.S. Carbon Dioxide Emissions: The Cost of Different Goals', in John R. Moroney (ed.), *Advances in the Economics of Energy and Natural Resources*, Vol. 7 JAI Press: Greenwich, Connecticut.

Joskow, Paul L., and Richard Schmalensee (1998), 'The Political Economy of Market-based Environmental Policy: The U.S. Acid Rain Program', *Journal of Law and Economics*, **41**(1), 37–83.

Joskow, Paul L., Richard Schmalensee and Elizabeth M. Bailey (1996), 'Auction Design and the Market for Sulfur Dioxide Emissions', Working Paper, MIT-CEEPR 96-007WP.

Kerr, Suzi (1998), 'Uncertainty, Renegotiation, and the Design of a Carbon Trading Program', Draft Paper, Resources for the Future.

Manne, Alan S. and Richard G. Richels (1992), *Buying Greenhouse Insurance: The Economic Costs of CO_2 Emission Limits*, Cambridge, Massachusetts: MIT Press.

Milliman Scott R. and Raymond Prince (1989), 'Firm Incentives to Promote Technological Change in Pollution Control', *Journal of Environmental Economics and* Management **17**, 247–65.

Noll, Roger G. (1989), 'Economic Perspectives on the Politics of Regulation' in *Handbook of Industrial Organization*, Vol. II, R. Schmalensee and R.D. Willig (eds), Elsevier: Amsterdam, 1234–87.

Nordhaus, William D. (1991), 'The Cost of Slowing Climate Change: A Survey' *Energy Journal*, **12**(1).

Nordhaus, William D. (1994), *Managing the Global Commons: The Economics of Climate Change*, Cambridge, Massachusetts: MIT Press.

OECD (1995), *Climate Change, Economic Instruments and Income Distribution*, Paris: OECD.

Parry, Ian W. (1995), 'Pollution Taxes and Revenue Recycling', *Journal of Environmental Economics and Management*, **29**(3), S64–77.

Parry, Ian W.H., Robertson C. Williams, Dallas Burtraw and Lawrence H. Goulder (1997), 'The Cost Effectiveness of Alternative Instruments for Environmental Protection in a Second-best Setting', Paper presented at NBER Summer Institute Workshop on Public Policy and the Environment, Cambridge, Massachusetts, August.

Poterba, James (1990), 'Is the Gasoline Tax Regressive?', MIT Working Paper 586, November.

Poterba, James (1991), 'Tax Policy to Combat Global Warming: On Designing a Carbon Tax', in Rudiger Dornbusch and James Poterba (eds) *Global Warming: Economic Policy Responses*, Cambridge, Massachusetts: MIT Press.

Repetto, Robert and Duncan Austin (1997), *The Costs of Climate Protection: A Guide for the Perplexed*, Washington, DC: World Resources Institute.

Smith, S. (1992), 'The Distributional Consequences of Taxes on Energy and the Carbon Content of Fuels', *European Economy Special Edition 1992*, No. 1, The Economics of Limiting CO_2 Emissions.

Stavins, Robert N. (1997), 'What Can We Learn from the Grand Policy Experiment? Positive and Normative Lessons from SO_2 Allowance Trading', *Journal of Economic Perspectives*, **12**(3), 69–88.

Tietenberg, Tom (1985), *Emissions Trading: An Exercise in Reforming Pollution Policy*, Washington, DC: Resources for the Future.

US Department of Energy, Energy Information Administration (1996), *Petroleum Supply Annual.*

US Department of Energy, Energy Information Administration (1997) 'Coal Production Industry Profile' Unpublished Report.

US Department of Energy, Energy Information Administration 'Oil and Gas Production Industry Profile' Unpublished Report.

Van Dyke, Brennan (1991), 'Emissions Trading to Reduce Acid Deposition' *Yale Law Journal*, **100**, 2707–26.

Vickrey, William (1961), 'Counterspeculation, Auctions, and Competitive Sealed Tenders', *Journal of Finance*, **16**, 8–37.

Wilson, Robert (1979), 'Auction of Shares', *Quarterly Journal of Economics*, **94**, 675–689.

13. Market-based Instruments for Environmental Policy in Developing Countries – from Theory to Practice with a Case Study of Sri Lanka's Recent Experience

Paul Steele

1. THE THEORY OF MARKET-BASED INSTRUMENTS

Market-based instruments (MBIs) are defined in this chapter as any policy which seeks to pass on the economic costs of environmental damage through the market mechanism. So economic incentives or market-based instruments (MBIs) are generic terms to describe a whole range of policy reforms that use the 'market' through either prices or ownership to provide incentives for sound environmental management. This is a broader definition than the simple extreme case of a pollution charge, and includes deposit refunds, resource rent taxes and environmentally beneficial subsidies.

MBIs have a different emphasis from the traditional regulatory approach, known as command and control (CAC) which focus on legal remedies for environmental management. CAC controls are mandatory with a legal limit on quantities of environmental damage. By contrast, MBIs are 'voluntary' since although the pollution charge must be paid, the firm or individual can choose whether to change their behaviour and reduce environmental damage in response to the charge.

This difference between MBIs and CAC gives rise to a number of theoretical advantages, which have been highlighted by the growing literature of environmental economics. The major advantages are the efficiency gains of MBIs and their potential to generate funds. The efficiency gains are both static and dynamic. Static efficiency arises because if society's scarce resources have to be allocated among competing users, then prices are more efficient than quantity rationing. Thus raising water prices is a more efficient way of reducing water demand than simple water rationing, or exhortations to use less water. The government does not need to know the cost curve for each water consumer as it would for efficient rationing; it simply sets the price and lets each consumer decide whether it is better to pay the high water fee or not.

The dynamic efficiency gains arise since market-based instruments provide continual incentives for reduced natural resource consumption and declining environmental damage. Returning to the simple example of water, once firms have complied with their water rationing, then they face no further incentive to reduce water demand. By contrast with a higher water price, they face a continual incentive to reduce demand until their cost of water saving is equal to the water price.

The revenue-raising potential of MBIs is advantageous since taxes on 'bads' such as resource use and pollution is economically optimal since it corrects a 'market failure', unlike conventional taxation on saving or labour, which has negative impacts on economic behaviour. In addition, the revenue from MBIs can be 'earmarked' to use for environmentally beneficial uses. Thus revenue raised from higher water charges can be used to invest in water-saving technologies.

2. MARKET-BASED INSTRUMENTS IN DEVELOPING COUNTRIES – FROM THEORY TO PRACTICE

In practice, the simple theoretical picture of the environmental economic textbook has some major shortcomings, particularly when applied to developing countries. This is for four main reasons. First, the simple distinction between voluntary and economic-related MBIs and legal and mandatory CAC is blurred in practice. Regulations with fines as penalties also have an 'economic' component, and many so-called economic incentives require legal support in that non-payment of the user fee or tax will result in some legal remedy, such as disconnection or ultimately imprisonment. Thus in practice, regulations with a high penalty attached may create more of an incentive for compliance than a low pollution tax. It is for this reason that non-compliance fees are considered in this chapter as a form of market-based instrument.

Thus the difference between market-based instruments and so-called command and control (CAC) policies is not always clear cut. There is a continuum running between the most extreme MBI of a Pigouvian tax to the most extreme CAC of a ban on some environmentally damaging activity. In between come non-compliance fines, subsidy removal, deposit refunds, user charges and environmental taxes.

The second major shortcoming from the textbook view is that in practice, few countries have prices that equal marginal private cost, so consideration of adding external social costs to price is a long way off. As a first step it is vital to ensure that price is equal to marginal cost by removing any environmentally damaging subsidies. Only then can the next step be taken to internalize environmental externalities by ensuring that price is equal to marginal social cost (or marginal social benefit) (Steele and Pearce 1994). Given this practical reality of underpricing, this chapter devotes most space to the removal of environmentally damaging subsidies through rises in user charges, removal of implicit subsidies through import controls and increases in resource rents.

The third major shortcoming with the textbook view is that it ignores the many political and institutional objections to market-based instruments. The most widespread of these is the perception that MBIs are regressive since they have an undue impact on poor households. This perception can be challenged and it is directly addressed in a later section of this chapter. However the fact remains that price rises are politically risky in a way that command and control regulations are not. This is mainly because of the very visible income effects of a price rise, compared with the much less transparent effects of regulations. There is also the related issue of rent seeking to retain environmentally damaging subsidies, which often uses the claims of impacts on the poor as a specious argument to justify existing subsidies. However, more research is needed both to test and if necessary challenge the regressivity hypothesis.

The fourth shortcoming with the traditional textbook view of MBIs is the focus on their efficiency gains over CAC regulations. While this is theoretically interesting, it misses the much more important practical point that subsidy removal saves revenue and pollution taxes generate revenue. For developing country governments facing budget pressures and state utilities being privatized this makes MBIs very attractive. It is the revenue-raising advantages of MBIs much more than their efficiency gains, which has been most responsible for their application in developing countries. If more research was available on this revenue-raising potential of MBIs, then their application might have been more widespread.

This chapter tries to remedy some of the perceived shortcomings of the more theoretical approach to market-based instruments by an empirical study of Sri Lanka, where a number of them have recently been implemented.

3. ECONOMIC–ENVIRONMENTAL LINKAGES IN SRI LANKA

Sri Lanka's rich tropical ecosystem is facing growing pressures from the drive for economic growth for the population of almost 18 million. Per capita income was estimated at $700 in 1997 and about one-third of the population is currently living in absolute poverty. However, despite the war situation in the north and east, the economy continues to grow at about 4 percent a year.

While current government policy emphasizes manufactured output, Sri Lanka's economy remains heavily dependent on natural resources. The main natural resource-dependent sectors are (with contribution to GNP in brackets): agriculture (17.6 percent), fisheries (1.8 percent), mining (2.5 percent), forestry (1.4 percent), tree crop processing (2.3 percent) and tourism (about 3 percent).

Together these sectors made up 28.6 percent of GNP in 1994 (Central Bank 1995). In addition, hydropower provides for over 90 percent of Sri Lanka's electricity. Thus even using conventional measures of GNP, Sri Lanka's dependence on natural resources is high, contributing between one quarter and one third of total GNP. This natural resource dependence also has implications for poverty alleviation since it is the rural and urban poor that are most dependent on natural resources for their livelihood. The poor are more likely to use wells or rivers for water, biomass for cooking, and mud and other natural resources for building materials.

Sri Lanka has rich water and land resources with a central mountainous plateau from which over 100 rivers drain. The country experiences two monsoons a year, although the rainfall is concentrated in the southwest of the country. This wide range of temperature and altitude in an island of only 6.5 million ha, has given Sri Lanka the highest density of biodiversity per unit of area in Asia. For example, 26 percent of the species of flowering plants, 76 percent of land snails, 60 percent of amphibians and 49 percent of reptile species found in the country, exist nowhere else.

With the expansion of the economy, the main environmental problems include soil erosion, mining of groundwater aquifers, deforestation in catchment areas, loss of flood-absorbing wetlands, untreated sewerage and solid waste in urban areas and pesticide run-off in rural areas.

While many of these problems are common to developing tropical economies, they can be reduced through appropriate policies, which seek to encourage economic growth while reducing impacts on the environment. This chapter seeks to identify the role of market-based incentives in this search for the right policy package.

4. ENVIRONMENTAL POLICY IN SRI LANKA: COMMAND AND CONTROL AND MARKET-BASED INSTRUMENTS

Traditionally, environmental policy in Sri Lanka has been dominated by command and control through the legal, regulatory and planning approach.

Even in the Constitution, Clause 28 states that: 'it is the duty of every person in Sri Lanka to protect nature and conserve its riches'. Sri Lanka, in common with many countries in South Asia, has very extensive environmental legislation, with many acts overlapping and even contradicting one another. Some of this, such as the Forestry Act, dates from the British colonial administration before independence in 1948. The bulk, however, came more recently, including the Coast Conservation Act of 1980, the National Aquatic Resources Act of 1981, and the National Environmental Act (1980 and amended in 1988).

The problem lies in the implementation of this legislation. Most acts follow the British colonial legacy in defining the state as the owner of resources with a strong enforcement mentality. Only very recently has the idea of a more participatory view of natural resource management developed. This ineffective 'policeman' approach of most environmental regulations combined with the budgetary constraints of the state have made most environmental laws unenforceable.

In response to these perceived failures as well as more general fiscal pressures, the government is focusing on the need to consider so-called market-based instruments in environmental policy. This has been institutionalized in the latest draft of the country's National Environmental Action Plan, which explicitly required the major sectoral assessments to consider 'the role of economic incentives' in improving environmental policy. This exercise has generated a number of important and innovative ways to introduce MBIs into the key environmental related sectors. Examples include selected subsidies for watershed conservation, proposals to reduce export restrictions on erosive crops and introducing a waste user fee. As a first step, the Ministry of Forestry and the Environment is sponsoring research with donor assistance on Economic–Environmental linkages. So far 19 different studies by Sri Lankan universities and other institutions are under way.

In this context, it is curious to note that Sri Lanka provides perhaps the world's first documented example of an environmental tax with an inscription outside the ancient ruined city of Anuradhapura from AD 65 stating that fisheries in large reservoirs were owned by the King and those he allowed to fish paid a tax.

In addition to this explicit focus on MBIs for environmental purposes, a number of market-based-type instruments have been adopted for more 'fiscal' macroeconomic reasons. Examples include price rises for gasoline, water and electricity, and the reduction of fishing subsidies.

The next section reviews key examples of MBIs with selected case studies of MBIs recently introduced, highlighting their environmental impacts, and some shortcomings in their effectiveness.

5. INCREASED NON-COMPLIANCE FEES

Non-compliance fees are related to CAC instruments in that they are generally fines levied for not complying with an environmental regulation. However, they have an economic impact depending on the extent to which the fine provides an economic incentive not to damage the environment. For this reason, non-compliance fees are considered in this review of MBIs.

Sri Lanka generally has suffered from low levels of non-compliance fees; thus incentives for compliance are reduced. This is partly the result of poor legal drafting as the level of the fine is included in the main body of the environmental law, instead of being set in separate regulations. The result of this is that since acts are only updated every ten years or so, the fines are swiftly made unrealistic due to inflation.

5.1 Case Study of Raising Non-compliance Fees: Increased and More Targeted Timber Fines

There are a whole host of forestry-related environmental laws, with some of the most important being bans on the illegal felling and transport of timber. However, until recently this system was enforced in a very bureaucratic fashion, with very low rates for those caught offending. A survey in one district of the country found that the value of the timber captured was significantly higher than the fines imposed. This provides little incentive against illegal timber extraction, particularly for the large illegal-logging operators. The fines may even have a negative incentive on afforestation as the regulations apply not only to trees illegally removed from the forest, but also to trees grown in homesteads for food and timber. Because of the difficulty of receiving a permit to fell and transport such legally grown trees, farmers are more reluctant to grow them.

In response to these shortcomings, a number of reforms are under way. The first reform which took place was to allow part of the timber fine to go towards those who detect the illegal timber. This provided forest officers and even local communities with much greater incentives to detect illegal logging.

The second reform was to raise timber fines. This has been done in the latest set of forestry regulations. The third and still controversial reform is to focus the regulations on those species of timber found only in the natural forest. This reform has been accepted on a technical level, but only partially implemented. One reason may be that those officers who currently require additional payments (or bribes) to issue a timber permit will lose out if these reforms were introduced to streamline the permit procedure. The environmental impacts of these reforms are unclear but, according to the data from the Forestry Department, detection of illegal logging is increasing. This would be expected if a simplified set of effective regulations allow forestry officers to focus on large-scale illegal deforestation.

6. RISE IN USER CHARGES FOR ENVIRONMENTALLY RELATED SERVICES

Until recently, many environmentally related goods and services were underpriced because of subsidies. Examples include water, electricity, sewage and waste collection, and are shown in Table 13.1. The subsidies were generally provided to residential consumers, often through a cross-subsidy financed by higher prices for business customers. Table 13.1 shows that the data available indicates that subsidies to farmers through the fertilizer subsidy have been the largest (US$27 million consumption subsidy in 1995), followed by the subsidy to domestic electricity consumers (US$18 million in 1992). There are also major capital subsidies to road users (capital subsidy of US$140 million), and to new water consumers (capital subsidy of about US$20 million per year). While the data is insufficient and for different base years, it does indicate the relative size of various subsidies.

The negative effects of these subsidies appear in the lack of funds for vital environmental infrastructure such as sewage and waste collection and disposal. There is growing concern over the lack of proper sewage collection and treatment in the Colombo Urban Area (CUA). The only large conventional sewage system within the CUA is that serving the Colombo Municipal Council (CMC) with main sewer extensions to Kolonawa MC and Dehiwala–Mt Lavinia MC. However this is discharged without any treatment by two ocean outfalls, and the system is not working adequately due to lack of maintenance, undercapacity and illegal connections. Presently about 482,000 people (about 25 percent of CUA) are connected to the sewage system. A further 60–65 percent are served by local sanitation systems (mainly septic tanks) and it is estimated that 10–15 percent of the total population in CUA has no sanitation facilities at all, primarily in low-income areas. The environmental impact of this is that in most of the canals and urban waterways of Colombo household pollution is the major source of organic pollution, with industrial pollution playing only a marginal role (UDA 1994).

Currently the sewage system of Colombo is financed partially by local government property taxes. But this covers a very small share of the true costs, hence the lack of maintenance or expansion. To fund improvements it is recommended that realistic targets for cost recovery are set, as well as for coverage of O&M costs and debt servicing. Three sources for funds have been identified: water bill surcharges on the bills for consumers connected to the system, more realistic property tax revenues and billing of local governments connected to the system.

Table 13.1. Underpricing of environmental-related goods and services

	Current pricing policy	Estimated subsidy
Electricity	Price recently raised but still below marginal cost	Cross-subsidy of O&M costs to domestic consumers in 1992 of Rs 900 million (US$18 million)
Domestic pipe-borne water	Price still below marginal cost for most domestic consumers, financed by cross-subsidy	Cross-subsidy in O&M to domestic consumers. Capital subsidy of about 1,000 million per year (US$20 million)
Sewage	Price not fully charged, financed partially out of local taxes	Rs 4,500 (US$90 million) million soft loan for expansion of sewer system in Colombo now under way
Waste collection and disposal	Price not fully covered, financed out of local taxes	Rs 62 million (US$1.2 million) per year spent by CMC, or about Rs 600 per household per year, rates generally less than Rs 300 per year
Irrigation water	Area based irrigation tax not properly collected	Subsidy of Rs 7/acre or Rs 10–15 million per year in 1996 (US$200,000–300,000)
Fertilizer	Fertilizer subsidised by 30% of world price levels since 1994	Total subsidy in 1995 was Rs 1.34 billion (US$27 million)
Roads	Only partially covered by vehicle revenue licence	Road-building plans in Colombo estimated as capital costs of Rs 7,000 billion (US$140 million)
Fishing boats	Coastal fisheries heavily subsidized until 1990s	Capital subsidy of about Rs 100–150 million per year (US$2–3 million) in 1980s

Note: Rs 50 = US$1 (average exchange rate during 1996/97).

The same lack of funding affects solid waste management. The Colombo Municipal Council has the right to collect a sum of Rs 100 per half barrel of garbage from an industrial site. However, of the 47 wards, only six wards were able to implement the regulation. The Municipal Council can also charge Rs 100 from each household when demolished building materials or felled trees are collected, but again this is poorly enforced (De Silva 1989).

The environmental effects are that there are no funds to develop a proper waste management system. Waste, including toxic waste is dumped in open dumps in residential neighbourhoods, leading to pollution of wells, flooding and the spread of diseases through mosquitoes, flies and vermin.

There are also environmental effects of water pricing since there is a cross-subsidy in place whereby domestic consumers pay rates of Rs 0.85 for 10-20 m^3 per month while commercial rates are Rs 11 per m^3 and hotels Rs 25 per m^3. The result is that urban consumers who are subsidized generally have high levels of usage of about 150 litres per capita per day. While hotels and commercial establishments prefer to avoid the relatively high rates altogether and so dig their own tubewells (ADB 1994). This indiscriminate and completely unregulated tubewell digging has led to problems of lowering the water table in coastal areas where there are large numbers of hotels. Thus all sources of water need to be properly priced. The current situation of charging higher prices for surface water, while leaving groundwater unpriced (other than the private cost of pumping), can be counterproductive.

The environmental effect of electricity pricing and the linkages with the environment are more complex still. The main factor is the environmental impacts of using other fuel sources and to what extent consumers switch to these other sources as electricity prices rise. At present only about 45 percent of the population has access to electricity, mostly used for lighting, while the remainder are largely dependent on kerosene for lighting, but kerosene has no major environmental impact. The more important environmental impact would arise with small-scale industry, which might be tempted to switch to unsustainable timber sources if electricity prices rose. However, a survey carried out in 1984 (Wijemanne et al.) found that those who did use electricity did so because it saved labour costs and improved the quality of output. The main issue was the relative price comparison between electricity and the wage rate. As wage rates have risen substantially this might offset any rise in electricity costs. As Wijemanne et al. state: 'There is little possibility of substitution between electricity and other sources of energy in the firms covered by the survey. In the face of a price increase in electricity, firms are unlikely to shift to other substitutes simply because they find the use of electricity efficient and convenient'.

In terms of overall electricity consumption, in Sri Lanka 70 percent of electricity production is hydropower. But the amount of coal fired power is expected to increase in the future as the available hydro has largely reached its potential. Thus peak load pricing which cuts down overall demand will have positive environmental impacts by reducing the need for additional fossil fuel power stations.

6.1 Case Study of Increased User Charges for Environmental Goods and Services for Consumers: Irrigation Water Pricing

Water pricing in irrigation can take two main forms, both of which reduce water use and therefore can be seen as environmentally beneficial:

1. It can cover the costs of Operation and Maintenance (O&M) of irrigation structures, thus reducing water loss.
2. It can indicate to farmers the scarcity of water as a resource.

In the former case of covering O&M costs, a flat rate fee (for example, based on the area irrigated) is sufficient. However, to indicate scarcity, a fee based on the volume of irrigation water consumed is most efficient. Because of the high transaction costs of metering hundreds of small rice farmers, volume-based irrigation fees have not been tried in Sri Lanka. By contrast, area-based irrigation fees have a long history dating from the colonial period. Even though the price paid in an area fee is not strictly related to irrigation water use, there may be an indirect effect on water use if funds generated for improved operation and maintenance lead to less water loss and wastage.

In 1984, there was a concerted effort to collect an Rs 100-acreage fee from irrigation farmers. Initially results were very positive with collection rates of about 60 percent. This compares very favourably in terms of repayment rates for government-sponsored credit and other such schemes. However, in exchange for such payments, farmers also demanded an improved service with cost-effective construction methods, transparent tendering of contracts and maximum use of cheap local labour. As stated in the National Policy Framework of the Ministry of Agriculture (1996): 'Sub standard construction work has been responsible for reduction of the envisaged life span and increased cost of rehabilitation'.

These demands met resistance from officials who were benefiting from ineffective and corrupt management of irrigation operation and maintenance. Disillusioned farmers then responded by not paying the irrigation fees and the collection system once again collapsed. Recovery of irrigation fees which had been covering 50 percent of the total O&M budget in 1984 fell to 3 percent in 1988 (ADB 1994). In order for farmers to pay for irrigation, they must truly be handed responsibility for the management of the irrigation system. This has now been recognized in the latest Amendment to the Irrigation Ordinance, which actually allows farmer organizations to collect irrigation payments directly and decide on how the money should be used. For example, in the Gal Oya irrigation system in the southwest of Sri Lanka, farmers review the budget and spending plans of the Irrigation Department and other agencies and as a result irrigation payment collection rates reached 80 percent.

6.2 Case Study of a Rise in User Charges: Subsidy for Boats Reduced and Refocused

One of the most environmentally damaging subsidies has been the subsidy given for fishery craft in the coastal fishery. This led to large increases in fishing effort as the number of motorized craft increased, with a resulting decline in the coastal fish stocks. The motorized craft as a proportion of the lagoon fleet increased from about 20 percent of the fleet in 1981 to 46 percent of the fleet in 1989. The result was generally declining yields per unit of effort.

However, in the mid-1980s the government began to correct this by shifting the subsidy away from the overcrowded coastal fishery and towards the relatively unexploited offshore fishery. The offshore fishery focuses on the large pelagic drift net fisheries of skipjack, yellowfin and other tuna and pelagic sharks; and the shrimp trawl fishery.

The environmental effects of this have been significant and are reflected in data for the major fishery areas of Sri Lanka. For example in Negombo, one of the largest coastal fisheries in the island, the number of large 3.5 ton day boats has halved from 1981 to 1995 from 304 to 128, with most of these converted into offshore multi-day boats. This same pattern is apparent in the fishing areas of Chilaw and Kalutara.

The shortcoming of this reform is that while the large 3.5 ton day boats have declined, the subsidy remained until recently for the small fibreglass mechanized craft. These boats have increased substantially in all areas. The government has now sought to correct this by allocating only Rs 4 million in subsidy for the coastal fishery in its latest budget and Rs 65 million for the deep-sea fishery.

7. REMOVAL OF IMPLICIT SUBSIDIES THROUGH IMPORT CONTROLS

A less obvious form of environmentally damaging subsidy is that of import and export restrictions or tariffs. By levying import duties, the price of the imported good goes up, so domestic goods, which might be too expensive without the duty, become competitive. Thus domestic production increases. If the production of the domestic good leads to environmental damage, then the import levy acts as an environmentally damaging subsidy. This is the case in Sri Lanka for tariffs on erosive crops such as tobacco and potatoes, and was for timber until the government abolished duty.

In the case of potatoes, the duty is now at 35 percent and Sri Lankan potatoes are now about three times world price levels. Quite apart from the negative consumer impacts, this tariff has been a major cause for soil erosion as potato production is expanding rapidly in the central hill country, where it has led to severe soil erosion. Potatoes are often grown by illegal settlers who also cut down forest for their plots and mine the soil for the high profits. These profits can be as much as five times that from pole beans and fifty times the profit from rice.

In addition, farmers on encroached land lack tenure, so they are unlikely to install soil conservation measures. Most of this production would be uneconomic without the enormous implicit subsidy provided by the import restriction. This is demonstrated by the large resistance to any removal of the duty from the potato growers. Like any rent seekers who earn supernormal profits, the landowners and financiers of the 'potato mafia' have used their political influence to keep the subsidy in place. The soil erosion from these lands washes down into major reservoirs which provide hydro power for the national grid. Estimates are that the Rantembe reservoir downstream of the main potato-growing area was 36 percent silted up in just seven years and silting up at almost 4 percent a year (Yatawera 1997).

The other important linkage between tariffs and the environment is if there are reduced tariffs for inputs to environmentally damaging activities. One of the main examples is the duty waiver on imported equipment and other tax holidays for the potentially environmentally damaging export industries of shrimp farming and ornamental fish exports. While neither industry has to be environmentally damaging if properly practised, the way they have been developed in Sri Lanka has been very detrimental to the environment. The shrimp industry has caused significant water pollution in certain lagoons and about one-third of the farms have been on areas where mangroves have been removed (Steele and Sivakumar 1997). The ornamental fish industry has been involved in large-scale export of freshwater and marine tropical fish at levels which appear unsustainable. Both industries require significant imports of equipment such as tanks, aerators, pumps and refrigeration and as they are export orientated they qualify for the government's export incentives. It would be more appropriate if the industry paid an export duty (known as a *cess* in the Sri Lankan context) which could be used to finance environmentally friendly practices and management. The linkages between tariffs and the environment are summarized in Table 13.2.

Table 13.2. Import/export duties and environmental impacts

Item	Environmental impact	Current policy
Potatoes	Soil erosion in hill country	35% duty on imports
Tobacco	Soil erosion in hill country	35% duty on imports
Timber	Leads to illegal deforestation	Formerly 10% duty on imports, in 1995 budget duty abolished
Shrimp	Leads to loss of mangroves and water pollution	Duty waiver on equipment (e.g., pumps, aerators) as export industry
Ornamental fish	Loss of biodiversity	Duty waiver on equipment (e.g., pumps, aerators) as export industry

7.1 Case Study: Removal of Duty on Imported Timber

The duty on imported timber was until recently set at 10 percent. This reduced imports and acted as an implicit subsidy to domestic timber. It is estimated that in 1994 about 22 percent of the supply of sawlogs in Sri Lanka was provided from natural forests, and only 1 percent imported (the rest was from homesteads and from rubber and coconut plantations). In response to these concerns, import duties were reduced in the 1995 budget. The effects of this reform in increasing timber imports and reducing dependence on the natural forest are not yet clear.

8. RISE IN RESOURCE RENTS FOR PRODUCERS OF ENVIRONMENTALLY RELATED GOODS AND SERVICES

Another form of environmentally damaging subsidy is low rents charged for natural resource extraction. The suppliers of natural resources are undercharged when the resource rent earned from natural resource extraction and harvesting by private concessionaires is not sufficiently captured by government through taxation. This resource rent, which arises for all renewable and non-renewable natural resources (for example, minerals, fisheries, timber or nature tourism sites) is the difference between the cost of extracting the resource and its price (also including a reasonable profit margin and possible risk premium). Since rent arises because of the scarcity value of a resource, even if it taxed to zero, it is still profitable to harvest the resource.

Table 13.3 summarizes the current policy on rent for a number of resources and the environmental impact of low rent collection. The main impact for all resources is resource depletion.

In most cases in Sri Lanka the rent fees are extremely low and clearly suboptimal. For example, it is estimated that sand extraction from river beds is almost double the natural rate of regeneration (from upstream siltation) and the sand resources will all be exhausted within 25 years. The other role of a rental charge can be to internalize any additional environmental impacts. In the case of sand mining, this will include riverbank erosion and salt water intrusion due to the lowering of the riverbed at the sea mouth.

Table 13.3. Nature resource rents and environmental degradation

	Current policy	Environmental impact
Sand	Flat rate fee of Rs 100 for one-month mining permit	Resource depletion, bank erosion, salt water intrusion
Coral	Sea coral mining is banned, inland coral charged at low flat rate	Resource depletion, sea erosion, loss of habitat
Clay	Low, flat rate charge	Resource depletion, unfilled pits, effect on hydrology
Timber	Stumpage fee recently raised by 10%	Resource depletion
Groundwater	Zero fee	Resource depletion
Nature sites	Department of Wildlife Conservation has realistic rate of $12 entrance fee for foreign tourists, but Forest Department still has low rate	Insufficient funds to promote biodiversity conservation
Gems	Low flat rate	Resource depletion, unfilled gem pits (mosquitoes etc.)
Deep sea fish (e.g. tuna)	Access fees generally not paid due to weak surveillance	Depletion of fishery

8.1 Case Study of Rise in Resource Rents: Introduction of Stumpage Fees

A standard example of rent taxes is stumpage fees charged on timber. The government has just introduced a stumpage fee for timber from state-owned plantations. Previously the price was very low with consequent lack of incentives to invest in plantations or to improve efficiency in the sawmill factories. The new fee should raise prices by about 33 percent.

Prior to this change, the State Forest Plantations provided the State Timber Corporation with very cheap timber, which does not reflect its market price. This means that the timber is sold off too cheaply, leading to wastage in the timber-processing industry, lack of development of the minor timber species and timber being acquired by consumers at well below its true cost, for uses such as construction.

8.2 Case Study of Rise in Resource Rents: Rise in Nature Park Entrance Fees

One of the most important natural resources is protected areas of natural beauty. As with any limited natural resource, such natural sites have a scarcity premium which can be taxed. This is particularly so for foreign visitors to national parks. If such 'rents' are not collected by the site owner, they either simply go to the consumer as consumer surplus, or are captured by the foreign tour operator in the cost of the package (Steele 1995). The environmental benefit is that this money generates funds for conservation and for employment creation (or more simply compensation) among local communities to prevent encroachment and hunting. Currently encroachment, particularly for agriculture is the major threat to Sri Lanka's protected areas.

This point is now gaining increasing acceptance in Sri Lanka among the major agencies responsible for protected areas. Already foreigners are charged higher rates than nationals, and the Department of Wildlife Conservation (DWLC) and the main Botanical Gardens at Peredeniya have recently increased their entrance fees, leading to significant growth in entrance fee revenue. DWLC revenue has increased ten times between 1991 and 1993, partly due to more visitors, but mostly due to much higher entrance fees levied since August 1992 (Ministry of Agriculture 1995). In 1993, revenue exceeded recurrent expenditure, suggesting that it could become a self-financing agency. In 1995, revenue from the DWLC was over Rs 56 million, a considerable increase from the 1993 figure of Rs 47 million.

However the Forest Department (FD), which controls a smaller number of parks, has yet to raise its entrance fees, which are 12 times lower than the DWLC fees (Rs 50 as against Rs 630). Sinharaja Forest in particular is a

UNESCO listed World Heritage site and as a unique example of Asian tropical rainforest, would generate a significant premium for the Forest Department. The FD has to invest in staff and facilities to collect entrance fees at the other parks. At Rittigala Sanctuary, it is estimated that the FD is losing from the estimated 2,000 foreign tourists at least Rs 100,000 a year, while at Knuckles Forest a minimum estimated annual visitation of 1,000 means a lost revenue of Rs. 50,000. In addition to providing revenue, the level of visitation must be carefully recorded by the main offices at DWLC and FD as it is a key management tool.

The other issue is that some of this revenue from entrance fees should be kept by the relevant authorities and invested in biodiversity management. This scheme currently operates at the DWLC, but not yet at the Forest Department or Peradeniya Gardens, although it is under discussion. At the DWLC, about, 85 percent of this revenue is sent to the Treasury, but about 15 percent or Rs 8 million in 1995, is kept by the DWLC in the Wildlife Fund. However, the DWLC has yet to invest this revenue fully and the Wildlife Fund has a large surplus.

9. DEPOSIT REFUNDS

Deposit refunds provide useful incentives to encourage environmentally friendly behaviour, and will be discussed below.

9.1 Case Study: Deposit Refunds for Mining

This has been introduced by the recently amended Mines and Minerals Act, which states that refundable deposits will be required before mining begins as a guarantee that the mine is rehabilitated after use. Prior to this act there were deposits but they were generally so low as to be ineffective. The current levels of deposit refund are now substantial for clay mines, since clay is mined on a commercial scale.

9.2 Case Study: Deposit Refunds for Paper and Glass

Sri Lanka, in common with many countries has had a traditional system of deposit refunds for paper and glass. This system existed as a financial measure by the monopoly paper and glass manufacturer who sought to lower raw material costs by reusing paper and glass. This system continues today with payments of Rs 5 for a glass bottle and Rs 5–200 per kg of paper depending on its quality. The deposit refund for paper has recently been increased significantly to prevent exports of waste-paper to India, which had been growing. The paper company reduces the transaction costs of administering this refund by appointing waste paper agents in key areas, who transport the waste paper in bulk to the paper factory.

The environmental impact of this deposit refund has been significant. At present in Sri Lanka, 450 tons of cullet (broken glass) is recycled annually by the monopoly Glass Company, out of which 350 tons is white glass and 100 tons is amber. This corresponds to a 35 percent recycled content for domestically produced glass.

According to the Glass Factory, the environmental benefits of this are that every ton of broken glass used in the production process saves 1.2 tons of virgin material, and every additional 10 percent of broken glass saves 2.5 percent of energy. In addition to these direct benefits, the use of broken glass helps to reduce the cost of production as it needs a lower temperature which leads to an increase in the lifetime of the furnace.

A higher level of recycling is found in the paper industry, where the recycled content of domestically produced paper is about 50 percent. However, of the total paper requirement in Sri Lanka of 147,000 metric tons, about 23,500 or 16 percent is collected for recycling mostly by the monopoly State Paper Company, but with a small amount exported. This figure is low because only 25 percent of Sri Lanka's paper is produced domestically.

While 35 percent recycling content of glass and 50 percent of paper are a good start, they could be much higher. The Paper Company plans to increase the use of waste paper up to 30,000 metric tons annually, which would mean domestically produced paper would have a recycling content of 80 percent, while the Glass Company plans to increase the quantity of white waste glass up to 500 tons and amber waste glass up to 150 tons, making a total recycled content of 50 percent. However the Glass Factory has a capacity to increase this quantity up to 60 percent. The main problem is that neither company has a well-planned, well-publicized scheme for administering the deposit refund. While the traditional informal house-to-house collection system is now breaking down, there is a need to harness the growing supermarket retail sector to encourage recycling. Glass also faces competition from cheaper and lighter plastic bottles, which are now being advertised on television with the slogan that the plastic is better as you do not need to carry it back to the supermarket to get a refund!

10. PROPERTY RIGHTS FOR THE COMMUNITY/PRIVATE SECTOR TO REDUCE OPEN ACCESS AND EXTERNALITIES

Property rights to an environmental good or service can be altered to improve environmental management. The main concern is to strengthen incentives to make efficient use of resources. Thus both private and public ownership must be optimally combined to create such incentives. This combination requires a subtle combination of regulation, ownership and other incentives (such as competition).

In some cases, a resource may currently have no owner. This is known as an open access resource since it is open to all to exploit. An example would be lagoon fisheries, which for some fishing gear were open to any fishermen. With the recent Fisheries Act amendment, the government has recognized the need to license fishermen. A similar process is under way at the island's most famous coral resort of Hikkaduwa where open access by 'glass bottom' boat operators has led to damage to the reef and reduced profits from the boat operators. The sustainable carrying capacity was fixed at about 60 boats. Unfortunately political pressures have led to this limit being exceeded. However, here the market-based approach is for the state to assist in regulating and controlling open access.

In other cases, property rights can be managed more effectively by local communities. In Sri Lanka, fishery rights are often hereditary and closely guarded. Beach *seine (madel)* fishermen will 'own' a stretch of the shoreline and will prevent overfishing by keeping outsiders out. In this case the government needs to intervene selectively to support local communities to ensure that ownership is not monopolized. Often the government has done the reverse and simply revoked these traditional rights. Once state bureaucracies have been set up and communities reduced their stake in resource management, it is difficult to return to a system of local management of resources. For example, the Forest and Irrigation Departments are notoriously reluctant to really assist in transferring control of resources to resource users: the Forest Department has now been persuaded of the advantages of community management of the mangrove resources, but is still negotiating the exact terms. Here the economic instrument is to support and encourage community ownership where it is more effective than government control.

A third type of property rights can be to ensure that property rights are secure with a reasonable time horizon. Since many environmental investments take time to pay off, this security of tenure is vital, whether ownership is by the state or the private sector. For example, if smallholder farmers do not have a reasonable time horizon when awarded land rights then they tend to use the soil as much as possible without being concerned about soil erosion. In Sri Lanka it had been government policy to grant encroachers in streambed reservations only a one-year renewable lease, but at the same to require them to grow tree crops to reduce erosion. However, it was realized that as these encroachers are always afraid of not receiving a licence renewal, they almost never plant tree crops, which take at least one year to bear fruit which can be sold. Now the government is discussing as a short-term policy measure (before long-term measures are taken such as making more land available) the possibility of providing five-year renewable leases. Here the policy instrument is to ensure that owners of environmental assets have sufficiently secure property rights.

A fourth type of ownership policy is to foster public–private partnerships of environmental goods and services, when pure government provision of resources is inefficient and undercharged. Examples might be the government provision of domestic sewage treatment or solid-waste collection and disposal. By transferring ownership to the private sector, the private sector will raise fees to cover costs (and their profit margin) which the government might find politically difficult. The private sector may also have access to funds for borrowing which the government does not have (without increasing inflation). Many countries are now installing environmental infrastructure, such as waste-treatment facilities, through public–private partnerships and build–operate–transfer (BOT) projects. Even environmental monitoring and inspection may be done more cheaply and effectively by the private sector. The government is now preparing a Terms of Reference to employ a private company to monitor compliance to the industrial pollution licensing programme (Steele and Pearce 1996).

11. ENVIRONMENTALLY BENEFICIAL SUBSIDIES

Environmentally beneficial subsidies can be used as a powerful instrument to encourage environmentally beneficial behaviour. Examples are shown in Table 13.4.

While subsidies are useful, there are a number of caveats. In particular, subsidies should be short term and less than 100 percent of the total cost to provide incentives for private producers and consumers to use the subsidy for economically viable investments. Community forests planted with complete subsidies have generally failed in Sri Lanka, as in India and elsewhere. It is far more efficient to subsidize seed banks and extension/marketing services, leaving the farmers to select what to plant, when to plant it and to actually care for the trees.

Table 13.4. Environmental subsidies

	Current policy
More efficient biomass stoves	Some subsidies
Afforestation	Some subsidies
Integrated pest management	Some subsidies
Alternative to sand and offshore coral	No subsidy
Energy conservation	Subsidy to low energy bulbs
Waste collection	Some subsidy for community collection
Relocation to industrial estates	Proposed regional incentives
Pollution abatement	Zero interest loans
Unleaded petrol	No subsidy
Soil-erosion investments	Low interest loans in one watershed

11.1 Case Study: Subsidy for Waste Treatment Technology

Lack of investment in industrial waste treatment was identified as a major problem, especially as about 80 percent of industry is focused in the Greater Colombo area, where about 15 percent of the population live.

While studies have shown that domestic water pollution is most serious in terms of biochemical oxygen demand (BOD) and chemical oxygen demand (COD), industrial pollution is significant for heavy metals and other toxics. While there is an industrial licensing programme in place (the Environmental Protection Licence) it has been largely ineffective in ensuring compliance. It was estimated that less than 15 percent of industries had waste treatment systems in 1995.

In response to this, the government introduced two major economic incentives to spur investment in waste treatment. First, the 1994 budget announced duty waivers for advanced technology, which was defined to include 'clean technology'. Second, one of the major development banks, the National Development Bank, introduced a soft loan scheme for clean technology, with a real interest rate of zero.

The environmental impacts have been quite significant. Over thirty enterprises have benefited from the scheme. Those benefiting include tanneries, hotels, textile plants and metal plants. More recently a number of prawn farms have applied for funds to install closed system water recycling schemes. The major shortcomings of the loans include initially poor publicity about the funds which limited their initial effect. This was corrected with a number of workshops with the local Trade and Industry Chambers.

11.2 Subsidy for Watershed Protection

A number of subsidies to watershed protection currently exist. The Ceylon Tobacco Company requires that its tobacco growers introduce soil erosion controls in order to be eligible for the generous input subsidies that the Company provides. In addition the major government agency responsible for the steep catchment areas, the Mahawelli Authority provides payments to cover the costs of installing gliricidia sticks which form a vegetative hedge along the contour. After the initial planting the farmer is given Rs 4.5 per metre, and additional Rs 2.5 per metre after proper maintenance. This scheme, along with awareness-raising activities, has been quite successful in popularizing vegetative erosion control methods.

12. ENVIRONMENTAL CHARGES

Environmental charges seek to raise prices to include environmental externalities by taxing (that is raising the price of) environmentally damaging behaviour through pollution fees. These fees can be charged both on inputs which produce pollution (for example, toxic chemicals, vehicles) or on the output of pollution (for example, tax on chemical effluent, tax on air emissions). An example of input charges (also known as product charges) is a tax on high-sulphur coal introduced by China, while Indonesia has a tax on each processed log to capture the environmental costs of deforestation. A more indirect product charge is a tax on vehicle use, which will reduce congestion and pollution from vehicles. A very indirect vehicle charge raises the price of owning a vehicle (for example, through high duty) while a more direct scheme raises the price of driving. This could include taxes on fuel (petrol or diesel), or charges on driving. The advantage of input taxes is that they are often easier to enforce and monitor than charges on polluting output. The disadvantage is that they are much less direct and so do not provide any incentive for reducing the pollution associated with a particular input. Charges on polluting outputs would cover charges on pollution emissions to air and water. Malaysia introduced a very successful scheme of effluent charges in 1978 to lower pollution from palm oil and rubber factories and used the revenue raised to fund research into cleaner technology. Palm oil processors reduced their discharges of BOD by almost 90 percent between 1982 and 1987.

12.1 Case Study of a Load-based Industrial Licensing Scheme

In Sri Lanka a study was conducted to examine the feasibility of introducing a load-based pollution charge (Steele and Hassan, 1996). The study recommended a charge to be levied on a load-based approach using an effluent fee on BOD per m^3 of wastewater discharge.

However, this scheme was felt to be too ambitious by the major pollution regulatory agency, the Central Environmental Authority, who were reluctant to abandon their purely command and control method of regulation. Thus it was agreed as an initial first step to introduce the concept of load-based fees by altering the pollution licence fee from a low flat rate fee to a higher load-based licence fee. Once this proved successful, the next step of a load-based effluent charge could be considered.

12.2 Case Study of Indirect Charges on Vehicle Use

In Colombo as in many cities, vehicles are the main source of air pollution. The lead in Colombo's petrol is very high, while the diesel contains high levels of sulphur. As a revenue-raising measure, the government heavily taxes the price of petrol and also charges a 100 percent duty on vehicles (all of which are imported). This has led to a reduction of motor vehicles, and of petrol vehicles in particular.

The problem is that while petrol is taxed, diesel is not and so diesel is about three times cheaper. In terms of the costs of production, there is little difference between the two fuels. From 1 September 1994, the government reduced the price of all diesels by Rp 1 – about an 8 percent price cut – while petrol prices stayed constant. This Rp 1 cut in diesel prices cost the government about Rs 900 million in lost revenue. This price cut means that a growing percentage of Sri Lankan vehicles run on diesel. This price cut will also have environmental consequences as diesel is one of the main sources of particulate and sulphur dioxide air pollution (Indraratna 1994).

The 1995 Budget proposed a tax on diesel vehicles, but this has now been amended so that only luxury cars will have to pay. The diesel–petrol price differential is defended primarily on grounds of poverty alleviation since it is claimed that if diesel prices increase, both public transport (all buses are diesel) and vegetable prices (since vegetables are brought from Nuwara Eliya by diesel trucks) will rise. The benefit of raising diesel prices would be reduced particulates and sulphur dioxides, and revenue increases.

13. CONCLUSIONS

The summary in Table 13.5 shows examples of the major MBIs discussed in this chapter. In addition, the table draws attention to areas where further MBIs are required. While some important first steps have been made, there is clearly room for much greater use of MBIs in the future. This review has shown that those MBIs that have been introduced have generally been successful in improving the environment.

Table 13.5. Existing MBIs in Sri Lanka and potential for future expansion

MBI	Already introduced	Potential for introduction
Rise in non-compliance fees	Timber fine increased	Non-compliance fines for other regulations for coastal and water pollution etc.
Rise in user charges	Irrigation fees introduced, removal of coastal fishing subsidy	Waste and sewage user fees, groundwater extraction charge
Export/import subsidy	Lowering of timber import duty	Remove potato and tobacco import tariff, introduce export charge for shrimp and ornamental fish
Raise rent taxes	Timber stumpage fee introduced, rise in entrance fee for parks run by Dept of Wildlife Conservation	Rise in sand, clay and gem rental taxes, rise in entrance fees for parks controlled by Forest Department, deep sea fishing access fees
Deposit refunds	Deposit refunds for paper and glass, and large-scale clay mining	Deposit refunds for car batteries and plastic waste
Improved property incentives	More secure tenure for smallholders	Community management of mangroves
Environmental subsidies	Subsidy for watershed protection, pollution-abatement control, low-energy light bulbs	Subsidies for relocation to industrial estates, and for alternatives to sand and offshore coral mining, subsidy for unleaded petrol
Environmental charges	Load-based pollution licence fee, product charges on vehicles	Load-based pollution charge, pesticide tax

The main resistance to the introduction of MBIs is from groups who will lose out from their introduction. The main claims are that subsidy removal and price rises will affect the poor, the cost of living (inflation) or affect international competitiveness. While these arguments may have some validity depending on the particular circumstances it is important to test for this empirically. Too often such claims are not so clear cut when actually examined. For example, the claim that user charges for waste collection, or sewage will impact the poor is rarely the case since the poor do not have access to such services in the first place. Often the existing subsidies give most benefit to the urban middle class (who also tend to be the public servants in charge of policy making!) and in fact such subsidies are at the expense of the true poor in urban and rural areas. It must also be remembered that it is the poor who suffer most from environmental pollution – they tend to live near polluted waterbodies and waste dumps, and in noisy areas (such as next to busy roads). So reducing urban environmental pollution can often benefit the poor most. These issues are discussed further below.

13.1 Market-based Instruments and the Poor

One of the main problems in the introduction of MBIs is the fear that they will have a negative impact on the poor. This arises from a mistaken view that while regulations are income neutral, price rises are not. In fact, both regulations and MBIs can have negative impacts on poverty depending on the way they are implemented. Forestry regulations in Sri Lanka are an example that anecdotal data suggest are regressive in that the poor face problems getting permits to fell cultivated timber, while the large illegal operators can bribe their way out of needing permits to fell natural timber.

A second mistaken assumption is that subsidies are pro-poor. Even though subsidies are often introduced or defended in the name of the poor, they generally benefit larger consumers more. Examples from Sri Lanka show that the poor often lack access to the subsidized goods. This is illustrated by Table 13.6. The table shows the relatively small section of the population that benefits from certain subsidies, often less than 50 percent of the population. The final column takes the data available to estimate the per unit level of the subsidy. Often the size of the subsidy, such as the subsidy to road users in Colombo or to coastal fishermen in the early 1980s, was quite significant. If it is indeed true that subsidy removal will affect the poor disproportionally, then it may be possible to provide the subsidy in a less distortionary fashion.

For example, instead of subsidizing public transport by providing low-price diesel, it would be more efficient to reduce the duty on imported spares and parts to public transport as this would only benefit public transport. In some other cases, the subsidy could be targeted to benefit just the poor. In this way, Sri Lankan subsidies for kerosene fuel were targeted by introducing fuel stamps for the poorest members of the population. Another approach is through cross subsidies, where charges are raised for the wealthier to cover the costs of the subsidy for the poor. This approach already exists in many countries where electricity and water charges increase as more units are consumed. This can be an effective way of protecting the poor while ensuring that the average price is sufficient to cover marginal costs.

Table 13.6. Underpricing of environmental-related goods and services

	Percentage of population served	Estimated subsidy	Subsidy per unit
Electricity	45% of population (mainly in urban areas)	Cross-subsidy of O&M costs to domestic consumers in 1992 of Rs 900 million (US$18 million)	US$3.3 per residential consumer per year (1992)
Residential pipe-borne water	18% of national population (3.2 million)	Cross-subsidy in O&M to domestic consumers. Capital subsidy of about 1,000 million per year (US$20 million)	US$6.2 capital subsidy per consumer per year (1996)
Sewage	25% of Colombo urban area	Rs 4,500 (US$90 million) million soft loan for expansion of sewer system in Colombo now under way	US$90 per capita capital subsidy
Waste collection and disposal	90% of Colombo Municipal Council served, but as little as 40% in other urban areas	Rs 62 million (US$1.2 million) per year spent by CMC, partially covered by property taxes	US$4 per capita per year
Irrigation water	69% of land served by irrigation	Subsidy of Rs 17.5 per ha or Rs 10–15 million per year in 1996 (US$200,000–300,000)	US$0.4 O&M subsidy per ha
Fertiliser	550,000 metric tons imported and locally produced	Total subsidy in 1995 was Rs 1.34 billion (US$27 million)	US$50 per metric ton
Roads	215,000 vehicles entered Colombo in 1993	Road-building budget for Colombo estimated at Rs 7,000 million (US$140 million)	US$651 capital subsidy per vehicle (1997)
Fishing boats	Estimated 78,000 active fishermen in 1985	Capital subsidy of about Rs 100–150 million per year (US$2-3 million) in 1980s	US$1,282 per fisherman

Note: Rs 50 = US$1 (average exchange rate during 1996/97).
O&M = Operations and Maintenance

13.2 Market-based Instruments and Government Bureaucracy

The second main obstacle to MBIs will be from sections of the government bureaucracy who may feel threatened by their introduction. Examples given in this chapter include forestry officials who resist more focused non-compliance timber fees, irrigation officials who resist greater scrutiny of their budgets and pollution-control enforcement officers who fear a loss of their regulatory control with the introduction of a pollution charge. Even if environmental agencies are not opposed to MBIs, they generally lack the economic experience and required skills to collect revenue and charge environmental taxes. It is important for thorough discussions to take place prior to the introduction of MBIs in order to allay such fears and build up support for the reforms.

As MBIs tend to focus on the efficiency role of prices and to generate revenue, an important agency that may be sympathetic to their introduction will be officials from the Treasury and other financial agencies. However, the finance agencies will resist the use of taxation for environmental measures due to a general resistance by the Treasury to 'earmarking' revenue from taxation as this reduces the flexibility of fiscal policy.

There is also concern that removing funds from parliamentary control can lead to increased corruption. Indeed for both these reasons, earmarking is generally viewed as not economically efficient as it means that government expenditure cannot be targeted according to national priority areas. However for this same reason, earmarking can safeguard areas such as environmental expenditure which may be cut in times of austerity. Thus if biodiversity is financed out of entrance fees to national parks this can be a continuous source of funds even after current donor interest in funding biodiversity subsides. Earmarking can also sometimes make environmental charges and taxes more politically acceptable. For example, industry may be more willing to pay an effluent charge if they know the revenue will be returned to them as subsidies for pollution-abatement equipment. However, with opposition by the Treasury to earmarking and lack of experience in fiscal issues by environmental agencies, introducing earmarked environmental charges is a difficult task.

REFERENCES

Asian Development Bank (1994), 'Comprehensive Water Resources Management in Sri Lanka', Draft Strategic Framework and Action Plan, January.

De Silva, M. (1989), 'Major Characteristics Associated with the Problem of Solid Waste in Colombo', *Sri Lanka Journal of Social Sciences*.

Indraratna, A.V (1994), *Environment and Economic Implications of Petrol/Diesel Pricing*, Natural Resources and Environmental Policy Project.

Ministry of Agriculture (1996), *Forestry Sector Masterplan*, Colombo.

Steele, P. (1995), 'Ecotourism: an Economic Analysis', *Journal of Sustainable Tourism*, **2**(1).

Steele, P. and Hassan, R. (1996), *Study on the Introduction of Effluent Charges as a Means of Controlling Industrial Water Pollution in Sri Lanka*, Institute of Policy Studies.

Steele, P. and Pearce, D.W. (1994), 'The Application and Potential for Market Based Instruments in the Asia Pacific Region', in *Financing of Environmentally Sound Development*, Manila: ADB.

Steele, P. and Pearce, D.W. (1996), 'Promoting Private Sector Financing for Sustainable Development in the Asia Pacific Region', for Third Expert Meeting of Financial Issues of Agenda 21, Asian Development Bank, 6–8 February.

Steele, P. and Sivakumar, M. (1997), 'Costs and Benefits of Mangroves', *Journal of Sri Lanka Association for Aquatic Resources*.

UDA (1994), *Environmental Management Strategy for Colombo Urban Area*, Vol. III, Urban Development Authority, March.

Wijemanne, E. et al. (1984), *Energy Pricing Policies in Developing Countries*, Energy Pricing Policy.

Yatawera, S. (1997), 'Upper Mahawlei Catchment Sedimentation Studies', Results and Conclusions, Paper presented at workshop of Sri Lanka Association for the Advancement of Science, 1997.

14. Environmental Taxation in Kenya

Collins Ayoo and Mohamud A. Jama

1. INTRODUCTION

Environmental degradation in Kenya is a serious and complex problem which in direct and indirect ways poses a real threat to the country's prospects for sustainable development. This contention is predicated on the now widely accepted fact that close links exist between the environment and the economy. Manifestations of the environmental degradation include the widespread destruction of forests to create more agricultural land and meet the high and rising demand for fuelwood and other forest products, large-scale loss of biological diversity, excessive soil erosion and consequent decline in the long-term productivity of the land, air and water pollution, water depletion, the draining of wetlands and overexploitation of fisheries.

These problems have been exacerbated by the high rate of population growth and a planning regime which treats environmental issues lightly. Besides contributing considerably to the vicious circle of poverty, they highlight the critical challenges between economic growth on the one hand and environmental protection and management on the other (Republic of Kenya 1995c). But they also reflect the shortcomings in the country's environmental policies which for a long time have been *ad hoc*, short term, sectoral, uncoordinated and of the command and control type.

As economic reforms continue to be implemented, the country's environmental policies need to be evaluated with a view to designing more appropriate instruments. In particular there is a need to explore the possibility of using pricing, taxation, financial incentives and subsidies for the management of natural resources and the environment. We need to point out here that the two categories of policies need not be mutually exclusive. Rather a mix of policies that will generate efficient outcomes, needs to be found. In other words, we need to design the least-cost approaches for controlling environmental damage. Our general concern in this chapter is taxation as it is undertaken in the Kenyan context. We make an attempt to analyze how some of the taxes relate to a variety of environmental issues.

In the next section we discuss in a broad way some changes which have recently been undertaken in Kenya's taxes. Section 3 then examines in detail the energy subsector focussing on the various taxes which have been levied on electricity and petroleum products and how these have been changing over time. The focus on the energy sector is due to the fact that many of the country's most serious environmental problems stem from commercial energy production and consumption. A discussion of the environmental effects of the various taxes is then undertaken in Section 4. We finalize the chapter in Section 5 with some concluding remarks.

2. TAX REFORMS IN KENYA

Improving the tax system has been a major concern to the government of Kenya since it started implementing economic reforms whose aims have been to reduce and eventually eliminate budget deficits, stimulate economic growth and stabilize prices. The key features in this tax modernization program have been the broadening of the tax base, the strengthening of controls to minimize cases of tax evasion, and the increasing reliance on indirect taxes as opposed to direct taxes. So far, value-added tax (VAT), import duties and excise duties have been the major sources of indirect taxes. For instance, in 1994/95 these contributed 37.8 percent, 28.7 percent and 29.8 percent, respectively, of the total indirect taxes

Further proof of the country's increased reliance on indirect taxes is the fact that their shares in the government revenue have been rising steadily over time and were 49 percent in 1973/74, 58 percent in 1985/86 and 63.8 percent in the 1989/90–1995/96 period. A breakdown of the revenues that the various categories of taxes generated to the government from 1989/90 to1995/96 is presented in Table 14.1.

The table indicates that the fiscal instruments used have at least succeeded in accomplishing their primary objectives. We see this in the steady rise in the gross receipt on the recurrent account from 1989/90 to 1995/96.

Besides enhancing the efficiency of revenue collection, the tax modernization program which the government of Kenya has been implementing has also been aimed at achieving other goals such as lowering the tax rates for those who bear a heavy burden, reducing double taxation and taxing benefits paid to high-income earners. For this reason the top marginal tax rates were lowered from 40 percent to 35 percent in 1995 while tax reliefs were increased by 50 percent.

A significant effect of the increase in reliefs was the exclusion of 23,000 employees from the payment of PAYE (pay as you earn). It is a progressive income tax paid by persons who are formally employed. The tax reliefs are the amount of income earned which is statutorily exempted from taxation. They can therefore be regarded as tax expenditure. Increases in reliefs imply the exemption of a greater proportion of income from taxation.

In 1996 further reforms were carried out. A personal relief of Kshs 7,200.00 was made to apply to all taxpayers, and, individuals with monthly incomes of up to Kshs 6,000.00 exempted from the payment of income tax. Measures were also instituted to reduce the number of middle-income earners falling in the top tax bracket. These latter reforms excluded an additional 140,000 low-income earners from payment of income tax. Again, we can see in these reforms a deliberate attempt by the government to reduce its reliance on direct taxes consisting mainly of income taxes. There can be no doubt that the above reforms resulted in declines in revenue. These declines in revenue have, however, been more than compensated by the introduction of more broad-based taxes and the increased efficiency of tax collection. Among the new taxes were VAT, which was expanded to the services sector, the road maintenance levy and transit toll levies, although the latter have since been abolished.

Table 14.1. Gross receipts on recurrent account 1989/90–1995/96 (Kshs per Million Pounds)

	1989/90	1990/91	1991/92	1992/93	1993/94	1994/95	1995/96
Direct tax							
Income tax	599.15	713.08	851.39	998.52	1838.36	2185.74	2,509.87
Indirect taxes							
VAT domestic	323.74	421.85	335.63	406.54	651.24	675.00	738.87
VAT imports	316.61	334.22	592.14	700.60	798.48	548.94	616.94
Import duties	347.67	344.68	255.93	459.15	739.64	929.91	1178.72
Excise duties	149.56	185.16	340.46	418.35	556.27	966.61	1062.56
Export duties	0.729	0.07	0.74	0.22	0.30	–	–
Trading licenses	9.05	10.25	13.57	11.28	11.01	23.63	25.24
Licenses fees under Traffic Act	16.62	16.09	16.31	16.26	19.53	28.31	33.65
Other taxes etc.	67.42	77.48	70.28	59.78	89.38	67.17	83.02
Total	1831	2102	2476	3071	4703	5425	6248
Share of indirect taxes	67.3	66.1	65.6	67.5	60.9	59.7	59.8

The introduction of the transit toll levies was motivated by the need to generate funds for maintaining and expanding the country's roads. The mode of collecting this levy was through toll stations erected at strategic points on the major roads. In a practical sense this was a form of user charge applied to motorists with the rates being dependent on vehicle size, the amount of load carried and the frequency of road use. The main weakness of this approach was its exclusive application to vehicle users transiting through toll stations. Charges were not levied on motorists using roads on which toll stations were not constructed.

The road maintenance levy was designed and introduced primarily to remedy this shortcoming. Instead of fees being collected at toll stations, the new system now entails collecting the levies at service stations where the charges are built into the cost of fuel. This is a sure way of maximizing revenue collection, eliminating evasion and curbing corrupt practices. A detailed treatment of this tax is reserved for Section 3.

For a long time Kenya's government had also relied on import duties as a source of revenue. Some of these duties have, however, been intended to protect certain strategic domestic industries from competitive pressures. The latter objective is an application of the 'infant industry argument' in international trade theory. The country's experience so far is that the import duties have acted as a disincentive to the enterprises which rely heavily on such imports. It is for this reason that the duty of 25 percent which was levied on all imports in 1994/95 was discontinued. However, import duty is still levied on selected items. The main sources of import duty are transport equipment, machinery and fuels. Estimates show that the yields from these items were 54 percent of the total duty collection in 1995 and 53 percent in 1994. In the period between 1994 and 1995 considerable improvements on duty collection were registered on transport equipment and machinery. Specifically, duty from equipment increased by 69 percent in 1995 while that from machinery increased by 50 percent over the same period. In Table 14.2 the import duty collections on commodities by end-use categories from 1991–95 are shown.

Table 14.2. Import duty collection, 1991–1995 (KShs Million Pounds)

End-use category	1991	1992	1993	1994	1995
Food, drinks and tobacco	6.82	5.59	17.88	56.35	70.98
Basic material	20.17	33.41	69.95	77.91	89.28
Fuels	32.19	1.51	102.34	195.13	187.18
Chemicals	62.73	50.83	108.80	115.29	121.18
Textile	5.63	4.97	27.53	29.24	37.16
Semi-manufacture	26.14	20.49	38.02	45.06	72.85
Metals	30.10	29.34	57.05	73.23	144.57
Transport equipment	41.20	19.08	80.54	151.45	255.46
Machinery	50.19	47.84	113.25	139.48	208.65
Miscellaneous commodities	9.16	9.63	27.49	39.39	49.87
Total	284.33	222.69	642.85	922.23	1,202.18

It is clear from table 14.2 that revenues from import duties on all the commodities considered have shown an upward trend since 1993. Plans to further lower both the maximum import duties and the income tax and VAT rates have not been implemented, because of the huge and increasing budget deficits which have continued to be recorded over the years.

With regard to excise revenue, more has been collected over the years from beer and spirits, and cigarettes than from all other commodities combined. The combined contributions of these items to the total excise revenue collected were 88.4 percent in 1993 and 92.7 percent in 1994. The duty on locally produced sugar was lifted in 1994. The estimates of the excise revenue generated by the above commodities over the period 1990–95 are presented in Table 14.3.

Table 14.3. Excise revenue by commodities, 1990–1995 (KShs thousand pounds)

	1990	1991	1992	1993	1994	1995
Beer and Spirits	23,781	54,581	194,849	255,923	289,585	332,274
Sugar	19,392	17,844	16,150	18,505		21
Cigarettes	91,540	91,321	117,651	164,764	193,873	211,033
Other Commodities	252	6,385	36,832	36,537	38,520	49,002
Total	151,965	180,131	364,482	475,729	521,708	592,330

As has been pointed out in the foregoing section, VAT has been a central feature in Kenya's taxation system since 1990. It was introduced to replace the old sales tax on imports and domestically manufactured goods. It has now been extended to services. Among the reasons for its introduction was the need to expand the tax base with particular emphasis being given to the taxation of consumption. This could then enable allowances to be made for reducing the tax on investment and thereby stimulating the country's economic growth. Structures such as zero rating have been widely used in the administration of VAT to ensure that exports are made without any tax content which would raise their prices and thereby make them uncompetitive internationally. The VAT Act also has provisions for compensating manufacturers by offsetting input taxes. This is aimed at avoiding double taxation which would undermine the competitiveness of the country's manufactured products. Over the years the VAT base has been systematically expanded and the revenue yield from VAT has increased substantially. The collection of VAT has, however, continued to be characterized by a high degree of evasion. This has been worsened by the complicated nature of the tax, particularly the application of different VAT rates to different goods and services.

To minimize VAT evasion, concerted efforts have been made to harmonize the VAT rates and simplify the procedures in its administration by placing all goods and services in the following four categories.

1. Zero-rated goods and services, for example, agricultural inputs and medicines.
2. Goods and services charged a VAT of 8 percent, for example, vegetable oils and restaurant services.
3. Goods and services charged a VAT of 15 percent.
4. Goods and services exempted from VAT, for example, rice, milk, maize, wheat and bread.

There is a difference between goods that are exempted from VAT and those that are zero-rated. For zero rated goods, their producers are entitled to a recovery of all their input tax while this is not the case for producers of commodities which are exempted from VAT. Increased collection is expected from these adjustments, given that measures are simultaneously being undertaken to lower income taxes.

Similar to the road maintenance levy is the service charge which was introduced in 1990. Its specific purpose was to generate the financial resources for improving the quality of services rendered by local authorities to the urban dwellers. It was started because urban environmental problems were worsening yet the local authorities lacked the resources for addressing these problems. Examples of the problems being referred to here include the accumulation of wastes and the deterioration of infrastructure. Although charges existed previously for meeting the costs of providing these services, these had over time become insufficient thus prompting the need for alternative sources of funds to finance their provision. So far the service charge has been very successful in terms of its ability to raise funds.

In a practical way, the service charge can be viewed as an attempt by government to compel the citizens to pay for some of the services which they enjoy. It is disturbing, however, that the introduction of the service charge has not been accompanied by appreciable improvement in environmental quality. In fact the environmental quality has continued to deteriorate but this could be due to the long-term time lags in this sector. There is a need to restructure the administration of the service charge so that priority is given to the provision of services and improvement of environmental quality.

In recognition of the link between environmental problems and the 'publicness' of environmental resources, a number of initiatives have been designed to privatize them. It is hoped that these measures will create the necessary incentives not only for their conservation but also for their efficient utilization. The recent listing of the coastal beaches by the Kenya Wildlife Service and the subsequent introduction of the beach management levy should be viewed from this perspective. Through the mechanism of gazettment what was formerly common property has now been transformed into private property, a necessary condition for the imposition of charges. The levies being presently charged are Kshs 100.00 per swim or Kshs 4,000.00 per person for an annual swimming pass. The revenue collected is intended for the conservation and protection of the coastal environment, the cleaning of the beaches, the provision of security to beach users and for controlling commercial activities along the beaches. The beach levy holds considerable promise as an instrument for protecting the endangered coastal environment by restricting access; it also poses a threat to the country's competitiveness. The move has, however, been strongly criticized on the grounds that it is likely to adversely affect local fishermen who have traditionally depended on marine resources for their livelihood. As most people are poor and have no other means of securing a livelihood, it is necessary that suitable alternatives be found.

In line with the government's policy of lowering duties on imported items, those on motor vehicles which ranged from 50–100 percent in 1991 have now been lowered to about 35 percent. Motor vehicles have as a result become cheaper and therefore more affordable. The recent sharp rise in the number of motor vehicles in the country can be attributed, in part, to this particular reform. But in the motor sector we can also identify a number of tax expenditures because the Value Added Tax Act and the Customs and Excise Act contain provisions exempting several groups from the payment of duty on vehicles. These groups include the Armed Forces, diplomatic missions, aid agencies, charitable institutions, members of the National Assembly, permanent secretaries, provincial commissioners, judges and university lecturers. It is therefore plausible to hold that the lowering of duties on vehicles (and the tax expenditures on their imports) has contributed to environmental problems such as air pollution, high lead exposures and traffic congestion. This impact is, however, likely to be small given that the total number of persons entitled to this benefit is small relative to the country's motor vehicle-owning population.

3. THE ENERGY SECTOR

Energy resources are an extremely important factor in Kenya's economic development. This is not surprising since historically economic development has been linked to increasing energy consumption per capita. In the light of this fact, due consideration needs to be given to the process of energy planning in the country. Indeed the achievement of short- and long-term development objectives critically depends on the availability of energy resources in adequate amounts and of the appropriate types to sustain the various sectors of the economy. In trying to meet such targets the environmental impacts of the different initiatives need to be borne in mind so that measures can be taken to minimize the negative externalities associated with the production, storage, transportation and use of energy.

The types of energy which Kenya relies on include woodfuel, petroleum fuels, electricity, ethanol, coal, wind and solar radiation. Wood, charcoal and crop wastes, however, are the dominant fuels used in the country. It is expected that the demand for energy, which is already high, will continue to grow rapidly due to the high rate of population growth and the fast urbanization. One projection for the supply of energy is shown in Table 14.4.

Table 14.4. Projections of Kenya's energy resource requirements (petrojoules)

	1980	2000
Wood		
for firewood	300.2	416.9
for charcoal	207.0	317.9
for industry	86.7	19.0
Oil		
Imported refined	94.7	169.6
Imported crude	1.2	161.2
Hydro	3.3	11.8
Geothermal	0.0	0.8
Electricity import	0.9	0.9
Coal	8.7	16.9
Total sources	409.3	1,121.1

Source: O'Keefe et al. (1984).

Woodfuel and petroleum demand are expected to contribute the largest share of the total demand. The supply on the other hand is projected to average only 26.6 million tons of oil equivalent per annum (Republic of Kenya 1995c). These figures suggest that Kenya is faced with a deficit in her energy budget which can in very real and direct ways undermine the prospects for economic growth. These are the core concerns which underpin the country's energy policy which aims at, among others, promotion of conservation of all forms of energy; intensification of exploration or prospecting for indigenous fossil fuels; development of hydro and geothermal electricity generation; increasing wood production on both farm and plantation systems; increasing the efficiency in woodfuel utilization; encouraging domestic fuel substitution and introducing alternative energy sources to broaden the national energy base and lessen reliance on imported energy. We focus now on woodfuel, petroleum and electricity since 63 percent, 24 percent and 10 percent of the country's energy needs are met from these energy sources.

3.1 Woodfuel

Woodfuel is Kenya's most important energy source which serves to meet about 63 percent of the country's domestic energy needs. It is used mainly for cooking, heating and lighting in the rural and urban poor households. The demand for woodfuel has been rising over the years causing increased pressure on wood resources. Some of the consequences of this increase in woodfuel demand have been deforestation, deterioration of soil conditions, sedimentation, extinction of species and decline in biological diversity, decline in agricultural productivity and increased time allocated by rural households to woodfuel gathering. These detrimental environmental outcomes need to be checked by first properly understanding the factors which determine the rate at which wood resources are exploited. In these endeavors it should be clear that wood is not a strictly renewable resource except under conditions of either natural abundance or properly devised management regimes (O'Keefe et al. 1984; Meir 1986). Its use in Kenya is clearly unsustainable since fuelwood is presently being consumed at about four times the annual rate of incremental production (Republic of Kenya 1995c).

The present scarcity of fuelwood in the country is a pointer to the existence of loopholes in the way this resource is priced. If attaining efficiency is the goal toward which we are striving, the prices need to be adjusted to reflect the real scarcity of the resources and thus influence the consumers to conserve it. This would require that prices be set at levels higher than the present ones of Kshs 1.60 per kg for fuelwood and Kshs 6.00 per kg for charcoal. One way of achieving this end would be through a tax. The possibility of levying such a tax is, however, severely constrained by the nature of the market for fuelwood. In many cases wood is harvested on communal lands and traded in informal markets. This suggests that institutional reforms may be needed to regulate the overexploitation of this vital resource. A crucial component in such reform would be defining property rights to lands on which fuelwood is harvested and putting in place mechanisms for enforcing such rights. In the short run this is likely to have adverse social effects since the poor households who rely on such environmental goods are likely to be denied access to the same. Indeed the shortage of fuelwood in several rural areas of the country has now reached crisis proportions and the use of dung and crop residues has become a common practice. Agriculture which relies on these resources also stands to be adversely affected if the practice continues unchecked.

3.2 Petroleum

Petroleum's importance in Kenya's economy is evident not only from the modern sector's heavy dependence on it, but also from the revenue it provides to the government through various taxes. The petroleum products being referred to here include liquefied petroleum gas, gasoline, kerosene, automotive diesel, heavy industrial diesel, fuel oil and bitumen. Because of Kenya's lack of her own exploitable reserves of petroleum and the significant bearing which petroleum imports have on the balance of payments, the government's policy on the petroleum subsector has been two-pronged, namely to ensure an adequate and secure supply of these products and to reduce the growth in their demand (Oginda 1987; Kimuyu 1988).

Table 14.5. VAT rates on petroleum products from 1989–June 1996

	1989	1990	1991	1992	1993	1994 (Feb.)	1996
Liquefied PG	1,093	1,142	3,075	3,575	3,946	5,396	3,000
Prem. gasoline	4,097	4,238	6,465	7,565	7,648	9,411	0
Regular gasoline	4,254	4,396	6,443	7,543	7,628	9,391	0
Illuminating kerosene	113	203	2,076	1,140	391	391	0
Automotive diesel	2,087	2,123	4,096	3,961	4,103	5,245	0
Industrial diesel	665	683	2,730	2,977	3,280	4,038	2,000
Fuel oil	335	3,421	2,330	3,202	3,152	3,870	2,000
Bitumen	435	474	2,352	3,352	3,161	3,716	3,715

The idea at the heart of this policy has been to ensure the continuation of economic activities which depend on petroleum fuels but in a sustainable way. The demand and consumption of petroleum products have, however, continued to grow with the expanding economy.

Table 14.6. Petroleum development levies, 1989–1996

	1989–91	1992–96
Liquefied petroleum gas	87	151
Gasoline, kerosene, diesel, fuel oil and bitumen	50	114

The factors which underlie the upward trend include the levels of real income, the prices of petroleum products, the utilization rate of automobiles, the stock and average fuel consumption of automobiles, the availability of public transport and the number of industries. Since the use of petroleum products is positively correlated to the production of emissions such as carbon dioxide, carbon monoxide, nitrous oxide, lead, sulfur dioxide and particulates, it is an important determinant of the extent of environmental degradation in Kenya, particularly air pollution. That the emissions can move great distances and even across national boundaries implies that they can also adversely affect the environmental quality in other countries. We feel, however, that this is insignificant in the East African context. Stemming from the arguments advanced above, the various taxes levied on petroleum products can be regarded as environmental taxes, although their express purpose has not been to achieve particular environmental goals. These taxes include VAT, the petroleum development levy, import duty, excise duty and the road maintenance levy. The rates of these taxes over the 1989–96 period are shown in Tables 14.5–9. The values in the tables are in KShs/m^3 except for liquefied petroleum gas and bitumen where they are per 1,000kg.

Table 14.7. Import duty on petroleum products

	1989 –91	1992 –93	1993 (Mar .)	1993 (June)	1994 (Feb.)	1994 (June)	1994 (Oct.)	1996 (June)
Liquefied PG	242	242	242	500	625	4,020	3,020	3,020
Prem. gasoline	653	653	726	2,000	2,500	2,500	2,500	2,500
Regular gasoline	653	653	726	2,000	2,500	2,500	2,500	2,500
Illuminatin g kerosene	204	204	204	204	204	0	0	3,000
Automotive diesel	454	454	484	2,000	2,000	2,500	1,900	2,080
Industrial Diesel	0	400	400	1,500	1,875	3,900	3,900	4,400
Fuel oil	0	400	400	1,500	1,875	3,850	3,350	3,350
Bitumen	121	121	121	1,500	1,875	1,875	1,875	1,875

Table 14.8. Excise duty on petroleum products, June 1994–June 1996

	June 1994	Oct 1994–June 1995	Feb 1996–June 1996
Premium gasoline	9,900	9,900	11,600
Regular gasoline	9,800	9,800	11,300
Automotive diesel	5,800	4,400	5,720

With regard to the VAT levied on petroleum products it can reasonably be generalized that for the 1989–96 period the rates exhibited an upward trend followed by drastic reductions with effect from June 1994. To be more exact the VAT on premium gasoline, regular gasoline, illuminating kerosene and automotive diesel were discontinued in June 1994. VAT was, however, retained for liquefied petroleum gas, heavy industrial diesel and bitumen, though, with the exception of bitumen, at lower rates. A significant development which needs to be borne in mind is that the discontinuation of VAT on the aforesaid products coincided with the introduction of the road maintenance levy and excise duty. The only exception was kerosene, on which these taxes were not levied.

Table 14.9. Road maintenance levies and collections, 1994/95–1996/97

	1994–1995	1995–1996	1996–1997
Premium and regular gasoline	1,500	2,000	2,000
Automotive diesel	1,500	15,000	1,000
Total collection Kshs pounds	67,632,860	120,000,000	158,969,874

The main reason for the introduction of the road maintenance levy was to generate the financial resources for maintaining and expanding the country's road network to stimulate economic activity. Its design was geared primarily to remedying the shortcomings of the road toll levies which had hitherto excluded a substantial proportion of road, gasoline and diesel users. Its major strength has been that the charges are built into the prices of the affected petroleum products. Thus they are automatically directly proportional to the quantity of fuel purchased. The revenues generated through the road maintenance levy over the 1994/95–1996/97 period are as shown in the fourth row of Table 14.9.

If we compare the VATs that were levied on premium gasoline, regular gasoline, illuminating kerosene and automotive diesel until June 1994 with the combined road maintenance levy and excise duty which were introduced at this time, it becomes clear that with the exception of kerosene the net taxes on these products were positive. This is demonstrated in Table 10.

Table 14.10. Comparison of VAT with combined road maintenance levy and excise duty on selected petroleum products (Kshs/m³)

	VAT	Road maintenance levy and excise duty	Net tax
Premium gasoline	9,411	11,400	1,989
Regular gasoline	9,391	11,300	1,909
Illuminating kerosene	391	0	0
Automotive diesel	5,245	6,800	1,555

One direct and immediate consequence of the positive net taxes on the above products was an increase in the prices faced by their users. We do not expect this to have caused a substantial decrease in the consumption of these products due to their low price elasticities of demand. The view that price elasticities of demand for these products was low is predicated on the conclusions of empirical studies which have been undertaken to analyze their demand. In Senga et al. (1980), the short-run price elasticity of demand for gasoline was estimated to range from –0.05 to –0.47 but tending to cluster around –0.2 while the long-run price elasticity was estimated to range from –0.24 to –0.82. In Kimuyu (1988) the price elasticity of demand for commercial energy (petroleum is Kenya's major source of commercial energy) was estimated to be about –0.1735. A study of Kenya's energy sector undertaken jointly by the United Nations Development Program and the World Bank (UNDP/IBRD 1980) also had similar results. The price elasticities for gasoline, aviation spirit and heavy diesel were found to be of –0.84, –0.07 and –0.82, respectively. The elasticities were, however, found to be higher for kerosene (–1.63), gasoline (–1.59) and liquefied petroleum gas (–1.97).

The low price elasticities for gasoline, heavy diesel and aviation spirit explain in part why these energy carriers have long been targets for higher government taxes. Kerosene's use in Kenya has largely been confined to low-income households. The low taxes levied on it reflect a central concern in the country's economic and social policies, namely, the protection of low-income households. This is why the price of kerosene was subsidized for a long time. As part of the economic reform process being currently undertaken, the subsidies on kerosene have been abolished with the result that the price of this fuel has risen, thus prompting many poor households to shift more and more to the use of woodfuel, crop wastes and animal dung.

Also to protect low-income households, kerosene was with effect from June 1994 exempted from duty. The unfortunate though not unexpected effect of this rebate was increased diversionary use and smuggling of the fuel to neighboring Tanzania and Uganda. The extent of kerosene smuggling has, however, been extremely difficult to estimate because of the illegal nature of the practice and its exclusive occurrence outside the formal channels. However, on the basis of the large price differentials which existed at the time under consideration, it is plausible to expect that the extent of smuggling was substantial. The incentives for smuggling were particularly strong given that the duty and taxes on kerosene charged in Tanzania and Uganda were 16 percent and 116 percent, respectively. These were the main reasons why an import duty of 18 percent was imposed on kerosene in June 1996. The price of kerosene was in the process raised by Kshs 3.00 per liter. From the price elasticity of kerosene, we can infer that the imposition of duty affected the consumption of this fuel substantially. It is among the factors which underlie the shift of more and more poor households to the use of woodfuels, which in turn has a deleterious effect on the environment.

3.3 Electricity

Electricity ranks second in importance to petroleum fuels as a source of commercial energy in Kenya. The bulk of it is generated from hydrothermal and geothermal plants and is used mainly in industrial and commercial establishments. Small amounts of electricity are also generated from wind and solar power (Republic of Kenya 1995d).

Although its generation, transmission and utilization entail considerable efficiency losses, electricity has the unique advantage of being highly versatile and therefore capable of being conveniently used as a source of both mechanical and thermal energy (O'Keefe et al. 1984). This is why rural electrification is a priority in Kenya's development strategy and more so at this time when the country is pursuing the goal of industrializing. Notwithstanding the fact that the installed capacity has risen over the years, the domestic supply of electricity has continued to lag behind the demand. Meeting the deficit has been primarily through imports from Uganda.

Since the generation of electricity is costly, it is the government's policy to encourage both its economic consumption and its conservation. There is considerable scope for using economic instruments to achieve this goal. We need to point out here that for a long time electricity use in Kenya was highly subsidized. This partly explains the wastefulness which characterized and has continued to characterize its use. It is further evidenced by the fact that the tariffs on electricity were and have continued to be much lower than the long-run marginal cost of electricity. It was to deal with this distortion that the government in its policy paper on environment and development (Republic of Kenya 1995a) declared that tariffs would be raised to 75 percent of the long-run marginal cost by the beginning of June 1996. Thereafter further adjustments would be effected to raise the tariffs to fully cover the long-run marginal costs. Like petroleum products, taxing electrical energy has been an important source of revenue to the government. The main tax levied on electrical energy has been VAT whose present rate is 8 percent of the taxable value of electrical energy consumed. The first 200 units under domestic consumption are, however, exempted from tax and therefore constitute tax expenditure. Broadly speaking we can regard the tax levied on electrical energy as an environmental tax since it has environmental ramifications. Although we do not have empirical evidence, we can plausibly hypothesize that high taxes on electrical energy will discourage its use for domestic purposes and increase the demand for woodfuels.

4. ENVIRONMENTAL EFFECTS ON TAXES

The discussions in the foregoing sections demonstrate that the overriding concern in Kenya's tax policies has been the generation of revenue to the government. The purpose has not been to bring about particular environmental outcomes. A number of the taxes can, however, be regarded as environmental taxes if by environmental taxes we mean those taxes introduced for non-environmental reasons, but which have environmental impacts (Sterner 1994a; OECD 1994). In at least two ways they can be a valuable instrument for protecting the environment. First, they can be used to induce shifts from activities and products that have harmful effects on the environment. This is the case when they are used to correct for negative externalities. These are economic activities whose effects are external to those who decide over them. They therefore generate social costs that are not fully translated into private costs. Such externalities usually result when decisions of the users of environmental resources are independent of the determinants of those decisions. When external costs are not internalized through appropriate mechanisms, suboptimal results can be expected with the level of environmental damage being excessive. So far the practice of this principle has not been attempted in Kenya.

The other way in which environmental taxes can serve the goals of environmental protection is by generating the resources for financing abatement measures. Levying taxes for such a purpose is consistent with the polluter pays principle, which requires that agents whose activities result in environmental damage meet the costs of clean-up. For optimality these taxes need to be set at levels equal to the marginal damage costs. Ascertaining such costs is therefore an important first step in designing environmental taxes. This, too, has not been attempted in Kenya.

The environmental effects which can be attributed to the various taxes in Kenya include

1. *Increased deforestation.* The country's energy sector has been heavily dependent on fuelwood whose use has risen steadily over the years. In fact there is presently an acute shortage of energy in the country. This, in conjunction with the open access character of several of the country's forests and woodlands, has culminated in widespread deforestation. But when considering the use of wood as fuel, we need to take cognizance of the fact that its demand is also dependent on, among others, the availability and prices of substitutes such as kerosene, liquefied petroleum gas (LPG) and electricity. The sharp rises in the prices of these substitutes over the years coupled with their relatively high price elasticities of demand can therefore explain the high rates at which the country's forests are being lost. Hence it is plausible to hold that macroeconomic factors such as devaluation of the Kenyan shilling, the removal of subsidies and imposition of taxes which underlie the increase in energy prices have had adverse effects on the environment. The assumption being made here is that the increases in energy prices have not induced significant technological innovations. Efficiency in energy use has therefore not been enhanced. For practical reasons, we can expect significant increase in energy use efficiency only in the medium to long term.
2. *Increased agrochemical use.* Kenya's supply of suitable agricultural land is limited, and increasing agricultural output has largely depended on improving the productivity. Towards this end, the policy of the government has been to promote the use of yield-increasing agricultural chemicals such as fertilizers, pesticides and herbicides through subsidies and low taxation or even exemption from tax altogether. Many subsidies have been abolished but the low taxes remain. This is clearly exemplified in the zero rating of agricultural chemicals in the VAT

schedule. The high fertilizer and pesticide use which has resulted from this policy is environmentally harmful, though yields have increased in the process.

3. *Improved quality of the coastal environment.* This was among the reasons given for the introduction of the beach management levy. It is a plausible outcome on two grounds. First, access to the beaches has been restricted. Second, the beach management levy is a mechanism for mobilizing the resources for clean-up. The beach management levy is obviously an environmental tax since its introduction was mainly for environment reasons. It is similar to the charge of Kshs 50.00 per month which local government authorities require urban dwellers to pay for services such as provision of waste bins. Like the service charge, this latter levy has not been put to its intended use as is manifested by the increased accumulation of waste, particularly in urban areas.
4. *Vehicle Use.* It is quite plain that the number of motor vehicles in the country and especially in the urban areas where their concentration is high is among the major determinants of the extent of air pollution. Factors which influence the prices of motor vehicles and the extent of their use are therefore important in this respect too. On the basis of these premises we can say that vehicle sales tax and road license fees have environmental impacts. Again it is appropriate to point out that it is fiscal and not environmental motivations which underlie the structure of these particular taxes.

5. CONCLUSION

Although Kenya's taxes are motivated primarily by fiscal considerations, we have tried in this chapter to associate some of them with particular environmental outcomes. To this extent, they can be regarded as environmental taxes. Among the taxes which fall in this category are those charged on motor vehicles, petroleum products, electrical energy, agricultural chemicals and the beach management levy. The service charge can also be regarded as an environmental tax if its use is confined to environmental concerns. These taxes are important because they can be used either to induce shifts from products and activities which have deleterious environmental impacts and/or to generate the resources for financing environmental protection. If, however, we want outcomes which are economically efficient, we need to design specific taxes which are at least equal to the value of marginal damage caused by the particular activities under consideration. For Kenya no empirical studies have been done to specifically assess and value the extent of environmental damage caused by particular activities. However, provisions exist in the country's laws for the imposition of penalties on the economic agents whose activities degrade the environment beyond the permitted limits. These penalties have largely failed to achieve their intended purpose because they have tended to be mild and also because of difficulties in enforcing the set standards. That some relation exists between certain taxes and environmental quality suggests that there is scope for using them to direct the county's development toward sustainable paths.

REFERENCES

Customs and Exercise Act. Chapter 472 of the Laws of Kenya.

Income Tax Act. Chapter 476 of the Laws of Kenya.

Kimuyu, P.K. (1988), 'Demand for Commercial Energy in Kenya 1963–1985: A Structural Investigation'. PhD Dissertation, Economics Department University of Nairobi.

Meir, P.M. (1986), 'Energy Planning in Developing Countries: An Introduction to Analytical Methods'. Energy Management Training Monograph Series.

Munasinghe, M. (1984) *Kenya: Energy Pricing and Demand Management* Boulder, CO: Westview Press.

OECD (1994), *Managing the Environment: The Role of Economic Instruments.* Paris.

Oginda, J.S. (1987), 'Demand for Gasoline and Light Diesel in Kenya'. Unpublished MA Thesis submitted to the University of Nairobi.

O'Keefe, P., Raskin, P. and Bernow, Stave (1984), *Energy and Development in Kenya: Opportunities and Constraints.* Stockholm: Beijer Institute.

Onjala, J.O. and Jama, A. Mohamud (1994), 'Energy Economy Interactions in Kenya'. Mimeograph.

Republic of Kenya (1995a), *Policy paper on Environment and Development: Policy, Objectives and Recommendations.* Nairobi: Government Printer.

Republic of Kenya (1995b), *Economic Survey.* Nairobi: Government Printer.

Republic of Kenya (1995c), *Statistical Abstract.* Nairobi: Government Printer.

Republic of Kenya (1996a), *Economic Survey.* Nairobi: Government Printer.

Republic of Kenya (1996b), *Kenya Gazette Supplement* No. 34, 18 June. Nairobi: Government printer.

Republic of Kenya (1996c), *Kenya Gazette* (**98**)36, 14 June. Nairobi: Government Printer.

Republic of Kenya (1996d), *Legal Notice* No. 9. The Wildlife (Conservation and Management) Act. Cap. 376, 31 January.

Republic of Kenya (1996e), *Finance Bill of 1996.* Nairobi: Government Printer.

Senga, W.M.W., House, J. and Manundu, M. (1980), *Assessment of Commercial Energy Supply and Demand in Kenya.* Study Commissioned by the United Nations

Department of Technical Cooperation for Development in conjunction with National Council for Science and Technology.

Sterner, T. (1994a), 'Environmental Tax Reform: Theory, Industrialized Country Experiences and their Relevance in Less Developed Countries'. Environmental Economics Working Paper 2 of 1994. Gothenburg University, Gothenburg.

Sterner, T. (ed.) (1994b), *Economic Policies for Sustainable Development.* Boston, MA: Kluwer.

UNDP/IBRD (1980), *Kenya: Issues and Options in the Energy Sector.* Report of the joint UNDP/World Bank Energy Sector Assessment Program.

15. Economic Instruments for Environmental Management in Tanzania: The Case of Environmental Taxes

Godius Kahyarara[1]

1. BACKGROUND

Since independence, Tanzania has experienced massive economic changes from market economy to state control in 1967, and from state control to market economy in the 1980s. Her economy depends largely on agriculture as it contributes over 70 per cent of total foreign exchange, 54 per cent of total GDP and provides employment to over 80 per cent of the labour force. Following poor performance of the economy in the 1970s and 1980s, Tanzania is undertaking economic reforms supervised by the World Bank and International Monetary Fund (IMF). During the economic reforms era, Tanzania is faced with the challenge of sustainable economy so as to meet the needs of the present generation without compromising the ability of future generations to meet their own needs.

In the context of changing economic and development environment, when environmental problems detract from sustainable development, they are increasingly coming to the attention of the government and the general public. This is vindicated by the government's policy to put all environmental issues under the Vice-President's office and to establish of the National Environmental Council. Tanzania was also represented in the 1992 Conference on Environment and Development held by the United Nations (UNCED) in Rio de Janeiro, and participated in the preparation of AGENDA 21, which recommends a global plan of action for achieving sustainable development. In implementing AGENDA 21, Tanzania has introduced a

[1] I am very grateful to Professor Thomas Sterner of Göteborg University in Sweden, Dr Flora Musonda, Mr Omary Kimweri, Mrs Albina Kasango and Stella Kemilembe all of the Economic and Social Research Foundation and the Government of Tanzania for their invaluable contributions to this chapter.

National Conservation Strategy for Sustainable Development (NCSSD) whose main focus is on sustainable utilization of natural resources with the aim of encompassing the goals and strategies of AGENDA 21. In addition, the government prepared the National Environmental Action Plan (NEAP) as a means to link and coordinate efforts in all sectors of the economy in fulfilment of national environmental plans and to ensure implementation of the AGENDA. According to this plan, the key policy instruments and strategies identified as important for achieving sustainable development are environmental legislation, environmental impact assessment, economic instruments, environmental indicators and standards public participation. The establishment of environmental taxes on permits, imports and domestic goods has been proposed as part of the economic instruments of environmental management. The areas earmarked for such kinds of taxation are air pollution, water pollution, protection of public health, land degradation and protection of wildlife.

In 1996, the government also revised the National Environmental Policy to cater for implementation of the AGENDA. In order to ensure effective channelling of financial resources to environmental conservation efforts, Tanzania has incorporated environmental aspects into the ongoing macroeconomic policy reforms, especially fiscal policies, financial sector reforms and other reforms in government revenue and expenditure. Investment in environmentally friendly technology and environmental conservation campaigns qualifies for various incentives such as low tax rates. Tanzania has also set out strategies to ensure availability of adequate and multidisciplinary training of skills in environmental issues. This has included introduction of environmental studies in various Training Institutes including the University of Dar es Salaam. Public awareness campaigns have also been applied as a means of spreading knowledge about the existence, extent and effect of, and solution to various environmental problems.

2. ENVIRONMENTAL PROBLEMS OF TANZANIA

Six major problems of environment have been identified by the National Environmental Action Plan of Tanzania. These are land degradation, lack of accessible water supply and poor water quality, environmental pollution, deterioration of aquatic systems, loss of wildlife habitats and bio-diversity, and deforestation. These problems appear in several forms discussed below.

1. Loss and deterioration of soils, degradation of water resources and damage to ecological process and life-support systems and deforestation. Between 300,000 and 400,000 hectares of forests are

cleared each year. It is currently estimated that about 35 per cent of Tanzania is suffering from desertification.

2. Water sources in Tanzania are threatened by pollution, posing hazards to life. Industrial effluent and sewage, turbidity and bacterial contamination are common in these water sources. Some aquifers contain excessive amounts of fluoride, salt, or objectionable minerals.
3. The management of wastes and emissions in many parts of Tanzania poses serious environmental problems. It is estimated that only 15–20 per cent of the residents in urban areas benefit from sewerage services, including septic tanks and soakways.
4. The pressure exerted by increasing poaching and encroachment endangering wildlife and genetic resources is one of the manifestations of environmental problems. Tanzania's elephant population recorded a decline from 316,000 in 1979 to 85,000 in 1987 and 52,400 in 1991 – an average loss of 60 elephants a day (Bagachwa and Limbu 1995).
5. Poor methods of farming, including failure to conserve the soil and water, urban agriculture with improper disposal of animal wastes, improper use of fertilizers (and overuse of pesticides, herbicides and fungicides), pressure by peasants to extend agriculture, and search for woodfuel, timber and so on have resulted in severe environmental problems, especially land degradation and loss of water sources.
6. Overgrazing of animals in the semi-savanna areas of northern and central Tanzania has resulted in the region's carrying capacity being exceeded by 200 per cent (DANIDA 1989). About two-fifths of the livestock population in Tanzania is concentrated in the three regions of Shinyanga, Arusha and Mwanza out of 25 regions in the country.
7. Overfishing and destruction of fish habitats, through the use of very small mesh sizes in freshwater fisheries, uncontrolled dynamite fishing and illegal sand quarrying in the river beds close to the coast are observable in Tanzania.
8. Motor traffic, exhaust fumes, industries and solid waste burning have resulted in high concentrations of carbon monoxide, sulphur dioxide, suspended particulate matter, nitrogen oxides, hydrocarbons and other pollutants, including lead.

3. ENVIRONMENTAL MANAGEMENT IN TANZANIA

Environmental regulatory systems in Tanzania are dominated by command and control principles. Provisions that are directly legally binding include statutes themselves, together with regulations made under a framework of the statutes. Other instruments, such as guidelines and codes of practice, have been in use to help enforce other legally binding provisions or conditions. In addition there are common rules such as torts of negligence and nuisance which are relevant to environmental protection. Tanzania's parliament also enacts statutory laws to deal with various aspects of the environment. These laws are known as principal legislation. There are about 50 principal laws related to environmental issues.[2]

Lack of environmental standards has been a limiting factor to the effectiveness of the existing environmental management framework. All three broad categories of environmental standards, that is, ambient and receptor standard, emission standard and specification standard, are either non-existing or not well defined in almost all sectors of the economy. Other reasons are administrative bottlenecks, and lack of environmental awareness.

Recently, discussion has focused on the possibility of replacing the command and control approach with one relying more on market-based instruments. Pollution taxes or deposit-refund systems, pollution rights or marketable permits to emit have been proposed by the National Environmental Action Plan for testing in Tanzania's conditions. The economic instruments are thus to take the form of incentives such as pricing, tax relief and subsidies and disincentives such as environmental taxes and resort to the polluter pays principle. These are to be supplemented by other measures such as public participation in the form of ensuring accessibility by the people to all relevant information on the environment.

4. ENVIRONMENTAL TAXES IN TANZANIA

Lower taxes on environmentally friendly technologies or products, and higher taxes on environmentally damaging processes, products as well as consumption patterns, is a strategic taxation policy in Tanzania for environmental protection. Maximum rates of excise and import duties are imposed on cigarettes, beer and other commodities which are perhaps not 'environmental' in the usual sense but are certainly harmful, and do cause external damage to others. In the mining sector, efforts to discourage artisanal mining which has a great impact on the environment, include granting zero tax on production equipment incorporating appropriate technology, until the year of production when they are charged 5 per cent import duty. Production taxes, property taxes, miscellaneous taxes and local taxes are also used as tools of environmental protection. Specifically, environmental taxes have been imposed on sectoral activities, depending on

[2] National Environmental Policy (1995).

the nature and the intensity of the environmental problems. Some of these taxes are discussed below.

4.1 Agriculture

Prior to the 1990s when there were massive implementations of agricultural and rural development programmes, the government subsidized the price of fertilizers. This resulted in excessive use of fertilizers, which badly affected the soil in many parts of the country, although increased productivity in the short run.

With economic liberalization, subsidies on fertilizers have been removed. Fertilizers are subject to a 5 per cent tax rate which has resulted in a rise in price and a decline in fertilizer use by about 40 per cent. The reduction in fertilizer use is said to have led to lower crop yield, which has forced farmers to encroach into forests (searching for fertile land,) with disastrous consequences for the environment. On the other hand, the decline in fertilizer use has led to a reduction in the negative effect of fertilizers on the soil. Also there are taxes in some livestock-keeping areas of Tanzania aimed at discouraging the keeping large herds of cattle, and for the purpose of revenue collection as well. These taxes, mainly under the provision of bylaws, are charged per head of livestock, see Table 15.1.

Table 15.1. Taxes on livestock in selected parts of Tanzania

Livestock	Morogoro (Tax per head, Tshs)	Dodoma (Tax per head, Tshs)	Mwanza (Tax per head, Tshs)
Cattle	500	200	150
Goat	500	100	100
Horse	–	100	–
Sheep	–	200	100
Donkey	–	–	150

Note: Exchange rate US$1= Tshs 600.
Source: URT (1997).

Table 15.1 indicates that tax rates applied vary considerably across the regions. Morogoro appears to have the highest rates (although Morogoro is not among the regions which have exceeded their carrying capacity in terms of livestock keeping) whereas Mwanza has the minimum rates. While the local governments rely heavily on these taxes as one of the revenue sources, it is also evident that such taxes have, to some extent, served the purpose of regulating the behaviour of livestock keepers. In areas where local governments are strong and every livestock keeper is forced to pay, farmers have responded by reducing the total number of livestock, thus reducing the pressure on land.

Hunting has so far had an adverse environmental impact on the wildlife sector of Tanzania. To counteract this effect, hunting licence fees have been introduced. Table 15.2 summarizes different rates of fees as applied to various groups of hunting operators.

Table 15.2. Licence fees applicable in the wildlife subsector

Type of operation	Type of fee	Amount in US$
Hunting safari by foreigners	Licence fee	3,000
Hunting safari by locals		1,000

Note: Exchange rate US$1 = Tshs 600.
Source: URT (1997).

The rates indicated in the table, show that the fees paid by licensed foreign hunters are low and affordable given the high cost of big game hunting. The impact on environmental protection is thus limited. Efforts are needed to introduce fees which will be prohibitive enough to regulate the behaviour of hunters, specifically by reducing their hunting activities.

4.2 The Existing Taxes in the Fishing Subsector

Table 15.3. Taxes applicable in fishing in selected areas of Tanzania

	District/regions (tax in Tshs)		
Type of fish	Kondoa	Newala	Mwanza
Sardines per sack	126	–	315
Dried fish per sack	500	630	–
A fish	–	–	107
Monthly tax	–	–	10,000

Note: Exchange rate US$1= Tshs 600.
Source: URT (1997).

In almost all fishing areas there exist certain forms of taxes which are administered by local governments. These are set for both revenue collection, and regulation of the behaviour of the fishermen and their fishing activities, so as to slow down the rate of environmental destruction and restore depletions associated with fishing. Some of the major problems targeted by these taxes in the subsector are the use of very small mesh sizes in fisheries which result in the catch of young fish, and a high concentration of fishermen around water bodies, which make the control of illegal fishing by the government difficult. Some of these illegal activities are uncontrolled dynamite fishing and the use of poisons in fishing, clearing of mangroves and other activities resulting in the pollution of coastal habitats. Table 15.3 summarizes tax rates applied to some fishing areas in Tanzania.

The tax rates in various places have been low, hence having less impact on environmental conservation. However, these taxes are supplemented by a total ban on the use of dynamite and poisons in fishing, although evidence suggests that illegal fishing is still carried on at an alarming rate.

4.3 Environmental Taxes for Counteracting Deforestation

It is estimated that between 300,000 and 400,000 hectares of forest are cleared each year in Tanzania through encroachment for fuelwood, timber, farming, and others, thus increasing deforestation. Several taxes on forest products exist as an attempt to slow down deforestation in addition to revenue collection. The main forest products which have been subject to tax include firewood, charcoal, timber and honey. Also since 1995 the government has banned export of hardwood, which was in danger of becoming extinct. Table 15.4 summarizes taxes as applied in some of the districts in Tanzania.

There are no clear criteria and the taxes are set arbitrarily by the local governments. For the case of charcoal there is a slight difference as it is subject to more than one tax. In the table, for example, it is shown that there is a tax for felling trees which are raw materials for making charcoal, and later the finished product (charcoal) is charged another tax in the market. This is the result of government efforts to educate the public on the danger associated with relying too much on charcoal as a source of fuel.

Table 15.4. Taxes on forest products in selected areas of Tanzania

District	Forest product	Cubic Metres	Amount in Tshs
Morogoro	Black wood	1 * 12 * 12	100
		1 * 8 * 12	126
		1 * 6 * 12	130
		2 * 8 * 12	130
		2 * 3 * 12	89
		2 * 2 * 12	63
Kondoa	Charcoal	NA	3150
	Wax	Kg	76
	Timber	Any size	208
Mwanza	Timber	Long timber	1575
	Honey	Per tin	630
	Felling tree	Per tree	144
	Charcoal	Per sack	76
	Timber	Per piece	76
	Firewood	Seven	2520

Source: URT (1997).

4.4 Mineral Sector

Mining activities in Tanzania have also left the country with some considerable environmental hazards such as deforestation, air and water pollution and land degradation. Different tax rates are applied in various mining areas, largely administered by local governments. Tax rates are levied on sand and quarry mining with the objective of combating beach erosion and other forms of land damage. These are summarized in Table 15.5.

Table 15.5. Taxes applied in sand mining areas

District	Type of mining	Size	Amount paid (Tshs)
Ulanga	Sand	1 lorry	630
	Stones	1 lorry	1,126
Dar es Salaam	Sand	1 lorry	3,870
Kilimanjaro	Sand	1 lorry	3,780

Source: URT (1997).

With these charges in place, the rate of sand mining has been lowered. Sand has become expensive to obtain compared to industrial construction materials such as bricks and so on which are made using environmentally friendly technology and cheaper materials. Nevertheless, these taxes are low in relation to the goal of reducing environmental hazards caused by mining activities.

In gemstone and gold mining there are a number of taxes both at the central and local government levels, which are either directly or indirectly related to environmental protection. Mineral dealers are supposed to pay about US$100 per month to the central government for a licence fee, and some of the money collected is used for covering open pits left by the small-scale miners. Miners also pay different types of taxes, which include royalties and withholding taxes. They are also charged a fee for every tree cut in their mining area. These charges are paid to the central government and they vary depending on the type of tree cut. Local governments in mining areas impose different forms of taxes and some of these are used to restore the damaged environment. In certain mining villages the money is used to hire youths, who cover the open pits left uncovered after the supply of minerals has been exhausted.

4.5 Water Pollution

Figures from the early 1990s reveal that more than 60,000 cubic metres of polluted water were released daily into the groundwater, 128,148 cubic metres into the sea and 5,058 into the ponds. Local governments and municipal authorities have initiatives for dealing with this issue. The Dar es Salaam Sanitary and Sewage Department (DSSD), for example, operates a tariff structure for sewerage with the assumption that 80 per cent of the water consumed is disposed of as waste.

Table 15.6. The current sewerage charge

Type of use	Amount paid (in US dollars) per month
Domestic	$12
Industrial	$48
Commercial	$13

Source: Dar es Salaam Sewage and Sanitary Department (DSSD), 1997.

These rates are supposed to reduce the pollution as they increase with the intensity of water use. For example, industries are shown to have the maximum rate whereas domestic consumers pay the minimum rate.

Evidence suggests that water is inefficiently used, especially in Tanzania's urban centers. In order to ensure efficient use of water, the tariff rates have been adjusted upward since 1997, see Table 15.7.

Table 15.7. Tariff rates applied to water consumers

Category of consumer	Water supply (in US$ per 1,000 gallons)
Domestic	$1.2
Institutions	$1.4
Industrial	$2
Brick making	$2.5
Irrigation	$2.5

Source: Dar es Salaam Water and Sewage Authority, 1997.

4.6 Air Pollution

The increasing number of cars and expansion of industrial activities in Tanzania especially during the mid 1980s and early 1990s have been a major cause of air pollution. In the 1997 budget speech, the government made amendments to the various taxes on different categories of small cars to ensure efficient use of fuel.

Table 15.8. Taxes on petroleum products

Type of product	Import duty(%)	Sales tax(%)	Excise duty
Motor spirit	5	30	–
Illuminating kerosene	5	5	18 Shs
Diesel oil	5	0	0
Fuels oil	5	0	0
Lubricating oil	5	0	600 Shs

Note: Exchange rate Shs 600 =US$1.
Source: URT Budget Speech, 1997.

Following the amendments, an excise duty of 30 per cent has been introduced for all station wagon cars, and the custom duty on all cars has been raised by 10 per cent. Apart from these amendments, certain energy taxes on petrol, diesel, heating gas oil and electricity exist in Tanzania which, among other objectives, are used to serve the cause of environmental protection. Some of the energy taxes on petroleum products were also adjusted during the last budget speech. For example, 5 per cent sales tax on gas oil, increased excise duty on liquefied petroleum gas (LPG) and an increase in excise duty on industrial diesel oil by 55 per cent. These measures are aimed at both raising government revenue and ensuring an efficient use of petroleum products, see Table 15.8.

5. CONCLUSIONS AND POLICY IMPLICATIONS

The tendency of the environmental problems in Tanzania to persist and increase over time is evidence that the existing environmental management framework is weak and insufficient. The current move by the government to focus on the possibility of replacing the command and control approach by one relying more on market-based instruments is thus justifiable. However, there are areas where physical control is still required.

The introduction of market-based instruments for environmental management, such as taxes, should be done very cautiously for several reasons. For example, the overall tax system in Tanzania has not been effective enough. Tax evasion is still high, and the tax system lacks clarity, uniformity and transparency. Environmental taxes are still very new even among the policy makers, and one major challenge is how to strike a balance between the conflicting objectives of revenue collection and environmental protection. The environmental taxes are administered mainly by the local governments which lack qualified personnel in tax and environmental economics. The rates are arbitrarily set and lack uniformity and clarity as mentioned above. The central government must take an upper hand in setting the rates and in administering some of these taxes.

The other important aspect to be considered is that tax exemption contradicts the aim of the World Bank and IMF of eliminating subsidies, and also the budgetary problems facing the country. Initially, imported, environmentally friendly, technology was granted zero tax but since last year it has been charged a 5 per cent duty. Despite these difficulties, economic instruments have a major role to play. This is evident from the fact that prior to 1985, trade policy in Tanzania was restrictive as the government resorted extensively to quantitative restrictions, to protect both the infant industry and external trade balance. Between the late 1970s and 1984, tariff rates were prohibitive, ranging between 0 and 300, resulting in a lower rate of consumption of various products, for example, petroleum products, cars and others.

Currently, prohibitive taxes are imposed on endangered hardwoods. This is supplemented by a total ban on exports of hardwood and these policies have been very successful. This shows that these instruments may be implemented at a lesser cost as they do not require cumbersome administrative or enforcement procedures. An appropriate environmental management framework will require the combination of both regulatory and economic instruments depending on the nature of the problem. A broad study would be required to design an appropriate environmental tax system for Tanzania.

REFERENCES

Bagachwa, M.S.D and Limbu, F. (eds) (1995), *Policy Reform and the Environment in Tanzania*, Dar es Salaam University Press.

Danish International Development Agency (DANIDA) (1989), *Environmental Profile: Tanzania*, Copenhagen: Ministry of Foreign Affairs.

Kulindwa, K. and Shechambo, C. (1995), 'Environmental Implications of Economic Reform Policies for Agricultural Development of Tanzania' in Bagachwa and Limbu (eds), pp. 89–118.

Mashala, Salome K. (1979), 'Vegetation as a Source of Fuel in Tanzania', MA Thesis, University of Dar es Salaam.

Mkenda, A and Kishimba, O. (1995), 'The Impact of Structural Adjustment Programs on Urban Pollution and Sanitation: Empirical Evidence From Urban Canters in Tanzania', in Bagachwa and Limbu (eds), pp. 125–96

Mnkeni, P.N.S. (1992), *Role of Soil Management in Enhancing Sustainability of Smallholder Cropping System in Some Agro Ecosystems in Tanzania. As (Norway)*: Ecology and Development Programme.

Mnzava, E.M (1981), 'The Wood Crisis in Tanzania: Policy Problems and Statics', Dar es Salaam Ministry of Natural Resources and Tourism (mimeo).

Mugurusi, E.K. (1995), 'Transitional Economic Policy and Policy Options', Paper prepared for Economic and Social Research Foundation.

Naho, A. (1995), 'The Link Between Public Policy and Deforestation: An Econometric Analysis of Tanzania', in Bagachwa and Limbu (eds), pp. 161–72.

Ndesamburo, J. (1993), 'Management of Liquid Wastes', Paper presented at a Seminar on Liquid Waste Management in Dar es Salaam.

United Republic of Tanzania (URT) (1997), *Financial Statement and Revenue Estimate*, Government Printer, Dar es Salaam.

United Republic of Tanzania (1989), *Tanzania Forest Action Plan, 1990/91–2007/08*, Dar es Salaam: Ministry of Land, Natural Resources and Tourism.

United Republic of Tanzania (URT) (1994), 'The National Environmental Policy' First Draft; Dar es Salaam Ministry of Tourism, Natural Resources and Environment.

16. The Role of Enforcement and Economic Instruments in Inducing Environmental Investment in a Transition Economy: The Water Sector in Romania

Clifford Zinnes, Cornel Tarhoaca and Mihaela Popovici[1]

1. INTRODUCTION

A principal challenge in transition economies is to stimulate an optimal level of investment in environmental compliance and abatement (Hughes 1991). The historical use in these economies of command and control methods for this purpose, though, has been shown to be costly, both in theory and in practice (Markandya 1994). Unfortunately, the conditions being placed on Eastern European countries for accession into the European Union include the achievement of even higher levels of environmental compliance (EDC 1997). Great attention has been focussed, therefore, on the choice and design of economic instruments with the aim of 'getting the prices right' so as to generate a more efficient allocation of environmental goods and services and to reduce the society-wide costs of environmental compliance (Panayotou 1994).

These policies presuppose that, once set, the prices will be paid. However, in the transition economies of Eastern Europe not even existing low prices for environmental goods and services are paid, let alone the presumably higher prices entailed by economic instruments set at allocatively efficient levels.

[1] Dr Zinnes is an institute associate at the Harvard Institute for International Development (HIID) and senior policy advisor for sustainable development to the Government of Romania. Prof. Tarhoaca is an assistant professor of economics at the Academy of Economic Studies, Bucharest, Romania. Ms. Popovici is executive director of the Center for Environmentally Sustainable Economic Policy in Bucharest, Romania. The authors express their gratitude to Secretary of State Viorel Raicu of the Water Department for whom this research was conducted and to Directors Cornel Predescu, Beatrice Popescu and Petre Serban for the cooperation of *Apele Romane*. Research was funded by the United States Agency for International Development through a cooperative agreement with the Harvard Institute for International Development (HIID). All opinions and errors are those of the authors.

Instead, compliance such as it is occurs through explicit and tacit negotiation and persuasion. Moreover, the region is undergoing massive privatization, the most powerful economic instrument of them all. While privatization leads to a greater responsiveness to price incentives (so a given level of pollution charges should lead to a higher level of environmental quality), the profit motive and competition encourage the privatized enterprise to take advantage of weak enforcement, thereby pushing regulatory limits.

The present chapter develops a decision-theoretic model of the enterprise non-compliance problem in the face of non-payment and where the probability of inspection on the part of the regulatory authority is endogenous. The model is then econometrically estimated, accounting for the degree of privatization, and used to analyze the role of enforcement and economic instruments in stimulating enterprise investment in abatement in the context of the water sector in Romania. The water sector is particularly good to study given that it takes on aspects of both a good as well as a service. Based upon these theoretical and empirical results, the chapter ends with a series of policy recommendations related to the introduction of economic instruments in a transition economy.

2. INSTITUTIONAL AND POLICY BACKGROUND[2]

Romania is a country of 23 million people. Water resources include the Danube River and 12 tributary basins, as well as the the 650,000-hectare Danube Delta – the largest wetland in Europe – and part of the Black Sea. In addition to having the largest old-growth forest reserves in Europe and abundant deposits of ferrous and non-ferrous metals, the country has reserves of oil, natural gas and coal. This resource abundance, however, has had its costs.[3] The country developed minerals, petrochemical, and metal-processing industries that are highly polluting, leading to economic, health and ecological impacts on an enormous scale. Such impacts have also stymied the development of activities with a potential future, such as tourism and fisheries.[4] While these costs are clear, weak economic growth during the transition has led to understandable trepidation about pursuing too quick or rigorous a program of environmental protection, and economic instruments in particular.

In 1997 and under the newly elected reformist government, an International Monetary Fund Financial and Enterprise Sector Adjustment Loan (IMF-FESAL) agreement launched the country on an ambitious privatization

[2] This section draws on, updates, and extends Zinnes (1997).
[3] This is not unusual internationally. Sachs and Warner(1995) show that countries with a greater abundance of natural resources have experienced *lower* long-run growth.
[4] A summary of the worst of these impacts by key economic sector and by health, ecological and economic effect is provided in Manea and Zinnes (1994).

program. Strong economic growth is expected as a result. These and other reforms will place new stresses on the environmental regulatory authorities at a time when budgetary austerity imposed by the FESAL will lead to a substantial reduction in personnel and equipment. While options are being considered on how to put regulatory finance on to a sustainable basis and though a comprehensive new set of environmental regulations has been drafted (Zinnes 1996), enforcement in the near term is certain to get worse. It is important to consider whether the privatization program will generate enterprise investment in environmental protection or will it lead to further environmental degradation as has been found elsewhere (Reed 1995).

At the same time, stimulated by (i) the new government's campaign commitment to set up an environmental fund, (ii) anticipation of World Bank loan conditionalities, and (iii) pressure to signal to the European Union Romania's seriousness to meet the environmental commitments of the legal approximation process of accession, there is a renewed interest in developing economic instruments. It is thus particularly germane to analyze in the context of Romania what the role should be of economic instruments and of command and control to elicit the necessary level of enterprise environmental investment in the future. In order to address these questions, we examine the effects that such polices have played so far in the privatization process on the water sector.

The water sector is regulated by the Water Department located in the Ministry of Water, Forests, and Environmental Protection (MAPPM). The Water Department supervises *Apele Române* (AR), a public utility with branches in each of the country's 12 river basins. AR is responsible for the management of 70,000 kilometers of rivers and 150 multi-purpose lakes and dikes. AR supplies 95 percent of the raw water to municipalities, industry, and agriculture. Local government is responsible for municipal water supply and wastewater treatment.

Water resources in Romania are administered according to the principles of integrated water management which links water quality and water quantity. This linkage is important because excessive abstractions lower underground and surface water levels, thereby increasing contaminant concentrations and creating the same deleterious environmental effects as effluent discharges. The permitting process, the heart of the regulatory system, incorporates this duality by issuing permits and assessing charges and fines both for water consumption and for effluent discharges. The 12 river basin branch offices of *Apele Române* issue permits based on the national water management strategy specifying the amount of water used or consumed, as well as the quantity and quality of effluents. Water management standards include effluent standards that limit the amount or rate of discharges. Ambient water quality standards also exist. These standards provide some flexibility, because they allow facilities to choose which technologies should be used to meet requirements.

For enforcement, the Water Department of MAPPM and AR can take legal action against non-complying facilities and levy fines and other sanctions – including closure – against violators. Compliance is monitored in many ways. First, AR conducts routine plant sampling and inspections, including the review of the facility's records (enterprises are responsible for monitoring and reporting their discharges). While the number of inspections are planned, the timing of the visit is not known to the enterprise. Second, AR carries out unplanned plant visits, usually based on concerns raised from other inspections. Third, when an accident is reported, AR does an immediate inspection. Finally, through its ambient program, AR also conducts periodic sampling from a series of sampling checkpoints along water bodies, both selectively for pollution-prone water bodies and according to predefined annual programs. Local environmental protection agencies also carry out some limited water monitoring.

Water charges exist in Romania and are collected by AR. They consist of prices for raw water abstraction and tariffs for discharges into water bodies.[5] Since abstractions can either be consumed or be discharged after use for cooling or for effluent removal, the charge system covers water as a 'good' and as a 'service'. They were introduced at the start of 1991 and rates are indexed quarterly.

Considering raw water prices first, these are set nationally based on type of water body (surface, subterranean, Danube) and category of user, with industry paying more than agriculture, and agriculture paying more than households. With little relationship to location-specific or temporal characteristics, however, this system does not accurately signal differences in water scarcity to economic agents. As a result, water-intensive activities may be undertaken in (socially) high-cost zones, though in principle AR may reject a construction permit request for such an activity. For the most part, however, plant location decisions under communism were not based on economic considerations. Water prices are also very low: rates per thousand cubic meters in 1996 for industrial users were 23,755 lei (US$4) from rivers, 2,851 lei (US$0.47) from the Danube, and 29,240 lei (US$5) from underground sources. Penalties of two to six times normal rates can be levied for abstractions *above* permitted limits, with the multiplier depending on the amount of the infraction and whether it occurred during a period of restricted consumption.

There are also charges for effluent discharges into water bodies. This charge system comprises two components, a *tariff* for within-permitted

[5] Discharges into sewage systems are contracted directly with the municipality owning the sewage works. Such services are not generally used by large enterprises.

discharge concentrations and a *penalty* (over and above the tariff) for above-permitted discharge concentrations. In 1996, for example, tariffs were levied only on two contaminants: a 7,850 lei/ton ($1.30) charged for suspended solids and a 31,750 lei/ton (US$5.30) charge for biochemical oxygen demands (BODs).

The penalty depends on both the volume of wastewater emitted and the *difference* between actual and permitted concentrations. For the *i*th pollutant, the formula used is $P_i = (C_i - C_i^*)\, V R_i$ where P_i is the total penalty assessed on the *i*th pollutant, C_i and C_i^* are, respectively, the actual and permitted concentrations of *i*th pollutant, V is the annual volume of wastewater discharged, and R_i is the rate for discharging the *i*th pollutant. In theory, for repeat offenders penalties are doubled each year until concentration standards are met.

Penalties are levied on twenty substances divided into two general categories. The first group (containing, for example, nitrates, BODs, chlorine and cadmium) is for those for which allowable levels are established to meet concentration standards. The second group (containing, for example, mercury, persistent pesticides, radioactive residues and carcinogens) is made up of substances for which no discharges are permitted and C_i* is zero. Rates are lower for the first group of pollutants (BODs at US$4.90 per metric tonne in 1995) than for the second group (mercury at US$13,000 per metric tonne in 1995).

3. THE STYLIZED FACTS IN THE WATER SECTOR

In spite of their low levels, revenue collection from water prices and discharge tariffs is a serious problem. Penalties assessed for effluent discharges and raw water abstractions *above* permitted limits in 1996 were 2.96 billion lei (US$1.5 million), yielding collections of 482 million lei. Worse, while revenues assessed in real terms in 1996 were 240 percent of those assessed in 1993, the collection rate had fallen from 24 percent in 1993 to 16 percent in 1996. Regarding water prices, while in 1996 AR regulated 5,000 industrial permit holders, it also was owed arrears from 3,000 of them.[6] Nevertheless, only three enterprises have been closed since 1991 because of water infractions.[7]

This relatively lax enforcement is perhaps not surprising. At least until recently, past governments regardless of the ministry have had an implicit 'take-it-easy' approach on enterprises, many of which were prohibited from

[6] The comparability of these two figures is in doubt since it is not clear whether the latter includes users without valid permits while the former comprises only permit holders. Information from personal discussions with AR officials.
[7] Information from personal discussions with AR officials.

borrowing and subject to other uneconomic restrictions. This has led to the authorities' inability to impose penalties or set prices for environmental goods and services at economic levels to achieve acceptable emissions, and to enterprises' indifference to operating with a valid permit. Therefore, two complementary approaches have also been taken, investment co-financing and compliance schedules.

The favored instrument of the government has been to augment the permit system with environmental abatement investment co-financing to stimulate enterprises to fulfill permit requirements. In 1994, for example, the national treasury provided the majority of environmental financing. In the country's 1996 National Environmental Action Plan, the budget's share of investment fell to 45 percent of all investments compared to 58 percent in 1994 (see MAPPM 1995). Under the 1997 FESAL agreement with the IMF, this mechanism is not likely to continue, with the burden being shifted on to economic agents themselves as the enterprises are privatized.

While the concept of compliance schedules was developed to create feasible plans for polluters to reach compliance, in practice they have been used in the water sector to work with the enterprises to simply improve their performance. As such, it is an open question for analysis as to whether their use has actually slowed down full compliance.

With the hope of increasing its collections of water charges, MAPPM implemented a phase-in program for payments of assessed penalties. It was announced that for 1991, 25 percent of the assessed penalty must be paid, 50 percent of what was assessed in 1992 should be paid, 75 percent in 1993, and 100 percent from 1994 onwards. Starting in 1996, fines owed must double each year until individual standards are met. Unfortunately, the schedule was not indexed for changes in prices and inflation averaged 175 percent per year during the period 1991 to 1996. Debts from early in the phase-in period were therefore highly discounted. In real terms the pressure on enterprises actually fell over time up until 1995 and only after the period of forgiveness ended did real penalty rates increase.

These broad impressions can be deepened by looking at two datasets. The first is a firm-level survey for 1996 administered as part of the present research effort. It comprises a random sample of 81, above-average,[8] industrial, water users possessing or in the process of receiving a water permit from AR.[9] The second contains data for the years 1993–96 on the fees

[8] Average consumption nationally for permitted industrial users was 25 m^3/hr. The rationale to restrict the sample to such firms was that, being the most polluting, they are the focus of regulatory enforcement such as it is.

[9] This dataset contains (i) general information related to location, ownership status, and type of activity, (ii) size and financial data, (iii) capacity utilization and technology vintage, (iv) detailed water consumption and discharge data, (v) source and destination information on water abatement investment, including the loan and/or subsidy terms, (vi) a description of existing abatement investment and the regulatory compliance situation, including measures of public

and fines assessed and collected from all of AR's 5,000 clients aggregated at the river basin level. Bivariate correlations from these two datasets tell a consistent, if surprising story leading to a set of stylized facts.[10]

Physically, water pollution and abstraction were unrelated to whether the enterprise was located in a big or small town (though smaller-town enterprises used older technologies). The greater the share of state ownership in an enterprise, the more likely it had a water purification station. While bigger enterprises abstracted and discharged more, concentrations of discharges were unrelated to enterprise size.

The penalty picture for abstraction was unexpected: no penalties were issued for excess abstraction for any enterprise in the sample. There simply was no above-permitted abstraction; in spite of the regulators' claims, the abundance of raw water was such that water allocations were not binding constraints for enterprises. This view is reinforced below when enterprise investment patterns are discussed.

Regarding penalty collection rates, the greater the number (as well as average and total value) of penalties assessed, the lower was the enterprise's penalty payment rate.[11] Examining their ability to pay, enterprises with higher (gross) profits had fewer penalties (in number) but a higher total value of penalties assessed. The number and average size of penalties were unrelated, however, to the profit *rate*. Looking at the relationship between penalties to inspections, the number of penalties was positively related to the number of unannounced inspections but not related to routine or accidental inspections. Total penalties assessed were related positively to both routine and unannounced inspections, but not to accidental inspections. Penalties paid, however, were positively correlated to accidental inspections while *not* related to routine and unannounced inspections. Thus, while most penalties were issued as a result of unannounced inspections, payment of these was generally ignored while only inspections as a result of accidents resulted in a fine actually being paid. In fact, the greater the number of unannounced inspections, the lower was the enterprise's penalty payment rate.[12] Regarding regulatory control strategies, the probability of being inspected was not related to the enterprise's location (perhaps not surprising since, as mentioned earlier, nor was pollution or abstraction). The number of total inspections had no relation to the economic size (for example, number of employees, revenues, equity) of the enterprise or its amount of abstraction. Finally, the greater the degree of state ownership (versus domestic private, or

pressure and (vii) information regarding the enterprise's foreign contacts.

[10] We use the arbitrary cut-off of less than 0.20 as the absolute value of the correlation coefficient to describe two variables as related or not.

[11] Keep in mind that the 'penalty' is really just the second component of the pollution charge representing the price for above-permitted discharges.

[12] The data itself generally indicate that if an enterprise paid any amount of the assessed penalty, it paid the full amount; unfortunately, about half the fined enterprises chose to pay zero.

foreign), the greater the probability of routine and of unannounced inspection and the higher the value of total and average penalties; the opposite was true the more ownership was domestic private.

Before continuing, we may draw two important conclusions regarding penalties, inspections and collections. First, there is a basic simultaneity between compliance and enforcement which needs to be disentangled to properly understand agency incentives. Second, the only way to understand the regulator's inspection program is to see that only unplanned inspections and 'accidental' inspections directly reflect non-compliance at the enterprise while routine inspections, established by bureaucratic inertia based on the number in the previous year (and thus only weakly related to current year compliance), represent the enforcement stance of AR toward the enterprise. These key insights allow the detailed econometric work below to be developed. Regarding the investment and finance picture, the level of investment in water-abatement was unrelated to the size of enterprise profits, equity, or turnover. State budget subsidies for water abatement investment were negatively related to enterprise profits, to whether it exported and had regular foreign contacts, and to whether the enterprise engaged in water pre-treatment. Higher capacity utilization was related to higher concentrations in discharges and, therefore not surprisingly, related to higher levels of water investment, particularly investment for improving water quality. Curiously, higher capacity utilization was also associated with higher levels of investment subsidies and less interaction with the foreign sector.

Regarding public participation, a quarter of the enterprises in the sample experienced some public pressure. Most was related to pollution, not to excess abstraction – perhaps not surprising given that in truth raw water was not scarce.[13] This pressure was more (less) likely to be on an enterprise, the greater the share of domestic private (of state) ownership. This is odd considering that the sample indicated that the higher the state ownership share, the higher were the pollution penalties.

Those firms with compliance schedules in force were much more likely to invest in abatement (though only financed through own funds) but such investment was related to water quality only (the compliance schedule being uncorrelated to water quantity investment). While the existence of a compliance schedule was independent of the penalty collection rate for a firm (the latter, perhaps, being a measure of the desire to comply), it was more likely for firms which experienced incidents leading to accidental inspections to have compliance schedules. Interestingly, while compliance schedules were also to be found more readily the higher the amount of penalties

[13] This is not as obvious as it may seem considering that most households in Romania do not have water 24 hours a day. The paradox is resolved by noting that municipal systems have 60 percent loss rates and pumps are turned off to reduce energy bills.

actually paid, they were *less* likely to be found the higher were *assessed* penalties. This suggests that regulators have succeeded in negotiating compliance schedules as a *quid pro quo* for leniency on penalty collection. Finally, compliance schedules were more likely to be found at firms with lower average penalties and a higher foreign share of ownership; this probably reflects the fact that minor problems (as suggested by the smaller penalty) are cheaper to fix, thereby facilitating the acceptance of a compliance schedule and that foreign investors have more money and are more interested in quickly improving their environmental image.

Looking across the eleven river basins in aggregate from 1993–96, a similar picture emerges regarding penalty and collection rates and enforcement. First, average penalties and collection rates over the period were negatively correlated (–0.22). This suggests that because returns to evasion are increasing in the value of penalties, higher penalties tend to reduce collections; smaller penalties therefore appear to be easier to collect.

In general, greater abundance of water resources was highly correlated to the number of penalties issued (0.68) and to the value of penalties paid (0.49) but, curiously, less so for the value of penalties assessed (0.28). The number of inspections was unrelated to the value of penalties assessed but correlated (0.27) to the value of penalties paid. The average penalty assessed by basin increased the *fewer* the number of users and amount of water resources per inspector, suggesting that increasing AR's financial and human resources would improve enforcement. While the number of users and amount of water resources had no effect on collection rates, the latter did increase the fewer were the resources per user. This complements the related finding on average penalties and suggests that as water scarcity increases, the user community does accept and take regulatory enforcement more seriously.

These river basin-level correlations aggregated over a tumultuous four-year period, however, hide some important temporal changes. First, while over the period 1993–95 the annual correlation between the collection rate and average penalty size fluctuated between –0.37 and –0.50, it fell to zero in 1996. Second, the correlations between the number of inspections, on the one hand, and the scarcity of water resources and the number of penalties, on the other, fall continuously and drastically from a high of 0.67 and 0.69 in 1993, respectively, down to a low of 0.18 and 0.17 in 1996. Furthermore, the correlation between users per inspector and the average penalty assessed fell from 0.67 to 0.36 over this period. Worse, regression analysis yielded a *negative* growth rate of inspection efficiency (number of penalties per inspection) of –33 percent over this period.[14] Since the number of

[14] The log of the inspection efficiency was regressed on time (with *t*-stat. = –3.1, adjusted R^2 = 0.69 and n = 41) using the dummy variable absorption technique with Huber standard errors as described later in this chapter.

inspections increased 50 percent over this period but staffing remained relatively constant, this is clear evidence for inspection quality being sacrificed for quantity as enforcement resources are squeezed during the transition period.

This plethora of stylized correlations, while intriguing, is far from definitive, primarily due to the extensive simultaneity and endogeneity of the various characteristics examined. Below, therefore, these stylized facts are investigated in three steps. First, we develop a theoretical model of the enforcement game between the enterprise and AR. This model is then used to disentangle the relationship between an enterprise's level of compliance and AR's level of control and enforcement. Finally, we use this information to examine the role of economic instruments and command and control to influence the enterprise's investment response to the regulatory regime.

4. THE MODEL

The decision facing the enterprise in the short term is how intensively to use (for consumption and discharge) the water resources – even if it means exceeding permitted levels – given the costs for doing so. The 'cost' may be directly financial due to an economic instrument or indirect through the imposition of additional regulatory oversight measures. A simple way to present this decision is to consider the enterprise as using an amount of water goods and services, W, as its only production input and to assume that AR has previously allocated the enterprise a maximum amount of it, W^o, as reflected in the enterprise's operating permit. In keeping with the situation in Romania, we further simplify the presentation by assuming that the expected costs of using water below permitted levels are zero and those above it are $P(W-W^o)\,\rho(N)$, where $P(.)$ is the penalty for exceeding permitted levels with $P' > 0$, $P'' > 0$ so that each additional amount in excess of permitted levels is relatively more heavily penalized, $\rho(N)$ is the joint probability that the infraction is discovered, the penalty assessed, and sum paid with $\rho' > 0$ and N is the number of inspections by AR. Thus, the penalty collection rate is captured inside ρ.

Letting the enterprise's production function and output price be $Q(W)$ and q, respectively, its decision problem is

$$\max W \quad [\, qQ(W) - P(W-W^o)\,\rho(N)\,] \tag{16.1}$$

and has as a first-order condition for $W^* > W^o$ of

$$\Omega \equiv qQ'(W) - P'(W - W^o)\,\rho(N) = 0$$

Thus, since $\partial\Omega/\partial N = -P'\rho' < 0$ and $\partial\Omega/\partial W < 0$ for profit maximization then

$$dW^*/dN = (\partial\Omega/\partial N) \,/\, (-\partial\Omega/\partial W) < 0 \qquad (16.2)$$

where W^* is the profit-maximizing level of water use. Thus, as one would expect, increasing the number of inspections tends to decrease the degree of excess water use.

The decision facing each AR branch in the short term is how to allocate the N_{AR} number of inspections it is capable of doing per period across the regulated community of $i = 1, ..., N_E$ enterprises so as to maximize the expected discovery of damages, $D^i\,\sigma^i$, from water use in excess of permitted levels where $D^i = D(W_i - W_i^o)$, $D^i_W > 0$ are damages, if discovered and $\sigma^i = \sigma(N_i, D^i)$ is the probability of discovery with $\sigma^i_N > 0$, $\sigma^i_{NN} < 0$, and $\sigma^i_D > 0$. This decision requires setting a number, N_i of inspections for each enterprise i. For simplicity we assume that each enterprise uses water from a different water body in the basin so that we may write the decision problem for AR as

$$\max_{\{N_i\}} \quad [\Sigma D(W_i - W_i^o)\,\sigma(N_i, W_i - W_i^o, S, N_E)] \text{ s.t. } \Sigma N_i \leq N_{AR} \qquad (16.3)$$

Here, S may be considered a vector of variables capturing the stress on or demand for the resource and N_E is the number of enterprises which the AR must inspect. The reason both N_i and N_E appear is that the more enterprises a given number of inspectors are responsible for, the shorter or less thorough is an inspection. With Ψ the Lagrangian and Ψ_i its partial with respect to N_i, the first-order condition for each i is

$$\Psi_i \equiv D(W_i - W_i^o)\,\sigma^i_N(N_i, W_i - W_i^o) - \lambda = 0$$

where λ is the LaGrange multiplier. If the expected discovery of damages is being maximized then the second-order condition, $d^2\Psi < 0$ requires that the principal minors of the bordered Hessian begin positive and alternate in sign. This is satisfied since $\sigma^i_{NN} < 0$ for all i by assumption.

Note that there is a relationship between σ in expression (16.3) and ρ in expression (16.1):

$$\rho(N_i, W_i - W_i^o) = \sigma(N_i, W_i - W_i^o)\,\theta$$

where θ is the probability that a penalty is actually applied or applied in full; as will be seen in the following section, θ will differ, depending on the strength of the enforcement regime in place in a given river basin.

Totally differentiating the first-order conditions, the response by AR to a change in enterprise *i*'s excess water use may be determined as

$$dN_i / dW_i = -(\partial\Psi_i / \partial W_i) / |H| > 0 \qquad (16.4)$$

where |H| is the determinant of the bordered Hessian. The positive inequality in (16.4) is due to $|H| > 0$ from the second-order condition, $d^2\Psi < 0$ and due to

$$\partial\Psi_i / \partial W_i = D^i{}_W \, \sigma^i{}_N + D^i \, \sigma^i{}_{NW} > 0,$$

where we have reasonably assumed that an increase in excess water use makes it easier for an additional inspector to find the infraction ($\sigma^i{}_{N\,W} > 0$).

The expressions $\Omega(N_i, W_i) = 0$ and $\Psi_i(N_i, W_i) = 0$ may be considered implicit form reaction functions. Given the signs in expressions (16.2) and (16.4), a stable (convergent) equilibrium is ensured if

$$-(dW_i / dN_i)|_\Omega > (dW_i / dN_i)|_{\psi i}$$

Reaction functions satisfying these conditions are illustrated in Figure 16.1.

5. EMPIRICAL RESULTS

The reaction functions of the enterprises and AR developed in the theoretical model above may be estimated econometrically for the case of Romania. This is done in Section 5.1. The results are then applied to Romania to analyze economic instruments, investment, privatization, perverse responses, and collection problems in the subsections that follow.

5.1 Compliance and Enforcement

Using the two datasets described in Section 3, the reaction functions of Section 4 are estimated from the following simultaneous equations econometric model:

$$\begin{aligned} \text{ENFORCE}_{ib} &= \text{F}[\text{E}(\text{NONCOM}_{ib}), \text{ARCAP}_b] \\ \text{NONCOM}_{ib} &= \text{G}[\text{E}(\text{ENFORCE}_{ib}), \text{POLCHRG}_b] \end{aligned} \qquad (16.5a,b)$$

where F and G are functions to be specified and estimated, 'E' is the expectations operator, *i* and *b* index the enterprise and the river basin, and $NONCOM_{ib}$, $ARCAP_b$, $ENFORCE_{ib}$, and $POLCHRG_b$ are, respectively, the enterprise's level of compliance with its permit, AR's total (basin) enforcement capacity, AR's degree of enforcement at an enterprise, and the basin-specific pollution charge for exceeding permitted (quantity and quality) levels.

Figure 16.1. Compliance and enforcement

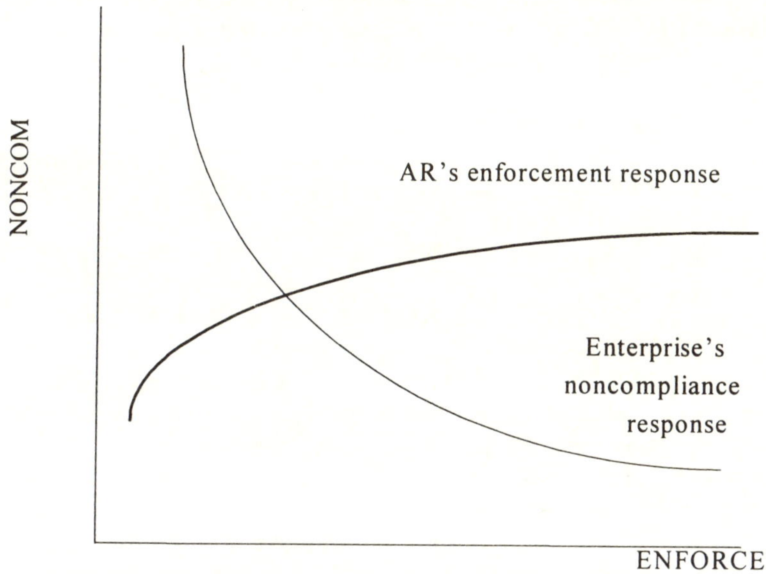

Considering the ENFORCE equation, expression (16.4) suggests that an enterprise would be submitted to a stricter enforcement regime, the worse is its expected compliance, (the 'enforcement curve' is upward sloping) and the greater is the AR's capacity for enforcement. Considering the NONCOM equation, expression (16.2) predicts that an enterprise's compliance improves the higher is the expected penalty and the stricter is the expected enforcement (the 'non-compliance curve' is downward sloping). The system is illustrated in Figure 16.1.

The variables. The key to estimating this system was a number of insights regarding good overall measures of the variables involved. First, as revealed in Section 3, AR's enforcement (ENFORCE) regime could be measured by the number of routine inspections set for each enterprise. This is because these are in fact pre-programmed based on expected enterprise performance and the amount of human resources available for inspection at the AR. Second, the number of unannounced and 'accidental' inspections reflect regulatory responses to compliance lapses at an enterprise and, thereby, reflect well an enterprise's actual compliance (NONCOM).[15] For a measure of AR capacity, ARCAP, the total number of inspections made was used. It is this number which had to be allocated in the theoretical model as well. Finally, since Romania has a single national pollution charge, *P*, if this were used then there would have been no variance for the economic instrument variable in question. Therefore, we constructed the variable POLCHRG to be equal to θP^N where θ as before is the conditional probability that a charge is collected, given that the compliance lapse is discovered and charged. Thus, while *P* is invariant nationally, POLCHRG varies approximately by river basin.

The estimation. Noting that this system is exactly identified, its reduced form may be solved and then estimated using indirect least squares (ILS) by individually regressing

$$\text{ENFORCE}_{ib} = a + b\,\text{POLCHRG}_b + c\,\text{ARCAP}_b + u_{ib}$$

$$\text{NONCOM}_{ib} = d + e\,\text{POLCHRG}_b + f\,\text{ARCAP}_b + v_{ib}$$

where a, b, c, d, e, and f are the parameters to be estimated and u_{ib} and v_{ib} are the standard, i.i.d. least-squares error terms. The structural parameters of the system in (16.5) may then be retreived using these parameters. In fact, the alternative used here was to recognize the equivalence between ILS and the standard two-stage instrumental variables approach. What is particularly appropriate about this equivalence is that the instruments for ENFORCE and NONCOM (denoted below with the 'IV' superscript) may be interpretted economically as the expected values of each variable. The results of the estimation are

$$\underset{}{\text{ENFORCE}_{ib}} = \underset{(0.17)}{0.34} + \underset{(2.6)}{0.94}\,\text{NONCOM}^{\text{IV}}_{i\,b} + \underset{(4.1)}{0.003}\,\text{ARCAP}_b + u_i,\ \text{Adj. } R^2 = 0.17$$

$$\text{NONCOM}_{ib} = \underset{(4.3)}{18.5} - \underset{(-3.3)}{1.53}\,\text{ENFORCE}^{\text{IV}}_{ib} - \underset{(-3.5)}{13.2}\,\text{POLCHRG}_b + v_i,\ \text{Adj.} R^2 = 0.12$$

where the *t*-statistics are in parentheses and the number of observations were 81 in each case. As is seen, the signs are as the model's theory predicts and illustrated in Figure 16.1.

[15] This is well borne out by the fact that the correlation between these sorts of inspections and concentrations of suspended solids and BODs were 0.92 and 0.88, respectively.

5.2 Economic Instruments and Investment

As shown above, the level of compliance of an enterprise is affected by both the signal of the pollution charge and AR's enforcement behavior. It is the aim of environmental policy that such effects should lead to enterprise investment. In this section, we examine whether any investment response can be detected and whether another economic instrument, the subsidy, which governments have often used in the past, has had any stimulative effect.

The model. The reduced-form relationship considered is based on the hypotheses that the level of an enterprise's investment (in 1996) was related to its industrial sector, the degree it used water goods and services, its financial ability to invest, its expected level of non-compliance, and any pre-existing investment program commitments.

The variables. The variable to be determined is the enterprise's investment in water quality in 1996 (WINV). The predicted values of NONCOM from Section 4 were used to measure expected non-compliance. We use the enterprise's total discharge (DISCH) as a proxy for water services used.[16] The enterprise's use of water *qua* good is taken as the amount of water consumed (CONS), equal to abstractions minus discharges. The enterprise's financial ability was measured by gross profits over turnover (PROF). Finally, past environmental financing commitments were taken as the sum in 1996 Romanian lei of investment in water quality in 1994 and 1995 (L_WINV).

The estimation. Investment is obviously highly linked to the particular industrial sector. Ideally a dummy variable would be appropriate for each sector. Unfortunately, we have only 81 observations available. Therefore, we have employed a linear regression method which 'absorbs' these sectoral dummies into one categorical factor but which produces robust standard errors based on Huber's formula for individual-level data, thereby allowing consistent standard errors to be estimated even if there is heteroscedasticity or clustered sampling.[17] The main drawback of this approach is that the individual coefficients of the dummy variables cannot be recovered. The estimation results are shown in Table 16.1.

The regression suggests that the effect of expected non-compliance leads to greater investment in water quality. The amount of this investment was greater, the greater was past investment. Profitability (PROF) here indicates an ability to pay and, as such, also has a positive effect on WINV. The negative coefficient on water discharges supports the hypothesis tested below that more polluting enterprises dilute their waste streams, thereby lowering

[16] The reason that a measure of pollutant discharges was not used here is that these are already picked up in the non-compliance variable, NONCOM.

[17] The description of this technique here draws on Stata Corporation 1995 and was first developed by Huber 1967 as well as independently by White 1980.

their average concentrations and subsequent requirements in water quality investment. Consumption, on the other hand is costly and triggers a positive investment response.

Table 16.1. Water investment regression with Huber standard errors

Variable	Coefficient	*t*-statistic
L_WINV	1.046705	10.589
CONS	16.20723	4.252
DISCH	–46.31995	–5.443
PROF	895,215.80	3.142
NONCOM (predicted)	36,318.18	1.742
Constant	–57080.24	–0.521
Industrial dummies	Absorbed (18 categories)	
Dependent variable: WINV	Number of obs = 76	
Grouping variable: river basin	Adjusted R^2 = 0.8456	

Without providing all the regression statistics, an identical regression was run including an additional term to capture the size of budget subsidies in 1996 SUBS. The results are the same as above with coefficients being even slightly 'more' significant, especially regarding NONCOM. However, though negative, SUBS was not statistically significant (*t*-statistic of –0.37). This suggests that subsidies had probably no stimulative effect in generating investment (and, if the sign is right, even a pacifying effect).

5.3 Privatization

Romania, like most other countries in Eastern Europe, is undergoing a massive privatization of its industrial enterprises. This raises the question about whether the ownership of an enterprise has been a missing factor in the above analysis. As argued at the outset of this chapter, privatization should have at least two effects in theory. First, the imposition of a 'hard' budget constraint should cause management to have a more pronounced response to the price incentives of economic instruments. Second, the new owners of privatized enterprises often have made additional investment commitments and have brought additonal sources of capital (as well as the ability to borrow it). While this may increase their ability to pay economic instruments on the one hand, it also may make them targets for the regulatory agencies whose compliance demands have historically been tailored to their perceptions of an enterprise's financial resources. The profit motive brings with it pluses and minuses. On the plus side, it causes enterprises to reduce all forms of waste, including waste in the form of pollutants in water discharges (which may even be potentially valuable if recovered). On the minus side, however, it leads enterprises to use relatively intensively those inputs whose relative prices are lowest. Since weak enforcement serves to reduce the perceived 'price' of the environment's waste assimilation services, the profit motive could encourage privatized enterprises to take advantage of weak enforcement, thereby stretching (or even ignoring) regulatory limits.

Table 16.2 Characteristics of higher state ownership share (SHRSTAT) using regression with Huber standard errors

Variable	Coefficient	*t*-statistic
VINTAGE	0.0143	4.366
PROFITY	0.1212	0.544
NUMEMP	7.94e–07	0.353
CAP_U	–0.1953	–1.667*
Constant	0.4658	4.738
Industrial dummies	Absorbed (18 categories)	
Dependent variable: SHRSTAT	Number of obs = 76	
Grouping variable: river basin	R^2 = 0.5082	
	Adj. R^2 = 0.3169	

Note: *Significant at the 90-percent level.

What is different about a privatized firm? Table 16.2 indicates the answer for the companies sampled for the present study. Here, we look at firm characteristics *after* accounting for the likely fact that the state's share of ownership (SHRSTAT) is probably sector-specific. We see that enterprises with older vintage equipment (VINTAGE) and lower capacity utilization (CAP_U) tend to have greater state ownership. These variables are indicators of efficiency (as well as pollution generation). However, surprisingly, greater numbers of employees (NUMEMP) or lower profitability (PROFITY) were *not* the mark of greater state ownership in this sample.[18]

We may now examine the effect of accounting for the share of state ownership on enterprise compliance and environmental performance. First, we examine how the compliance–enforcement relationship is affected by the level of state ownership. This can be done by re-estimating the model in

[18] This illustrates the importance of using the Huber regression method. Without accounting for the state's propensity to be in certain sectors, the statistical significance results (with *t*-statistics in parentheses) are reversed with profitability becoming so and capacity utilization no longer so:

$$\underset{}{SHRSTAT_i} = \underset{(5.24)}{0.59} + \underset{(2.03)}{0.007}\, VINTAGE_i - \underset{(-1.65)}{0.222}\, PROFITY_i - \underset{(-0.948)}{0.120}\, CAP\_U_i + u_i \qquad \text{Adj.}R^2=0.12,\ N=76$$

Section 5.1 and including the share of state ownership (SHRSTAT) as an explanatory variable.

$$\text{ENFORCE}_{ib}=\underset{(0.70)}{1.37}+\underset{(2.33)}{0.76}\ \text{NONCOM}^{IV}{}_{ib}+\underset{(3.98)}{0.003}\ \text{ARCAP}_b+u_i,\quad \text{Adj.}R^2=0.15$$

$$\text{NONCOM}_{ib}=\underset{(3.5)}{16.0}-\underset{(-3.2)}{1.49}\text{ENFORCE}^{IV}{}_{ib}-\underset{(-3.5)}{12.8}\text{POLCRHG}_b+\underset{(1.33)}{3.11}\text{SHRSTAT}_i+v_i,\quad \text{Adj. }R^2=0.12$$

where the number of observations were 81 and the t-statistics are in parentheses. As is seen, none of the signs of the variables' coefficients change though there is a minimal fall in their magnitudes. Statistically significant at the 81 percent level, the positive sign on SHRSTAT suggests that non-compliance is higher, the greater is the level of state ownership.

This finding is strengthened when we look at how the performance of enterprises with greater state ownership influences the assessed penalty component of the pollution charge. Again using the Huber regression method to account for the possibility of state pre-selection into more polluting sectors, the following equation suggests how the average penalty assessed (AVGPEN) is influenced by the ownership structure of the firm (SHRSTAT):

$$\text{AVGPEN}_i=\underset{(0.21)}{242}+\underset{(1.88)}{3067}\ \text{SHRSTAT}_i+\underset{(\text{absorbed})}{h\,\Sigma_i^{N-1}d_i D_i}+u_i,\quad \text{Adj. }R^2=0.57,\ \text{No. Obs.}=25$$

With SHRSTAT statistically significant at the 90 percent level, this equation helps to strengthen the earlier results by indicating that higher levels of state ownership tend to lead to higher average penalties, *ceteris paribus*.[19]

A third interaction related to enterprise ownership will be shown below when the issue of collection rates is discussed.

5.4 Perverse Responses: Dilution Effects

As is always the case with government intervention, even of the economic instruments type, it can lead to perverse incentives and unwanted side-effect behavior if improperly designed. Consider the case of charging for pollutants based on the discharge concentration. By diluting the effluent stream, the

[19] The sample for this regression was restricted to enterprises which were assessed penalties. When rerun with the full sample (setting AVGPEN = 0 when no penalty was assessed) the regression resulted in, not surprisingly, a smaller coefficient of 715 for SHRSTAT though at a lower level of significance (t-statistic of 1.5). A simple regression of AVGPEN on SHRSTAT ignoring industry dummies but on the full 81-observation sample, resulted in a SHRSTAT coefficient of 2,570 and a t-statistic of 1.77.

polluter can reduce the total tariff charges (or the threat of command and control oversight). In Romania, although pollutant concentrations are monitored together with the total volume of water discharged, the actual computation procedure may still distort behavior. This is because the total payment is based on the number of hours of factory operation times a technical coefficient of discharge per hour of operation times the monitored concentration. Thus, by exceeding the technical discharge rate, the enterprise can reduce the level of the monitored concentration. The only additional cost for this sort of defensive action is to increase the enterprise's abstraction costs. Thus, if the discharge tariff is sufficiently high relative to the abstraction charge, behavior may become distorted.

To test for this possibility, the following simple short-run dilution decision model is utilized.[20] Given a level of (assumed exogenous) water consumption, Q^c, and pollutant generated, L, the enterprise chooses a level of discharge, Z, which minimizes the combined costs of abstraction, A (whose water price is w), plus pollution tariffs (assessed at a rate of t) which are calculated based on monitored concentration, L/Z, in excess of permitted levels, c^* times the technically computed discharge, Z^T:

$$\min_{Z} \; \{ Z^T[(L/Z) - c^*]t + (Z + Q^c)w \}$$

Solving this minimization problem for Z and putting the result into the abstraction identity, $A = Q^c + Z$ leads to the equation:

$$A = Q^c + (Z^T Lt/w)^{1/2} \tag{16.6}$$

This equation may be estimated using water consumption (WCONS) for Q^c, suspended solids (SUSSOL) for L and water abstraction (ABS) for A. As before, since all enterprises face the same tariff rates, we used the concept of expected tariff payment (TARIFF) where the national tariff has been multiplied by the enterprise's rate of tariff payment. The results, again using the Huber regression method with industry dummies, B_i, are:

$$\underset{}{\mathrm{ABS}_i} = \underset{(-3.71)}{-4018} + \underset{(7.52)}{2.45}\ \mathrm{WCONS}_i + \underset{(3.69)}{5888}\ \mathrm{TARIFF}_i +$$

$$\underset{(18.9)}{7.71}\ \mathrm{SUSSOL}_i + \underset{(\text{absorbed})}{\mathrm{h}\,\Sigma_i^{N-1} b_i B_i} + u_i \qquad \text{Adj. } R^2 = 0.91,\ N=25$$

[20] We say 'short-run' because the state of the transition means that the alternative to dilution, namely production process changes, has not been carried out yet.

Inspection reveals that all the variables have the signs implied by equation (16.6). The estimated equation, therefore, suggests that, once (exogenous) water consumption is accounted for, an enterprise's abstraction is influenced by the degree of pollutants it discharges, the more so the higher the (firm-specific) tariff rate.[21] As predicted by the model, since higher charges lead to greater abstraction, the pollution charges have created a perverse incentive to abstract water in excess of what is needed to meet permit concentration requirements.

5.5 Collection Rates and Inspections

Clearly, in order for economic instruments to have an incentive effect, not only do they need to be raised to economic levels, but the sums assessed must also be collected. As presented in Section 3, however, collection rates are very poor. This calls into question the efficacy of raising pollution rates further. In this section, we look at a number of contributing factors at both the basin and enterprise levels. These include ability-to-pay issues, ownership, and the strength of regulatory enforcement.

At the basin level, we examine whether the average size of the assessed pollution charge influences the collection rate of the AR branch, once other factors are accounted for. Two key factors include the state of the economy (as measured by real GDP growth rate, RGDPR) to capture the general ability to pay of enterprises in the basin and the regulatory load of AR in the basin (as proxied by the amount of water resources per number of inspectors, BREGLOAD) to capture the strength of regulatory enforcement. We would expect that basins with higher average charges would lead to lower rates of repayment. Using the following reduced-form equation to regress river basin collection rates (BCOLRATE) on the average pollution charge (BAVCHARG) in the basin (with *t*-statistics in parentheses), we see that this is borne out:[22]

$$\ln(\text{BCOLRATE}_{bt}) = \underset{(3.26)}{9.79} - \underset{(-5.06)}{1.04}\ln(\text{BAVCHARG}_{bt}) - \underset{(-2.95)}{0.99}\ln(\text{BREGLOAD}_{bt}) +$$

$$\underset{(1.93)}{33.8}\,\text{RGDPR}_t + u_{bt}, \qquad N=30,\ \text{Adj. } R^2=0.46, \quad \text{AR}(1)=0.55\ (t\text{-stat}=4.17)$$

This relationship is estimated for the period 1993 to 1996 using the standard Cochrane–Orcutt iterative procedure for first-order autocorrelation

[21] The model estimation did not generate results when BODs were included instead of suspended solids.

[22]. Recall that charges comprise two components, the 'tariff' for below-permitted levels and the 'penalty' for above-permitted levels.

correction. The results indicate that increases in the average charge are associated with lower collection rates *ceteris paribus*. Moreover, results show that collection rates would improve if additional resources were allocated to enforcement and if the state of the economy were to improve.[23]

Turning to the enterprise level and accounting for regulatory load (proxied by REGLOAD, the ratio of enterprises per inspector) the following two regressions further illustrate the effect of higher pollution assessments in 1996 (POLBILL) on collection rates for enterprise i in basin b, the first equation taking into account ownership structure and the second profitability (PROFITY):[24]

$$\underset{}{\mathrm{COLRATE}_{ib}} = \underset{(4.17)}{1.93} - \underset{(-2.5)}{0.897}\ \mathrm{SHRSTAT}_{ib} - \underset{(-2.45)}{0.002}\ \mathrm{REGLOAD}_{ib} - \underset{(-1.73)}{2.11}\ \mathrm{POLBILL}_{ib} + u_i, \qquad \text{Adj. } R^2 = 0.31, N{=}25$$

$$\mathrm{COLRATE}_{ib} = \underset{(4.15)}{1.49} + \underset{(2.27)}{2.01}\ \mathrm{PROFITY}_{ib} - \underset{(-2.86)}{0.003}\ \mathrm{REGLOAD}_{b} - \underset{(-2.68)}{3.29}\ \mathrm{POLBILL}_{ib} + u_i, \qquad \text{Adj. } R^2 = 0.33, N{=}25$$

These more micro-level relationships reinforce the basin-level insights above. First, the larger is the pollution charge bill, the lower is the tendency to pay in full. Second, the state of the economy effect on repayment in the basin-level regression probably reflects the enterprise's lack of ability to pay, as proxied here by profitability. Finally, we see that privatization will improve enterprise payments of pollution charges – regardless of profitabilty. While this is helpful in its own right, it portends another more important development. Since privatized enterprises will try to minimize input costs, the fact that they tend to pay more of the charges they are assessed indicates that they

---

23 We wondered how far one could improve collection rates by adjusting the pollution charge. This was checked using the following regression (where Δ indicates that the variable has been first-differenced):

$$\Delta\mathrm{BCOLRATE}_b = \underset{(2.00)}{0.217} - \underset{(-4.32)}{0.659}{*}\Delta\mathrm{BAVCHARG}_b - \underset{(-2.50)}{0.392}{*}(\Delta\mathrm{BAVCHARG}_b)^2 + u_b, \qquad N{=}33, \text{Adj. } R^2 = 0.73$$

The negative sign on the squared term indicates that (i) the collection rate cannot be increased indefinitely by lowering the size of penalties and (ii) a revenue-maximizing average penalty size exists.

24 Recall that for the current sample, profitability and state ownership share capture very different characteristics, with no correlation between the two.

will be more responsive to existing (low) pollution charge rates; thus, privatization should lead to reduced pollutant flows.

6. POLICY IMPLICATIONS

Based on the analysis above, a number of policy conclusions may be drawn. First, although pollution fees are extremely low and rarely assessed, they do have some value in signaling to enterprises when the authorities are fed up with the enterprise's low compliance. As such and probably only indirectly as a result, higher fee rates do seem to generate an improvement in compliance. On the other hand, enterprises' acceptance to pay these fees falls, the higher is the overall fee bill. Still, it is possible to discern an effect of these fees on enterprise investment behavior, even after controlling for the level of water authority enforcement efforts.[25] Subsidies, on the other hand, were found to have no influence on water sector investment.

As suspected, privatization so far has had an influence on the use of water assimilation services and consumption. Since this chapter has shown that enterprises with a lower private ownership share are assessed higher penalties, display lower compliance, and are less likely to pay the pollution fees assessed, privatization is likely to improve enterprise compliance in spite of the many forces mentioned in this chapter which might encourage profit-maximizing firms to operate to the contrary.

As is true with any government interference in the market, pollution charges can generate perverse incentives if improperly implemented. In Romania we show that this is the case in the water sector. Enterprises apparently have an incentive to dilute their effluents in order to reduce pollution tariffs and additional regulatory oversight measures. However, at least in this case, a modified procedure involving the monitoring of discharge amounts (instead of using preset technical parameters) would correct the problem.

We ended our analysis by recognizing that it is the *expected* pollution charge on which economic agents base their compliance decision and that the expectation was related to the rate of collection of the pollution charges assessed. We therefore, examined the collection problem. We show that nonpayment of pollution charges is inversely related to the level of the assessment and that enterprise nonpayment is exacerbated, the more over-stretched is the enforcement agency and the weaker is the economy while it is

[25] While not developed in this chapter, the data have helped resolve a longstanding dispute regarding water scarcity in Romania: no abstraction penalties were assessed, let alone collected. The reason? In spite of all the hype, water is so abundant that abstraction permit levels may be set so high so that no enterprise need exceed– never mind have to pay for– 'excessive' (above-permitted) abstraction.

ameliorated the more profitable are enterprises. Finally, regardless of profitability, greater state ownership increases nonpayment. As such, the lower is the enterprise's ability to pay and the higher is its assessed bill, the lower will be its rate of payment of charges that do get assessed. These results, however, point to solutions: enterprise privatization and greater financial resources to the regulatory authorities. Moreover, since privatized firms also seek to minimize input costs, the fact that they are more likely to pay their assessments corroborates our earlier result that they will also improve their environmental compliance.

REFERENCES

EDC, Ltd. and EPE, Asbl. (1997), 'Estimation of Compliance Costs for the Approximation of European Union Legislation in Central and Eastern European States: Guidelines for Country Studies', European Commission, DG XI, September.

Huber, P. (1967), 'The Behavior of Maximum Likelihood Estimates Under Non-standard Conditions', *Proceedings of the Fifth Berkeley Symposium on Mathematical Statistics and Probability*, vol. 1, pp. 221–33.

Hughes, G. (1991), 'Are the Costs of Cleaning Up Eastern Europe Exaggerated? Economic Reform and the Environment', *Oxford Review of Economic Policy*, 7(4), Winter.

Manea, G. and C. Zinnes (1994), 'An Overview of the Impact of the Most Polluted Sectors in Romania', Harvard Institute for International Development, International Environment Program, Working Paper.

MAPPM (1995), *Report Regarding the National Action Program for Environmental Protection (Synthesis)*, Ministry of Waters, Forests and Environmental Protection.

Markandya, A. (1994), 'Environmental Taxation: A Review of OECD Country Experience and Prospects for Economies in Transition', Paper No. 1, Budapest: Regional Environmental Center.

Panayotou, T. (1994), 'Economic Instruments for Environmental Management and Sustainable Development', United Nations Environment Programme, Environmental Economics Series Paper No. 16, December.

Reed, D. (1995), *Structural Adjustment Programs and their Environmental Impacts*, Geneva: World Wildlife Fund.

Sachs, J. and A. Warner (1995), 'Natural Resoure Abundance and Economic Growth', Harvard Institute for International Development, Development Discussion Paper No. 517a.

Stata Corporation (1995), *Stata Reference Manual, Release 4*, College Station, Texas: Stata Press.

White, H. (1980), 'A Heteroskedasticity-consistent Covariance Matrix Estimator and a Direct Test for Heteroskedasticity', *Econometrica*, **48**, pp. 817–30.

Zinnes, C. (1996), 'Environmentally Friendly Investing', *Romania In Review*, Issue 11, pp. 24–5.

Zinnes, C. (1997), 'The Road to Creating an Integrated Charge and Permitting System in Romania', in R. Bluffstone and B. A. Larson (eds), *Economic Instruments in Environmental Policy in the Transition Economies of Eastern Europe*, Cheltenham: Edward Elgar.

17. Design and Performance of Economic Instruments for Waste Management and Air Emission Control in Hungary

Glenn Morris, Péter Kaderják and András Kis

1. INTRODUCTION

Development and implementation of cost-effective or, better still, economically efficient environmental protection policies is critical for transition countries such as Hungary. Transition countries have, roughly speaking, only one-fifth the economic resources of Western countries and the history of serious environmental abuse extends well into the later quarter of this century. They simply cannot afford to waste resources or make serious policy mistakes, even or especially in the name of environmental protection.

Most transition countries, as part of their adoption of, and adaptation to, market economies, have sought to introduce market-based instruments or market-like processes as an important component of their environmental policy. In this chapter we examine the design and, where appropriate, the implementation of selected market instruments and market-like procedures in Hungary. We describe and analyze three 'product charges' that have already been introduced in Hungary and a proposal for emission charges to be levied on three major air pollutants. For each of these economic instruments we assess their merit as cost-effective or economically efficient approaches to the environmental problems they were designed to deal with and suggest changes that would likely improve their current or projected performance.

2. THE RECENT HISTORY AND DESIGN OF ECONOMIC INSTRUMENTS

Policy forms that looked like economic instruments, mostly in the form of penalties or fines, have a long history in transition economies. Klarer (1994), Morris and Lehoczki (1996), and the various papers in Bluffstone and Larson (1997) offer various reasons for this fact, but most relate to the inherent weakness of market-based incentives in a non-market system. In Hungary, contemporary use of economic instruments began with raising the profile of the Central Environmental Protection Fund (CEPF) and increases in the transport fuels tax, part of which were earmarked for use by CEPF. We discuss the transport fuels charges and an associated gasoline tax differential in favor of unleaded fuel below.

In the mid-1990s Hungary developed and implemented a set of four 'environmental product charges' on consumer products whose disposal posed environmental threats. These charges covered refrigerators, batteries, tires and product packaging. Each of these product charges had unique elements, but the common features of their design were:

- the product charge varied roughly with the degree of hazard posed by the type of battery, tire, packaging and so on being taxed;
- while 25 percent of the revenue of the product charge was sent to the central budget, the remainder went to the CEPF and was, to a large extent, earmarked for reducing the environmental damage produced by the product's disposal; and
- the selected product charge rate was anchored more on anticipated financing needed for prospective solid waste collection and treatment facilities than on an examination of the benefits of reducing or improving the associated product's waste stream.

As part of a 'comprehensive' approach to environmental protection Hungary developed and passed the Environmental Framework Law (EFL) in 1995. This law provides the legal basis for most environmental protection law and regulation. The EFL codified the elements of environmental policy, provided the legal basis of new rules and regulations, and confirmed many of those environmental policy initiatives already undertaken. There are two fundamental problems with the EFL as a basis for design and use of economic instruments. First, the EFL does not codify the principle that cost should play a role in shaping environmental policy. Second, EFL does not describe how various policies are to be coordinated or prioritized, thus creating the possibility that the economic instruments that are instituted will simply be a costly or ineffectual redundancy.

The economic instruments specifically identified in the EFL are: environmental load fees (emission charges), user charges, product charges, deposit refund systems, and exceedence fines. As noted above, the Ministry of Environment and Regional Planning (MoE) had already undertaken the development of a set of product charges. The MoE is currently designing additional charges covering lubricants, solvents, and paper. Prompted by the EFL, the MoE has also been developing innovative legislation with the aim of introducing a system of environmental load fees (ELF), covering pollutant discharges into (i) air, (ii) surface water, and (iii) soil. The proposed approach, as it stands now, is quite extensive and covers a wide range of pollutants while varying the design to account for regional, administrative, technical, and media differences. In this chapter we shall examine in more detail that part of the proposal which aims at regulating air pollution; the air emission charge (AEC). The MoE continues to operate the exceedence fine system inherited from the earlier regime and has not, as yet, determined how it will design a user charge system. Currently the government also collects fees, possibly construed as user charges under the EFL, from harvesting timber on public lands, mining minerals, and abstraction of water.

2.1 Performance Criteria

There are a variety of measures one could use to evaluate the design of all policies for environmental protection, including economic instruments. Among the more obvious candidates is: does it improve the quality of the environment? A more sophisticated criterion is whether the policy is cost effective, that is, is it the least-cost way among all feasible alternatives of providing a given level of environmental improvement? Finally, there is a policy measure that reflects economic efficiency: have we introduced a policy where the additional benefits of extending the policy are equal to the additional costs (including administration costs). We note with regard to this criterion the importance of linking the incentive for control with the value of environmental services damaged by the pollutant. If the policy improves economic efficiency, then the policy will in all likelihood be successful under the other two criteria. Consequently, we prefer to analyze the performance of Hungarian economic instruments using the economic efficiency performance standard. Unfortunately, however, while researchers have started to experiment with environmental valuation (most often contingent valuation) in and for the Central and Eastern European countries (see, for example, Markowska and Zylicz 1996; DeShazo 1996; Powell et al. 1997; Harrison et al. 1996), the lack of reliable information on the benefits of environmental improvements is still such as to seriously limit the use of economic efficiency as a performance standard. This is why, when analyzing the following regulatory designs, we usually rely on 'lower-level' criteria, especially one or another variant of cost-effectiveness, in evaluation of the selected Hungarian economic instruments.

3. PRODUCT CHARGES IN HUNGARY

3.1 General Design Issues

Product charges usually address environmental problems in two ways: by taxing a good or service that is closely associated with the environmentally damaging activity and by using all or part of that revenue to assist in mitigating the environmental damage caused. In the case of motor fuels, driving the vehicle creates air pollution, noise, and congestion. In the case of tires and batteries, undirected disposal of used products produces solid waste with particularly troublesome health and amenity problems. The product charge contrasts with a tax imposed directly on the emission of pollutants an effluent charge on water pollutants: a 'Pigouvian' tax.

A Pigouvian tax is, in principle, more economically efficient than a product charge because it links to all the opportunities available for controlling pollution. The product charge, by contrast, does not provide a direct incentive to reduce pollution, only an incentive to reduce use of the product. If pollution and the product are perfectly correlated, then product charges and Pigouvian taxes can be equivalent economic instruments. In general, the better the correlation between the product and associated pollution, the more efficient the product charge. Even product charges on products that are not nearly synonymous with pollution can be preferable to Pigouvian taxes on grounds of economic efficiency if the act of polluting is costly to identify and measure and/or administration of the Pigouvian tax is expensive.

3.2 Administration

In general, the product charges in Hungary are collected by the Customs Office when a product is imported or by the Tax Collection Office when the product is produced domestically. These Offices receive a share of 5 percent of the revenues set aside for administrative purposes to cover their expenses. The Customs Office also collects the product charge when the product is embodied in an imported vehicle or piece of equipment such as the product charge on tires and batteries when a car is imported. The CEPF is responsible for rebating the product charge when a product is subsequently exported without having been used in Hungary. The product charge is calculated before value-added tax (VAT), so that, with a 25 percent VAT, the VAT tax makes the effect of the product charge 25 percent higher than its nominal value. Product charge legislation aimed at solid waste problems contain provisions for 50 percent reductions in the product charge if a product qualified for an 'eco-label' as an environmentally friendly product. This provision, however, has prompted enterprises only to a small extent to develop 'green products'.

3.3 Environmental Product Charge on Transport Fuel

The environmental product charge on transport fuel was in fact the first economic instrument (aside from generally ineffectual exceedence fines) developed expressly as part of Hungarian environmental policy. Its introduction in May 1992 aimed at increasing the tax on the consumption of a product for environmental protection purposes. In the case of mobile source air pollution the administrative costs associated with the direct taxation of emissions are prohibitive. The charge imposed on transport fuel can be viewed as a close substitute for a direct emission charge, first, because the amount consumed and the pollution caused are highly and positively correlated, and second, because of the significantly lower administrative costs of the latter regulatory regime (Lehoczki and Balogh 1997).

One environmentally beneficial effect of this product charge is any associated reduction in the demand for transportation fuel. With the tax component comprising from 60–70 percent of consumer prices, this effect has probably been significant even assuming a demand elasticity for motor fuels considerably less than 1. The 2 HUF/liter component of the charge earmarked for environmental protection and damage mitigation is only 1.3–1.5 percent of the retail price of fuels as of November 1997 (see Table 17.1). According to the law, the earmarked portion of the product charge is to provide financing for projects to address those environmental problems which are caused by the use of the product in question. The performance of this part of the motor fuels product charge depends on the effectiveness (or efficiency) of use of these funds.

While a full and systematic analysis of the use of fuel product charge revenues remains to be accomplished, there is some recent work which provides an indication of the effectiveness of the earmarked spending. Among the early, earmarked spending priorities of the CEPF were: diesel bus engine replacement projects, a catalytic converter installation program for used cars, and the development of a combined rail-road service in which the state-owned railroad company has a considerable presence. Raucher et al. (1991) and Kaderják (1992) concluded that diesel bus engine replacement is on the top of cost-effective options to reduce transport-related air pollution in Hungary. At the same time, the cost effectiveness of the catalytic converter program is questionable. Finally, the railroad project attacks one of the most urgent transport-related environmental problems in Hungary, namely air and noise pollution by commuter traffic.

Table 17.1. Composition of the price of motor fuels in Hungary as of November 1997

	Unleaded 95 gasoline		Leaded 98 gasoline		Diesel	
	HUF per liter	% of total price	HUF per liter	% of total price	HUF per liter	% of total price
Net price	48.40	33.40	48.30	31.80	47.86	35.74
Road fund	15.40	10.63	15.40	10.14	15.40	11.50
Excise tax	48.30	33.33	54.00	35.55	40.00	29.87
Environmental product charge	2.00	1.38	2.00	1.32	2.00	1.49
Fuel reserves charge	1.82	1.26	1.82	1.20	1.86	1.39
VAT (25%)	28.98	20.00	30.38	20.00	26.78	20.00
Total tax	96.50	66.60	103.60	68.20	86.04	64.26
Gross price	144.90	100.00	151.90	100.00	133.9	100.0

3.4 Environmental Product Charge on Tires

The problem with tire disposal in Hungary is that, of the annually generated 40–50 thousand tons of used tires, only a small portion is disposed of in environmentally preferable ways. The rest is littered, stored or illegally landfilled together with municipal solid waste. These alternatives raise problems for a variety of reasons:

- Littered tires often end up in forests and rivers or on the roadside, and will stay there for a long time, since tires are extremely slow to decompose. The material of tires is foreign to the natural environment and their sight both reduces the aesthetic value of the area and encourages the disposal of other litter at the same site.
- Tire storage sites are at risk of serious fire, resulting in severe air and possible water pollution. Extinguishing tire fires is one of the most difficult and costly tasks facing fire departments.
- Tires in a community landfill provide shelter for rodents and pathogens. Whole tires often spring back to their original shape after compaction and tend to work their way to the surface during settling, disrupting the protective cap of a landfill. Potential damage arises from water infiltration through the disrupted cap, possibly resulting in leaching of polluting materials from the landfill. Landfills that dispose of whole tires are subject to prolonged fires, which are also a source of air pollution.

The MoE decided to address these problems through the introduction of a product charge on tires. According to the MoE, the product charge serves primarily to generate revenues to finance environmentally friendly disposal of scrap tires. The tire product charge was enacted together with three other solid waste-related product charges in the middle of 1995 (Act LVI of 1995). Morris and Kis (1997a&b) have analyzed this instrument to see how effectively this product handles the scrap tire problem and the opportunities for improvement.

The basis of the product charge is the weight of the tire. The product charge rates are 30 HUF/kg for new tires and for a limited number of used tires which are imported exclusively for retreading purposes, and 120 HUF/kg for imported used tires. Domestically produced retreaded tires are not subject to the product charge directly, but their input, imported used tires, is subject to the product charge. The product charge itself, together with the base price of the commodity, is subject to a 25 percent VAT. While the product charge provides revenue to the CEPF, the VAT component accrues to the Central Budget of Hungary. A large part of the tire product charge revenues of the CEPF are earmarked to finance scrap tire collection and disposal schemes. A smaller share covers the expenses of CEPF operation and the costs of more general environmental projects.

In Table 17.2, the unit product charges and the supplementary VAT are transformed into a potential price increase per tire. The actual price increase will diverge from these values, the extent of such divergence depending on market reaction. The price (in 1995) of a new automobile tire was between HUF 4,500 and 10,000, used automobile tires cost about HUF 1,500. New truck tires were sold for HUF 22,000 to 80,000, while the price of a used truck tire was about HUF 8,000. The percentage change in price due to the product charge and VAT is in parentheses.

Table 17.2. Potential price increase per tire due to the product charge and VAT

	Price increase of an automobile tire (HUF)	Price increase of a truck tire (HUF)
New tires	270 (or 3–6 percent)	2,000–2,300 (or 2.5–10 percent)
Used tires	900 (or 60 percent)	7,500 (or 2,590 percent)

The tire product charge regulation can be viewed as an environmental protection program with three elements: (i) a tax or product charge on the production or import of tires, (ii) use of part of the product charge revenues to finance scrap tire collection and disposal, and (iii) use of the balance of the product charge revenues for a variety of environmental projects and general government programs. Morris and Kis made a detailed examination on the first two elements because they are most specific and amenable to objective analysis. In doing so they examined the costs and benefits associated with taxing the tires, administrating the product charge system and disbursing tire product charge revenues to the scrap tire disposal market. These components and the most important benefits and costs associated with them are depicted by Figure 17.1.

Figure 17. 1. Schematic of a Framework for evaluating the Performance of the Tire Product Charge.

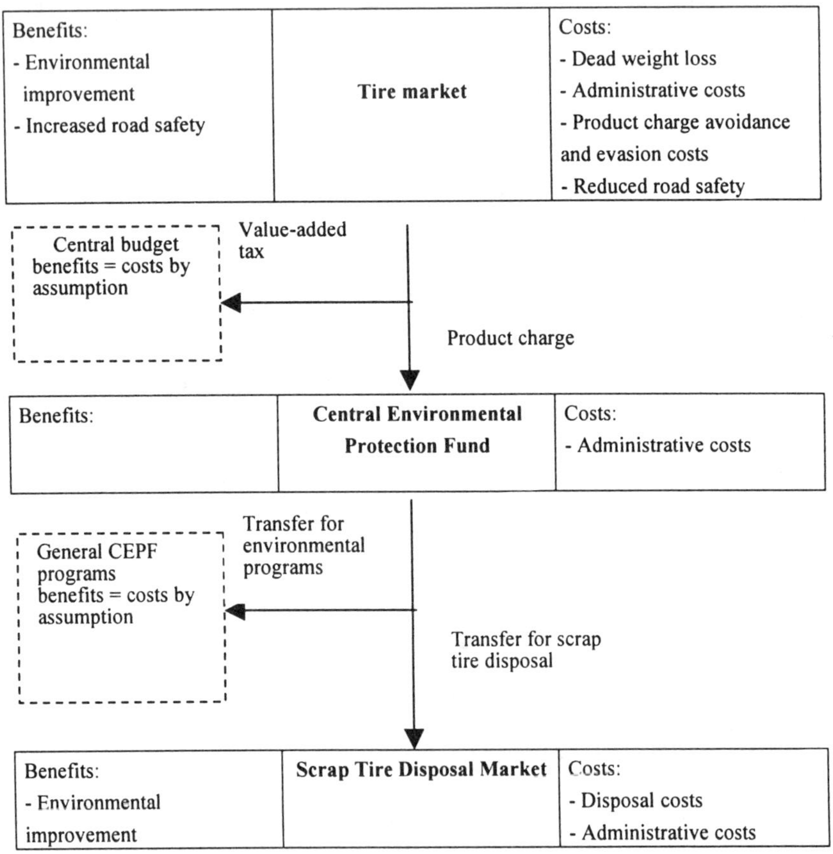

The Morris and Kis analysis of the tire market estimated the following changes as a result of the tire product charge. Total tire consumption decreased by about 4 percent for smaller-sized passenger car tires and by about 1.3 percent for larger truck tires. The composition of tire consumption also would change: a significant number of customers would switch from purchasing used or retreaded tires to buying new tires. From an environmental perspective the changes in aggregate quantity are welcome; the less tires are consumed, the less tires will need to be disposed. These environmental benefits may be counterbalanced by a potential reduction of road safety, however, if the reason for a reduced tire consumption is longer use of bald or structurally weakened tires. As the market adjusts to the product charge, some consumers will experience a loss in their welfare. Morris and Kis found that the total economic welfare loss of the product charge in the tire market is between HUF 50 and 65 million per year. Another HUF 60 million would be spent by the CEPF for administering the product charge. Thus the total economic burden of collecting annual tire product charge revenues of HUF 1.2 billion is about HUF 120 million, or 10 percent of anticipated revenue. Both the welfare loss and the size of the revenue are dependent on avoidance or evasion of the product charge. There is a general presumption that a significant portion of the product charge due is not collected.

Morris and Kis also examine the scrap tire disposal market. The product charge legislation together with the law on the CEPF channels a large part of the tire product charge revenues to scrap tire disposal and, together with the annually published disbursement guidelines, establishes the rules for disbursement. Scrap tire collecting, transporting and disposing facilities can apply for subsidy at the CEPF according to these rules. These rules, however, do not satisfy the criterion of cost-effectiveness. Morris and Kis identify the following changes that could lead to major improvements in cost-effectiveness and, probably, efficiency:

- As opposed to present practice and regulation, landfilling of chopped tires could be included among the supportable disposal alternatives, since it is a less expensive option which results in the same (or more) environmental benefits as some other, supported disposal alternatives.
- Present disbursement rules promote discrimination among applications based on the geographical location of the activity or the amount of scrap tires to be disposed. Nonetheless, there should be no discrimination among applicants based on regions or size because that may create regional monopolies and less cost-effective choices. For efficient performance, the applicant offering the better bid should be supported *ceteris paribus*. This would also create the possibility for measuring all applications against each other by some common measure such as unit cost/subsidy.
- Only disposal should be directly supported; not the collection and transportation of scrap tires, without proper disposal. When applicants calculate their subsidy need, they would have to keep in mind the cost of

collection and transportation including the cost of inducing organizations or individuals to bring used tires to the disposal site or a common collection area. By paying for scrap tires, disposing facilities create a competitive and efficient market for collecting and transporting scrap tires.

Furthermore, the CEPF, the MoE, and the regional environmental inspectorates would experience lower management costs, since they would have to administer applications for disposal only, but not for collection and transportation.

The present system of the tire product charge takes care of only half of the scrap tire problem of Hungary. By improving the scope and procedures of the disbursement system, Morris and Kis believe the cost effectiveness of the tire product charge program would increase substantially. Nevertheless, it is useful to remind ourselves that even if all components of the tire product charge program were as effective as theoretically possible, there is no guarantee that the tire product charge is an efficient policy instrument. To be able to assess economic efficiency of the program, we need to know the marginal monetary benefits of the associated environmental improvements and, for the time being at least, such estimates are not available. Furthermore, while a well-designed product charge appears to be a good instrument to handle the scrap tire problem of Hungary, a deposit-refund system is an alternative to the product charge that is also worth examination.

3.5 Environmental Product Charges on Automotive and Commercial Batteries

This product charge was implemented in January 1996 and covers secondary cell (rechargeable) batteries such as the lead acid and alkaline batteries used to start or drive commercial or transportation equipment. It has the same general design features as the tire product charge.

Lead-acid batteries posed the biggest environmental problem because they constitute over 90 percent of the market by weight and roughly 60 percent of this weight is lead, a hazardous substance when inhaled or ingested. Fucskó (1997) estimates that lead-acid battery waste stream is currently about 17,000 tons per year, that 30–70 percent are collected and shipped abroad for recycling, and that the balance are either stockpiled by households and businesses, littered, or disposed of in municipal landfills or incinerators.

The battery product charge is 38 HUF/kg. We found nothing in the legislative record or supporting analysis to indicate that this rate was selected on the basis of damages arising from the existing pattern of battery disposal. On a typical automobile battery this adds about HUF 550 or roughly 7 to 9 percent to the retail price. The MoE anticipated HUF 700 million annual revenue from the product charge on batteries would flow to the CEPF.

Given that battery demand is highly price inelastic (a notion seemingly confirmed in the Hungarian battery market when the product charge was folded into battery prices), the product charge's dominant pathway for improved battery disposal will be funding of improved collection and disposal activities. The goal of developers of the battery product charge appears, to quote Fucskó (1997), 'to generate enough revenue ... to finance the chosen scheme of ... subsidized collection and full domestic reprocessing of waste batteries'. In the product charge legislation itself, there are guidelines that direct financial support toward a few, select 'program masters' who would be franchised to improve collection and disposal on an exclusive basis either regionally or nationally.

Table 17.3. Design of air emission charges

Pollutant	Scenario A (HUF/kg)	Scenario B (HUF/kg)	Estimated benefit range* (HUF/kg)
SO_2	15	30	61–435
NO_x	30	60	93–1,386
CO	15	15	n.a.
TSP	15	15	0–379
Toxic I	750	750	n.a.
Toxic II	75	75	n.a.

Notes: Scenarios A and B are the official proposals of the MoE as of November 1997. The current exchange rate is: US$1 = HUF 197.
* The zero lower bound estimate originates in the fact that available abatement-cost estimates for TSP were suspected to be too high.
Source: Kaderják et al. (1996).

The CEPF subsequently established 18 criteria for awarding investment and operating subsidies for battery collection and disposal, many of them subjective, some of them contradictory, and some emphasizing a preference for domestic participation. The concern (indeed the conviction) of some potential waste collectors and processors was that the selection process was highly politicized and that only those who were 'close' to the MoE had a chance of winning a franchise and financial support (Fucskó 1997). Public information on the proposals received by CEPF and the awards made to date is scant, but recently it was announced that financing was being provided for construction of a large-scale national lead-acid battery reprocessing facility in northeast Hungary.

Fucskó's 1997 study identifies changes likely to improve the cost effectiveness of the current design.

- One alternative involves modifying the current strategy of product charge disbursement. He argues that since there appears to be excess battery recycling capacity in Europe and that a commercial scale battery recycling facility (about 30,000 Mg/year capacity) far exceeds the flow of used batteries in Hungary, it makes both environmental and economic sense to drop domestic processing and concentrate on collection and export of used batteries for reprocessing elsewhere.
- Fucskó further argues that economies of scale in collection do not justify regional franchises and that support should be provided to any collection entity that shows that they have collected used domestic batteries for export and recycling.
- And lastly, a different alternative is to re-cast the product charge as a deposit-refund system. In this case the purchaser would receive the product charge back when turning in the used battery at a collection center. Financing of the collection centers and assurance that the batteries they collect are properly disposed could be supported with part of the 'deposit', in which case this would be a hybrid deposit-refund and product charge system. Again, to make this a more competitive and economically efficient system, support would be provided to any collection center in proportion to the amount of waste battery volume they properly handle.

4. DESIGN OF AIR EMISSION CHARGES

We refer to proposed Hungarian environmental load fees on air pollutants as air emission charges (AECs). As noted earlier, the AEC is part of an ambitious and innovative legislative proposal to introduce extensive, emission-based environmental taxes into the environmental policy of Hungary. Among the general features of this proposal are:

- gradual phasing in of the environmental load fees (emissions taxes) over a five-year period;
- coordination with exceedence fines so that the combination results in a two-stage emission tax;
- upgrading the monitoring and enforcement systems with an incentive for local authorities (usually environmental inspectorates) to enforce in the form of a 5 percent share of revenues;
- a substantial percentage reduction in the load fees assessed if, under a negotiated and monitored agreement with the local environmental inspectorates, the polluter invests in environmental protection equipment or programs;

- annual adjustment of the rates to, at a minimum, reflect inflation and, possibly, to reflect the most up-to-date estimates on the value of environmental damages due to air pollutants; and
- self-reporting of emission as currently exists within the system of exceedence fines and selected monitoring by environmental inspectorates as part of administration and enforcement.

4.1 Features of the Air Emission Charges

The AEC would be a unit charge levied on each kilogram of SO_2, NO_x, CO, total suspended particulates (TSP) and an extensive list of toxic pollutants – divided into highly toxic (Toxic I) and lower toxicity (Toxic II) groups emitted from point sources. The current proposal does not cover mobile sources of pollution.

The AEC proposal has generous rebate or forgiveness provisions; from 50 to 80 percent of the assessed fees will be forgiven if the source makes an equivalent investment in environmental control over a five-year period. There is also a special penalty provision for large sources (> 50 MW) in the energy sector that increases the AEC by a factor of five if the source exceeds its emission limit (calculated on a base of emissions exceeding that limit). Most of the revenues ultimately collected as a result of these AECs will accrue to the CEPF and are extensively earmarked.

4.2 Selection of the Charge Rate

Kaderják et al. (1996) carried out an economic impact assessment of the proposed AEC. They tried to roughly estimate economically efficient AEC rates (that is, rates where marginal abatement costs and marginal benefits of abatement would roughly coincide) for SO_2, NO_x and TSP. Even given data limitations and assumptions that yielded a wide range of estimates, they concluded that the AEC rates proposed by the MoE are far below the levels which could be judged as roughly economically efficient (see Table 17.3, last column). Subsequently, in hearings during November 1997, the MoE committed itself to apply the lower (Scenario A) rates.

Kaderják et al. (1996) also doubted that the rates considered were high enough to induce any noticeable abatement activity in the Hungarian industry. This conclusion might be due to the abatement-cost data they used as well as to the partial equilibrium nature of their analysis. In a more recent study, which applied a general equilibrium model of the Hungarian economy and used more detailed information to assess abatement costs, Morris et al. (1997) found a sizable incentive effect at the level of the officially proposed rates. That study, however, was not able to fully factor in the expected impact on behavior of AEC conditional reduction provisions or exceedence penalties. Still, international evidence supports the notion that *ex-ante* abatement-cost estimates most often overestimate *ex-post* costs, partly because *ex-ante* cost estimates are not usually able to reflect all the cost-saving input, process, and end-of-pipe control innovations discovered only after the financial incentive to reduce costs becomes real. This evidence, along with the fact that Hungarian industry is undergoing significant and widespread modernization, strengthens the expectation that AECs, even at currently considered levels, could induce significant emission reductions from point sources.

By using the benefit estimates developed by Kaderják et al. (1996), Morris et al. (1997a&b) also concluded that the introduction of the AEC proposal of the MoE would result in a benefit/cost ratio of two to four. This means that the AECs, while their introduction would just mildly affect national income (GDP is estimated to decrease by 0.15 percent), are expected to have a positive impact on economic welfare in Hungary. Morris et al. (1997a&b) also found that introduction of AECs would have the biggest immediate negative impact on the electricity-generating sector: in case of compliance its AEC payment (Scenario A) would equal 3.9 percent of the 1995 value added. The same impact measure for other affected industries is 2 percent for mining and a value of about 1 per cent for non-ferrous materials and metallurgy. In sum, these estimates support the argument that introduction of a pure AEC system in Hungary is probably both cost effective and highly efficient. There are still, however, numerous institutional and design issues that qualify this conclusion. Now we turn to discuss potential problems posed by some of the other design issues found in the current AEC and other environmental policy proposals.

4.3 Air Emission Charges and Policy Coordination

4.3.1 Air emission charges and best-available technology standards

The proposal to introduce AEC is just one element of a more elaborate regulatory initiative: the new Hungarian 'Clean Air Act' proposal. According to the proposal, the principal tool for protection of air quality will be a detailed set of technology-based emission standards, specific to major industrial activities by pollutant, sector, and/or technology. These standards are planned to be as strict as their counterparts in Germany and may be summarized as best-available technology (BAT) standards. The proposed Hungarian BAT standards for sulfur-dioxide emissions from large combustion plants are, in some cases, stricter than those included in the Second Sulfur Protocol. In the case of industrial polluters, different emission standards are proposed for existing versus new point sources. However, in the case of the power-generating sector, strict emission standards are planned to apply both for new and existing sources (with a five-year waiting period for the latter), despite the possibility of applying more cost-effective solutions than BAT to existing plants. As argued by Klassen (1997), '[in CEE countries] emission standards for existing plants should be avoided, set at lenient levels, or more flexible approaches such as offsets and bubbles should be offered as alternative means of meeting these standards. Such approaches are allowed in the EU directive on large combustion plants and under the Second Sulfur Protocol'.

The objective that some environmental policy makers have in mind is minimization of emissions rather than maximization of social welfare. By way of illustration, the proposed regulation envisions an aggregate emission limit of SO_2 from the power sector (combustion facilities with thermal power input greater than 50 MW(th) equivalent to 150 thousand tons in 2004 in Hungary. If this goal is achieved, total SO_2 emissions of Hungary could be estimated to be about 300 thousand tons in 2004. At the same time, in the Second Sulfur Protocol, Hungary agreed to cut SO2 emissions by half by the year 2005 (to 816 thousand tons from 1,632 thousand tons in 1980). Thus, the goal set by the proposal is more than twice as strict as the already aggressive obligation Hungary undertook under its international agreements.

According to the ideas of some MoE representatives, these two approaches, AEC and BAT standards, are envisioned as complements, rather than substitutes. In a fundamental misunderstanding of the efficiency rationale for AEC, some policy makers view the AEC as a 'temporary' regulatory measure that will motivate the polluters to take actions that, in turn, will better prepare them to comply with strict emission standards in the future. In their study, Morris, et al. (1997a&b) found that under joint AEC and BAT policy, the BAT-based emission standards dominated economic choices so much that the burden on the economy was substantially increased relative to the associated improvement in environment, GDP was estimated to drop by 5 percent more than with AEC alone. Again, using the damage values estimated by Kaderják et al. (1996), Morris et al. (1997a&b) computed a benefit/cost ratio of the joint AEC and BAT design as being substantially less than 1.

4.3.2 Other technologies

Note, finally, that if no comparable regulatory measures were taken in order to internalize the external costs associated with the disposal of nuclear waste, the implementation of the AEC regulation would put fossil fuel-based electricity production into a disadvantageous position in Hungary.[1] Given the prevailing conditions of the Hungarian power-generating sector, this

[1] Note that about 50 percent of electricity produced in Hungary is provided by the country's single nuclear power plant.

disadvantage could have far-reaching consequences for future developments in this principal economic sector. Note, however, that from the beginning of 1998, a special charge is built into each kWh electricity produced on nuclear bases in Hungary. The charge is dedicated to a fund to finance the costs of disposal of nuclear waste. The fund is estimated to receive about HUF 7 billion from charge payments in 1998.

4.4 Monitoring and Enforcement

The assessments of the proposed AEC regimes, including, for example, charge revenue predictions carried out by MoE experts and Morris et al. (1997a&b) are based on estimated emission data derived from energy use and current control and production technology. If the AEC is implemented as proposed, payments will be based on self-reported emissions. Underreporting of emissions is already a widespread phenomenon in Hungary. For example, Kaderják and Csermely (1997), while analyzing available 1990 emission data for manufacturing, found that, based on energy usage, emission data for industrial SO_2 emitters (exclusive of the power-generating sector), was 4.34 times higher than the self reported emissions for the same group of polluters. Kaderják et al. (1996) also found significant inconsistencies between estimated and self-reported emissions using 1994 data from manufacturing and the power sectors: self-reported emissions for SO_2, NO_x, and TSP were, respectively, 47 per cent, 58 percent, and 88 per cent of official estimates. Without significant investments in monitoring and information systems and strengthening the power to enforce the findings of independent emission estimates, the proposed AEC regulation will probably produce less revenue and fail to satisfy its potential for efficient environmental protection.

5. CONCLUSION

Environmental policy makers in Hungary have been trying to take advantage of the recent changes that have been made in the economic and political life of the country to establish a new group of regulatory instruments for environmental protection. A remarkably large number of those instruments capitalize on the power of economic incentives in this new setting to provide efficient means and levels of environmental protection. We applaud environmental policy makers for the outstanding progress they have made and identify a number of instances in which economic instruments have been reasonably efficient in design and implementation. At the same time, however, we have also identified many instances where the specific policy elements adopted fall short of using these economic instruments to best advantage. We note the following significant problems:

- While it is common in Hungary to use, or to propose use of taxes, charges and so on to provide incentives to reduce, directly or indirectly, environmental damages, the charges are set, or proposed, at levels that are not well supported by available economic evidence (or any evidence at all in some cases) of the benefits that would be achieved. The rates, in some cases, seem to be derived from investment or operating programs dear to the hearts of some policy makers rather than notions of budgetary effectiveness or economic efficiency.
- The design of the existing economic instruments, mostly product charges, has been very good on the 'revenue side'. As far as we can say, they impose little direct welfare loss relative to the revenues collected and administrative costs are low. The totality of the designs is, unfortunately, seriously weakened by disbursement strategies that do not encourage the efficient use of the revenues. In some cases these problems can easily be remedied with specific reforms suggested by economic analysis of the economic instrument. More generally, there is a need to make the disbursement process more open and market-like through competitive bidding or cost–benefit comparisons of proposed options.

Hungary, in its eagerness to improve environmental quality, has moved to adopt a wide variety of both economic and non-economic policy instruments and to make policy interventions at multiple points in the economic system. We have a serious concern that efficiency properties of well-designed economic instruments will be lost due to concurrent use of redundant and/or conflicting environmental policy instruments.

REFERENCES

Bluffstone, Randall and Bruce Larson (eds) (1997), *Controlling Pollution in Transition Economies: Theories and Methods*. Cheltenham, United Kingdom: Edward Elgar.

DeShazo, J.R. (1996), 'Urban Environmental Services in Transitional Economies: The Case Study of Iasi, Romania', Harvard University, Policy Brief Series, Draft, April.

Fucskó, József (1997), 'Battery Waste Management and the Role of the Battery Product Charge in Hungary'. Harvard Institute for International Development, Budapest. Final Draft.

Harrison, K., A. Krupnick, E. Nickell and M. Toman (1996), 'The Value of Health Benefits from Ambient Air Quality Improvements in Central and Eastern Europe: An Initial Assessment', *Environmental and Resource Economics*, 7 (4), 307–32.

Kaderják, Péter (1992), *A Study on Mobile Source Air Pollution Problems in Hungary*. Prepared for US AID, Washington, DC.

Kaderják, Péter, Gábor Bartus and László Székely (1996), *An Economic Impact Assessment of Air Emission Charges, Ministry for Environmental and Regional Planning* (in Hungarian) Budapest: QuercusCoop.

Kaderják, Péter and Ágnes Csermely (1997), 'Direct Impacts of Industrial Restructuring on Air Pollutant and Hazardous Waste Emissions in Hungary', in Péter Kaderják and John Powell (eds), *Economics for Environmental Policy in Transition Economies: An Analysis of the Hungarian Experience*, Cheltenham: Edward Elgar.

Kaderják, Péter and Erzsébet Páczi (1997), 'Environmental Impacts of Industrial Privatization in Hungary', in Péter Kaderják and John Powell (eds), *Economics for Environmental Policy in Transition Economies: An Analysis of the Hungarian Experience*, Cheltenham: Edward Elgar.

Klaassen, Ger (1997), 'Practical Experience, International Agreements and the Prospects for Emission Trading in CEE', in: Péter Kaderják and John Powell (eds), *Economics for Environmental Policy in Transition Economies: An Analysis of the Hungarian Experience*, Cheltenham: Edward Elgar.

Klarer, Jurg (ed.) (1994), *Use of Economic Instruments in Environmental Policy in Central and Eastern Europe*, Regional Environmental Center for Central and Eastern Europe, Budapest.

Kovács, Péter, Glenn E. Morris and József Tiderenczl (1997), 'Environmental Emission Charges and Air Quality Protection in Hungary: Recent Practice and Future Prospects', in Bluffstone and Larson

Lehoczki, Zsuzsanna (1993), 'Experiences of Using Economic Instruments: Summarizing Report', prepared for the Hungarian Ministry of Finance. Harvard Institute for International Development, Budapest. December.

Lehoczki, Zsuzsa (1997), 'Coordinating Environmental and Fiscal Policy in Hungary: Possibilities and Constraints', Presented at the Conference on Green Budget Reform – Prospects in Central and Eastern European Countries. Lake Bled, Slovenia. April.

Lehoczki, Zsuzsa and Zsuzsanna Balogh (1997), 'Hungary', in B. Moldan and J. Klarer (eds), *The Environmental Challenge for Central European Economies in Transition*.

Lehoczki, Z. and G.E. Morris (1996), 'Environmental Fund Disbursement: Incentives for Performance in Central and Eastern Europe', Environmental Discussion Paper, Harvard Institute for International Development. July.

Markowska, A. and Zylicz, T. (1996), 'Costing an International Public Good: The Case of the Baltic Sea', Paper presented at the Seventh Annual Meeting of the EAERE, Lisbon, Portugal.

Morris, Glenn E. and András Kis (1997a), *The Design and Assessment of an Environmental Product Charge on Tires in Hungary.* Harvard Institute for International Development, Budapest. June.

Morris, Glenn E. and András Kis (1997b), *A Policy Oriented Analysis of the Tire Product Charge.* Harvard Institute for International Development, Budapest. English and Hungarian. July.

Morris, Glenn E., Tamás Révész, Erno Zalai, and József Fucskó (1997a), 'Integrating Environmental Taxes on Local Air Pollutants with Fiscal Reform in Hungary: Simulations with a Computable General Equilibrium Model', Harvard Institute for International Development, Budapest. Draft. July.

Morris, Glenn E., Erno Zalai, and Tamás Révész (1997b), 'Integrating Environmental Taxation with Fiscal Reform in Hungary: Simulations with a Computable General Equilibrium Model', Harvard Institute for International Development, Budapest. Draft. January.

Powell, John and Péter Kaderják and Frank Verkoijen (1997), 'Empirical Benefit Estimates for Improving Air Quality in Hungary', in Péter Kaderják and John Powell (eds), *Economics for Environmental Policy in Transition Economies: An Analysis of the Hungarian Experience*, Cheltenham: Edward Elgar.

18. Do Pollution Charges Reduce Emissions in Lithuania?

Randall A. Bluffstone[1]

1. INTRODUCTION

A variety of economic instruments are used throughout the world, but in no region are pollution charges as widely employed as in Central and Eastern Europe (CEE) and the former Soviet Union (FSU).[2] This concentration is in large measure a legacy of the communist period when charges were introduced primarily for raising revenues to finance environmental protection and as a mechanism for compensating citizens for the pollution generated by state-owned enterprises. Most countries' systems are linked with pollution permits, and they are also often connected with mechanisms for providing environmental finance.[3] An overview of pollution charge systems in CEE and the FSU taken from Vincent and Farrow (1997) is given in Table 18.1.

It is somewhat surprising given the theoretical appeal of pollution charges (for example, see Baumol and Oates 1971) that as of 1995 in OECD countries there were only five cases where charges were levied on measured or reported emissions (Fournier 1995).

[1] The author would like to thank the US Agency for International Development for providing funding for this research under cooperative agreement EUR-00040A-00-4014. The author would also like to thank officials of the Ministry of Environmental Protection of Lithuania for allowing him the opportunity to conduct the work. Research assistance was provided by Jurate Varneckiene.

[2] In this chapter a pollution charge is defined as a charge levied on the actual or reported emissions (in tons per year) of a particular pollutant.

[3] Extensive discussions of the implementation of pollution charge systems in Central and Eastern Europe and the and the former Soviet Union can be found in RandallBluffstone and Bruce A. Larson, (eds), *Controlling Pollution in Transition Economies: Theories and Methods*, Cheltenham: Edward Elgar.

Table 18.1. Charge systems in European transition economies 1994

Media	System type	Goal	Penalty multiple	Revenue distribution	# of pollutants charged	Revenue leaders	Rates vary by region?	Factors determin-ing charge rates	Rates indexed	Country
Air	2U	PPP	15	SF-90	>150			CC,D,PR,R	X	Belarus
Water	2U	PPP	15	NF-10	>150			CC,D,PR,R	X	
Air	U	C	n.a.	NF-70	16	SO_2 BOD/		CC		Bulg.
Water	U	C	n.a.	SF-30	27	COD		CC		
Air	2U	R	1.5	NF-	90	SO_2		CC,D,PR,R		Czech.
Water	2P	C	5	100	5	BOD		CC,D,PR,R		
Air	2P	PPP	5-500	NF-50	139	SO_2	X	CC,R	X	Est.
Water	2P	C	5-1000	SF-50	8	BOD	X	CC,R	X	
Air	P	C	n.a.	NF-70	150	SO_2	X	X CC,D,PR,R		Hung
Water	P	C	n.a.	SF-30	32	n.a.	X	R		
Air	2P	PPP	1-10	SF-65	>100	n.a.	X	CC,PR,R	X	Kazak.
Water	2P	PPP	1-10	NB-20	>100	n.a.	X	CC,PR,R	X	
				NF-15						
Air	2U	C	4	SB-70	7	SO_2		D,PF		Lat.
Water	2U	C	4	NB-30	10	BOD		D,PF		
Air	2P	C_E	10	SF-70	All	n.a.		CC,D	X	Lith.
Water	2P	C_E	10	NB-30	All	n.a.		CC,D	X	
Air	2U	C	10	SF-64	62	SO_2	-	D,R	X	Pol.
Water	2P	C	about 4	NF-36	6	BOD/ COD	X	D,R	X	
Air	2U	R	5	SF-54	>100	n.a.	X	CC,PR,R	X	Russ.
Water	2U	R	5	NF-36	>100	n.a.	X	CC,PR,R		
				NB-10						
Air	2P	C	1.5	NF-	123	Particles		CC,PR,R		Slov.
Water	2P	C, R	3	100	5	BOD		CC,PR,R		

Notes
System type: 2U Uniform two-tiered structure; 2P Progressive two-tiered structure; UUniform non-compliance penalty system; P Progressive non-compliance penalty system.
Goals: C Encourage compliance; C_E Cost-effectiveness; PPP Polluter pays principle; R Revenue raising.
Revenue distribution: NB National budget; NF National environmental fund; SBsubnational (regional or municipal) budget; SF subnational (regional or municipal) environmental fund.
Charge rate determinants: CC Compliance costs; D Damage to environment; PF Political factors; PR Enterprise profitability; R Government revenue needs.

Source: Vincent and Farrow (1997).

A consequence of this relative lack of international experience is that less is known about the operation of pollution charges than, for example, tradable emission rights or environmental product charges. The goal of this chapter is to take a modest step toward understanding the effects pollution charges have had in one country in the region of the world where they are most intensively used. Support for the use of pollution charges is somewhat mixed. On the one hand, the policy environment has been strongly supportive. Countries are working actively to refine existing systems, and the regional scope for the use of pollution charges is, if anything, expanding (Bluffstone and Larson 1997). International institutions have also weighed in positively.

For example, the Environmental Action Program for Central and Eastern Europe endorsed the increased use of economic instruments in transition countries and recommended that 'countries [build] on existing frameworks of pollution charges' (Environment for Europe 1994, p. 78). A recent document produced by the Committee on Environmental Policy of the UN Economic Commission for Europe gives substantial mention to pollution charges and makes several recommendations for improved performance (UN-ECE 1998). At the same time, however, important questions have been raised about whether the pollution charges that are so extensively used in CEE and the FSU are actually doing anything. For example, Smith and Zylicz (1994), reporting on an OECD workshop held in 1993, noted that 'taxes levied on measured emissions are unlikely to be worthwhile during the transition phase'. Vincent and Farrow (1997), Anderson and Fiedor (1997) and others have claimed that pollution charges have little effect because the rates are too low.[4] Questions have also been raised about the utility of raising rates, because of 'J curve' effects related to poor monitoring and enforcement in the region (Anderson and Fiedor 1997; Zinnes 1997). Concerns have also been expressed that polluters do not know their abatement options and costs, and are therefore unable to respond efficiently to appropriately set pollution charge rates (Smith and Zylicz, 1994).

Given these legitimate concerns, it seems useful to empirically evaluate the effects pollution charges have had on environmental performance. The goal of the rest of this chapter is therefore to estimate these effects using firm-level data from Lithuania. To provide some background, the following section briefly overviews the regulatory system in Lithuania. Section 3 presents an analytical model of polluter behavior within that regulatory framework, and Section 4 discusses the data used to estimate a structural form of that model, as well as some key econometric issues. Section 5 presents the results of the analysis and Section 6 concludes the chapter.

---

[4] At the same time, however, UN-ECE (1998) advises that 'countries with low initial marginal pollution abatement costs will be able to achieve abatement objectives with relatively low tax or charge rates'.

2. THE LITHUANIAN REGULATORY STRUCTURE

Lithuania became independent from the Soviet Union in 1990. Economic transformation has been under way since that time and by 1996 the economy had changed from one based on agriculture, mining and manufacturing to one with a substantial service sector. A consequence of that transformation has been a sharp decline in industrial output. In 1994, for example, 75 percent of the enterprises analyzed in this chapter were producing at least 30 percent below and 50 percent were at less than half of pre-independence levels.[5] These economic changes were certainly good for the environment, and air quality, particularly, has improved substantially since independence. Emissions of sulfur dioxide, nitrogen dioxide, carbon monoxide and dust all fell by at least two-thirds between 1989 and 1996 (Ministry of Environmental Protection 1997).

Environmental protection is the responsibility of the Ministry of Environmental Protection and its 55 regional departments. The environmental regulatory system in Lithuania, as in most CEE and FSU countries, combines facility-level permits and pollution charges levied on reported emissions monitored through periodic spot-checks. In the sample used in this chapter, air polluters were checked on average every 6.3 months. The most important section of a permit is an annual facility limit that specifies a facility's target emissions of each permitted pollutant. Limits are renewed once every five years, but are changed infrequently.

Good environmental performance is defined as emitting at or below this limit, which is abbreviated in Lithuanian as DLT. These limits are set in the case of air pollution to divide a total air pollution load among all enterprises in a region such that ambient air quality goals are met.[6] If firms emit over their limits they are subject to a substantially higher charge rate. Firms that are judged to have no hope of meeting their DLT limits can apply for more lenient LLT standards if they also agree to achieve DLT levels within a predetermined time period. Among air polluters, approximately one-third of all polluters have LLT limits (Semeniene et al. 1997).

Limits are tailor-made for each facility. They are not only set based on estimated environmental effects, but are also calibrated to take into account differing sizes of facilities, types of products, vintages, production technologies used, and qualities of existing end-of-pipe controls. They

[5] As was noted by Fischer et al. (1996) Lithuanian GDP fell by 61 percent during the period 1989–94.

[6] This mapping of enterprise emissions into ambient concentrations is done by using dispersion models. As of 1996, ambient standards had been developed for approximately 800 pollutants. Of these, 151 substances had pollution charge rates.Semeniene et al. (1997) provide a discussion of the details of the system in Lithuania.

therefore encapsulate a large amount of technical information into one number.

The pollution charge rate structure that is linked to these limits is rather complicated. There are a total of 151 *base* rates defined for different pollutants, and the charge rates owed depend on the type of limit and the *ratio* of facilities' emissions to their limits. Because different polluters are assigned different limits, this rate structure means that polluters pay different rates for emissions of the same pollutants.

As Table 18.2 suggests, average charge rates for key pollutants are quite low. For example, Lithuanian charge rates for sulfur dioxide, nitrogen dioxide and dust in 1994 were only 15–25 percent of those levied in Poland.[7] The charge in Sweden that is applied to nitrogen oxide emissions by power plants is more than 500 times that found in Lithuania. Also as shown in Table 18.2, the annual charges paid by firms are generally low.

Table 18.2. Charge rates levied and annual payments for pollutants analyzed in this chapter, 1994

Air pollutant	Mean charge rate (US$/ton)[2]	Mean annual charges paid (US$/annum)	Median annual charges paid (US$/annum)	Number of facilities in sample
SO_X	$12.05	$4665.25	$24.90	102
NO_X	$21.75	$1086.45	$24.33	127
Dust[1]	$10.58	$111.40	$11.90	83
M_n	$4,345	$22.51	$7.57	56
CO	$0.675	$65.44	$3.14	115

Notes:
[1]Mean and median charge rates are similar.
[2]There are actually eight categories of dust that are charged. The main category is called organic and inorganic dust, but there are also separate categories for coal, cement, limestone, gypsum, clay, talc and mica dusts. For the purpose of this paper, the five specialized dusts that were charged the same base rate as organic and inorganic dust in 1994 were considered to be the same pollutant. It is only these six dusts that are examined here.

Source: Author's calculations.

But as shown in Table 18.3, these payments do not necessarily correspond with those the legislation says should be paid. Stated otherwise, just because a firm is supposed to pay a particular rate does not mean it actually pays it. There is a certain lack of formalism in enforcing this system and one example of this tendency is that charge rates paid often deviated from those

[7] It should be noted that a real doubling of charge rates occurred on July 1, 1995 when full inflation indexing was adopted.

specified in the Law on Pollution Charges of 1991. Perhaps not surprisingly, overcharging often occurred when facilities were entitled to rates that were low or zero. Those who were required to pay high rates often did not pay them and in both cases there was a tendency for firms to pay rates equal or very close to base rates.

With a system in which central controls on regional behavior are relatively weak, relations between inspectors and polluters are often long term and sometimes also close, with a rate structure that is complicated and time-consuming to check, it is not surprising there is room for negotiating charge rates that both regulator and regulated regard as 'reasonable'. One possible way to interpret this behavior is that 'too-low' or 'too-high' charge rates are viewed as unfair in Lithuania, resulting in a system that is somewhat analogous to that of a market in which limited price negotiation takes place. Anecdotal evidence also suggests that there is substantial inertia in the system. Firms therefore can expect that the rate they pay will not vary substantially from year to year, and can plan their emissions accordingly.

Table 18.3. Extent of over- or underpayment per ton emitted in 1994 for pollutants analyzed in this chapter ($1.00= Lt. 4.00)

	Number of firms under-paying by more than Lt. 1.00 per ton emitted (min. In litas in parentheses)	Number of firms over-paying by more than Lt. 1.00 per ton emitted (max. in litas in parentheses)	Average over or under-payment per ton emitted (in litas per ton)	Number of firms in sample
NO_2	28 (–6426)	43 (237.30)	–62.84	123
SO_X	16 (–6027)	38 (341.65)	–107.37	101
Dust	11 (–568.5)	35 (117.85)	2.30	83
M_n	20 (–25653)	29 (187,137)	6973	56
CO	17 (–10,041)	27 (78.90)	–99.95	108

Source: Author's calculations

3. A MODEL OF POLLUTER BEHAVIOR

In order to motivate the empirical work to follow, this section discusses a highly simplified model of polluter behavior. Equation 18.1 presents the maximization problem of a representative firm, where the firm chooses its emissions within the regulatory environment described above. Output (*Q*) in this problem is exogenous, as are output and input prices. There is one choice variable, reported emissions (*E*), which is a function of environmental investments made in the past (*I*) and the exogenously determined monitoring frequency of the regulator (M). Emissions are scaled by a predetermined facility standard (S). P_0 is the price of output (Q), and C_i is a standard input cost function that depends on output (Q) and a vector of input prices (P_i). C_E is the emissions charge rate function defined in the legislation, which depends on E/S, and the limit type (L).

$$\max\Pi = P_0Q - C_i(Q,P_i) - \left[C_E(\frac{E(I,M)}{S},L) - C_X\right]\frac{E(I,M)}{S} \qquad (18.1)$$

$$C_E \geq 0; E \geq 0; S \geq 0$$

$$\partial C_E \Big/ \partial \frac{E}{S} > 0; \partial E/\partial I < 0$$

The firm also faces an exogenous positive or negative excess charge rate (C_X), which it pays for each unit of E/S that it emits.

Maximizing equation 18.1 with respect to E/S gives the first-order condition in equation 18.2.

$$\frac{-\partial\Pi}{\partial C_E}\frac{\partial C_E}{\partial(E/S)}\frac{E(I,M)}{S} - C_E(\frac{E(I,M)}{S}) - C_x = 0 \qquad (18.2)$$

To better understand the implications of this first-order condition, let us assume a linear functional form for C_E such that $C_E = a + b*E/S$. For simplicity this form omits the complication associated with differing permit types (DLT versus LLT), but otherwise reflects key aspects of the Lithuanian legislation reasonably well. If we define the first term in equation 18.2 as the positive number 'd', the explicit form of equation 18.2 is given in equation 18.3.

$$db\frac{E(I,M)}{S} - (a + b\frac{E(I,M)}{S}) - C_x = 0 \qquad (18.3)$$

If we then abstract from modeling the link between E and the predetermined and exogenous variables I and M to focus on the relationship between E/S and C_X, we get the solution in equation 18.4. With d clearly less than one, because C_E *is a rate per ton*, $\partial\{E/S\}/\{\partial\partial C_X\}$ is negative. Increases in excess charge rates are therefore expected to improve environmental performance.

$$\frac{E(I,M)}{S} = \frac{a + C_x}{b(d-1)} \qquad (18.4)$$

This result is useful, because it establishes our hypothesis with regard to the effect of differing levels of C_X on polluter behavior. We also see from the solution that because C_E is just *E*/*S* in disguise, it is not in itself helpful for estimating the demand for pollution in Lithuania; indeed, despite the differing charge rates the legislation assigns to different polluters, this variation is no more useful than if each polluter was charged the same rate.

In reality, of course, a number of factors affect the optimal choice of *E*/*S*. At the very least, for a given firm there is an unknown function that links *E*/*S* and the predetermined and exogenous variables *I* and *M*. The limit type should also be included in our C_E function, therefore influencing the equilibrium *E*/*S*. In reality, therefore, the structural form of the optimal solution is substantially more complicated than equation 18.4. At minimum our equation to be estimated should look something like equation 18.5, where the expectation is that $\{\partial(E/S)/\partial C_X\} \leq 0$; $\{\partial(E/S)/\partial I\} \leq 0$; $\{\partial(E/S)/\partial M\} \geq 0$. In addition, firms with more stringent DLT standards are predicted to be closer to their limits (that is, *E*/*S* is larger) than facilities with LLT limits.

$$\frac{E^*}{S} = \frac{E}{S}(C_x, I, M, L) \tag{18.5}$$

4. DATA AND SOME ECONOMETRIC ISSUES

Equation 18.5 is the basic equation to be estimated in this chapter, with *E*/*S* the measure of environmental performance. This scaling of emissions is viewed as appropriate, because that is what is specified in the legal framework. Because limits are set as much as five years in the past based on a variety of observable and unobservable firm-specific variables, this predetermined variable also allows us to adjust for important cross-sectional differences such as size, technology vintage and so on. Without this scaling, it would be impossible to explain even a small fraction of the variation in emissions.

Given the special circumstances of the Lithuanian system, if we want to estimate the demand for pollution, instead of asking the question 'by how much do firms reduce emissions (or equivalently *E*/*S*) when charge rates rise?', equation 18.4 suggests that we must ask 'how much do firms reduce emissions when they are overcharged by one unit?'. The coefficient on C_X is therefore useful for calculating the short-run elasticity of demand for pollution.

This result is somewhat intuitive, because unless C_X were to dominate in the equation $C = C_E + C_X$ (which empirically is not the case), charge rates and emissions are determined simultaneously. The firm is therefore a price maker facing a preannounced supply schedule and we would already know the relationship between *E/S* and charge rates. The correlation would have to be a positive one, because that is the relationship that is specified in the legislation. Charge rates help us estimate the supply of pollution, but it is only because of the existence of excess charge rates that we have the opportunity to estimate demand.

The functional form of the relationship between excess charge rates and the variable *E/S* is unknown. The form most consistent with theory is perhaps one in which as emissions fall, demand becomes less elastic (that is, $\partial(E/S)/\partial C_X \leq 0$; $\partial^2(E/S)/\partial^2 C_X \geq 0$). Given the low average charge rates in Lithuania, however, it is possible that elasticities could rise as excess charge rates increase. To allow for this possibility, squared and cubed excess charge rates were included as independent variables.

The data to conduct the analysis come from a 366-enterprise random sample of all point source-air and water polluters reporting emissions to the Ministry of Environmental Protection in 1994. Official data include emissions, charges paid, permit types and annual facility standards. This sample was then surveyed in three areas: firm characteristics, current and expected future pollution reduction measures and sources of information regarding pollution reduction options.

Table 18.4 presents the variables used on the left- and right-sides in the regression equations. In addition to the excess charge rate variables, in the base regressions an attempt was made to adjust for the most important factors likely to affect *E/S*. The independent variables in all equations included variables in four areas:

1. The regulatory environment (for example, annual facility limits, monitoring frequencies).
2. Activities undertaken by facilities to reduce emissions (for example, net annualized expenditures on air pollution reduction projects, number of projects completed).
3. Basic firm information (for example, output, percentage state ownership, employees and so on).
4. Indications of firm innovativeness and environmental awareness (for example, environmental staff, business plan with environmental component, plans for projects in future).

The way in which excess charge rates are determined is unknown. On the one hand, C_X may be only very loosely within the control of the enterprise (that is, it is exogenous as proposed in the analytical model), but it is also possible that firms have some control over the degree of excess charges they pay (that is, C_X is endogenous). To allow for both cases, models were estimated by both OLS and 2SLS.

Because priors suggested the presence of heteroscedasticity in excess charge rates, standard error estimates were adjusted using the method of White (1980).

Table 18.4. Variable definitions

Variable Name	
E/S	Ratio of annual emissions to the facility standard (dependent variable in regressions)
C_x	Excess charge rate paid by facility (litas/ton/year)
C_x^2	Square of excess charge rate (litas/ton/year)
C_x^3	Cube of excess charge rate (litas/ton/year)
L	Dummy for permit type (1 = DLT)
*Netcostcrit**	Summed net annualized investment costs of all projects completed in 1993 or 1994 that reduced emissions of the criteria air pollutants NO_2, SO_2, CO, CO_2 and also responses labeled 'air pollutants'
Netcostdust	Summed net annualized investment costs of all projects completed in 1993 or 1994 that reduced emissions of dust
Critair	Total number of projects completed (including those during the soviet period) that reduced emissions of the criteria air pollutants NO_2, SO_2, CO, CO_2 and also responses labeled 'air pollutants'
Dustair	Total number of projects completed (including those during the soviet period) that reduced emissions of dust
Q	Output in 1994 as a percentage of 1989
Employees	Number of employees in 1994
EnergyInt	Estimated ratio of energy cost per unit of main output to price per unit of output
MinMon	Frequency of monitoring by the ministry of environmental protection (number of months between checks)
FirmMon	Frequency with which the facility itself measures its emissions (number of months between checks)
Envstaff	Total number of employees at the facility who are regularly involved with environmental issues
Stateown	Percentage of state ownership (0%–100%)
Energy	Dummy – heating or electric plant
Airplans	Number of air pollution reduction projects planned for the facility
Busplan	Dummy – 1 = Enterprise controlling the facility has a business plan that includes an environmental component

**Note*: The formula for calculating *Netcostcrit* and *Netcostdust* was the sum for each project '*I*' implemented in 1993 or 1994. Projects completed before 1993 were omitted because of currency changes that occurred in 1993. $Netcost_i = I_i * \{r/[1-(1+r)^{-t}]\} + O - R$. '*I*' is the level of investment made in period zero. '*r*' is the annual discount rate (assumed to be 12%). '*t*' is the lifetime of asset '*I*' (assumed to be 10 years). '*O*' is the operating cost of the asset and '*R*' are resources the firms saved by making the investment.

To accommodate the use of 2SLS, instruments were added that were believed to affect the degree of excess charges firms paid. These included variables that captured whether facilities were in large cities, how well connected firms were with other industrialists, the academic community and Ministry regional departments, and whether facilities came from known 'clean' industries (see Table 18.5).

For three of the five pollutants analyzed, including facilities with emissions greater than annual standards exerted an inordinately strong influence on the R^2 of equations. This is not itself a problem, but it did raise concerns that this tendency was related to the particular form for calculating C_E defined in the Lithuanian legislation. In all cases very few facilities were over their limits, but omitting over-limit observations typically reduced the R^2 by half, while leaving coefficient estimates for the variables of interest unchanged. To be sure these few observations did not drive results, above-limit firms were dropped from the sample.

Table 18.5. Additional variables (included exclusively as instruments for use in 2SLS regressions)

Variable name	
Clean	Dummy – 1 = service/natural resource industry
City	Dummy – 1 = facility located in one of the five major cities
Inffirms	Ranking (1–5 with 5 as the highest value) of other firms as a source of information on pollution prevention and waste reduction
Infmin	Ranking (1–5 with 5 as the highest value) of ministry of environmental protection regional departments as sources of information on pollution prevention and waste reduction
InfSem	Ranking (1–5 with 5 as the highest value) of ministry of environmental protection regional departments as sources of information on pollution prevention and waste reduction

5. RESULTS

Table 18.5 presents the 2SLS regression results for each of the five pollutants analyzed. The table gives only the final regressions after variables were tested out of equations using standard t-tests and F-tests. OLS results where not reported because they were very similar. The coefficients on excess charge rates always have the expected signs (negative) and are typically significant at the 99 percent level whether OLS or 2SLS was used. The coefficients on the variables '*Netcostcrit*' and '*Netcostdust*' also have negative signs and are significant at least at the 90 percent level, indicating that long-run environmental performance is not generally costless or profitable.

Table 18.6. 2SLS regression results

Variable	NO_x 2SLS	SO_2 2SLS	Dust 2SLS	CO 2SLS	Mang. 2SLS
Constant	0.65 (0.085)***	0.85 (0.068)***	0.52 (0.11)***	0.45 (0.098)***	0.83 (0.088)***
C_x	–0.34 (0.00084)***	–0.0039 (0.0031)	–0.011 (0.0030)***	–0.19 (0.041)***	–0.000023 (0.49 E–05)***
C_x^2			0.43 E-04 (0.000017)***	0.0023 (0.00054)***	
L			0.31 (0.11)***		
Netcostcrit	–0.00096 (0.00034)***	–0.0026 (0.00058)***		–0.00094 (0.00052)*	
Netcostdust			–0.00091 (0.00032)***		
Critair		–0.096 (0.049)**			
Q	0.0016 (0.0010)			0.0043 (0.0013)***	
Employees					0.0071 (0.0037)**
MinMon		–0.0077 (0.0071)		0.012 (0.01)	–0.038 (0.01)***
FirmMon		–0.15 (0.085)*	–0.15 (0.080)*		
Envstaff	0.11 (0.063)*	0.12 (0.068)*			
Stateown	–0.0022 (0.0013)*		0.004 (0.012)***	–0.0013 (0.0013)	0.0029 (0.0014)**
Energy	0.31 (0.12)***				
Busplan	0.075 (0.056)		–0.26 (0.11)***		
N	66	63	49	54	36
Adj. R^2	0.30	0.33	0.20	0.24	0.40

Notes:

Dependent variable '*E/S*' (standard errors in parentheses).

***, **,* Significant at 99% , 95% and 90% level using a two-tailed test.

Table 18.7 presents estimates of the charge rates (that is, $C = C_E + C_x$) required to achieve 10, 25 and 40 percent emission reductions. The elasticities of demand associated with those reductions are also given. It should be emphasized that these results are for a representative firm, where being 'representative' means that in the base case (that is, without any increase in charge rates) the firm pays a total charge rate per ton equal to the mean of the sample, has the mean level of C_X and all other regression variables are also set equal to their means.

*Table 18.7. Estimates of demand elasticities and charge rates required to achieve various emissions reductions ($US 1995 per ton per year)**

	0% Reduc. (Base Case)	10% Reduction in Emissions		25% Reduction in Emissions		40% Reduction in Emissions	
Pollutant		Using OLS	Using 2SLS	Using OLS	Using 2SLS	Using OLS	Using 2SLS
SO_2	$12.80	$25.38 (-.21)	$42.24 (- .15)	$37.12 (-.44)	$80.00 (-.36)	$53.44 (-1.05)	$118.08 (-.68)
NO_X	$23.65	$58.88 (-.17)	$59.20 (-.15)	$106.56 (-.39)	$117.12 (-.37)	$152.96 (-.70)	$165.76 (-.67)
CO	$0.81	$1.04 (-.47)	$1.00 (-.55)	$1.34 (-.83)	$1.26 (-.88)	$1.61 (-1.4)	$1.54 (-1.2)
Dust	$13.78	$47.36 (-.095)	$17.95 (-.40)	Non Achieve	$24.93 (-.63)	Non Achieve	$32.67 (-.92)
Manganese	$4333	$7684 (-.22)	$7770 (-.25)	$12,992 (-.44)	$11,910 (-.46)	$18,400 (-.80)	$16,464 (-.83)

Notes:

Point elasticities at the given levels of reductions are in parentheses.*The representative facility simulated is assumed to be average in all ways. Its base emissions are consistent with the mean value of E/S. It pays the mean charge rate as well as the mean *excess* charge rate.

Elasticities from the estimated demand functions were applied to proportionate increases in total charge rates to get the rates needed to achieve the different levels of reduction. If we start the simulation from the base case as defined above, this means that the elasticity of demand associated with an initial 10 percent increase in C_X is assumed to be the same as an initial 10 percent increase in the charge rate paid per ton. The same assumption is then made for the second 10 percent increase, the third 10 percent increase and so on.

What we see in Table 18.7 are elasticities that are consistent with what one might expect given the low overall levels of charge rates and charges paid in Lithuania, but these estimates also contradict our priors regarding the expected shapes of demand functions. Instead of becoming relatively less elastic as charge rates rise, elasticities are relatively low for small rate increases – typically in the –0.20 to –0.50 range – but increase in absolute value as rates rise. To achieve, for example, a 25 percent reduction in emissions, charge rates must typically at least be doubled. As rates rise to levels consistent with 40 percent reductions, estimated elasticities approach or even exceed –1.0.

6. CONCLUSION

This chapter used pollution charge information at the firm level to estimate the demand for air pollution in Lithuania, with the goal of ultimately determining whether pollution charges are having any effect. The evidence indicates that Lithuanian firms are indeed responding to pollution charges. Because at least on average charge rates are quite low, these results also suggest that low rates do have an effect. Perhaps not surprisingly, as shown by the low elasticities (–0.15 to –0.40), at rates close to base levels these effects are small. To achieve significant (for example 25 percent) reductions in emissions from 1994 base levels, it was estimated that average rates would have to rise by 50–100 percent depending on the pollutant. This would imply, for example, a per ton charge for NO_x of about $100.00.

The effectiveness of pollution charges is predicted to increase rapidly as charge rates rise, with elasticities of demand approaching –1.0 when charge rates are doubled or tripled. We would not expect this result to be observed forever, however, and eventually polluters' responses to increasing charge rates should decline. Monitoring and enforcement costs are also expected to be increasing at an increasing rate as pollution charge rates rise.

In conclusion, we would like to emphasize that we do not consider deviating from legislation, as seems to have taken place in Lithuania, to be a good idea – indeed, the establishment of systems that ensure a clear and fair application of the law is perhaps the most important policy step that can be taken by countries in transition – but the existence of these deviations did prove useful and effectively allowed the analysis to take place. Given that other transition countries are also struggling with similar challenges, there may be opportunities for conducting similar analyses in other transition countries.

REFERENCES

Anderson, C.D. and B. Fiedor (1997), 'Environmental Charges in Poland', in Randall Bluffstone and Bruce A. Larson, (eds), *Controlling Pollution in Transition Economies: Theories and Methods*, Cheltenham: Edward Elgar.

Baumol, W. and W. Oates (1971), 'The Use of Standards and Prices for Protection of the Environment', *Swedish Journal of Economics*, March, pp. 42–54.

Bluffstone, R. (1997), 'Are the Costs of Pollution Abatement Lower in Central and Eastern Europe? Evidence from Lithuania', Development Discussion Paper No. 610, Harvard Institute for International Development, November.

Bluffstone, Randall and Bruce A. Larson (1997), 'Implementing Pollution Permit and Charge Systems in Transition Economies: A Possible Blueprint', in Randall

Bluffstone and Bruce A. Larson (eds), *Controlling Pollution in Transition Economies: Theories and Methods*, Cheltenham: Edward Elgar, pp. 253–69.

Environment for Europe (1994), *Environmental Action Programme for Central and Eastern Europe*, World Bank, March.

Fischer, S., R. Sahay and C. Vegh (1996), 'Stabilization and Growth in Transition Economies: The Early Experience', *Journal of Economic Perspectives*, **10**(2), Spring.

Fournier, B. (1995), *Environmental Taxes in OECD Countries*, Paris: OECD.

Ministry of Environmental Protection (1997), *Air Protection Division Database*, Vilnius, Lithuania.

Semeniene, D., R. Bluffstone and L. Cekanavicius (1997), 'The Lithuanian Charge System: Evaluation and Prospects for the Future', in Randall Bluffstone and Bruce A. Larson (eds), *Controlling Pollution in Transition Economies: Theories and Methods*, Cheltenham: Edward Elgar.

Smith, S. and T. Zylicz (1994), 'Rappateurs' Report of the Workshop on Taxation and Environment in European Economies in Transition', in *Taxation and Environment in European Economies in Transition*, Paris: OECD, pp. 6–15.

United Nations Economic Commission for Europe (1998), *Report on the UN-ECE/OECD Workshop on the Role of Economic Instruments in Integrating Environmental Policy with Sectoral Policies*, Committee on Environmental Policy, UN-ECE, January.

Vincent, J. and R.S. Farrow (1997), 'A Survey of Pollution Charge Systems and Key Issues in Policy Design', in Randall Bluffstone and Bruce A. Larson (eds), *Controlling Pollution in Transition Economies: Theories and Methods*, Cheltenham: Edward Elgar.

White, H. (1980), 'A Heteroskedasticity-consistent Covariance Matrix Estimator and a Direct Test for Heteroskedasticity', *Econometrica*, **48**, May, pp. 817–38, May.

Zinnes, C. (1997), 'The Road to Creating an Integrated Pollution Charge and Permitting System in Romania', in Randall Bluffstone and Bruce A. Larson (eds), *Controlling Pollution in Transition Economies: Theories and Methods*, Cheltenham: Edward Elgar, pp. 232–52.

19. Issues in Designing an Effective Solid Waste Policy: The Israeli Experience

Ofira Ayalon, Yoram Avnimelech and Mordechai Shechter

1. BACKGROUND

The aim of this study was to analyse alternative options for municipal solid waste (MSW) disposal in order to delineate economically efficient and environmentally sound MSW policies, taking into consideration political constraints involved in implementation (such as local political pressures which might block rational choices), the level of environmental awareness of the citizenry, and the physical characteristics of the system (such as the composition of waste). A rational solid waste policy should attempt to select an option which would minimize total direct and indirect (that is, external) costs.

Israel, is a densely populated country (average population density, excluding the sparsely populated, arid Negev region, is more than 550 people per km^2, compared with 350 in the Netherlands, Japan and Belgium). The country is undergoing a gradual closure of poorly regulated or inappropriately-sited dump sites of MSW and the opening of new sites that conform to strict environmental standards. This adjustment process is aggravated by the familiar NIMBY (not in my backyard) problem. In 1993 the Israeli government mandated the closure of most existing dumps and their replacement with five national and 14 smaller regional, state-of-the-art landfills. According to the Ministry of the Environment (MoE), (*Israel Environment Bulletin*, 1997), recycling rates of post-consumer domestic waste leaped from 4 per cent to 10.5 per cent. These figures are due to increased costs of waste transportation to more remote, approved landfills; higher tipping fees at the new sites; opening of new sorting plants; local initiatives for collection and recycling of specific wastes; and public awareness.[1] Although we have reason to believe that these figures are somewhat overestimated, they nevertheless indicate a degree of price-responsiveness on part of consumers and other waste generators, and suggest that the introduction of market incentives might move the system towards economic efficiency.

In order to promote recycling, the MoE has advocated a mixture of command and control (CAC) and financial instruments: regulations requiring municipalities and businesses to meet specific recycling and waste reduction goals; restriction or prohibition of import of cheaper recycled waste materials (for example, plastics); subsidies to recycling plants; a charge of 0.25 per cent of total package cost on producers of one-trip soft drinks containers. On the other hand, due to political pressures of local municipalities, the MoE has subsidized the additional costs incurred because municipal wastes need to be moved to the new officially approved, better-managed but more remote landfills. This, of course, enables the affected towns to avoid raising municipal taxes. Clearly, this policy in turn would render landfilling the least-cost option for waste management, and acts to limit the development of new enterprises and other disposal options.

Following the selection of an efficient option, an appropriate mix of economic incentives and regulations should accompany its implementation. Studies from a number of countries on the use of market incentives (mainly bag-based fees) have shown a positive response to the fee. Thus, a volume-based fee was followed by a 37 per cent decrease by volume (14 per cent by weight) in Charlottesville, Virginia (Kinnaman and Fullerton 1994). Similar results were reported for other US municipalities (Cuthbert 1994): a 10 per cent increase in MSW tax was followed by a 2 per cent decrease in the amount of household waste. Several studies have shown price elasticity of demand for MSW management services to be on the order of –0.12 to –0.6, depending on covariates such as income, perceived benefits from recycling, size of household, degree of urbanization and weather conditions (see, McFarland et al. 1972; Wertz 1976; Jenkins 1993). One should note, however, that the introduction of a fee-based system is more appropriate and more easily implemented in neighbourhoods with single-family units; in cities of multi-family housing (and with a populace not strongly motivated towards environmental issues), the problem of 'free riding', illegal dumping and burning could pose a serious obstacle (Kinnaman and Fullerton 1994), creating social costs which cannot be overlooked.

[1] For example, the city of Rishon Le'Zion enforced the use of cardboard compactors in medium and large commercial businesses. If compactors are used, the business gains a reduction in municipal taxes. The cardboard is collected by a private haulier for a lower price than the rest of the waste, which is collected by the municipality. The cardboard is recycled in a paper mill. A reduction of more than 15 per cent (by weight) of MSW transferred to the landfill was achieved.

2. ASSUMPTIONS AND METHODS

2.1 Delineating Waste Management Options

We have analysed in this study what we believe to constitute four 'viable' options for MSW policy: (i) landfilling of the total amount of the waste; (ii) sorting mixed waste at a MRF (material recovery facility); (iii) curbside collection of recyclables; and (iv) wet/dry separation at home. A detailed description of these options is given in Appendix 19A.1. The choice of an optimal MSW policy should be based upon considerations of direct disposal costs as well as the indirect environmental costs (but should not overlook public sensitivities with regard to issues such as siting). In Israel, a flat, uniform waste disposal charge is included in the monthly municipal tax bill (*not* as a separate item); therefore, there is a complete absence of any incentive for the households to separate or reduce the waste stream. One of the intricate policy problems is to design an efficient incentive system in order to encourage households to initiate or improve source separation (if *that* were shown to be the optimal option).

Accordingly, a number of important facts should be taken into account in the case of countries like Israel. First, each person produces on average 1.14 kg of garbage per day. Population growth combined with rising incomes and living standards would give rise to a growth rate of 2–3 per cent annually of total MSW (by weight). Furthermore, about half of the Israeli MSW is composed of *wet* food waste (including yard waste and disposable diapers), due to a diet rich in vegetables and fruits (coupled with lack of sink garbage disposal devices[2]), compared with about 7 per cent in the US and 30 per cent in Europe (Table 19.1). On the other hand, the 'classic' recyclables (paper, glass, plastics and metals as secondary raw materials) comprise less than 30 per cent of total MSW. Thus, even under ideal conditions regarding participation rates, collection, sorting and recycling of these recyclables, this component would not be expected to divert more than 20 per cent of the waste stream – much lower than in Western Europe or the US. On top of all of this, population density along the urban coastal plain (on top of the coastal aquifer which supplies about one fifth of the country's fresh water), where most of the population resides, is among the world's highest. Consequently, the availability of land for landfills (except in certain areas of the southern Negev desert[3]) is severely limited.

---

[2] To be soon prohibited by law in order to conserve water and prevent overloading of sewage treatment plants.

[3] Even in this region a good portion of it could not accommodate landfills because of potential groundwater pollution or military needs.

Table 19.1. Solid waste composition in Israel, the US and Europe (composition (%) on dry weight basis)

Material	Israel 1995 (*)	US 1995 (**)	Europe (average) 1989 (***)
Food waste	45.3	6.7	30.0
Paper and cardboard	19.4	39.2	32.0
Plastics	13.1	9.1	12
Glass	3.0	6.2	7.0
Metals	5.4	7.6	6.0
Yard waste and wood	3.0	21.4	
Disposable diapers	5.0		
Others	5.8	9.8	13.0

Sources
* Israel Ministry of the Environment (1997).
** US Environmental Protection Agency, 1992. Characterization of MSW in the US: 1992 Update. EPA/530-R-92-019.
***Abfaelle in der Schweitz, Auszug aus der Publikation 'Umweltbericht Schweitz 1990' (Vorabdruck).

2.2 Data

2.2.1 Cost of alternative MSW options

To compare direct and indirect costs across management options, we assembled and analysed technical and cost data from recycling companies, municipalities, and other relevant sources, as well as data on potential environmental impacts and the associated external costs[4] of the different MSW management options. We next compared costs of the different solid waste management scenarios for a 'representative' town, generating 500 tons per day (tpd) of MSW. Apart from the customary collection and hauling costs, in the case of the separated recyclables collection, an additional charge of 5 per cent was added, and in the case of the wet/dry option the cost of the additional bins needed for collecting the separated waste was incorporated.[5] Under all options, the opportunity cost of households' time devoted to waste separation was not taken into account. We surmise that in any case the time needed for wet/dry separation is less than that needed for sorting recyclables.

[4] Economic evaluations of environmental impacts were obtained from a research conducted by EMC Ltd. for the Israeli Ministry of the Environment in 1996. Evaluations of external costs from air pollution (caused by transportation and landfill gas) and leachates from landfills were obtained from DoE Report (1993).

[5] Some of the data were obtained from private firms engaged in recycling as 'black boxes' – that is, 'bottom-line' figures only. Therefore, it was not possible to conduct a full-scale sensitivity analysis for all parameters, for example, distances to remote landfills, revenues from selling recyclables, and so on.

2.2.2 Survey data

Applying economic incentive schemes in the context of MSW management must take cognizance of the aforementioned fact that households have not faced any explicit price for waste collection and processing. This can, therefore, be viewed and studied as a new service, in a manner not altogether different from that which is applied to new products. However, in this case we deal with a non-market service, because there customarily do not exist markets for municipal waste collection services. Households' demand schedules for these services must be inferred by means of a CV-type survey. Alternatively, we could have analysed the process of source waste-separation in the framework of a household production function, combining time and labour inputs (as well as some capital costs in the form of additional containers and bags) to produce sorted waste. Here, the price of the service could be in the form, say, of a penalty if the waste were not thus separated. We opted for the first alternative. The data were obtained from a survey conducted at the end of a one-year source separation pilot project.

In a project lasting through 1994, 6,000 families in the cities of Ra'anana and K'far Saba in central Israel were asked to separate the waste into wet and dry streams. To evaluate the project's performance, a follow-up telephone survey of heads of households (husband or wife, randomly selected) of 600 of these families was carried out when the project terminated. Altogether, the questionnaire[6] contained 28 questions, dealing with the household familiarity with and attitude towards waste separation and recycling, participation rates, demographics, and a contingent valuation (CV) scenario. Table 19.2 gives the socioeconomic and demographic characteristics of the 600-household sample.

Table 19.2. Socioeconomic characteristics of the towns of Ra'anana and K'far Saba

Characteristic	Ra'anana	K'far Saba	Avg.
No. of people interviewed	296	309	
No. of habitants in a household	4.39	3.88	4.1
Single-unit homes (%)	42	28	35
Multifamily homes (%)	58	72	65
1 car per family (%)	55	68.8	62
2 cars per family (%)	38	28.8	34
Education (of respondent) (years)	14.2	13.74	14
Income (%) (equals or higher than average)	86.8	77.8	82.3
Occupation (of respondent)			
Employee (%)	53.4	59.4	56.6
Self employed (%)	17.3	9.73	13.5
Spouse occupation			
Employee (%)	61.67	65.42	63.6
Self-employed (%)	25.83	18.75	22.2

[6] A pre-test of about 25 household heads was carried out prior to the survey.

In the CV part, respondents were queried on their willingness to pay (WTP) for municipal services which would enable source (that is, at home) waste separation, in order to facilitate the recycling component in the various MSW options. The CV scenario is given in Appendix 19A.2.[7]

2. RESULTS AND DISCUSSION

3.1 Comparing Costs of Alternative Waste Management Options

The results of the cost analyses of the different options for a 'representative' town are presented in Figure 19.1 and Table 19A1.2. The least-cost solution involves the disposing of waste to a nearby landfill, *if* one is available. This, as elaborated above, is fast becoming an infeasible solution. The externality costs of landfilling due to leachates and landfill gas are in the range of 5.75 US$/ton (DoE Report 1993). When external costs attributable to transportation (congestion, road accidents, noise and pollution) are added, the total external costs could increase total disposal costs by more than 10 per cent (Table 19A1.2). According to an analysis conducted by the US Environmental Protection Agency (EPA), (Glebs 1989), the expected costs of a well-operated sanitary landfill are about 20 US$/ton. Therefore, if tipping fees are higher than 20 US$/ton, external costs – mainly road related – could raise total disposal costs by about 6 per cent, NIMBY 'costs' notwithstanding.

As noted above, recycling of 'conventional' recyclables (paper, plastics and glass) is often viewed by decision makers. There is no doubt that using recycled materials, compared with incineration or landfilling, conserves natural resources and sometimes energy (for example, aluminium recycling). Therefore, recycling has a high rate of public acceptance (Chilton 1993). However, in Israel, conventional recycling methods – curbside collection of recyclables – does not reduce the need for landfilling, since, due to its composition, this option would still leave 80 per cent of the waste to be landfilled.

Regarding the other solutions, it can be seen that as long as tipping fees (TF) are relatively low, less than 20 NIS/ton (about US$5), there is a cost advantage to sorting mixed waste at a material recovery facility (MRF). This option includes collection of unsorted, wet, sticky and fermenting waste, the waste being mechanically sieved for the organic fraction and manually sorted for recyclables. These characteristics of the waste impose several environmental and economic disadvantages: the compost might be contaminated with heavy metals and broken glass (which are sieved as well);

[7] On the CV method and the issues and problems associated with its application, see Mitchell and Carson (1989).

the ability to sort the waste is limited (due to the wetness and stickiness of the waste); and the quality of recyclables is reduced (with a corresponding decline in marketability and price).

Figure 19.1. Cost of waste management alternatives (direct + external costs)

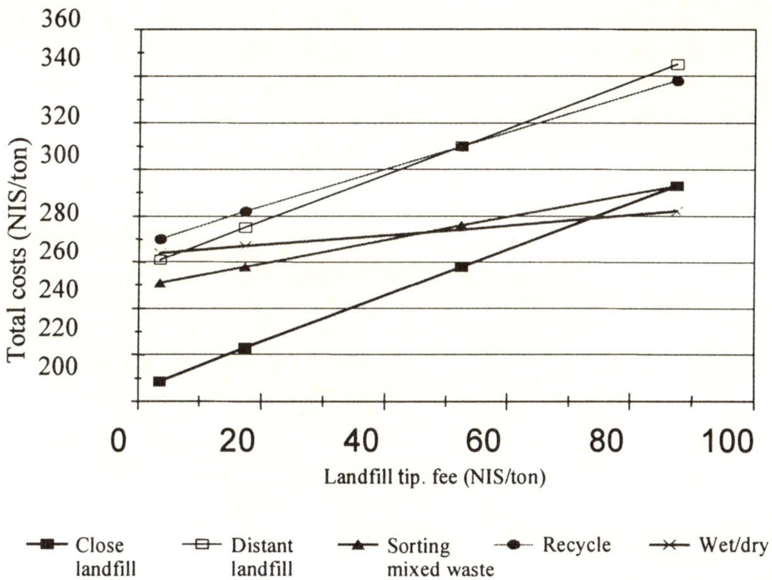

When TF are above NIS 55 (about US$15), the cost-effective solution is the wet/dry source separation, which would also promise to keep the highest ratio of waste away from landfills. In this option, 40 to 50 per cent of the waste is directly composted and the clean compost is applied to the soil, increasing crop yields and improving soil structure. A further 10 to 20 per cent of the waste is recycled, and about 10 per cent may be used as refuse-derived fuel (RDF). Only 20 to 35 per cent of the waste would be delivered to a landfill.

3.2 Factors Affecting WTP for Waste Separation

About 40 per cent of the surveyed sample population refused to pay any sum for the introduction of a recycling option, a slightly higher percentage than that usually encountered in CV studies (usually in the 20–35 per cent range), although not unexpected given that garbage collection is customarily viewed as a basic and essential public service, paid for by our municipal taxes. Three separate analyses of WTP responses were carried out: WTP = 0 versus WTP > 0 responses, WTP > 0 responses, and a combined analyses of these two response groups.

First, the customary logistic regression analysis of zero versus non-zero responses (Table 19.3) indicates that the probability of a zero response is higher if the person is a salaried employee, the household owns only one car (an indicator of *relatively* lower income level in the case of these two rather affluent suburban towns), is older, and resides in a single-unit home. Except for the latter, the explanatory variables may be interpreted (in the present framework) as proxies for less affluence. Not surprising, the higher the bid, the higher is the probability of getting a WTP of zero, noting that the addition of INS 20 to the monthly municipal bill amounts to almost 50 per cent increase in the aforementioned flat charge for waste handling presently incorporated in it.

Table 19.3. WTP regressions. K'far Saba and Ra'anana telephone survey, December 1994

Variable	logistic regression P (WTP) = 0		Ln (WTP) WTP > 0	
	Coeffic.	Prob.	Coeffic.	Prob.
Intercept	–2.1422	0.0035	1.219	0.0001
No. of cars	–0.509	0.0099		
Age	0.0295	0.0018		
Occupation (self-employed)	–0.3481	0.0198		
Spouse occupation (self-employed)			0.1487	0.068
House (multi-family)	–0.5457	0.0157	–0.189	0.0108
City (Ra'anana)			–0.1117	0.076
Ln (bid)	0.7462	0.0002	0.591	0.0001

Next, the *positive* WTP responses were analysed with a semi-log regression equation, which performs better when money is the dependent variable. The analysis indicates that WTP is higher if the spouse is self-employed, the family lives in a single-unit housing, resides in the town of K'far Saba, and is randomly assigned a higher bid level (the familiar 'anchoring' effect). Thus, again, the regression results suggest that a higher WTP to help introduce and operate the recycling option is associated with a higher level of affluence.

Finally, given the high percentage of zero responses, we applied a mixture 'spike' model (Reiser and Shechter 1997), which has been designed to analyse the combined WTP response distributions. The mixed model assumes that the population of interest could be considered to be composed of two sub-populations. One sub-population is not willing to pay for the good or service in question, while the other sub-population is willing to pay and has a continuous WTP distribution. That is, the model does not compel the investigator to assume that both groups are drawn from the same population in terms of preferences and other relevant attributes, when combining the two groups, as is the case with standard analyses of CV data.

In applications of this kind, one usually is made aware of the fact that due to the strong covariate effects, examining the overall mean (or median) of the sample may be misleading. Consequently, rather than the customary overall sample means, we present in Table 19.4 means for a number of particular sub-groups, representing different combinations of socioeconomic and demographic covariates. For example, given a bid of NIS 10, the probability of WTP = 0 (last column in Table 19.4) is higher if the household (in the case of a salaried employee) owns only one car instead of two or (for self-employed) if the head of the household is older.

Table 19.4. Mixed model regression results (at bid =NIS 10)

Age	Car	Spouse occup.	City	House	E(WTPi)	MEDi	P(WTP = 0)
40	2	Employee	Ra'anana	Multi-fam.	8.81	5.4	0.308
40	2	Employee	K'far S.	Multi-fam.	9.91	6.0	0.308
40	2	Employee	K'far S.	Multi-fam.	11.29	7.8	0.211
40	1	Employee	K'far S.	Multi-fam.	8.22	3.5	0.425
21	2	Self-employed	Ra'anana	Single	12.41	7.6	0.305
63	2	Self-employed	Ra'anana	Single	7.1	0	0.6

This of course would be reflected in the mean and median of the corresponding subgroups. Thus, in analysing the entire sample WTP responses in a consistent manner, this model is expected to provide a more accurate representation of the relevant population, and, in our case, the range of the community's responses to the introduction of an MSW incentive scheme. We believe that this kind of information is important in designing a workable incentive scheme, such as a per-bag fee, since it might indicate, for instance, neighbourhoods where there might be tendencies towards less cooperation. In such cases, more events of illegal dumping or other forms of non-cooperation would be more likely to occur and, therefore, should be taken into consideration prior to the launch of the incentive scheme.

3.3 Economic Incentives as a Reflection of WTP

To illustrate how one might go about converting expressed WTP into a (hopefully...) workable incentive scheme, we computed mean WTP of each community using the mixed model (that is, averaging for each place of residence over all responses) and used it as a basis for calculating a per-bag fee – the economic incentive proposed to promote separation at source. That fee is intended to 'internalize' disposal externalities, moving the system to operate closer to the optimal disposal scheme. In Table 19.5 we present mean monthly WTP with and without the zero's for the two towns.

Table 19.5. Mean monthly willingness to pay

	K'far Saba	Ra'anana
WTP > 0	NIS 14.65 (NIS 176)*	NIS 13.62 (NIS 163)
WTP ≥ 0	NIS 7.17 (NIS 86)	NIS 7.69 (NIS 92)

**Note*: Annual payment is given in parenthesis.

Given that an average family generates approximately 2 tons of solid waste per year, the lowest WTP value of NIS 7 per month implies that each family would be willing to pay an extra fee (that is, marginal WTP) of about 40 NIS/ton of MSW. The relevance of this specific value in the present case will be shown momentarily.

Figure 19.2 shows the three 'runner-up' options: 'Close landfill', 'Sorting mixed waste', and 'Wet–dry source separation', but with a 'cosmetic uplifting' of the first alternative via a vertical upwards shift of its cost schedule by NIS 40. This shift causes the second alternative, namely, 'sorting mixed waste', to become the cost-effective solution at a TF of NIS 7–8 (the point where the two cost schedules intersect). One could interpret this shift as representing the shadow price, or the implicit marginal supply cost of in-situ waste disposal services, following the aforementioned national policy of closing 'close' municipal landfills.

However, we argue that the next best option, the separation at the source to wet and dry fractions, merits a closer examination. It has already been noted that if the TF were to rise to about 55 NIS/ton, it will become the cost-effective solution. Now, in Appendix 19A1 it is argued that, compared with the 'wet–dry' solution, the 'sorting mixed waste' option produces an inferior

Figure 19.2. Cost of waste management: use of economic incentives

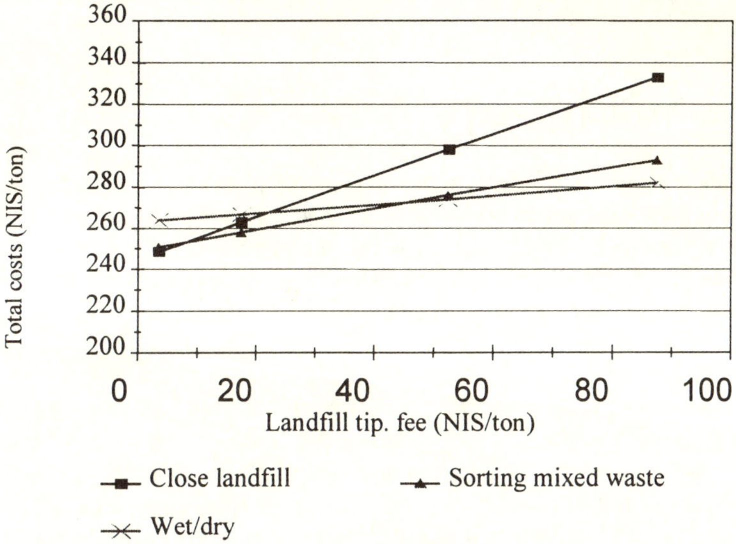

quality compost and recyclables. But as no price tag was attached to either the production of compost (of any quality) or to the quality component of the recyclables stream, one may surmise that if these aspects were taken into account (causing a corresponding *downwards* vertical shift of the relevant curve in Figure 19.2), the "wet–dry" option could turn out to be the most cost-effective solution, intersecting the 'close landfill' schedule at a point near that where the 'sorting mixed waste' curve now intersects it.

Consider now the marginal WTP of 40 NIS/ton calculated above: given the closure of 'close' landfills, this WTP turns out to equal the marginal supply cost of the most cost-effective option(s). If municipalities were willing to pass over this added supply cost to the citizenry, through some form of a decentralized incentive payment, the system could reach the desired optimal solution in a decentralized fashion. In that case, the numbers above would translate into a fee tag of 0.6 NIS per bag[8] in a home-sorting waste scheme, accompanied, of course, by an appropriate monitoring and enforcement scheme. (If the authorities decide that bag price should also reflect current collection and disposal costs, its price would rise from NIS 3.90 to NIS 4.50[9])

[8] NIS 40 divided by 70, the number of waste bags needed for 1 ton of waste.
[9] Average collection and disposal fees are about 270 NIS/ton; dividing by 70 (the number of waste bags per ton) = 3.90 NIS/bag.

This approach could substitute for (or at least supplement) command and control-type regulations, or subsidies to municipalities (to cover the added cost of centralized sorting facilities) financed by the general tax–paying public.

3. CONCLUSIONS

MSW policy should be adjusted to the unique characteristics of any country. MSW in Israel contains more organic kitchen waste and less paper and cardboard than the European and US waste; the populace, in general, is less motivated to voluntary 'environment-friendly' behaviour; the typical residential pattern of more than 70 per cent of the dwelling units is one of small apartments (including small storage space in kitchens) in multi-apartment buildings.

Our results show that sorting mixed waste and the wet/dry options, involving recycling of both the dry and organic fractions, are the most cost-effective as well as social welfare optimizing solutions. Our findings call for the establishment of a 'pay-per-bag' incentive scheme, namely, a tax of NIS 0.6 per bag, which will induce households to internalize the optimal solution. This price would not constitute too heavy a burden on households and will not induce non-cooperation or illegal dumping. Furthermore, in arriving at a suitable solution to MSW policy, we should avoid adopting 'politically correct' solutions. In both, popular and political circles, recycling – rather than the total management of the solid waste stream – is often considered a 'politically-correct' national priority. Green lobbies have often argued that recycling is *the* solution to the MSW problem,[10] promoting 'nobler' goals such as 'saving raw materials, energy, and land resources', often – sadly – regardless of the associated cost tab or other indirect environmental costs, such as the pollution generated by additional collection vehicles, or water and energy needed to wash reusable glass bottles. Countries like Israel should learn from other nations' mistakes, and try to avoid repeating them. This is particularly true in regard to the hasty imposition of CAC rules and regulations (for example, the packaging ordinance in Germany) prohibiting landfilling, which have proved to be economically inefficient (Anonymous 1993a, Anonymous, 1993b).

[10] To quote from a recent newsletter of 'Man, Nature, and Law', the Israeli Union for Environmental Defense: 'Recycling should be viewed as a national objective [underlined in the original text] without constraining its execution by economic considerations, or at least by narrow economic tests. Recycling is an expression of important values, such as preventing squandering of resources, saving of natural and energy resources, and treating land resources with respect'. Not unexpectedly, the newsletter goes onto advocate more stringent command and control regulations, stiffer laws, and the subsidizing of recycling.

REFERENCES

Anonymous (1993a), 'Waste and the Environment'. *Economist*, May 29.

Anonymous (1993b), 'Putting Responsibility on Industry (German Green Dot System)'. *BioCycle* **34**(6): 60–63.

Avnimelech, Y., A. Cohen and D. Shkedi (1990), 'The Effect of Municipal Solid Waste Compost on the Fertility of Clay Soils'. *Soil Technology* **3**: 275–84.

Avnimelech, Y., A. Cohen and D. Shkedy (1993), 'Can We Except a Consistent Efficiency of MSW Compost Application?' *Compost Science and Utilization*, Autumn: 7–14.

Avnimelech, Y., M. Kochva and Y. Yotal (1994), 'The Use of MSW Compost for the Reclamation of Saline and Alkaline Soils'. *Compost Science and Utilization*, Summer: 6–11.

Chilton, K. (1993), 'Municipal Solid Waste Reduction and Recycling: Implications for Federal Policymakers'. *Resources, Conservation and Recycling* **8**(1,2): 21–37.

Cuthbert, R. (1994), "Variable Disposal Fee Impact'. *BioCycle* **35**(5): 63–65.

DoE Report (1993), *Externalities from Landfill and Incineration.* A study by the Center for Social and Economic Research on the Global Environment, Warren Spring Laboratory and Economics for the Environment Consultancy, Edinburgh: HMSO press.

Glebs, R. (1989), 'Subtitle D: How Will It Affect Landfills?' *Waste Alternatives* **1**(3): 56–79.

Israel Ministry of the Environment (1995), *MSW in Israel: Composition, Heating Values and Estimations.* Jerusalem.

Israel Ministry of the Environment (1997), 'Integrated Solid Waste Management. Israel'. *Environment Bulletin* **20**(2): 2–6.

Jenkins, R. (1993), *The Economics of Solid Waste Reduction: The Impact of User Fees.* Cheltenham, UK: Edward Elgar.

Kinnaman, T.C. and D. Fullerton (1994), 'Household Demand for Garbage and Recycling Collection with the Start of a Price Per Bag" National Bureau of Economic Research, Working Paper #4670. 40 pp.

McFarland, J.M et al (1972), "Comprehensive Studies of Solid Waste Management' Report for the US EPA, University of California, Berkeley, May.

Mitchell, R.C. and R.T. Carson (1989), *Using Surveys to Value Public Goods: The CVM.* Washington, DC Resources for the Future.

Reiser, B. and M. Shechter (1997), 'Incoporating Zero Responses in the Analysis of CVM Valuations'. Working Paper. Haifa: Natural Resource and Environmental Research Center, University of Haifa.

Wertz, K.L. (1976), 'Economic Factors Influencing Households' Production of Refuse'. *Journal of Environmental Economics and Management*, **2**: 263–72.

APPENDIX 19A1. ALTERNATIVES FOR MSW MANAGEMENT IN ISRAEL

In this study, four alternatives for waste management in Israel are presented. It must be emphasized that each solution has to meet the accepted environmental standards (EPA, EC standards and so on) or charged for the environmental impacts whenever they are not internalized within the tipping fee (TF): that is, sanitary landfilling should prevent soil, water and air pollution as well as ensure landscape rehabilitation, or charges for any environmental damages.

A qualitative comparison of the methods is given in Table 19A1.1 An economic comparison among the alternatives is give in Table 19A1.2. The alternative of incineration was not taken into account, since the waste in Israel contains more than 50 per cent water, the caloric value of MSW in Israel is, thus, lower than MSW in the US or Europe and therefore, this fact makes this alternative technologically and economically doubtful.

The first two methods listed, total landfilling and MRF (material recovery facility) for mixed waste do not demand any change in life style, collection systems or need for public education.

1. *Total landfilling* of the waste. The vast majority of waste in Israel is being disposed of at close landfills, which are, practically, dumps, with no environmental protection standards. The landfills are operated by the municipalities, and the land is public, therefore, the tipping fees are at the range of 1–5 US$/ton. It must be emphasized that landfilling may be a reasonable solution from the economical point of view as long as it is managed in a way that environmental damages are minimized. It should be environmentally accepted and land must be available. Israel needs about 50 ha/year to dispose of all its waste (Anonymous 1993a), but there is public opposition to open new sites, unless they are sited in remote locations in the desert. The major drawbacks of this method are the need to carry the MSW to remote locations, the difficulty to approve suitable locations and a low public acceptance (NIMBY syndrome). Two schematic landfill alternatives were evaluated in this study: a close landfill (20 km) and a remote one (100 km).
2. *MRF-mixed waste.* The waste, not sorted at home, is being transported to a mixed waste sorting facility. Organics, separated by sieving, are composted and the rest of the waste is manually sorted for recyclables. The residues can be either incinerated or disposed of at a landfill. Sorting mixed waste is unpleasant due to odours and constant presence of leachates. Possibilities to mechanize the sorting are poor since the mixed waste is sticky, especially with the high moisture content of the Israeli

waste. The quality of the end products or secondary materials for the recycling industry is questionable; the compost is contaminated with heavy metals and broken glass and the secondary materials for recycling are dirty and wet, and therefore the revenues from the recycling industry are lowered.

The next two alternatives are based upon separation of the waste at home.

3. *MRF–recyclables.* The rationale of this method is to get clean stream of recyclables, as secondary raw materials, and to dispose of the rest. The residents are required to sort the recyclables into a special bin. The commingled recyclables are collected and transported to an MRF, to be sorted and sold to the scrap industry. The rest of the waste is collected separately, and transported, through a transfer station, to a landfill. The major disadvantage of this option is that at its maximum output this method will lead to a solution for only 20 per cent of the MSW in Israel. Most of the MSW will have to be landfilled.
4. *The wet/dry system.* The wet/dry home sorting is aimed first at the production of high-quality compost from the wet stream. It is essential to accept a clean wet stream, free of heavy metals and glass. (The presence of diapers may be accepted, since proper composting will sanitize the product, plastic sheets and bags can be separated rather easily following the composting.) The dry stream can be sorted easily, even mechanically, at an MRF for recyclables. The residues can be either incinerated or disposed of at a landfill. The viability of this option depends on the demand for compost. Extensive research conducted in our laboratory has shown that using compost as a soil amendment improves soil structure and fertility, especially in the semi-arid, organic-low soils of Israel. The application of MSW compost is expected to increase yields at a rate of 10–20 per cent above that obtained following optimal application of fertilizers (see Avnimelech et al. 1990, 1993, 1994). In Israel, the wet/dry separation seems to have the maximum potential for diverting waste from landfills and reusing most of the waste (50 per cent for compost, 20 per cent for recycling, which leaves only 30 per cent to be landfilled or incinerated). It must be emphasized in our study that the price of the compost is zero at the gate of the composting plant.

Table 19A1.1 summarizes the advantages and disadvantages regarding different criteria for the comparison of the alternatives for waste management in Israel.

Table 19A1.1. Advantages and disadvantages in MSW management alternatives in Israel

Criterion	1 Landfilling	2 MRF-mix	3 MRF-recyc.	4 Wet/ dry
Changes in lifestyle	–	–	+	+
Need for public education	–	–	+	+
Home collection convenience	++	++	+	+
Changes in collection system	–	–	+	+
Need for MRF	–	+	+	+
Sorting at the MRF-Convenience to workers & potential mechanization	=	–	++	+
Correcting home sorting mistakes	=	=	easy	+/–
Recyclables quality as secondary raw materials	=	low	high	medium
Recyclables quantity	=	20%	20%	20%
Quantity landfilled (w/o RDF)	100%	50%	80%	30%
Energy recovery (through recycling)	=	+	+	+
Land needed for composting plant	=	ca. 1 ha/ 100 tpd	=	ca. 1 ha/ 100 tpd
Quality of compost	=	poor	poor	high
Yield increase	=	10–30% (200$/ha wheat)	=	10–30% (200$/ha wheat)
Change in hedonic prices and WTP	7,700$/km from landfill	10,300$/km from MRF	10,300$/km from MRF	10,300$/km from compost plant

Notes:
* : possible but not essential.
= : irrelevant.
+/–: easy for the dry fraction, impossible for the wet.

Table 19A1.2 Calculations of social cost for different waste management options (disposing of 500 tons of waste)

	CLOSE LANDFILL			DISTANT LANDFILL			SORTING AT MRF				CURB COLLECTION				WET/DRY			
	Landfill 100% 500 tons			Landfill 100%			Landf 50%, Rec 15%, Comp 35%				Landf 80%, Rec 20%				Landf 30% Rec 20%, Comp 50%			
	Km	$/ton	total	Km	$/ton	total	ton	Km	$/ton	Total	ton	km	$/ton	total	ton	Km	$/ton	total
Cost of City collection		44	22,000		44	22,000	500		44	22,000	400		40	16,000	250		44	11,000
											100		70	7,000	250		44	11,000
Bins															250		10	2,500
Cost of trpt to transfer site				20	3	1,500								1000				
Cost trpt to recyc.							500	50	8	3,750	400	20	3	1,200	250	50	8	1,875
Cost of trpt to MRF											100	50	8	750	250	50	10	2,500
Cost transport to landfill	20	3	1,500	100	15	7,500	250	50	incl. in TF		400	100	15	6,000	150	50	Incl. in TF	
TF landfill		1	500		1	500												
TF transfer station		5.0	2,500		5.0	2,500					400		5.0	2,000				
TF mixed waste							500		16.5	8,250	400		1	400	250		14.0	3,506
TF MRF / TF compost.											100		15	1,500	250		15	3,750
Total quant. Landfilled							250				400				150			
TOTAL DIRECT COSTS		*53.0*	26,500		*68.0*	34,000			*68.0*	34,000			*71.7*	35,850			*72.3*	36,131
EXTERNAL COSTS																		
Transport	20	0.40	200	20	0.40	200	500	20	0.40	200	400	20	0.40	160	500	50	1.00	500
	100	0.20	100	100	0.20	100	500	30	0.06	30	400	100	0.20	80				
Landfilling		5.75	2,875		5.75	2,875	250		5.75	1,438	400		5.75	2,300	150		5.75	863
NIMBY		0.27	135		0.27	135	500		0.36	180	500		0.36	180	500		0.36	180
							250		0.27	68	225		0.27	61	150		0.27	41
TOTAL EXTERNAL COSTS		6.6	3,310		6.6	3,310			3.8	1,915			5.6	2,781			3.2	1,583
TOTAL COST WASTE MANAGEMENT		***60***	***29,800***		***75***	***37,300***			***72***	***35,900***			***77***	***38,600***			***75***	***37,700***

APPENDIX 19A2. THE CV SCENARIO

Respondents were asked the following question:
Q1: The current fee for waste management is 50 NIS (New Israeli Shekels) per family per month. In order to accommodate separation of waste at home and recycling afterwards, additional municipal investments (in collection equipment) would be needed.
Would you be willing to pay a monthly fee of X[11] *NIS in order to help establish such a recycling scheme?*
[If 'yes' go to Q2, else go to Q3].
Q2: If needed, would you be willing to pay a higher sum?
[If 'yes'] *Please state the highest sum you would be willing to pay ________ NIS.*

Q3: Would you be willing to pay a lower sum?
[If 'yes'] *Please state the highest sum you would be willing to pay ________ NIS.*
[If 'no' go to Q4].
Q4: Please state the reason(s) for your refusal to pay for the recycling scheme?

---

[11] The participants were randomly assigned to four bid groups (5, 10, 15 or 20 NIS).

20. Waste Management and Recycling

Thomas Sterner[1]

1. INTRODUCTION

During the last decade or so, politicians have started to react to the waste issue and a number of policies have been tried. These include various forms of waste treatment, waste reduction, separation and recycling or reuse. All these activities are useful options and may be necessary ingredients in an overall policy. However, there are occasions when actions appear to have preceded analysis so that apparently 'paradoxical' setbacks occur.

Examples of this include the newspaper reports of 'scandals' when there is no demand for the 'valuable' paper or glass that citizens have been persuaded to collect for recycling.[2] The reason it cannot be sold is that cheap recycled paper is imported from Europe. Particularly in Germany there has been much more collected than there is demand for paper and so the paper was sold to Sweden. Similar stories have occurred with other materials such as batteries which no-one wants to recycle and it caused a scandal when the collected batteries were dumped. The batteries were in fact deposited in a seemingly responsible way with barriers to stop leakage and so on, but there was still an outcry because people thought they were going to be recycled.

The point here is not necessarily that collection is wrong, but we must be clear about what to collect and for which reason. In the above cases, people have been persuaded to collect used material with the argument that there is a lack of material and that the collected material is a valuable resource. When there is no demand and the collected materials are not saleable, this motivation clearly appears to be erroneous and indeed misleading. This is not the place to judge whether or not batteries should be recycled but we should

[1] Research assistance from Anna-Carin Fahlberg is gratefully acknowledged.

[2] The local paper *Göteborgs Posten* reported (94/03/22) how the municipality ofStenungsund was forced to use taxpayers' money (SEK 140,000) to pay for the disposal of paper collected locally which cannot be sold. According to another newspaper article (*GP* 94/05/29) the municipality of Linköping was making a considerable loss on its collection of glass which was costing sek 600,000 per year while the glass manufacturers were only prepared to pay SEK 250,000 for the collected glass.

recognize that at least in principle it might be better to dispose of them in a safe way and that this does not necessarily mean that their collection separately from household waste was ill-founded.

In many cases there may indeed be good reasons for collecting certain types of waste. The reason, however, need not be their inherent value – if they were very valuable they would indeed not be considered waste. Gold is a good example; we do not hear about piles of used gold as a waste disposal problem since it is valuable and thus the market 'recycles' it automatically. This happens with car batteries, too, but other materials (such as smaller batteries) are not commercially valuable as a source of raw material; however, it might still be valuable from an environmental viewpoint to collect them in order to control the release of toxic elements into nature. By so doing, the treatment of the remaining waste stream may also be facilitated (composting, landfill and incineration may become cheaper and more environmentally acceptable).

According to economic theory, an excessive amount of waste will be produced in an economy where the environmental damage caused by disposed products is not reflected, either in the price of the products or in specific disposal costs. This is usually called a 'market failure'; prices fail to reflect the full social costs of production and consumption of products. In other words the assimilative services of the environment have been under-priced; the true cost of disposal, either in landfills or through incineration, has not been reflected in the price of the product.

Economic policies can be used to stimulate a more economical management of natural resources. The task of the environmental economist is to design policy instruments such as taxes and charges, for instance making it economically sensible for households to sort their waste to an optimal extent, increasing the volumes of relatively homogeneous material available for commercial use or appropriate waste management. The choice of instrument is complicated since there are other instruments such as deposit-refund schemes, subsidies, tradable permits, green labeling and so forth to choose from. Another example, relevant for the waste management area, is the new policy of successive imposition of producer responsibility for taking back and finally disposing of used goods.

This chapter is divided into four sections. We start by looking at some theoretical aspects: first the importance of rising income for recycling and how the design of waste management fees is connected to the use of deposits for hazardous waste which might otherwise be dumped illegally. The next section looks at the experience of deposit-refund schemes in Sweden. It shows that economic incentives are quite important for recycling but are far from being the only significant variable. Ease of collection as well as habit formation are strong factors too. In the final section some local solutions such as recycling centers in Gothenburg are discussed.

2. THE VALUE OF MATERIALS AND THE EFFECT OF RISING INCOME

Figure 20.1a illustrates how we usually perceive of our economy. Income, *Y*, measured in nominal terms rises very fast, prices, *P*, also rise but not so fast. Some price might of course be an exception, but on average the price of industrially produced goods (including raw materials which are more or less industrially produced) will grow less fast than income. This is a result of technical progress and capital accumulation and is the driving force behind our increased material well-being. According to Hotelling-type theory of scarcity, scarce goods would experience a faster than average rate of growth but so far there is little actual empirical evidence that this happens with any of the major raw materials.

The two lower curves of Figure 20.1a show another common representation where (average) prices are kept constant (P_{fix}) and we measure real income growth $Y_{p\text{-}fix}$. This growth (in real, deflated, income) is of course the difference between the growth rates for nominal income and average prices $Y_{p\text{-}fix} = Y/P$.

Figure 20.1. Income and price changes over time

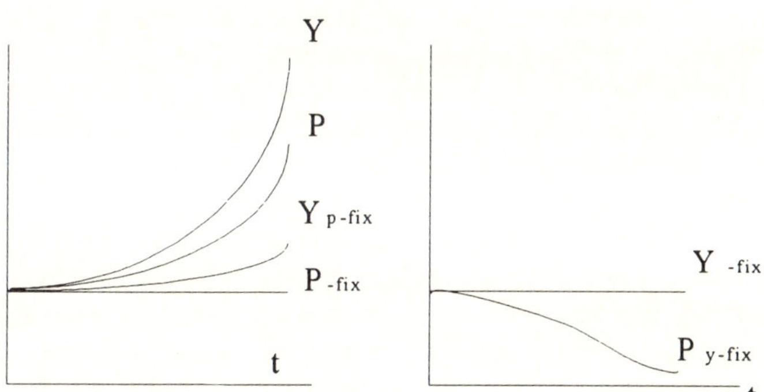

a) Nominal and fixed prices b) Fixed income

Figure 20.1b shows another way of representing these processes. Here we normalize prices by (average) income. Thus income Y_{fix} is kept constant and a price index for constant income can be calculated as $P_{y\text{-}fix} = P/Y$ which thus typically falls over time. This picture shows us clearly how declining real prices of the average (manufactured) good is a mirror image of increasing income.

Figure 20.1 can help us understand the apparent paradoxes of recycling in modern society. Because the price of goods is declining, people will be inherently less inclined to recycle. There is simply no reason to take the trouble if new products are becoming continually cheaper. The price of a product measured with income as a deflator gives us a measure of value in terms of our own time: the time it would take to earn money to buy a new product will determine how much time we are willing to spend on repairing or recycling an old one. In addition, there are secondary factors: products tend to become more complicated and difficult to repair without extensive knowledge about the product. Spare parts are marketed in small series and are often relatively expensive. The cost of repairing and replacing damaged parts is often greater than the cost of a new product. Furthermore, even the environmental characteristics of some new products evolves so fast that repairing and maintaining old ones may be a very inferior option (cars are a prime example).

Thus the first point to note here is that we need to understand the mechanisms behind price formation in order to discuss recycling. Some products will have such a high price that the market 'recycles' them. We have already mentioned the case of gold, and this applies to several metals. If a particular good is scarce, then its price would increase and there would be increasing incentives over time for reuse and recycling. But on average, goods that can be produced industrially and for which our normal assumptions concerning technology and so on apply, will have a decreasing price (at least measured as above in terms of income – or time).

This is one of the major problems with recycling. If there is no demand for recycled goods, the market mechanism will not work. People wonder what would be the use of collecting used products if they are just dumped into a nearby landfill. It is almost inevitable that a country with rising income will produce more waste over time, and a government that insists on recycling will not only have to deal with promoting recycling but also with establishing and maintaining a market for recycled goods.

We should not recycle out of a misconceived preconception that everything is becoming scarcer and that all resources have some inherent value that the 'market' does not understand. There are, however, good reasons for collecting some categories of waste even if they have no value, in order to avoid contamination if they contain toxic substances.

To take a concrete example: the reason we should collect products that contain cadmium and mercury is not that these elements are scarce and valuable – on the contrary. If they were sufficiently scarce and valuable there would be no problem. However, their price is relatively low compared to their toxicity and that is the reason why there is a market failure. It is because these elements are toxic to nature that we should undertake a series of measures to minimize their leakage into the biosphere. This has implications for the type of policy instrument necessary. If there is no market for the waste collected in these cases, this should not in any way be seen as a failure for the policy undertaken since its purpose is not to economize on cadmium and mercury but simply to reduce their release into nature.

As a result of the environmental costs of different methods of handling the solid waste problem, many official environmental agencies have embraced a so-called 'waste hierarchy' approach to waste management, giving priority to source reduction and particularly reduction of the hazardous components. If that is not possible then recycling, and only as a last option, landfills or incineration should be considered. For an economist it is not clear that this should be the correct order. Economists would suggest that costs (including external costs and scarcity rent and so on) should be minimized and we would generally see it as an empirical issue which of the disposal or reuse options best fulfills these goals in different circumstances.

The issue of what to do is related to the issue of how to do it. As long as engineers and lawyers have dominated, they tended to promote control and command policies such as legislation to enforce recycling, that is, to mandate the use of recycled materials in finished products.

Market-based instruments seek to modify behavior through the price mechanism. Policy alternatives include (i) waste collection charges at the point of disposal; (ii) retail disposal charges at the point of sale; (iii) raw material taxes in the production process; (iv) deposit-refund systems; and (v) pure subsidies. As a first rule of thumb the tax, charge, subsidy or other policy instruments should be levied as closely as possible to the activity that actually causes the externality. Only when this is not possible or excessively costly will it be preferable to levy charges at earlier or later stages in the product chain.

A natural starting point when discussing economic policy instruments is the Pigouvian tax which in the area of waste management would correspond to a disposal charge. If there were no illegal dumping, then the only way to avoid producing waste would be to increase recycling or reuse, increase useful life of products or buy less-waste-containing products. Under these conditions, consumers ideally would calculate future disposal costs when they made purchases and therefore producers would have an incentive to design products so as to economize on waste production (longer useful life, less environmentally hazardous and more easily recyclable materials for components and packaging and so on).

A motivation for disposal charges for waste disposal is that they explicitly link household costs to the real costs of collection and disposal. The charge can be based on either toxicity, volume, weight or some combination of these. Experience suggests that properly designed programs should work for household waste in general (multi-family buildings may represent a special type of problem). There is, however, some concern that unit charges might result in increased household disposal of toxic waste such as cadmium and mercury. The problem is that the optimal Pigouvian tax on these metals should be equal to the marginal damage and because this would be quite an astronomical figure, then the risk of illegal dumping becomes a real concern. Notice that these risks might be more easily controllable for an industrial enterprise where the sheer size of operations and their concentrated nature might make monitoring costs reasonable in relation to environmental costs. In the case of the individual household, however, the monitoring system necessary to detect the disposal of a few grams of mercury from, say, a thermometer, would be excessively intrusive, complex and costly. Here in fact we may even argue in the exact opposite direction. It is so valuable for the environment to avoid this type of dumping that we may even be prepared to provide free or low-cost disposal at transfer stations or even monetary rewards for the collection of certain hazardous materials. While disposal charges or taxes would be the natural Pigouvian policy instrument, monitoring and information costs may thus push us in the direction of subsidies or deposit-refund systems instead.

A second approach that is directly intended to address the potential problem of illegal dumping, administers the disposal costs at the point of product purchase. This could be done by introducing a retail disposal charge on the sale of items, reflecting their disposal costs. Note, however, that these charges can only discourage total consumption but cannot encourage recycling or other responsible waste management.

Sometimes it is not the product but one specific ingredient or raw material that causes environmental damage and in these cases it would be more appropriate to levy the costs directly on the raw materials. Certain elements, such as cadmium, are highly toxic. By taxing virgin production at the mine, the value of recycled cadmium would be increased and this would discourage disposal. Unfortunately this would require global coordination which makes it administratively much more difficult to decide on and implement. Both retail and raw material charges suffer from the same defect that their only incentive effect is to economize on total use. Once the good has been purchased there is no further incentive with respect to waste management. Deposit refund systems (DRS) can be a cost-effective way to manage some categories of toxic wastes. They give the agents incentives to find safer substitutes and to recover and recycle used material. DRS are a combination of a front-end charge (deposit) and a refund, payable when the substance in question, or part of it, is turned in for recycling or proper disposal. The refund gives an incentive both to follow the rules for proper disposal and to minimize substance loss during production. DRS are particularly useful when the improper disposal of waste, rather than its generation *per se*, is of concern. The initial charge can be levied either as the material enters production or at any point in the manufacturing or distribution process.

It can be shown (see, for instance, Fullerton and Kinnaman 1995, and also Bohm 1981) that if the 'Pigouvian' tax on dumping cannot be applied to dumping itself (because monitoring is not available) it must be applied to all goods at purchase and thus becomes a general consumption tax. If, however, a good is recycled, then this tax is 'refunded'. Similarly if the good is left for waste disposal then the new waste disposal 'tax' is actually composed of two terms which is the old waste disposal tax minus the new 'refund' term. This is equal to the difference in externality between dumping waste illegally and disposing of it through the proper systems. We have assumed that the latter is always better from an externality viewpoint and thus this whole term is negative. Whether it is sufficiently large to outweigh the time cost of municipal disposal or not is an empirical matter but in that case the total fee to the consumer for waste management might become zero or even negative. Thus we have effectively created a type of 'deposit-refund' system in which recycling is paid a subsidy and (municipal) waste collection is also subsidized (the fee is lower than actual costs and may be even zero or negative).

A remaining problem is to identify the appropriate deposit level. From a theoretical point of view, the deposit should be set equal to the Pigouvian level, that is, the social value of the recycling activity as compared to the alternative of disposal. If it is too low, there is insufficient incentive to return the waste and the deposit essentially becomes a tax on that product. If it is too high, however, various types of abuse are possible. These would include the direct production or import with the sole purpose of claiming the refund. In practice, however, it may not be necessary to make the deposit equal to the Pigouvian tax level. The main function of the deposit is that it should be high enough to motivate the public (which does not necessarily have to be the people who actually bought the product, but could also be other individuals or organizations that collect the waste) to return the products.

We are therefore interested in how the public reacts to different deposit-refund levels. Preferably we should have looked at environmentally hazardous wastes but since there are few relevant experiences we shall look at the various goods for which deposit-refund systems are currently used.

3. ECONOMIC INCENTIVES AND RECYCLING IN SWEDEN

Internationally there have been a number of experiments with differentiated waste fees and other incentives for waste minimization, recycling and increased composting. This applies particularly to some of the more densely populated areas of Europe such as the Netherlands. According to one study, the results vary a lot and depend very much on the exact implementation of the program as well as on local demographic factors (Fullerton and Kinnaman 1994), see also Repetto (1992) and Sterner and Bartelings (1998). This study, however, will not deal with waste management fees but with other determinants of recycling such as deposits and convenience.

The use of deposit-refund systems has been increasing somewhat in accordance with what might be expected from the theoretical considerations discussed above. There are several interesting aspects here. One is their changing role: historically they were used mainly for glass bottles and actually reflected a market value. Now they are increasingly being used as an economic incentive. However, it is clear that collection of some items such as paper occurs on a very large scale without any deposit. It is therefore valuable to understand what role deposits have compared to that, for instance, of ease of deposition (comfort) or of information, opinion, values and habit.

This is particularly relevant since there have been several disagreements as to who should have the responsibility for collection, the municipalities, the producers, the retailers or the consumers. In the case of nickel-cadmium batteries, the industry has organized collection in an attempt to stop charges on cadmium which were being proposed by the government.

In the case of aluminum cans, industry and trade have been under pressure to prove that they can achieve a high rate of recycling to avoid pressure to ban the use of aluminum cans. As can be seen from Figure 20.2, this has been quite successful, recycling rates have passed 90 percent and it appears that the increase in nominal deposits from 25 to 50 öre (Swedish 'cents') in 1987 has played a role. The fact that the real value of deposits has fallen since then does not, however, seem to have reduced collection. Maybe there have been changes in attitude and information or ease of deposition. Lately there have been increasing numbers of machines that compact the cans and make deposition easier. The number of shops accepting cans for refunds may have increased too. However, we have no access to any data that describe this type of convenience factor quantitatively. Perhaps deposits are important just as signals to change behavior, which then has its own inertia.

Figure 20.2. Level of deposit and recycling rate for aluminum cans

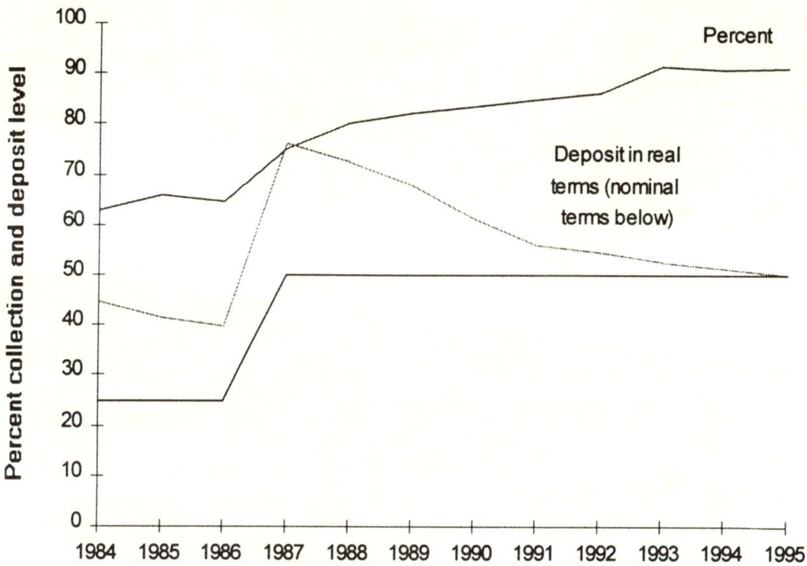

We have not drawn a diagram for the case of soft drink bottles, since recycling has been fixed at 98 percent since 1970 and it seems that these are recycled irrespective of the level (although perhaps not existence) of the deposit. Presumably habit and ease of deposition are important here: it is relatively easy to return the empties to your closest shop when you go shopping. It is not as easy to do this for alcoholic beverages since these are sold in special shops in Sweden and there are fewer of them (see Figure 20.3). There is also the added difficulty that only some (in fact a decreasing number) of wine bottles and so on are refundable. However, it seems from the evidence that increasing levels of deposit have been successful in eliciting higher levels of recycling.

The nominal deposits rose from just 15 öre to 2.00 SEK/bottle. In real terms the increase has been more than 100 percent since 1970. It appears that the recycling rate goes up each time the nominal deposit rises.

Figure 20.3. Level of deposit and recycling rate for wine and liquor bottles

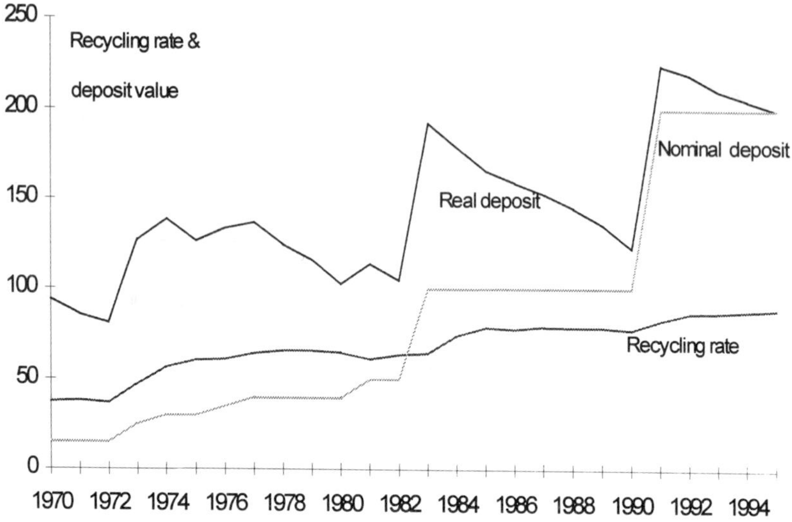

Figure 20.4. Collection of paper and glass without deposits as an incentive

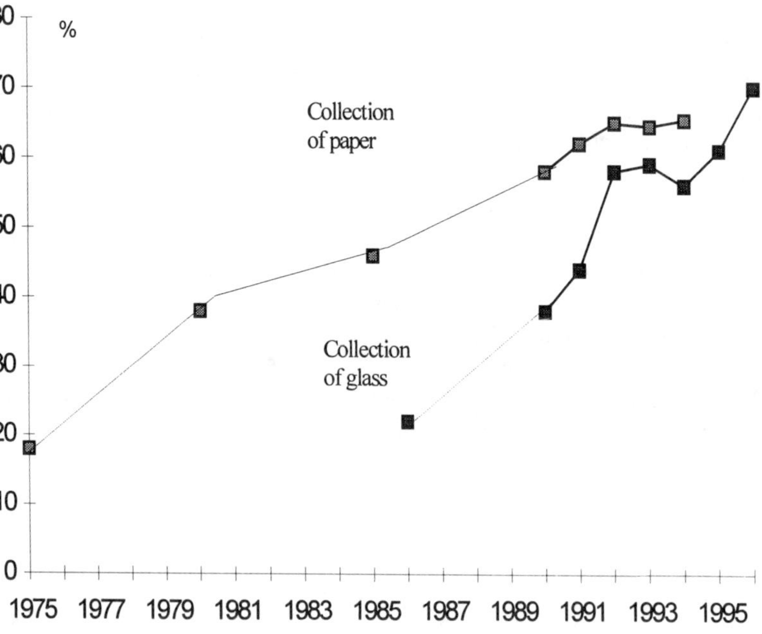

By way of comparison, Figure 20.4 shows the estimated collection of paper and disposable glass which is collected without any deposit. Within a decade collection rates have soared from 20 to 70 percent for glass in spite of the absence of any economic incentive.

It is clear, however, that considerable efforts were made during this period to facilitate and encourage the collection of various types of waste, as will be discussed in the next section. In fact by way of anecdotal evidence it is clear that many people are so keen on being environmental that they throw bottles into the glass collection that are actually refundable. Clearly these people care more for the environment than for the deposit since they are prepared to make the effort to bring the bottles to the glass collection points but not to separate out the refundable ones! By contrast, and as a result of increasing unemployment and harsher economic conditions, there is also another, rapidly growing group of people who are to be found collecting refundables from these disposal centers.[3]

Figure 20.4 also shows the percentage collection of paper which has increased in much the same way as for glass although spread over a longer period of time. It would seem that the collection of paper has become a habit which is fairly well rooted. As we shall see in a later chapter, older people particularly are prone to collecting paper. However, it has been questioned whether this collection makes environmental sense. Clearly it is not a major priority from an environmental viewpoint since if paper is deposited or burned then the environmental damage is modest. Obviously there is even a certain amount of energy and wood that is saved and some external costs associated with the production of paper (and of the energy). However, compared to the relatively low levels of recycling of some items of hazardous waste such as fluorescent light strips (which contain mercury), the importance of collecting paper is small. Furthermore, if the hazardous waste and compostable fractions were removed then burning the remaining trash might be an environmentally attractive option – particularly if it has a high paper content, which would give useful energy!

Estimating the recycling rates for different types of batteries is rather difficult since the statistics on the number of batteries bought and recycled are incomplete, particularly in any detail. Also, for some batteries such as nickel cadmium ones, there is an element of delay since the batteries are used for several years and then perhaps not disposed of immediately. Collection of

---

[3] I interviewed a gentleman who was unemployed and wanted to remain anonymous who worked full-time collecting refundable bottles from glass disposal centers (and others thrown into wastepaper baskets, parks and so on). He had earned $6,000 in half a year and estimated that there were another 50–80 persons like himself – although many of them less hard working since they only collect enough to buy a bottle or two! Still, this suggests that refundable bottles and cans with a value of hundreds of thousands of dollars are discarded annually in Gothenburg, many of them in bins for free (non-refund) glass disposal.

these batteries has increased lately with a collection of 106 tons in 1995 compared to 48 tons in 1992. It is estimated that this corresponds to 35 percent of new batteries which is an increase from an estimate of 20 percent in 1991 but still far from the official goal of 90 percent! When it comes to car batteries, the estimated recycling is actually somewhat over 100 percent, which perhaps indicates that a few unanticipated batteries from abroad find their way into the Swedish market. The incentive here is the scrap value of the lead. There are no data series on other types of batteries but an official estimate for 1989 indicates 89 percent of mercury oxide batteries were collected compared to 29 percent for ordinary alkaline batteries. The same source (*The Environment* 1992), however, gives 49 percent for cadmium, which appears high compared to the above figures. We should note that mercury batteries are the very small type found in watches and so on. Very often customers take their equipment to the shop where the new battery is installed, which makes collection of the old one very easy! This may be the main factor explaining the high collection rate in this case.

Figure 20.5 shows how the scrapping of cars has varied and that there appears to be some response to changes in the deposit offered through scrapping premiums, which were scaled to 100 in 1995.

Figure 20.5. Scrapping rates and premiums for automobiles

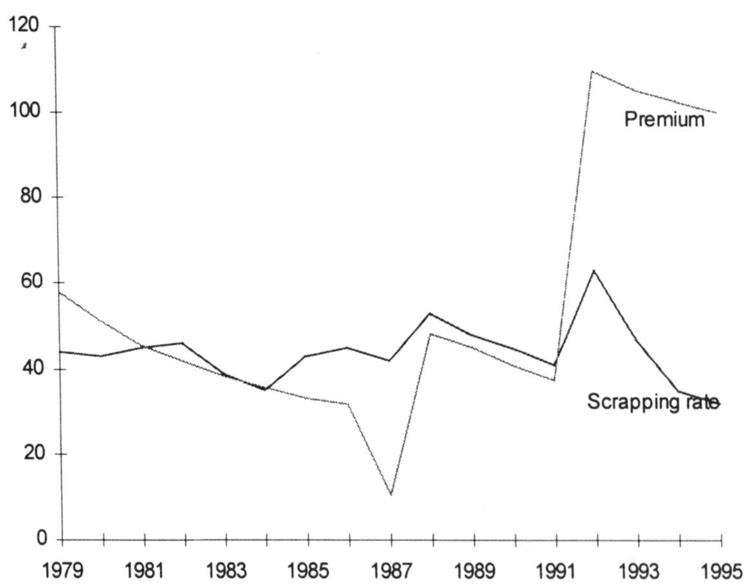

It is very hard to summarize the above evidence since it is indeed quite diverse. We have, however, found that deposits appear to have helped to increase collection rates for alcoholic beverage bottles and aluminum cans. On the other hand there has been an increased collection of paper and glass without any deposit. There are also high rates of collection for some items like mercury batteries but they are low for others such as fluorescent lighting, which seems to indicate that higher deposits may indeed be a powerful instrument to increase collection rates but that they are far from being the only one. Comfort, habit, attitudes and information are just as important and possibly the main function of the deposit is in fact as a signal to focus attention on social priorities.

One way of analyzing this type of information is by linear regression (see Table 20.1). Although it is uncertain whether we have sufficient data for a good analysis of more than one or two types of refundables, we can at least see regressions as an alternative way of summarizing our data. However, we are constrained to using price, year and dummies as our only variables which is clearly unsatisfactory. 'Price' is only the unit price and takes no account of the size, weight and so on of the item. 'Year' obviously captures some change in our attitudes and in the ease or efficiency of the necessary infrastructure but in a very aggregate and imperfect way. We have analyzed cans, beer bottles, wine bottles and car hulks separately and furthermore run pooled regressions for all these categories (except car hulks which are obviously very different).

The regressions used have been of the type:

$$R = a + bP + cT + dD \tag{20.1}$$

$$LnR = a + bLnP + cT + dD \tag{20.2}$$

where R was recycling rate, P real price (deflated), T was an index of time and D was a vector of dummies (in the pooled regressions).

We had one dummy for each type of refundable and one common dummy for the two non-refundables. The regressions were run in both linear and log-linear form when this was possible (zero prices precluded the use of the log-linear model when non-refundable items such as paper were included). In the case of the linear equation (20.1) the parameter for T can be interpreted as change in percentage points per year. For instance, this was 1.7 for wine and liquor bottles or 2.7 for aluminum cans.

In the case of the loglinear equation (20.2) the parameter for T can be interpreted as (the natural logarithm of) percentage change per year. Thus in the case of wine bottles collection rates increased on average by $e^{0.024} = 2.4$ percent per year. (Note that this is percent change, not increase in percentage points!)

Table 20.1. Regressions explaining collection of refundables

	Price	Time /(growth)	Dummies	R^2
Wine/liquor bottles (Loglinear)	0.22 (1.9)	0.024 (5.7)		0.86
(Linear)	0.05 (1.4)	1.7 (8.4)		0.91
Aluminum cans (Loglinear)	0.19 (5.7)	0.034 (18)		0.97
(Linear)	0.22 (4.6)	2.7 (17)		0.97
Beer /soft drink	–	–		
Wine, beer and cans pooled (Loglinear)	0.35 (11.5)	0.019 (14)	Al=0.38 Beer=0.54	0.92
(Linear)	0.18 (10)	1.1 (12)	Al=21 Beer=39	0.93
All previous pooled (Linear, separate intercepts)	0.18 (7.6)	1.2 (11)	Al=20 Beer=39 Nonref.=1	0.91
All previous pooled (Linear, separate intercepts and growth for non-refundables)	0.18 (8.4)	1.1 (10) but 2.3 for nonref.	Al=21 Beer=39 Nonref.=–109	0.93
Car hulks	0.03 (0.4)	–0.004 (0.4)		0.02

We note that for all the items studied there was an increase by a couple of percent per year (except car hulks in which there were no significant results, and beer bottles for which there was no change at all over the period studied and hence estimations were impossible). When looking at the pooled regression with all the items together (except car hulks) and when we allow for different parameters for time, the non-refundables were found to have collection rates which rose more rapidly than the refundables: 2.3 percent points per year as compared to 1.1.[4]

When it comes to price elasticities it is easier to interpret the logarithmic models (20.2) (no effort has been made to test one type of model against another or to do any more fancy modeling since the quality of data hardly warrants it). The price elasticities found were all around 0.2 except in one

[4] The model used here was $R = a + bP + cT + dD + eD_n{}^*T$. The estimate of change over time for the non-refundables was thus $c + e$ whereas the change over time for the refundables was c.

pooled regression for the refundables only when it was 0.35.[5] These values seem clearly indicative of the limited but still significant role of the deposit.

The conclusion of the above is that refunds seem to have an important effect at least as far as attention goes. They send a signal that society considers this recycling important. Obviously the purely economic component also exists but is limited. Other factors such as comfort or ease of collection may be very important. For many items that are particularly important from an environmental viewpoint there are no national statistics and we shall therefore in the next section turn to the case of hazardous wastes in Gothenburg.

4. THE IMPORTANCE OF CONVENIENCE FOR RECYCLING HAZARDOUS WASTE

As can be seen from Table 20.2, the late 1980s was a period when the collection of hazardous waste really started in earnest. From 1985 to 1989 the collected quantities increased ten times. Naturally there was a good deal of uncertainty about how to collect hazardous waste and considerable efforts were made to inform the public and so forth. A number of different methods for collection were also tried. A couple of large recycling centers were set up in Gothenburg where employees took care of whatever (hazardous and other) waste the public cared to hand in. Furthermore, smaller recycling stations were set up to receive oil, solvents, car batteries and so on. These were generally located at (and run by) petrol stations or small yacht harbors. Passive deposits (boxes and so forth) were set up for the collection of, for instance, batteries. These could be set up both in the streets (for example, close to collection points for glass and paper) or in appropriate shops and so on.

In order to collect waste from these deposits and from the recycling stations the environmental authorities needed a collection van. The latter was also used for some time as a special neighborhood service van. The environmental van drove around according to a special schedule and visited every single neighborhood at some specific time.

The idea of this was to increase the comfort or ease with which households would be able to deliver hazardous waste. Without having to drive to a recycling station or center they would be able to hand the waste in practically at their own doorstep. The environmental van also had specially trained personnel who could advise on storage/handling of chemicals and so on. They could thus also perform an educational role. During 1992 we carried

[5] For car hulks we also found a very small and insignificant price elasticity.

out a special evaluation of this environmental van, on which this section is based (see Dahlin and Kuhlin 1992).

Table 20.2. Hazardous waste collected from households in Gothenburg, 1985–1991 (kgs)

	1985	1988	1991
Car batteries	13,000	185,900	144,400
Waste oil	5,600	24,000	73,000
Waterbased paints	4200	25,000	59,100
Synthetic paints		22,000	71,800
Solvents	600	15,100	20,100
Spraycans	300	1,200	1,600
Acid/alcaline	225	1,500	668
Pesticides	200	1,030	594
Medicine	600	1,000	500
Fluorescent tubes	900	11,000	40,300
Photo. Liquids	200	1,500	6,930
Asbestos	200	500	40,500
Other chemicals	200	344	1,659
Mercury	–	190	388
Small batteries	27,600	76,000	88,040
Total	54,000	366,000	550,000

Table 20.3 provides a disaggregation by three different types of collection and shows that for some items such as car batteries, oil and asbestos, the recycling stations were particularly important. This is not surprising for car batteries and oil, since these stations were actually in many cases petrol stations. The passive deposits are not shown in the table but they were particularly important for batteries and for fluorescent lighting.

*Table 20.3. Specification of some waste items, 1991**

	Recycling centers	Recycling stations	Neighborhood coll.
Paints	24,065	6,138	4,755
Solvents	3,364	1,035	858
Aerosol cans*	3,303	844	1,828
Alkalines	465	130	283
Acids	432	215	103,5
Pesticides	779	163	219
Other chemicals	1,846	701	808
Waste oil	2,250**	5,545	1,821
Car batteries*	137	1,079	576
Small batteries	6,351	741	926
Waterbased paint	21,175	2,853	3,912
Plastics	271	337	1,178
Medicines	239	122	378
Thermometers*	114	31	219
Asbestos	26	117	60
Electronic scrap	9	37	115
Other	535	521	864

Notes

* Number of items. Otherwise Kgs.

** Waste oils have special containers at the recycling centers which are not included here.

Table 20.4. Cost efficiency estimated for various collection methods (SEK/Kg)

Collection method	Total hazardous waste
Neighborhood collection	33
Recycling stations	44
Recycling centers	28
Deposits	18

For some items the environmental van's neighborhood collection was particularly useful: for instance this applied to medicines, thermometers, plastics, and electronic and 'other' waste. The latter are perhaps more typical household items and it may be a good example of how the neighborhood collection succeeded in reaching new groups of consumers and focussing attention on new types of hazardous waste. It has presumably been used more frequently by housewives and elderly persons without cars while the recycling stations and centers have required access to a car.

Acquiring information on the costs that the local authorities have for collection was far from easy since they are not always available in the form we would have needed. Nevertheless, we were able to carry out a very rough estimate of the collection costs in kronor per kg of waste. Table 20.4 shows that the passive deposits (mainly for batteries) were the most cost effective with recycling centers as second and the neighborhood collection as third. The recycling stations were the most expensive. However, we should emphasize that this is a rough calculation which takes no consideration of the relative toxicity of the different items collected or of the existence of joint production or cost sharing. The latter was quite important since the same personnel and equipment were being used for the neighborhood collection and for collection from the deposits and centers. The neighborhood collection trips were, however, generally in the evenings or at weekends and the personnel costs may have been underestimated above since we only had total wages. Furthermore, external costs of the collection itself should be considered.

All in all the impression of the personnel we interviewed was that the vans were poorly utilized during the neighborhood collection trips. Very often people seemed unaware of when the van would come since it came very infrequently – as a result of the ambition to visit as many different neighborhoods as possible. Thus generally only a very small number of persons would come to visit the van, and this appears in the end to have been the main factor why this service was discontinued.

On the whole the environmental vans do seem to have fulfilled some niche function in waste collection and were presumably important as part of a campaign for awareness creation. It is possible that they could have had a continued role to play. On the other hand, the number of recycling stations has increased dramatically, implying that the average distance for most people has been reduced anyway. One lesson from this experience is that ease of handling and comfort are indeed important. However, keeping track of a complicated schedule and then actually going off with your hazardous waste at a certain pre-specified time once every couple of months may not be more 'comfortable' than having to carry it a little further but being able to do so whenever it suits you, for instance when fueling your car! Nevertheless, it might have been interesting to ascertain the effect of a deposit or simply an economic premium for certain types of waste. If, for instance, the recycling centers or the environmental van had paid a certain price for, say, particularly hazardous chemicals (such as those containing mercury) then it is conceivable that collection rates would have increased more than enough to offset the presumably rather small increase in total costs of collection!

5. SUMMARY

In this chapter we started by reviewing a few fundamental theoretical concepts. We showed that contrary to the general perception, recycling is not a 'new' idea that will gather impetus of its own accord. On the contrary, increasing productivity and income will imply a strong bias against recycling. There are, however, situations when collection of certain types of material or waste is necessary and recycling may be an option. This is particularly the case when materials are very toxic or when production of virgin material implies serious environmental or other problems. In many of these cases economic instruments should be used rather than mandatory recycling programs. We also discussed combinations of (differentiated) waste management fees and deposit refunds (or other instruments such as taxes) on toxic or hazardous waste materials.

In the empirical part of the chapter we reviewed some experiences from a few Swedish deposit-refund systems and from the collection of hazardous waste. These indicate that economic incentives such as deposit-refund systems can work for quite a wide range of products and do have some effect but also that the consumer-friendliness of the systems are important. The price elasticity of collection with respect to the deposit appears to be quite low (about –0.2).

REFERENCES

Baumol, W.J. and Oates, W.E, (1988), *The Theory of Environmental Policy*, Cambridge: Cambridge University Press.

Bohm, P. (1981), *Deposit-refund Systems: Theory and Applications to Environmental, Conservation and Consumer Policy*, Baltimore, MD: Johns Hopkins University Press.

Copeland, B.R. (1991), 'International Trade in Waste Products in the Presence of Illegal Disposal', *Journal of Environmental Economics and Managment*, (**20**), pp. 143–62.

Dahlin, A. and Kuhlin, A. (1992), 'Miljöfarligt Avfall – styrmedel, insamling och effektivitet', Project paper for the BSc degree 1992:1, Unit for Environmental Economics, Department of Economics, University of Göteborg.

Duggal V.G., Saltzman, C. and Williams, M.L (1991), 'Recycling: An Economic Analysis', *Eastern Economic Journal*, (**17**)3, pp. 351–58, July–September.

Fullerton, D. and Kinnaman, T.C. (1994), 'Household Demand for Garbage and Recycling Collection with the Start of a Price per Bag', National Bureau of Economic Research Working Paper 4670.

Fullerton, D. and Kinnaman, T.C. (1995), 'Garbage, Recycling and Illicit Burning or Dumping', *Journal of Environmental Economics and Managment* **29**(1), pp. 78–91.

Hong, S., Adams, R.M. and Love, H.A. (1993), 'An Economic Analysis of Household Recycling of Solid Wastes: The Case of Portland Oregon', *Journal of Environmental Economics and Management*, **25**, pp 136–46.

OECD (1989), *Economic Instruments for environmental protection*, OECD Report, Paris.

Repetto, R., et al (1992), *Green Fees: How a Tax Shift Can Work for the Environment and the Economy*, Washington: RWI.

Sterner, T. and Bartelings, H. (1999), 'Household Waste Management in a Swedish Municipality', *Environmental and Resource Economics*, **13**(4), July.

21. The Effectiveness of the UK Landfill Tax – Early Indications

Dominic Hogg[1]

1. INTRODUCTION

This chapter seeks to shed some light upon the changes which have occurred in the behaviour of waste producers and waste operatives following the introduction of the UK Landfill Tax. It illustrates the fact that the tax has had an important effect on the UK waste management industry, but that its effects on waste producers vary considerably. On the basis of our observations (which are, to some extent, preliminary), we have made some recommendations as to how the effectiveness of the tax might be improved.[2]

1.1 Background to the Introduction of the Tax

Waste management in the UK is dominated by the practice of landfilling. Some 90 per cent of all household waste, and 70 per cent of all controlled waste, is disposed of in landfill sites (DoE and WO 1995, p. 4). The dominance of landfill has partly historic roots, but under current institutional arrangements, disposal to landfill is the cheapest option for waste disposal.

A number of concerns have arisen regarding the practice of landfilling.

---

[1] Senior Consultant, ECOTEC Research and Consulting, Priestley House, 28-34 Albert Street, Birmingham B4 7UD, UK.

[2] The original work was funded by the European Foundation for the Improvement of Living and Working Conditions and was Part II of a study addressing the economic, employment and environmental implications of the UK Landfill Tax. This tax was introduced in October 1996, and its overall costs to business were to be offset through a reduction in employers' higher rate National Insurance Contributions (NICs) from 10.2 to 10 per cent. Part 1 of the study was an *ex ante* assessment of the employment effects of the tax undertaken by Cambridge Econometrics (see EFILWC, forthcoming). This chapter highlights some of the major conclusions of Part II of the Study programme, as well as some of the recommendations of an ECOTEC Report commissioned by Friends of the Earth, UK, regarding the tax's environmental effectiveness (for a fuller treatment, see EFILWC forthcoming and ECOTEC 1997).

Principal among these are problems associated with leachate, migration of gas generated through the rotting of putrescible materials, and a feeling that simply filling up holes in the ground *ad infinitum* cannot be sustained in the longer term. Furthermore, the cheapness of landfilling has constituted a break on initiatives designed to make waste producers more aware of the costs of wasted raw materials since the marginal costs of disposal per ton of waste are relatively low, and in many cases, zero.

Reflecting some of these concerns, an intention to introduce the Landfill Tax was announced in the November 1994 Budget. In March 1995, a consultation paper was issued by HM Customs and Excise (responsibility for the tax was given to Customs and Excise because of their experience with indirect taxes and existing links with the industry through VAT). The consultation paper elicited responses from some 720 bodies. Once the details of the tax were finalized, it was eventually introduced in October 1996.

The consultation process was undertaken to elicit the views of industry, environmentalists and local authorities. Its major outcome, as confirmed in the announcement in the November 1995 Budget, was a change in the tax from an *ad valorem* to a weight-based instrument. Furthermore, it was intended that there should be no exemptions from the tax. The tax was set at two rates, the standard rate of £7 per ton for non-inert wastes, and the lower rate of £2 per ton for inert wastes specified in the HM Customs Qualifying Materials Order (HM Customs and Excise 1996). Exemptions from the tax were eventually awarded for dredgings removed from inland waterways and harbours, mining and quarrying waste (which typically resides in the mine itself), pet cemeteries and waste arising from the clearance of contaminated land (for further details, see HM Customs and Excise 1997).

The tax was supposed to be revenue neutral. HM Customs and Excise (HM C&E) estimated initially (November 1994) that the tax would generate some £500 million, based, it should be said, on the very limited statistics that are a feature of the waste industry in the UK. The overall costs to business were to be offset through a reduction in employers' higher rate NICs from 10.2 to 10 per cent. In addition, an element of 'hypothecation' of revenue was made possible through the channelling of funds to groups registered as environmental bodies under a new organization named ENTRUST.[3]

---

[3] Strictly, the environmental bodies scheme is not hypothecation. Indeed, the scheme would not have arisen were that the case since the UK Treasury is not positively disposed to the idea. The scheme allows landfill operators (and through them, third parties) to make a contribution to an environmental body, which must be a non-profit distributingorganization, and must be required to register with a body named ENTRUST established specifically for this purpose. The operator essentially receives, in return, a tax credit to the tune of 90 per cent of that contribution. The voluntary commitment of funds is the reason why this is not seen as strict hypothecation.

1.2 The Tax as a Means for Achieving Environmental Objectives

On the surface, the tax seemed to be a rarity, a popular tax (Wakelin 1997). Yet there are good reasons for questioning the way the level of the tax was set. Furthermore, the reasons for setting it at the eventual level have been subject to some misunderstanding, with the Treasury apparently believing that the tax was designed to capture the difference in externalities between incineration and landfill, and with different personnel in the Department of the Environment (DoE, now the Department of the Environment, Transport and the Regions) holding differing opinions as to whether the tax was set on the basis of an absolute measurement of externalities associated with landfill, or on the difference between externalities associated with landfill or incineration. This raises a number of issues concerning presentation.

The setting of the tax should clearly reflect the intentions behind the tax, and should, presumably, influence future decisions as to whether or not the tax should change, either in its magnitude or its scope. The aims of the tax as set out in the UK Waste Strategy are:

> to ensure that landfill costs reflect environmental impact thereby encouraging business and consumers, in a cost effective and non regulatory manner, to produce less waste; to recover value from more of the waste that is produced; and to dispose of less waste in landfill sites. (DoE and WO 1995, p. 12)

From this, it seems clear that the aim of internalizing externalities is the primary one, with the aims of increasing recycling and valorization of waste, and reducing disposal of wastes to landfill subordinate to this aim.

A number of points are worth raising at this juncture. The first is that it would seem odd to tax disposal to landfill without at the same time taxing routes of disposal other than landfill, such as incineration (which currently plays a relatively minor role in waste disposal in the UK, but which may well play a more prominent role in the future, particularly if the Landfill Directive is introduced in its mid-1997 form). One of the reasons this was not considered at the time of introducing the landfill tax was that the work carried out to measure the external costs of landfill (CSERGE et al 1993), which also sought to measure the external costs of incineration, estimated the latter (excluding disamenity costs, and the benefits forgone through not recycling) to be negative (the externalities were positive). An important assumption made in this work was that the energy generated by incineration from waste plants would displace energy from coal-fired power stations, so that incineration would be displacing pollution from these plants. This assumption is questionable in the UK where the 'dash for gas' (the replacement of coal-fired power generation with less-polluting gas-fired sources) has assisted the UK in meeting its greenhouse gas targets.[4] Furthermore, the study placed a zero value on the externality associated with toxic atmospheric pollution, an assumption which is extremely contentious even in the context of tighter standards for emissions on new incineration plants.

Second, the externalities associated with waste disposal have been measured on the basis of the disposal of a typical ton of waste. Quite apart from the fact that in the UK, waste statistics are so poor that one cannot seriously claim to know what a typical ton of landfilled waste looks like, to the extent that the composition of waste disposed to landfill or incinerators changes over time, and to the extent that the externalities of each are heavily influenced by the capacity of each to generate energy, these will actually change over time as the composition of the waste stream changes. Indeed, if recycling rates were to increase, and if putrescible wastes continued to be disposed of in landfill sites, the efficiency of energy production from landfill sites could increase as that from incineration fell. The conclusion which one is forced to draw is that if one was to seek to base waste disposal taxes on the basis of externalities alone, one would be faced with a dynamic problem, with the tax liable to fluctuate with changes in the residual (that which is not re-used or recycled) waste stream and in the market shares of different energy sources.

These concerns raise questions as to the wisdom of the strategy of setting the level of the landfill (or any other environmental) tax on the basis of a measurement of externalities. Indeed, it seems that only in the UK have waste taxes been set with the aim of measuring and internalizing externalities. This pursuit of the Holy Grail, the optimal tax, has been referred to by Daly (1997, p. 18) as an exercise in 'crackpot rigour', and he goes on to eulogize persuasively on the merits of using blunter tools to shift taxation away from labour and on to environmental bads. Such an approach has much to recommend it, particularly in the context of UK waste management where the Landfill Tax could have been used as a tool to meet targets which were set out in the Waste Strategy. After all, where taxes are set on the basis of externalities alone, policy makers may find their hands have been tied by the unwarranted emphasis on internalizing externalities once these have, as far as can be discerned, been captured in their entirety. At present, the UK approach would appear to be leading to an overemphasis on a technocratic approach which denies the yawning gaps which exist between the real world and that of theory.

[4] The basis for this assumption was called into question by later work conducted by CSERGE in association with Coopers & Lybrand (Coopers & Lybrand and CSERGE 1996).

2. ENVIRONMENTAL IMPACT OF THE TAX

2.1 Response and Behaviour of Waste Operatives

ECOTEC surveyed a number of companies in the waste management industry. The major landfill operators vary in the extent of their geographical representation. The largest companies operate collection fleets as well as landfill sites, whilst the medium and small-sized landfill operators tend to rely on waste carriers for their custom. Even where companies have both landfills and collection fleets these tend to operate as different cost centres within a given company so that it is by no means the case that waste collected by one company will be disposed of in a landfill of the same operator. Generally, collection centres will seek the lowest cost route of disposal.

2.2 Pass-through of the Tax

All landfill operators interviewed had passed on the tax in full to their customers. Some had increased charges by an amount greater than the tax, reflecting incremental investment costs associated with administering the tax. Thus, whilst the tax itself was levied at the rates of £2 and £7 per ton, the actual increase in charges for disposal of each ton of waste may have been greater than these figures.

It is important to appreciate the significance of the separation of collection and disposal services. As far as waste producers are concerned, the crucial issue regarding incentives for reducing waste is whether or not waste is weighed at the point of its production, not at its point of disposal. To have the appropriate incentive effect, a tax on landfilled waste would ensure that the tax was levied on the amount of waste being generated by each producer. At present, on-vehicle weighing facilities are the exception rather than the rule and waste is likely to be weighed (if at all) only at the point of disposal, when it has often been aggregated with the waste of other producers.

Many have criticized the lack of any compulsion upon landfill operators to install weighbridges. Even where they are used the fact remains that waste producers will remain largely ignorant of the weight of waste which they produce simply because it is not weighed at the point of collection. Although it was recognized, in advance of the tax, that pass-through of the tax in a form which gave incentives to reduce waste production at the margin would not be possible in the case of household waste (see below), few seemed to appreciate the extent to which this also affects commercial and industrial waste producers.

The tax has had some impact on the way in which companies charge for the collection of waste. Broadly (and it should be noted that the way in which waste collection fees are calculated is far from uniform) the move has been from charging for a container-full of waste, towards a fee which reflects, in some way, the weight of waste produced. For example, one waste management company weighed the containers of its customers from which it was collecting in advance of the tax and assigned them a tax element based on whether their waste was heavy, medium, or light in weight. It will be appreciated from the above that individual companies are not having the tax conveyed to them in such a way as encourages them to reduce waste production at the margin. Two companies in our survey were motivated by the tax to ask for their wastes to be weighed at the point of collection.

Those who see the tax most clearly are the companies who landfill 'in-house'. These operators landfill their own waste and see the impact of the tax directly. The amount of waste disposed of in this manner is believed to be approximately one-third of all waste landfilled.

2.3 Effects in Terms of Waste Management

It is not easy to de-couple the effects of the Landfill Tax on waste management companies from the effects of other policy initiatives affecting waste management. Especially important in this regard are the Packaging Waste (Producer Responsibility) Regulations which require certain obligated companies to achieve targets for the recovery of packaging waste on the basis of the waste that they themselves produce. Yet if it is difficult to do this when the tax is originally implemented, it is probably more difficult when the tax has been in place for a longer period of time, and this may be one of the merits of carrying out an early survey of companies' changes in behaviour resulting from the tax. Evidently there is the danger that one fails to capture the changes which might occur over longer periods of time, but it is clear from our survey that the majority of the sample (see below) were aware of the tax in advance (albeit with differing periods of advance notice).

A number of companies are investing in Materials Recovery Facilities (MRFs). These essentially separate recoverable fractions of waste into component waste streams for use by materials reprocessors. It seems fair to say that these investments are motivated by the landfill tax, but also by schemes designed to help customers meet their obligations under Producer Responsibility. Of eleven companies interviewed, seven reported investment in MRFs. Several applied for planning permission in advance of the tax, and though some companies were moving in this direction anyway, the tax has clearly made investments in MRFs more attractive. Recovery activity is also carried out at transfer stations and landfill sites.

Landfill operators wishing to do so can apply to have part of their site designated as a tax-free area for purposes of sorting and separation of waste. Landfill operators separating materials at the front of their sites can, if they separate inert from active fractions, effectively gain £5 (the difference between the rates for inert and active wastes) for every ton of inert waste separated from a mixed fraction (mixed wastes are, except under specific circumstances, supposed to be treated as active wastes for the purposes of the tax). Similar sorting operations are believed to be occurring in undesignated areas in 'backyard' sites near residential areas (ENDS 1997a, p. 20).

2.4 Experience Regarding Waste Arisings

Landfill operators have been quite vocal concerning the drop-off in inert materials, principally construction wastes, arriving at landfill sites (ESA 1997; Environment Business 1997). These wastes have traditionally been accepted at low or zero charge, but now, they are subject to the tax even if they are used on site. On the basis of a survey of its members, the Environmental Services Association (ESA) estimates that the quantity of construction wastes 'disappearing' from landfill sites will amount to 18 million tons (of an estimated total of 42 million tons – the estimate is from the DoE for 1994) over the course of the first year of the tax's operation. Landfill operators confirm the reduction almost universally. This would appear to have been by far the most important change in landfilled waste tonnages resulting from the tax.

The argument runs that this is an environmentally damaging side-effect of the landfill tax. Two reasons in particular have been given:

1. the lack of inert wastes arriving at landfill sites forces companies to use virgin materials for engineering site roads, hardstanding, screening bunds, and so forth, so increasing resource usage (Wakelin 1997). The same applies with regard to daily cover materials. Alternative cover technologies such as Geohess liners (which use virgin fibre) are more expensive. Similarly, even if these wastes are not used in landfill engineering, the fact that they are simply buried for no particular use prevents them being used in alternative ways; and
2. where inert-only sites are operated, they are becoming (some have already become) unprofitable to run. This may lead to unfilled sites being abandoned, and becoming eyesores.

However, not all landfill operators have incurred costs as a result of this reduction. Indeed, some comment that the reduction in inert wastes has had a beneficial impact in terms of reducing the supply of materials which generate low charges and take up considerable volumes of void space. The potential arises, thereby, for operators to generate greater value from their available void space.[5]

Apart from the issue of inert wastes, landfill operators had little to say concerning the changes in waste disposed to landfill since the tax took effect. Broadly, most landfill operators interviewed seemed to have few problems with the Landfill Tax beyond the issue of inert wastes. Indeed, the tax is welcomed by many larger operators who recognize that the nature of the industry is changing quickly. The latent efforts of the industry to move to more sustainable waste management practices are thus being aroused. Many operators are happy to see the tax increase as it will move the industry into more service-oriented, higher value-added activities, involving, for example, on-vehicle weighing, provision of advice concerning waste minimization, and provision of other services and facilities, especially with regard to recycling.

3. RESPONSE AND BEHAVIOUR OF WASTE PRODUCERS

The following section outlines the responses of the sample of 72 waste producers.

3.1 Awareness of the Tax

Seven companies, or 10 per cent of the sample, stated that they were unaware of the tax in advance. None of these respondents analysed the tax's impact. Of those who showed awareness of the tax in advance (90 per cent the of sample), approximately a third (32 per cent of the total sample) carried out no analysis of the tax's impact. The remaining 58 per cent of the sample analysed the tax's impact in some way. Thus, 42 per cent of the total sample did not examine the impact of the tax in advance. From the responses obtained, there was clearly substantial variation in the advanced knowledge of the tax which companies had. Some companies were aware as much as two years in advance, whereas others became aware only a month or so in advance. It is clear from the responses that at least three waste management companies ran seminars in advance of the tax to inform customers of the tax and how to cope with it. Trade journals and associations were also mentioned as sources of information.

[5] The 'disappearance' of these materials raises questions as to where it actually ends up. Anecdotal evidence points to the use of much of the 'missing' inert wastes inactivities which are exempt from waste management licensing. These include uses for landscaping, bunding, contouring golf courses, farmland improvement, or in construction projects, and other activities.

3.2 Tracking of Waste Costs and Quantities

A number of respondents in our survey were unable to give any reliable indication of the tonnage of waste which they produce. The extent of knowledge shown by companies in our survey is shown in Figure 21.1. There are a large number (44 per cent) of companies who do not know the quantity of waste they produce.[6] Of these 44 per cent, around half (21 per cent of the total) do not know the costs of waste disposal either. They represent the majority of those who do not know the costs of waste disposal.

Figure 21.1. Extent of knowledge of waste tons and waste disposal costs

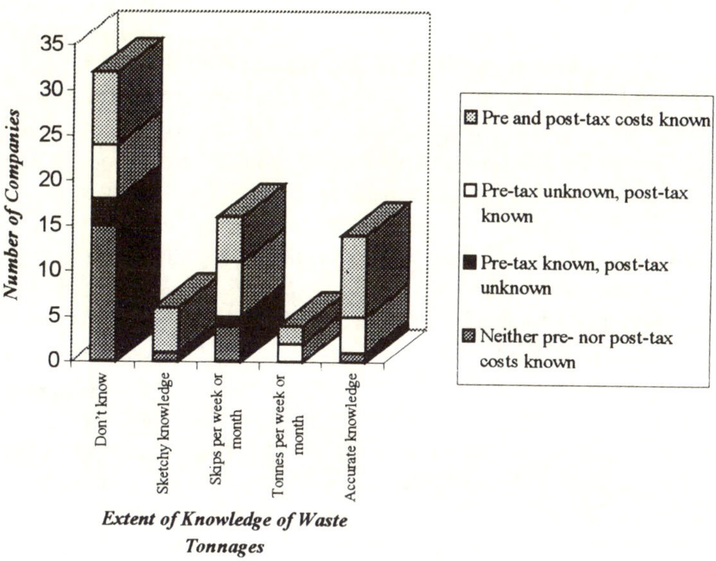

Interestingly, 25 per cent of companies who had no knowledge of the quantity of waste of which they disposed (11 per cent of the total sample) knew both their pre- and post-tax disposal costs. Indeed, 40 per cent of the sample knew their pre-and post-tax disposal costs. By contrast, only 19 per cent were able to give any accurate data about the weight of the wastes which

---

[6] Coincidentally, this is exactly the same figure which was arrived at in an earlier survey conducted for Biffa in advance of the landfill tax. This estimated that although waste was costing UK industry £2.6 billion, some 44 per cent of UK firms did not keep track of waste costs, and over half had no plans for waste minimization (Biffa Waste Services 1994).

they generated, reflecting the limited extent of on-vehicle weighing at present.

Only 6 per cent of the sample were aware of pre-tax costs, but not post-tax costs, but 25 per cent of the sample were aware of post-tax costs but not pre-tax costs. This might be taken as evidence of companies' heightened interest in waste disposal costs in the wake of the tax. There is a suggestion from Figure 21.1 that, consistent with the lack of on-vehicle weighing, more is known about costs than is known about weights. The reaction of some companies to the tax, therefore, has been to simply minimize costs through seeking alternative means of disposal, or separation (of inert and active waste) rather than through waste reduction, re-use and minimization.

3.3 Behavioural Changes in Response to the Tax

Reflecting the picture we have gained of the waste management industry, Figure 21.2 is offered as a way of explaining how the tax has tended to modify waste producers' behaviour. Essentially, because the tax point is the point of waste disposal, it is only at the landfill site that the tax is charged on a per ton basis. Even here, since only 800 or so of more than 1,900 sites registered for the tax have weighbridges installed, rules of thumb have been formalized as a means of assessing the weight of vehicle loads arriving at landfill sites (HM Customs and Excise 1997). Thus, a per ton tax is, as we have seen above, paid only by those delivering the waste to the landfill site (including those who own their own landfill sites), though in some cases, industrial waste producers will be charged at a rate which reflects the marginal cost of each ton of waste produced. The types of pre- and post-tax charging structure employed by the waste carriers were broadly confirmed in the survey of waste producers.

In Figure 21.2, one can visualize the tax's incentive effect as being attenuated by the intermediate collection phase associated with waste management. For most waste producers the cost of producing extra waste is not reflected in the charging structure. Even where a waste producer is billed in part on the basis of some assessment of the weight of waste produced, the waste is probably not, in the majority of cases, weighed at the point of collection to assess the per ton element of disposal costs (for example, a waste carrier may collect waste from a number of waste producers and invoice the waste producers on the basis of the average contribution to the total weight once this has been assessed, not necessarily through weighing, at a landfill site).

Figure 21.2 also shows the behavioural responses open to companies in the wake of the tax taking effect. There are links between the waste producers and collectors, as well as the landfill operators. The information which flows between these actors may affect their respective responses. For example, a waste management company which is more pro-active in its approach to the tax may give advice on waste minimization, or at least, separation of inert and active wastes. Similarly, a waste producer that is well-informed about the tax and its workings may ask to have its waste weighed, or ask to have separate skips for inert and active wastes, presumably reserving the right to switch contractor (assuming the nature of the contract allows this) if responses are unsatisfactory.

Figure 21.2. Behavioural responses to the tax

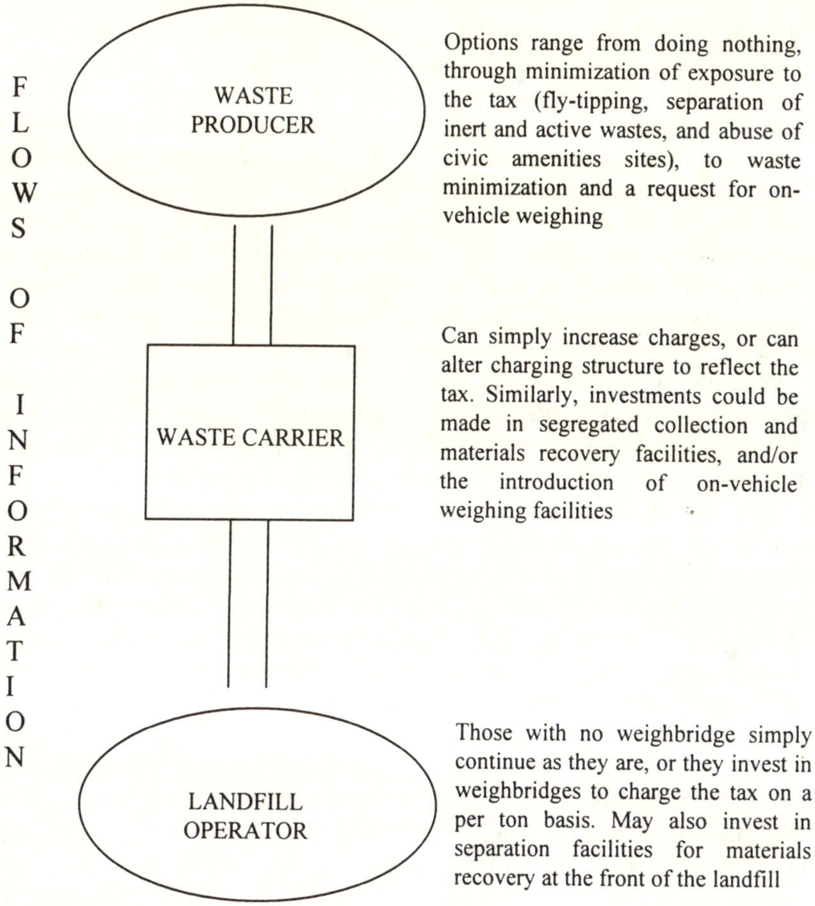

The incentive provided by the tax, which is levied at the site of disposal, is dependent on the nature and quality of the information exchange between the landfill operator and the waste carrier, and the waste carrier and the waste producer. The charging structure and the costs of waste disposal constitute, therefore, but one part of a range of information which the waste producer may receive. The charging structure determines the extent to which the existence of a weight-based tax becomes opaque as far as the waste producer is concerned.

The exchanges of information, and the actors' response to them, will give rise to a variety of arrangements. At one end of the spectrum, one could envisage a site operator with no weighbridge, who assesses weights on the basis of the vehicle used. The carrier conveys limited information concerning the nature of the tax to its customer, and charges the waste producer a fee based primarily on collection of waste and partly on some notional weight-based element supposed to reflect the tax. This weight-based fee will not change on the basis of the weight of waste produced for the simple reason that it cannot because it is never weighed. At the other end of the spectrum, the landfill operator always uses a weighbridge. The carrier conveys good information to customers about the tax and its workings, as well as advice on waste minimization. There is a strengthened rationale for embarking on waste minimization since the benefits of reduced waste accrue to those undertaking the activity. If not already receiving such a service, the waste producer might ask for its waste to be weighed at the site of production.

Whilst the survey sought to understand how far round the virtuous circle companies were, such an exercise does not capture the dynamic response to the tax itself which is of greater interest in the current context than simply discovering how far companies are down the road to waste minimization.

The range of responses prompted by the tax thus far, even in this small sample, is quite considerable. Thirty-one per cent began or stepped up efforts in waste minimization, re-use and recycling, yet 40 per cent of the sample have done nothing in this regard. Five companies implemented waste minimization schemes as a result of the tax. It was notable how, in the foundry sector, the tax prompted investments in attrition, and thermal reclamation units which typically had payback periods of about a year and a half.

Fifteen companies in the survey mentioned the Packaging Directive when asked about other issues concerning waste that were affecting their outlook. Obligated companies are required to recover a percentage of the wastes that they produce under the Producer Responsibility Obligations (Packaging Waste) Regulations. This is leading to a heightened awareness of the need to recycle packaging wastes. Thus, it seems that some of the increased recycling activity is due not to the landfill tax *per se*, but to the combined effect of the tax and the Packaging Regulations.

3.4 Regional Variation

One of the reasons for conducting the survey in different regions at different ends of the landfill charging spectrum was to investigate the extent to which the effect of the tax on behaviour was a reflection of the proportional change in waste disposal costs. The evidence in this regard is examined below and should be placed in the context of the small size of the survey sample. There appears to be some regional variation in the response of companies to the tax (see Figure 21.3). In particular, in the low charge regions, one sees the most positive responses to the tax. This may be a manifestation of the fact that companies' behavioural response to the tax is determined not by the absolute magnitude of the tax *per se* but by the percentage change in disposal costs which this brings about. Further research would be required to confirm whether or not this is the case, and to confirm more rigorously than we were able to do that the nationwide variation in landfill charges is clearly reflected in collection charges.

However, the companies surveyed in Cumbria, one of the lowest landfill charge areas in the country, seemed to be furthest advanced in terms of recycling and waste management in advance of the tax. This highlights the complexity of the issue of behavioural responses to the tax. A number of issues may be significant in determining how companies respond to the challenge of waste management, of which landfill, and more generally, disposal charges are likely to be only one. Indeed, even with full pass-through of the tax, one would not expect a completely 'pricist' view to prevail. From interviews with national companies with large numbers of sites, it seems clear that even within a given company, and even where that company has 'nationwide' guidelines, it is the attitude of individual managers and staff that determines exactly what practices will be followed as regards waste management. To the extent that it is true for different sites within any one company, this is almost certainly true of different companies. Lastly, some regions are believed to be better informed, and better at informing, on waste matters than others through various local authority, and other bottom-up initiatives. One of these, Bristol, actually performs rather badly on the basis of our survey, again cautioning against drawing firm conclusions from such a small survey sample.[7]

[7] Given the interest in the influence of firm size expressed in some of the literature, we did look at companies' responses by firm size in terms of both turnover and number of employees. There was no systematic variation in the sample as a whole by either measure. We did not test (because the sample size was too small) for variation by size accounting for industrial sector.

Figure 21.3. Company behavioural responses disaggregated by region

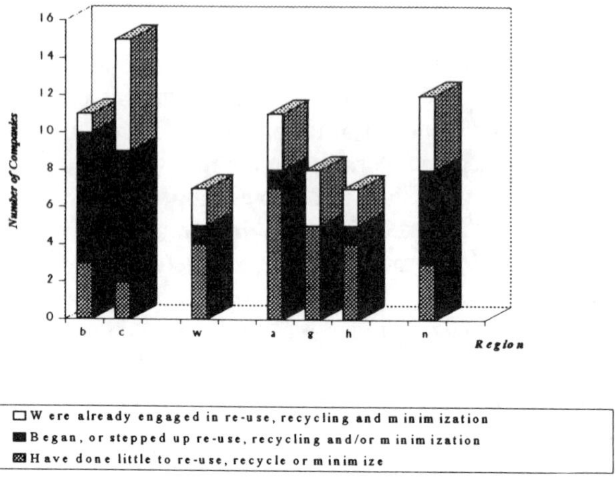

Notes: a = Bristol (high charge), b = Bedfordshire (low charge), c = Cumbria (low charge), g = Greater Manchester (high charge), h = Hampshire (high charge), n = National, w = West Midlands (intermediate charge).

3.5 Effects on Final Product Demand

One of the indirect ways in which the tax would reduce waste arisings would be through its impact on demand for the final product. The extent to which the tax affects demand for any final product will depend on the price elasticity of demand for the product. A principal concern which arises from the study is that the tax is simply lost as noise in the overall cost structure of a given enterprise. Several firms made comments of the type that the tax simply comes off the bottom line reflecting increased disposal costs.[8] No company reported an impact on product pricing outside the construction industry, which internalized the tax either by inclusion at the tendering stage or, in the case of one concrete manufacturer, as a result of a levy. In the food industry, competitive pressures were cited as being such as to make passing costs on impossible, whilst one food retailer commented that the period was one of price deflation in the industry.

The observation that so few cases exist where producers are passing the tax

[8] Other things being equal, this would influence the net revenue generated by the tax through reducing revenues from corporation tax.

through in final product pricing is confirmed by work undertaken by Coopers and Lybrand (Boulton 1997). The reasons for this are easy to see when one appreciates the impact of the tax relative to companies' total turnover. In advance of the tax, rough estimates were provided by MEL (1995) as to the impact of a £5 Landfill Tax on total costs. Typically, the estimated impact was a 0.05 per cent increase in costs. Our results suggest that MEL's estimates were, if anything, on the high side. Table 21.1 gives some figures for industries sampled in our survey. Typically, the tax increases disposal costs by between 50 and 85 per cent (this is not reflected in the average figures), but the cost of waste disposal is of the order of a thousandth of a percent of company turnover.

Table 21.1. Survey results concerning waste disposal costs as a percentage of total costs

Food	0.00029 (0.00027–0.0003) (pre-tax) (2)
	0.0005 (0.0001–0.0009) (post-tax) (4)
Metal goods	0.0035 (0.0007–0.009) (pre-tax) (4)
	0.0038 (0.0002–0.01) (post-tax) (7)
Construction	0.0038 (pre-tax) (1)
	0.004 (0.0009–0.0075) (post-tax) (4)
Education	0.0011 (0.0005–0.0018) (pre-tax as % salaries) (5)
	Two increases reported were 17% and 70%
Clothing and leather	0.0004 (0.0001–0.0006) (pre-tax) (2)
Manufacturing	0.00017 (0.00004–0.0003) (pre-tax) (2)
Mechanical	0.0002 (pre-tax) (1)
Engineering	0.0003 (post-tax) (1)
Non-metallic mineral	0.0007 (pre-tax) (1)
Products	0.006 (0.00075–0.015) (post-tax) (3)
Retailing	0.025 (0.0072–0.033) (post-tax) (3)

Note: Figures given are in the form: average (range)(pre- or post-tax)(number of data points).

Note that the figures for the metal products and construction sectors are higher than in all other sectors but one, retailing. In the metal goods industry, fairly dramatic gains were made due to waste minimization. In construction, there has been some pass-through of costs, especially from small builders. Many retailers are now seeking to reduce wastes they landfill, not least because the larger ones are obligated to recover substantial quantities of packaging waste under Producer Responsibility. Thus, a good deal of back-of-store recycling occurs in which the packaging of materials received at the site are separated so as to meet recovery targets.

It is interesting to reflect on the way the tax has affected waste producers' behaviour. The tax is minuscule in terms of company turnover, yet it has caused approximately one-third of the survey sample to step up activities in minimization, recycling and re-use of wastes. On top of this, other companies have altered behaviour in ways that reduces their exposure to the charge, but does not change the weight of waste disposed to landfill. Examples of such activity include switching waste management company and separating inert and active fractions of waste. It seems surprising that such a small tax, measured in terms of company turnover, can generate such behavioural changes, and this once again suggests that it may be the percentage change in waste disposal costs that drives behavioural response.

4. LOCAL AUTHORITIES

The response of householders to the Landfill Tax was not expected to be significant since householders do not see the tax as such and have little incentive to change their behaviour. The cost to Local Authorities (LAs) of waste disposal is met through residents' payment of a Council Tax, but the Council Tax is an annual payment which is based on the value of the payee's property and (to some extent) income. The Council Tax is intended to cover the costs of a variety of services provided by local government of which waste collection and disposal is only one. The extent to which incentives are awarded to householders to reduce the generation of waste is likely to reflect, in part, the Council's perception of the benefits or costs of embarking on minimization schemes and recycling initiatives.

Two fundamental problems exist in this respect. The first relates to the way in which local government is funded. Many LAs are currently operating at capping limits regarding their annual expenditure, and to spend more on waste management would require them to reduce expenditure on other services. Yet landfill, even with the landfill tax in place, still remains (according to most studies – see Table 21.2) the cheapest option for LAs in most areas (the exceptions being those high-charge areas where the tax has made incineration directly competitive with landfill). Partly for this reason, recycling rates in UK LAs remain low – about 7.5 per cent – despite a target for LAs, set in the Waste Strategy, of 25 per cent.

In terms of altering their behaviour in response to the Landfill Tax, LAs are constrained by the contracts which they have entered into with waste collection and disposal companies in the past which may lock them in to the provision of quantities of waste for disposal over a period of years, or guarantee minimum payments on the basis of a specified amount of waste. This is less an issue of the length of time for which the contract runs – the duration is now set as between 6 and 10 years – more one of the targets and contractual agreements contained within these. However, it is decidedly unhelpful, given the duration of these contracts, that the evolution of the landfill tax should be shrouded in so much uncertainty. Already cash-strapped councils face considerable uncertainty as to the relative costs of different waste management options even as they seek to let contracts which will carry them well into the next millennium.

Other key issues which LAs were expected to face were those related to fly-tipping (illegal dumping on highways, in hedges, on agricultural land and so on) and the abuse of Civic Amenity (CA) sites.[9] NAWDO's survey, to which just over half of the WDAs responded, identified 11.2 million tons of household and commercial waste of which an estimated 99 per cent was landfilled. The average pre-tax landfill charge was £11.93 per ton. The average recycling rate envisaged for the year 1998/99 was 10.5 per cent for 24 Waste Disposal Authorities responding to the question (NAWDO 1997), a level which is well below that of the most advanced European countries.

The survey also suggested that of the 33 returning authorities, only eight indicated increases, or suspected increases in fly-tipping (illegal disposal) whilst nine reported abuse of their civic amenity sites.

Of the six LA regions which ECOTEC surveyed, four gave adequate responses. The structures within which LAs function, alluded to above, appear to be of greater significance than the tax itself. However, all authorities reported increases in the use of CA sites due to their abuse by traders. The picture regarding fly-tipping is less clear. The evidence remains, therefore, largely anecdotal in this respect, partly because the problem had not received any thorough examination before the tax was implemented (though an attempt to do so was made – see Tidy Britain Group 1996). There is, finally, a suspicion that, partly because the incentive to reduce waste is not passed through to those on the municipal collection round, the total waste arisings have increased in three of the LAs interviewed. These issues confirm that the predicament of LAs, which are not entirely devoid of blame for the situation in which they find themselves, is perhaps the most intractable and serious problem facing policy makers in the UK at the end of the millennium. It has to be said that this is due mainly to the lack of attention given to waste matters in past years.

---

[9] CA sites are sites where householders only are allowed to take bulky wastes for disposal free of charge. The abuse has come through small tradespeople using these facilities for (illegal) disposal of trade wastes.

Table 21.2. Cost of alternative waste disposal options (£/ton)

	Cost per ton (£)				
Option	Coopers & Lybrand (1993)		MEL (1995)[4]	Holmes (1996)[5]	W.S. Atkins (1993)
	Current	Future			
Landfill (pre-tax)			1–3 (inert) 8–10 (ind & comm) 5–8	8–10 (gen. Comm and ind) 5–8 5–8	7.50–22.50
Urban high cost	22.5	31–47[1]			
Rural high cost	15	22–35[1]			
Urban low cost	10	15–24[1]			
Rural low cost	7.5	11–18[1]			
Incineration				18	
Mass incineration	15–20	20–25[2]			
WTE incineration with NFFO	20–30	20–25[3]			20–25 (17.50–28.80)
Without NFFO	(25–30)-(35–40)	(25–30)-(30–35)			30–35 (26.53–39.09)
Recycling					
Bring	16–36	16–36			
Blue box	85–175	85–175			
Green bin	55–70	55–70			
Green bag	55–75	55–75			
Composting	35–50	35–50			

Notes :

1 Range of landfill costs over next ten years see Section II of the Coopers report.
2 Likely costs if existing incinerators are fitted with the emission control equipment required after 1996.
3 The figures for future costs assumed that NFFO would continue to be available; without NFFO, the estimates would have been £5 to £10 per ton higher.
4 MEL's estimates were based on work by Howard Humphreys (inert wastes), WDA sites in the Midlands (commercial and industrial wastes and other hard core, foundry sand and soil).
5 Landfill figures are for LAWDCs and private sites in the West Midlands. Incineration figure from LAWDC plant for industrial and commercial waste.

5. DATA FOR THE DATALESS INDUSTRY

Before the tax was brought into force, there was some conjecture that Department of the Environment figures, which had remained largely static for a number of years, were off target. One spokesperson for one of the major waste management companies suggested that the weight of waste being landfilled would be something of the order of 70–80 million tons rather than the 100 million or so estimated by the DoE.

A major positive spin-off of the tax is that it is generating revenue data, from which can be calculated the weight of waste currently being landfilled. Recent revenue statistics from HM C&E are shown in Table 21.3.

Table 21.3. Revenue raised by the landfill tax and imputed tons

	£ Millions			Millions of tons		
	Standard Rate	Lower Rate	Total	Standard Rate	Lower Rate	Total
Original forecast	420	80	500	60	40	100
Anticipated returns	356	74	420	51	37	88

Source: ENDS (1997b)

The tax revenue is clearly below that which was anticipated in advance of the tax due to the fact that the active waste fraction, and to a lesser extent, the inert wastes too, have been lower than anticipated. The optimistic view is that this is entirely a consequence of the stimulus given to recycling, re-use and minimization. More realistically, the pre-tax guesstimates relied more on 'guess' than 'estimation', and there are significant problems when one tries to square existing statistics with those being generated by the Landfill Tax. This appears to have given added impetus and urgency to the exercise of gathering statistics concerning UK waste arisings and disposal.

6. INCREASING THE TAX'S EFFECTIVENESS

Environmental taxes are likely to create new problems, and in some cases, exacerbate old ones, largely through encouraging activities that amount to evasion of the charge. This is one of the drawbacks associated with the use of economic instruments which is all too rarely mentioned in discussions concerning the relative merits of regulatory and market-based approaches to environmental policy. Viewed in isolation, market-based instruments create incentives which encourage actors to change their behaviour in environmentally beneficial ways. Yet these instruments do not work in isolation, and in the context of the overall incentive structure, which is composed of regulations, laws and price-based incentives (to mention only the main influences), the same instruments encourage actors to seek loopholes which can nullify attempts to create incentives for positive changes as regards the environment.

It also seems likely that complementary instruments will be necessary to lubricate the wheels of behavioural change which economic instruments seek to encourage. Elasticities are not set in stone. They are amenable to manipulation through the use of such instruments. Examples of ways in which the effectiveness of the tax could be increased are considered below.

1. *Using the tax explicitly as a means to encourage behavioural change so as to meet waste strategy targets rather than a means of internalising prices*. Targets for reduction in landfilled waste exist in the UK's Waste Strategy. A target-based approach gives policy makers leeway to alter the level of the tax (and they are currently reviewing the level). Logical consistency would demand that, since the tax has been set on the basis of externalities, then since these have already been internalized, the level of the tax should not be changed.
2. *Tax other disposal routes, specifically (if the landfill tax is to increase), in the short term, incineration.* The costs of landfilling vary across the UK. With the landfill tax in place, incineration is becoming price competitive in high-cost (of landfill) areas. Many fear that local authorities, with responsibility for disposal of domestic waste, will simply switch their reliance away from landfill and towards incineration. If the landfill tax is to be truly a tax on waste, the intention must be expressed to tax incineration if the landfill tax increases. This would send a clear signal to local authorities and help them in their financial planning.
3. *Review current banding to revoke 'exemptions' (those categories of waste which, due to effective lobbying, were taxed at the lower rate as opposed to the standard rate)*. In the political negotiations leading up to the setting of landfill tax rates, several types of waste were granted exemptions from the higher rate of the tax. These should be reviewed with a view to phasing some of them out in the short to medium term.
4. *Review the activities currently exempt from Waste Management Licensing, so as to encourage re-use of construction and demolition wastes.* The government is in the process of considering the virtues of a tax on virgin aggregates with a view to, amongst other things, increasing the extent of recycling of construction wastes. A major loophole exists at present whereby, within certain limits, such wastes can be buried under ongoing developments even where this results in the loss of potentially recyclable material (and landfill tax revenue) to spurious uses of the

material. Anecdotes concerning elaborately landscaped golf courses and houses being built higher off the ground have emerged over the last year or so. Neither the landfill tax, nor the aggregates tax, will be able to stimulate recycling of construction wastes unless present exemptions are removed or revised.

5. *Stimulate the recycling market by setting targets for use of recycled materials, especially within government procurement policy.* The government could seek to stimulate the market for recyclables through making the use of recycled materials a necessary component of any successful bid for government contracts. Without such stimulation, the UK recyclables market is likely to experience a crisis as recovered material outstrips re-processing capacity.
6. *Change the primary legislation to allow local authorities to embark upon variable charging schemes.*[10] It is clear that several LAs are already interested in these schemes, and a positive Resolution in this regard has already been passed in Bath and North East Somerset. A number of countries now have experience with unit pricing of municipal waste (Miranda et al. 1994, 1996; McLellan 1994; Skou Andersen 1997). Experience with these schemes has been varied, but one condition that seems necessary, though not sufficient, for their successful operation is the functioning of aggressive recycling schemes. A number of issues are worthy of close attention, including those of the physical practicalities of such schemes, and problems of collection of such charges. However, such schemes are already attracting the attention of some local authorities who are currently unable even to pilot these schemes.
7. *Earmark a portion of the tax for regulatory activities.* The Environment Agency has responsibility for policing on waste related issues. As mentioned above, economic instruments, whilst having the potential to drive positive innovation, also drive innovative behaviour regarding the evasion of taxes and charges. There are currently concerns relating to fly-tipping, the spreading of organic wastes on agricultural land, and the abuse of civic amenity sites. Although (given the paucity of good statistics) some of these concerns are largely conjectural at present, some of the tax revenue might usefully be earmarked for the regulatory work of the Environment Agency.

[10] It might also be desirable to take expenditure on waste management out of the Council Tax umbrella so that aims to recover costs of waste disposal options which are currently more expensive need not have negative effects on other local services.

7. CONCLUSION

The account above suggests that the Landfill Tax has been successful in pushing some 30 per cent of firms towards more responsible approaches to waste matters. Indeed, in our survey, some firms are taking significant steps not just to reducing their disposal costs, but reducing the wastes they generate in the first place. A number of other firms indicated that they were already moving in this direction, so presumably, the tax simply made these efforts more worthwhile. However, waste disposal costs are still a tiny fraction of companies' total costs. Slightly less heartening, therefore, but somewhat understandable, is the fact that this is only one end of a spectrum of responses which includes a number who indicate little or no willingness to reduce the wastes they produce. The gulf between best and worst practice, even between apparently similar firms in a given industry, is huge. Even so, the Landfill Tax has been important in bringing about a change in attitudes regarding waste management in the UK. Most significantly, it is the type of policy instrument that more forward-thinking waste management companies have been keen to see implemented to move their activities towards the higher value-added end of the spectrum.

Problems with the landfill tax relate to the increase in abuse of civic amenity sites, the anecdotal evidence that suggests increased fly-tipping, the problems facing local authorities in terms of funding waste management, and the issues surrounding the disappearance of inert, and possibly other wastes through activities exempt from waste management licensing. The review of the tax currently under way after a year of its operation takes place following a commitment made in the new government's first Budget to re-visit the tax. There is recognition that the tax is not without its problems, and that there is much that could be done to improve its environmental effectiveness.

However, these changes will need to be located within a more coherent policy regarding waste management for the UK as a whole. For rather too long, the UK approach has amounted to filling holes in the ground. The Waste Strategy contains a number of targets, but commitment to meet these has been lacking, despite the fact that they are far from onerous. The Landfill Tax is one of a few national initiatives undertaken since the Strategy was launched and it has the potential to play an important role in the future of UK waste management if it evolves in an appropriate manner in the context of complementary instruments.

REFERENCES

Anon (1997), 'Agency Accused of Chasing its Tail in War Against Flytippers', *The Waste Manager*, May, p.7.

Biffa Waste Services (1994), *Waste: A Game of Snakes and Ladders: A Benchmarking Report on Waste and Business Strategy*, High Wycombe: Biffa Waste Services.

Boulton, Leyla (1997), 'Landfill Tax Fails To Reduce Amount of Waste', *Financial Times*, Friday 6 June.

Coopers & Lybrand (1993), *Landfill Costs and Prices: Correcting Possible Market Distortions*, London, HMSO.

Coopers & Lybrand and CSERGE (1996), *Cost–benefit Analysis of the Different Municipal Solid Waste Management Systems*, Final Report, March, Luxembourg: Office for Official Publications of the European Communities.

CSERGE, Warren Spring Laboratory and EFTEL (1993), *Externalities for Landfill and Incineration: A Study by CSERGE, Warren Spring Laboratory and EFTEL*, London: HMSO.

Daly, Herman (1997), 'Reconciling Internal and External Policies for Sustainable Development', in Andrew K. Dragun and Kristin M. Jakobsson (eds), *Sustainability and Global Environmental Policy: New Perspectives*, Cheltenham, UK, and Lyme, US: Edward Elgar, pp. 11–31.

DoE and WO (Department of the Environment and the Welsh Office) (1995), *Making Waste Work: A Strategy for Sustainable Waste Management in England and Wales*, London: HMSO.

ECOTEC (1997), *Effectiveness of the Landfill Tax in the UK: Barriers to Increased Effectiveness and Options for the Future*, A Final Report for Friends of the Earth, Birmingham: ECOTEC.

European Foundation for the Improvement of Livng and Working Conditions (forthcoming), *Employment and Sustainability: The UK Landfill Tax*, Dublin: EFILWC.

ENDS (1997a), 'Pluses and Minuses From the Landfill Tax', *ENDS Report* **265**, February, pp.18–21.

ENDS (1997b), 'Less Waste Than Expected Leaves £80 Million Hole in Landfill Tax Revenue', *ENDS Report* **274**, November, p.13.

Environment Business (1997), 'Construction Waste: Treasury Loss – £36 m/yr.', *Environment Business*, 8 May, p.4.

ESA (Environmental Services Association) (1997), 'Press Release: Treasury "Loses" £36 Million Landfill Tax Revenue as Government's Fiscal and Environmental Policies Conflict', 1 April.

HM Customs and Excise (1996), 'Landfill Tax: The Landfill Tax (Qualifying

Material) Order 1996', *Statutory Instruments*, No. 1528.

HM Customs and Excise (1997), 'Landfill Tax: A General Guide to the Landfill Tax', *Notice LFT1*, February.

Her Majesty's Stationary Office (1994), 'The Waste Management Licensing Regulations 1994', *Statutory Instruments*, No. 1056, Environmental Protection, London: HMSO.

Holmes, John (1996), *The United Kingdom Waste Management Industry Report 1996*, London: Institute of Waste Management.

McLellan, D. (1994), 'Weight Based Rates: Collecting Wastes Canadian Style', *World Wastes*, **37**(3), March, pp.32–5.

MEL (1995), *Analysis of Industrial and Commercial Waste Going to Landfill in the UK*, London: HMSO.

Miranda, M..L., Everett, J.W, Blume, D and Roy, B.A. (1994), 'Market-based Incentives and Residential Municipal Solid Waste', *Journal of Policy Analysis and Management*, **13**(4), pp.681–698.

Miranda, M.L. Bauer, S.D. and Aldy, J.E. (1996), *Unit Priclng Programs for Residential Municipal Solid Waste: An Assessment of the Literature*, Research Products from US EPA Cooperative Agreement #CR822-927-010, Durham, NC: School of the Environment, Duke University.

National Association of Waste Disposal Authorities (1997), NAWDO 'Landfill Tax Questionnaire', Unpublished survey.

Riley, C.J. (1996), 'The New UK Landfill Tax', in EFILWC (European Foundation for the Improvement of Living and Working Conditions), *Environmental Taxes and Charges: National Experiences and Plans: Papers from the Dublin Workshop*, Dublin: European Foundation for the Improvement of Living and Working Conditions, pp.231–42.

Skou Andersen, Mikael (1997), 'The Danish Waste Tax: The Role of Institutions for the Implementation and Effectiveness of Economic Instruments', Paper presented at the International Workshop on the Institutional Aspects of Economic Instruments for Environmental Policy, Eigtveds Pakhus, Copenhagen, 20–21 May.

Wakelin, Ian (1997), 'The Landfill Tax: Effects and Developments Within Industry', Presentation to Parliamentary Group on Sustainable Waste Management's Annual Conference 'Regulations, Directives and Markets', 5 June.

W.S. Atkins (1993), *An Assessment of Mass Burn Incineration Costs*, A Report for Energy and Technology Support Unit Prepared by W.S. Atkins Consultants, ETSU B RI/00341/REP.

22. Environmental and Economic Implications of Market-based Instruments in Portugal – Discussion and Examples

Rui Santos, Paula Antunes and Sandra Martinho

1. INTRODUCTION

In this chapter the current key environmental issues in Portugal and the environmental policy approach followed in the last decade are described, focussing on the current use of market-based instruments, obstacles to implementation and potential for greater use. Two case studies about, respectively, the tax reduction on low-sulfur content fueloil and on unleaded gasoline, are also presented, as well as a prospective view of the impact of the application of the tax on solvents to reduce volatile organic compound (VOC) emissions in three Portuguese industries: pharmaceutical, paint and printing.

1.1 State of the Environment[1]

Environmental quality in Portugal is generally good and important natural endowments are still available, more as a result of the development stage of the country than effective environmental policy. However, degradation of water, air, soil and coastal ecosystems has arisen, primarily as a result of unplanned land use and inadequate environmental management practices, associated with the increased density of population and economic activities in the coast. Although the situation still compares favorably with many EU Member States, the recent fast economic growth and the need to maintain it

[1] Sections 2, 3 and 4 are partially based on a previous work by the authors Santos andAntunes (1998), 'Using Markets to Manage the Environment in Portugal', in*Making Markets Work for the Environment*, Edited by Frank Convery and Sheenagh Rooney, Environmental Institute, University College Dublin, Ireland.

in the future require a particular attention to environmental policy in order to guarantee a sustainable development in the country.

Current key environmental concerns can be summarized in the following:

- Inadequate quantity and quality of water in certain areas, as a result of unfavorable climatic conditions, with a non-uniform distribution in time and space, high spatial concentration of water needs, poor management of the resource (for example, absence of wastewater treatment facilities and of consideration of the full social cost into individuals' and firms' decision making), and dependence on water courses from Spain. This is one of the main environmental concerns of the general public in Portugal.
- Increased production of solid and liquid wastes, as a result of the recent economic growth and changing consumption patterns, requiring a fast increase and improvement in collection, disposal and treatment infrastructures, including the eradication of unregulated landfills and uncontrolled effluent discharges in water bodies.
- Degradation of air quality in some urban and industrialized centers. The rapid increase in road traffic in many urban centers is worrying, as is the increase in emissions per unit of GDP, caused by the combustion of fossil fuels.
- Increased soil erosion, mainly in the south, as a result of climate conditions associated with inadequate agricultural and forest practices. Also increase in fertilizer use by farmers contributes to soil contamination, eutrophication of lakes, and pollution of water courses.
- Increased pressure for tourism and urban development in coastal areas, threatening the equilibrium in some coastal ecosystems, such as dune strips and wetlands, which have a high nature conservation value.

2. ENVIRONMENTAL POLICY

2.1 Framework and Goals

Portuguese environmental policy began officially in 1971, with the creation of the National Environmental Commission. The 1976 Portuguese Constitution made environmental protection a civic duty, guaranteeing the citizens a 'right to the environment', which can be invoked before the courts, but environmental policy was only fully recognized in 1987 with the approval of the Basic Environmental Law. The Ministry for the Environment and Natural Resources was created in January 1991.

Since 1987, the basic legal framework was created, followed by legislation for the different environmental sectors incorporating environmental quality and emission standards, together with provisions for charging for resource use. Most of these laws are not a consequence of an environmental strategy guided by the principles of the Basic Environmental Law (for example, the polluter-pays and user-pays principles), but were prompted by the country's accession to the European Community. However, their regulation is not yet fully completed and associated with the lack of enforcement capacity, this has constrained their application and environmental efficacy. Recently, an Environmental Inspectorate, coordinated by a Magistrate, was created to improve enforcement capabilities.

The first Portuguese National Environmental Policy Plan, presented in 1994, considers the attainment of sustainable development as the strategic environmental policy goal. Although it is acknowledged that environmental policy should be essentially preventive, existing situations of poor environmental quality have forced authorities to focus their attention on their recovery and on the adoption of emission-control actions based mainly on end-of-pipe approaches.

Recognizing the economic and technological difficulties that many industries face in order to comply with environmental regulations, priority has been given to the adoption of sectoral agreements, which establish scheduled targets and incentives to comply.

2.2 Current Use of Economic Instruments

The application of economic instruments for environmental policy in Portugal is still at a very early stage, where most instruments are still being assessed. In current use are the following:

- The single explicit product-oriented economic instruments currently applied are the fiscal incentives (tax reduction) on unleaded gasoline and on low-sulfur content fueloil. The government decided from 1991 to grant a deduction in the tax on petrol-based products (ISP) to unleaded gasoline, relative to the value charged to leaded gasoline. A tax reduction on ISP was also established in order to promote the substitution of high-sulfur contents (HSC) fueloil by low-sulfur contents (LSC) fueloil. Mineral oils obtained from recycling of used oils also have a fiscal incentive which is implemented through the application of a zero ISP tax.
- Legislation from 1990 sets down the authorization to tax point source atmospheric emissions, through an earmarked charge whose revenues are allocated to the implementation of emission-control technologies and improvement of the air quality monitoring network. However, these charges have not yet been applied because the specific regulations were

not produced. There is also a tax incentive for the installation of equipment and technologies for emission control, decided on a case-by-case basis.

- The water resources management laws (from 1990) establish general emission standards, penalties for non-compliance and refer to the user-pays principle. The economic and financial regimen for the use of the public water domain, defining the charges for water and inert material extraction, occupation of terrains or water plans, and wastewater disposal was published in 1994, but the unit charge values for some uses (such as effluent discharges) have not yet been established, being equal to zero to other uses (for example, water extraction), thus negating its efficacy. That law also establishes that all users of the public water domain should have a use license to which the payment of a charge is associated. Specific economic incentives for the installation of equipment and the development of water pollution-control technologies were also established. Municipalities charge water consumption, based mainly on the desire to combine socially oriented concerns with an average pricing approach, not taking into account the resource scarcity and its time and space variation. A tax on domestic wastewater discharge also exists in many municipalities, often calculated as a function of the property value, without any relation to the effluent flows and pollutant loads. A tax on wastewater discharge in municipal sewerage systems by industries is also sometimes applied, usually calculated in order to cover average O&M costs of existing facilities. This type of charge is also applied in some cases for the use of joint (or regional) treatment plants. The studies for the Watershed Management Plans that are under preparation will provide information about the users, the scarcity value of water and the damage caused by water uses, useful for the application of market-based instruments for water resources management.
- Solid waste policy has been related mostly to the transposition of EC Directives for domestic and hazardous wastes and packaging materials. The National Plan for Solid Waste Management, from 1997, considers as a priority the implementation of the full-cost principle in the collection, disposal and treatment of solid waste, through the application of municipal solid waste charges with incentives for separative collection. Some municipalities have already set user charges for solid waste disposal, calculated usually in order to cover O&M costs of existing collection and treatment services.
- A number of programs provide financial incentives to promote the adoption of single or joint solutions for pollution control at the industrial and/or municipal level (for example, the Regional Development Plan, 1994–99; PEDIP II Program – Strategic Program for the Dynamization

and Modernization of Portuguese Industry; POA – Operational Program for the Environment).

- Currently there is a fiscal incentive for the acquisition of tools, machines and other equipment for solar or geothermal energy generation, for the generation of energy from wastes, for the use of natural gas and for pollution measurement or control costs, which is expressed as a reduced value-added tax rate of 5 percent. Personal expenditure on renewable energy forms also has some fiscal benefits, translated into a small deduction in income tax (up to a defined ceiling).

3. POTENTIAL FOR, AND OBSTACLES TO, THE INCREASED USE OF ECONOMIC INSTRUMENTS

In Portugal a rapid economic growth is taking place, with the corresponding pressure on the environment, but financial resources for environmental protection are scarce. In this context, the application of economic instruments is essential to improve the efficiency and effectiveness of environmental policy, but some key issues have to be addressed, such as the fiscal approach, sectoral policies, environmental regulations, environmental information and attitudes.

3.1 Fiscal Approach and Structure and Integration with Other Sectoral Policies

Tax reform in Portugal has been aimed at improving administrative efficiency and decreasing tax evasion. The goal is not to promote an eco-tax reform, which should be considered a fundamental issue in the implementation of an integrated environmental management approach, but instead to assure the maintenance of the revenue base through traditional sources. Nevertheless, there are some factors favoring the introduction of economic instruments from a fiscal point of view:

- The control of the general budget deficit and public debt are governmental priorities, which increase the attractiveness of environmental taxes as new sources of revenue.
- The improvements achieved in the efficiency of fiscal administration associated with large experience in the collection of indirect taxes, could reduce the initial costs of the eco-tax systems.
- The high value of taxes on labor, social security and income, creates the potential, for instance, to move the taxes from labor to the use of environmental resources, attaining a 'double dividend'.

- The increasing role of regional and local bodies in environmental policy can improve the acceptability of a policy based on charging the full cost for resource use.

Apart from these, some other factors have hindered the introduction of economic instruments, such as the lack of cooperation between ministries, and the fear within the administration that such an approach would adversely affect the competitiveness of Portuguese economic agents, which is not compatible with the objective of avoiding any risk to economic growth efforts. The difficulties of integration with sectoral policies, namely industrial, agricultural, transport and energy should also be mentioned.

3.2 Existing Environmental Regulations

Current EC and national environmental legislative framework based on a command and control approach, imposing emission and technological standards, can also be seen as a constraint to the acceptance and operationalization of market-based instruments. This framework should be made more flexible in order to improve compatibility with market mechanisms.

3.3 Environmental Database and Monitoring System

Lack of information about environmental quality, resources scarcity, damage valuation and the estimated economic impact of market-based instruments, are other factors which constrain the adoption of a market-based environmental policy. For example, the systematic economic evaluation of environmental impacts has not been adopted in Portugal, although for some specific projects, namely those financed by the European Regional Fund, cost-benefit analysis (CBA) was performed. Additional studies and improvements in the monitoring network are fundamental to supply better environmental/ economic information for decision making.

3.4 Stakeholders and Public Attitudes

Surveys of Portuguese attitudes toward the environment (Dunlap 1994; Barata 1998) showed the increased recognition of both the importance of a high-quality resource base for future development and economic growth, and the requirement to increase prices of products to pay for this.

However, until now the application of market-based incentives has not had the support of economic agents and the government. Economic agents, for example in the industrial sector, have been objected to the application of emission taxes or tradable permits, arguing that these would entail extra production costs with effects in competitiveness due to the economic and technological difficulties faced by some major activity sectors. This argument is generally accepted by the government.

Public companies and agencies usually follow an average cost pricing approach, for example for infrastructures services. Sometimes the generated revenues do not even fully cover capital costs, since the main objective is to charge operation costs. The pricing rules are also based on income redistribution objectives, which are usually dominant over the economic efficiency criterion.

4. TAX DIFFERENTIAL ON UNLEADED GASOLINE AND LOW-SULFUR CONTENT (LSC) FUELOIL

4.1 LSC Fueloil

Under Portuguese SO_2 emission control policy, an economic incentive was established in order to promote the substitution of HSC fueloil (with more than 1 percent sulfur) by LSC fueloil, thus contributing to a pollution source reduction approach. This incentive was implemented as a reduction of the tax on oil products (ISP) for LSC.

Table 22.1. Evolution of fueloil prices (in PTE $/kg)

	1994		1995		1997		
	July 1	Oct 6	Apr 3	Aug 8	Mar 6	April 3	May 29
HSC Fueloil	26.3	25.5	28	26	32.5	31.5	31
LSC Fueloil	31	28	29	28.5	35	34.5	33.5
Tax differential	3	3	3	3	3	3	3
ISP/HSC price (%)	21	21.6	19.6	21	16.9	17.5	17.7
ISP/LSC price (%)	8.1	9	8.6	8.8	7.1	7.2	7.5

Sources: Directorate General for Energy (DGE) – 'Estatísticas Rápidas' and 'Preços da Energia'; DGE, Statistical Department.

From 1991 to 1996, the market transactions of HSC fueloil were conditioned to a maximum market price system (MMP) and LSC fueloil price had a free price regimen. In the period 1991–94, the ISP unit tax for HSC was calculated indirectly from the fixed MMP and was variable within a range of PTE $1–10/kg.[2] Unit ISP tax for LSC fueloil had a reduction of PTE $3/kg. After July 1994, a fixed ISP unit tax system was established, with a value of PTE $2.5/kg for LSC, and PTE $5.5/kg for HSC fueloil, thus maintaining the tax differential.

The legislator assumed that 'in what concerns low sulfur contents fueloil, it is justified to keep the existing differential, which is sufficient to assure its progression in the market, compared with the most polluting product'. New legislation from 1996, abolished the MMP system maintaining the values of ISP for LSC and HSC fueloil, thus keeping the fiscal incentive.

A sample of the average fueloil sale prices, computed by the General Directorate for Energy (DGE), for the period between July 1994 and May 1997 is presented in Table 22.1, showing also the tax differential value, and the weight of ISP on HSC and LSC prices. The share of taxes (including VAT) in the market price in July 1997 was about 28.4 percent for HSC and 18 percent for LSC.

In spite of the fiscal incentive, LSC fueloil average sales price is PTE $2–4/kg higher than HSC prices. The fiscal incentive has not been fully translated into a market price differential, which is the relevant variable for consumers' decision making. This can be justified by differences in production costs and profit margins.

Table 22.2 shows the evolution of LSC fueloil domestic market share between 1990 and 1995, according to data from Petrogal, the largest Portuguese oil company.

Table 22.2. Petrogal data for fueloil domestic market (in ktons)

	1990	1991	1992	1993	1994	1995*
LSC fueloil	–	49	180	284	315	393
HSC fueloil	3,506	3,604	4,305	3,256	2,835	3,166
LSC market share (%)	–	1.30	4	8	10	11

**Note*: Forecast.

Source: Petrogal (1995).

Since the introduction of the incentive, LSC fueloil sales have increased considerably (for example, 267 percent in 1991–92 and 58 percent in 1992–93), compared to HSC fueloil. DGE statistics did not distinguish between LSC and HSC fueloils before 1994, but according to data from the period 1994–97, LSC fueloil has an increasing but still low market share (Table 22.3).

[2]An indicative exchange rate ECU $1 = PTE $195 can be considered.

Table 22.3. DGE data for fueloil domestic market (in ktons)

	1994	1995	1996	1997*
LSC fueloil	273	339	380	216
HSC fueloil	2,781	3,310	2,345	1,109
Total	3,054	3,649	2,725	1,325

**Note* January–June 1997: preliminary data.

Source: DGE, Statistical Department (1995).

Data concerning fueloil imports and exports are presented in Table 22.4. The commercial balance of fueloil products is in deficit (1,353 ktons). LSC fueloil accounted for 60 percent of total exports. LSC imports in the same period were very low, since about 80 percent of LSC supply in the domestic market comes from Petrogal refineries, and only the remaining is imported by the other two companies in the LSC fueloil market: Shell (and Leacock), with a 15.6 percent market share, and CEPSA with 4.5 percent. There are a larger number of suppliers of HSC fueloil, although 83 percent of domestic market is shared by the two biggest companies: Petrogal and Shell (and Leacock). Oil companies are interested in promoting LSC fueloil sales, since they can provide higher profit margins when compared to HSC.

Table 22.4. Fueloil imports and exports (in ktons)

	Imports			Exports		
	1,994	1,995	1,996	1,994	1,995	1,996
LSC Fueloil	52	51	111	964	629	246
HSC Fueloil	1,341	1,813	1,035	640	244	327
Total	1,393	1,864	1,146	1,604	873	573

Source: DGE, Statistical Department.

On the demand side, the Portuguese Electrical Company (EDP) is the major consumer of fueloil, for power generation. Table 22.5 shows that EDP has a very significant share in the domestic market, consuming only HSC fueloil, with 3.5 percent sulfur content and, in some circumstances, with about 3 percent sulfur, in order to comply with emission standards. EDP is exempt from ISP and so the fiscal incentive is not effective in this case.

Table 22.5. Domestic demand (in ktons)

	1990	1991	1992	1993	1994	1995	1996*	1997*
1.Industry	1,564	1,599	1,603	1,625	1,831	2,059	2,220	1,170
LSC fueloil		49	180	284	315	393	–	–
HSC fueloil		1,551	1,423	1,341	1,516	1,666	–	–
2.EDP	1,942	2,054	2,882	1,915	1,319	1,500	758	315
Domestic market (1+2)	3,506	3,653	4,485	3,540	3,150	3,559	2,978	1,485
EDP Market share (%)	55.4	56.2	64.3	54	42	42	25.4	21.2

**Note*: Data from DGE (1997): preliminary data for January–June.

Source: Petrogal (1995) and DGE.

Cogeneration units are the major consumers of LSC fueloil, with a significant increase in demand in the last years. Almost all units are linked to the REN (National Electrical Network), and therefore do not pay ISP, adopting LSC fueloil because of technological constraints.

In 1994, 20 percent of LSC fueloil sales (about 50 ktons) from Petrogal were exempt of ISP. If this is considered together with the 1,319 ktons consumed by EDP, at least a total amount of 1,369 ktons of fueloil, corresponding to 43 percent of the total market, were exempt of ISP. This is a low estimate, since it does not take into account LSC fueloil sales by the other two oil companies to cogeneration units.

The detailed assessment of the environmental efficacy of this instrument is not possible with the available data, due to the lack of information regarding SO_2 emissions from fuel consumption and difficulties in identifying changes in consumption patterns induced by the tax incentive. Table 22.6 shows the values of SO_2 emissions adopting an average HSC fueloil sulfur content of 2.83 percent, and the reductions attained with the introduction of LSC fueloil between 1990 and 1993.

The figures presented show that fuel substitution already has some impact on total SO_2 emissions. However, the estimated potential for emission reductions from fuel substitution, assuming that all consumers could adopt LSC fueloil, in 1993, is 130 ktons, from which only 10.5 ktons (8 percent) were attained.

Table 22.6. SO_2 emissions and reduction (in ktons)

	1990	1991	1992	1993
SO_2 total emissions	282.3	290.1	345.9	290.3
Obtained reduction	0	1.8	6.6	10.5
Reduction (%)	0	0.62	1.92	3.6

Source: Institute of Meteorology (1995).

In summary, in spite the ISP tax reduction, the average LSC price is higher than the HSC price, and so unless the operational performance of LSC is better, no rational consumer will prefer it. The power generation sector is tax exempt and so does not benefit from the tax advantage associated with LSC fueloil, which still has a very low market share, although its sales have increased considerably since the introduction of the incentive. In the future the efficacy and need for this instrument will tend to be reduced with the adoption of new EC regulations which will impose the adoption of a maximum sulfur content of 1.5 percent.

Oil companies' commercial policy, as well as technological constraints on the demand side, seem until now to have had a more effective role in the promotion of LSC fueloil consumption than the economic incentive provided by the ISP tax reduction. In fact, the relevant increases in LSC consumption have been in those segments – cogeneration, glass industries, and so on – where there are technological constraints.

4.2 Unleaded Gasoline

Unleaded gasoline was introduced in Portugal in 1989, and until 1991 both leaded and unleaded gasoline were under a maximum market price (MMP) regime. In 1991, in order to reduce lead emissions, the government eliminated the MMP regime for unleaded gasoline and granted a deduction of PTE $12/liter in the tax on petrol-based products (ISP), relative to the value charged to leaded gasoline (determined indirectly, according to a defined formula, after the MMP has been fixed, but with the restriction to be between PTE $77–109 per liter).

Legislation from 1994 fixed the ISP unit taxes for leaded (in the range PTE $77–99 per liter) and unleaded gasoline (PTE $71–93), and reduced the fiscal incentive for unleaded gasoline to PTE $7/liter, based on the argument that its consumption was already approaching the EU average. In 1996 unleaded gasoline was also included in the MMP regime. In June 96 the tax differential was reduced again to PTE $6.3/liter, but in December ISP for both leaded and unleaded gasoline increased, to recover revenues lost with gasoil taxes (VAT and ISP), and the differential increased also to PTE

$6.8/liter. Table 22.7 shows the ISP unit taxes applied to unleaded and leaded gasoline, since 1991.

Table 22.7. ISP applied on unleaded and leaded gasoline (in PTE $/l)

	1991[a]	1992	1993	1994[b]	June 96[c]	Dec 96[d]
ISP Unleaded	81–86	77–88	74–81	84	90.7	91.5
ISP leaded	93–98	89–100	86–93	91	97	98.3
Tax differential	12	12	12	7	6.3	6.8

Notes
[a] DL 261-A/91. Data for 91, 92 and 93 correspond to the range of values really verified.
[b] Portaria 326-A/94 – ISP starts to be fixed.
[c] Portaria 224-B/96.
[d] Portaria 769-A/96 recover ISP tax revenues.

The share of taxes (including VAT) in the market price in July 1997 was about 72 percent in leaded, 70.7 percent in unleaded 95 and 68.7 percent in unleaded 98.

The described fiscal incentive has not been fully translated in a market price differential, the relevant variable for consumers' decision making, as shown in Table 22.8, which depicts the evolution of market prices between 1990 and 1997 (not accounting for variations along the year).

Table 22.8. Leaded and unleaded gasoline prices (in PTE $/l)

	1990	1991	1992	1993	1994	1995	1996	1997
Unleaded 95	131	137	136	141	152	153	158	163
Unleaded 98	–	–	–	151	155	156	164	169
Leaded	137	147	146	151	155	155	163	168

The difference between market prices for unleaded 95 and leaded gasoline ranges from PTE $2/liter in 1995 to PTE $10/liter in the 1991/93 period, being throughout the 1991/97 period lower than the corresponding tax differential. Differences in production costs can partially explain this behavior. Nevertheless, a more in-depth analysis shows that from 1991 to 1993 the price differential accounted for 83.3 percent of the tax differential, but this value has fallen to 42.9 percent and 28.6 percent respectively, in 1994 and 1995, and recovered again to 73.5 and 79.3 percent in 1996 and 73.5 percent in 1997. These figures indicate that the commercial strategy of oil companies also has an important role.

Unleaded 98 was introduced in 1993, and its price evolution reinforces this last argument. Although it has the same fiscal incentive as unleaded 95, the market price (free to fluctuate) was equal to leaded gasoline until 1995 and

PTE $1/liter higher since then. Therefore, the changes in the tax differential did not have any impact in the price differential between leaded and unleaded 98. This fact, associated with the evidence that almost all retailers have been charging the same prices (even though only leaded gasoline has an MMP regime),[3] reveal that the oil companies' strategic behavior, as they act in an oligopolistic market, has mitigated the potential impact of this environmental policy instrument since they incorporate part of the tax incentive as increased profit margins.

The share of both unleaded gasolines increased from 1.8 percent in 1990 to 41.4 percent in 1996. It is difficult to identify the role of the tax incentive on the described evolution of the market share. Palma (1996), using data on the monthly evolution of market shares for 1991, did not find a clear response of consumers to tax benefit, since the pattern of unleaded gasoline market share increase remained unchanged after publication of the legislation. Therefore, the rise in the market share reflected more a slow increase in the number of potential users (new cars) than a response to the price difference.

Table 22.9 shows the evolution of market sales for the three types of gasoline, from 1990 to 1996.

Table 22.9. Domestic market (in ktons)

	1990	1991	1992	1993	1994	1995	1996
Unleaded 95	23	127	221	329	358	370	456
Unleaded 98	–	–	–	65	190	294	362
Leaded	1,241	1,331	1,464	1,401	1,303	1,217	1,156
Total	1,264	1,458	1,685	1,795	1,851	1,881	1,974
% unleaded	1.8	8.7	13.1	21.9	29.6	35.3	41.4

Source: DGE.

The analysis of annual data shows a slow increase of unleaded market share, which is still below that achieved in most other European Countries, and which was not affected by the tax differential reduction of 1994, indicating that the increase in the number of cars that can use only unleaded gasoline, and for which the incentive is not relevant,[4] perhaps has a more important role in market evolution than the tax incentive.

Unfortunately, no data are available on the number of cars which could use unleaded gasoline when the tax incentive was introduced in 1991, or on its market share evolution since then. This information could help in clarifying some of the presented issues. Palma (1996), assuming unofficial information

[3] There are a few stations which are applying lower prices, but they are not relevant in the country context.

[4] Cars that can use both leaded and unleaded gasolines have been sold in Portugal since the second half of the 1980s and cars with catalytic converters have been sold since 1991. All cars sold from 1993 must have this equipment installed.

from four car manufacturers, estimated the unleaded potential users as representing 41 percent of the market in 1995 and concluded that some of these potential users did not switch to consume unleaded gasoline.

In summary, the impact of the tax differential on unleaded gasoline is not very clear, but it is evident that it has decreased from 1993, and will decrease faster in the future, as the share of catalytic converter equipped cars increases. It must also be stressed that the oil companies' commercial policy has mitigated the potential impact of this environmental policy instrument since they incorporate part of the tax incentive as increased profit margins.

5. A PRODUCT TAX ON SOLVENTS

Volatile organic compounds (VOC) emissions, which contribute to ozone formation in the atmosphere, are a priority issue of the European Commission's environmental policy. Solvents constitute an important source of VOC emissions, but the reduction of emissions due to solvent use in Europe is a complicated policy problem because of the large variations in solvent applications, the availability of alternatives and abatement techniques, the relative importance of VOCs as a policy problem, and the instruments used to address the problem (Oosterhuis et al. 1996, 1998).

In the scope of a study to address the feasibility of applying a Europe-wide tax on solvents to reduce VOC emissions (Oosterhuis et al. 1996), the potential impact of a tax on solvents on three Portuguese industries, printing and ink, pharmaceutical and paint, was evaluated. This section presents a brief synthesis of the conclusions of that study. Data for these three industries were collected on the availability of abatement and substitution options, as well as on the share of solvent costs in the total production value of the industry. The expected impact of the tax on production costs in the case where there are no abatement or substitution options which could become profitable due to the tax (in which case solvents will continue to be used and the full tax will have to be paid) is also presented.

5.1 Printing and Ink Industry

The printing and ink industry sector was responsible, in 1991, for about 2.4 percent of total VOC emissions from solvent use in Portugal, of which only 4.9 percent was from ink manufacture. The market of printing inks reveals a high concentration in the supply side.

Major technologies available for recovering and/or reducing VOC emissions in the ink industry are: recycling of used solvents, cooling/aeration systems of the mixer tanks, evaporated solvent recovery, through condensation (which is a costly process) or through absorption (with a higher efficiency), technological substitution (reduction of the average organic solvent content in inks), and implementation of 'good housekeeping'.

Some companies' strategy to reduce VOC emissions is based on the development of a package of internal policies, namely using dispensing and blending systems to minimize emissions and developing closed production systems. Other companies have been adopting strategies based on technological substitution (producing water-based inks – without organic solvents – and 'fat inks' or offset inks – without solvent vapor emissions) and recycling residual solvents by distillation (with efficiency from 40 percent to 60 percent).

In 1991, the estimated average share of solvent costs in production value of the ink industry amounted to 6.7 percent[5] and a VOC tax of 1 ECU/kg (PTE $195/kg) would increase this share to 13.7 percent, assuming that ink prices and quantities remain constant. On the other hand, if the increase in production costs is fully incorporated in the final price of inks, it will increase by about 7 percent.

A large variety of organic solvents are usually incorporated into the production process with prices ranging widely (for example between PTE $58 and $634/kg). The level of dependence on solvent-based inks varies among companies and thus a solvent tax would lead to differentiated impacts on the firms. However, the impact of the tax on the cost structure is in both cases very significant.

In the printing industry, solvent consumption includes not only the 'direct' incorporation of solvents into the process (for example, as an additive) and in cleaning operations, but also the 'indirect' incorporation through inks consumption, which accounts for about 95 percent of emissions in this sector and 2.3 percent of Portuguese total emissions from solvent use.

VOC emissions in the printing industry depend on solvent contents in inks, the type of solvents used before printing to liquefy inks and to aid the drying process, and solvents used in equipment cleaning. Available technologies for reducing VOC emissions differ according to the printing technique.

Offset is the most important technique used in Portugal, namely by the large newspaper and periodical printers. Use of solvents in cleaning printing equipment is the major source of VOC emissions. Development toward VOC emission reduction follow three directions: to increase the use of vegetable oil-based inks; to implement systems to collect and incinerate organic vapors; and to improve housekeeping in cleaning operations.

The market share of vegetable oil-based inks, used mainly in newspaper printing, is increasing slowly, since their performance is usually worse than mineral oils for the other uses. However, in sheet-fed offset, vegetable oils

[5] For the two largest companies the solvent share in production value is about 5.7and 6.6 percent, respectively.

have a performance as good as mineral ones, with similar costs, and so they are both used.

Technological constraints are the major barrier on the demand side for water-based color inks, since existing equipment does not allow their use and new technology requires high investments. The few water-based inks on the market with a performance similar to solvent-based options, are more expensive. Therefore, it can be expected that a tax on solvents will improve the market share of low-solvent inks.

Thermal incineration of VOCs is already applied in heatset dryer installations, with an environmental efficacy of about 98 percent. The investment costs in these installations were very different, according to the plant's size and characteristics, and there are no figures about unit costs per kg of VOC emissions avoided. VOC emission reductions are also being obtained by good housekeeping in cleaning operations, with negligible costs.

Rotogravure printing technique is applied exclusively in the packaging sector. The main emission control measures that have been applied are the change from chemical to electronic gravure (with a reduction in ink consumption of about 20 percent and a higher capacity to remove the solvents and inks used), the experimental use of water-borne inks (although their low performance and slow drying rate, which limits production capacity, justify, nowadays, the use of solvent-based printing inks), and recycling solvents (this system often has a low efficacy, about 3–6 percent).[6] In flexographic printing, the use of water-borne inks is the main measure that has been applied for VOC emission control.

For the three main offset printing companies, the share of ink consumption costs amounts to 3.1–8 percent of the production value, and the share of indirect solvent costs is 0.21–0.54 percent. A tax of ECU $1/kg solvent would increase this share to 0.42–1.1 percent, respectively, if the increase in production costs is totally incorporated in ink price and supported by the printing producer. Since the direct solvent consumption as an additive represented about 0.14 percent of the production value for one of the leading companies, and a tax of ECU 1 per kg will increase it to 0.36 percent, the share of the total solvents in production value after tax remains low.

In rotogravure printing, the share of (direct) solvent costs in production value can be estimated at about 4.2 percent and a tax of ECU 1 per kg will increase it to 8.2 percent if the increase in production costs is totally supported by the producer. On the other hand, if the increase is fully incorporated in the final price it will increase by about 4 percent.

---

[6] Nowadays, a leading printer is considering installing a new solvent recycling system with an efficacy of about 100 percent.

5.2 Pharmaceutical Industry

According to the CORINAIR'90 database, the pharmaceutical industry was responsible for the emission of only about 18 tons of VOCs (0.03 percent of Portuguese total emissions), but this value is underestimated since the amount of organic solvents incorporated in only one of the Portuguese companies production process in 1995 (Cipan) was 323 tons with emissions of about 65 tons.

The Portuguese pharmaceutical industry is engaged in two main manufacturing activities: production of bulk pharmaceuticals, drug intermediates and active ingredients; and formulation of finished drugs and medicines.

There are three manufacturers of drug intermediates and active ingredients which produce exclusively for foreigner markets. This subsector is responsible for a large share of VOC total emissions in the sector, and it was possible to get information from two of the three corporations established in Portugal. VOC emissions in the production process are about 20 percent of total solvents incorporated, the remaining 80 percent being lost in chemical reactions, recovered, or incorporated in products.

The remaining pharmaceutical companies do not develop the chemical process in-house, but import the active ingredients to formulate the final preparations and dosages. VOC emissions in these processes are not significant, although it is not possible to have a figure for the whole subsector.

Usually, in the pharmaceutical industry, technological substitution is not a feasible measure for VOC emission reductions, since solvents are used according to the final product chemical composition, thereby constraining the substitution of any solvent incorporated.

The use of recycled solvents can correspond to 50 percent of the total solvent use in production. Wastewater generated in the process is often harmful to the environment, mostly due to organic solvents, but valuable through a recycling program (PTE $78.7 per kg of recovered solvents).[7] Incineration costs of wastes that cannot be recovered are not relevant.

The high level of competitiveness and dynamics of the pharmaceutical industry, with continuous changes in product formulation and production processes, requires the frequent adaptation of pollution-control processes demanding high investments for small payback periods.

In 1990, the estimated share of solvent costs in production value would be about 0.015 percent. A VOC tax of ECU 1 per kg would increase this rate to 0.04 percent. Nevertheless, it must be stressed that emissions from the

[7] Data obtained from Hovione–Sociedade Química, S.A. (1996).

CORINAIR'90 database are underestimated and, consequently, the solvent uses estimated for 1990.

According to one of the companies, the share of solvent costs in total costs of raw materials incorporated into the production process is about 20 percent (valuing solvents to market prices) and 6.6 percent of production value.[8] Nevertheless, this share varies according to the product specification of the firm. For instance, for an antibiotics producer, the solvent shares in production costs range from 1–2 percent to 10–12 percent. For this company the average share of solvent costs in the production value, in 1995, amounted to 2.1 percent and the proposed VOC tax would increase it to 5.3 percent, if the final products price remains constant. On the other hand, the final price will increase by about 3.1 percent, if the increase in production costs is fully incorporated.

5.3 Paint Industry

In 1991, the paint sector was responsible for about 38 percent of Portuguese total emissions from solvent use, from which 94 percent result from paint use. Currently, four companies own about 75 percent of the domestic market share in Portugal, although there are a large number of paint suppliers (about 220 firms), of which 27 percent are construction firms producing for self-consumption.

The construction industry is the major paints consumer (including household consumption), accounting for 70 percent of total demand, using water-based paints almost exclusively (64 percent water-borne paints, 4 percent enamels, 2 percent other solvent-based paints). The remaining 30 percent are consumed by industry, namely by the automobile and marine sectors.

The market share of water-based paints, decreased by 9 percent from 1991 to 1992, according to official data from the National Institute of Statistics (INE). Nevertheless, consumption of water-based paints has been growing slowly, but steadily, since 1992. The use of solvent-based paints for non-industrial application (for example, building, household use) is decreasing.

Low-solvent paints are usually a little more expensive than the traditional high-solvent ones, due to higher technology requirements and incorporated raw material costs. For instance, in the paints for metals the market price of low-solvent products is about 21–27 percent higher.

However, in some cases, such as for backgrounds and anti-fouling, the prices are similar. In those cases the products with a higher solvent content have a better performance, and in some market segments product

[8] However, this data concerns only the amount of solvents purchased, it does not take into account the recovered solvents incorporated.

performance is considered more important than price in the formation of consumer preferences (for example, fishermen are still using tin-based anti-fouling, which has a solvent content of 40 percent, in spite of the prohibition of its use on small vessels and the rule that it can only be sold in large amounts).

Two types of measures have been applied in the Portuguese paint sector to reduce VOC emissions in the production process: (a) improved housekeeping in cleaning operations and (b) technological substitution (reducing the organic solvent content in the final product through the use of alternative ingredients).

On the supply side, financial constraints are quoted by producers as the major barrier to a more rational use of solvents and VOC emission control, arguing that this kind of measure requires investments in new equipment and changes in the production technology (for example, an activated carbon system technology for waste treatment with solvent recycling requires a high investment and provides negligible savings from the use of recovered solvents, due to the low price of most solvents).

The main producers target different market segments, which have a corresponding dependence on solvent-based paints. Thus the tax will have varying impacts.

Robbialac is one of the largest paint suppliers for the construction sector, and, in 1994, water-borne paints accounted for 80 percent of its production. However, it incorporates 52 organic solvents in the final products. The share of solvent costs in the production value amounts to 6.1 percent, and a VOC tax of ECU 1 per kg would increase this share to 15.6 percent if paint prices remain constant. On the other hand, if the increase in production costs is fully incorporated into the final price it will increase by about 9.5 percent.

Hempel is the largest paint supplier for the marine sector, also offering a wide range of products for industries and construction. In 1995, the solvent cost share in production value was 9 percent.[9] Solvent content in paint ranges between zero and 70 percent and solvent prices between PTE $60 and 300. A VOC tax of 1 ECU/kg over solvents purchased, if fully incorporated, would increase the paint price by 29.3 percent. Since Hempel has a higher dependence on solvent-based paint than Robbialac, a solvent tax would lead to a higher impact on the production costs.

General data regarding the paint sector for 1991, show that solvent costs amounted to 7.7 percent of production value. Assuming an average price of PTE $120 per kg of solvent, the proposed VOC tax would increase the share of solvent costs to about 20.7 percent, assuming that the price remains

[9] Although Hempel produces 50 different products, which demand different solvent combinations and incorporation needs, this share has remained relatively stable.

constant. The final price of paints will increase for about 13.2 percent, if the increase in production costs is fully incorporated.

Considering the low prices of most solvents used in this sector and the share of solvent costs in the total production costs, a solvent tax of ECU $1/kg would introduce a significant change in the price structure, increasing the incentive to reduce solvents consumption.

In summary, the impact of a possible tax on solvent use will vary considerably across sectors, and between companies within the same sector, depending on the nature of the production processes, uses and technological control options, as well as the market conditions. Table 22.10 summarizes the main issues identified for the sectors analyzed above.

Table 22.10. Summary of results

	Ink	Printing	Pharmaceutical	Paint
Share of total VOC emissions from solvent use	2.4%	Indirect (inks) – 2.3%	> 1%	38%
Share of emissions in manufacture stage	4.9%	High	bulk: ±20%	6–10%
Variety of solvents used	High	Low	High	High
No. of control technologies available	High	Differ according to the printing technique – medium/high	Medium	Low
Efficiency of control technologies	High	Low/high	Medium	Medium/high
Constraints	Demand requirements	Product technology constraints to use water-based color inks	Technological substitution is not available	Consumer preferences Price Financial constraints
Level of dependence	Varies among companies	High, but varies among printing techniques	High	Varies among companies
Price of solvents	High range PTE $58–$634/kg	Low range PTE $125–200/kg average PTE $187/kg	High range	High range PTE $50–$300/kg
Average share of solvent costs on product value	6.7%	Indirect: 0.2–0.6% direct: 0.14% rotogravure: 4.2%	< 0.1% in general 2.1–6.6% for two companies	6.1–9%
Expected impact of tax in the cost structure	Very significant	Low for offset significant for rotogravure	Low/medium	Very significant

6. FINAL REMARKS

The adoption of a market-based environmental policy, creating the economic and financial instruments for the application of the user-pays and polluter-pays principles, for the creation of a market of environmental resources and for the change in citizen behavior patterns, is one of the major stated goals of current environmental policy in Portugal. The integration of sectoral policies (for example, energy and transport) with environmental concerns can be promoted by the use of economic instruments. Market-based instruments can improve efficiency and create an incentive to innovation.

To move from intentions to actions it is necessary to change the perspective and practices of decision makers, professionals and economic agents, namely through education and training on environmental economics and management principles and methodologies for those generations with a poor background in these fields at the government and firm levels. Environmental education of the general citizen is also a priority of Portuguese policy.

The case studies described show the difficulties that arise when applying economic instruments in practical policy problems and some of the factors that hinder their effectiveness such as unsuitable design (for example, insufficient incentive, misevaluation of target agents), imperfect market structures (for example, oligopolistic markets), and lack of coordination with existing or 'in the pipeline' regulations.

The successful design of new economic instruments is an essential condition for improving their acceptance by decision makers and economic agents as efficient and effective instruments in environmental policy. The thorough evaluation of their environmental and economic impacts should be made before implementation, which requires the availability and analysis of appropriate information, as was shown in the solvent tax case study, and the collaboration of experts from several disciplines such as economists, technology experts and environmental professionals.

REFERENCES

Barata, P. (1998), 'A Atitude dos Portugueses Terante o Ambiente', Seminario Politica de Ambiente, Reforma Fiscal e Mercados, DCEA–FCT/UNL, Lisboa.

Dunlap, E.R. (1994), 'International Attitudes towards the Environment', *Green Globe Yearbook*, Oxford University Press.

Oosterhuis, F., Olsthoorn, X., Antunes, P., Santos, R., Kaderjak, P. and Sejak, J. (1998), 'Reducing VOC Emissions from Solvents in Europé: The Potential Role of Economic Instruments', *European Environment*, In press.

Oosterhuis, F., Olsthoorn, X., Santos, R., Antunes, P., Seják, J. and Kaderják, P. (1997), *Harmonization of Environmental Charges in Europe: The Case of VOC Emissions from Solvents*, Report E-97/3, Phare-Ace Program, IVM, Free University of Amsterdam, The Netherlands.

Palma, C. (1996), 'Differential Tax of Unleaded Petrol', in European Commission DGXI Report on *The Use and Potential of Fiscal Instruments in the Cohesion Countries*, Environmental Institute, University College Dublin.

Santos, R., Martinho, S. and Antunes, P. (1996), 'Differential Tax on Low Sulfur Fuel Oil - Effectiveness and Potential in Portugal', European Commission DGXI Report on *The Use and Potential of Fiscal Instruments in the Cohesion Countries*, Environmental Institute, University College Dublin.

Index